GREVISSE

Sbdd, M.

CORRECT FRENCH

a practical guide

Preface by André Chamson
of The French Academy

English version by
Christopher Kendris

First U.S. edition

**BARRON'S
EDUCATIONAL SERIES, INC.**
Woodbury, New York / London / Toronto

© Copyright DUCULOT PUBLISHERS, PARIS-GEMBLOUX 1973, 1979
© Copyright Barron's Educational Series, Inc. 1982 with respect to the English
language version. Title in France: LE FRANÇAIS CORRECT. ISBN 2-8011-
0223-7

All inquiries should be addressed to:
Barron's Educational Series, Inc.
113 Crossways Park Drive
Woodbury, New York 11797

Library of Congress Catalog Card No. 82-1757

Paper Edition
International Standard Book No. 0-8120-2169-X

Library of Congress Cataloging in Publication Data

Grevisse, Maurice.
  Correct French.

  Translation of: Le français correct, 2nd ed. 1979.
  Includes index.
  1. French language—Idioms, corrections, errors.
I. Kendris, Christopher, 1923-   II. Title.
PC2460.G63513   1982   448.2   82-1757
ISBN 0-8120-2169-X (pbk.)   AARCR2

PRINTED IN THE UNITED STATES OF AMERICA
2345   049   987654321

CONTENTS

PART THREE
CORRECT FRENCH IN SUBORDINATE CLAUSES

ABBREVIATIONS

Ac. or *Acad.* The French Academy

adj. adjective

adv. adverb

art. article

auxil. auxiliary

c.-à-d. c'est à dire (that is, that is to say)

cf. compare

cit. cited by

colloq. colloquial

condit. conditional

conjug. conjugation

dev. devant (in front of)

e.g. (Latin, *exemplī grātia*) for example

etc. (Latin, *et cetera*) and others, and so forth, and so on

f. or *fem.* feminine

fam. familiar

ff. and the following

fut. future

geom. geometry

id. (Latin, *idem*) the same as previously given or mentioned

i.e. (Latin, *id est*) that is; French, *c'est à dire* that is, that is to say

imper. imperative (command)

imp. or *imperf.* imperfect

ind. or *indic.* indicative

infin. infinitive

interj. interjection

m. or *masc.* masculine

mythol. mythology

no. number

p. page

par. paragraph

parf. parfois (at times)

part. or *partic.* participle

pers. person

pfois. parfois (at times)

pl. or *plur.* plural

pr. or *prés.* present

qq.ch. quelque chose (something)

qqn quelqu'un (someone, somebody)

qque quelque (some)

qualif. qualifier

s. simple

sing. singular

subj. subjunctive

suppl. supplement t. tome

(volume) or terme (term)

PREFACE

For more than half a century, I have been using our language daily, as a potter who uses clay every day or an artist who uses paints and brushes. Yet, my interest is still aroused by a work like this practical guide to correct French by Maurice Grevisse which is being published today.

This little book contains a treasure of good usage coming from afar [printed in Belgium, to be exact]. It plunges into the depths of a collective experience—or better put—a common experience in the proper meaning of the word. In it, you will find a sense of commitment, observations made on all the new adventures our language experiences and all the problems that the life of our language faces, whether they are usual or new. Each observation made is illustrated with examples cited from the writings of good authors of French and each decree has, behind it, lengthy authoritative evidence.

Whether in the category of correct French vocabulary or correct French grammar, I would not dare to claim that I am like a fish in water; on the contrary, I am like a fisherman fishing in a sea full of fish, a fisherman who never casts his line into the water in vain.

André Chamson
of The French Academy

TRANSLATOR'S NOTE

This is an English version of *Le français correct: guide pratique* by Maurice Grevisse, second edition, revised, 1979. It is being published in English for the first time in this country by Barron's Educational Series, Inc. The French editions of 1973 and 1979 were issued by Editions J. Duculot, Paris-Gembloux.

It was a joy for me to do this translation from the French of an author who is known internationally in the field of French language. Surely you must be familiar with some of his other major works in French—*Le Bon usage, Précis de grammaire française, Problèmes de langages, Dictées françaises, Savoir accorder le participe passé,* and *Quelle préposition?*—all of the highest quality. For a long time, teachers and students who speak French or English (or both) have been aware of the high value of Grevisse's books about the French language. I know I have.

After each French entry (identified by a number), I have generally inserted in brackets its English equivalent, its meaning or explanation, or even its definition (if appropriate), except those entries that are the same as in English; for example, the entry ACCENTS, which is entry no. 3, is the same word in English and has the same meaning as presented in the entry; hence, no English is given in brackets. At other times, no English appears in brackets after an entry if the French word or words are obsolete or archaic, if the entry has no exact equivalent in English, or if the entry is defined, explained, or translated into English in the discussion that follows each entry. Also, no English is given in brackets after an entry if it is in the process of changing in meaning or if it has different meanings—in which case these matters are pointed out in the body of an entry.

This translation into English also includes the textual content that follows each entry. The author generally gives examples, definitions, or explanations of what is correct or incorrect about the use of an entry. He tells us how to use the French words or phrases correctly and what should be avoided. The author also makes distinctions between the different meanings of an entry, if there are any, and gives exceptions (if there are any) and comments on them. I have translated the author's complete discussion after each entry into English.

At the end of each entry, the author cites examples from a multitude of sources he has found; they consist of complete sentences, phrases, or fragments of sentences—all taken out of context, of course. After each example, the author cites the source, which is indicated in parentheses; for example, *(Grand Larousse)*, a reference book, or (Flaubert), the name of the author who wrote the example. The examples the author gives illustrate the correct or incorrect use of an entry, sometimes both. I left those examples as they are in French so you could see them in actual use; in this way, you may scrutinize and analyze them if you wish, keeping in mind the observations and comments contained in the body of each entry, which I have translated into English.

Finally, at times the author uses an ellipsis (. . .) to indicate that he has omitted a word or some words which are not needed to convey the meaning of what is presented. I have done the same.

The value that you will derive from this book is immeasurable. It contains something of interest and value for every English-speaking person who knows French in various degrees of proficiency; for example, teachers and students of French in schools and colleges at the intermediate level and beyond, graduate students in universities majoring in French to become teachers, career people who desire to improve their use of correct French, and others who have a knowledge of French and want to know how to use the language correctly.

There is one special feature in the appendix of this book which you must not overlook. It is the complete text of grammatical / spelling changes allowed, as contained in the latest decree of the French Ministry of Education, issued by René Haby, Minister of Education. I found it extremely interesting and, I must say, shocking. Every teacher and student of French must be aware of it. The English language is undergoing changes, whether we like them or not. Similarly, changes are being made in the French language today, whether we like them or not. Read the French ministerial decree and the *Annexe* in the appendix and you, too, will be shocked.

I am sure that you will learn something of lasting value from Grevisse's work. I hope you enjoy using this book as much as I enjoyed preparing an English version for you.

Christopher Kendris

The Albany Academy
Albany, New York

PUBLISHER'S NOTE

Christopher Kendris, who wrote the English version of this book, has worked as interpreter and translator for the U.S. State Department at the American Embassy in Paris. At present, he is a teacher of French language and literature at The Albany Academy, Albany, New York. He is also a teacher of Spanish. His credentials are as follows.

Dr. Kendris earned his B.S. and M.S. degrees at Columbia University in the City of New York, where he held a New York State scholarship, and his M.A. and Ph.D. degrees at Northwestern University in Evanston, Illinois. He also earned two diplomas with *Mention très Honorable* at the Université de Paris (en Sorbonne), Faculté des Lettres, École Supérieure de Préparation et de Perfectionnement des Professeurs de Français à l'Étranger, and at the Institut de Phonétique, Paris.

He has taught French at the College of The University of Chicago as visiting summer lecturer and at Northwestern University, where he held a Teaching Assistantship and Tutorial Fellowship for four years. He has also taught at Colby College, Duke University, Rutgers—the State University of New Jersey, and the State University of New York at Albany. He was Chairman of the Foreign Languages Department at Farmingdale High School, where he was also a teacher of French and Spanish. He is the author of numerous school and college books, workbooks, dictionaries, and other language aids. Among his most popular works are *201, 301,* and *501 French Verbs Fully Conjugated in All the Tenses; 201, 301,* and *501 Spanish Verbs Fully Conjugated in All the Tenses* (with special features); *French Now!* (Level One textbook and workbook); *How to Prepare for the College Board Achievement Test in French; How to Prepare for the College Board Achievement Test in Spanish;* and two workbooks, *Beginning to Write in French* and *Beginning to Write in Spanish*—all of which have been issued by this publisher.

Dr. Kendris is listed in *Contemporary Authors* and *Directory of American Scholars.*

Barron's Educational Series, Inc.

PART ONE

CORRECT FRENCH IN VOCABULARY

1 ABASOURDIR [to dumbfound, to stupefy, to slay *(colloq.)*] (from [slang] *basourdir*, "to kill," and *basir*, same meaning). Correct pronunciation: *a-ba-zour-dir*. [Pronounce *s* as *z*.]

2 ACCAPARER [to monopolize] cannot be used as a reflexive verb. Do not say: *Il s'est accaparé de toute la production*. And do not say: *Il s'est accaparé toute la production*. Say: *Il a accaparé toute la production*.

3 ACCENTS
   (a) Do not write an accent mark, either acute (é), grave (è), or circumflex (ê), on the vowels in boldface in the following words:

appas	*cyclone*	*miserere*
axiome	*débucher*	*momerie*
bailler (donner)	*dégainer*	*otage*
bateau	*déjeuner*	*phylloxera*
Benoit (Pierre ~)	*demiurge*	*pretentaine*
besicles	*dessouler*	*pupitre*
boiter	*dévot*	*raclée*
boiterie	*diplomatique*	*ratisser*
boiteux	*disgracier*	*receler*
Bremond (abbé ~)	*disgracieux*	*receper*
brome	*drolatique*	*refréner*
bucrane	*égout*	*registre*
cela	*égrener*	*rengainer*
chalet	*fantomatique*	*repartie (réponse)*
Chalon-sur-Saône	*féerie, -ique*	*retable*
chapitre	*fibrome*	*rembucher*
Chateaubriand	*futé*	*revolver*
chatoyer	*gaine*	*roder (user)*
chebec	*gelinotte*	*secrétaire*
chechia	*gnome*	*seneçon*
chenet	*goitre*	*senescence*
chrome	*gracier*	*senestre*
cime	*haler (tirer)*	*senior*
Clemenceau	*havre, Le Havre*	*sorbetière*
compatir	*Heredia*	*sur (aigre)*
compatissant	*home*	*symptomatique*
conifère	*infamant*	*tatillon*
cote (de coter)	*infamie*	*Valery (Larbaud)*
coteau	*inversement*	*Vendryes*
craniologie	*mater (dominer)*	*Venezuela*
cru (vin)	*Megève*	*zone*

(b) Write an accent mark, either acute, grave, or circumflex, on the vowels in boldface in the following words:

abrégement	deçà	pèlerin, -inage
afféterie	déficit	pèlerine
aimé-je	déjà	il plaît
alêne	delà	pêne (de serrure)
allégement	détritus	piqûre
allégrement	diplôme	pluviôse
antéchrist	dussé-je	poêle
arène	écrémer	poème
arôme	emblème	poète
bâiller	emboîter	puissé-je
bâillon	empiétement	rébellion
barème	eussé-je	réglementer
bohème (vagabond)	événement	sécréter
çà (interj.)	faîte	sécrétion
chaîne	il gît	soûl
châlit	grêlon	spécimen
Châlons-sur-Marne	hâler (brunir)	surcroît
châssis	holà	symptôme
châtiment	icône	tempétueux
il clôt	infâme	ténacité
côlon (intestin)	Liège	théâtre
crème	liséré	trêve
crémerie	mémento	ventôse
crémier	nivôse	voilà

4 (1) Littré, the *Dictionnaire général,* and *Robert* write: *assener;* the *Grand Larousse encyclopédique* and the *Grand Larousse de la Langue française* write: *assener* or *asséner.*

(2) Littré, the *Dictionnaire général,* and the *Grand Larousse encyclopédique* write: *bélître;* the Academy: *belître;* the *Grand Larousse de la Langue française: bélître* or *belître.* The word *criterium* is written with no accent mark by Littré and the Ac.; an acute accent mark (*critérium*) is optional for *Robert* and the *Grand Larousse de la Langue française.*

(3) The Academy and the *Grand Larousse encyclopédique* write: *faine* (fruit of the beech tree); Littré and *Robert* write: *faîne;* the *Dictionnaire général* and *Lexis* write: *faine* or *faîne.*

(4) The Academy writes: *referendum;* the *Grand Larousse encyclopédique* and *Lexis: référendum; Robert: referendum* or *référendum.* Pronunciation: *ré-fé-rin-dom'.*

(5) Littré, the *Grand Larousse encyclopédique,* and J. Rostand use the French element *-genèse* (without an acute accent mark on the 1st syllable), which corresponds to the Greek element

genesis (production, creation, [birth]), in learned compound words, e.g.: *Parthénogenèse, glycogenèse, ovogenèse,* etc. Others put an acute accent mark there (which is not justified): *Parthénogénèse* (Ac.; *Robert*), *glycogénèse (Robert), ovogénèse* (A. Chamson).

(6) The Academy writes: *reviser, revision;* Littré: *reviser,* but *révision;* the *Dictionnaire général,* the *Grand Larousse encyclopédique,* and *Robert: reviser* or *réviser; revision* or *révision.*

(7) In learned words ending in *-iatre* (Greek *iatros,* doctor) or in *-iatrie,* a circumflex accent mark must not be placed on the *a: pédiatre, pédiatrie, psychiatre, psychiatrie,* etc.

(8) The Academy writes: *assidûment, congrûment, continûment, crûment, dûment, goulûment, incongrûment, indûment, nûment.*

The Academy writes with no circumflex: *absolument, éperdument, ingénument, résolument,* etc. (the Ac. does not recognize: *prétendument);* the Ac. writes with an acute accent: *exquisément;* with no acute accent: *intimement, opiniâtrement.* For several of these adverbs, usage varies; you will find: *éperdûment, exquisement, ingénûment, opiniâtrément, prétendûment.* Recommendation: adhere to the spelling of the Academy.

(9) The Academy writes: *senescence; Robert* and various *Larousse* sources: *sénescence.*

5 ACCEPTATION [acceptance] is the accepting, the fact that something is accepted. Do not use this word for *acception* [acceptation], which denotes the generally accepted meaning of a word. Do not say: *dans toute l'acceptation du terme* [in the full acceptance of the term]. Say: *dans toute l'*ACCEPTION *du terme* [in the full acceptation of the term]. *Ce mot a plusieurs* ACCEPTIONS (Academy).

6 ACCIDENTÉ [uneven, bumpy]. The traditional meaning is "presenting unevenness; rough, broken ground; moving, eventful": *une région* ACCIDENTÉE; *une vie* ACCIDENTÉE.

Now this word has a neological meaning [i.e., a new meaning for the established word] which is: "something or someone who has been in an accident": *une voiture* ACCIDENTÉE (J. Orieux); *Devant l'*ACCIDENTÉ *à panser, à recoudre* (É. Henriot).

The Academy does not recognize the verb *accidenter.* In the meaning of "to wound by accident" or "to damage, to injure," it belongs especially to informal French: *En roulant trop à droite, il* A ACCIDENTÉ *un cycliste (Grand Larousse de la Langue française).*

7 ACCOUTUMÉ [accustomed]. *Avoir accoutumé de* + inf. means *avoir pour habitude de (faire qq.ch.)* [to be in the habit of doing some-

thing]. The use of this term has become a little outdated: *Ce qu'on*
A ACCOUTUMÉ *d'appeler le théâtre du boulevard* (Fr. Mauriac).

8 ACHALANDER. According to strict opinion, *achalander* means
"to have [to provide] buyers," that is to say, "customers": *Ce
marchand est fort* ACHALANDÉ (Ac.). In today's use, *achalander* (especially in the past participle form) is used not only to mean "to
obtain numerous customers," but also to mean "to stock in merchandise"; this slip in meaning, condemned by the French Academy (notice issued Feb. 18, 1965), seems quite irreversible: *Boutique bien* ACHALANDÉE *(Petit Robert). L'épicerie Borange (. . .)
mieux* ACHALANDÉE *comme papeterie et librairie* (M. Proust, in Robert, Suppl.).

9 ACHEVÉ DE [completed], **COMMENCÉ DE** [begun] + inf. The
ways in which a verb expresses, with the infinitive that follows it,
the idea of completion or commencement of an action (e.g., *ache-
ver, finir, commencer de bâtir* [e.g., to complete, to finish, to begin
building]) allow a passive construction. The passive idea, which
logically concerns each one of the two elements of the verbal unit,
is expressed only in the first: *Il n'est pas encore* ACHEVÉ D'HABILLER
(Ac.). *Le petit volume (. . .),* ACHEVÉ D'IMPRIMER *le 2 janvier 1670,
parut dans le mois* (Sainte-Beuve); *Les lettres* FINIES DE LIRE
(P. Loti); *Une nouvelle petite Fiat qui est juste* FINIE DE RODER (J.-L.
Vaudoyer); *Ma robe est* COMMENCÉE DE GARNIR (F. Brunot).

10 ACOMPTE [installment, payment on account] / **ARRHES** [pay-
ment of a deposit]. An *acompte* is a partial payment on account
toward an amount that is due; *donner des arrhes* means to give a
sum of money as a deposit at the moment a contract is concluded
or when a business deal is agreed upon and which is lost if the
contract or deal happens to be broken.

11 ACQUIS [experience, knowledge acquired] / **ACQUIT** [acquittal,
relief from, quittance]. Distinguish clearly between *avoir de
l'*ACQUIS [to have a fund of knowledge, experience acquired] and
par ACQUIT *de conscience* [i.e., solely to avoid a regret] or *pour
l'*ACQUIT *de sa conscience* [for the release or relief of one's con-
science], and *faire qq.ch. par manière d'*ACQUIT [to do something
negligently, neglectfully]. [cf. *acquitter.*]

12 ACTER, an Old French word, is mentioned as a term of practice
in Bescherelle *(faire des actes),* in La Châtre *(faire, rédiger* [to draw
up, to edit], *signer des actes),* in the Supplement of Littré *(prendre*

acte [to note a fact]), and in the *Larousse du XXe siècle (prendre acte).* You sometimes find it used by journalists and in juridical language, notably in Belgium: *agriculteurs européens ont* ACTÉ *avec satisfaction la volonté du Conseil européen de Brême d'arriver à une stabilisation monétaire.*

[In Canada: *acter* = *agir; acter* (in the theater) = *jouer* (in the theater).]

13 ACTIVER [to activate, to stir up, to start up], in the form of a reflexive verb, *s'activer,* is rejected by purists: "I know very well that currently people are saying *s'activer* or *s'affairer;* but the first is detestable and means nothing because one can activate [start] a work or a fire, but one does not activate oneself [one does not start oneself]" (A. Hermant, *Chroniques de Lancelot,* t. I, p. 294). However, *s'activer* is in use today: *Elle admirait les fondrières où* S'ACTIVAIENT *les ouvriers* (R. Dorgelès).

The same for *s'affairer* [to busy oneself, to stir about, to fuss over] (which neither Littré, the *Dictionnaire général,* nor the Ac. mention): *Tandis que certains* S'AFFAIRAIENT *auprès de la présidente* (A. Gide, cit. Le Gal).

14 AFFABULATION, in its strict and etymological meaning, designates the morality of a fable, of an apologue. Its meaning in that sense is outdated and today the word means "the plot of a story or of a play." In modern usage, no clear difference has been determined between *affabulation* and *fabulation* (this last word, much less frequent than the other, is not recognized by Littré, by the *Dictionnaire général,* or by the Ac.): *À mesure que j'avançais dans le travail de* FABULATION [storytelling], *je voyais croître mon embarras* (R. Martin du Gard).   *L'*AFFABULATION *de ce roman est dramatique* (É. Henriot).

15 AFFAIRES [personal belongings, personal things] is used in the sense of "objects, clothing, personal effects": *Ranger ses* AFFAIRES *(Robert).   Elle eut vite fait de préparer ses valises en les bourrant à grands coups de poings sans même plier ses* AFFAIRES (A. Chamson).

16 AGONIR [to agonize, to torment] / **AGONISER** [to be in agony]. Do not confuse these two verbs; *agonir* means "to overwhelm (with reproaches, with insults, etc.)": *Elle m'a presque* AGONIE *de sottises* (Balzac, in *Petit Robert).*

The verb *agonir* is conjugated like *finir: j'agonis, il agonit, nous agonissons, j'agonissais, que j'agonisse,* etc. Certain authors improperly conjugate it like *agoniser;* examples cited by A. Goosse: *Vos publicistes* AGONISENT [should be *agonissent*] *le néophyte de propos vertueux* (M. Barrès).   *Ils étaient fâchés avec leurs voisins parce que la mère Tuvache les* AGONISAIT [should be *agonissait*] *d'ignominies* (Maupassant).

Agoniser means "to be in agony": *L'abbé se meurt; il* AGONISE (Sévigné).

17 **AGRÉATION** (from *agréer*, which means to accept as good, to approve, to ratify). Littré lists this word in its Supplement, but the two examples given are taken from the *Journal officiel*, a Belgian publication. In Belgium, the word is used in the meaning of "official recognition, acknowledgment"; for example, regarding nominations, ratification of certificates of studies. Do not confuse this word with *agrégation*, which is the admission of a candidate after competitive examination to the title of *agrégé*, qualified to hold the rank of professor at a lycée, an atheneum, or a faculty.

18 **AGRESSER** [to assault]. This "annoying and useless neologism," according to Dauzat, is an old word taken into use again at the end of the 19th century; it has been accepted by the *Grand Larousse encyclopédique*, by the *Grand Larousse de la Langue française*, by *Lexis*, as well as by *Robert* (Suppl.); the latter gives these examples: *Deux individus l'ont* AGRESSÉ *la nuit dernière.   Passant* AGRESSÉ *dans une rue déserte.*

19 **AJOUTE, RAJOUTE** [an addition, something extra added] are not accepted in good usage. Although *une ajoute* is listed among the Additions in Littré ("that which one adds to an engine") and you will come across it sporadically in use in France, it does not belong to conventional French: *C'est donc* UNE AJOUTE *toute gratuite* (Gabriel Marcel).   [Use *un ajout* or *un rajout*, but not *une ajoute*, *une rajoute*.]

You can choose from among: *ajout, rajout, ajouté, addition, adjonction, allonge, rallonge, supplément, surcharge, annexe, complément, correctif,* etc: *Il chargea les épreuves de repentirs et d'*AJOUTS (A. Maurois).   *Quand il y avait* UN RAJOUT *au bout de l'article* (M. Cohen). *Mettre* UNE RALLONGE *à une table* (Ac.).

20 **ALLONGER** [to lengthen]. Along with Littré, purists condemn *les jours allongent* and they want us to say: *les jours s'allongent* [using the reflexive form *s'allonger*, not *allonger*]; however, this faulty way is used by excellent authors: *Les jours* ALLONGEAIENT (Hugo).   *Comme les jours* AVAIENT ALLONGÉ. . .(Fr. Mauriac).

Allonger, as an intransitive verb, is at times also used in the concrete meaning of "to take on more length": *Ses cheveux* AL-LONGÈRENT (Fr. Mallet-Joris).

21 ALLUMER [to light]. Since one certainly does say *éteindre la lumière* [to extinguish the light] (Ac.), one can also say *allumer la lumière* [to turn on the light], like *faire la lumière: Elle referma la porte et alluma la lumière électrique* (J. Green).

Compare: *Je vais allumer l'éclairage au néon* (G. Duhamel). *J'allumai l'électricité* (P. Guth).

Allumer is also used in its absolute meaning: *Il alluma et tenta de lire* (A. Maurois).

22 ALTERNATIVE, in a strict sense, means "a succession of two things which come back by turns" or "one option between two courses, two sides to choose from": ALTERNATIVE *continuelle d'espérance et d'alarme* (Hugo). *C'est un fumiste ou un fou, nulle autre* ALTERNATIVE (M. Proust).

The word is often used improperly, even by excellent authors, to mean "one of two *or several* terms to choose from." This use, condemned by Littré and by the Academy (notice made known on Nov. 19, 1964), is spreading: *Entre ces deux* ALTERNATIVES: *les vivres coupés ou bien un départ immédiat pour Paris* (M. Prévost). [Note: in correct French, as in correct English, there is *only one* alternative that can be chosen from between two things or from among more than two things; there cannot be two or more alternatives.] *En lui montrant deux* ALTERNATIVES: *ou se laisser traîner dans les prisons de la terre ou porter le fer et le feu dans le palais d'Ialdabaoth* (A. France). *De là enfin la conclusion qu'il y a trois* AL-TERNATIVES (. . .). *Mais la vérité est qu'il y en a une quatrième* (H. Bergson). In sentences of this sort, instead of using the word *alternative*, in correct French the following words are used, for example: *éventualité, parti, solution, issue,* or *possibilité.*

Recommendation: Use the word ALTERNATIVE only in its strict meaning, as indicated in the beginning of this entry [i.e., as a single alternative between two choices]. [See also entry no. 182.]

23 ALUNIR [to land on the moon], **ALUNISSAGE** [a moon landing]. These neologisms have been the subject of much discussion: two *l*'s or just one? *alunir* or *atterrir sur la Lune?* The Academy (communication dated Feb. 17, 1966) rejected *alunir* and recommended *atterrir sur la Lune* [to land on the moon]. But, in today's usage, *alunir* and *alunissage* seem to have won the battle, and they are listed in the *Grand Larousse encyclopédique,* in the *Grand Larousse de la Langue française,* in *Lexis,* in *Robert* (Suppl.), in *Petit*

Robert, and in *Dictionnaire Bordas.* Examples: *Mais* ALUNIR *signifiera pour lui [pour l'homme] freiner les deux ou trois kilomètres-seconde qui ont anéanti Lounik* (Charles-Noël Martin). *Il y aura peut-être des expériences manquées, des* ALUNISSAGES *pénibles, mais la réussite n'est qu'une question d'années* (A. Maurois).

24 **AMBIANCE** [environment, atmosphere, surroundings]: "a material or moral atmosphere which surrounds a person, a group of persons" *(Petit Robert). Telle ou telle* AMBIANCE *peut améliorer ou déformer un caractère* (Ac.). *La tante disait qu'une* AMBIANCE *familiale est plus efficace qu'un repas d'affaires* (R. Sabatier). The general meaning of AMBIANCE, therefore, is one of "milieu (surroundings), climate, atmosphere" in their figurative use.

AMBIANCE is used in informal French for "an atmosphere of merriment, of liveliness, of fun and good cheer": *Il y a de l'*AMBIANCE *ce soir (Robert,* Suppl.).

25 **AMENER, RAMENER.** Used in their proper meaning, these verbs, according to the Academy (notice dated Nov. 18, 1965), should be used only to mean "to lead or conduct while guiding" and you would not say: *J'ai ramené une montre de Suisse.* [In that example, *J'ai ramené* is not correct; *J'ai rapporté* is correct.]

More than one good author uses these two verbs to mean "*apporter* [to bring], *rapporter* [to bring back] something with oneself, while coming back to the place that one has left": Robert Le Bidois cites (but at the same time condemns) these examples: *Les vêtements (. . .) qu'il n'avait pas voulu* AMENER *à la maison* (J. Giraudoux). *Mon père* RAMENA *le panneau à la maison* (A. Chamson). *La bibliothèque* RAMENÉE *d'Argelouse* (Fr. Mauriac). *Il s'agit d'un hareng qu'un vieux Juif* RAMENAIT *chez lui pour nourrir sa famille. . .* (H. Troyat).

Recommendation: Accept the advice of the Academy [given in the 1st par. of this entry].

26 **AMERRIR / AMÉRIR** [to land on a sea, on a body of water]. The spelling *amérir* would conform to the rules of derivation, the radical being *mer,* and the suffix *-ir.* "This neologism," Thérive writes, "is very much under discussion. In any case, it should be written as *amérir;* to use a double letter [r] would be absurd. However, *amerrir* is so much in use already that it is necessary, I believe, to sanction it."

At times, you will come across it as *amérir: Il décolla,* AMÉRIT, *décolla,* AMÉRIT *sans répit* (J. Kessel). But *amerrir* has been adopted by the Academy and this spelling is justified by analogy with *at-*

terrir [to land on ground]. It should be noted that *amerrir* or *amérir* means not only "to land on a sea" but also, by extension, "to land on a surface of water" [as on a lake, for example]: *L'hydravion* AMERRISSAIT *difficilement* (Ac.).

27 AMIDONNER, EMPESER. Grammarians make a distinction between *amidonner* "to coat with amidin" and *empeser*, which is more precise according to them: "to stiffen by applying amidin, by applying starch." As a matter of fact, people say without any appreciable difference: *du linge* AMIDONNÉ or *du linge* EMPESÉ: *Une blouse blanche bien* AMIDONNÉE (J. Green).   *Toutes les femmes (. . .) étaient ainsi vêtues de blanc, de lingeries fines* AMIDONNÉES (M. Genevoix).   *Étranglé par son col* AMIDONNÉ (M. Pagnol).   *De courtes robes de mousseline* EMPESÉES *comme du carton* (Maupassant).   *Les grands cols* EMPESÉS *que lui seul n'avait pas abandonnés* (P. Morand).

28 AMITIEUX (from *ami* [friend]). In Belgium, this word means affectionate, lovable, caressable: *Cet enfant est* AMITIEUX *comme tout!* [Note that the *t* in *amitieux* is not pronounced as an *s;* pronounce it as in the word *amitié.*]

29 AMODIER. To rent (land, a mine. . .) by a contract including a periodic allowance in kind or in money. Do not confuse this verb with *amender* [which means "to improve land"]: AMODIER *sa terre pour tant de blé, ou tant d'argent* (Ac.).

30 ANNOTER [to annotate a text] means "to accompany it with notes, with remarks, with critical annotations": *Il a* ANNOTÉ *les ouvrages de Pline, de Tacite* (Ac.).   Make a clear distinction between *annoter* and *noter*. Do not say: *Annoter une adresse dans son agenda.* Say: *Noter une adresse. . .*

31 ANNUAIRE [yearbook, directory]. An annual publication of a book that contains necessary information about an administrative or other type of organization: *l'*ANNUAIRE *des téléphones.*
    You can also say: *le bottin des téléphones* [the telephone book]; *Chercher un numéro dans le* BOTTIN (*Robert*, Suppl.).

32 ANOBLIR / ENNOBLIR. Distinguish between the meaning and use of these two verbs. *Anoblir* means to confer a title of nobility on someone. *Ennoblir* means to raise to a height of moral greatness or grandeur [e.g., to lionize, to glorify].

33 ANTAN (*d'*~). This expression, which serves only as a complement of a noun, is used to refer to the year preceding the current year. This is the only meaning given by the Academy: *Elle parlait d'une arche de Noé qu'elle m'avait donnée le premier janvier* D'ANTAN [i.e., January first of last year] (A. France, cited by Deharveng). But this meaning has been somewhat forgotten and, in modern usage, D'ANTAN is taken to mean "formerly, in years gone by": *Je paie aujourd'hui mes dénis* D'ANTAN, *de ce long temps où me paraissait indigne de réelle attention tout ce que je savais transitoire* (A. Gide, in *Grand Larousse de la Langue française*).

34 ANTICIPATIF / ANTICIPATIVEMENT. You find *anticipatif* in *Larousse du XXᵉ siècle* and in *Lexis*, but no other *Larousse* publication and no other dictionary mention it. *Anticipativement* is not accepted by any lexicographer. Instead of saying *un versement anticipatif*, you should say: *un versement* ANTICIPÉ. Instead of saying *payer anticipativement*, you should say: *payer* PAR ANTICIPATION.

35 AOÛT [August]. This word is pronounced *oo* rather than *ah-oo*, according to the Academy. A complacent opinion! "The pronunciation *ah-oo*, says Martinon, "is also outdated and should appear just as ridiculous as pronouncing *paon* [peacock] in two syllables instead of one." The letter *t* "is not supposed to be pronounced in the word *août* any more than in the word *debout* [upright, standing (up),]," says Martinon, "despite its use in certain provinces." As a matter of fact, many people in France pronounce the *t* in *août*, even in "distinguished" use.

36 APAISEMENT [appeasement]. People do say, "*avoir, donner tout apaisement, des apaisements, (tous) ses apaisements.*" The general meaning is "to be assured" or "to reassure": *Le spécialiste ne peut manquer de vous donner toute lumière et tout* APAISEMENT (G. Duhamel). *Il me faut apporter des* APAISEMENTS *aux esprits que le sous-titre pourrait étonner* (Id.). *Vous pouvez donner tous les* APAISEMENTS *à M. le Supérieur* (Fr. Mauriac). *Vous avez vos* APAISEMENTS (J. Romains).

37 ARBORÉ, in the meaning of "planted with trees, covered with trees," is found in the works of M. Bedel: "la savane *arborée* du Katanga." But in conventional French, *arboré* means "elevated, raised, straight up like a tree" or "worn, displayed ostentatiously": *Drapeaux* ARBORÉS *le 14 juillet, décorations fièrement* ARBORÉES, etc.

38 ARCHELLE designates, in regional French, in Belgium and in various regions in France (Picardy, Manche, Champagne, etc.), a kind of shelf used to expose plates and on which to hang pots, jars, and different culinary utensils. According to Hanse (see: *Revue belge de Philol. et d'Hist.*, t. XXVIII, no. 2, 1950), this word is related to *ais* (= plank, board) and has perhaps been attracted into the realm of *arche*. In Artois and in Picardy, it has the following equivalent words: *potière, barre à pots*. Technicians and antique dealers also say *potière-corniche, archelle potière*.

39 ARDOISIER. This word is used to describe a person who exploits or works in a slate quarry. Make a distinction between this word and *couvreur*, which is a roofer, a worker who makes or repairs roofs made of slate, tile, zinc, etc.

In this regard, it should be observed that in the expression, *le vivre et le couvert* [room and board—*le vivre* means board, food; *le couvert* means room, shelter], the word *couvert* signifies "a lodging where a person has shelter, is under cover."

40 ARÉOPAGE [Areopagus]. This word is from the Greek *Areios pagos*, the hill of Ares. [*Areios*, of Ares + *pagos*, hill: the hill of Ares, west of the Acropolis in ancient Athens]. Do not mispronounce this word as if it were spelled *aéropage*.

41 ARIA. This word is not recognized by the Academy. It is used familiarly to mean "care, trouble, frustration, burden, worry." [Do not mistake or misuse this word, which is a masculine noun, for the feminine noun *aria*, which is an aria, an air, a melody.] *À quelque temps de là il assiste à la libération de Paris, à laquelle il participe allégrement sans perdre de vue son journal, dont les feuillets heureusement conservés au milieu de tant d'*ARIAS, *nous valent un des plus vivants récits de témoin sur ces pathétiques et confuses journées* (É. Henriot).

42 ASSEOIR (s'~). When asking someone to sit down, say: *Asseyez-vous, Prenez place*, or *Mettez-vous là*. Or, in a polite, somewhat formal tone, you can say: *Donnez-vous la peine de vous asseoir*, or *Prenez la peine de vous asseoir*. Do not say: *Mettez-vous*, which is used in southern France. And do not say: *Remettez-vous*.

43 ATTENDRE UN ENFANT [to expect a child]. In talking about a woman who is expecting "a blessed event," one ordinarily says: *être enceinte* [to be pregnant] or *attendre un enfant*. The following is a familiar way of expressing this and is somewhat outdated: *être dans une position intéressante* [to be in an interesting condition]. The expression *une femme grosse* is outdated. [In Canada: *être en famille* or *tomber en famille* (= *être enceinte*).]

Do not say: *Elle a eu une portée pénible*. Instead of saying *une portée pénible*, say: *une grossesse pénible*. Or, in medical terms, you can say: *une gestation pénible*. The word *portée* [litter] is used to refer to the total number of young brought forth at one time by quadrupedal female animals (Ac.).

44 AUBETTE. In Middle High German the word is *hûba*; in Old French, it is *hobe*, which is a shelter, a hut or shed. It is a regional French word, current in Belgium, known also in western France (Nantes, Rennes, Brest, Saint-Malo). The word designates a newspaper stand or a shelter for people who are waiting for a streetcar, bus, etc. The word AUBETTE would be a useful replacement, as M. Piron has noted, for the term *kiosque à journaux* [newspaper stand or covered stall], which is a periphrasis [circumlocution]. This pretty word would merit being admitted into universal French, but it will remain, without doubt, confined to marginal French. *Lexis* has welcomed this word as being dialectal.

45 AUTARCHIE [autarchy] / **AUTARCIE** [autarky]. The word *autarchie* (= autonomy) has had, since the end of the last century, a certain usage: *Dans une société où l'*AUTARCHIE *économique conduit logiquement à l'*AUTARCHIE *intellectuelle* (G. Bernanos). But in order to designate the state of a nation that is sufficient unto itself and lives in a closed economy, the word AUTARCIE is used today: *Une ère d'*AUTARCIE *et de misère s'est ouverte* (R. Kemp). *L'économie sans débouchés, l'*AUTARCIE *semi-villageoise que s'était établie aux temps carolingiens, a duré un peu plus d'un siècle* (P. Gaxotte).

46 AU TEMPS! This term is used in gymnastics or military drills in order to give an order to return to the preceding position for the purpose of doing the movement all over again. According to Thérive, *au temps!* "might possibly be merely a pedantic spelling [for *autant*], whose origin would be rather recent." However, the spelling *au temps!* is the one which has imposed itself: AU TEMPS! *cria Brague. Tu l'as encore raté ton mouvement!* (Colette.)

47 AUTOMATION. This word is to be proscribed, according to the Academy (communication dated April 20, 1967). It will be replaced by *automatisation* or by *automatique*, according to the case.

48 AUTOROUTE [express highway, freeway, thruway], a feminine noun, has superseded the word *autostrade*.

49 AVANT-MIDI [before noon] is at times used in Belgium, either as a masculine or feminine noun, for *matinée* [morning]: *Nous aurons aujourd'hui un bel (une belle)* AVANT-MIDI.

50 AVANT PLAN is very seldom used in France. It is not mentioned in Littré, the *Dictionnaire général, Robert,* or by the Academy. It is listed in the *Grand Larousse encyclopédique* but normally *premier plan* [foreground, downstage] is used.

51 AVATAR [avatar]. In the Hindu religion, this word designates each of the ten incarnations of Vishnu. [In Hindu theology, Vishnu is the second member of the trinity.] This word is properly used to mean "metamorphosis, transformation": *Thénardier, à qui les* AVATARS *étaient aisés, saisit cette occasion de devenir Jondrette* (Hugo). *Les* AVATARS *d'un politicien.*

Today, despite what purists say, AVATAR is frequently taken to mean adventure, misadventure, mishap, trouble, worry, inconvenience, etc. It is undoubtedly necessary to accept this slip in meaning: *Il m'arrive, notamment après une série d'*AVATARS, *d'avoir envie de me défaire de ma voiture* (P. Daninos). *À cause de ce retard, il n'arriva à Rio que le lendemain vers midi. Malgré cet* AVATAR (. . .), *Mermoz souriait. . .* (J. Kessel). *Ils (. . .) riaient volontiers de ses* AVATARS *de fortune* (A. Chamson). *Et comment évaluer l'effet produit sur l'état matériel et moral de toutes les autres unités allemandes par les* AVATARS *des convoirs, du ravitaillement, des liaisons?* (Ch. de Gaulle.)

52 AVÉRER [to aver, to affirm, to allege as a fact]. This word is used especially as a reflexive verb, *s'avérer* (= to be truly, to reveal itself, to manifest itself) and as a participial adjective, *avéré: La soif s'*AVÉRAIT *redoutable* (M. Genevoix). *C'est un fait* AVÉRÉ (Ac.) [*un fait* AVÉRÉ: an established, confirmed fact].

Certain authors (although grammarians do protest) are not afraid to join the adjective *faux* [false] to *s'avérer* or to *avéré.* If one wished to justify them, one could say that in modern usage people are no longer aware of the etymology of the word *s'avérer* (cf. Latin *versus,* French *vrai,* [English, true]). To say *cela s'avère faux* does not appear to be more shocking than to say *cela est vraiment faux* [that is truly false]: *Bien que ses calculs* S'AVÉRASSENT *faux* (Montherlant). *Jusqu'au jour où il est* AVÉRÉ *qu'il* [*un objet d'art* (an art object)] *est faux* (Id.). *Quand tous les calculs compliqués* S'AVÈRENT *faux* (M. Yourcenar). *Les vues de l'homme* S'AVÈRENT *toujours fausses* (Fr. Mauriac, cited by Georgin).

53 AVEU [avowal]. Do not say: *être en aveu(x), entrer en aveu(x)*. In good French usage, we are expected to say: *avouer, faire des aveux, passer aux aveux*, or *entrer dans la voie des aveux* [to avow, to make avowals, to confess, to admit frankly]: *Crainquebille eût* FAIT DES AVEUX *s'il avait su ce qu'il fallait* AVOUER (A. France). *Le coupable est* ENTRÉ DANS LA VOIE DES AVEUX? (H. Bernstein.)

54 AVOIR AFFAIRE, AVOIR À FAIRE [to deal with, to have to do (with)]. The two ways of writing this are good, but the first is undoubtedly the most frequently used: *Il a eu* AFFAIRE *à moi pour une question de passeport* (J. Romains). *Il faut que l'on ait* À FAIRE *à quelque vainqueur* (Sainte-Beuve). *Qu'ai-je* À FAIRE *avec le génie?* (J. Cocteau.)

55 AVOIR FACILE. The construction *avoir* plus an adjective is not outmoded in France: *Il a eu* FACILE *de me reprendre les bibelots* [said a music hall girlfriend] (Colette). *Les médecins ont bien* FACILE (G. Lenôtre, cited by Deharveng). *Saint Gorgon ne l'a pas eu si* AISÉ (Bossuet, cited by Hanse). *J'aurais plus* COURT *de rester à Paris* (A. Dumas, cited by Deharveng).

In normal French, instead of saying: *Il a facile de le faire* [It is easy for him to do it], say: *Il lui est facile de le faire*, or *Il le fait facilement*, or *Il n'a aucune difficulté à le faire*.

56 AVOIR GARDE. An ordinary use: *n'avoir garde de* + infin. = not to have the willingness or capability to, to be quite distant from: *Il n'a garde de tromper, il est trop honnête homme* (Ac.). *Il n'avait garde de contredire sa fille* (Mérimée). It is also used about things: *Cette permission n'avait garde de lui être refusée* (Ac.).

To express the same meaning, the affirmative construction is at times used: *avoir garde de* + infin. [= *faire en sorte de ne pas. . .* (to do so as not to. . .)], but this construction is not recommended because it creates confusion: *Nous avions garde de l'aborder brusquement* (Th. Gautier). *J'ai garde surtout de m'aveugler sur les tares du régime capitaliste* (Fr. Mauriac).

57 AVOIR LIEU DE [to have reasons for, to have reason to]. "I accept," wrote Gide, "the use of this locution only in the neuter [*il y a lieu de. . .* (there is reason to. . .)]. *J'ai lieu de. . .* shocks me, and even more so because Littré seems to accept it."

There is no basis for Gide's opinion: *Vos prêtres, je veux bien, Abner, vous l'avouer / Des bontés d'Athalie* ONT LIEU *de se louer* (Racine). *Tout ce que* J'AI LIEU *d'écrire aujourd'hui* (A. Hermant).

58 AVOIR SOIN DE [to take care of]. Do not say: JE SOIGNERAI *pour vous, pour cette affaire* [I shall care for you, I shall (care for) take care of this matter], which is a Germanism. Say: *J'aurai soin, je prendrai soin de vous* [I shall take care of you], *de cette affaire* [of this matter], *je m'en occuperai* [I shall take care of it], *j'y veillerai* [I shall watch over it].

59 AZIMUT [azimuth]. This is a word used in astronomy. In general usage, the term TOUS AZIMUTS [all angles] is used informally as an epithet having the value of "being suitable in all cases, being applicable in all eventualities."

60 BACCHANAL, BACCHANALE(S). The first of these words is masculine and means "loud noise, uproar": *Faire du* BACCHANAL (Ac.) *Au milieu de ce* BACCHANAL [in the midst of all this carousing] *la belle Marco restait muette* (Musset).

The *bacchanales* [Bacchanalia] were, among the ancients, the festivals celebrated in honor of Bacchus [name which the Romans used for Dionysus, god of wine and revelry]. *Bacchanale*, in the feminine form, is used either for a noisy and tumultuous dance or for a debauchery (an orgy) made with a lot of noise: *J'ai connu aussi un écrivain à la mode qui passait pour présider chaque nuit de fameuses* BACCHANALES (A. Camus). *Mais huit ans aussi de* BAC-CHANALE *organisée, et de* BACCHANALE *qu'on savait qui était couverte par le fric paternel* (Montherlant).

61 BAGOU(T) [glibness; *avoir du bagou(t)*, to have the gift of (the) gab]. Littré, the *Dictionnaire général*, and the Academy write this word as *bagou*. The spelling *bagout* is fairly frequent: *Il avait ce qu'on appelle à Paris* DU BAGOUT (A. Hermant). *Papa se mit à parler d'abondance, forçant son maigre* BAGOUT *à occuper le silence* (H. Bazin).

62 BALADE. [stroll] / **BALLADE** [ballad]. Make a distinction between these two words. *Balade* (not recognized by the Academy) is a word used familiarly [i.e., informally] meaning "to take a walk in an idle, leisurely way without going to any particular place in mind." *Ballade* is a short poem written in a certain form; it is a story in verse that tells about historical or legendary traditions.

63 BALLOTIN. This masculine noun is of the same family as *un ballot* [a bale, a bundle] and *une balle* [a ball]. Currently, in Belgium, it designates a small box, container, or carton used in wrapping (especially for what the Belgian people call *pralines*). In France, they say *des chocolats* or *des crottes de chocolat* [chocolate drops].

The word *ballotin* is in use in Paris and other parts of France. [See also entry no. 113: *chocolat.*]

64 BARBOUZE. This word was at first used for *une barbe* [a beard]; later, it was used to mean *agent d'une police parallèle*, a secret agent, because of the fake beard worn by such an agent as a disguise.

65 BARON. This word denotes a certain cut of meat and this is the usual spelling. *Baron d'agneau* [bottom round of lamb] consists of two legs of mutton and two fillets *(Robert)*.

Some people spell this word as *bas-rond* [bottom round]: *Le* BAS-ROND *d'agneau proposé à l'admiration des convives* (G. Duhamel).

66 BASER, SE BASER (= *fonder* [to base], *se fonder* [to be based]). These two words [*baser* and *se baser*] are not recognized by the Academy. There is no doubt that they have been sanctioned through usage: *Dès que les dramaturges ont* BASÉ *leurs ouvrages sur ce qui était* (G. Duhamel).   *Que cet ensemble auguste où l'insensé* SE BASE. . . (Hugo).   *Le marché des jeux,* BASÉ *sur la tolérance policière, était le champ ouvert aux compensations faciles* (Aragon).   *Il serait plus sérieux de tenter une classification des peuples en* SE BASANT *sur leur façon de s'interpeller* (A. Chamson).

67 BEC DANS L'EAU. The real meaning of *tenir qqn le bec dans l'eau* is "to keep someone waiting for something, to keep someone hoping, to keep someone in doubt by not giving the person a positive answer" (Ac.). The essential idea is, therefore, "to wait in vain." [The literal translation of this expression is to have your "beak (or snout, i.e., your nose) in the water"]: *C'est que si je veux, moi aussi, libérer de jeunes esprits, dès octobre, je ne peux pas rester* LE BEC DANS L'EAU. *Mon dévouement doit être utilisé* (R. Benjamin).   *On ne lésine pas en boucherie; tuer ce qu'on aime, tuer ce qu'on hait, on s'y précipite: on ne craint pas de rester ensuite* LE BEC DANS L'EAU (J. Giono).

68 BÉER [to be opened, with mouth wide open, agape]. This verb is a variant of *bayer* (pronounced as *ba-yer*). It can be used in its complete conjugation: *On a l'impression que l'enfer s'ouvre tout à coup et* BÉE (J. Green).   *Les narines* BÉAIENT *sous l'arête du nez décharné* (M. Genevoix).   BAYER *aux corneilles.   La servante vint nous annoncer qu'Auguste* [*un jeune canard*] BAYAIT *du bec* (J. Duché).

69 BÉNÉFICIER [to benefit]. Do not say: *Cette mesure vous bénéficie* [This measure benefits you]. Say: *Vous bénéficiez de cette mesure* [You benefit from this measure]. The verb *bénéficier* can have as its subject only the person or thing that benefits (French Academy's notice dated Feb. 18, 1965).

70 BÉNÉFIQUE [beneficial, propitious]. Littré, the *Dictionnaire général,* and the Academy do not recognize this word. It was used in the 16th century as a term in astrology. Nowadays, it is current: *Le retour aux sources est parfois* BÉNÉFIQUE (A. Maurois). *Renoncer à ce «farniente»* BÉNÉFIQUE (P.-H. Simon). *Quel événement,* BÉNÉFIQUE *ou funeste, pourrait-il affecter les hommes sans déclencher à la fois cette foie et ce désespoir?* (A. Chamson.)

71 BESOGNEUX [needy]. The spelling *besoigneux* is obsolete. The word means someone "who is in straits, in a position of difficulty, in need" [based on the French word *besoin*] (Ac.): *Femmes portant des paquets, hommes au col relevé, au nez soucieux, toute une humanité* BESOGNEUSE, *pressée, mécontente de vivre* (H. Troyat). The word, carelessly associated with *besogne* [task, work, job], is often taken today to mean "performing a mediocre job, poorly paid": *Gratte-papier* BESOGNEUX (Petit Robert).

72 BESOIN *(avoir ~ de).* Do not say: *Ce* QUE *nous avons besoin* and do not say: *Il n'a plus* RIEN *besoin."* There, a direct object is not correct. Say: *Ce* DONT *nous avons besoin* [that *which* we need, i.e., what we need] (Littré). Say: *Il n'a plus besoin* DE *rien* [he no longer needs anything, i.e., he no longer has need *of anything*] (Ac.). [The following are taken from the letters of Madame de Sévigné: *Tout ce que vous aurez besoin* (her letter dated Jan. 19, 1674) and *On me demande ce que j'ai besoin* (her letter dated April 8, 1676); the use of this term as a direct transitive construction remains confined in popular usage.]

Avoir besoin can well be used with *que* and the subjunctive: *Il n'a pas besoin qu'on lui dise deux fois la même chose* (Ac.).

With *être besoin* (which is impersonal), you can say, in negative or interrogative sentences: *Est-il besoin* DE *le dire?* [Is it necessary to say it?] or: . . . QUE *je le dise?* [. . .that I say it?]; *Il n'est pas besoin* DE *le dire* [There is no need to say it]; *Il n'y eut pas besoin* QU'*on excitât Paris* (J. Bainville, cited by Deharveng).

73 BEST-SELLER (English *the best,* le meilleur, and *to sell,* vendre): a book that is printed in large quantities and has great sales success in bookstores.

74 BÉTONNIÈRE. People say: *une bétonnière* [cement mixer]: *Il y a une* BÉTONNIÈRE *aussi* (F. Marceau). And people do say (although its use is criticized): *une bétonneuse: On découvrait des tracteurs, des* BÉTONNEUSES (J. Kessel).

75 BI-, TRI-. When these prefixes are on adjectives to indicate periodicity, they express:
(a) At times, the idea of division of a lapse of time: *biquotidien* (which takes place or appears twice a day), *bihebdomadaire* (twice a week), *trihebdomadaire* (three times a week), *bimensuel* (twice a month), *trimensuel* (three times a month).
(b) At other times, the idea of a multiple lapse of time: *bimestriel* (every two months or for a duration of two months), *trimestriel* (every three months), *bisannuel* (every two years), *trisannuel* (every three years).

Usage has strayed from the opinion expressed by Littré, for whom *bihebdomadaire* means "which is done or appears every two weeks" and for whom *bimensuel* means "every two months." For Littré, the idea of "appearing twice a week or twice a month" is expressed by *semi-hebdomadaire* or by *semi-mensuel*.

76 BIDULE. In slang, *un bidule* is an object of some sort, a gadget, a "doodad," a "thingumajig."

77 BILLE (pertaining to a railroad). The word *bille*, in terms of the arts, is a "piece of wood the thickness of a tree, separated from the trunk by two thrusts of a saw and intended to be cut up in quarters and made into planks, etc." (Ac.).

The word *une traverse* [railway tie] is ordinarily used [not *une bille*] to designate each one of the pieces of wood (or of iron, or of reinforced concrete) placed across the tracks and to which the rails are attached: *Les* TRAVERSES *d'un chemin de fer* (Ac.). In this sense, the word *bille* is correct, according to Thérive (see *Ne dites pas. . .*[Do not say. . .] *Dites. . .* [Say. . .], by Englebert / Thérive, p. 59). But this opinion would have to be supported by usage.

78 BILLET [ticket] (railroad, subway, etc.). *Prendre un* BILLET *d'aller et retour* [to get (buy) a round-trip ticket]. BILLET *de métro, de quai.* Do not say: *un* COUPON *de chemin de fer* [a railroad "coupon"]. Also note the use of the word *ticket* [masc.]: *ticket de chemin de fer, de métro, d'autobus . . .*, etc. [railroad (train) ticket, subway ticket, bus ticket . . ., etc.].

79 BISER. In Belgium, this verb is used in talking about cattle that are running wildly, their tails in the air, furious because they have been bitten or stung by flies: *L'orage venait; les vaches, harcelées par les taons,* BISAIENT *dans la prairie.*

80 BISTRO or BISTROT. A wine merchant who maintains a café; a small café, a modest restaurant. It is a popular or familiar word. The two spellings are used: *La petite salle de* BISTRO *s'emplit de monde* (H. Troyat).   *Tu as eu envie de t'asseoir à la terrasse du petit* BISTROT *pour manger des huîtres?* (Colette.)   *Aller manger ensemble dans un* BISTROT (A. Chamson).

81 BLINQUER. In Belgium (from the Flemish language, *blinken*), this verb is used to mean *briller* [to shine], *reluire* [to glow]: *Allons! frottez bien, que ça blinque!*

82 BOUGER [to budge, to move, to stir]. This verb can be used intransitively [i.e., with no direct object]: *Il ne* BOUGE *pas plus qu'une statue* (Ac.). *Il ne* BOUGE *pas du cabaret* (Id.).   *C'est une bête égarée, dit-il, ou morte, car elle ne* BOUGE (G. Sand).

This verb can be used transitively [i.e., with a direct object], especially in familiar, informal usage: BOUGER *la main, le pied* (*Grand Larousse de la Langue française*).   *Sans* BOUGER *le visage* (A. Malraux, cited by Baiwir).

The reflexive verb, *se bouger*, is somewhat archaic: *Et personne, Monsieur, qui* SE *veuille* BOUGER (Molière).

Do not say: *bouger à qq. ch.* Say: *toucher à qq.ch.*

83 BRAS DE CHEMISE. People say *en bras de chemise* [in shirt-sleeves] as well as *en manches de chemise.* [Note that *un bras* is an arm and *une manche* is a sleeve.] Examples: *Il était assis* EN BRAS DE CHEMISE *à côté de moi* (Colette).   *D'un bout à l'autre de l'année, il restait* EN BRAS DE CHEMISE (A. Chamson).   *Justin,* EN MANCHES DE CHEMISE, *emportait un plat* (Flaubert).

People also say *en corps de chemise: De braves types en espadrilles et* EN CORPS DE CHEMISE, *jouant à la pétanque* (A. Billy).

84 BRIQUAILLONS. In Belgium, this word means "fragments or remains of bricks," "remains of an excavation," "rubble": *Des* BRIQUAILLONS *encombraient le chantier.*

85 BROUILLAMINI, EMBROUILLAMINI [mess, muddle]. Both words [masculine nouns] are good, but the first is somewhat outdated: *Il y a bien du* BROUILLAMINI *dans cette affaire* (Ac.).   *Quel*

BROUILLAMINI! (A. Hermant.)   *Un* EMBROUILLAMINI *dans lequel il n'était plus nécessaire que j'aille mettre le nez* (J. Giono).

86 BUSE. This feminine noun is used currently in Belgium for *tuyau de poêle* [stovepipe] or for *un chapeau haut de forme* [stovepipe hat, opera hat, black silk top hat, gibus]. The word also designates a failure in an examination or in an election.

87 BUT [goal, target, mark, aim] (*poursuivre un ~, remplir un~*) [to pursue a goal, to fulfill a goal]. Because purists allege that UN BUT [a goal] is generally fixed, they condemn the term *poursuivre un but*. But if the word *but* is taken metaphorically to mean "an end that a person sets for himself / herself," then *poursuivre un but* is not any more strange that *poursuivre une fin*. The expression is perfectly acceptable because of usage: *Poursuivre un but* (Ac.). *On passe sa vie à* POURSUIVRE UN BUT (Renan).

Purists also reject the expression REMPLIR UN BUT. However, as illogical as it may seem, this expression is used by many: *J'ai toujours rempli mon but* (Stendhal).   *Il a pensé que nulle troupe mieux que la vôtre ne remplirait ce but* (Th. Gautier).

It is somewhat rare to use the expression *réaliser un but: Cet esprit (. . .) réalise le but qu'il se propose. . .*(Pasteur Vallery-Radot).

For a comment about *dans le but,* see entry no. 1140.

88 BUTTE (*être en~à*). Be careful of the spelling: *en butte.* The meaning of *être en butte à* is "to be exposed to": *Être en butte à la raillerie* [To be exposed to raillery] (Ac.).   The meaning of *mettre en butte à* is "to expose to": *Je vous mettrai* EN BUTTE *à vos contradictions.*

89 CADRES [officials of an administrative staff]. This word is used in the plural to designate the entire staff of personnel officials or directors of a firm or administration: *Le représentant des* CADRES *au comité d'entreprise (Grand Larousse de la Langue française).* It is used somewhat popularly in the singular in order to designate a member of such a personnel staff: *C'est un cadre moyen; il est passé* CADRE (*Robert,* Suppl.). In a notice dated May 20, 1965, the French Academy declares that *cadre* in the singular is an improper use.

90 CAFETERIA. A public place where coffee is served, or other nonalcoholic beverages, or dishes of food prepared and ready to serve. Variations of this word are: *cafétéria, caféteria, cafetaria: Après un lunch à trente cents dans une* CAFETERIA (J. Romains).

People also say *caféterie* (a form which is highly recommended): *Françoise (probablement en visite à la* CAFÉTERIE *. . .)* (M. Proust, cited by A. Goosse).

91 CALCAIRE [calcareous] (= which contains lime). Do not say: *Terrain calcareux, zone calcareuse.* Say: . . . *calcaire.* Examples: *Terrain* CALCAIRE (Ac.). *Roche* CALCAIRE *(Robert). Comme l'eau de Megève était très* CALCAIRE . . . (H. Troyat).

92 CANULAR [hoax, prank, trick, hazing]. Formerly, the word *une brimade* was commonly used at the École normale supérieure. Nowadays, it means a hoax, a droll farce, a joke: *Romains s'était rendu célèbre à l'École normale par de ces mystifications que l'on appelle* CANULARS (G. Duhamel).

Some people have written the word as *canulard* (but this spelling has been completely abandoned): *Le* CANULARD *n'avait pas tenu très longtemps* (A. Chamson).

93 CAPARAÇONNER. This verb means to cover a horse with caparison, with trappings. Do not pronounce it as *carapaçonner* by reversing *p* and *r*. The word *caparaçon* [caparison] is from the Spanish *caparazón*, from *capa*, meaning *manteau* [coat, cloak], a kind of covering put on horses.

94 CARITATIF. This word is from the Latin *caritas*, French *amour du prochain*, meaning "love for one's neighbor." This word means "concerning charity, something which is said or done out of the goodness of one's heart." It is a word "in the swim" [in active use] and does not appear in any dictionary. It is used currently in Belgium, especially in ecclesiastical circles, when talking about works of charity: *Aider les institutions* CARITATIVES *de la paroisse.*

95 CARROUSEL. Correct pronunciation is: *ka-roo-zel.* Pronounce *s* as *z*.

96 CARTABLE. To designate a bag, a satchel in which school children put their books, notebooks, etc., people generally say: *un cartable, une serviette* [briefcase], *un portefeuille, une carnassière, une sacoche* [satchel], or *un sac* [bag]: *Un enfant qui revient de l'école, son* CARTABLE *dans les jambes* (Fr.-R. Bastide). SERVIETTE *d'avocat, de professeur, d'écolier* (Ac.). SACOCHE *d'écolier (Robert).*

Anatole France uses the word *une gibecière: C'est un petit bonhomme qui, les mains dans les poches et sa* GIBECIÈRE *au dos, s'en va au collège en sautillant comme un moineau.* And François Mauriac uses the word *une giberne: Ma* GIBERNE, *gonflée de livres, était moins lourde que mon coeur.* [In Belgium, according to the region: *un calepin* (in Brabant), *une mallette* (in Liège).]

97 CARTE POSTALE / CARTE-VUE [picture postcard]. This is a card where on one side there is space for a message and the address of the person to whom it is being sent. On the other side there is a picture of a place, a landscape, a monument, etc. In ordinary use, it is called *une carte postale;* at times, it is described as *une carte postale illustrée* or simple *une carte: Sa chambre était tapissée de* CARTES POSTALES *représentant l'Elbrouz* (H. Troyat). CARTE POSTALE or CARTE *(Petit Robert).   Comment se fait-il que vous avez eu sous la main* UNE CARTE-VUE *de Paris?* (Simenon.)   However, the term *carte-vue* (current in Belgium) is not used in standard French.

98 CASUEL is a word used for "fragile, brittle" in popular French. In refined French, you should be careful not to say, for example: *Attention! Ce vase est casuel!* [In this example, instead of saying *casuel,* say *fragile* or *cassant.*]

99 CATASTROPHÉ [wrecked, ruined, come to grief, sore at heart]. In familiar language, it means: "overthrown, thrown down, wiped out by a catastrophe or by some incident considered, hyperbolically, as a catastrophe": *Ces soirs-là il revenait plus* CATASTROPHÉ *que d'habitude* (P. Daninos).   *Il n'a pas piloté un avion lourd depuis son procès, ni un avion de chasse depuis son départ de l'armée italienne. Il est . . .* CATASTROPHÉ (A. Malraux).

100 CAUSER [to chat]. This verb is used to mean "to have a talk, a conversation in familiar terms with someone": *Ils ont été une heure à* CAUSER *ensemble* (Ac.). CAUSER *de littérature, de voyages* (Id.).   Do not say: *causer à qqn;* say: *causer* AVEC *qqn* (See entry no. 1121, in the section about prepositions): *Je cause français* À *la Vierge* [I am chatting in French *to* (should be AVEC, *with*) the Virgin] (P. Claudel).

The use of *causer (l')allemand, (l')anglais,* etc., is at times found in literature: *Ainsi l'on peut demeurer dans ce magnifique hôtel,* CAUSER ANGLAIS *avec Madame votre épouse, allemand avec Monsieur votre fils, français avec vous, moyennant sept francs par jour?* (L. Veuillot.)   But, in careful French, people say: PARLER *(l') allemand, (le) français,* etc.

101 CENSÉ / SENSÉ. Do not confuse these two words. *Censé* means deemed, considered, regarded, reputed: *Celui qui est trouvé avec les coupables est* CENSÉ *complice* (Ac.).   *Il est* CENSÉ *être à Paris (Robert).*

Sensé (which is the opposite of *insensé* [senseless, mad]) means having good common sense, reason, judgment or conforming to good sense, to reason: *C'est un homme* SENSÉ (Ac.).   *Ce projet n'est pas* SENSÉ (Id.).

The same distinction is made between *censément* [supposedly, apparently] and *sensément* [sensibly, wisely, in a sensible manner], which is very little used.

102 CERVICAL. The following is from the works of A. Billy: *À dix-huit mois, il a eu des convulsions; il lui en reste (. . .) une irritation de l'écorce cervicale. . . .*   And in the works of J. Dutourd, you will find: *Où se cachait tout cela? Dans quel frisottis de quelle lointaine circonvolution cervicale?* Instead of saying *écorce cervicale* [A. Billy] or *circonvolution cervicale* [J. Dutourd] (which is an unfortunate confusion caused by the influence of the word *cerveau* [brain]), what should have been used is: *écorce cérébrale* or *circonvolution cérébrale.*

Cervical (Latin *cervix, -icis,* meaning neck, nape) pertains to the nape of the neck, to the region of the neck: *Muscle* CERVICAL (Ac.).   *Cérébral* (Latin *cerebrum* French *cerveau*) refers to *le cerveau,* the brain: *Congestion* CÉRÉBRALE.

103 CHANCE [luck, fortune, chance] / **RISQUE** [risk, hazard]. *Chance* is used for any effect, favorable or unfavorable, resulting from a given order of things: CHANCE *de succès* (Ac.).   *Il n'a pas de* CHANCE (Id.).   *Il y a moins de* CHANCES *de se faire tuer là-bas que d'avoir ici un accident de voiture* (R. Ikor).

Risque, risquer are used in talking about an eventual danger, a dangerous hazard: RISQUE *de guerre,* RISQUE *d'incendie.*   *Au* RISQUE *d'être tué. N'allez pas vous* RISQUER *dans cette entreprise* (Ac.).

Do not say: *Prenez un billet! Vous risquez de gagner le gros lot!* Say: *. . . vous aurez des* CHANCES *de. . . .*

104 CHANGER, SE CHANGER. In talking about clothing or linen to be changed or replaced by others, these two verbs are good: *Je suis rentré chez moi pour* CHANGER (Ac.).   *Elle se retira dans sa chambre pour se* CHANGER (H. Troyat).

People do say: *changer qqn: Il faut* CHANGER *cet enfant* (Ac.).

105 CHAPEAUX DE ROUES *(sur les ~).* Drivers of automobiles say: *prendre un virage* SUR LES CHAPEAUX DE ROUES or to cut a curve "on two wheels," that is to say, at a very high speed. The expression is used figuratively in the meaning of "in a rapid rhythm," "with much liveliness." [See also entry no. 319.]

106 CHARRUER. This verb, which means to labor with the plough, to drive a plough, is not listed in Littré or in the *Dictionnaire de* *l'Académie*. This rural word is old or literary: *Les rats, les mères, les enfants, les chats pêle-mêle, tout le tas se fond encore vivant dans la terre* CHARRUÉE (R. Ikor).

107 CHASSE AUX SORCIÈRES [witch-hunting]. This locution, borrowed from the American playwright Arthur Miller *(Les Sorcières de Salem) [The Crucible]*, an absurd lesson in favor of liberty and sang-froid), denotes pursuits made against certain persons professing political opinions considered as subversive.

108 CHAUD-FROID. This culinary term refers to food prepared from poultry and game surrounded or covered with gelatin or mayonnaise: CHAUD-FROID *de mauviettes* (Ac.). *Le plateau chargé de* CHAUDS-FROIDS (H. de Régnier). Some people write it as one word, *chaufroid* or even *chaufroix* (as does Bescherelle), which is from the proper name Chaufroix, the chief cook at Versailles in 1774: *Aimera-t-elle le* CHAUFROID *de pintades?* (R. Dorgelès.) CHAUFROIX *de poularde en bordure* (in a menu of the Belgian Court, July 22, 1919, cited by Deharveng).

109 CHAUSSER. People currently say: *mettre ses lunettes* [to put on one's eyeglasses] (Ac.).   In familiar style, you can say *chausser ses lunettes* ["to slip on" one's eyeglasses]: *Elle avait* CHAUSSÉ *des lunettes à branches de fer* (M. Arland).   *Il fallait mieux* CHAUSSER *ses lunettes* (Littré).

110 CHAUSSE-TRAP(P)E [trap]. This word is a modification (from *chausser* and *trappe*) of the old word *chauchetrepe*, composed of *chaucher* [to trample underfoot] and of *treper* [to tread down, to trample]. The traditional spelling is: *chausse-trape*. The Commission of the *Dictionnaire de l'Académie* decided (on Nov. 30, 1961) that in the new edition of the *Dictionary*, the word is to be written as *chausse-trappe*, with two *p*'s.
  In the plural: *des chausse-trap(p)es.*

111 CHECK-UP. This Anglicism denotes a complete medical examination, which can be called, in good French, *un bilan de santé.*

112 CHEMISE [file folder]. This word is used to mean a cover made of paper, cardboard, etc. in which are inserted various documents, papers from a file, a brief, etc.: *Mettez* UNE CHEMISE *à cette liasse, à ce dossier* (Ac.).   *Les pièces étaient classées et réunies sous* UNE CHEMISE *blanche* (H. Bordeaux).   *Tout cela repose dans une* CHEMISE (R. Benjamin).

113 CHOCOLAT. To denote pieces of chocolate more or less thick, in a rectangular shape, such as those which are sold in stores, there are the following words [all of which generally mean "bar"]: *tablette, table, barre, plaque, plaquette, bille, rai(s), raie, bâton, cran: Il m'a donné encorce* UNE TABLETTE *de chocolat* (G. Duhamel).   *Il me passe la moitié d'une grosse* TABLE *de chocolat*   (J. Schlumberger). *Je glissai dans ma musette (. . .) deux* BARRES *de chocolat. . .* (M. Pagnol).   *Il daigna accepter (. . .) quelques* PLAQUES *de chocolat* (M. Bordeaux).   *De la* PLAQUE *de chocolat, le popotier (. . .) détache une* BARRE *. . .* (R. Ikor).   *Xavier avait repris une* BILLE *de chocolat* (G.-E. Clancier).   *Les papiers argentés qui enveloppent les* RAIS *de chocolat* (Fr. Mauriac).   [In Belgium, at times the following word is used: *une ligne.*]

When it is a question of "chocolate [covered] candy," people say: *des crottes de chocolat, des bonbons de chocolat, des bouchées de chocolat,* or simply: *des chocolats, des bouchées: Volodia (. . .) lui offrait des* CHOCOLATS (H. Troyat).   *Une boîte de* CROTTES DE CHOCOLAT (A. Billy).   *Un jour, après avoir croqué un* CHOCOLAT *à la liqueur, il fut ivre* (Béatrix Beck).   *Il lui mit dans la bouche des* CHOCOLATS (M. Van der Meersch).

In this regard, it should be noted that *une praline* (current in Belgium for *une crotte de chocolat*) is "an almond browned in sugar" (Ac.).   *Des* PRALINES *bouillonnant dans un chaudron de cuivre* (R. Sabatier). [See also entry no. 63.]

114 CLENCHE. The word *une clenche* or *clenchette* designates a door latch. A distinction is made between this and *la poignée* of a door, which is a door handle: *Il enleva la* CLENCHE *de la porte qui donnait sur la rue* (R. Queneau).   *Il avait posé la main sur la* POIGNÉE *de la porte* (H. Troyat).   [In Belgium: *cliche* or *clinche* for *poignée.*]

Le bouton of a door is a doorknob made of iron, copper, etc., ordinarily round or oval, which is used simply to open or close a door.

115 CLIMATÉRIQUE [climacteric]. In its strict meaning (which is the only one listed in Littré), this word pertains to one of the ages in a person's life (years in multiples of seven or nine) regarded as critical: *La 63ᵉ année est la grande* CLIMATÉRIQUE. *L'année 1836 fut* CLIMATÉRIQUE *pour Gogol. En plein succès, sa vie s'empoisonne* (E.-M. de Vogüé).

This word has had a slip in meaning and it also means "pertaining to the climate"; this word has thus become a synonym of *climatique: Les conditions* CLIMATÉRIQUES *d'un pays* (Ac.).

The word *climatologique*, which properly pertains to climatology, is taken, by extension, to mean "which depends on the climate": *Influences* CLIMATOLOGIQUES (Ac.).

116 CLOCHE [blister]. According to Bescherelle and the French Academy, *une cloche* can denote a small bubble filled with serous [watery] fluid that forms on the outer skin: *Il lui est venu des* CLOCHES *aux mains à force de travailler* (Bescherelle). The Academy notes that these days people say *une cloque* rather than *une cloche*: *Les pieds pleins de* CLOQUES (Verlaine). Another synonym is *une ampoule*. In medical terms, the word is *une phlyctène* [phlyctena].

117 CLORE, CLÔTURER. These two verbs can mean "to declare closed, terminated": CLORE *une discussion,* CLORE *le débat dans une assemblée délibérante* (Ac.). *La retraite pascale qui fut* CLÔTURÉE *par leur archevêque* (Fr. Mauriac). *Parce qu'il* CLÔTURAIT, *sur une note funèbre, une manifestation . . .* (P.-H. Simon). Note that the Academy does not mention CLÔTURER, either in the meaning of "to surround with an enclosure" or "to terminate." The Academy rejects CLÔTURER *un débat, une séance, un congrès* [you should say: CLORE *un débat, une séance, un congrès*] (Academy's notice dated Nov. 5, 1964).

118 CLOU [furuncle, a boil]. This word can be used to mean a boil, a furuncle: *Je m'aperçois que j'ai un autre petit* CLOU *qui commence* (J. Cocteau).

119 COBAYE [guinea pig]. To pronounce this word correctly, the second syllable should be sounded as in the French vowel *a*, not as if it were spelled with *è*. Pronounce: *ko-BAH-y.*

120 COLLE DE FARINE [flour paste]. This soft and sticky preparation, obtained by mixing flour in water and heating the mixture until it thickens, is called *colle de farine* or *colle de pâte*. [See also the entry **PAPE,** no. 335.]

121 COLLÈGUE / CONFRÈRE. The distinction between these two words, made in H. Bénac's book *Dictionnaire des synonymes*, is quite clear: "*Les collègues* [colleagues] are named officially to exercise a public function or to fulfill a common mission (ministers, deputies, officials, civil servants of the same rank, military officials); *les confrères* [confrère, fellow-member of the same society] belong to the same body, to the same liberal profession, or have the same profession without being officials, without acting in the name of the same administrative body, e.g., academicians, lawyers, doctors, artists, priests, ecclesiastical members of the same order."

In southern France, *collègue* is used for *camarade: Ça va, collègue?* [See also entry no. 500.]

122 COLLOQUER [to collocate]. In legal terms: "to arrange or rank (creditors) in a prescribed order for payment." By extension: "to be relieved of a person or a thing": *Il m'a* COLLOQUÉ *un objet sans valeur* (Ac.).

This verb is also used to mean "to place somehow or other": COLLOQUER *un ami sous les combles (Robert). Provisoirement on les* COLOQUA *dans l'auberge* (Flaubert).

In Belgium, *colloquer* is taken incorrectly to mean *interner* [to confine, to shut in], *séquestrer* [to keep in confinement], *incarcérer* [to incarcerate]: *Il faudrait* COLLOQUER *ces étrangers suspects,* ~ *cet aliéné. Le bandit a été colloqué.*

123 COLLUSION / COLLISION. Distinguish between these two words: *une collusion* is a conspiracy, a secret understanding [for fraud] between two (or more) parties to the detriment of a third. *Une collision* is an impact of two bodies, a violent encounter of two sides, a clash, a struggle.

124 COLMATER. Its first meaning is to raise a low-lying ground or terrain, allowing the water, laden with deposits of slime, to remain there. By extension, the word has taken on the meaning of *boucher* [to cork, to plug], *fermer* [to close, to clog]: *Un trou de purin qu'il fallait* COLMATER. . . (M. Genevoix). *Si nous n'arrivons pas à* COLMATER *cette brèche, nous risquons de perdre la guerre* (A. Maurois).

125 COMMÉMORER [to commemorate]. This word means "to recall, by a ceremony, the memory of a person or a fact."

For the Academy, in its notice dated Feb. 18, 1965, "*commémorer* does not apply to an anniversary but to the event itself which is commemorated by celebrating the anniversary in a festive occasion." An opinion to reform; current usage is to say: *commémorer un anniversaire,* as in this example: *Pour* COMMÉMORER *le dixième anniversaire du traité de Rome* (Charles de Gaulle, May 17, 1967).

Une commémoraison is a ceremony recalling the memory of a person or an event. *La commémoration des morts* is a feast day that the Catholic Church celebrates on All Souls' Day, or it is the mention that the priest makes of deceased persons during the mass for the dead. *Une commémoraison* is the word formerly used for *une commémoration*, which is the word used today.

126 COMMOTIONNER [to shock]. This word is a neologism: *La décharge électrique, cette émotion l'a fortement* COMMOTIONNÉ *(Petit Robert).   Le vieux avait l'air simplement* COMMOTIONNÉ (H. Troyat).

127 COMPENDIEUSEMENT [compendiously, concisely]. (Latin, *compendium;* French, *abrégé* [abridged, condensed]). This word does not mean "abundantly, wordy [or] full of detail"; it means "in abridged form, concisely, succinctly": *Pour quelques-uns qui savent exposer clairement et* COMPENDIEUSEMENT *l'objet de leur visite, combien d'autres qui se perdent dans d'interminables détails oiseux* (Henri-Robert).

As Brunot has observed, because of the length of this word, it is at times taken to mean "lengthily, at length, with all details," which is the complete opposite of its real meaning. The *Dictionnaire général* welcomes this doubtful usage, but you should be careful not to use it in this way.

128 COMPLICITÉ [complicity]. This word means "participation in the misdemeanor or crime of another" (Ac.). At times, this unfavorable meaning fades away and, by extension, the word takes on the meaning of "a deep, spontaneous and often unexpressed understanding between persons" *(Petit Robert);* it then becomes almost a synonym of "concurrence, collaboration, cooperation, agreement": *Pour bien réussir une convalescence, il y faut la* COMPLICITÉ *du printemps* (A. Gide, in the *Grand Larousse encyclopédique).   Avec mes proches, je vis dans une transparente* COMPLICITÉ (S. de Beauvoir).

129 COMPRESSER [to pack (familiar use)]. This is an old word which is trying to make a comeback: *La scène en cellulose pure,* COMPRESSÉE *à 250 atmosphères* (G. Duhamel).   *En pénétrant dans l'ascenseur, elle crut étouffer entre tant de chairs* COMPRESSÉES (H. Troyat).

130 CONCERNÉ [concerned, affected]. In its passive participial form, this word has been contested. Littré cautions against it and so does usage: *Votre ami est* CONCERNÉ *dans cette affaire* (Littré).   *Les intérêts* CONCERNÉS *par cette mesure. . .* (Id.).   *Un Grec était* CONCERNÉ *par ses héros historiquement* (A. Maurois). [See also entry no. 279.]

131 CONCRÉTER, CONCRÉTISER. The Academy gives only *se concréter*, a term in chemistry. *Concréter* [to concrete] is rather rare: *Qui pouvait mieux sculpter et peindre les idoles, mieux* CONCRÉTER *ce rêve?* (G. Duhamel.)   *Concrétiser* [to put in concrete form] is what is used: CONCRÉTISER *magnifiquement l'indicible* (É. Henriot).

132 CONDITION *(être en ~).* In talking about a person who serves in the capacity of servant in a house, people say: *être (mettre, se mettre, entrer, rester,* etc.) *en condition,* or *en place,* or *en service.*

133 CONDOLÉANCE(S). This word is written either with or without final *s* in *une lettre de* CONDOLÉANCE, or *une lettre de* CONDOLÉANCES (Ac.).

134 CONFÉRENCE [lecture]. People say: *faire, donner, prononcer une conférence* [to give or deliver a lecture]: *Hier, j'ai* FAIT *une conférence non loin d'ici* (J. Green).   *Raymond Lefebvre me demanda de* DONNER *une conférence* (G. Duhamel).   *Douze conférences que M. André Maurois* PRONONÇA *en Amérique* (R. Kemp).

135 CONFIANCE *(faire ~ à)* [to trust]. This locution, in spite of purists, has become widely accepted in good usage since the beginning of the 20th century: FAISONS CONFIANCE *au choix des siècles* (A. Maurois). *Je lui* FAIS CONFIANCE (J. de Lacretelle). FAITES CONFIANCE *au sommeil* (Alain).

136 CONGÉ *(donner ~)* [to give leave]. People say: *donner congé* (of an apartment, for the term, etc.): DONNER CONGÉ *à un locataire* (Robert).   *J'avais* DONNÉ CONGÉ *de mon appartement* (H. Bordeaux). *L'appartement du deuxième étage pour lequel on m'a* DONNÉ CONGÉ (G. Beaumont).

  You can say: *renoncer à mon appartement* [to give up my apartment] but not: *renoncer mon appartement.* And do not say: *donner son renon.* [See also the entry *renon,* no. 398.]

137 CONJECTURE / CONJONCTURE. Distinguish between these two words. *Conjecture:* a probable judgment, an opinion based on appearances, a surmise, supposition, conjecture: *Se perdre en* CONJECTURES (Ac.).   *Conjoncture:* a situation resulting from a combination of circumstances, a particular state of affairs, a conjuncture, a predicament: *Se trouver dans des* CONJONCTURES *difficiles* (Ac.).

138 CONSÉQUENT. This word properly means: "which reasons or acts logically, with thoughts that are connected consequentially," or "which is the consequence, result, outcome of something": *Cet homme est* CONSÉQUENT *dans ses discours* (Ac.). *Sa conduite est* CONSÉQUENTE *à ses principes* (Id).

The word *conséquent* has taken on the meaning of "important," "considerable," which is widely found in popular language and, at times, in literature, in spite of Littré and many grammarians: *Envoyez-moi le fauteuil couvert de cuir noir et pour un derrière aussi* CONSÉQUENT *que le vôtre* (Stendhal). *Il n'y avait pas dans les environs de Combray de ferme si* CONSÉQUENTE *que Françoise ne supposât qu'Eulalie eût pu facilement l'acheter* (M. Proust). *C'est une des plus belles pages de la biographie des deux chefs, et pour Foch, (. . .) l'une des plus* CONSÉQUENTES (L. Madelin).

Those who love to use "carefully polished" French will be careful not to use *conséquent* in the meaning of *important* or *considérable* (this use was rejected by the Academy in its notice of Nov. 19, 1964).

139 CONSIDÉRER [to consider, to regard, to look upon]. This verb, in the meaning of *juger* [to judge], *réputer* [to repute, to deem], regularly requires the attribute and the direct object to be introduced by *comme* [like, as]: *Ses soldats le* CONSIDÉRAIENT COMME *un père* (Ac.). *Je* CONSIDÈRE *cette promesse* COMME *sacrée* (A. Maurois).

However, you will find in literature the use of *considérer* with an attribute but without using *comme* to introduce it, even though this was condemned by the Academy (on Feb. 24, 1965): *Je ne pus me considérer dégagé d'un grand poids* (É. Henriot). *Attitude spécifiquement française que je ne considère certes pas élégante* (G. Duhamel). If you are careful of the way you use the French language, you will be careful not to use *considérer* incorrectly, as in these last two examples where *comme* should have been used [*comme dégagé; comme élégante*].

140 CONSTELLÉ [constellated, star-studded]. Certain authors, forgetting the etymology of the word (Latin, *cum*; French, *avec*; *stella, étoile*, star), have added the complement *d'étoiles* to *constellé* [which is redundant]: *Un plafond bleu* CONSTELLÉ D'ÉTOILES *comme le ciel* (Th. Gautier). *Un manteau d'azur* CONSTELLÉ D'ÉTOILES (A. France). *Les vastes cieux de sombre azur,* CONSTELLÉS D'ÉTOILES *par myriades* (É. Henriot).

141 CONTACTER [to contact]. This Anglicism, which is "hideous and weak," says R. Kemp, is condemned by the Academy (notice dated May 20, 1965), which recommends: *se mettre en rapport,* or *prendre contact avec, rencontrer, toucher,* or *s'entretenir avec.* The word is being introduced: *C'est toujours "Chez Dupont" qu'on* CON-TACTAIT *les gars. . .* (P. Vialar).

142 CONTROUVER properly means "to make up or to fabricate entirely" or "falsely, untruthfully": *Certains chansonniers ont* CON-TROUVÉ *un peuple imaginaire* (A. Thérive).

Some authors use the word improperly by giving it the meaning of *démentir* [to give the lie to, to belie, to contradict, to refute] or of *contester* [to challenge, to dispute]: *Hypothèse aujourd'hui controuvée. . .* (A. Dauzat). *La sagesse des vieillards est sans doute aujourd'hui une des notions les plus* CONTROUVÉES (R. Kanters). *Ce point a été souvent* CONTROUVÉ (S. de Beauvoir).

143 CONVOLER, for the Academy, means "to contract a new marriage, in speaking of a woman." It is a definition that does not conform to the etymology of the word or to its actual use. *Convoler* simply means "to get married" or "to marry again" and applies to a man as well as to a woman: *Enlever par force de la maison des pères les filles qu'on menait marier, afin qu'il ne semblât pas que ce fût de leur consentement qu'elles* CONVOLAIENT *dans les bras d'un homme* (Molière). *En dix ans, neuf cent soixante et une «filles du Roi» gagnent la colonie et y* CONVOLENT (J. Chastenet). *Cette grande dame avait déjà* CONVOLÉ *à l'âge de quinze ans* (J.-P. Chabrol). *Il est probable qu'il* [Hannibal] *ne consentit à se marier qu'après son élévation au poste suprême. Alors il* CONVOLA *en justes noces avec une Espagnole . . .* (J. Carcopino). *Le gros Luther* CONVOLANT *au sortir du cloître entre les bras d'une nonne* (M. Yourcenar).

144 COTER [to mark, to grade]. This verb is used in talking about an assignment, a piece of written work, a student's exercise; in the same way, the noun *la cote* [the grade, the mark] is used: *la* COTE *d'un devoir* [the mark on a written assignment]: [Alain] *pouvait le moins étant capable de plus; mais il eût dû se garder—comme on voudrait lire ses copies de concours!—de le laisser voir trop tôt! Les meilleures pages des "Dieux" eussent été mal* COTÉES (R. Kemp). *La composition française a été* COTÉE *19* [19 out of 20] (Cl. Farrère). *La* COTE *d'un devoir* (Robert).

In France, most often the verb *noter* is used instead of *coter* and *une note* is used instead of *une cote: Il avait tenu à me* NOTER *20 sur 20* (Cl. Farrère). *J'eus la* NOTE *20* (Id.).

145 COU(P) *(monter le~).* Theoretically, it would be desirable to make a distinction here between *monter* and *se monter* and to write *mon-*

ter le coup à qqn [to take someone in, to frame (American idiom)] when the meaning is *lui en faire accroire* [to impose upon, to delude], *l'abuser* [to take advantage of someone]. But *se monter le cou* is used when one wants to express, more or less, the following ideas: *se monter la tête* [to get excited, to get worked up] (= *s'exalter* [to exalt oneself, to grow excited], *se faire des illusions* [to deceive oneself, to labor under a delusion]) or *se hausser du col* [to set oneself higher than someone else] (= *afficher de l'orgueil, des prétentions, se mettre en colère* [to display or flaunt one's pride, pretentions, to become angry]) [Cf.: *Les maisons collées contre le rocher avaient l'air de se monter le col*] (J. Giono).

But, in actual use, there is a good deal of confusion [in the use of these terms] and writers are seldom careful to make a distinction: *Vous vous laisseriez* MONTER LE COU *par ces gens qui ne cherchent qu'une chose, c'est à vendre* (M. Proust). *L'homme* SE MONTE LE COUP. *Il idéalise la femme* (Aragon). *Cela roule. Mais il ne faut pas trop* SE MONTER LE COUP *pourtant* (M. Barrès). *Je ne me suis jamais* MONTÉ LE COU *sur cette famille* (A. Chamson).

146 COUPE SOMBRE. *Une coupe sombre* is "the action of diminishing only the thickness, the density of a forest" (Ac.); in other words, to cut down only some of the trees. According to that, in its figurative meaning, *faire une coupe sombre dans un écrit* [to make cuts in a piece of writing] would logically mean "to remove *some* sentences, *some* passages." But usage has decided otherwise and the Academy notes that *une coupe sombre* applies, especially in a figurative sense, to cuts made in a text, to a good number of deletions made in a piece of writing. It is used similarly in speaking of other things besides writings: *Peu de mois après notre séparation de juillet 1914, d'affreuses* COUPES SOMBRES *avaient clairsemé nos rangs* (M. Genevoix). *On a fait* UNE COUPE SOMBRE *dans le personnel de l'entreprise* [A cut was made in the personnel of the firm] (i.e., *on a licencié beaucoup d'employés* [a purge was carried out, many employees were dismissed, laid off] *(Robert)*.

147 COUPER, DÉCOUPER. People say: *couper* or *découper* [to cut] the pages, the leaves of a book (along the edges in order to separate the pages): *On lui apporta l'ouvrage sans être* COUPÉ (Chateaubriand). *Il aimait à* COUPER *les feuillets des livres* (A. France). *Il suffit de lire les cinquante premières pages et de* DÉCOUPER *le reste* (J. Renard). *Nous* DÉCOUPIONS *les premières livraisons de la "Nouvelle Revue Française"* (P.-H. Simon). *Sarrazin prit le volume (. . .). Je ne le* DÉCOUPERAI *pas, si vous voulez, dit Frayssinous en riant* (L. Martin-Chauffier).

When it has to do with a fragment clipped from a newspaper, a book, etc., you can say *couper* or *découper, une coupure* or *une découpure: Je* COUPE *le dernier article du journal* (Stendhal). *Un quatrième correspondant* DÉCOUPE *dans un journal et m'envoie ce titre. . .* (A. Hermant). *La concierge, en passant, lui remit* UNE COUPURE *de revue* (R. Rolland). *Nous ne croyons pas inutile de copier ici, sans commentaires, ces* DÉCOUPURES (A. Gide).

148 COUPER *qqn.* From *couper la parole à qqn* [to cut short someone's words], it has been possible, in familiar language, to go a step further and say *couper qqn* [to cut someone short]: *Si vous trouvez que je divague, allez-y carrément,* COUPEZ-*moi* (M. Genevoix). *Ils détournent vite la conversation à moins qu'ils ne vous* COUPENT *brutalement* (Montherlant). This use of *couper* [i.e., *couper quelqu'un*, to cut someone off] is criticized by the Academy in its communication dated Nov. 13, 1969.

149 COURBATU [stiffness of a person], **COURBATURÉ** [stiff, ache all over]. Both words are good (the Academy does not recognize the second): *Je me couchais le soir, heureux,* COURBATU (G. Duhamel). *Le jour suivant, je me réveillai* COURBATURÉ (A. Gide). *Il était tout* COURBATURÉ (A. Chamson).

150 COURRERIES. This noun (from *courir*, to run) is used currently in Belgium in the meaning of "running errands," "doing a lot of foot work," "much running around from place to place"; the word implies the general idea of a lot of legwork for nothing.

151 COURS [course], **CLASSE** [class], **LEÇON** [lesson]. Say: *faire un cours,* or *donner un cours,* or *professer un cours, avoir cours, avoir un cours, il y a cours: Hier, j'ai* FAIT *mon premier cours à des officiers* (J. Green). *Charles Richet* DONNAIT *son cours* (G. Duhamel). PROFESSER *un cours* (Ac.). *Dans l'après-midi, je n'*AVAIS *pas cours* (P. Guth). *Nous* AVONS *un cours de littérature anglaise ici même* (J. Green). IL Y A COURS *de droit canon* (A. Billy).

As for *une classe* or *une leçon,* there are the following expressions: *faire la classe, faire classe, il y a classe, avoir classe, avoir une classe; faire une leçon, donner leçon, donner une leçon, prononcer une leçon: C'est la dernière fois que je vous* FAIS LA CLASSE (A. Daudet). *Il n'est pas habitué à* FAIRE CLASSE (Littré). IL Y A CLASSE *aujourd'hui* (J. Renard). *Pourvu qu'on* AIT *lecture et pas* CLASSE! (G. Cesbron.) *Il a* FAIT AUJOURD'HUI UNE LEÇON *sur Spinoza* (Ac.). *Il (. . .)* FAISAIT *cette* LEÇON *sans prononcer un seul mot* (A. Chamson). *Il ne pourra lui* DONNER LEÇON *comme il faut* (Molière). *Il me souvient*

d'avoir PRONONCÉ *(. . .) une* LEÇON *sur la médecine et l'étatisme*
(G. Duhamel).
Do not say: *donner classe, donner la classe.*
Un interclasse is the short interval between two classes: *Au lycée,*
pendant les INTERCLASSES. . . (R. Ikor). In Belgium, teachers and
professors say: *une fourche.*

152 COURT. "To go by the shortest route" can be expressed by *cou-*
per au court or *prendre au court, au plus court, par le plus court,*
prendre le plus court: Pour couper AU COURT *à travers les bois* (Nerval). *Le fameux Drouet (. . .) prit* AU COURT *par les bois*
(M. Barrès). *Pour couper* AU PLUS COURT *dans le taillis*
(G. Bernanos).   *Elle prendra* PAR LE PLUS COURT (J. Schlumberger).

153 COURTISER, FRÉQUENTER. *Courtiser* a woman or a girl is "to
be with her regularly, to try to please her, to court her": *Il a épousé*
cette jeune fille qu'il COURTISAIT *depuis longtemps* (Ac.).
In the same meaning, people say: FRÉQUENTER *une femme, une*
jeune fille (which is a provincialism): *Je suis fâché que tu n'aies pas eu*
le courage de renoncer à la FRÉQUENTER (G. Sand, in *Petit Robert*).
It is also a provincialism to use these two verbs without a direct
object in the meaning which has just been indicated: *Si jeune en-*
core, il COURTISE *déjà; il (or elle)* FRÉQUENTE *déjà. Elle est trop jeune*
cette petite; je ne veux pas qu'elle FRÉQUENTE! *(Robert.) Ma mère apprit*
bien vite que je FRÉQUENTAIS (B. Clavel).   *Un jour sur deux, le gros*
Jules plantait quatre poteaux. Le lendemain, il disparaissait jusqu'au
soir, il FRÉQUENTAIT (J.-P. Chabrol).
If it is only a matter of puppy love or having "a crush" on
someone, generally without deep feelings, people use *flirter* [to
flirt], *avoir un flirt (une amourette, un béguin)* with this boy or that
girl.

154 COUSSIN [cushion]. This word is used for *un oreiller* [pillow] not
only in Belgium, but in several regions in France.

155 CRACK. An English word, meaning "champion" or "ace," especially in sports.

156 CRAMIQUE. In Belgium, this word is a sort of bread with sugar
and Corinth grapes.

157 CRÉATIVITÉ. This word is fashionable. It designates an aptitude
to create, to invent something. It appears, in particular, in peda-

gogical circles: *Ce sont les écoles qui feront trouver à la* CRÉATIVITÉ *son vrai langage.*

158 CRESSON [cress, watercress]. The correct pronunciation is: *kré-son*. The pronunciation of the vowel *e* as if it were mute (which, according to Martinon, is used at least in Paris and in part of northern France), or the pronunciation of the vowel *e* as if it were open *è* [as in père], is less frequent.

159 CROCHE-PIED [the skillful art of tripping someone]. *Un croche-pied* is not listed in Littré or the *Dictionnaire de l'Académie*. These days, it is commonly used: *L'art difficile du* CROCHE-PIED (M. Pagnol). *Qu'on lui épargne les* CROCHE-PIEDS *et les pinçons!* (H. Troyat).

160 CRU [raw]. In talking about the weather, *cru* (for "cold and humid") is a provincialism used in Belgium, northern France, and Canada: *L'air est* CRU *dans ces mines* (P. Gascar).

161 CULBUTE [somersault, tumble]. *Une culbute* is a physical stunt in which one thrusts one's body one full revolution either forward or backward head over heels. There are various words for *une culbute* depending on the region, for example: *cumulet* (very current in Belgium), *coupèrou* (in Liège), *cutourniau* or *cutrumiau* (in Mons, Tournai, etc), *cud'boûré* (in Gaume), *cumariot* (in Champagne), *faire la cupesse* (in Switzerland), etc.

Note also that the following two expressions are in good French: *faire des cabrioles* and *faire des galipettes* [to turn somersaults], the second of which is used in familiar language. *Un roulé-boulé* is a somersault one makes while one's body is rolled in a ball in order to deaden the shock.

162 DÉCADE, DÉCENNIE. Etymologically, *une décade* (Latin, *decas, -adis;* from the Greek, *dekas, -ados;* French, *une dizaine*) is ten or about ten. The word is used to designate a period of ten years: *Pendant la* DÉCADE *1860–1870* (A. Maurois). *La dernière* DÉCADE *du XIXe siècle* (G. Duhamel).

But *une décennie* has come into competition with *une décade* in designating a period of ten years: *La* DÉCENNIE *1920–1930* (A. Maurois). *La* DÉCENNIE *tragique 1940–1950* (P.-H. Simon).

It would be desirable to make a distinction between *décade* (period of ten *days*) and *décennie* (period of ten *years*), but in present use the two words are still in competition when it is a matter of a period of ten years. Note that the French Academy (in a notice dated Nov. 18, 1965) declares that to indicate "a period of ten years," *une décennie* [a decade] is the word that must be used.

163 DÉCRISPER [to thaw social or political relations]. This verb is based on the verb *crisper* [to contract, distort facial expressions, to get on one's nerves]. The word is especially favored by people in politics. The same is true of the noun *une décrispation*, which is equivalent to *une détente* [a relaxing of tense feelings].

164 DÉDOUBLER. The Academy's definition of this word is "to re-store to a single unit what was double." This meaning is now somewhat rare. In current use, the word means "to divide into two, to make two parts out of one": DÉDOUBLER *une classe, dans un lycée* (Ac.). *Dédoubler un train,* i.e., to convert one train into two.

165 DÉFICIENCE [deficiency]. The word *une déficience* is not listed in Littré or in the *Dictionnaire de l'Académie*. The word came from English at the beginning of the 20th century and it is in current use: *Il est étrange qu'un écrivain bénéficie quelquefois de ses manques, de ses* DÉFICIENCES (Fr. Mauriac).

166 DÉFINITIVES *(en~)* [in a word, in short]. People used to say *en définitif:* EN DÉFINITIF, *je dois prévenir Votre Excellence que . . .* (Stendhal).   But this form has fallen into disuse and now *en définitive* is used: EN DÉFINITIVE, *que voulez-vous? que prétendez-vous?* (Ac.)

167 DÉGINGANDÉ [lanky, gangling]. This adjective means having something out of proportion in one's tall stature or out of joint in one's way of walking. Correct pronunciation of *dégin . . .* is as in *dé-jin. . . .*

168 DÉGUSTER [to taste, to sample food or drink, to sip, to relish]. This word is used not only in the meaning of *to drink* but also in the meaning of *to eat with great pleasure:* DÉGUSTER *de l'eau-de-vie* (Ac.).   *Un certain civet à l'ancienne qu'il était impatient de* DÉGUSTER (J.-L. Vaudoyer).

169 DÉJETÉ [warped, buckled, crooked, off its natural direction]: *Le bois de ce meuble s'est* DÉJETÉ (Academy).   *Sa colonne vertébrale s'est un peu* DÉJETÉE (Id.).

By analogy, people say: *Cet homme est tout* DÉJETÉ [that is to say, his body is curved, bent over, deformed]. But people should not say, as they do in Belgium: *Tout est* DÉJETÉ *chez lui* to mean *Tout est* EN DÉSORDRE *chez lui.*

170 DÉMYSTIFIER, DÉMYTHIFIER. There is good reason to distinguish between these two words (Academy's notice dated Oct. 21, 1965): *démystifier* is "to free the victim from a perplexity, to clear up the error, the deception." *Démythifier* is "to remove [from a word, an idea, etc.] its misleading value of a myth": DÉMYTHIFIER *une notion, un personnage* (*Robert,* Suppl.). Since both these words imply a certain idea of deceit and of error, they are often confused in usage and that is regrettable. The Supplement to *Robert* notes that *démythifier* is used in the meaning of *démystifier.*

The same observations can be made about *démystification* and *démythification.*

171 DENTITION, DENTURE. Strictly speaking, there is a distinction between *une dentition* [dentition], which is the formation of teeth at various stages in life, and *une denture* [denture], which is a set of teeth. But in modern usage, *dentition* is currently used (accepted by the Academy) as a synonym of *denture: La bouche profite d'une forte* DENTITION (Colette). *Ses épaisses lèvres de Bambara découvraient une* DENTITION *canine* (Fr. Mauriac).

172 DÉODORANT. This word is an Anglicism and, for the Academy, it is badly formed (Academy's notice dated Feb. 17, 1969). One ought to say: *un désodorisant;* nevertheless, *un déodorant* is very much in use today: *Ils faisaient une consommation régulière de crèmes pour la peau, lotions astringentes, fonds de teint,* DÉODORANTS *et même poudre* (J.-L. Curtis). However, there is a distinction between the two words: *déodorant* for care of the body; *désodorisant* for a more general use, e.g., to get rid of unpleasant odors.

173 DESIGN. This English word, which comes close to meaning "a project or creation of new forms," (whether it be *le dessein* [the design] leading to *le dessin* [the drawing or sketch]), has taken hold notably in the fields of industrial arts, furniture, furnishing, decorative arts, and fashion.

174 DÉSUET, DÉSUÈTE [obsolete, old-fashioned, antiquated]. This adjective (which Thérive ranks among the words of "symbolard" style [pejorative way of saying symbolist style]) was entered in the 8th edition of the *Dictionnaire de l'Académie* in 1935. Today it is commonly used: *Deux poèmes médiocres du symbolisme le plus*

DÉSUET (J. Romains, in *Robert*).   *La grâce* DÉSUÈTE *qui émanait de ce lieu* (É. Estaunié).

At times, one hears the word pronounced as *dé-zuet*, but that is not the general pronunciation: the Academy points out that, in this word, the *s* is pronounced hard (as in *penser*). That is also the opinion of the *Grand Larousse encyclopédique* and of Warnant.

175 **DÉTONER** [to detonate, to explode] / **DÉTONNER** [to jar, to clash (colors), to sing or play out of tune, to be out of place]. Distinguish between these two words: *détoner* is to explode with a noise, producing a detonation; *détonner* is to be out of tune, not to be in harmony: *Il y a dans ce livre des choses qui* DÉTONNENT (Ac.).   *Cet individu* DÉTONNE *dans un tel milieu* (Id.).

176 **DÉTRITUS** [detritus, rubbish, refuse]. The *s* is pronounced.

177 **DÉVIATION** [deviation, detour]. At times, one sees road signs which indicate, with the word *détournement*, that it is necessary to make a detour. In France, the word *déviation* is used: *M. Édouard Bonnefous a inauguré hier (. . .) la* DÉVIATION *de Rambouillet sur la route nationale n° 10* (in *Le Figaro*, July 3, 1957).

Évitement [shunting, railroad switch] is a railroad term: *une voie d'évitement* is a railway track where trains and railroad cars are shunted to a siding to allow the main track to be clear.

178 **DIFFÉRENT** [different] / **DIFFÉREND** [disagreement in opinion]. Distinguish between these two words. *Différent* is an adjective, meaning something which differs, which is not the same thing; whereas *différend* is a noun, meaning a disagreement in opinion, a debate, a dispute: *Ils ont eu* DIFFÉREND *ensemble* (Ac.).

179 **DIFFICULTUEUX** [fussy, unaccommodating]. This adjective means "inclined to raise or create difficulties at every moment about anything, [a person who is] unaccommodating": *C'est un homme fort* DIFFICULTUEUX (Ac.).   Do not use this word in the meaning of "involving difficulties" [for example, a difficult lesson is *une leçon difficile*]. By extension, one can say: *une opération difficultueuse*.

180 **DIGEST.** This English word (which is pronounced either in the English or French way) means "a summary" or "an abridgment." It is used to describe a book, a publication which is presented in the form of a résumé. It can also designate a publication containing such résumés.

181 DIGESTE. This word, in the meaning of "which is digested easily," is not listed in Littré or by the Academy, which give only *digestible* [digestible] meaning, "that which is digested easily." *Robert* (Supplement) does list *digeste;* the *Grand Larousse encyclopédique* does also: *La chair de poisson est* DIGESTE. *Lexis* lists it also.

182 DILEMME [dilemma]. In its strict meaning, this word means: a reasoning whose major premise states a disjunction (often introduced by *ou bien. . ., ou bien. . .* [either. . ., or. . .]) and in which the two alternative terms lead to the same conclusion.

The following is a type, according to Aristotle: *Ou bien il ne faut pas philosopher, ou bien il faut philosopher; s'il ne faut pas philosopher, pour montrer qu'il ne faut pas philosopher, il faut encore philosopher.*

Another type: *Ou bien tu étais à ton poste ou bien tu n'y étais pas; si tu y étais, tu n'as pas donné l'alarme qu'il fallait donner; si tu n'y étais pas, tu as manqué à ton devoir; dans les deux cas, tu mérites la mort.*

Such is the usual meaning of the word. But in current usage, *dilemme* is often taken in the meaning of "an alternative containing two proposals which are opposite or contradictory, between which one must make a choice": The word, then, becomes a synonym of the word *alternative: Il refuse de résoudre le* DILEMME: *"Détruire Notre-Dame de Paris ou la petite fille qui joue au cerceau sur le parvis"* (R. Kemp). *La guerre ou la paix? Une question de jours, une question d'heures—et le* DILEMME *terrible sera résolu. . .* (J. Kessel).

You must be careful not to pronounce and not to write the word as "dilem*n*e." [Victor Hugo used this form several times in his personal notebooks.] [See also entry no. 22.]

183 DISCOUNT. This is an American word [whose equivalent in French is *une remise, un escompte*]. It designates a reduction which is used in the language of publicity to denote sales containing considerably reduced prices made possible by a lowering of general costs.

184 DISPOSABLE. In the medical field, this word is used to describe an object, e.g., a syringe, tweezers, tongs, which is thrown away after use: *détruire les* DISPOSABLES. A good substitute for this Anglicism would be *un jetable* [a throwaway]. [Canadians, at times, use the word *uniservice: détruire les uniservices.*]

185 DOPAGE [stimulant, dope]. This word is used in the sports world to refer to certain stimulants. *Le dopage* would advantageously replace the word *le doping.*

186 DOSE. In Belgium, this word means an eruption, a redness on the skin: *Il a le dos plein de* DOSES.

187 DOUBLER, REDOUBLER *une classe.* These two verbs are good. [*Redoubler une classe*—more commonly used than *doubler une classe*—means to be kept back or down for a year; to repeat (in U.S.A.)]: *M. le Procureur. . . l'envoya à Paris pour qu'il* DOUBLÂT *sa rhétorique au collège d'Harcourt* (A. France). *Au lycée, il avait dû* REDOUBLER *successivement deux classes* (J. de Lacretelle).

The student who repeats a class is called *un doublant* or *un redoublant.* [In Belgium: *doubleur, redoubleur*].

188 DOUILLE [socket (for an electric bulb)]. *Une douille* is the part attached to one end of an electric cord where the base of a light bulb is inserted. In Belgium and Canada, the word commonly used is *socket.* In good French, the word is *une douille.*

189 DRACHE. This noun is used currently in Belgium for *une averse* [a shower, downpour]. *Dracher, pleuvoir à verse: Quelle* DRACHE! *Il va* DRACHER! [*Une drache* is from the Dutch, *draschen*, as listed in *Petit Robert.*]

190 DRÈVE. In Belgium and northern France, *une drève* (from the Dutch, *dreef*) is used for *une allée bordée d'arbres* [a path bordered with trees]: *La belle drève de Mariemont.*

191 DRINGUELLE. This word is a Germanism: *trinkgeld. Une dringuelle* is used in Belgium for the word *un pourboire* [a tip], *une gratification: Cela mérite une bonne* DRINGUELLE. [In Canada: *un bon* TIPE; TIPER = to give a tip].

192 DRUGSTORE or **DRUG-STORE.** (From the Anglo-American words "drug," *une drogue*, and "store," *une boutique.*) *Le drugstore* is a store open to all, with bar and restaurant, where pharmaceutical products, stationery, books, bibelots [knick-knacks], beauty creams, eaux de toilette, etc. are sold.

193 DUCASSE. This word is a popular form of *dédicace* [dedication]. The word is used in northern France and by Walloons [in southern and southeastern parts of Belgium and adjacent regions in France]: a village feast, a parish feast, a kermesse [a village fair, charity fair].

194 DUPLEX. For professional real estate agents and brokers: an apartment of "high standing" generally equipped with all the comforts, built on two floors connected by an inner stairway and creating, more or less, an atmosphere of a private home in a large building.

195 ÉCRITURE [writing, style]. This word is in common use today; it means "the manner of writing" and is a synonym of *le style:* L'ÉCRITURE *artiste des Goncourt. L'étrange roman! (. . .)* L'ÉCRITURE *en est excellente. Elle serait meilleure encore sans de menues fautes de grammaire* (A. Billy).   *C'est une pièce bien faite, d'une* ÉCRITURE *assez ferme* (P. Gaxotte).

196 EFFICIENCE (derived from the English word "efficiency"). *L'efficience* means "efficacy, effectiveness, having the capacity to yield or produce efficient output or service." It is a neologism, in common use today: *Le monde moderne ne reconnaît d'autre règle que l'*EFFICIENCE (G. Bernanos).

197 ÉGAILLER *(s'~).* This verb means "to scatter, to disperse." It came from dialects in western France and it is in use today. At times it is used when speaking of a person in the meaning "to stray away from the proper direction," "to draw aside from," "to go off in another direction," or "to drift away": *Ces soldats* S'ÉGAILLÈRENT (Ac.).   *Volontiers elle* S'ÉGAILLAIT *dans les prés voisins* (H. Bordeaux).

As for the spelling of this verb, do not confuse it with *égayer* [to cheer up, to enliven].

198 ÉLANCER [to give stabbing pains], **ÉLANCEMENT** [stabbing or shooting pain]. These two words are used when speaking of a sharp, acute pain: *Une douleur lui* ÉLANÇA *dans une molaire* (H. Queffélec).   *Il attendait que ses* ÉLANCEMENTS *à la tête fussent un peu calmés* (M. Proust).

In this meaning, do not use: *lancer, lancement.*

199 ÉMÉRITE. This word is used in the meaning of "retired, pensioned off, honorary, emeritus," but in this sense it has become obsolete: *Professeur* ÉMÉRITE [Professor emeritus] (Ac.). In ordinary use today, it means "remarkable in some field of knowledge or in the practice of something": *Philologue* ÉMÉRITE [remarkable philologist], *buveur* ÉMÉRITE [remarkable drinker] (Ac.).   *Nous ne devons pas oublier que Jean Rostand est aussi un moraliste* ÉMÉRITE (G. Duhamel).

The quality, privilege, and honor of the person who, according to certain rules, keeps the title of a function after having ceased practicing it, is called *honorariat: Conférer l'*HONORARIAT *à un ancien notaire, à un ancien professeur* (Ac.).   *Éméritat* is used in Belgium (but very seldom in France?) and is listed in Littré: "status, prerogatives of a professor emeritus."

200 ÉMOTIONNER [to stir, to move, to thrill]. This verb, which Littré finds to be "in rather bad style," but "regularly used" (just as in the use of the verbs *affectionner, illusionner,* etc), has become current. Unlike the verb *émouvoir* [to move, to stir, as in a moral and emotional impression], the verb *émotionner,* whose conjugation is very easy [not so with *émouvoir*], is very widely used now. As Littré notes, *émouvoir* applies to that which is touching, sad, etc.; whereas *émotionner* is used for minor perturbations or anxieties in daily life: *Ton arrivée m'a tant* ÉMOTIONNÉE (A. Daudet).

201 EMPRISE. In administrative terms, this word designates the action of taking land by expropriation. In current usage, it has taken on the meaning of "upper hand, influence, authority, power": *L'*EMPRISE *de cet écrivain sur la jeuneese. . .* (Ac.).   *Quelle* EMPRISE *Père exerce encore sur nous!* (R. Martin du Gard.)

202 ENCOURIR *(s'~).* The reflexive verb *s'encourir* (or *s'en courir*), *se mettre à courir* [to start to run], was commonly used in the 17th century: *À la fin le pauvre homme /* S'EN COURUT *chez celui qu'il ne réveillait plus* (La Fontaine).   The word has remained alive in Belgium.

203 ENGINEERING. This word is an Anglicism which the French Academy, in its communication dated April 20, 1967, proposes to replace by *génie industriel.*
As a substitute for *engineering,* it has been recommended to use *ingénierie* (= the application of an engineer's art in the construction of tools and equipment).

204 ENNUYANT [annoying] / **ENNUYEUX** [annoying]. In ordinary usage, these two words are confused. Of the two, *ennuyeux* is used more. Strictly speaking, *ennuyant* means "which annoys occasionally" and *ennuyeux* "which causes annoyance constantly." As Littré says, *un homme ennuyant* cannot at all be *ennuyeux.*

205 ENTIÈRETÉ. This Old French word, which was still in use at the beginning of the 17th century [it is found in Cotgrave (1611), in

Oudin (1640), in Richelet (1680)], is used from time to time in France. It has survived in Belgium. As for substitute words, you may choose—according to the situation—from among: *la totalité* (of one's wealth); *l'intégrité* [the completeness, the entirety] (of a work, of a territory); *l'intégralité* [completeness, wholeness] (of an income, of a revenue); *l'ensemble* [the whole] (of legislation); *composer un tout* [constitute a whole]; *rapporter un passage dans son entier* [to relate, to give an account of a passage in its entirety]; *la plénitude (d'un droit)* [the fullness (of a law)].

206 ENTRAIDE [mutual help] / **S'ENTRAIDER** [to help each other or one another]. To each of these two words, do not add the word *mutuelle* or *mutuellement* because it would create a pleonasm: *Les hommes doivent* S'ENTRAIDER (Ac.).

207 ENTRE. Concerning elision in this word [i.e., whether to drop the final *e* and add an apostrophe or omit an apostrophe in a compound word, or to leave the word as *entre*], the French Academy has welded the compound elements in: *s'entraccorder, s'entraccuser, entracte, s'entradmirer, entraide, s'entraider, entrouverture, entrouvrir.*

It is not understood why the Academy has not done the same for the following five verbs: *s'entr'aimer, entr'apercevoir, s'entr'appeler, s'entr'avertir, s'entr'égorger.*

Without an apostrophe: *entre eux, entre amis, entre autres,* etc.

208 ÉPINGLE [pin]. People say: *une épingle de sûreté* [a safety pin] or *une épingle de nourrice;* at times, *une épingle à nourrice;* less often, *une épingle anglaise* or *une épingle double: Rafistoler une jaquette avec des* ÉPINGLES DE SÛRETÉ (Aragon). *[Ils] avaient fixé la doublure des manches de son pardessus avec des* ÉPINGLES DE NOURRICE (Daniel-Rops). *Un brassard fixé par une énorme* ÉPINGLE À NOURRICE (A. Lanoux).

For an altogether different use: *une épingle à linge* [clothes pin] or *une pince à linge.*

209 ÉPOUX [husband, spouse] / **ÉPOUSE** [wife, spouse]. These two words are used especially in administrative language: *Consentez-vous à prendre pour* ÉPOUX. . . ? . . .pour ÉPOUSE. . . ? [Do you consent to take for your husband. . . ? . . .for your wife. . . ?] In other situations, the use of these two words is somewhat stilted or affected and lacks simplicity and naturalness (unless they are used in a joking way or to express irony). In ordinary usage, say: *mon mari* [my husband], *ma femme* [my wife].

Do not say: *J'ai rencontré un tel avec son* ÉPOUSE, *avec sa* DAME, *avec sa* DEMOISELLE; say: . . .*avec sa* FEMME, *avec sa* FILLE [with his wife, with his daughter]. For example, while speaking to Mr. Durand, do not say: *Comment va votre* ÉPOUSE? or *Comment va* MA-DAME? Say, according to the degree of familiarity: *Comment va votre* FEMME? *Comment va* MADAME DURAND?

A husband, in speaking about his wife, would not say: MA-DAME *m'accompagnera.* He would say: MA FEMME *m'accompagnera.* But if he is speaking to a servant, he will say: MADAME *vous appelle.*

210 ERREMENTS. This word properly means "a course usually taken" [a usual way of behaving]: *Suivre les anciens* ERREMENTS (Littré). In modern usage, this word is often taken to mean "a manner of behaving which is blameworthy, unreasonable behavior, an error." This use was rejected by the French Academy in its notice dated May 20, 1965: *Le retour aux* ERREMENTS *qui ont failli jeter la République aux abîmes* (Ch. de Gaulle).   *Quand je pense à tout le temps que j'ai gâché, à tout le temps que j'ai perdu en* ERREMENTS, *en fautes, en futilités.* . . (H. Troyat).

This word is rare in the singular: *Les prêtres du Parc connaissaient cet* ERREMENT (Motherlant).

211 ESCABEAU, ESCABELLE. A seat made of wood without arms or a back. The two words, for the Academy, are synonymous, but the second is seldom used in the meaning of the word *escabeau.* [These two words are synonymous when they mean "stool," "footstool."]

Nowadays, *escabeau,* other than the meaning indicated, has taken on the meaning of "a sort of stepladder or a pair of steps which one uses like on a ladder" *(Robert).*

In household furnishings, *un marchepied* is the word for a sort of low stepladder containing two convergent risers, which often slide in and out, equipped with wide steps.

212 ESCALIER. Littré declares that "in some provinces, people say *escalier* [stairway, flight of stairs, stairs] for *degré* [stair, step]: *monter* LES ESCALIERS *quatre à quatre. C'est une faute."* The "error" that Littré is talking about results from a confusion between *escalier* and *degré* or *marche* [step]. As a matter of fact, in general usage, this "error" is not an error: *Il est tombé en descendant* L'ESCALIER OU LES ESCALIERS *(Robert).   Les domestiques que, dans ce récit,. . . on n'aperçoit jamais qu'en fuite et redescendant* LES ESCALIERS *quatre à* *quatre* (M. Proust). *Cinq enfants bondissaient dans* LES ESCALIERS *à sa rencontre* (A. Maurois, in *Petit Robert*).

Of course, when it is a matter of several partial stairs, the word is used in the plural: *Les différents* ESCALIERS *d'une maison* (Littré).

213 ESCAVÈCHE. In Belgium, this is a culinary term denoting a sort of food made of fillets of fish or eels, diversely seasoned: *Des harengs à l'*ESCAVÈCHE.

214 ESSUYER [to wipe] *ses pieds* [one's feet]. It is very logical to say: *essuyer ses chaussures* [to wipe one's shoes] *(sur un paillason)* [on a door mat]; *Personne n'essuie plus ses* CHAUSSURES *à la porte des maisons* (M. Jouhandeau). But people also say: *essuyer ses pieds* [to wipe one's feet]: *Essuyez en entrant vos* PIEDS *au paillasson* (Hugo). *Joseph, après s'être essuyé les* PIEDS *sur un confortable tapis brosse, heurta le battant de la porte* (G. Duhamel).

215 ESTIVANT [summer resident, vacationer]. This word is used commonly to designate a person who spends a summer vacation in a country resort: *Hivernant* [winter resident, vacationer] *ou* ES-TIVANT, *le touriste arrivait en train* (A. Siegfried). *Quelques* ESTI-VANTS *débouchaient sur la Promenade des Planches* (H. Troyat).

People also say: *vacancier* [vacationer] (broader meaning: a person who spends his vacation in some place): *Les habitants de Saint-Tropez se plaignent de l'afflux des* VACANCIERS *(Robert).*

Villégiateur [a vacationer in the country] (already in the Supplement to Littré) is used less. For the verb that corresponds to it, there is *villégiaturer:* VILLÉGIATURER *à Biarritz (Robert);* Thérive finds this verb "ridiculous" and, according to him, people normally say: *être* (or *aller*) *en villégiature.*

216 ESTUDIANTIN. People use the word *étudiant* as an adjective (when referring to students): *Parce que la révolte* ÉTUDIANTE *confondait le meilleur et le pire* (Fr. Mauriac). *La mentalité* ÉTUDIANTE *actuelle* (A. Billy). But people also commonly say *estudiantin:* *L'horreur du genre* ESTUDIANTIN (Motherlant). *La contestation* ES-TUDIANTINE (J. Mistler).

217 ETC. This abbreviation is from the Latin *et cetera*, which means "and others," "and the rest," "and so forth," "and so on." Pronounce it as *èt-sé-té-ra* (and not as *ek-sé-té-ra*, nor *èk-sé-tra*, nor *èt-sé-tra*).

Although *etc.* is, etymologically, neuter and refers to things, it can come after names of persons: *Dans Montluc, Brantôme, d'Aubigné, Tavannes, La Noue, etc.* (Mérimée).

218 EXACTION [extortion]. This word properly means "the action of demanding what is not due or more than is due"—especially in speaking of a public agent: *Ce gouverneur a commis d'horribles* EX-ACTIONS (Ac.).

This word, because of an unfortunate slip in meaning, is used today to mean "bad deeds, [crimes], of a moral kind: assassinations, murders, violations, rape, massacres, etc." *Que l'amitié de deux communautés, de deux races qui s'entretuent depuis tant d'années ait chance de survivre aux* EXACTIONS *de toutes sortes, aux assassinats, aux ratonnades, aux tortures, il m'arrive d'en désespérer* (Fr. Mauriac). *En 1957, il y avait en Algérie, en moyenne tous les mois, 2000* EXACTIONS *de toutes sortes* (Ch. de Gaulle).

The Academy, in a notice sent on Nov. 18, 1965, declares this slip in meaning as unacceptable.

219 EXCUSER. Strictly speaking, *s'excuser de faire une chose* [to excuse oneself from doing something] is "to give reasons to be exempted from something": *On m'a prié de solliciter pour lui;* JE M'EN SUIS EX-CUSÉ (Ac.).

If you mean: *je vous demande pardon de faire telle chose, je vous présente mes excuses, je vous exprime mes regrets de la faire ou de l'avoir faite,* then you should say: *Excusez-moi* or *veuillez m'excuser.* But you can also say: *je m'excuse* [a usage accepted by Thérive, in *Clinique du langage,* p. 26, and wrongfully reputed to be incorrect by Paul Léautaud (in *Mercure de France,* Nov. 1955, p. 387; as well as by *Petit Robert*)]: JE M'EXCUSE, *Messieurs, d'un si long abus de votre courtoise patience* (P. Valéry). *Je me suis jeté sur vous, Monsieur, comme sur une proie:* JE M'EN EXCUSE (A. Hermant). *Claude* S'EXCUSE *de ne pas descendre* (A. Chamson).

Faire excuse, which means to contradict politely, is somewhat outdated: *Je vous* FAIS EXCUSE (Ac.). *Pour vous, je ne veux point, monsieur, vous* FAIRE EXCUSE (Molière). FAITES EXCUSE, *mon bourgeois, disait le marchand d'eau* (M. Druon).

Demander excuse, which means to beg one's pardon, is an old locution and has survived only as a provincialism: *Je vous* DE-MANDE EXCUSE, *a-t-il dit, et j'ai tort* (La Fontaine). *Je vous* DEMANDE EXCUSE *de mon impertinence* (Sévigné). *Je dois vous* DE-MANDER EXCUSE *de mon indignation de l'autre jour* (Stendhal).

220 EXEMPLATIF. This neologism, which is used especially in the expression *à titre exemplatif,* is pedantic. Let us say: *à titre d'exemple* [by virtue of, by way of, as a. . .].

221 EXERGUE. This word means "a small space reserved on a [coin or] medal in which to insert a date, an inscription" or "the inscription itself." The word is also used, by extension, to mean "that which presents, explains the subject of a *tableau,* the contents of a text"; thus, it takes on the meaning of *épigraphe: Il eût été sage d'inscrire "Libre Opinion" en* EXERGUE *de l'article* (Fr. Mauriac). *Mettre un proverbe en* EXERGUE *à un tableau, à un texte (Robert).*

For the Academy, it is necessary, in usage, to maintain a distinction between *un exergue* and *une épigraphe* (cf. *Défense de la Langue française,* Nov. 1969, p. 5).

222 EXHAUSTIF. Some people take this word to mean *épuisant* [exhausting] (i.e., removing all strength): *Quand elle [la soif immatérielle] se fit jour avec la violence la plus* EXHAUSTIVE. . . (J. Kessel). *Une fatigue* EXHAUSTIVE (G. Duhamel). But in ordinary use it means: "which exhausts a subject by not forgetting any detail": *Une analyse qu'on peut qualifier d'*EXHAUSTIVE (A. Billy).

223 EXPRÈS. People say: *une lettre portée* PAR UN EXPRÈS [that is to say, by a courier, by a messenger], *une lettre* PAR EXPRÈS: *Cette lettre a été portée par exprès* (Ac.). People also use *exprès* as an invariable adjective and they say: *Une lettre* EXPRÈS *(Robert).* Do not say: *lettre express, lettre par express. Un express* or *un train express* is a rapid [express] train.

It should be noted, incidentally, that *un train express, un train rapide,* or *un train direct* has its opposite: *un train omnibus (un omnibus),* which is a train that stops at all stations.

Un train de banlieue is a train that makes stops at suburban stations of a city.

224 FAIBLE *(tomber~).* This expression is used in Belgium, in various regions of France, and in Canada (with its different dialectal forms: *toumer flawe* in Liège, *cair flaive* in Picardy, *cherre fiauve* in the Vosges, *tomber feube* in central France, etc.). This expression is not acceptable in good French usage. For a good French expression, you can choose from among the following: *tomber en faiblesse* [to fall into a weakness, a faint], *tomber en défaillance* [to fall into a faint, a swoon], *tomber en syncope* [to fall faint], *tomber en pâmoison* [to fall into a swoon]; *avoir une faiblesse, avoir une défaillance, avoir un évanouissement; s'évanouir, faiblir, défaillir; tomber sans connaiss-*

ance, se trouver mal. Two expressions that are synonymous (but used in informal French) are: *tomber dans les pommes* and *tourner de l'oeil.*

225 FARD. The root of this word is the same as that of *farder* [to paint (someone)]. Write it as *piquer un* FARD (not: *un phare*) or *piquer un* SOLEIL, both expressions meaning "to blush with emotion or confusion": *Ah! tu as peur de piquer un* FARD (Montherlant). *Mais à peine avait-il dit ces mots que le duc piqua ce que l'on appelle un* SOLEIL (M. Proust).

226 FAUTE *d'(in)attention.* When talking about an error that someone made, do not say: *C'est une faute d'attention.* Say: *C'est une faute d'inattention;* or, even better: *C'est une faute commise par inattention* (Littré). *Armand Lanoux a fait cependant deux fautes d'*INATTENTION (H. Bazin). *On y trouve beaucoup trop de ces fautes d'*INATTENTION *qu'il appartient à un éditeur de gommer* (Fr. Nourissier).

Do not confuse *faute d'inattention* [an *error* committed because of carelessness] with *faute d'attention,* which means "by lack of attention": *Faute d'attention, il a employé trois fois le même mot dans cette phrase.*

227 FAUTER. According to Block-Wartburg, this verb, already attested in the 16th century to mean "to make a mistake," came into use in the 19th century with the special meaning of "to allow oneself to be seduced" when speaking of a woman. It is used in familiar language.

228 FAUTIF. This adjective, in the meaning of "failed," is rejected by Littré. The word is currently used to mean "at fault," "guilty": *Il se sentait* FAUTIF (Ac.). *Je me sentais rougir et me troubler comme un enfant* FAUTIF (A. Gide).

229 FERMETTE. *Une fermette,* according to its etymology, is a "small farm." But, as a matter of fact, you will find in real estate advertising that *une fermette* is generally a country house more or less fallen into disuse as a country home, of modest size, which the person who acquires it furnishes according to his/her tastes, depending on the idyllic image he/she has of a "secondary residence."

230 FESTIVITÉ(S). This word is used especially in the plural. The Academy does not recognize this word. Littré (the Supplement) defines it as "characterized by a feast" [but should have added: "feast(s), rejoicing, merrymaking festivities"].

In the 16th century, *festivité* meant "feast, feast day, holiday" or "cheerfulness, gaiety"; after its disappearance during the classical period, it came back into use after the beginning of the 19th century, especially during the middle of that century.

Hanse has thoroughly studied the history and the uses of the word *festivité(s):* In accepting it in the meaning of "feast(s), rejoicing, merrymaking festivities," the word is in current use, not only in Belgium but also in France: *Cette* FESTIVITÉ *avait lieu dans un vaste hémicycle* (A. Gide). *Jusqu'à l'instant où sonnerait l'heure des* FESTIVITÉS *d'Asterabad* (P. Benoit). *Sa curiosité sympathique pour les* FESTIVITÉS *de saint Roch, à Bingen* (R. Kemp). FESTIVITÉS *sur* FESTIVITÉS. *Avant-hier, visite de la Reine à Québec. Hier, la Saint-Jean.* . .(H. Bazin).

231 FEU *(faire long~).* Properly used, *faire long feu* [to fizzle out, to misfire] refers to a weapon whose shot is slow in firing: *L'amorce était mouillée, le fusil* FIT LONG FEU (H. Pourrat).

In a figurative meaning, this locution expresses the idea of a long duration: *Un petit miracle en somme et qui devait* FAIRE LONG FEU *dans les saints propos de la famille* (H. Bazin). It can also express the idea of a failure, a vain attempt: *Persuadés que tout ce qu'ils entreprendront* FERA LONG FEU. . . (A. Hermant).

Used in the negative, *ne pas faire long feu* expresses almost exclusively the idea of "not to last a long time": *Que Pierre ait à se battre quinze jours avec la vie, et les balivernes de M. Menuise* NE FERONT PAS LONG FEU (J. Romains).

232 FIABLE, FIABILITÉ. *Fiable* is an Old French word meaning "worthy of faith, trust (confidence), capable of being trusted." The word was taken up again in modern technical language to describe material [a product] which one could trust, have confidence in, and whose chances of failing or breaking down are slim. From *fiable*, in that sense, the word *fiabilité* has been derived, which denotes the quality of reliable material.

233 FIEU. In Picardy, this noun is a form of *fils* [son]. The plural would normally be *des fieux.*

234 FIXER. In the meaning of "to look at fixedly, i.e., to stare," this word has been condemned by Littré. The Academy does not point out this acceptation in meaning, which is, however, used by better authors cautiously: *Oh! cette porte, je la* FIXAIS *maintenant de mes pleins yeux* (P. Loti). *Thérèse sourit, puis le* FIXA *d'un air grave* (Fr. Mauriac). *Je me mettais alors à* FIXER *le vieux notaire* (A. Chamson).

235 FLAT. This English word is used by Belgian real estate agents and brokers to denote a small modern apartment of "high standing" with certain comforts and conveniences; it is a single room that contains a living room area, a dining area, a corner with sleeping accommodations, a kitchenette, and a bathroom, usually separated from the main area. The word *studio* is also used for such an apartment.

236 FLOCHE. Littré defines this noun as follows: "a small shred fraying out." Littré gives this example: *Prenant du vêtement de chacun une* FLOCHE *imbibée de leur sang, il en frotte sept pierres* (P.-L. Courier).

For *Larousse du XXᵉ siècle, une floche* is "a small silk flossy tuft used as decoration on attire, such as what is placed in the upper part of an ankle boot" or "the tassel of a police cap worn by Belgian soldiers."

What the Belgian people call *une floche* is called *un gland* [tassel] in France: *Des* GLANDS *de rideaux, de draperies* (Ac.).   *Les* GLANDS *d'un coussin* (Id.).

237 FLOTTEMENT. When talking about currency whose value is not fixed, people say that it "floats" [*flotte*]; hence, according to the Academy, *le flottement* [floating] *de la monnaie* (and not: *flottage,* nor *flottaison,* nor *flottation*).

Fluctuation would designate a variation of weaker amplitude than *un flottement* and it would be said of currency without fixed parity.

238 FOND, FONDS. Observe the spelling of the word *fonds* in: *bâtir sur son* FONDS [to build on one's funds], *un* FONDS *de commerce* [business house, business establishment], *prêter à* FONDS *perdu,* etc. [to lend without security, etc]. The word is always in the plural when used for an amount of money [funds]: *être en* FONDS [to have funds], *manier des* FONDS *considérables,* etc. [to handle large funds, large amounts of money, etc.].

When it concerns the characteristics or resources peculiar to a thing or to a person, the word is normally written as *fonds: Cela prouve un grand* FONDS *de savoir* [fund of knowledge] (Ac.).   *Un excellent* FONDS *de santé* (Id.).   *Cela part d'un* FONDS *de probité.* (Id.).   *Un* FONDS *de candeur* (J. Schlumberger).

At times, you will find the spelling in the singular, but this is not recommendable: *Ce* FOND *de lucidité, de santé* (J. Kessel).   *Un* FOND *de sympathie* (A. Sorel). [See entry no. 330 (1).]

239 FORMULE [printed form], **FORMULAIRE** [formulary]. *Une for-*

mule is used to designate "a sheet of paper printed in numerous copies, containing instructions and intended to be filled in briefly" *(Robert): Il remplissait une* FORMULE *de dépêche pour moi* (M. Proust). *En fouillant dans mon bureau pour y trouver une* FOR- MULE *imprimée . . .* (G. Bernanos).

Un formulaire, strictly speaking, is a collection of forms, form- ulas: FORMULAIRE *des notaires,* FORMULAIRE *pharmaceutique* [. . ., pharmaceutical formulary]. But in its present use, *formulaire* is also used in the meaning of FORMULE indicated above: *Tandis que je remplissais le* FORMULAIRE *qu'on m'avait tendu. . .* (Vercors). *Comment remplir un* FORMULAIRE *fiscal* (A. Dauzat). *Remplir en triple exemplaire un* FORMULAIRE *de quatre pages* (P. Daninos).

240 FORTUNÉ. This word can mean "favored by fate, a person who is at the height of happiness": *amants* FORTUNÉS [blissful lovers] (Ac.). *Siècle* FORTUNÉ [prosperous century] (Id.).

The word also has the accepted meaning of "rich, possessing a fortune": *Nous passions pour* FORTUNÉS, *parce que nous avions . . . de belles terres et pierres au soleil* (H. Bordeaux). PAS TRÈS FOR- TUNÉS, *cette maman et ce grand-père: ne possédant guère qu'une mai- sonnette en ville et un petit bien de campagne* (P. Loti). *C'est la famille* LA PLUS FORTUNÉE *du pays* (Ac.).

241 FOU has the meaning of "out of order, disordered, inaccurate, out of balance, disturbed, deranged": *Balance* FOLLE, *roue* FOLLE (Ac.). As an invariable adverb or as a variable attribute: *tourner fou: La société américaine, présentée comme une mécanique qui tourne* FOU (R. Las Vergnas). *La roue des comparses, qui tourne* FOLLE, *reste seule digne d'intérêt* (R. Kemp).

242 FOULTITUDE. This word is formed by combining *une foule* [a crowd, throng] and *une multitude;* it is used in familiar, hu- morous language: *Une* FOULTITUDE *de raisons* [Heaps of reasons] (cited by V. Hugo, as an example of "the jargon used by duchesses"). *Dans l'église assombrie, j'imaginais (. . .) les ombres, noircissant de leur* FOULTITUDE *empressée ce vaisseau. . .* (La Varende).

243 FOURCHETTE. In the language of statisticians and economists, this neologism designates the gap between two extreme values in a forecast, an estimate.

244 FRANQUETTE. People say familiarly: *à la bonne franquette* (i.e., simply, without any frills, without ceremony): *Recevoir des amis à la bonne* FRANQUETTE. In all dialects, you will find the form: *à la bonne flanquette.*

245 FRAPPER *à la porte* [to knock on the door]. People ordinarily say: *frapper à la porte* or merely *frapper. J'entendis donc* FRAPPER *à la porte de ma chambre* (G. Duhamel). You can also say: *heurter,* or, in familiar usage: *toquer.* At times you will hear: *cogner. Elle . . .* TOQUA *de l'index à la porte vitrée* (Fr. Mauriac). *On* COGNA *à la porte* (H. Troyat).

246 FRICADELLE. In Belgium, *une fricadelle* is a deep-fried seasoned meatball; in certain regions, it is called: *vitoulet* or *vitolet.*

247 FRISELIS [rustle, rustling]. *Un friselis* is "a slight rustling, quivering sound" [usually of leaves]; it is from the verb *friser* [which has several meanings, two of which are "to skim, to graze"]: LE FRISELIS *clapotant du flot* (M. Genevoix). *Il y avait toujours* LE FRISELIS *des buissons* (B. Clavel). People also say, but less frequently: *le frisselis* (influence of the word *le frisson* [shivering, shuddering]). The French Academy does not recognize these two words [*le friselis* and *le frisselis*]: *Ce n'était pas ce* FRISSELIS *que j'entendais en moi* (H. Bosco). *Un nouveau* FRISSELIS (P. Guth).

248 FRITERIE, FRITURE. According to the Academy, *la friture* is the action of frying; it is also the word used to refer to butter, olive oil, or grease used in frying or to food that is fried.

To designate a place, a merchant's shop, booth, or stall where fried potatoes are sold, in Belgium the word in current use is *une friture.* This word is found in the works of Taine: *Une* FRITURE *de pommes de terre sous des colonnes antiques.* But in France people say: *une friterie* or at times *une friturerie* [for the place] (the Academy does not recognize these words): *Les* FRITERIES *sont campées sous toutes les portes cochères* (G. Duhamel, cited by *Robert*). *La vieille trotte vers la* FRITERIE (R. Queneau). *Des cafés, des débits de vin, des* FRITURERIES (E. and J. de Goncourt).

Theoretically, the word FRITURE, when printed on a sign, could be justified as well as VINS ET LIQUEURS, or CHAUSSURES (shortened from "Here, fried food is sold; Here, wines and liqueurs are sold, Here, shoes are sold"). But Belgian people do not interpret a sign with the word FRITURE printed on it to mean fried food; in their mind, FRITURE is short for *Ici on vend des frites* [Here, (French) fries (chips) are sold]. On the other hand, note that FRITERIE, printed on a shop sign, is hardly ever used in France, it would seem. [In other words, it would seem that people in France buy *friture* (fried food) in a *friterie* (if there is such a shop with such a sign); whereas, people in Belgium buy *frites* in a *friture!!*

249 FROMAGE DE TÊTE. This is a variety of pâté made of minced pork (head, feet, ears) prepared in gelatin. In Belgium, it is called: *de la tête pressée*.

French white cheese is called, in certain regions of Belgium, *maquée: de la bonne* MAQUÉE. The French regional word is: *jonchée*.

250 FRUSTE. The proper meaning of this word is "whose relief has been effaced by use, by rubbing, by the weather" or even, according to *Robert*, "whose relief is rough, coarse": *une médaille* FRUSTE [a worn (out) medal].

For the French Academy, *fruste* used in the meaning of "rough, unpolished, coarse" is utterly incorrect, and *manières frustes, un homme fruste* would express the opposite of what one means. Nevertheless, current usage (under the influence of *rustre* [rustic, country bumpkin, boorish] has admitted *fruste* in the meaning condemned by the Academy: *La vie* FRUSTE *et mal dégrossie des hommes* (M. Proust). *Villèle avait un frère siamois, Corbière,* HOMME FRUSTE (A. Maurois). [*Hérésie*] *à la portée des esprits* FRUSTES (P. Gaxotte). *Ces personnages* FRUSTES *et puants n'en étaient pas moins admirables* (H. Troyat).

Do not say: *frustre* (influence of *rustre* and *frustrer*).

251 GADGET. The *t* in this word is pronounced. This Americanism designates in familiar use (as a synonym of *"machin, truc, bidule"* [thingumajig, doohickey, contraption, gimmick]) a small practical invention, an amusing object, which is ingenious and intended especially for household use.

252 GAGEÜRE [wager, bet, stake]. This word is pronounced *ga-jûr*. Similarly, *mangeüre* is pronounced *man-jûr; rongeüre*, as in *ron-jûr;* and *vergeüre*, as in *ver-jûr.* [They rhyme with *jure*.] [See also entry no. 330 (4).]

253 GAGNER *une maladie* [to be afflicted by, to come down with an illness]. People say: *La gangrène a gagné rapidement* (Ac.).   *La scarlatine se gagne* (Id.).   Also, you can use *gagner*, without being incorrect, in speaking of an illness, as an attack, etc., which one comes down with, which one contracts, which one catches: *Une fièvre qu'elle* GAGNA *en traversant un pont chargé de cadavres. . .*

(Nerval). [*Un père qui*] *a* GAGNÉ *une maladie naguère encore sans remède* (R. Kemp). *J'ai* GAGNÉ *un rhumatisme dans le bras droit* (J. Green).

254 GALOCHE. *Une galoche* is "a kind of shoe whose upper part is made of leather, whose sole is of wood, and which is worn over a slipper or a shoe." (Ac.).

Footwear made of rubber which is worn over shoes, generally in snowy weather, is called *caoutchoucs* (or: *snow-boots*) [rubber overshoes, rubbers, galoshes]. The following example is from Duhamel's works: *Chacun doit remettre, avant de sortir, ses lainages, ses fourrures, son bonnet, ses bottes ou ses* GALOCHES DE CAOUTCHOUC.

255 GEÔLE [gaol, jail]. Pronounce as *jôle* (not: *jé-ôle*).

256 GESTION. Pronounce as *jès-tyon* (not *jes-sion*).

257 GOULET [narrow passage, gully] / **GOULOT** [neck of a bottle]. Make a distinction between these two words: *un goulet* is "a narrow passage in the mountains, a narrow entrance to a port." *Un goulot* is "the narrow neck of a container" [as the neck of a bottle]. (To convey this meaning, people used to say *le goulet*.)

258 GOÛTER [to taste, to sample, to try]. To appreciate the taste, savor, or flavor of food or drink, say: *goûter d'un plat, goûter d'un vin, goûter à un plat, goûter à un vin*. Do not say: *Ce plat me goûte*. Also, do not say: *Est-ce que ça goûte?* You should say: *Ce plat est à mon goût* [This plate of food suits my taste]; *est-ce qu'il vous plaît?* [Do you like it?]; *est-ce que vous le trouvez bon?* etc. [Do you like it? Do you find it good? etc.]

Also, do not say: *Ce vin goûte le bouchon*. Say: *Ce vin a un goût de bouchon*, or: *Ce vin sent le bouchon* [This wine has a taste of cork]. Also, do not say: *Ce pain goûte le moisi*. Say: *Ce pain a un goût de moisi*, or: *Ce pain sent le moisi* [This bread tastes moldy]. *Le vin* SENTAIT *le bouchon* (A. Daudet). *Ce plat a le goût d'épinards* (Stendhal).

259 GOUTTER [to leak, to drip]. *Goutter* (a verb which is not recognized by the French Academy) means "to allow to flow drop by drop." This verb is in common use: *Les toits* GOUTTENT (Littré). *Mouchez-vous, votre nez* GOUTTE (Id.). *Des larmes* GOUTTAIENT *une à une le long de ses joues* (M. Prévost). *Tiens! le robinet* GOUTTE *toujours* (J.-J. Gautier).

260 GRAVE *(blessé~), blessé léger.* These two expressions are rejected by purists because, they claim, it is not the *blessé* [wounded person] who is *grave* [serious] or *léger* [slight]; it is *la blessure* [the wound] which is either serious or slight.

Nevertheless, the transfer of epithet is not really incorrect French. Note, for example, the following: *un malade imaginaire* [an imaginary invalid, sick person], *un instituteur primaire* [a primary (school) teacher], *un critique littéraire* [a literary critic], etc.: *C'étaient des mutilés* GRAVES (G. Bernanos). *Un mort, deux blessés* GRAVES, *tous les autres blessés* LÉGERS (A. Malraux). *Une trentaine de blessés* GRAVES (H. Troyat). *Une rixe qui, par miracle, ne fit pas de blessés* GRAVES (Y. Gandon).

261 H aspirate. A word beginning with an aspirate *h* prevents making an elision or liaison. Therefore, it is not possible to write or to say: *l'hareng, cet hareng, les-z-harengs.* Since the *h* in the word *hareng* is aspirate, we must write or say: *le hareng, ce hareng, les harengs.*

Other words and their derivatives that begin with an aspirate *h* are:

ha!	halot	harangue
habanera	halotechnie	haras
hâble*	halte	harasser
Habsbourg	halurgie	harceler
hache	hamac	harde
hagard	hameau	hardes
haie	hampe	hardi
haïe	hamster	harem
haillon	had	hareng
Hainaut	hanap	hargneux
haine	hanche	haricot
haïr	hand-ball	haridelle
haire	handicap	harnais
halage	hangar	haro
halbran	hanneton	harpe
hâle	Hanovre	harper
haler	hanse	harpie
haleter	hanter	harpon
hall	happe	hart
halle	happelourde	hasard
hallebarde	happer	haschich
hallier	haquenée	hase
halo	haquet	haste
haloir	hara-kiri	hâte

hâtelet	hisser	hourd
hâtier	ho!	houret
hauban	hobereau	houri
haubert	hoc	hourque
hausse	hoca	hourra!
haut	hocco	hourvari
hautain	hoche	houseaux
hautbois	hocher	houspiller
Hautesse	hockey	houssaie
havane	holà!	housse
hâve	Hollande	housser
havir	hom!	houssine
havre	homard	houssoir
havresac	home	houx
hayer	honchets	hoyau
hé!	hongre	huard
heaume	Hongrie	hublot
hein	honnir	huche
héler	honte	hucher
hem	hop!	hue!
henné	hoquet	huer
hennir	hoqueton	huette
Henriade	horde	huguenot
héraut	horion	huhau!
hercher	hors	huis clos
hère	hospodar	huit
hérisser	hotte	huitaine
hernie	Hottentot	hulotte
héron	hou!	hululer
héros	houblon	humer
herse	houe	Hun
hêtre	houille	hune
heurt	houle	huppe
hi!	houlette	hure
hibou	houlque	hurler
hic	houp!	Huron
hideux	houper	hussard
hie	houppe	hutin
hiérarchie	houppelande	hutte
hile	hourailler	

H mute. On the other hand, words that begin with a mute *h* permit making an elision or a liaison, e.g., *l'homme, cet homme, les-z-hommes.*

(1) Note that the following words do begin with a mute *h:*
*hanséatique; héraldique, héraldiste; héroïde, héroï-comique, héroïne,
héroïque, héroïquement, héroïsme; huis, huissier.*

(2) Note also that it is bad usage to treat the word *handicapé*
(English: *hand in cap*) as if the *h* were mute and to say 'or to
write: *l'handicapé, un-n-handicapé, les-z-handicapés.* The word
handicapé begins with an aspirate *h;* hence: *le handicapé. un /
handicapé, les / handicapés.*

The original meaning of the word *handicapé* designated a game
of chance; in the 18th century it was used in horse races.
Among sports persons, the word was formerly used to settle
differences or disputes by drawing from a hat (cap; "hand in
cap"). But even among educated people, there seems to be a
tendency to make a liaison or elision: *l'handicapé, un-n-handicapé, les-z-handicapés.*

Recommendation: Treat the *h* in the word *handicapé* as aspirate.

262 HABITAT. This word properly means "a geographic environment which combines the conditions necessary for the existence
of animal or vegetable species": L'HABITAT *d'une plante, d'un animal.* For this word, this is the only acceptation in meaning
pointed out by the Academy. However, by extension, *habitat* has
taken on broader meanings: "man's way of planning and settling
the environment where one lives" *(Robert): Habitat rural, habitat
urbain, habitat sédentaire, habitat nomade.* "Habitat is the totality of
living, of dwelling" *(Robert): Amélioration de l'habitat. Je me disais
que l'*HABITAT *rural n'a guère varié depuis le XVIII* siècle
(A. Maurois).

In a notice dated Feb. 18, 1965, the French Academy declares
that *habitat* "does not mean *habitation.*"

263 HACHER [to hack, to mangle, to chop, to cross-hatch, to hachure
a design] / **HACHURER.** *Hacher avec le burin, hacher avec le crayon,
hacher avec la plume* (Ac.).   HACHER *une estampe (Robert).*

Hachurer is not listed by Littré nor by the Academy. However,
this word is used today: *Le plancher était déjà tout* HACHURÉ *à
l'endroit où il frappait* (R. Dorgelès).   *La brèche aux bords* HACHURÉS
s'ouvrait devant lui (H. Troyat).

264 HAUT-DE-FORME, HAUTE-FORME [top hat, silk hat, opera
hat, topper]. People say: *un chapeau haut de forme,* or *un haut de
forme,* or *un haute-forme* (with or without hyphens; the use of hy-

phens is indecisive). People also say: *un gibus* [a crush-on opera hat, a folding hat] or *un huit-reflets: Sous le chapeau* HAUT-DE-FORME *de tel ou tel* (R. Martin du Gard).   *Il a mis son chapeau* HAUTE FORME (J. Renard).   *Il tenait son* HAUT DE FORME *à la main* (Fr. Mauriac).   *Le vieux Mérivet, en* HAUTE-FORME *et longue blouse grise* (A. Daudet).   In Belgium, the word is: *chapeau buse.*

265 **HINDOU** [Hindu] / **INDIEN** [Indian]. There is reason to distinguish between these two words: *Un Hindou* is a person who belongs to the Brahmin social system, to the Brahmin religion (Hindu religion), to Brahmin civilization. *Un Indien* is an inhabitant of India; this word, therefore, is more general, and, as Deharveng says, an Indian who practices Hinduism is a Hindu.

266 **HIPPIE** (or **HIPPY**). An American word. *Les hippies* are young people, generally students, "initiates," "on the scene." In principle, they protest the way of life and the uses that society makes of consumer goods. They preach nonviolence and ask for moral and social freedoms, complete liberty in choosing what they wear.

267 **IL N'EST QUE DE.** When this expression is followed by an infinitive, it is used in the meaning of "the best [thing] is to" (classical usage); it also has the meaning of "all you have to do is. . ., it suffices to. . ., the only thing to do is. . .": IL N'EST QUE DE *jouer d'adresse en ce monde* (Molière).   *Quelques vers restaient à composer;* IL N'ÉTAIT QUE DE *s'y mettre* (G. Duhamel).

268 **IMPASSIBLE** [impassive, unmoved, unperturbed] / **IMPAVIDE** [fearless, impavid]. Do not confuse these two words. *Impassible* (Latin, *pati;* French, *souffrir;* English, to suffer) means "not susceptible to suffering; or to be in control of oneself so as not to show one's physical or emotional sufferings" (Ac.). *Impavide* (Latin, *pavor;* French, *peur;* English, fear) means "not feeling or revealing any fear."

269 **IMPECCABLE** [impeccable, faultless; ecclesiastical meaning: sinless]. Etymologically, this word means "not capable of sinning" (Latin, *peccare;* French, *pécher;* English, to sin). For Abel Hermant and for purists, the word is used only for persons—a refuted opinion because, according to current usage, the word is also used for things that are flawless: *Tenue* IMPECCABLE, *toilette* IMPECCABLE (Ac.).   *Elle me rapporta un texte* IMPECCABLE (A. Maurois).   *Demeure* IMPECCABLE (J. Green).

270 **IMPENSABLE** [unthinkable, inconceivable, unbelievable]. This word is rejected by purists. What one calls *impensable,* they claim, cannot be thought up; consequently, how can one declare it to be not thinkable?—an insidious reason, which usage does not take at all into account. The word is used currently in the meaning of *inconcevable* [inconceivable], *incroyable* [unbelievable]: *Il y a là pour moi, de l'inadmissible, de l'*IMPENSABLE (A. Gide). *Cette* IMPENSABLE *folie* (Fr. Mauriac). *Cela nous paraît* IMPENSABLE (Ph. Erlanger).

271 **INCLINAISON, INCLINATION.** One can, along with Littré, the Academy, and others, make the following distinction: *inclinaison* [incline, slope] is the state in which something is on an incline, on a slope: L'INCLINAISON *d'un toit, d'un mur,* etc. [the incline of a roof, a wall, etc.]. *Inclination* [bowing, bow (of a body), nod (of a head), inclination] is the action of inclining, and in particular, the action of nodding one's head or bending (bowing) one's body as a sign of acquiescence or deference or an affective movement toward someone or something: *Elle répondit par une* IN-CLINATION *de tête* (H. Troyat). *Gêner, combattre les* INCLINATIONS *d'une personne* (Ac.). *Mariage d'*INCLINATION [a love match].

But a distinction between these two words is risky; in modern usage, people commonly say: *une* INCLINAISON *de tête ou de corps: En faisant une légère* INCLINAISON *de tête. . .* (A. Billy). *Barois approuve d'une simple* INCLINAISON *de tête* (J. Romains).

272 **INDEMNITÉ** [indemnity], **INDEMNISER** [to idemnify, to compensate]. Pronounce the first *e* as if it were written *è* [as in *père*]. The pronunciation of that first *e,* as if it were written as *a,* is still used but it is becoming outdated. [Pronounce the *m* and the *n.*]

273 **INDIFFÉRER.** This word was formed by regressive derivation. Progressive French (humorous, whimsical) incorrectly used certain adjectives, such as *indifférent* [indifferent], *insupportable* [intolerable, unbearable], *urgent, insouciant* [heedless, not caring] and formed verbs from them, such as *indifférer* (condemned by the Academy in a notice dated May 20, 1965), *insupporter, urger, insoucier: Le mécanisme de l'enseignement m'*INDIFFÈRE (R. Kemp). *Je crois qu'Albertine eût* INSUPPORTÉ *maman* (M. Proust). *Les littérateurs, race qui l'*INSUPPORTE. . . (Montherlant). *Mais comme, après tout, la présence du matou n'*URGE *point* (Colette). *Les plus sincères d'entre nous ne peuvent tout à fait* S'INSOUCIER *de ce qu'on pense d'eux* (La Varende).

274 **INFARCTUS.** This word was formed irregularly; it should be

written as *infartus* [without the *c*]. Etymologically, it is related to the Latin *farcire* [to fill, fulfill, stuff]; *fartus* [that which fills or stuffs]. *Infarctus* has nothing in common with the family words of *fracture* (Latin *frangĕre* [to break, to shatter]. Do not pronounce *infarctus* as *infractus*.

275 **INGAMBE.** This word (from the Italian *in gamba*, French *en jambe*) means "alert, having nimble legs, capable of walking briskly": *Ce vieillard est encore* INGAMBE (Ac.).

276 **INGRÉDIENT.** Pronounce this word as *in-gré-dyan*, and not *in-gré-dyin*.

277 **INLASSABLE** [untiring (efforts), tireless, indefatigable]. "To say *inlassable*," Faguet declared, "is very *inlogique* [the prefix *in* is deliberately written incorrectly; should be *illogique*]: *inlassable* is not French; I would be *illassable* to say it." In spite of purists, *inlassable* and *inlassablement* have become implanted in use: *L'*INLASSABLE *dévouement* (G. Clemenceau). *Pareils à des insectes* INLASSABLES (G. Duhamel). *Dans cette fuite* INLASSABLE *du temps* (J. Guitton). *Contemplant* INLASSABLEMENT *le lent travail rotatoire d'un oursin* (A. Gide).

278 **INSTANCE.** From the original meaning of "a pressing (urgent) request," this word has been able to move into a juridical meaning: instance, suit, proceedings.

The word has also passed into a neological meaning: "an authority holding the power of making a decision." This meaning (the word is most often used in the plural) has been rebuffed by purists but, as Thérive has said, "one cannot be astonished or shocked enough upon seeing the meaning of this word broadened to include 'jurisdictional powers' that are not judiciary." Be that as it may, the word *instances*, in the meaning criticized by purists, is frequently used today: *La Tunisie se tourne aujourd'hui vers les* INSTANCES *internationales* [Today, Tunisia is turning to international decision-making powers] (A. François-Poncet). *Les plus hautes* INSTANCES *de l'Église* [The highest decision-making powers of the Church] (L. Leprince-Ringuet). *Les* INSTANCES *officielles se refusèrent à tout changement* [The official decision-making authorities refused any change] (Ch. de Gaulle).

279 **INTÉRESSER** [to interest]. This word cannot be used in the meaning of *concerner* [to affect], as noted in the French Academy's communication dated Nov. 19, 1964. For example, you would not

say: *Les régions* INTÉRESSÉES *par la grêle*. [You should say: *Les régions concernées*. . . .] [See also entry no. 130.]

280 JOUETTE. In Belgium, this word is often used in the meaning of "who loves to play too much" when speaking of children, ordinarily: *Cet enfant,* JOUETTE *comme il est, devient insupportable.*

281 JUGULER. For Littré, *juguler* means "to cut the throat of, to butcher, to slaughter" or "to cause a great loss, a ruin" or "to annoy excessively, to torment, to inconvenience." For the Academy, it means "to squeeze the throat" [to strangle]. In these various meanings, *juguler* is hardly used today.

For Thérive, *juguler* could only mean "to assassinate." This is a false opinion; today, the living meaning of *juguler* is "to control, to check [to stop], to interrupt the development of": *Un fou que nous n'avons pas su* JUGULER (Fr. Mauriac).   *Afin que le plaisir qu'il se donnait ainsi* JUGULÂT *sa mauvaise humeur* (Montherlant).   *Laisser un Tzar sur le trône de Russie, quitte à* JUGULER *son pouvoir par une constitution* (H. Troyat).

282 JUKEBOX. An American word. An electrophone [record player], a "music box"; you put a coin in the slot and the box grinds out a tune.

283 KLAXON [horn (of a vehicle)]. This word is written in various spellings: *Leur impertinent* KLAKSON (R. Boylesve).   *Une camionnette. . .faisait retentir son* CLAKSON (É. Estaunié).   *Un énorme coup de* CLAXON (G. Duhamel).   *La troupe des* CLACKSONS (J.-J. Gautier).   [*Il*] *enfonça le* KLACKSON (H. Bazin).

The spelling that prevails is *klaxon*.

284 LAC [lake]. *Tomber ou être dans* LE LAC [To fall into or to be in the lake (i.e., to fall on one's face, to go "down the drain," to fail)]. This expression is used familiarly in the meaning of "to fail": *Tomber dans le* LAC *(Robert).   Son projet est dans le* LAC *(Id.).*

There are certain purists who want us to say and to write: *dans le lacs* [rather than *dans le lac*], i.e., *dans le lacet* [in the snare], *dans le piège* [in the trap]; but that is an old expression, not in use today. [Use: *tomber dans le lac* or *être dans le lac*.]

285 LETTRE CLOSE / LETTRE MORTE. *Lettre close* is an expression used for ideas or feelings which are foreign to you, something whose meaning you do not understand: *Je ne comprends rien à ce que vous m'écrivez; c'est pour moi* LETTRE CLOSE (Ac.).

Lettre morte is an expression used for a title [right], an agreement [contract], a testament, etc., which has lost all its legal value, all official authority; or, by extension, something which is useless, without effect: *Les recommandations qu'on lui fait sont pour lui* LETTRE MORTE (Ac.). *Tous les commandements de la politesse, de la charité, sont* LETTRE MORTE *pour cet homme pressé* [*l'automobiliste*] (G. Duhamel).

286 **LEVER** [to raise, to lift] / **SOULEVER** [to lift up]. In hunting, the term *lever un lièvre* [hare] means "to make a hare start to run." In its figurative meaning, *lever un lièvre* means "to raise unexpectedly a question which is embarrassing or compromising for someone" [to open a can of worms]: *Il ne fallait pas* LEVER CE LIÈVRE-LÀ (Ac.).

Since one says *soulever une question, une difficulté,* etc. [raise a question, a difficulty, etc.] it would seem by analogy that one could say *soulever un lièvre* in a figurative meaning, parallel to *lever un lièvre*. Examples of this use: *Sartre a* SOULEVÉ *là un gros lièvre* (J. Cocteau). *Cette petite question, qui* SOULÈVE, *comme on dit, un lièvre énorme* (M. Chapelan). *Le mari en question ne devait pas être bien reluisant, pour que la jeune femme mît autant de soin à le cacher et elle s'était gardée de* SOULEVER *ce lièvre* (J.-J. Gautier).

This use, nevertheless, remains generally criticized by theorists of good language.

287 **LICHETTE** (at times, **LICHE**). In Belgium, *une lichette* is used to mean an attachment, a small cord, sometimes a small chain, used to hang an article of clothing.

288 **LIMITE D'ÂGE.** Quite illogical as it may be, the passive expression *atteint* (or *touché*) *par la limite d'âge* [reached or affected by age limit] is used in administrative language; it is also found in ordinary usage: ATTEINT PAR LA LIMITE D'ÂGE, *il toucherait sa retraite à partir de l'année suivante* (M. Van der Meersch). *Il ne quitta son haut poste qu'en 1955,* ATTEINT PAR LA LIMITE D'ÂGE (H. Torrès). *C'était un bon officier, destiné normalement à être* TOUCHÉ PAR LA LIMITE D'ÂGE *comme chef de bataillon* (Montherlant).

289 **LINCEUL** [shroud, winding sheet]. Pronounce this word as *lin-seul*, not *lin-seuil*.

290 **LOQUACE, LOQUACITÉ.** The traditional pronunciation of these two words is: *lo-kwass, lo-kwa-si-té.* Today's pronunciation, which is commonly used, is: *lo-kass, lo-ka-si-té.*

291 MACHINE. This word is commonly used to designate a locomotive engine: *Les wagons sont tout petits, la* MACHINE *grosse comme
celle d'un tramway* (Maupassant). *La* MACHINE *avec son sifflement,
sa fumée et le grand bruit qui accompagne le train* . . . (Taine).
Jeanne. . .vit fulgurer les cuivres jaunes de la MACHINE; *l'ombre des
wagons glissa sur ses épaules* (M. Genevoix).

292 MACHINISTE. According to the Academy, this word designates
"someone who places or moves the décor [scenery, settings],
stage props, theater equipment" [stage hand, scene shifter]. For
Robert, it is seldom used in the meaning of "someone who drives
a locomotive, a vehicle used in public transportation": *Il courut à
l'avant du tramway et s'entretint, pendant quatre ou cinq minutes, avec
le* MACHINISTE (G. Duhamel). The word *mécanicien* is generally
used in this sense: *Depuis plus de quinze ans, le nommé Marc Lefort /
Est* MÉCANICIEN *sur la ligne du Nord* (Fr. Coppée). People also say
le conducteur: CONDUCTEUR *d'autorail, de locomotive électrique (Petit
Robert).*

293 MAGISTER / MAGISTÈRE. Distinguish between these two
nouns: *Un magister* is a pedant [an ostentatious person of learn-
ing]: *Les leçons d'un* MAGISTER *ridicule. Un magistère* is the doctrinal,
moral, or intellectual authority imposing itself in an absolute way:
Exercer un MAGISTÈRE (Ac.). *J'ai cessé de croire au* MAGISTÈRE *spirituel des pays les plus développés* (P. Emmanuel).

294 MAJUSCULES [capitalization of words].
   (a) **Write with a capital letter:**
      1. Names designating *la Divinité* [Divinity (God)] or *Jésus-
      Christ,* names of mythological divinities, names of stars,
      planets, names of holidays: *Le Créateur, la Providence, le
      Seigneur* [the Lord], *le Tout-Puissant* [the Almighty], *le Messie*
      [the Messiah]; *Jupiter, Sirius, Uranus; la Toussaint* [All
      Saints' Day], *à Noël.*
        As for the word *ciel* [sky] designating the Divinity, usage
      is indecisive. In current usage, the following words are not
      capitalized: *le soleil, la lune, la terre.* But when they have to
      do with cosmography: *le Soleil, la Lune, la Terre.*
      2. Proper names of people of a nation, of families, of dynas-
      ties: *les Français, les Bourbons, les Capétiens.* However, do not
      capitalize the adjectives that correspond to those nouns: *les
      auteurs français, la monarchie capétienne.*
      3. Proper names of religious, scholarly, or political societies,

orders of chivalry: *l'Église, l'État, la Chambre des députés, le Sénat, l'Académie française, la Légion d'honneur.*

As for names of religious orders, usage is indecisive: *les jésuites* or *les Jésuites, les franciscains* or *les Franciscains, les carmélites* or *les Carmélites.* The following are also undecided: *Le révérend père. . .*(Ac.). *L'élixir du Père Gaucher* (A. Daudet). *La vie de l'abbé de Rancé* (A. Maurois). *L'Abbé de Mondésir* (Id.).

4. Names of the cardinal points [north, south, east, west] when they designate very special geographical regions: *Les plus belles fourrures viennent du Nord* (Ac.). *Les départements de l'Ouest. Les gens du Midi.*

Usage is indecisive in cases like the following: *Le vent souffle du nord* (Ac.). *Le vent soufflant du Nord* (A. France). *L'ouest de la France (Dictionnaire général). Faire une tournée dans l'Ouest de la France* (Ac.).

5. Proper names of streets, monuments, vessels, ships, etc.; titles of works, works of art, etc.: *La rue du Bac, le Parthénon, le Titanic, les Misérables de Hugo, les Glaneuses de Millet.*

6. Names of titles and high rank: *Sa Majesté.* Be sure to use a capital letter when you address yourself to the person himself / herself: *Il est tard, Monsieur Coûture.* (Fr. Mauriac). *J'ai l'honneur, Monsieur le Président, de. . . . Daignez agréer, Monsieur le Ministre. . . .*

(b) **Some special cases:**

1. Symbols of units: Use a capital letter when the symbol comes from a proper noun. Use a lower case letter when it comes from a common noun: *10 h [heures], 6 A [ampères], 60 W [watts], 10 kW [kilowatts].*

2. *Saint:* Use a lower case letter if referring to the saint himself / herself: *Le supplice de saint Sébastien.* Use a capital letter in all other cases: *La rue Saint-Paul, la Saint-Nicolas* [Saint Nicholas Day], *né à Saint-Cloud.*

3. The following are written as shown: *le bon Dieu, la Sainte Vierge, l'École polytechnique, l'École militaire, la mer Méditerranée, l'océan Atlantique, le mont Blanc, le golfe Persique.*

4. As for the Middle Ages, the French Academy writes it as *le moyen âge.* But there are some variations; certain authors write: *le Moyen-Âge,* or *le Moyen Âge,* or *le moyen-âge.*

295 MANAGEMENT. This word is an Anglicism which is taken to mean "*direction, conduite* [of a matter, a factory, etc.]'' (in the Supplement to *Robert,* which considers this fashionable word to be useless). Pronounce this word in the French way [the ending -*ment* is nasalized].

In the same word family: *manager* (pronounce as *ma-na-djèr* or *ma-na-djeur*), a person who manages the organization [planning] of a theatrical performance, a match [in sports], etc., or who manages the interests of an artist, a sportsman / sportswoman.

296 MAPPEMONDE. In its strict and etymological meaning (compare the Medieval Latin *mappa mundi*, which is a map of the world), *une mappemonde* is a flat map "representing all parts of the terrestrial globe divided into two hemispheres, each enclosed in a great circle" (Ac.).

A slip in meaning has occurred and *une mappemonde* is commonly used today for *un globe terrestre* (a sphere representing the terrestrial globe) or, figuratively speaking, *mappemonde* is used for "a large ball": *C'est comme si Hector Servadac et Ben Zouf . . ., enlevés par une comète, regardaient de loin leur planète, de nouveau, comme une* MAPPEMONDE *illuminée* (R. Kemp). *À mes pieds s'arrondit une* MAPPEMONDE (A. Billy). *Au milieu de la pièce, une* MAPPEMONDE *de verre* (H. Bosco). [*Les chevaux*] *tournaient, dociles et calmes, sous la main qui leur claquait la croupe,* MAPPEMONDE *de chair rebondie* (M. Genevoix).

In a notice dated Feb. 18, 1965, the Academy condemned this slip in meaning.

297 MARIE-JEANNE [Mary Jane]. This is a familiar name for *marijuana*, a hallucinogen from Indian hemp, which a person smokes to obtain euphoria.

298 MARIER. This verb means "to unite a man and a woman in a marriage bond": *Le maire, le curé de la paroisse les a mariés* [. . .married them]. Or, this verb may also be defined as "to bring about or to arrange a marriage, either by paternal authority or by friendship": *Son père l'a* MARIÉ *avantageusement* (Ac.). *Il a fort bien* MARIÉ *sa nièce* (Id.).

Do not say: *Pierre a marié Nicole* if you mean that Pierre united himself in marriage with Nicole. Say: *Pierre a épousé Nicole.*

The use of *marier* instead of *épouser* is current in France, Canada, and elsewhere in many popular or vulgar ways.

299 MARIOL, MARIOLLE, MARIOLE. You will find these three spellings used. This term is used in very familiar language and, according to André Castelot, it has probably come from a soldier named Mariole "who, one day, presented arms to the emperor not with his rifle but with a coin worth a few pennies—from which the following expression has come: *Ne fais pas le mariole.* . . [Don't act like a show-off]" (in *Le Figaro littéraire*, Jan. 13–19, 1969). *Voici un galopin qui vient jouer les* MARIOLES (J. Perret). *Il aurait bien pu attendre h̊uit jours avant de faire le* MARIOL (Aragon). *Mon petit pote, fais pas le* MARIOLLE (R. Ikor).

300 MARKETING. This word denotes the technique and methods of studying the market. This Anglicism is used in the world of commerce and industry. In a communication dated April 20, 1967, the Academy proposes to replace *marketing* by *commercialisation*.

301 MARTYR / MARTYRE. Make a distinction between this: *Saint Étienne est le premier* MARTYR [. . .is the first martyr]; *sainte Cécile, vierge et* MARTYRE [. . ., virgin and martyr]—and this: *souffrir le* MARTYRE [to suffer martyrdom]; *le* MARTYRE *de saint Étienne, de sainte Cécile* [the martyrdom of Saint. . .].

302 MASSACRER. This verb can be used not only for several persons (who are killed, slaughtered without being able to defend themselves), but also for one person (who is put to death or who commits suicide): *Si tu dis un seul mot, mon roi, je* ME MASSACRE (Hugo). *Si les Maures demain ne me* MASSACRAIENT *pas* (Saint-Exupéry). *Vous seriez* MASSACRÉ *sur-le-champ* (Montherlant).

303 MASS MEDIA. This "fashionable" expression, which came from America not too long ago, designates the dissemination of propaganda, communication and information through a very broad system, including varied technical and psychological means, audiovisuals, newspaper, radio, television, and publicity on a massive scale. Its abbreviated form is *media*.

304 MATINAL / MATINEUX. The Academy defines *matinal* as "someone who got up early, or who is in the habit of getting up early." The Academy defines *matineux* as "someone who is used to getting up in the morning." In today's usage, *matineux* is outdated and *matinal* has both meanings. *Matinal* also means "which takes place or happens in the morning": *Vous êtes bien* MATINAL *aujourd'hui* (Ac.). *La brise* MATINALE (Id.). *Gymnastique* MATINALE.

  Matinier is used only in the expression *l'étoile matinière* [Venus].
  Matutinal, "which pertains to the morning," is more poetic and is hardly ever used.

305 MÉCONDUIRE *(se~)*. *Larousse du XXe siècle* lists this verb as old. It is practically not in use in France, although current in Belgium; however, compare: *Comme s'il la rendait responsable de la* MÉCON-DUITE *de sa fille* (J.-L. Curtis). The normal expression is *se mal conduire* or *se conduire mal* [to misbehave].

306 MEILLEUR *(prendre le~sur)*. At times, people say familiarly: *avoir le meilleur sur*, and frequently, in the language of sports: *prendre le meilleur sur* [to have an advantage over, to have the upper hand, to outshine]: *Il entrera en concurrence (. . .) avec André Bardot, sur lequel, pense-t-il, il* AURA LE MEILLEUR (Tr. Bernard). *L'Ajax a* PRIS LE MEILLEUR *sur l'Inter*.

307 MELON *(chapeau~)*. *Un chapeau melon* [a derby hat, a bowler] or *un melon* is a hat made of felt, which is round and bulging in shape [like a melon]. In France, people used to say: *chapeau cape* or *cape: Leclerc, maigre singe en combinaison, mais en* CHAPEAU CAPE (A. Malraux, cited by Baiwir). *Coiffé du haut de forme ou de la* CAPE (J. and J. Tharaud, cited by Baiwir). In this sense, *cape* is no longer used today. In Belgium people say: *un chapeau boule* [compare the English word, *bowler*].

308 MENTALITÉ [mentality]. This word has been rebuffed by Thérive (who recommended *humeur* [mood, disposition, temperament], *caractère, tour d'esprit, nature*). The word is very commonly used: *La* MENTALITÉ *de la génération nouvelle* (Ac.). *Parce que nous ne nous représentons pas une différence de* MENTALITÉ *si profonde entre les Allemands et nous* (J. and J. Tharaud).

309 MESDAMES ET MESSIEURS [ladies and gentlemen]. People say: *Bonjour, Madame et Monsieur*, or *Mesdames et Messieurs*, or *Madame, Monsieur*, or *Mesdames, Messieurs*. Say: *Bonjour, Messieurs, dames (m'sieu dames)*, or popular usage is: *Bonjour, Messieurs et dames*. *Dégagez, Messieurs-dames* (Ionesco).

310 MESSE [mass (church)]. People say: *servir la messe* (i.e., *dire les réponses, présenter le vin et l'eau*, etc.) [(i.e., to say the responses, present the wine and water, etc.)]: *L'aumônier, dont il* SERVAIT *tous les matins la messe. . .* (R. Vercel). The following is also said: *répondre la messe: J'étais consciencieux à* RÉPONDRE *la messe* (Alain). *J'ai* RÉPONDU *la messe comme un autre* (G. Bernanos).
    Do not say any of the following: *aller à messe, faire la messe, une*

messe d'année, une basse messe. Say: *aller à la messe, dire* or *célébrer la messe, une messe de bout de l'an, une messe basse.*

311 METTRE AU NET, METTRE AU PROPRE [to make a correct copy]. Both expressions are good: *Une petite fille silencieuse mettait ses devoirs* AU NET *près du comptoir* (Colette). *Votre fils. . .me confia même le soin de mettre* AU PROPRE *pour lui les copies elles-mêmes* (J. Giraudoux). *Il fallut recopier le texte* AU PROPRE (H. Troyat).

312 MINÉRALOGIQUE *(numéro ou plaque~)* [mineralogical number or plate]. This expression denotes the entire group of letters or numbers that constitute the registration number, the numerical order of a motor vehicle. This curious expression is explained by the fact that in France automobiles were originally linked with the Bureau of Mines.

313 MIXITÉ [mixed, coeducational]. This word indicates the state or quality of what is mixed. It was introduced in order to designate, in particular, the characteristic of educational institutions that admit students of both sexes. This new word has not been coined well: from the word *mixte*, it would have been normal to coin the word MIXTITÉ; the following words would not be suitable in this case because they have special uses: *mélange, mixage, mixture, mixtion*. In spite of everything, *mixité* is in current use; it is listed in the Supplement to *Robert* and in *Lexis*.

314 MOEURS [customs, manners]. Pronounce the *s* in this word. Not to sound the *s* is an outdated pronunciation and is less commonly used. In the expression *bonne vie et moeurs* ["clean living," good conduct, and good morality], the *s* is pronounced.

315 MONTRE *(faire~de).* This expression means, in a strict sense, and often considered disparaging: "to make a parade of, to show with ostentation": *Le père Léonard aimait à* FAIRE MONTRE *de sa richesse* (G. Sand).
    This expression can also mean, without any idea of ostentation, "to display, to show proof of," as in the following examples: *Aussi voit-on maint pauvre curé de campagne* FAIRE MONTRE *d'un savoir bien supérieur aux besoins journaliers de ses ouailles* (A. Billy). *Je souhaiterais. . .que nous* FASSIONS MONTRE *d'autant de prévisions que les circonstances l'exigent* (Fr. Mauriac). FAIRE MONTRE *de patience.*

316 MOUROIR [deathbed]. *Le mouroir* is used for *lit de mort: Arriver* *au* MOUROIR (Bescherelle). In a broader sense, this derivation of *mourir* (cf. *parler*, PARLOIR; *laver*, LAVOIR, etc.) designates a place where sick persons are confined to an inevitable fate and abandoned because of a terminal illness and a pitiable end of life: *Dans l'argot des camps nazis, un sanatorium était aussi un* MOUROIR (P. Daix). *Les rues des villes [sous Philippe VI de Valois] sont des* MOUROIRS (M. Druon).

317 MOYEN-ORIENT. This expression is improper, says the Academy in a communiqué dated Oct. 2, 1969, to designate riverain or neighboring countries in the eastern part of the Mediterranean Sea. One ought to say: *Proche-Orient* [Near East]

318 NATIF [native]. People say: *Il est* NATIF *de Paris, de Lyon* (Ac.). *Le bonhomme Piédeleu était Beauceron, c'est-à-dire* NATIF *de la Beauce* (Musset).

Né natif [native born] is used in popular language.

319 NÉGOCIER *un virage.* The expression is not, according to Sauvageot, derived from the English *to negotiate a curve;* it originates from a metaphorical use of *négocier* (*négocier un traité, un arrangement*, etc.) [to negotiate a treaty, an arrangement, etc.]. One can say, without being incorrect: *négocier un virage* [to execute, to make a turn in a car, to bank an airplane]: NÉGOCIER *montées et descentes infernales* (J. Kessel).

Nevertheless, the expression remains criticized. Robert Le Bidois rejects it and recommends sticking to *prendre un virage.* [See also entry no. 105.]

320 NÉGRITUDE. This is a word coined by Aimé Césaire, writer and political leader in Martinique, pertaining to the black race, to the totality of values of civilization in the black world: *Le sentiment religieux jaillit des profondeurs de la* NÉGRITUDE.

321 NIVEAU *(au~de)* [at the level of]. This expression properly marks "the degree of elevation, regarding a horizontal plane, a line, or a plane which is parallel to it" (*Dictionnaire général*). In its figurative meaning: *Cet écolier n'est pas* AU NIVEAU *des enfants de son âge* (Ac.).

In today's usage, *au niveau de* has been astonishingly favored. It has become a vicious habit in the press and elsewhere, for example: . . . *au niveau des finances publiques,* . . . *au niveau de la gestion du pays,* . . . *au niveau du style,* etc.

Recommendation: Do not use this expression improperly. Substitutes, according to the case, are: *dans le rang, à l'échelon, dans le domaine de, en ce qui concerne, en matière de, pour ce qui est de.*

322 NOM *(petit~).* In familiar usage, *petit nom* is used for *prénom* [first name]: *Quel est votre* PETIT NOM? (M. Achard.)

323 NOTABLE [notable, noteworthy] / **NOTOIRE** [acknowledged]. Distinguish between these two words. *Notable* is worthy of being pointed out: *Parole* NOTABLE. *Dommage* NOTABLE. *Différence* NOTABLE. *Les* NOTABLES *de la ville.*

Notoire is generally known, generally manifest, obvious, evident: *C'est une vérité* NOTOIRE (Ac.). *Voilà une preuve* NOTOIRE *et convaincante* (Id.). *Je crois avoir rendu quelques* NOTOIRES *services; j'ai définitivement purgé la terre de maints tyrans, bandits et monstres* (A. Gide).

In the same order of ideas, distinguish between *notabilité* and *notoriété*. *Notabilité* is characterized by that which is notable: *Sa* NOTABILITÉ *est incontestable* (Ac.). Or: *Personnage notable. Les notabilités de la ville* (Id.). *Notoriété* [notoriety] is general public knowledge of a fact: *Cela est de toute* NOTORIÉTÉ, *de* NOTORIÉTÉ *publique* (Id.).

324 NUISANCE. Littré says that "this word, which used to be a French word long, long ago, is now taken up again from the English who retained it from the Normans." *Nuisance* (not recognized by the Academy) "is characterized by that which is harmful." It has been rather seldom used since the middle of the 19th century and today the word has been taken up again with great vigor, notably in texts that are about the environment or pollution.

325 OBSERVANCE / OBSERVATION. The word *observance* is used to designate the practice of a rule or a law in a religious matter: *L'observance de la règle dans les maisons religieuses* (Ac.). *L'observance du jeûne* (Id.). At times, it is also used when speaking about a rule which is not religious: *J'avoue avoir attaché à cette condition* [*l'euphonie des vers*] *une importance première, et avoir sacrifié beaucoup à son* OBSERVANCE (P. Valéry).

In this last meaning (a rule that is not religious), the word *observance* is generally replaced by *observation:* L'OBSERVATION *de sa parole, de sa promesse* (Ac.).

326 Œ-. This is pronounced as *é* in: *Œcolampade, Œdipe, Œnone, Œta,*

Mœris, Pœcile, fœtus, œcuménique, œdème, œnologie, œsophage. Pronounce the *œ* as *eu* (like in *feu*) in German or Scandinavian nouns, such as: *Björnson, Gœthe, Gœring* (or *Göring*), *Gœbbels, Jönköping, Kœnig, Malmö, Œrsted, Tromsœ,* etc.

327 ŒUVRER [to work]. This old verb is frequently used today when one wants to tint the idea of *travailler* [to work] with a noble tone and to evoke courageous efforts, a noble task, the pursuit of an ideal, etc.: *Souhaitant une victoire et* ŒUVRANT *pour y aider* (P.-H. Simon). *Les biologistes soviétiques de l'école mitchourinienne ont* ŒUVRÉ *dans la bonne route* (J. Rostand).

328 OLYMPIADE [Olympiad]. This word designates, in terms of Greek antiquity, the period of four years between two celebrations of Olympic feasts. That is the only meaning given by the Academy. However, in spite of purists, *olympiade* can also designate the Olympic games themselves. (In Greek, *olympias* had the double meaning of "celebration of Olympic games" and "period of four years.") Nevertheless, these days, to designate the games themselves, *jeux olympiques* is almost always used.

329 OPTION. This is a word *dans le vent* ["in the swim"] which many people, especially in politics and journalism, consider to be more elegant than the good old word *un choix* [a choice]: *La meilleure des* OPTIONS *proposées au pays.*

330 ORTHOGRAPHE [spelling].
  The latest attempt to reform our spelling was made by René Thémonnier in his two works, *Le Système graphique du français* (1967, revised in 1976) and *Code orthographique et grammatical* (1970). This author centered his analysis on the "problem of homonyms," on the "phonetic-graphic constants" (accentuation, double consonants, unstable consonants), on the "prefix, suffix, and verbal series," and on the "irregular families of words."
  The French Academy, always prudent, has until now retained only very little of the few hundred modifications proposed by the Conseil international de la Langue française. Jean Mistler, permanent secretary of The French Academy, in *Banque des mots* (issue no. 12, dated 1976, pp. 145–148), makes it known that The French Academy has, in the past, made decisions of which the following is the main substance:
  (1) Etymological regularization: *bonhommie, boursouffler, boursoufflure, chausse-trappe, combattif, combattivité, cahutte, charriot, déciller, embattre, imbécilité, innommé, persiffler, persifflage, persif-*

fleur, prudhommie, sottie, ventail, appâts, fond [for *fond* and
fonds], *tréfond, relai, cuisseau, levreau, ognon, encognure.*
(2) Standardization of the endings *-èle* and *-ète* in all verbs ending
in *-eler* and in *-eter: je harcèle, j'attèle, j'étiquète, je halète,* etc.
(3) Accentuation conforming to the pronunciation in *affèterie,
allègrement, empiètement, évènement, règlementaire, règlementaire-
ment, règlementation, règlementer, assener, belître, bésicles, chébec,
démiurge, gélinotte, phylloxéra, recépage, recépée, recéper, séneçon,
sénescence, sénestre.*
(4) Dieresis *(tréma)* on the vowel *(a, i, u)* which is pronounced in
aigüe, ambigüe, ambigüité, cigüe, exigüe, etc., *argüer, gageüre,
mangeüre, rongeüre, vergeüre.* [See also entry no. 252.]

These new written forms, for the French Academy, are official as of the present time. From now on, they are used in
the texts in preparation for the next edition (the ninth) of its
dictionary. They will be offered parallel to the old ones, which
will be regarded equally as correct until such time in the future when the old spellings will progressively disappear.

Regarding certain grammatical or orthographical variations that
are permitted, see the Haby decree on p. 353; in the correction of examination or competitive tests in elementary or secondary teaching, the decree prescribes that "they will not be
counted as errors" in a series of cases (about thirty).

331   Be sure that you spell correctly the words as indicated on the
following list:

The spelling indicated here is, generally, the one that is given
in the last edition (1935) of the *Dictionnaire de l'Académie.*

abattage	*acolyte*	*allier* [*chasse*] *ou*
abattant	*acquiescer*	*hallier*
abattis	*affoler*	*allonger*
abbaye	*agglomérer*	*alourdir*
abhorrer	*aggraver*	*amande (fruit)*
aboiement	*agrafe*	*amende (taxe)*
abréviation	*agrandir*	*améthyste*
absinthe	*agréger*	*amphitryon*
acanthe	*agresseur, -ssion*	*anaglyphte-glypte*
accalmie	*agripper*	*ananas*
accessit	*aire (nid)*	*anoblir*
accoler	*ais (planche)*	*anonyme*
accommoder	*alaise ou alèse*	*antécédent*
accourir	*aligner, -gnement*	*anthologie*
accroc	*alizés (vents ~)*	*anthrax*
accueil		*anthropophage*

antipathie
apercevoir
aplanir
aplatir
aplomb
apocryphe
aposter
appas (charmes)
appât (pâture)
appeler
appendice
appui-main ou
   appuie-main
après-diner ou
   après-dînée
aquilon
araignée
arête
arithmétique
arôme
arrhes
aruspice ou
   haruspice
ascension
ascète
asphalte
asphyxie
asseoir
assonance
assujettir
asthme
astrakan ou
   astracan
athée
athlète
atmosphère
attraper
aulne ou
   aune (arbre)
authentique
auxiliaire
aventure

babil

bâbord ou bas-bord
baccalauréat
baccara (jeu)
badigeon
bafouer
bahut
balai
ballotter
balluchon ou
   baluchon
ban (publication)
banderole
bandoulière
banlieue
bannière
barboter
barcarolle
baril
baronnie
barrage
barrette
barricade
barrique
baryton
bazar
beffroi
besicles (sans
   accent)
besogneux ou
   besoigneux
betterave
biais
bibliothèque
bicyclette
bien-aimé ou
   bienaimé
bifteck
bizarre
boîte
bonace (t. de
   marine)
bonasse
bonhomie
bonifier

bougeoir
bouledogue
boulevard
bouleverser
bourgmestre
boursoufler
boussole
boute-en-train
brocard (raillerie)
brocard (t. de
   chasse)
brocart (étoffe)
brouillon
budget
buffle
buté (obstiné)
buter (~contre)

câbleau ou câblot
cachottier
cahot (secousse)
cahute
calembour
calepin
calotte
campanile
camphre
cannelle
canonnade
canonnier
cap (de pied en~)
cape (de~et d'épée)
carafe
cari ou kari (carry,
   cary, curry)
carotte
carrefour
carrosse
carrousel
carrure
cataclysme
catafalque
catarrhe
catéchisme

catéchumène
catégorie
céans (ici)
cellule
cène (repas)
censé (supposé)
cercueil
cerfeuil
certes
chaire (d'église)
chant (brique posée
    de~)
chaos (confusion)
chariot
charrette
chas (d'aiguille)
chère (bonne~)
chloroforme
chœur (d'église)
choléra
chrême (saint~)
chrétienté
christe-marine ou
    criste-marine
chromolithographie
chrysalide
chrysanthème
ciguë
cilice (chemise)
circonstanciel
circumnavigation
circumpolaire
cithare
clapoter
clapper
clef ou clé
cleptomane ou
    kleptomane
clerc
clown
cœliaque ou
    céliaque
coing (fruit)
colonel

colza
combatif
comparution
concurrence
confidentiel
connexion
consonance
contravis
contrecoup
contrordre
coquerico ou
    cocorico
à cor et à cri
    (sing.)
coreligionnaire
corolle
corridor
courir
courrier
cravate
crypte
cueillir
cuiller ou
    cuillère
cuisseau (de veau)
cuissot (venaison)
cyclone
cygne
cylindre
cyprès

dahlia
dam
damner
datte (fruit)
daurade (dorade
    désigne un autre
    poisson)
davantage
débarrasser
débris
déclencher
décrépi (mur~)

décrépit
    (vieillard~)
dégingandé
dégoutter (de
    goutte)
délétère
dénouement ou
    dénoûment
dénuement
dépens (aux ~ de)
derviche ou dervis
désarroi
dessein (projet)
dessiller
détoner (faire
    explos.)
détonner (sortir du
    ton)
deuil
développer
[au] diable vert ou:
    au diable au
    vert—ou: au
    diable vauvert
dièse
différend
    (contestation)
dilemme
dionysiaque
diphtongue
diptyque
dissonance
distinct
dithyrambe
dizain, dizaine
dollar
don (dev. prénom
    d'un noble
    d'Espagne [vieux:
    dom]
dorloter
dortoir
douairière
douceâtre

ductile
dysenterie

ecchymose
ecclésiastique
échafaud
échalote
échauffourée
écho
échoppe
écot (quote-part)
écueil
eczéma
égoutter
égrener ou égrainer
élytre
embarrasser
embatre
embonpoint
emmitoufler
emphysème
emphytéotique
empyrée
encoignure
encyclopédie
engrener
enliser (s'~)
enorgueillir
entérite
enthymème
entraccorder (s'~)
entraccuser (s'~)
entracte
entradmirer (s'~)
entraide
entraider (s'~)
entr'aimer (s'~)
entr'apercevoir
entr'appeler (s'~)
entr'avertir (s'~)
entr'égorger (s'~)
entrelacs
entrouvrir
entre autres

entre eux
entregent
envi (à l'~)
épithète
époumoner
ère (époque)
Érinnyes
erroné
érysipèle ou
    érésipèle
esbroufe
essaim
essor
essoufflé
essue-main
esthétique
étaler
état civil (sans trait
    d'union)
état-major
êtres (dispos. des
    lieux)
étude (salle d'~,
    maître d'~)
étymologie
exaucer
excédent
exceller
exception
exciter
exclu
exhaler
exhausser
exhiber
exhorter
exhumer
exigeant
exigence
exorbitant
expansion
exsangue
extension
exubérant

faix (fardeau)
familier
fanfaronnade
faon
faramineux (pha-)
farniente
fascicule
fatigant (adj.)
fatiguant (part. pr.)
fer-blanc
féverole
filigrane
final ou finale
    [musique]
flottille
flux
fœtus
folklore (folk-lore)
fondé de pouvoir(s)
fonts (baptismaux)
football
for (~ intérieur)
forcené
fourmilière
fourrure
fusilier (~ marin)

gageure
gaiement
gaieté
gargote
gaufre
gaze (étoffe)
gentleman
geôlier
gifle
glycérine
gouffre
grâce ou grâces
    (rendre~)
grand-mère
grelotter
griffonner
grignoter

groom
groseillier

haire (cilice)
hameçon
harassé
hasard
haschich ou
   hachisch
hécatombe
hemicycle
hémorragie
héraut (messager)
hère (pauvre~)
heurt (coup)
hiéroglyphe
Hippolyte
homéopathie
homonyme
hôtel de ville
hourra
hydropisie
hydrothérapie
hygiène
hyperbole
hypnotisme
hypocrisie
hypoténuse
hypothèque
hystérie

idylle
imaginer
imbécillité
imbroglio
inclus
indemniser
innomé
innommable
inonder
intéresser
interstitiel
irascible
isthme

jaquemart
jaquette
javel (eau de ~);
   abusivement:
   de javelle
joaillier
jockey
journaux
juvénile

kyrielle
kyste

labyrinthe
lacs (lacet)
lai (frère~)
langage
La Palice ou La
   Palisse
laper
la plupart
larynx
legs (don fait par
   testament)
léthargie
leurre
levraut
Libye
lieue (mesure itin.).
ligoter
lis ou lys
lourdaud
lycée
lynx

maraud
marguillier
marionnette
marqueterie
marronnier
martyr (personne)
martyre
   (tourments)
Méditerranée

mélèze
mess (table des
   offic.)
métempsycose
milliard
millionième
millionnaire
milord
misanthrope
misogyne
mite (insecte)
moelle (sans tréma)
moellon (id.)
mœurs
monolithe
moricaud
mors (du cheval)
mourir
mufle
mufti ou muphti
mûrir
myope
myosotis
myriade
myrmidon ou
   mirmidon
myrrhe
mythe (récit)

néanmoins
nénuphar
néophyte
nickel
niguedouille ou
   niquedouille

occulte
occuper
occurrence
odyssée
œcuménique
œsophage
œuvre
oignon

olympiade
opinion
opiniâtre
ores (d'~et déjà)
orgueil
ormaie ou ormoie
orthodoxe
orthographe
oxygène

pagaïe ou pagaille
  ou pagaye
paiement ou
  payement
paillote
pamphlet
panaris
panégyrique
panthère
pantomime
pantoufle
paon
papilionacé
papillonner
papillote
papilloter
papyrus
parafe (-phe)
parallélipipède
parcimonie
parlote
parmi
paroxysme
pathétique
patronage
patronal
patronner
patronnesse
peluche ou pluche
pénitentiaire
pépin
percussion
péristyle
péronnelle

persifler
pervenche
phalanstère
phantasme (fan-)
philanthrope
philtre (breuvage)
phlegmon
phtisie
phylloxera
physique
pilotis
pithécanthrope
pivert ou pic-vert
plaidoirie
plain-chant
plain-pied (de~)
plébiscite
pléthore
pli
plinthe
polychrome
polyptyque
poney
pore (de la peau)
porphyre
posthume
pouding ou
  pudding
poulailler
pouls (battement
  des artères)
presbyte
printanier
professeur
profiterole
pronunciamiento
prosélyte
prud'homme
pseudonyme
psychanalyse
psychiatre
psychologie
puits
pulluler

punch
pygmée
pyramide

quant à
quincaillier
quinconce
quintessence

raccommoder
raccourcir
raffiner
raffoler
ragaillardir
ralliement
ramoner
rancœur
rastaquouère
ratiociner
raz ou ras
recueil
rédhibitoire
réflexion
reflux
réhabiliter
relais
remblai
remerciement
  parfois: -îment
remords
remous
rêne (courroie)
repère (point de~)
résilier
résipiscence
résonance
ressusciter
retors
rets (filet)
réveille-matin ou
  réveil
révérenciel
rhapsodie
rhétorique

rhinocéros
rhubarbe
rhum
rhumatisme
ribote
ris (de veau)
rite
romand (Suisse)
rougeole
rythme
sabbat
salami
salmis
saoul ou soûl
sarcophage
satire (attaque)
satyre (mythol.)
saynète
schah (de Perse)
sceau (cachet)
scène (de théâtre)
scission
sciure
séance
seau (récipient)
sébile
seing (signature)
servile
sibylle
siffler
siffloter
silhouette
site
sixain ou
    sizain
smalah
sofa
soi-disant
sotie
souffler
souffleter
soufre
soupente
sous-pied

speech
sphinx
spleen
steamer
substantiel
succinct
suranné
surseoir
sursis
sybarite
symétrie
sympathie
symptôme
syncope
synecdoche ou
    synecdoque
synonyme
synthèse
taffetas
tannin ou
    tanin
taon (insecte)
teck ou tek
téléphérique ou
    -férique
térébenthine
thaumaturge
théologie
thérapeutique
thésauriser
thon (poisson)
thym
tilleul
timonier
tintamarre
tissu
toast
tocsin
torticolis
traditionalisme
trafiquant
tranquillité
transcendantal
transept

transfert
trappe
trapu
tréfonds
trembloter
tricycle
triptyque
trombone
trompeter
truffe
truquage (trucage)
tympan
typhoïde
typhus
typographie
tyrannie
uhlan
ukase
vaciller
vaisselier
valkyrie ou
    walkyrie
vantail (de porte)
ventail (d'un
    casque)
véranda
verglas
vermouth
    parf.: vermout
verni (adj. ou
    partic.)
vernis (nom)
versatile
vif-argent
viscère
voirie
voisiner
vol-au-vent
volontiers
whisky
whist
zéphyr
zoologie

332 PAGAILLE [muddle, jumble, clutter, mess]. This word means "in great disorder." The Academy gives the following three spellings: *pagaïe, pagaille, pagaye*. In usage, the spelling *pagaille* is the one that prevails.

333 PANACÉE [panacea, cure-all]. This word is from the Greek *pan*, French *tout*, English *all* plus the Greek *akeia*, French *remède*, English, remedy. Theoretically, the expression *panacée universelle* is a pleonasm, but when you consider that few users are really aware of the etymological value of *panacée*, you can, with a certain complaisance, allow the epithet *universelle* to be added to this word, However, one can become provoked by a fairly frequent usage: *Chimie du moyen âge, qui. . .cherchait la* PANACÉE UNIVERSELLE (Littré, under the word entry *alchimie*). *Ne croirait-on pas que j'ai dans ma boutique la* PANACÉE UNIVERSELLE? (Musset.) *Cette* PANACÉE UNIVERSELLE *gardée dans les magasins du Gouvernement* (A. Daudet).

334 PANIQUER (or **SE PANIQUER**) [to panic]. This neologism has become current in the meaning of "to find oneself in a state of panic." Etymologically, this word is in harmony with *terreur panique* [sudden and violent terror, like the one provoked by the god Pan in the fields]: *Cet étudiant* (SE) PANIQUE *dès qu'il pense aux examens.*

335 PAPE. Used in Belgium [cf. the Flemish word, *pap*]: pap, porridge, oatmeal, farina. *Faire manger sa pape à un enfant.* [See also the entry **COLLE DE FARINE**, no. 120.]

336 PAPIER [paper]. The paper used to cover walls is called *papier peint* [wallpaper], *papier-tenture, papier de tenture, tenture de papier,* or simply *papier: Manufacture de* PAPIERS PEINTS (Ac.). *Le* PAPIER DE TENTURE *était lie de vin* (Fr. Mauriac). *Je me retrouve dans cette petite chambre aux* TENTURES DE PAPIER *blanc et rose* (É. Henriot). *Il a renouvelé les* PAPIERS *de son appartement* (Ac.).
   Do not say: *du beau tapis.* Say: *du beau papier peint.*

337 PAPIN. In Belgium, this is a cataplasm, a poultice: *Un* PAPIN *bien chaud de graine de lin fera mûrir le furoncle* [A very hot poultice made of linseed will bring the boil (furuncle) to a head]. A dialectal word. It is found in *Thrésor de Nicot* (1606) [*cibus est infantium = c'est une nourriture des enfants* (it is baby food)]; in Richelet ["*mot vieux et provincial au lieu duquel à Paris on dit* BOUILLIE. *Faire, donner, manger du* PAPIN" ("an old and provincial word in place of which in Paris they say *oatmeal.* To feed with pap, farina, oat-meal")]; in Trévoux [same definition]; in Bescherelle [*"farine bouillie dans de l'eau ou dans du lait. Faire manger du* PAPIN *à un enfant"* ("farina boiled in water or milk. To have a child eat pap")]; in the Supplement to Littré ["the name, in Douai, for farina paste"]; in *Larousse du XX*ᵉ *siècle* [*"bouillie pour les enfants"* ("pap, oatmeal, gruel for children")]. [See also entries nos. 120 and 335.]

338 PARENTAL. This word, which first appeared in the language in the 16th century, came into general use only six or seven decades ago. Along with André Goosse—who gives, in *Libre Belgique,* issue dated April 20, 1970, examples of this word from the writings of Aragon, Montherlant, J. Leclercq, J. Rostand, Th. Maulnier, and Ph. Hériat—one can ascertain that the word *parental* is in full use today.

339 PARTITION [sharing, partition, allotment, demarcation]. This word is used when speaking of a country or of a territory. It is (as the Academy pointed out in its communiqué dated May 20, 1965) a useless duplicate of the word *partage.*

340 PARUTION [appearance (of a publication)]. This word is not recognized by the French Academy and it is rebuffed by purists who prefer to use *une publication, une mise en vente,* or *une apparition* to designate the appearance of a publication in bookstores.

The word is in current use: *Dès sa* PARUTION [*d'une revue*] (G. Bernanos). *La* PARUTION *d'un ouvrage illisible* (M. Aymé). *Depuis la* PARUTION *du tome X* (A. Billy).

341 PASSAGER. The adjective *passager* can be used in speaking of a street, a place frequented by people, where many persons pass through: *Dans les rues* PASSAGÈRES *et marchandes* (A. Vandal). *Au Jardin public, dans le coin le moins* PASSAGER (É. Henriot). For Thérive, the adjective *passager* [busy, crowded], in this meaning, is justified as well as *passant.* But it is this last adjective that is ordinarily used: *Chemin* PASSANT (Ac.). *Rue* PASSANTE (Id.).

342 PASSATION [drawing up and signing (of an act)]. In its strict meaning, this word denotes the action of putting through a contract, an act, an accounting entry.

In a neological meaning (20th century), it is also used in speaking of handing over power: *Lors de la* PASSATION *des pouvoirs* (L. Treich). This use is condemned by the Academy (cf. *Défense de la Langue française,* Nov. 1969, p. 5).

343 PEAU DE POULE [gooseflesh]. At times, you will hear: *Cela me fait venir la peau de poule,* or *Cela me donne la peau de poule* [That gives me gooseflesh (goose bumps); that makes my skin crawl; that makes me shudder]: *M. Thomas accepte, sans enthousiasme, "affectionner" qui me donne la* PEAU DE POULE. . . .*Que ceux qui préfèrent "chair de poule" relisent Anatole France. . .et Jean-Jacques Brousson* (R. Kemp).

The usual expression is *chair de poule: Cela fait venir la* CHAIR DE POULE (Ac.). *J'en ai la* CHAIR DE POULE (Id.).

344 PECCAMINEUX [sinful]. This word is from the family of the Latin verb *peccare,* French *pécher,* English "to sin." For Wartburg: from the Italian word *peccaminoso,* derived from Vulgar Latin (ecclesiastical) *peccamen.* Along with André Goosse [*Libre Belgique* dated March 19, 1979], it can be ascertained that *peccamineux* (like the Italian *peccaminoso*) apparently comes from Vulgar Latin (ecclesiastical) *peccaminosus.* In moral theology, the word applies to that which has the characteristic of a sin. It is rare in ordinary usage: *Une tendance* PECCAMINEUSE *qui va vers la destruction de soi* (G. Bernanos). *N'y prend-il pas une délectation peccamineuse?* (P.-H. Simon.) *Quand il s'agit de lui [du Peau-Rouge], aucune tromperie, aucune pratique corruptrice, aucune violence ne sont réellement* PECCAMINEUSES (J. Chastenet).

345 PÉCUNIER. The word is pointed out (and not condemned) by Littré, noting the following under the entry *pécuniaire:* "Sometimes *pécunier* is used." At times, it may be found in literature: *La chose* PÉCUNIÈRE (D'Aubigné). *Des indemnités* PÉCUNIÈRES (Stendhal). *Des difficultés* PÉCUNIÈRES (Lévis-Mirepoix).

An argument, however, cannot be drawn from the rare examples found, and a person will use the word *pécuniaire,* which has the same form in the masculine and the feminine: *Des embarras, des difficultés* PÉCUNIAIRES.

346 PEINTURER [to lay a coat of paint on, to daub, to dab]. This verb means "to coat with one or several colors of paint without any other purpose than to remove the natural color of the object: PEINTURER *un treillage, un lambris"* (Littré). In this use, the word is old. In current usage, this verb means "to paint in a crude way." It is almost a synonym of *peinturlurer.*

347 PENTHOUSE. This is an Anglo-American word. For professional real estate agents and brokers, it is an apartment built on the top floor (or just below the top floor) of a modern (apartment) building; it is set back from the façade's alignment, thereby allowing a spacious private roof garden and terrace. It is generally regarded as an apartment of "high standing," the most prized in the building. [See also entry no. 435.]

348 PERDURER. This verb means "to last indefinitely." It is an old verb, not listed in any dictionary except Bescherelle, who declares it to be "not in use." It is rarely used in France; it is used in Belgium where it means "to continue, to persist." For Deharveng, the word is useless. [It is also listed in *Petit Robert*, 1977.]

Perdurable means "eternal. . .everlasting." It is, according to Littré, "an outdated word, but could be taken up again."

349 PÉRIL EN LA DEMEURE. In the expression *Il y a péril en la demeure* [There is danger in the delay] or *Il n'y a pas péril en la demeure* [There is no danger in the delay], *demeure* means "lateness, postponement, delay" and the meaning conveyed is: "the least delay may (or may not) cause a great harm."

350 PÉRIPÉTIE [peripeteia, episode; *in the plural*, vicissitudes, ups and downs]. This word means: "a sudden and unforeseen change from one state of being to another" or, by extension: "an unforeseen event": *Toutes les* PÉRIPÉTIES *de cette agonie* (R. Martin du Gard, in *Robert*).   The Academy, in a communiqué dated Oct. 2, 1969, notes that *péripétie* cannot be taken to mean "a minor event."

351 PÉRIPLE [periplus, long and complicated journey]. This word is from the Greek *periploûs*, from *peri*, meaning "around," and *ploûs*, "navigation." The etymological meaning is: "navigation around a sea or the coasts of a country, of one part of the world, etc." Purists and the Academy (see its notice in *Défense de la Langue française*, June 1972, p. 59) keep the original meaning of the word.

By extension, in modern usage, *périple* has wrongfully taken on the meaning of "great voyage, an outing, [to go on] tour, a long excursion, etc." by any means (water, land, air) and the movement can be circular or not: [*La Terre*] *dans son* PÉRIPLE *autour du Soleil* (A. Billy).   *Au terme d'un* PÉRIPLE *qui les eût menés de Mende à Draguignan, de Draguignan à Digne. . .* (P. Guth).   *On s'était passionné pour le* PÉRIPLE *atlantique de Lindbergh et de sa femme* (J.-P. Chabrol).   *Le* PÉRIPLE [*un voyage de Turin à Lyon*] *fut à la fois magnifique et joyeux* (Ph. Erlanger).

In its notice, the Academy allows the word *périple* "to have the broad meaning of *voyage circulaire*."

352 PIÉTON, -ONNE, PIÉTONNIER, -ÈRE. These adjectives are used when speaking of a street, path, road, way, space, etc. to mean "reserved for *piétons*" [pedestrians]; these adjectives are also used to refer in some way to pedestrians: *Une rue* PIÉTONNE or PIÉTONNIÈRE. *À gauche, la porte* PIÉTONNE, *petite* (V. Hugo). *Des habitudes* PIÉTONNIÈRES.

353 PISTOLET. This word is very commonly used in Belgium to designate a small bread in a somewhat round, oval, or oblong shape (varying according to geographical location), slit in the middle, and often garnished like a sandwich with ham, cheese, and/or cold cuts. The word is listed with this meaning in the *Dictionnaire général*, in the *Grand Larousse encyclopédique*, in *Robert*, and in *Lexis*. The word is in use, particularly in southern France, notably in the southwestern region. Deharveng notes the use of this word in a novel by F. Fabre (*Ma Vocation*, p. 143), whose action takes place in Montpellier: *Quantité de* PISTOLETS, *petits pains longs à croûte vive.*

It is also used in a novel by É. Henriot (*Les Temps innocents*, p. 159), where the action takes place near Bordeaux: *Aller chercher le pain chez Escartefigue, ce pain tout brûlant encore, et fleurant la farine honnête, façonné en couronne mince, nommé "coque" ou bien en petits pains, dits* PISTOLETS.

354 PLAINTE [moan, groan, complaint, protest]. In speaking of a complaint (grievance) brought to the courts, the following are used: *porter plainte* or *déposer une plainte contre quelqu'un* [to file a grievance against someone]. The Academy, in a communiqué dated Oct. 2, 1969, condemns the expression *déposer plainte.*

355 PLAN(T): *rester en plan(t)* or *laisser en plan(t)* [to abandon, to leave in the lurch]. Littré considers these locutions as belonging to the family of the word *planter* (cf. *planter là*) [to abandon one's spouse, to leave in the lurch] and lists EN PLANT. Some writers use this spelling: *[Poèmes] qu'elle laissait en* PLANT (J. Maritain). *Joseph . . . me laissa en* PLANT (M. Blancpain).

Usage has clearly established the term as *en plan: Rester en* PLAN (Ac.). *Laisser en* PLAN (Id.). *Je ne peux pas laisser tout en* PLAN *comme ça* (H. Troyat).

In Belgium, *tirer son plan* is used in the meaning of *se débrouiller, se tirer d'affaires, se tirer d'embarras* [to manage, to get out of trouble, to get out of an embarrassing situation]: *Laissez-le faire; il tirera bien son plan.*

356 PLANTER, SEMER *des pommes de terre.* People say: PLANTER *des pommes de terre* [to plant potatoes]. *Je* PLANTE *des pommes de terre* (G. Duhamel). *Leur faire* PLANTER *des pommes de terre* (É. Henriot). It is less ordinary to say *semer* [to sow] *des pommes de terre: Le gardien. . .a profité du terrain vide pour y* SEMER *des pommes de terre* (Flaubert).

357 PLASTIC / PLASTIQUE. Distinguish between *le plastic* and *le plastique. Le plastic* (borrowed from the English language) is an explosive gelatine: *Attentat au* PLASTIC.

Le plastique [plastic] is a mixture containing a base material that can be molded or shaped [used in plastic arts and commercially made plastic goods]: *Il déteste les fermetures-éclair, le nylon, le* PLASTIQUE *sous toutes ses formes* (É. Henriot).

358 PLAT DE CÔTES [top ribs]. In a butcher's language, *plat de côtes* is the flat part of beef ribs: *J'ai demandé du* PLAT DE CÔTES (Ac.). The Academy notes that *plates côtes* is also used.

359 POIGNER. This verb, haphazardly formed under cover of *poignant* (from the verb *poindre*, which means *piquer* [to sting, to prick]) was drawn into the orbit of *poigne* [grip, grasp] and *empoigner* [to grab, to grip, to grasp]. *Poigner* has been used by some writers to mean "to clench, to squeeze, to wring one's heart": *Un sentiment profond de regret a* POIGNÉ *mon coeur* (Chateaubriand). *Un nouveau malaise le* POIGNA *au ventre* (H. Troyat).

Opinion of Littré: "There is no such verb as *poigner.*" The Academy, in a notice dated Nov. 13, 1969, states: *"poigner* is a barbarism."

360 POIL DE LA BÊTE *(reprendre du~)* [to buck up, to have another go, another try]. Formerly, people believed that the bite of a dog could be cured by a hair from the animal's tail—hence, the meaning "look for the remedy of an illness in the very thing that caused it": *Quand on est fatigué pour avoir trop couru à la chasse, il faut* REPRENDRE DU POIL DE LA BÊTE (Bescherelle).

Today, this expression means: "to recover oneself, to regain one's self-control, to pull oneself together, to regain one's energy, to start over again": *Après une période de découragement, il* A REPRIS DU POIL DE LA BÊTE (Ac.). *Loin de sa femme, ce petit quadragénaire gras* REPRENAIT DU POIL DE LA BÊTE (Fr. Mauriac, in *Robert*).

361 POINT DE VUE [point of view]. If one believed certain purists, the expression *point de vue* could not be used to mean "a personal opinion, an estimation, an appreciation." You must not believe them [because] people certainly say: *Je ne puis partager le* POINT DE VUE *optimiste* de Schlumberger (Fr. Mauriac). *La délégation française expose alors son* POINT DE VUE (A. Maurois). *Vous m'avez fait connaître votre* POINT DE VUE (Ch. de Gaulle).

In the meaning of "point of view, i.e., way of seeing," the word *optique* is frequently used today: *Son* OPTIQUE, *c'est curieux, est déjà celle du provincial* (G. Duhamel, in *Lexis*).

362 POLICLINIQUE, POLYCLINIQUE. If one takes into account the etymology of these two words, there is a distinction: *Polyclinique* (Greek, *polus;* French, *nombreux;* English, numerous, many) is a general clinic where all types of care are given. *Policlinique* (Greek, *polis;* French, *ville;* English, city) is "an establishment where medical teaching is given and medical care is administered, but where the sick persons are not hospitalized; a clinic established or functioning at the expense of *une commune*" (*Robert*).

But in practice, because of the common idea of "where care is given," the two words are often confused, and that is understandably excusable. Moreover, since the Greek element *poly-* (many) is found in numerous technical terms (*polygone* [polygon], *polyèdre* [polyhedron], *polyvalent,* etc.), it appears probable that the spelling *polyclinique* will replace *policlinique*.

363 POLITICIEN [politician]. *Un politicien (une politicienne)* is a person who, either in the government or in the opposition, exercises a political action.

According to the Academy, the word *politicien* "is taken in an unfavorable light." This is not necessarily so, however: *Elle excelle . . .à débrouiller en* POLITICIENNE *accomplie le dessous compliqué des affaires* (É. Henriot, in *Robert*).

But in fact, the word is most often taken in a pejorative meaning: *Tous les* POLITICIENS *retors qui se partagent le pouvoir en Europe* (R. Martin du Gard, in *Robert*). *Alfred Capus se présenta contre Léon Bourgeois et triompha de ce* POLITICIEN *banal et fastidieux* (H. Bordeaux).

The following term has no pejorative connotation: *un homme politique*.

364 PORT D'ARMES [bearing arms]. This expression is used for "the right to bear arms for hunting" or for "an administrative document verifying that a person has the right to hunt" (Ac.): *Il lui venait l'idée d'aller en Amérique pour être libre,. . .chasser en terre vierge et sans* PORT D'ARMES (E. and J. de Goncourt). In this meaning, the following is also used: *permis de chasse* [hunting license]: *Sans le certificat du curé,. . .point de* PERMIS DE CHASSE (Taine).

365 PORTE [door]. People certainly say: *la porte de la rue* [the front (street) door]: *On frappa rudement à* LA PORTE DE LA RUE (Mérimée).

At times people say: *trouver porte de bois* [to find a door made of wood], that is to say, not to find anyone in, or not to be received in the house where one is knocking: *C'est un plaisir que tu aurais eu plus tôt si je n'avais pas trouvé cinq ou six fois* PORTE DE BOIS (M. Pagnol). But the normal expressions [for not to have a door opened after knocking] are: *trouver visage de bois* [to find a wooden face], *trouver porte close.*

366 POSE / PAUSE. In the *Dictionnaire de l'Académie*, you find: "*Pause*: suspension, momentary interruption of an action: *Dans un long travail, il faut des* PAUSES." "*Pose*: the action of placing, of putting in place."

There is a small difficulty in spelling: when it is a matter of duration of work, does a person take *une pause* or does a person stay put, as to take *une pose*? Which word conveys the proper meaning? This may be problematic, since *pause* and *pose* both come from the Latin *pausa*. As André Goosse notes, the form *pose* can be preferred "if one considers. . .that in such a case *pose* indicates staying put in place as well as the time during which the *pose* takes place."

As a matter of fact, confusion often arises. In the following examples, instead of *pose*, one could write PAUSE: *Élie de Nacre fit une* POSE *tandis qu'un express, sans doute, semblait traverser le tunnel de sa cervelle. Il reprit:* . . . (Fr. Jammes). *Il fit une* POSE . . . *et enchaîna* . . . (Vercors). *En attendant que le rideau se relève sur la nouvelle troupe, je fais une* POSE (Fr. Mauriac).

367 POSER UN ACTE [to pose an act, to perform a deed, to accomplish an act or deed]. This expression is frequent not only in Belgium but also in France in ecclesiastical language (cf. ecclesiastical Latin, *ponĕre actum*). It is also found in general literature: [*Le docteur Ramsey*] *rendait visite à Paul VI.* . .POSANT *ainsi l'*ACTE *le plus important accompli depuis la Réforme dans le sens d'un rapprochement de l'Église anglicane et de l'Église romaine* (J. Daniélou). *Je n'avais pas l'intention de* POSER UN ACTE *universel* (P. Boulogne). *Il* POSE *librement* DES ACTES *bons et méritoires* (J. Maritain). L'ACTE *qu'il va* POSER. . . (H. Guillemin). POSER DES ACTES *méthodiques* (P.-H. Simon).

In traditional usage, one says: *faire un acte* or *accomplir un acte.*

If the act (or gesture) is blameworthy, one says: *commettre un acte* [to commit an act]. If it is a criminal act: *perpétrer* [to perpetrate].

368 POSTER [to mail, to post]. People say, when speaking of a letter that has been entrusted to the postal service: *la mettre à la poste, la jeter à la poste* [to post it, to mail it at the post office], *la mettre* or *la jeter à la boîte, dans la boîte* [to put it or to deposit it in the mailbox]. In this sense, the verb *poster* has been solidly implanted since the end of the 19th century: *En allant* POSTER *une lettre affolée* . . . (R. Kemp). *Une lettre. . .*POSTÉE *à Odessa* (A. Maurois). *Il avait* POSTÉ *à la gare les deux lettres* (Montherlant). In Canada: MALLER *une lettre.*

369 POUSSIÈRES. The utensil that is used to pick up dust, sweepings, refuse, rubbish, etc., is called *une pelle à poussière* or *une pelle à ordures* or *une pelle à balayures* [a dustpan]: *Il attendait, une* PELLE À ORDURES *à la main, que Mme Alexandre fût sortie de la cour pour y lancer ses balayures* (M. Druon). *Un ramasse-poussière, une ramassette* are provincialisms used in Belgium and northern France.

Do not say: *prendre les poussières.* Say: *épousseter* [to dust], *ôter, enlever, essuyer* [to pick up or to remove, or to wipe], or *aspirer* [to vacuum] *la poussière, les poussières* [the dust].

In familiar usage, the small accumulations of dust which are formed in fluffs under furniture are called *moutons* or *chatons;* in Switzerland, they are called *minons* or *mougnons.* At times, in Belgium: *plumetions.*

Regarding *une pelle à ordures,* the following should be noted: In Belgium, terms are used that correspond to the usual common French indicated right after them: UN BAC *à ordures* for *une poubelle* or *une boîte à ordures* [dustbin, garbage can]; UN BAC *à charbon* for *une boîte à charbon* or *un coffre à charbon* [coal bin] (*Larousse du XXᵉ siècle* and *Grand Larousse encyclopédique* both give *un charbonnier*); UN BAC *à fleurs* for *une jardinière* [flower stand or garden cart]; UN BAC *de bière* for *un casier de bière* [beer keg].

370 POUVOIR [to be able (to), may, can]. Do not say: *Entrez! Le chien aboie, mais il ne* PEUT MAL. Say, for example: *il ne mord pas* [he does not bite] or *il n'est pas méchant* [he is not mean] or *il n'y a aucun danger* [there's no danger].

In Flanders, they say: *Je ne peux pas de mon père* for . . . *je n'ai pas la permission de mon père.*

371 PRÉMICES [first fruits] / **PRÉMISSE** [premise]. Distinguish between these two words: *Prémices* (Latin *primitiae*), a plural noun, means "first fruits," the first products from the earth or livestock which were offered to the Divinity. Its figurative meaning is *début* [beginning]: *Abel offrit à Dieu les* PRÉMICES *de ses troupeaux* (Ac.).

Prémisse [premise, premiss] (scholastic Latin *praemissa*, implying *sententia*, meaning a proposition stated at the outset): used in deductive reasoning (a syllogism), where a conclusion is reached from each of the two propositions.

372 PRENDRE À PARTI(E). People used to say: *prendre quelqu'un à parti*, i.e., to take issue with someone, to charge someone with the harm that was brought about, to find fault with someone, to take someone to task. This form of the expression is now found only rarely: *Il n'ose* PRENDRE À PARTI *saint Jean de la Croix* (R. Kemp).

The modern expression is *prendre à partie*: [*Il*] *n'attendait plus que l'occasion de* PRENDRE À PARTIE *le camarade mal inspiré qui l'avait pistonné pour ce poste de choix* (R. Dorgelès, in *Robert*).

373 PRÉSENTER *(un examen).* In a notice dated Nov. 5, 1964, the Academy states that *présenter un examen* should not be used for *se présenter à un examen* [to sit for an examination].

374 PRÉSENTER, REPRÉSENTER. People do use the reflexive form of the verb: *Cette personne* SE PRÉSENTE *bien* [that is to say, this person makes a good appearance (impression) because of his / her physical appearance, posture, clothing, manners, and general appearance].

People also say, using the intransitive form of the verb, not only: *Cette personne* REPRÉSENTE *bien* but also *Cette personne* PRÉSENTE *bien: Ce général a un air martial; il* REPRÉSENTE *bien* (Littré). *Un grand seigneur que est un homme du royaume, qui* REPRÉSENTE *le mieux* (Montesquieu). *J'avoue qu'il ne* PRÉSENTE *pas mal* (J. Cocteau). *Vous avez fait une grande impression sur un jeune homme* PRÉSENTANT *bien* (H. Troyat).

375 PRESTATION, PRESTER. The noun *prestation* (meaning "the action of lending, of furnishing"), used in government administration or in sports, is often taken in a broad sense to express the idea of "being of service," "participating in the activity of a team": *Les* PRESTATIONS *de plus de 40 heures par semaine seront mieux rétribuées. Ce boxeur a fourni une* PRESTATION *exceptionnelle.* In Belgium, the verb *prester* has been formed, following the same order of ideas: *Les employés qui* PRESTERAIENT *plus de 40 heures par semaine.* For professional real estate agents and brokers, *les pres-*

tations of an apartment building include various luxury extras which add to its "standing" [status], e.g., major home electric appliances, use of marble in the bathroom, wall to wall carpeting, the use of tile, extension phones, intercoms, basement parking, etc.: *Un appartement aux* PRESTATIONS *luxueuses.* [See also entry no. 435.]

376 **PRÉTEXTE** [pretext, excuse]. *Un prétexte* is a reason that a person gives in order to cover the real motive of an action, a plan. The word implies an idea of falseness and *faux prétexte* is pleonastic.

377 **PROLONGATION.** This noun means the action of prolonging in time. Distinguish this word from **PROLONGEMENT,** which is the action of prolonging in space.

378 **PROMENER** *(aller se~).* People use the reflexive form of this verb and say: *Allons* NOUS *promener* (and not: *allons promener).* *Aller* SE *promener* (Ac.). *Allons, dit-il* NOUS *promener un peu sous bois* (G. Duhamel).

If you are displeased with someone or if you want to get rid of someone, you can say, in a spirited way: *Va te promener* or *Allez vous promener* [Go take a walk]. Similarly: *C'est un importun; qu'il aille se promener* (Ac.).

With *envoyer,* people say: *envoyer quelqu'un promener* (i.e., to send someone to the devil): *Je l'ai envoyé promener* (Ac.). *Envoyer quelque chose promener* (i.e., to knock it over violently) [to send something flying, to throw something out]. [See also entry no. 395.]

379 **PSYCHÉDÉLIQUE** [psychedelic]. This neological adjective has come from across the Atlantic [U.S.A.]. According to the Supplement of *Robert,* its etymology is from the Greek *psukhê,* French *âme,* English *soul,* plus the Greek word *dêlos,* French *visible, manifeste.* Properly, it means "which manifests the psyche." A fashionable word, it is used for the psychic state resulting from the absorption of hallucinogenic drugs or drugs that cause such a psychic state. It also applies to things that evoke visions during such a psychic state, for example, drawings, special lighting effects, etc.

380 **PYLÔNE** [pylon]. Abel Hermant upheld that *pylône* can mean nothing other than "the forepart [of a structure] in the shape of a four-angled pyramid with an opening cut out for a door" or, by extension, "a monumental door, a portal." He claimed that there

is no relationship between *un pylône* and *un pilier* [a pillar]. This is an opinion of a narrow-minded purist.

The word *pylône* is certainly used, not only for "each of the four-angled pillars that decorate the entrance to an avenue or a bridge": *Les* PYLÔNES *du pont Alexandre III, à Paris (Robert),* but also for a structure intended to support a scaffolding, cables, etc: *Là-bas, une armature de* PYLÔNES *géants. . . . C'est une station de T.S.F.* [It's a radio-station tower] (J. de Lacretelle). *Quand les vents d'hiver ou les orages déclenchaient les disjoncteurs des* PYLÔNES *de la vallée* (A. Chamson). *La voiture avait heurté un* PYLÔNE *de béton* (H. Troyat).

381 QUASI [quasi, seeming, seemingly (almost, nearly)]. Pronounce as *ka-zi* (not: *kwa-zi*). When associated with a noun that follows, it is joined with a hyphen: QUASI-*contrat* [quasi contract], QUASI-*délit* [quasi misdemeanor], QUASI-*totalité*. No hyphen is used in other cases: *Il est arrivé* QUASI *mort* (Ac.). *Des poires* QUASI *mûres. Il ne vient* QUASI *jamais. J'aime ceci* QUASI *autant que cela.*

This word is becoming outdated. It is generally replaced by *presque* [almost] or by *pour ainsi dire* [so to speak].

Quasiment is familiar and is becoming outdated: *Je suis* QUASI-MENT *tombé* (Ac.). QUASIMENT *dépouillé du produit de son labeur* (P. Gaxotte). *Sous le vieux béton* QUASIMENT *incorporé à la terre, il régnait une humidité parfumée de cathédrale souterraine* (J. Dutourd).

382 RACKET. An American word that designates an association of racketeers who extort, through blackmail or violence, large amounts of money; racketeering is a form of "organized crime": *Certains* RACKETS, *en Amérique, sont allés jusqu'au meurtre.*

383 RAI, RAIE, RAIS *(de lumière).* Of these three spellings, the French Academy mentions only the first: *Un* RAI *de lumière entrait dans la chambre par les volets mal clos.*

The other spellings are also used: *un rais* or, less often, *une raie:* LE RAIS *lumineux d'une lampe* (J. Renard). *De la poussière de sciure . . .dansait dans* UN RAIS *de soleil* (M. Genevoix). *Elle eut la surprise de voir* UNE RAIE *de lumière sous la porte* (J. Green).

(1) The word *raie* is used to indicate the separation of hair (part) made on the top of one's head, ordinarily with a comb: *Porter la* RAIE *au milieu, de côté* (Ac.). Do not say, as is often done in Belgium: *porter la* LIGNE *au milieu.*

(2) Regarding the hair, let us note: *crolle, croller, crollé* are used in Belgium for: *boucle, boucler, bouclé, frisé: Un bel enfant* CROLLÉ *comme un mouton.*

384 -RAMA. This element, taken by apheresis from the Greek *orama* (spectacle, sight), abounds in publicity: *discorama, cinérama,* etc., etc. Its use was denounced by the Academy in a communiqué dated Feb. 17, 1966.

385 REBATTRE *(les oreilles)* [to deafen one's ears]. People say: *Il m'en a* REBATTU *les oreilles* (Ac.). Do not say: *rabattre les oreilles.* Do not imitate the following example: *La musique et les choeurs d'Évolution-progrès, dont on nous rabattait les oreilles* (L. Daudet, *Le Stupide XIXe siècle,* p. 262). [See also the Academy's communiqué dated Oct. 21, 1965.]

386 RÉCIPIENDAIRE. This word (m. or f.) designates a person received in some company, some corporate body or association, with a certain amount of ceremony: *À l'Académie française, le* RÉCIPIENDAIRE *prononce un remerciement* (Ac.). *Le Roi vint féliciter la* RÉCIPIENDAIRE (G. Bauër, cited in the Supplement to *Robert*).

The word is also used for "a person who receives a university diploma, who has been recently nominated, etc." *(Robert).* To designate the man or woman who sits for an examination, the word *candidat(e)* is used: *Les* CANDIDATS *au baccalauréat* (Ac.). *Le* CANDIDAT *a fort bien répondu à son examinateur* (Id.). CANDIDAT *admissible, reçu;* CANDIDAT *refusé,* CANDIDAT *retoqué,* CANDIDAT *ajourné (Robert).*

387 RÉCIPROQUER. This is an old French verb, used as early as the 16th century, with the meaning of *rendre la pareille* [to return the same], but it has gone out of use completely in France. It has remained in Belgium where it is used to return an expression of best wishes during the New Year holiday. Abel Hermant declared: "No matter what authoritative source anyone cites in favor of this verb, I deny without any pity the right to perpetuate the life of this verb by using it." [In place of *réciproquer* use *échanger,* etc.]

388 RECONDUIRE. In the language of jurisprudence, *reconduire* [to renew] [Juridical Latin, *reconduĉere*] is used in the meaning of "to renew," in speaking of a contract, a lease.

Reconduire and *reconduction* [renewal] are used currently today in the language of government administration and politics to express the ideas of "to renew (renewal)," "to continue (continuation)," "to extend (extension)": *M. Pinay a décidé à ne plus* RECONDUIRE *la taxe civique (Le Figaro). La taxe civique ne sera pas* RECONDUITE. *. .beaucoup de contribuables craignent une* RECONDUC-

TION (Id.). *J'étais sûr que son projet,* RECONDUIT *par la Métropole, n'y aurait même pas un commencement d'application* (Ch. de Gaulle). *Il semble toutefois que le gouvernement soit décidé à* RECON-DUIRE *une nouvelle fois ce délai (Le Monde).*

389 REÇU *(au~de).* Theorists of good language condemn the expression *au reçu de votre lettre* [on receipt of your letter] and they want us to say *à la réception de.* . . . This is an opinion contradicted by usage: *Soyez donc assez bon pour me répondre sur ce point* AU REÇU *de ma lettre* (Nerval). *Au* REÇU *de la nouvelle* (É. Estaunié). *Au* REÇU *de cette lettre* (A. Billy). *Au* REÇU *de la lettre, il dit à sa femme. . .* (M. Druon). *Au* REÇU *donc de cette bonne lettre* (Montherlant).

390 RECYCLER. This is a fashionable word which means "to put someone back in the cycle of renewed activities in his / her profession": *Beaucoup de professeurs ont dû* SE RECYCLER.

390^{bis}RÉGENT, RÉGENTE, RÉGENDAT. In Belgium, *un régent, une régente* is a person who is *un agrégé (une agrégée)* [a person who has been successful at the *agrégation*—i.e., a qualified candidate who has passed a competitive examination to hold a teaching position in *lycées* at the lower secondary level]. In order to become *un régent / une régente,* a person participates at *une école normale moyenne* (or *Section*) in *le régendat,* which is a poorly coined word; *régentat* would be a slightly better term. The word *la régence* is also used, but a better term would be *les études de régent(e).*

391 RÉGRESSER [to regress]. This neological verb came into use in the 20th century: *La douleur est en train de* RÉGRESSER (N. Sarraute, in *Petit Robert*). *Art qui progresse, fleurit et* RÉGRESSE *(Robert). Pourquoi elle a* RÉGRESSÉ *pendant les premières années de son mariage, elle l'a compris* (S. de Beauvoir). *La consommation du vin a* RÉGRESSÉ *en janvier (Le Monde).*

392 REGRET *(être au~de)* [to feel sorry about, to regret]. People do say: *Je suis* AU REGRET *d'avoir dit, d'avoir fait cela; j'en suis* AU REGRET (Ac.). *Je suis bien* AU REGRET *d'avoir dû tailler et couper à travers la magnifique dissertation. . .* (H. Bremond).
This expression in the plural, *être aux regrets,* which is still in the *Dictionnaire de l'Académie* (1878), is old.

393 RELANCE; RELANCER [revival, resumption, restarting; to revive, to resume, to start again, to stimulate]. These words are used frequently today, especially in the language of journalists, when referring to the resumption of a project (plan), to the revival of an idea, of an activity that has been dormant: LA RELANCE *du pacte de Bagdad (Le Monde)*. RELANCER *un écrivain* (M. Chapelan). *Pour. . .*RELANCER *l'économie* (Génér. Béthouart).

394 RELAXER; RELAXATION. The traditional meaning of these two words is used when speaking of a prisoner who has been freed. *Relaxation* is used also, especially in medical terms, to mean "slackening, relaxation, loosening, suppression of a tension": RELAXATION *des muscles*.

In a neological meaning, *se relaxer* and *relaxation*, which are Anglicisms, are used currently to mean "to relax the body, to rest"; "a relaxation, a rest": *Alors chacun peinera pour* SE RELAXER *dans les règles* (P. Gaxotte).   *Vient cet âge où il est bon de s'asseoir toutes les fois qu'on le peut, de* SE RELAXER, *comme disent les Anglais* (É. Henriot).

395 REMBARRER *quelqu'un* [to turn someone away, to drive someone off]. This means to turn down someone harshly by a refusal, by an unkind reply. In familiar use it means: *l'envoyer promener* [to send someone walking, to tell him / her to go take a walk], *l'envoyer au diable* [to send him / her to the devil]. Popular expressions for this term are: *l'envoyer dinguer* [to turn someone out], or *l'envoyer bouler* [to send someone packing], or *l'envoyer paître* [to send someone to eat grass], or *l'envoyer coucher* [to send someone to blazes], or *l'envoyer valser* [to send him / her waltzing, to kick someone out].

In popular language, people incorrectly use *remballer* [to bully, to snub, to rate (someone)] in place of *rembarrer*. [See also entry no. 378.]

396 REMETTRE. (1) Classical writers used to say SE REMETTRE *quelqu'un* to mean *s'en rappeler le souvenir, le visage* [to remember someone's face]: *Vous ne vous remettez point mon visage?* (Molière). After the reflexive pronoun was dropped: *remettre quelqu'un* [to recognize someone]: *Vous ne me* REMETTEZ *pas, monsieur Auguste?* (Flaubert).   *Vous ne me* REMETTEZ *pas? Que si, que si, je te reconnais* (M. Arland).

(2) Do not say: *Commerce à* REMETTRE. Say: *Commerce à céder* [Business for sale].

(3) Do not say: *Il a* REMIS *tout son déjeuner* [He vomited all his lunch]. Do not say: *J'ai envie de* REMETTRE [I feel like vomiting]. Good French is: *Il a* RENDU *tout son déjeuner. J'ai envie de* RENDRE (or:. . .*de* VOMIR, or: *j'ai des* NAUSÉES).

397 RÉMUNÉRER [to remunerate]. (Latin, *remunerare;* from *munus, -eris,* meaning *faveur, récompense* [favor, recompense]: *Il a été justement* RÉMUNÉRÉ *de son travail* (Ac.).

Be careful not to pronounce or to write as *rénumérer* by reversing *m* and *n*. That is an influence of the verb *énumérer* [to enumerate].

398 RENON [an abbreviated form of *une renonce,* from the verb *renoncer* (to renounce, to give up, to abandon)]. The noun *un renon* is used in Belgium to mean *une résiliation* [cancellation] (of a lease, for example): *donner son renon.* It is also used in card playing: *Avoir un renon en pique.* In good French, the word is *une renonce: Je me suis fait* UNE RENONCE *en pique, à pique* (Academy).

The following are also used: *résilier,* or *rompre,* or *annuler un bail* [a lease], *un marché* [a business deal], *un contrat* [a contract], *un pacte* [a pact, an agreement]: CASSER *un contrat* (Acad.). ROMPRE *un engagement* (Id.).   *Le propriétaire du chalet suisse, manquant d'argent pour les réparations urgentes,* DÉNOUA *le bail* (Colette). [See also entry no. 136: *donner congé, renoncer à un appartement.*]

399 RENSEIGNER [to inform]. This verb means "to give information": *Il me* RENSEIGNA *fort mal* (Ac.).

In Belgium, *renseigner* is currently used, but incorrectly, to mean "to point out," "to indicate," "to make known"; for example: *Pouvez-vous me renseigner un bon chirurgien?* [Can you let me know of a good surgeon?]. *Ce livre renseigne les meilleurs moyens de placer son argent* [This book indicates the best ways to invest one's money]. *Renseignez-moi l'adresse de ce libraire* [Let me know the address of this bookseller]. *Ce lexique renseigne beaucoup de canadianismes* [This dictionary points out many Canadianisms].

It is probable that this use of *renseigner* is explained by a survival of the intensification of the verb *enseigner* (by adding the prefix *re-* shortened to just an *r*), whose meaning (to indicate, to make known) is today somewhat outdated: ENSEIGNANT *un logis à Paris* (Vaugelas).   *On m'*ENSEIGNE *la demeure* (Le Sage).   [*Le portier*] ENSEIGNE *volontiers aux profanes des adresses de cafés-concerts et de tripots* (J. Bainville).   The Walloons have perhaps also exercised their infleunce: In Liégeois, the following statement: *ac'sègnîz-m' li pus coûte dès vôyes* means in French, *enseignez-moi le plus court des chemins* [point out to me the shortest road]; *s'fé rac'sègnî = se faire "renseigner" (son chemin)* [to inform oneself, to get information about the right route, road].

400 RENTRER. The fundamental meaning of this verb is *entrer de nouveau* [to enter again]: *on entre dans une maison* [a person enters a house]; *on y* RENTRE *après en être sorti* [a person goes back in after having gone out of it].

This verb has other meanings that do not convey the idea of returning or an action that is iterative: *s'emboîter* [to fit (into)], *pénétrer* [to penetrate], *être enfoncé dans* [to be sunken into], *être contenu dans* [to be contained in]: *Les tubes de cette lunette d'approche* RENTRENT *les uns dans les autres* (Ac.). *Le cou lui* RENTRE *dans les épaules* (Id.). *Un nombre suffisant de fables étant composé par un La Fontaine, tout ce qu'on y ajoute* RENTRE *dans la même morale* (Voltaire). *[Certaines attitudes] qu'il n'est pas facile de faire* RENTRER *dans les cadres du système. . .* (Daniel-Rops). RENTRER *le ventre* [to draw in one's stomach].

In addition to the examples cited in the above paragraph of other meanings of the verb *rentrer*, there is a strong tendency (which is very old) to use the prefix *re-* on the verb *entrer* to indicate an instantaneous action, as opposed to an action that lasts, and to say *rentrer* instead of *entrer*: *C'est tout à fait comme au bal, quand les lumières vous* RENTRENT *dans les yeux* (Taine). *Tout l'hiver va* RENTRER *dans mon être* (Baudelaire). *On peut très bien se suicider pour deux raisons. Non ça ne leur* RENTRE *pas dans la tête* (A. Camus). *Et ce métro qui passe tout le temps que le bruit vous en* RENTRE *dans le corps* (P. Vialar). *C'était fou cette idée de vouloir* RENTRER *dans les musées [pour s'y faire une situation]* (A. Chamson).

This use is very well explained, but not condemned, by Vendryes in *Le Langage*, p. 130.

401 REPARTIR / RÉPARTIR. Distinguish between these two verbs. *Repartir* is "to leave again, to start off again"; it also means "to reply in a lively way, to retort." *Répartir* means "to share."

402 REPOUSSER. This verb can be used in the neological meaning of "to postpone to a later date, to delay": *Je vais téléphoner au bureau de* REPOUSSER *le rendez-vous de quarante-huit heures* (H. Troyat). *Certains de ceux-ci préférèrent disparaître subrepticement par le fond de la tente,* REPOUSSANT *à plus tard de s'expliquer* (M. Druon).

403 REPRENDRE. Do not say: *Ces noms sont* REPRIS *dans la liste ci-dessus*. And do not say: *Les cas* REPRIS *dans tel article du Code*. The verb *reprendre*, as used in those two examples in place of *mentionner* [to mention] or *indiquer* [to indicate], is a provincialism used in Belgium and in northern France.

404 RESSEMBLER [to resemble]. People say: *Ces deux personnes se ressemblent comme deux gouttes d'eau* (Ac.).

Purists condemn the structure *Il lui ressemble comme deux gouttes d'eau* because, as Martinon says, *"deux gouttes d'eau ne peuvent pas* LUI RESSEMBLER" ["two drops of water cannot look like him / her"].

Of course, there is an ellipsis there, but we must not interpret [the omission] the way Martinon does, which is: . . .*comme deux gouttes d'eau* [LUI *ressemblent*] [. . .like two drops of water which (resemble *her/him*)]. What must be understood is: . . .*comme deux gouttes d'eau* [SE *ressemblent*] [. . .like two drops of water which (resemble *each other*)].

This structure has been used by many excellent authors: *Il me ressemble comme deux gouttes d'eau* (Molière). *Il ressemblait comme deux gouttes d'eau à un petit homme qui se portait parfaitement bien* (Sévigné). *Cela ressemble à un tailleur comme deux gouttes d'eau* (Diderot).

405 RESSOURCER *(se~)*. This neologism, which means "to return to the sources," is currently in use in the language of theologians and people of the Church: *Ainsi le présent et l'avenir* SE RESSOURCENT *au passé* (P. Riquet). *Les théologiens* SE RESSOURCENT *en saint Paul et en saint Jean* (J. Guitton). *Tout au long de ce XVIᵉ siècle où nous la voyons [notre ancienne langue] . . .se rajeunir tout en* SE RESSOURÇANT *à la fontaine antique . . .* (J. Duron).

A parallel word is *un ressourcement* [a return to the origins, to the sources]: *Un peuple qui se relève par un* RESSOURCEMENT *profond de son antique orgueil* (Ch. Péguy, in *Robert*). *Le protestantisme est obligé, par cette nécessité de regroupement, à une nécessité de* RESSOURCEMENT (J. Guitton).

406 RESTER. When this verb is used to mean "*demeurer* [to reside], *loger* [to lodge, to live], *habiter* [to inhabit]," it belongs to popular or provincial French: *C'est ainsi que Françoise [une servante] disait que quelqu'un "RESTAIT" dans ma rue pour dire qu'il y demeurait* (M. Proust). *Mme Toullier* RESTE *au troisième* (J. Vallès). *Elle vient de m'acheter un brin de cresson pas plus tard qu'hier, raconte le verdurier à Mme Grosjean. Elle* RESTE *là-bas, vers la fontaine* (B. Beck).

407 RÉTICENT, RÉTICENCE. If one abides by the etymological value of these two words—(Latin *reticēre*, from *tacēre*; French *(se) taire*; English "to remain silent"; Latin *reticentia*; French *silence obstiné*; English "obstinate silence"—they both properly imply the idea of "silence," of "remaining silent"; and *réticence* means "a voluntary omission of a thing which one could or should say," or "the thing omitted," or "silence": *Dans le récit qu'il m'a fait, il a mis beaucoup de* RÉTICENCE (Ac.). *Dans cet acte, il y a une* RÉTICENCE *frauduleuse* (Id.). *Il [un pendu] s'ajoutait à toutes les farouches* RÉTICENCES *de la nuit* (Hugo). *Des phrases atténuées et* RÉTICENTES *(Robert)*.

Since a person who is *réticent* (the idea of "silence") is generally so because he / she is hesitant or reserved, and because *réticent* undergoes a paronymous attraction of "resistant" and "restive," a slip in meaning has been produced; thus, the words *réticence* and *réticent* often imply, in today's usage, in spite of purists, the ideas of "reserve," "hesitation," "resistance": *Ce n'est pas sans* RÉTICENCE *qu'ils ont, au début, consenti à "faire un papier"* (J. de Lacretelle). *Nul d'entre eux n'acceptait son lot sans* RÉTICENCE (G. Duhamel). *Ma mère était plus* RÉTICENTE *pour me laisser sortir le soir* (H. Bazin).

408 RETOUR *(point de non~)*. This is from the English "point of no return." It is the point beyond which it is no longer possible to bring bombardiers armed with nuclear weapons back to their base; the point beyond which a rocket launched from Earth no longer undergoes terrestrial attraction. In its figurative meaning: a matter whose destiny can no longer be changed.

409 RETRAITÉ. *Un retraité* [a person who has retired] is someone who is *à la retraite* [in retirement]; or, people also say: *en retraite*. When the retired person receives a retirement pension, that person can be called *pensionné* [pensioned]: *Les* PENSIONNÉS *de guerre* (R. Martin du Gard). *Les* PENSIONNÉS *du gouvernement. Homme de lettres* PENSIONNÉ *(Robert)*.

In saying *retraité*, the essential idea expressed is "who has stopped carrying out his / her duties, activity"; in saying *pensionné*, the essential idea expressed is "who benefits from a pension."

Pensionnaire can designate a man or woman who receives a pension from a state (government), a private source, etc.: *Il est* PENSIONNAIRE *de l'État, du gouvernement* (Ac.). But in this meaning the word is outdated and one generally uses the word *pensionné*.

410 RÉTROACTES. People say: *rétroagir* [to retroact; to act on the past], *rétroaction, rétroactivement, rétroactivité*. In Belgium, *rétroacter* is used: *étudier les* RÉTROACTES *d'une affaire*. In France: . . . *les* ANTÉCÉDENTS *d'une affaire*.

411 ROBE DE CHAMBRE *(pommes de terre en~)* [potatoes in jackets]. Certain theorists of good language think that people should say: *pommes de terre* EN ROBE DES CHAMPS to designate potatoes cooked in their jackets. To say *en robe des champs,* as *Robert* notes, seems to be a distortion (or a willful correction) of *pommes de terre en robe de chambre,* because it did not come into use until later.

Littré, the *Dictionnaire général, Larousse du XXe siècle,* and the *Grand Larousse encyclopédique* write it as *pommes de terre en robe de chambre. Robert, Grand Larousse de la Langue française,* and *Lexis* list both expressions. There is no doubt that *en robe des champs* is used: *Un mets rare, par exemple des toasts de caviar après des pommes de terre* EN ROBE DES CHAMPS (M. Toesca). But general usage is to say *en robe de chambre: Une petite tête d'enfant chaude comme une pomme de terre* EN ROBE DE CHAMBRE (J. Renard).

412 RUTILER, RUTILANT. These two words are used when speaking either of things that are a radiant fiery red (the only meaning pointed out by the Academy) or brilliant things, like gold. Regardless of what some purists say, these two words are also used for brilliant things—no matter what the color is (and that was used in Latin): *Cet uniforme* RUTILANT *passé aux couleurs nationales* (J. Giraudoux). *Il lui prête [à un fleuve] des beautés* RUTILANTES (A. Maurois). *[Deux brillants]* RUTILAIENT *sur sa main sèche de ménagère* (Fr. Mauriac). *La mer bleu sardine* RUTILAIT *au soleil* (H. Queffélec). *Rouges, jaunes, verts [des fruits confits], comme des pierres précieuses. Leurs chaudes couleurs* RUTILAIENT *sous le givre du sucre* (P. Guth). *En un dîner* RUTILANT *de clarté. . .* (M. Proust). *Ma voiture. . .,* RUTILANTE, *rechromée, pimpante. . .* (P. Daninos).

413 SAC À MAIN [handbag]. The small bag that a woman carries in her hand, holding money, keys, papers, cosmetics, etc., is called *un sac à main* or just plain *sac: [Elle] tira un mouchoir de son* SAC À MAIN (J. Green). *Elle sortit une glace de son* SAC (M. Druon). Do not call it *une sacoche,* which is a bag made of leather or strong canvas, equipped with a strap, allowing it to be carried over the shoulder or on the back: SACOCHE *d'encaisseur, de livreur* [A cashier's pouch, a delivery person's bag]. People also say: *sacoche de cycliste, sacoche d'écolier, sacoche de motocycliste* (containing various tools).

Un réticule for *sac à main* (and distorted, at times, as *ridicule*) is outdated today: *Dans le* RÉTICULE *de l'une d'elles, on a retiré une lettre d'amour* (H. Bordeaux). *Amélie ouvrit son réticule* (H. Troyat).

Note that *un sac à dos* [back pack, knapsack] is a bag made of canvas with straps like suspenders which is carried on one's back, in which sportsmen and sportswomen, mountain climbers, and others put their personal items, provisions, etc. There is also the word *un havresac* [haversack].

414 SALAUD, SALOP [scoundrel, swine, filthy beast]. These two words belong to popular and vulgar language. *Salaude*, the feminine form of *salaud*, is used very little. The masculine form *salop* (which is listed in *Robert* as a variant spelling of *salaud*) is not recognized by the Academy, which gives the feminine form, *salope*.

415 SANCTIONNER [to sanction, to approve]. This word means "to confirm by sanction, to approve legally or officially": SANCTION-NER *une loi. L'usage a* SANCTIONNÉ *telle expression.* In a communiqué dated Oct. 2, 1969, the Academy declares that it is wrong to use *sanctionner* to mean *punir* [to punish].

416 SAVEZ-VOUS. The Belgian people have often been mocked about the expression *savez-vous*, which they use and misuse in conversation to convey the idea of *n'est-ce pas?* or *n'est-il pas vrai?* [isn't that so? isn't that true?] or merely to give fullness to an idea.

There is nothing faulty about this French expression: *C'était une belle émeute,* SAVEZ-VOUS! (Hugo.) *Je chanterai dans les choeurs,* SAVEZ-VOUS! (Musset.) *Il est plus de midi,* SAVEZ-VOUS? (Mérimée.) *C'est une forte tête,* SAVEZ-VOUS, *le Docteur* (P. Valéry).

Advice to the Belgian people: use it, but do not abuse it, and do not make a bad habit of it.

417 SAVOIR [to know how] / **POUVOIR** [to be able]. A distinction must be made between *savoir* and *pouvoir* when followed by an infinitive:
(a) *Savoir faire qq.ch.* [to know how to do something] is to have the knowledge, the skill, the means to do something, or to be accustomed or to have the aptitude to do something: SA-VOIR *jouer du violon* (Ac.).   *Je* SUS *bientôt lire couramment* (Ch. Péguy). *Cette sublime figure de songeur n'a jamais* SU *s'accommoder du quotidien* (E. Jaloux).

The subject of the verb *savoir* cannot be the name of a thing. You cannot say, for example: *Ma voiture sait faire du 200 à l'heure* [My car knows how to go 200 kilometers an hour].
(b) *Pouvoir faire qq.ch.* [to be able to do something] is to have the ability or the permission to do something or to be in

condition to do something: *Il n'a* PU *réussir dans cette affaire* (Ac.).   *Vous* POUVEZ *partir; je vous y autorise* [You may leave; I authorize you]. *Des visages que je reconnaissais sans* POUVOIR *les nommer* (A. Camus).

(1) The distinction [between *savoir* and *pouvoir*] can be seen in the following example: *Ceux qui ne savent* [*les illettrés*] *ou ne peuvent lire* [*par exemple, les aveugles*] *ne pourront faire de dispositions dans la forme du testament mystique (Code civ., art. 978)* [Those who do not know how to (the illiterate) or cannot read (for example, the blind) will not be able to . . .] (Civil Code, art. 978).

(2) Since a person who knows how to do *(sait faire)* a thing, can *(peut)* generally do it, there are certain overlappings between *savoir* and *pouvoir* that take place at times in negative sentences with a simple *ne* and with no *pas: Il n'a* SU *en venir à bout* [He wasn't able to get through it / He didn't know how to get through it] (Ac.).   But nowadays this sort of thing is found only in the conditional: *Je n'aurais* SU *dire de laquelle j'étais jalouse* (A. Gide). *Il n'aurait* SU *dire pouquoi* (G. Duhamel).

418 SECOUSSE SISMIQUE. This locution is pleonastic because *sismique* [seismic], according to its etymology—(Greek, *seismos;* French, *tremblement de terre;* English, earthquake; from *seiô* in Greek, *je secoue* [I shake])—already implies the idea of *secousse* [shaking]. However, it has been accepted into usage: *Les dégradations, dues à un tassement de la muraille, ou plus probablement à une* SECOUSSE SISMIQUE . . . (A. France).   *Une sorte de* SECOUSSE SISMIQUE (A. Thérive).   *Il y a trois jours, une* SECOUSSE SISMIQUE *a été ressentie à Paris* (J. Green).   *Ce ne serait quand même pas une* SECOUSSE SISMIQUE? (R. Ikor.)

If you find it distasteful to use the term *une secousse sismique,* then you should say: *une secousse tellurique,* or *un séisme,* or *un tremblement de terre* [all of which mean earthquake].

419 SENS DESSUS DESSOUS [upside down] / **SENS DEVANT DERRIÈRE** [hind side before, backward]. In these two expressions, the word *sens* is a modification of the old form *cen,* which is a variant of *ce.* Littré writes it as *c'en dessus dessous, c'en devant derrière.* Some authors have written it as: *Tout va* C'EN *dessus dessous* (É. Faguet).   *La maison était* C'EN *dessus dessous* (H. Pourrat).   *Comme, à force de réformer, on a mis l'Université* C'EN *dessus dessous (ainsi doit-on écrire), je ne sais plus très bien ce qu'est aujourd'hui l'école primaire* (P. Gaxotte).

But usage has very clearly established the expression to be written as SENS *dessus dessous,* SENS *devant derrière: Tous mes papiers sont* SENS *dessus dessous* (Ac.).   *Il a mis son chapeau* SENS *devant derrière* (Id.).

420 SEPTEMBRE [September]. The *p* is pronounced. [In Belgium, the pronunciation *sè-tembre* is in use.]

421 SERVEUR, SERVEUSE [waiter, waitress]. These two words, which designate the person who serves people at a table, especially in a restaurant or in a café, are in use: *Ce père avait eu deux enfants d'une* SERVEUSE *de bar* (Daniel-Rops).   *Le* SERVEUR *du wagon-restaurant nous servait le café* (Y. Gandon).

422 SEULS. People certainly say: *se trouver* SEULS [to be alone] (two or more persons) when the meaning is "without any other person": *Quand ils furent* SEULS, *tous les deux. . .* (Flaubert).   *Ils étaient* SEULS *tous les deux* (N. Sarraute).

423 SÉVÈRE. The use of *sévère* [severe] to mean "grave, heavy, important" is an Anglicism which was introduced into the French language during World War I. Although it has been criticized, it has found its place in the language of journalists and sports writers and at times in literature: *Un échec* SÉVÈRE (H. Troyat).   [*Les convois aériens*] *n'atteindraient pas leur but sans subir des pertes* SÉVÈRES (A. François-Poncet).

424 SKATEBOARD or **SKATE-BOARD.** An Anglo-American word [skate, *patin;* board, *planche*]. This *planche à roulettes* has been very popular among boys and girls for several years.

425 SOLEIL [sun]. People say: *Il fait du soleil* (Ac.), *il fait déjà grand soleil* (Id.). But you can also say: *Il fait soleil* (Littré). *Il fait soleil maintenant* (Fr. Mauriac).

426 SOLUTION DE CONTINUITÉ. In this expression, *solution* means "the action of interrupting, of separating, of cutting" (cf. Latin, *solvěre = dénouer* [to untie, to unknot], *rompre* [to break]). There is, therefore, *une solution de continuité* when, in the domain of concrete or abstract things, there is an interruption, a cutting off, a separation of the parts: *Il faut une* SOLUTION *brusque* DE CONTINUITÉ, *une rupture avec le mode* (H. Bergson, in *Robert*).

427 SOLUTIONNER. This word came into use at the beginning of this century; it has spread especially into parliamentary language and the language of journalists. It has also entered into literary usage: *Pour les solutionner [les problèmes de l'existence]* . . . (L. Pergaud). *Pour le* SOLUTIONNER *définitivement [le problème "du Mal et du Progrès"]* (P. Teilhard de Chardin). This word remains criticized, but since it is easier to conjugate than *résoudre* [to solve], it has good chances of living on and prospering.

428 SOMPTUAIRE. This adjective (Latin, *sumptuarius*, from *sumptus*, expense) properly means "relating to expenses" and it is used concerning laws which restrain or regulate expenses in feasts, ceremonies, clothing, buildings, etc.: *Louis XII l'ayant défendue [l'orfèvrerie] dans son royaume par une loi* SOMPTUAIRE *indiscrète, les Français firent venir leur argenterie de Venise* (Voltaire).

But the word *somptuaire* [sumptuary], because of a paronymous attraction, falls into the semantic orbit of the word *somptueux*. The word *somptuaire* is generally taken to mean "*somptueux* [costly, sumptuous], which displays an excessive taste for what is magnificent, luxurious"—especially as an epithet of *dépenses* [expenses]: *Point de dépenses* SOMPTUAIRES (A. Maurois). *Il ne songera plus au bas de laine, mais à des dépenses* SOMPTUAIRES (G. Duhamel). *On parle de dépenses somptuaires* (A. Siegfried). *La capitale. . .voluptuaire et* SOMPTUAIRE *d'un grand pays* (P. Valéry).

This neological meaning of *somptuaire* is condemned by the French Academy in a notice dated Oct. 2, 1969.

429 SOUFFRETEUX. This adjective is used to mean "sickly, in ill health": *Il trouvait une analogie entre le sort de cette bête* SOUFFRE-TEUSE *et le sien* (R. Rolland). *Un tout jeune homme, voûté, malingre, au visage doux et* SOUFFRETEUX (J. Kessel). *Je l'ai trouvé hier tout* SOUFFRETEUX (Ac.).

430 SOUS-TASSE (SOUTASSE) [saucer]. This word is not a Belgianism. It is a popular French word very normally formed (from *sous* and *tasse*), as is *une soucoupe* [saucer]. *Sous-tasse* has been accepted by *Grand Larousse encyclopédique*, by *Lexis*, by the Supplement to *Robert*, and even by *Grand Larousse de la Langue française*, which permits the two spellings: *une sous-tasse* and *une soutasse*.

431 SPEAKER [announcer]. This Anglicism (fem. form, *une speakerine*), which is, moreover, an Anglicism only in part (because English-speaking people use the word *announcer*), designates the person who, on radio and television, presents broadcasts, announces programs, and gives the news. The word is in common use, but some people use *un annonceur / une annonceuse, présentateur / présentatrice.*

432 SPECTACULAIRE [spectacular]. This neologism is used very readily today to describe what is striking to one's eyes, a spectacular sight, a theatrical performance which makes an impression on one's imagination: *Juste ce qu'il fallait d'exhibition pour faire plus* SPECTACULAIRE . . . (M. Genevoix).

433 SPÉCULAUS (SPÉCULOOS, or at times: **SPÉCULATION).** In Belgium, this is a kind of "cracker" or "biscuit" made with brown sugar.

434 STANDARD [standard, standard design, standard pattern, type]. This English word (= *étalon, type*) is used as an invariable adjective: *Des modèles* STANDARD [standard models]. The Academy, in a communiqué dated April 20, 1967, proposes to replace it with the adjective *normalisé.* If the word is taken as a noun, the Academy suggests substituting *norme,* except for the expression *standard téléphonique* [telephone switchboard], which has been established by usage.

435 STANDING. This English word designates the rank *(le rang)* that a person occupies in society, the social or economic position, and standard of living. It is especially used in real estate announcements: *appartement de grand* STANDING, *de haut* STANDING (= outstanding comforts, every modern convenience). [See also entries no. 347 and no. 375.]

436 STUPÉFAIT [stupefied, amazed, astounded]. This word is used as an adjective: *Il demeura tout* STUPÉFAIT (Ac.).   It can have as a synonym the participial adjective *stupéfié: Je suis encore tout* STUPÉFIÉ *de votre intrépidité* (Voltaire).

This word has been able to give rise to the verb *stupéfaire* [to stupefy] (which is listed in *Robert* and mentioned in *Grand Larousse de la Langue française*), but it is used only in the third person singular of the present indicative and in the compound tenses: *Cela me* STUPÉFAIT (Flaubert).   *Une chose par-dessus tout m'*A STUPÉFAIT (Fr. Mauriac).   *Ses confidences qui . . .* AVAIENT STUPÉFAIT *Herbillon* (J. Kessel).

Advice: If you are tempted to use the verb *stupéfaire,* remember that the correct verb is *stupéfier: Cette nouvelle l'a* STUPÉFIÉ (Ac.).

437 SUBVENTIONNER, SUBSIDIER. The verb *subsidier,* in the meaning of "to support financially" (a newspaper, a political party, a university, a city, a theater, etc.), has not been accepted in normal usage. In good French, the verb *subventionner* is used: *Judas aurait probablement* SUBVENTIONNÉ *des sanatoria, des hôpitaux* . . . (G. Bernanos). *On* SUBVENTIONNE *des entreprises moribondes* (A. Maurois).

Subsidier [in place of *subventionner*, to subsidize] is very rare in France: *Les auteurs de l'envoi sont* SUBSIDIÉS *par un mystérieux malfaiteur* (Ch. Maurras, cited by Deharveng).

438 SUCETTE [lollipop, lollie]. *Une sucette* is candy attached to one end of a small stick: *Trois* SUCETTES *à la menthe* (R. Sabatier). The word also designates a small nipple (teething ring or pacifier) which is given to an infant to prevent it from sucking its thumb. This word is not recognized by the French Academy.

439 SUICIDER *(se~)*. Considered literally, this word contains the reflexive pronoun twice: *se* and *sui* (Latin, meaning *de soi*, of oneself), which amounts to *soi tuer*. That does not prevent *se suicider* [to commit suicide, to kill oneself] from being used [more popularly than *se tuer* (to kill oneself)]: *C'était par désespoir, comme on* SE SUICIDE (Flaubert). *Les gens qui vont* SE SUICIDER (J. Giraudoux).

440 SUITE À . . . The style *Suite à votre lettre* . . . [With reference to your letter. . .] belongs to commercial language. It is much better to say; *En réponse à votre lettre*. . . or (if you insist on using the noun *suite*), then say: COMME SUITE À *votre lettre:* COMME SUITE À *votre demande*. . . (R. Catherine). COMME SUITE À *la lettre que vous m'avez fait parvenir*. . . (J. Chaban-Delmas). COMME SUITE À *sa demande*. . . (R. Dorgelès).

It is rare to say *En suite de:* EN SUITE DE *l'entretien que vous avez bien voulu me demander* (Montherlant).

441 SUPPORTER. Pronounce this noun as *su-por-tère*. This Anglicism is very much in use in the language of the sports world. The Academy (communiqué dated Feb. 23, 1967) is of the opinion that we must say: *supporteur* or *partisan*. But will common usage listen?. . .

In the meantime, let us observe that it is not correct to say: *supporter une équipe* for *encourager, soutenir une équipe*.

442 SUSCEPTIBLE. For Littré, the words *susceptible* and *capable* must not be confused. Littré says that "a person is *susceptible* to receiving, feeling, undergoing; but a person is *capable* of giving or of doing." The Academy is of the same opinion (cf. its notice dated Feb. 24, 1965).

In practice, people hardly take into consideration this distinction in meaning and the best authors use *susceptible* to express a possibility: *Une vérité* SUSCEPTIBLE *d'affaiblir le bras qui combat* (A. Gide). SUSCEPTIBLE *d'accomplir de très grandes choses* (É. Henriot). *Les quelques généraux* SUSCEPTIBLES *de diriger une armée* (P. Gaxotte).

Note that *susceptible* can have a passive infinitive as a complement: *Je ne tiens pas la société. . .pour* SUSCEPTIBLE *d'être améliorée* (A. Malraux).

443 SUSPENS(E). This word, borrowed from the English *suspense* (which is actually from the French word *suspens*), has been in use for about twenty years. It designates, especially in mystery novels or in films, a suspension of action which brings about an unrest and a distressing feeling of expectation. Thérive thought that the word should be feminine: *une suspense.* In place of *suspense,* some people prefer *le suspens.* As for the pronunciation of *suspense,* some say *sus'-pèn'-s,* while others pronounce it as *sus'-pen-s'* [i.e., *pen* nasalized and final *s* pronounced] which is preferred: *Le* SUSPENS *est bien ménagé* (É. Henriot). *Dans le* SUSPENS *mystique* (P. Valéry). *Il n'y a plus de* SUSPENSE (Fr. Mauriac). *Ce qu'on appelle aujourd'hui "le* SUSPENSE" (J. Kessel).

There is a word that has a stronger meaning than *suspens(e):* the English word *thriller,* which makes a person shiver, which scares a person.

444 SYMPOSIUM. Etymologically, *un symposium* is a banquet, a feast (Greek, *sumposion,* from *sumpinein;* French, *boire ensemble;* English, "to drink together"). Certain people, not without pedantry, use this word (introduced through the intermediary of the English word) to designate a conference of philosophers, scholars, specialists who treat a topic of discussion.

The following French words are preferred: *congrès, colloque, carrefour,* or even simply: *réunion, entretien, rencontre: En vue de la préparation du "XIe* CONGRÈS *international de l'Organisation scientifique"* (A. Siegfried).

445 TABOU [taboo]. This word properly signifies the sacred and inviolable nature of certain things. The word, as an adjective (invariable or variable according to gender and number), serves to qualify a thing or a person whose prestige or authority is unquestionable: *Il y a, dans notre civilisation, bien des sujets* TABOUS.

L'appellation est TABOU (R. Georgin).   *Des livres complètement nuls deviennent tout à coup* TABOUS (N. Sarraute, in *Lexis*).

446 TÂCHER MOYEN DE. This term is used popularly for *tâcher de* [to try to], *faire son possible pour* [to do one's best to]: *Tâchez moyen de me rapporter un peu de fric* [Try to find some way to bring me back a little jack (money)].

Another term in popular language is: *Il n'y a pas moyen de* MOY-ENNER [There's no way to find a way]; that is to say, *la chose est impossible* [the thing is impossible—no way].

447 TAILLEUSE. This word, which is listed in Littré, means *une couturière qui coupe les vêtements de femmes* [a dressmaker]. It is a provincialism: *Les tailleurs et les* TAILLEUSES *du village ou du bourg voisin faisaient les habits et les robes* (A. Dauzat).

In standard French the word is *une couturière* [dressmaker, seamstress].

448 TAISEUX, TAISEUSE. In Belgium: a person who does not talk much; in common French: *taciturne*.

449 TAPIS CLOUÉ [fitted carpet, i.e., nailed-down carpeting]. In Belgium, people use the term *un tapis plain*. It is not, strictly speaking, incorrect. The word *plain* (from Latin, *planus;* French, *uni, égal;* English, plain, simple, even, equal) is used simply as an adjective of mode. You will find in Hugo's works: *Sa robe de drap brun* PLAIN.

But in France the term *un tapis plain* is not in use. What is used is *tapis cloué* or *moquette* [wall-to-wall carpeting]: *Sur le* TAPIS CLOUÉ . . . *il y avait une carpette* (Aragon).   *Elle s'élança sur la* MOQUETTE *beige, uniforme et moelleuse* (R. Martin du Gard). [In Canada: *tapis mur à mur.*]

450 TARTUFE. The Academy, as well as Littré, the *Dictionnaire général*, and the *Grand Larousse encyclopédique*, write this word as: *tartufe, tartuferie. Tartuffe* was the spelling used by Molière. Both spellings are listed in *Robert, Lexis,* and *Grand Larousse de la Langue française.*

451 TÉLÉ [T.V., TV].   This is a familiar abbreviation for the word *la télévision*. People say *la télé: C'est bête qu'on n'ait pas la* TÉLÉ (H. Troyat).   *Regardez la* TÉLÉ (H. Bazin).   Often, people also use *tévé, TV* or *T.V.: Se produire à la* TV (P. Daninos).   *Hier soir à la* T.V., *de Gaulle* (J. Green).

452 TÉMOIGNER [to testify, to show, to display, to bear witness].
Do not say: *Touchés des* MARQUES *de sympathie que vous leur avez*
TÉMOIGNÉES. It would be redundant to use the word *marques*
because *témoigner* does include the idea of *marques* (*témoigner*
= *marquer*). Say: *Touchés des marques de sympathie que vous
leur avez* DONNÉES or *Touchés de* LA SYMPATHIE *que vous leur avez*
TÉMOIGNÉE.

453 TENDRESSE / TENDRETÉ. *La tendresse* is used only in a moral
sense; it is related to affection, friendship, love: *La* TENDRESSE *d'un
père pour ses enfants* (Ac.).   *Elle a le coeur plein de* TENDRESSE *pour
lui* (Id.).

   La tendreté is used almost solely in a physical sense, e.g., when
speaking of meats, fruits, vegetables: *La* TENDRETÉ *d'un gigot* (Ac.).
La TENDRETÉ *de ces fruits, de ces légumes* (Id.).

   Rare: *Je te parle, malgré la* TENDRETÉ *de ton âge, comme à un homme*
(A. Arnoux).

454 TIERS MONDE [third world]. This is an expression that came
into use at the end of World War II. It designates the countries in
the process of development but which are not associated with
either the capitalist bloc or the Soviet bloc: *Les pays du* TIERS-
MONDE *forment les "non-alignés."*

455 TIRER [to draw, to pull]. The impersonal expression, *ça tire* [it
draws], frequently used in Belgium, means: "There is a very cold
current of air blowing (through a full or slight opening)"; "there
is a very strong draft." They also say: *ça chasse.*

456 TORCHON [dish cloth, kitchen cloth]. *Un torchon* is "a sort of
towel made of heavy material which is used to wipe dishes,
kitchen equipment, furniture, etc." (Ac.) Such a towel is also
called *un torchon de cuisine;* at times, *une lavette.* In Belgium, the
word *un essuie* is used.

   In France, the coarse material used to wash tile floors is called
serpillière, or *torchon,* or *toile à laver,* or merely *toile,* or *wassingue*
which is used less often, although it is popularly used in northern
France. In Belgium, this type of cleaning cloth is called, according
to geographical location: *loque à reloqueter,* (or *loque* for short), *drap
de maison, reloquoir, loquetoir, reloquetoir, ressuwô, clicote, wassingue, wite.* In the French Ardennes, the word *gobîye* is used; in
Vendée: *cince.* In Switzerland: *panosse.*

   As for wiping dust off furniture, people use the word *un torchon
à poussière* [dustcloth], or simply *un torchon,* or *un chiffon.* In

French commercial language, the following words are used: *chamoisette, chamoisine,* etc.

457 TOURNEMAIN, TOUR DE MAIN *(en un ~)* [in a twist of the hand]. These expressions mean "in as little time as is needed to twist one's hand." According to Littré and the Academy, *en un tournemain* is outdated, but it is still in use: *En un* TOURNEMAIN, *il s'empara d'un plaid* (H. Bazin). *Elle. . .fait bouillir l'eau en un* TOURNEMAIN (A. Lanoux). *Comme s'il suffisait que les gens soient morts pour qu'on les mette dans sa poche en un* TOURNEMAIN (C. Bourniquel).

458 TRAFIC [traffic]. For the Academy, *le trafic* means "trade, business, commerce dealing in merchandise." The word is used figuratively with a bad connotation to refer to the profit that is made from the "traffic" of certain items: *Les* TRAFICS *honteux qu'il a faits.*

In today's usage, the word *le trafic* (because of the English word "traffic") has taken on the meaning of "general movement of trains" or "of vehicles": *Les routes de grand* TRAFIC (G. Duhamel). *Les vieilles portes ogivales. . .sous lesquelles ne passait plus aucun* TRAFIC (A. Arnoux). *Le* TRAFIC *Ouest-Est. . .est plus lourd que l'autre* (A. Siegfried).

459 TRAIT D'UNION [hyphen]. A hyphen is used between elements in many compound words and, in particular, in certain words beginning with a prefix, such as, *après, arrière, avant, contre, entre, extra, sans, sous, ultra, vice;* for example, *arc-en-ciel, aveugle-né, aigre-doux, vis-à-vis, après-midi, avant-coureur, contre-attaque, sans-gêne, sous-préfet,* etc.

Special Observations

460 Demi, mi, semi, nu. Observe how the following are written: *demi-heure, à mi-chemin, semi-circulaire, nu-tête,* etc. [See also entry no. 660.]

461 Noms de rues [Names of streets]. In France, administrative usage is to place a hyphen between the first name and the last name when the name of a person is the name of a street, a lycée, etc. This is also done in literature: *Professeur au lycée Blaise-Pascal* (M. Barrès). *J'ai vu, avenue Victor-Hugo, un Gaveau d'occasion* (G. Marcel).

This use (faulty according to A. Dauzat) is poorly justified.

Many people, not without reason, do not follow it [i.e., they do not use a hyphen].

462 Noms de nombre [Numbers]. Regarding the use of the hyphen in numbers used as adjectives, see entry no. 682.

463 Verbe et pronom personnel [Verb and personal pronoun]. A hyphen is placed between the verb and the inverted personal pronoun subject (or *ce* or *on*): *Dis-je. Viens-tu? Était-ce? Dit-on.*

A hyphen is placed between the imperative form of a verb and the personal pronoun object when they form a single breath group: *Crois-moi, dites-lui, prends-le.*

Observe the use or nonuse of the hyphen in the following examples: *Dites-le-moi, allez-vous-en, faites-le-moi savoir, laisse-moi te raconter ceci; viens me le raconter; daignez nous le pardonner, veuille me suivre, ose le dire.*

464 Saint. Use a hyphen between the word *saint* and the name that follows when a designation is made as to locality, holiday, street, etc. Do not use a hyphen if a saint's name is not used in such designations: *La ville de Saint-Quentin, la rue Saint-Paul, la Saint-Nicolas.* No hyphen and no capital *s* in the word *saint* if the saint's name is not the name of a place, holiday, street, etc. [that is, when reference is made to the name of the saint only]: *La charité de saint Martin* [The charity of Saint Martin].

465 Prénoms [A person's first names]. A hyphen often used to be placed between the different first names of a person: *Louis-Charles-Alfred de Musset (Larousse du XXe siècle).*

Nowadays, the use of the hyphen has dropped, particularly in the records of vital statistics: *François René Théodore Durand.*

However, the hyphen is used to join two first names when they are considered to be one name: *Jean-Jacques Rousseau, Marie-Anne d'Autriche, Louise-Marie d'Orléans, Jean-Pierre Dupont.*

466 Pas de trait d'union [No hyphen]. No hyphen is used in the following locutions: *tout à coup, tout à fait, tout à l'heure; en dehors, en dedans, en deçà, en delà, en dessus, en dessous.* But the hyphen is used in: *au-dehors, au-dedans, au-delà, au-dessus de, au-dessous de.*

467 Pas de trait d'union [No hyphen]. No hyphen is used in *Alexandre le Grand, Charles le Téméraire,* etc.

468 TRAMINOT [streetcar employee]. Using as a model the word *un cheminot* [railroad employee], the word *un traminot* has been formed, based on the popular word *un tram* (short for *un tramway* [a streetcar]), designating a streetcar employee: *Cinq mille* TRAMI-NOTS *en grève à Lodz* (*Le Figaro*, Aug. 14, 1957). In Switzerland, *un tramelot* is also used: *Les tramelots de la ligne Moillesulaz-Anne-masse font grève aujourd'hui* (*Journal de Genève*, Aug. 8–9, 1953).

468ᵇⁱˢTRANQUILLE. Pronunciation: *tran-kil* [it rhymes with *ville*, not *fille*].

469 TRANSFERT [transfer, transference]. This word, which means "the action of transfering," that is to say, to pass from one place to another (and which belongs, also, to the language of commerce, finance), is used in speaking of a dead body, relics, etc.: *Le* TRANSFERT *du corps d'un mort* (Ac.). *Le* TRANSFERT *des cendres de Napoléon* (*Robert*). TRANSFERT *de populations* (Id.).

La translation is used in the same meaning: *La* TRANSLATION *des restes de Napoléon* (Chateaubriand, in *Robert*).

Do not say: LE TRANSFERT *d'un fonctionnaire*. Say: LE DÉPLACEMENT *d'un fonctionnaire* or LA MUTATION. . . .

Le transfèrement is used only when speaking of prisoners who are transported according to required formalities.

470 USITÉ. The adjective *usité*, in the meaning of "practiced commonly," is outdated: *Cela est fort* USITÉ *dans ce pays* (Ac.). In the meaning of "used, in use in a language," it is current: *Ce mot n'est guère* USITÉ (Ac.).

The passive participle *usité* (from the verb *usiter*) is archaic: *Une langue savante, ou pure,* USITÉE *par les professeurs et les fonctionnaires* (A. Maurois).

471 VACUITÉ [vacuity, emptiness] / **VIDUITÉ** [viduity, widowhood]. Distinguish between these two words. *Vacuité* is from the Latin, *vacuus*; French, *vide*; English, empty: *La* VACUITÉ *de l'estomac cause des tiraillements* (Ac.). *La* VIDUITÉ is from the Latin *vidua*; French, *veuve, veuvage*; English, widow, widowhood [the state of a widow or widower who does not remarry]: *Demeurer en* VIDUITÉ (Ac.).

At times, the word *viduité* is improperly used as if it were related to the word *vide*: *Ils sont bruissants à la manière des grosses caisses dont ils se servent; leur sonorité vient de leur* VIDUITÉ (Flaubert, in *Robert*). *Nous passions des jours sans échanger une parole; l'affreuse* VIDUITÉ *des heures ne le décourageait pas* (C. Lemonnier).

472 VALABLE [valid, good, acceptable]. The French Academy points out the following meanings of this adjective: "which is acceptable, well founded": *Une excuse* VALABLE; "which has the required conditions to produce an effect": *Ce billet est* VALABLE *pendant quinze jours;* "which ought to be received justly": *Quittance* VALABLE.

In today's usage, the word *valable,* undoubtedly under the influence of the English word "valuable," is often taken to mean "legitimately worthy, of value, remarkable": *Daurat sut leur faire comprendre. . .que leur tâche de paix était aussi belle, aussi* VALABLE (J. Kessel). *Sans doute y a-t-il des récits de voyages* VALABLES, *écrits par des explorateurs authentiques* (A. Billy).

The French Academy condemned this slip in meaning in a notice dated Feb. 18, 1965.

473 VÉHICULAIRE *(langue~).* Robert, the *Grand Larousse encyclopédique,* the *Grand Larousse de la Langue française,* and *Lexis* list this neological expression in which *véhiculaire* [vehicular] has the meaning of "which serves as a vehicle, as a means of communication among people of different languages in the world."

Purists rebuff the expression *une langue véhiculaire,* but if we accept A. Thérive's statement which is, *Notre langue fut alors le véhicule des gens cultivés* [Our language was at that time the vehicle of cultivated people], why, then, would we condemn a statement such as, *Le français fut alors la* LANGUE VÉHICULAIRE *des gens cultivés* [French was, at that time, the vehicular language of cultivated people]? The expression, accepted by linguists, is also found in current use: *Il ne comprend que le "kiswahili," la* LANGUE VÉHICULAIRE *de tous les Noirs à qui l'usage des langues européennes est interdit* (M. Bedel).

474 VERSER [to pour]. In certain places in Brussels, you can see official signs that say, *Défense de verser* ["Do not litter"]. What is understood is: ". . .it is unlawful for the public to dump garbage and refuse here."

475 VIDANGE [emptying, draining]. This word is used in Belgium in the plural, meaning "empty containers, bottles [returnable with deposit or not]": *On ne reprend pas les* VIDANGES ["Empties not returnable"].

476 VISITE *(rendre~).* Abel Hermant has justifiably said, "I therefore see no reason that prevents me from paying a visit [*rendre visite*] to someone who has not yet visited me [*faire visite*]." The expression [*rendre visite*] is perfectly correct and the idea of reciprocity has nothing to do with it here: *Il les avait à peine aperçus, trop jeune, trop novice pour oser leur* RENDRE VISITE (A. Billy).

People also say: *faire visite* or *visiter: Il n'y avait que Robert qui venait me* FAIRE VISITE (A. Chamson).   *Un de ses coreligionnaires (. . .) vint le* VISITER *dans son cachot* (J. and J. Tharaud).

477 VOLATIL / VOLATILE. Distinguish between these two words. The adjective *volatil* (feminine form: *volatile*) means "susceptible to being changed into vapor, gas": *Alcool volatil* (Ac.).   *Substance* VOLATILE (Id.).

The masculine noun *volatile* (which can be used as an adjective) is an animal that can fly: *Cet animal est du genre des* VOLATILES (Ac.).   *Les insectes* VOLATILES (Id.).

478 VOLCANOLOGIE, VULCANOLOGIE. In a communiqué dated April 20, 1967, the Academy made a distinction between these two words. *Volcanologie* is the science that studies volcanic phenomena. *Vulcanologie* is the treatment of rubber or substances possessing analogous properties. *Vulcanologie* used to be used in speaking of volcanoes and the *Grand Larousse encyclopédique* still gives *vulcanologie* and *volcanologie* as being synonymous. However, it is proper to make the distinction between these two words as given above by the French Academy.

479 VOULOIR *(se~)*. With an attribute, *se vouloir* is now sometimes used in the meaning of "to regard oneself / itself as, to consider oneself / itself as, to see oneself / itself as. . .": *Une institution qui* SE VEUT *pacifiste* (J. Benda).   *Il* SE VEUT *objectif* (A. Maurois).   *Tout cela qui* SE VEUT *jeune sent la poussière* (R. Kemp).

480 VOUSSOYER, VOUSOYER, VOUVOYER [to use the *vous* form with a person]. These three verbs, as well as the three nouns *voussoiement, vousoiement, vouvoiement* (all of which are not recognized by the French Academy), are in current use: *Il tutoie sa femme et* VOUSSOIE *ses enfants* (Littré).   *Elle s'était mise à les* VOUSOYER (Ph. Hériat).   *Jamais il ne cesse de* VOUVOYER *ses hommes* (M. Druon).   *Comme ce* VOUSSOIEMENT *épistolaire est solennel!* (P.-H. Simon.)   *Ce* VOUVOIEMENT *entre époux confondait Amélie* (H. Troyat).

481 VULGUM PECUS [the common masses]. This locution is from the Latin *vulgus* (French, *la foule, le vulgaire*; English, crowd, masses, vulgar) and from the Latin *pecus* (French, *troupeau*; English, herd, flock). The expression is undoubtedly based on the Latin *servum pecus* [*servum:* slave, servant; French, *troupe servile;* English, servile flock] of Horace.

It is an expression used in familiar language and is generally expressed in italics or in quotation marks: *Passer outre aux traditions en usage dans le* "VULGUM PECUS" (G. Courteline).   *Assis sur les bancs de l'amphithéâtre avec le* VULGUM PECUS (Vercors).

482 WAGON [train car]. This word is pronounced *va-gon*. Because of this, some people have advocated (at times, adopted) the spelling *vagon: En* VAGON, *l'autre jour, les portières fermées, je regardais un insecte* (A. Daudet).   *Je passe ma jeunesse dans les cabines de* VAGONS (A. Thérive).

However, the spelling *wagon* is widely used: WAGON *de marchandises* (Ac.).

483 WATERZOOI. In Belgium, this is a food whose origin is in Ghent; it is a kind of matelote [which is a highly seasoned fish stew made with white or red wine]: *Savourer un bon* WATERZOOI *de volaille* [. . .made with fowl].

PART TWO

CORRECT FRENCH IN GRAMMATICAL CATEGORIES

CHAPTER 1

NOUNS

I. MASCULINE / FEMININE

484 The following nouns are masculine:

abaque
abîme
acabit
acrostiche
adage
aéronef
aéroplane
age
agrumes
air
alambic
albâtre
amadou
amalgame
ambre
amiante
anathème
anchois
anévrisme
animalcule
anniversaire
anthracite
antidote
antipode
antre
apanage

aphte
apogée
apologue
apostème
apostume
après-dîner
arcane
armistice
aromate
arpège
artifice
asphalte
asphodèle
astérisque
asthme
astragale
athénée
atome
attique
augure
auspice
autoclave
autographe
automate
balustre
bastringue

bow-window
braque
camée
campanile
capitule
capuce
caramel
cénotaphe
centime
cèpe
cerne
chevesne (chevaine)
chrysanthème
cippe
cloporte
codicille
colchique
concombre
conifère
crabe
cytise
décombres
denticule
échange
édicule
élastique

ellébore	holocauste	ophicléide
éloge	hôpital	opprobre
emblème	horoscope	opuscule
émétique	hospice	orage
emplâtre	humour	orbe
empyrée	hyménée	orchestre
empyreume	hypogée	organe
encombre	incendie	orifice
en-tête	indice	ouvrage
entracte	insigne	ovale
entrecolonne	intermède	ove
épeautre	interrogatoire	ovule
éphémère	interstice	pagne
épiderme	intervalle	parafe (-phe)
épilogue	involucre	pastiche
épisode	isthme	pénates
épithalame	ivoire	pétale
équilibre	jade	pétiole
equinoxe	jujube (pâte)	planisphère
ergastule	jute	platine (métal)
érysipèle (érésipèle)	langes	pore
esclandre	légume	poulpe
escompte	leurre	prêche
espalme	libelle	quadrige
évangile	lignite	quinconce
éventail	limbe	quine
exemple	lobule	rail
exergue	losange	rifle
exode	mânes	salamalec
exorde	mastic	scolie (géom.)
fastes	mausolée	sépale
fuchsia	méandre	sévices
girofle	midi	socque
globule	millefeuille (gâteau)	stade
glomérule	mimosa	stipe
granule	monticule	tentacule
haltère	moustique	térébinthe
hand-ball	naphte	thyrse
harmonique	narcisse	trèfle
hectare	obélisque	trille
héliotrope	obstacle	triqueballe
hémisphère	omnibus	trope
hémistiche	ongle	trophée
hiéroglyphe	opercule	trottin

tubercule   uretère   viscère
tulle   ustensile   vivres
ulcère   vestige

485 The following nouns are feminine:

abside   chausse- trap(p)e   hypallage
absinthe   clepsydre   icône
acné   clovisse   idole
acoustique   conteste   idylle
affres   coquecigrue   immondice
agrafe   créosote   impasse
alcôve   dartre   imposte
alluvion   dent   insulte
amibe   drachme   loutre
amnistie   dynamo   malachite
amorce   ébène   mandibule
amulette   ébonite   météorite
anagramme   écarlate   millefeuille
ancre   ecchymose   molécule
anicroche   échappatoire   montgolfière
ankylose   écharde   moufle
antichambre   écritoire   mousson
apostille   égide   moustiquaire
apothéose   énallage   nacre
appog(g)iature   encaustique   oasis
après-dînée   enclume   obsèques
arabesque   éphémérides   ocre
argile   épigramme   office (cuisine)
arrhes   épigraphe   offre
artère   épitaphe   omoplate
astuce   épithète   once
atmosphère   épître   opale
attache   équerre   optique
autoroute   équivoque   orbite
avant-scène   escarre   oriflamme
azalée   estafette   ouïe
bakélite   estompe   outre
besicles   extase   palpe
bodega   fourmi   paroi
bonace   gemme   patenôtre
campanule   glaire   patère
câpre   hécatombe   périssoire
caténaire   hydre   piastre

prémices	*scorsonère*	*tranchefile*
prémisse	*spore*	*urticaire*
primeur	*stalactite*	*vêpres*
primevère	*stalagmite*	*vésicule*
pulpe	*stèle*	*vicomté*
réglisse	*synopsis* [*pfois: m.*]	*virago*
sandaraque	*ténebres*	*vis*
scolopendre	*topaze*	*volte-face*

486 Certain nouns of persons, which ordinarily apply only to men, do not normally have a feminine form in French. At times, however, in order to indicate the feminine gender, the noun *femme* is added to the noun. [See entry nos. 495, 506, 537.] Some examples are:

acolyte	*échevin*	*médecin*
apôtre	*écrivain*	*ministre*
architecte	*fantassin*	*modèle*
assassin	*fat*	*monstre*
automate	*filou*	*oppresseur*
avant-coureur	*flandrin*	*otage*
bandit	*forçat*	*peintre*
bâtonnier	*galant homme*	*pionnier*
bourgmestre	*géomètre*	*possesseur*
bourreau	*gourmet*	*professeur*
censeur	*grognon*	*sauveur*
charlatan	*guide*	*soldat*
chef	*hurluberlu*	*successeur*
chevalier	*imposteur*	*témoin*
cocher	*imprimeur*	*terrassier*
condisciple	*ingénieur*	*tyran*
défenseur	*juge*	*vainqueur*
déserteur	*littérateur*	*valet*
diplomate	*magistrat*	*voyou,*
disciple	*manœuvre*	*etc.*

You will find feminine forms such as: *bandite, bourrelle, charlatane, écrivaine, fantassine, forçate, nourrissonne, pionnière, valette,* etc. These have been created, for the most part, for *badinage* (banter, teasing) or out of sheer caprice.

487 AIGLE [eagle]. This word is ordinarily masculine when it refers to the eagle as a bird of prey, a man of genius, a decoration, a lectern in a church, paper in a large format [elephant]. The word is feminine when it expressly designates the female bird or refers to a banner, a standard, or armorial bearings: *L'aigle est* FURIEUSE *quand on lui ravit ses aiglons* (Ac.).   *Les aigles* ROMAINES. *Il porte sur le tout d'azur, à l'aigle* ÉPLOYÉE *d'argent* (Ac.).

488 ALVÉOLE [alveolus, bee cell]. This word is masculine (Littré, *Dictionnaire général*, the French Academy, *Robert*, *Grand Larousse de la Langue française*, *Grand Larousse encyclopédique*). However, there is some hesitation in usage because some authors have used it as a feminine noun: UNE *alvéole vide* (R. Martin du Gard).   *Sur l'alvéole* LAISSÉE *dans la terre* (A. Malraux).

489 AMATEUR. The feminine form, *amatrice*, has been used at times (by saint François de Sales, J.-J. Rousseau), but it has not been accepted into usage: *Elle venait à son hôpital, un peu en* AMATEUR (H. Bordeaux).   *La cuisinière* AMATEUR (J. Green).

490 AMBASSADEUR. The feminine form, *ambassadrice*, is the wife of an ambassador or, familiarly, a woman entrusted with some message: *Une* AMBASSADRICE *de joie* (Molière).   When it has to do with a woman sent in an ambassadorial capacity by a country, either the masculine or feminine form of the word is in use: *Madame X,* AMBASSADEUR or AMBASSADRICE. (The masculine form seems to prevail because the function is considered rather than the sex of the person.)

491 AMMONIAQUE [ammonia]. This is a solution of ammonia gas. It is a feminine noun: *dégraisser avec de* LA BONNE *ammoniaque* [to remove grease with good ammonia]. The Academy notes that at times it is used as a masculine noun: CET *ammoniaque est très* FORT [This ammonia is very strong]. To designate ammonia gas, the word is used elliptically in the masculine, *de l'ammoniac: L'ammoniac* LIQUÉFIÉ *sert à la production du froid* (*Grand Larousse encyclopédique*).

492 AMOUR [love]. This word is masculine when it has the general meaning of affection, attachment or when the meaning is "a representation of the god of Love": *Amour* MATERNEL; UN VIOLENT *amour des richesses.   Peindre, sculpter de* PETITS AMOURS (Ac.).

When this word means "passion of one sex for the other," in the singular it is generally masculine; it is only in poetry when it is at times feminine: *Mais combien fait mal* UN AMOUR *qui meurt!* (P. Loti.) *Mais pour désaltérer* CETTE *amour* CURIEUSE. . . (P. Valéry).   In the plural, it can be either masculine or femi-

nine: *L'antique océan qui berça les* PREMIERS *amours de la terre*
(A. France). *Ces hommes de l'Empire . . . parlèrent de leurs* PRE-
MIÈRES *amours* (Musset).

493 APRÈS-GUERRE, AVANT-GUERRE, ENTRE-DEUX-GUERRES
[postwar, prewar, between two wars]. These are either masculine
or feminine: *L'humaniste optimiste du* PREMIER *après-guerre* (P.-H. Simon). CET *avant-guerre* (P. Emmanuel). *La* DERNIÈRE *après-guerre*
(Fr. Mauriac). *On est toujours en retard d'*UNE *après-guerre* (A. Chamson). LA DERNIÈRE *avant-guerre* (G. Bernanos). *Dans l'*INDÉCIS(E)
entre-deux-guerres.

494 APRÈS-MIDI [afternoon]. This noun is either masculine or feminine. The French Academy uses it in the masculine: *Pendant* TOUT
l'après-midi (A. Chamson). UNE *après-midi* (J. Green). *Le milieu
d'*UNE BELLE *après-midi d'octobre* (Fr. Mauriac).

495 AUTEUR [author]. This noun does not have an official feminine
form. The feminine form, *une autrice,* which was used at one time
by Étienne Pasquier, Brantôme, Chapelain, and Restif de la Bre-
tonne [and others], is very rare today. The feminine form, *auto-
resse* (taken from the English word, *authoress*), is also rare. Normal
usage is: *Cette dame est l'*AUTEUR *d'un fort joli roman* (Ac.). *Une*
FEMME AUTEUR (Id.). [See also entry no. 486.]

496 AUTOMNE [autumn, fall]. This noun has been used in the feminine: *Que vous allez passer* UNE JOLIE *automne!* (Sévigné.)
L'automne est DOUCE (A. de Châteaubriant). Today, it is almost
always used in the masculine: *Les* BEAUX *automnes* (R. Rolland).
UN CHAUD *automne* (Colette).

497 BATEAUX *(noms de~)* [names of boats]. In France, official usage
is to make the definite article agree with the name of the boat and
to keep the gender of the noun as it is in ordinary language.
However, in present-day usage, this is not always observed; in
the field of journalism, the masculine form is used: *À bord de* LA
Médée (P. Loti). *Nous étions embarqués sur* LA *"France"* (G. Hanotaux). LE *"Normandie"* (A. Gide). *Je recalfaterai* LE *"Marie-Hélène"*
(H. Queffélec). *Quand nous l'avons envoyé [le panneau de la Joconde]
aux États-Unis, il est parti sur* LE *"France"* (A. Malraux).

498 BORGNE [blind in one eye]. The feminine form, *une borgnesse,*
has a pejorative meaning and is little used. When no pejorative
meaning is intended, the form *une borgne* is used: *Vous aurez affaire*

à UNE BORGNE (Y. Gandon). [The figurative meaning of *un borgne / une borgne* is "suspicious," "shady."]

It must be noted that the expression *borgne de l'oeil droit* (Hugo) means "who no longer can see with the right eye." It must also be noted that one says, although rarely, *aveugle d'un oeil* [blind in one eye]: *En devenant temporairement* AVEUGLE D'UN OEIL. . . (A. Maurois).

499 CHROMO. This is an abbreviated form of the word *la chromolithographie* [chromolithograph / chromolithography]. *Chromo* would logically be feminine, but in actual usage its gender is undecided, although the masculine seems to be used most of the time: *Comme* UNE *chromo* (Saint-Exupéry). UN *assez* VILAIN *chromo* (G. Bernanos).

500 CONFRÈRE [confrère, fellow-member of the same society]. Flaubert wrote: *Madame et cher* CONFRÈRE, *Ma chère* CONFRÈRE. Jules Renard wrote: *Il y avait aussi une jeune* CONFRÈRE.

When referring to a woman member of *une confrérie* [a confraternity], *une consoeur* is ordinarily used: *La plus brillante de nos* CONSOEURS *en critique* (R. Kemp). [See also entry no. 121.]

501 DÉBITEUR, DÉBITRICE [debtor]. *Un débiteur / une débitrice* is a debtor, a person who owes.

Un débiteur is also a person who spreads news; the feminine form is *une débiteuse: C'est une grande* DÉBITEUSE *de mensonges* (Ac.).

Une débiteuse is also a woman who, in department stores, escorts customers to the cashier. In this sense, the Academy says that people use the word *une débitrice* improperly when they should say *une débiteuse*.

502 DÉLICE [delight, great pleasure]. This noun is masculine when used in the singular, feminine when used in the plural: *La lecture de cet ouvrage est* UN *délice* (Ac.). *L'imagination m'apportait des délices* INFINIES (Nerval).

503 DÉMON [demon]. Some writers have used the feminine form, *démone: Que faisait à cela mon* ÉLÉGANTE DÉMONE? (Chateaubriand.) UNE DÉMONE *des bois et des rivières* (E. Jaloux).

504 DIABLE [devil]. The feminine form is *une diablesse: C'est une* DIABLESSE (Ac.).

In the following two examples *diable* is used as an adjective: *Cette* DIABLE *de Vendée* (Hugo). *Quelle* DIABLE *d'idée!* (Flaubert.)

In the following two examples *diablesse* is used as a noun: *Votre* DIABLESSE *d'imagination* (Voltaire). *Sa* DIABLESSE *de femme* (Stendhal).

505 DISPARATE [disparity, incongruity, clash of colors]. For the Academy, this is a feminine noun, meaning "shocking dissimilarity": *Quelle disparate* CHOQUANTE! [What a shocking clash of colors!] But in actual usage, it is often a masculine noun: CE *disparate est inconcevable* (Flaubert). LE *disparate des matériaux* (P. Gaxotte).

506 DOCTEUR. This is a title given to a person who achieves the highest university degree. It has no feminine form: *Une fille* DOCTEUR *en philosophie* (A. Billy).

According to the Academy, *une doctoresse* (a woman who holds the degree of Doctor of Medicine) is not used much and "for the most part, people say *une femme docteur, une femme médecin* or simply *docteur.*" Nevertheless, *doctoresse* is not rare: *Une sorte de maladie nerveuse que la* DOCTORESSE *soigne selon une méthode toute nouvelle* (A. Gide).

When speaking directly to a woman doctor, use *docteur.* [See also entry no. 486.]

507 EFFLUVE [effluvium, emanation]. According to dictionaries, this noun is masculine: *Effluves* ODORANTS (Ac.). However, there is a tendency to use it in the feminine: *Effluves* RAYONNANTES (Th. Gautier). *Des effluves* ENIVRANTES (R. Rolland).

508 ÉLYTRE [elytron]. This noun is masculine but, as the Academy notes, some people use it in the feminine: *Les élytres* FENDUES (Colette). *L'élytre* DROITE (J.-H. Fabre).

509 ENQUÊTEUR [investigator, inquirer, researcher]. The usual feminine form is *une enquêteuse.* The *Grand Larousse de la Langue française, Lexis,* and the Supplement to *Robert* give *enquêtrice* as a variant of *enquêteuse* for the special neological meaning of "a woman whose job it is to conduct a survey in the field of social or economic problems."

510 ENTRECÔTE [rib steak, rib of beef, sirloin steak]. This noun was masculine for a long time and it can still be: *Il piqua sa fourchette dans* UN *entrecôte* (J. Green). But, nowadays, it is most often used as a feminine noun: UNE *entrecôte* GRILLÉE (Ac.). UNE *entrecôte* JUTEUSE (P.-H. Simon).

511 ENZYME. The gender of this noun has not been settled: AUCUN *enzyme* (J. Rostand).   *Grâce à l'intervention d'*UN *enzyme* (J. Monod). *La cellule a donc besoin de* CETTE *enzyme* (J. Carles).   The Academy, in a notice dated Feb. 5, 1970, regards it as feminine.

512 ESPÈCE DE [sort of, kind of, "a certain"]. In popular usage, and at times in literary works, this term (which expresses a nuance of approximation or of depreciation) takes on the masculine gender, by assimilation, when it is followed by a masculine noun. In this way, *un espèce de* seems to become the equivalent of "a certain": *La phrase s'achève en* UN *espèce de murmure* (G. Bernanos).   TOUS *ces espèces d'Arabes* (J.-J. Gautier).   UN *espèce de vallon* (M. Pagnol).

In a notice dated Nov. 18, 1965, the Academy condemned this usage.

Regular use is in the feminine: *Les deux autres hommes étaient, l'un* UNE *espèce de géant, l'autre* UNE *espèce de nain* (Hugo).

513 ESQUIMAU [Eskimo]. According to *Robert: une femme* ESQUIMAU or ESQUIMAUDE. The feminine form *esquimaude*, has come into use: *Les mamans esquimaudes* (R. Kemp).   *Une vieille* ESQUIMAUDE (R. Vercel).

514 FOUDRE [thunderbolt]. This noun is generally used in the feminine: *La foudre est* TOMBÉE. *Les foudres de l'excommunication furent* LANCÉES.

It is masculine in *foudre de guerre, foudre d'éloquence*, or in heraldry, or when it designates Jupiter's [Zeus's] thunderbolt: *D'argent à* UN *foudre de sable; Jupiter . . . lance* UN *foudre à l'instant* (La Fontaine).

515 GARANT [guaranteeing, vouching for]. When applied to persons, this word has the feminine form, *garante: Cette marchande s'est rendue* GARANTE (Littré).   *Elle est, elle se porte* GARANTE *de ma conduite* [She can vouch for my behavior (conduct)]. [*Se porter garant(e) de* means "to guarantee, to vouch or to answer for."]

When applied to things, it is always in the masculine: *Sa conduite passée vous est* UN SÛR GARANT *de sa fidélité pour l'avenir* (Ac.).

516 GENS [people]. This is a plural collective noun in the masculine: TOUS *les gens* QUERELLEURS (La Fontaine).   QUELS *sont ces gens?* (J. Romains.)   QUELS *que soient ces gens-là, il faut les aider.*

However, when this word is immediately preceded by an adjective that does not have a single form for both genders, all the adjectives placed in front of it are written in the feminine; but the words placed after it (and whose agreement it demands) are written in the masculine: TOUTES *les* VIEILLES *gens* (Ac.). *Ce sont les* MEILLEURES *gens que j'aie* CONNUS. *J'écris pour ces* PETITES *gens d'entre* LESQUELS *je suis sorti* (G. Duhamel). QUELLES *que soient ces* VIEILLES *gens, je veux m'occuper d'*EUX.

The adjectives that precede *gens*—only because of a reversed order—remain in the masculine: INSTRUITS *par l'expérience, les* VIEILLES *gens sont* SOUPÇONNEUX (Ac.).

Gens, when followed by the preposition *de* and a noun designating a quality or a state, is in the masculine form: *De* NOMBREUX *gens de lettres, de robe, de finance, d'épée, de mer,* etc.

Gendelettre(s) is pejorative: GENDELETTRE *dans l'âme* (M. Proust).

Gent (race) is feminine: LA *gent canine* (Colette).

517 H.L.M. Because this abbreviated form stands for *habitation à loyer modéré* [lodging at a moderate rental], the feminine would be justified by the noun *une habitation.* As a matter of fact, some people say: *une H.L.M.* But most users, undoubtedly because of the attraction of the masculine noun *un bâtiment, un immeuble,* or *un ensemble,* use *H.L.M.* in the masculine: *Habiter* UN *H.L.M. (Robert,* Supplement).

518 HÔTE. In the feminine: *Une hôtesse* [hostess] is a woman who receives someone; *une hôte,* is a woman who is received [guest].

519 HYMNE [hymn]. This noun is masculine in its ordinarily accepted meaning, but it is generally feminine when it means hymns that are sung in church: *Les cieux sont* UN *hymne sans fin* (Lamartine). *Seigneur,* QUELS *hymnes sont dignes de vous?* (Ac.) *Les hymnes* CHRÉTIENNES (Id.). TOUTES *les hymnes de cet admirable office* (Fr. Mauriac).

520 INTERVIEW. This noun is sometimes used in the masculine: CE NOUVEL *interview* (A. Hermant). *Un interview* RÉCENT (J. Green). But the word is normally feminine (cf. *une entrevue*): *Donner* UNE *interview* (Ac.). UNE *interview sur le film* (J. Cocteau).

521 LAIDERON [ugly person]. The gender of this noun varies. The French Academy and most modern authors use it in the masculine: *Cette fille est* UN LAIDERON *(Petit Robert). Pour danser avec* UNE LAIDERON *comme moi* (G. Sand).

522 LETTRES *(noms des~)* [names of letters of the alphabet]. Traditional usage has been to refer to the following letters of the alphabet in the feminine: *f, h, l, m, n, r, s: Le pluriel met* UNE S *à leurs meas culpas* (Hugo). UNE *h un peu aspirée* (J. Renard).

But it has become current usage to refer to the consonants of the alphabet—no matter which ones—in the masculine: *L'l double qui est* MOUILLÉ. . . (A. Hermant). UN *H majuscule* (G. Duhamel).

523 MERCI [mercy]. This noun is feminine when it means "good will, mercy": *C'est un homme sans merci, qui ne vous fera* AUCUNE *merci* (Ac.). *Être à* LA *merci du vainqueur* (Id.).

It is masculine when used to mean "thank you," in such expressions as: GRAND *merci* (Ac.). In the plural: *Mille* MERCIS.

524 MINUIT [midnight]. This word used to be feminine and is still used in that gender, but it is archaic (written as *mi-nuit* or *minuit*): *Jusqu'à* LA *mi-nuit* (Montherlant). *Vers* LA *minuit* (G. Duhamel).

525 MULÂTRE [mulatto]. The feminine form of this word is *une* MULÂTRESSE (Ac.). At times, also: *une* MULÂTRE.

526 OEUVRE [work]. This noun is always feminine in the plural and generally feminine in the singular: *Les* DERNIÈRES *oeuvres d'un auteur*. TOUTE *oeuvre* HUMAINE *est* IMPARFAITE.

It is masculine when it designates the whole of the works of an engraver, an artist, at times also of a writer, or the search for the philosopher's stone: LE GROS *oeuvre est achevé* (É. Fabre). TOUT *l'oeuvre de Callot* (Ac.). *Dans l'oeuvre* ENTIER *de Flaubert* (Fr. Mauriac). *Travailler au* GRAND *oeuvre* (Ac.).

527 ORDONNANCE [an officer's military orderly]. This word is often used in the masculine: UN *des ordonnances* (A. Maurois). *Son* ANCIEN *ordonnance* (M. Druon). For Littré, the Academy, and for the *Dictionnaire général*, the word is feminine: *Mon* ANCIENNE *ordonnance* (A. Maurois). *Un secrétaire et* UNE *ordonnance* (G. Duhamel). [Note that today officers no longer have orderlies.]

528 ORGE [barley]. This noun is feminine: *De* BELLES *orges*—except in *orge mondé* [hulled barley] and *orge perlé* [pearl barley].

529 ORGUE [organ (music)]. This noun is always masculine in the singular and when it has to do with several musical instruments: *L'orgue de telle église est* EXCELLENT (Ac.). *Les deux orgues de telle église sont* EXCELLENTS.

The plural form, *orgues*, designating a unique instrument

[grand organ] is in the feminine: *Les* GRANDES *orgues* (Ac.). *Cela ressemblait aux sons d'orgues* LOINTAINES (R. Boylesve).

530 PALABRE [palaver (a long parley, a long discussion)]. For the French Academy, this noun is of both genders. In fact, it is most often used in the feminine: *Sans* AUCUNES *palabres philoso-phiques* (P. Claudel). *J'en ai assez de* TOUTES *ces palabres* (R. Martin du Gard). *Moyennant de* LONGUES *et rudes palabres* (Ch. de Gaulle).

531 PAMPLEMOUSSE [grapefruit]. Fruit of *le pamplemoussier* [grape-fruit tree]. The fruit is also called *pomélo* or *grape-fruit*. The word is used at times in the feminine: UNE *pamplemousse* DÉROBÉE *aux offrandes* (P. Claudel). Current usage makes it masculine: *La tête comme* UN *pamplemousse* (Vercors). *Mangé à midi (. . .)* UN *pample-mousse* (M. Aymé).

532 PÂQUE. As a Jewish holiday [Passover], it is feminine: *Des gâteaux de* LA *Pâque* JUIVE (A. Maurois). *Notre-Seigneur célébra* LA *pâque avec ses disciples* (Ac.).

Pâques, a Christian holiday, is masculine and singular when speaking of the feast day: *Quand Pâques sera* VENU (Ac.).

However, it is feminine when accompanied by an epi-thet, when it designates the Easter communion, in *Pâques fleuries, Pâques closes,* and in the greeting *Joyeuses Pâques: Ils se rappelaient (. . .) les* **Pâques** ÉCLATANTES *de soleil* (Hugo). *Faire de* BONNES *Pâques* (Ac.). *Ô mes Pâques* ENFANTINES, *à Vincennes* (M. Droit).

533 PARTISAN. The feminine form *partisane* is used today: *Les loges grillées (. . .) dont elle était* PARTISANE *déclarée* (Ph. Hériat). *Vous n'êtes jamais* PARTISANE *de rien* (J. Giono).

Partisante is used in popular language.

534 PERCE-NEIGE [Botany: snowdrop (a low, spring-blooming herb)]. This noun is feminine for Littré, the *Dictionnaire général,* for the French Academy, for the *Grand Larousse encyclopédique,* and for *Lexis.* Current usage makes it masculine: LE PREMIER *perce-neige* (Colette). *Les* PREMIERS *perce-neige* (J. Giono).

535 PÉRIODE [period (of time)]. This noun is ordinarily feminine but masculine when it designates the degree at which a person or thing has arrived: *Démosthène et Cicéron ont porté l'éloquence à son plus* HAUT *période* (Ac.). *Cet homme est à son* DERNIER *période* (Id.).

536 PHALÈNE [phalaena, moth]. According to Littré, the Academy, and *Lexis*, this noun is feminine but, as a matter of fact, it is of both genders (usage varies): *Des vols de* GRANDES *phalènes* (A. Daudet). *Comme l'aile d'*UNE GRANDE *phalène* (M. Genevoix). LE *phalène* DORÉ (Musset). *Comme* UN *phalène dans la nuit* (M. Barrès).

537 POÈTE [poet]. People say *une poétesse* for the feminine form: *Sapho est une* POÉTESSE *illustre* (Ac.). People also say *une femme poète* or simply *poète* (in the masculine): LE GRAND *poète Anna de Noailles* (J. Rostand). It is very rare with the feminine article and masculine form of the noun: UNE *jeune* POÈTE *blanche* (Chateaubriand). [See also entry no. 486.]

538 PRIÈRE D'INSÉRER [please publish (insert) in your columns]. The gender varies: *Comme le dit selon l'usage* LE *prière d'insérer* (A. Billy). LA *prière d'insérer des "Bostoniennes"* (Fr. Mauriac).

539 RELÂCHE [relaxation, rest, respite]. This noun is traditionally masculine in the meaning of "interruption of a tiring activity" or "temporary closing of a theater": *Son mal commence à lui donner* DU *relâche* (Ac.). *Les relâches sont* FRÉQUENTS *à ce théâtre* (Id.).

In modern usage, *relâche*, in these two meanings, is quite often feminine: *Nul répit,* NULLE *relâche* (R. Rolland). *J'y pensais, sans* LA *moindre relâche* (G. Duhamel). *Voyant tout à coup sur l'affiche du théâtre (. . .) l'annonce lamentable d'*UNE *relâche* (Huysmans, in *Robert*).

Relâche is feminine when it means the action of *relâcher* [to loosen, to slacken, to relax, to abate], or when it refers to the place where a boat is in port of call.

540 SANDWICH. Some people regard this word as feminine, but most often it is masculine: UNE *sandwich au foie gras* (H. Bordeaux). UN *sandwich au jambon* (Ac.). *De* PETITS *sandwichs* (Colette).

541 SAUVAGE [savage, wild]. As a noun, this word can be written in the feminine form as *une sauvagesse*, but generally people say *une sauvage: Ce ne sont point des* SAUVAGESSES *qu'on a* DÉGUISÉES *là* (P. Loti). *J'étais* UNE *sauvage* (J. Green).

542 SNOB. In the feminine, people say *une snob: Contre* UNE SNOB (M. Proust). *Jeunes femmes* SNOBS (Id.).

Feminine forms in familiar language are *snobette, snobinette*.

Observe that for the plural of *snob* when it is used as an adjective, there is some indecision in usage: *Dans quelques cercles* SNOB

(Montherlant). *Ces gens sont un peu* SNOB (M. Pagnol). *Ils sont un peu* SNOBS (H. Bordeaux).

543 SOLDE. Distinguish between *la solde* and *le solde*. *La solde* is the pay that a soldier receives. *Le solde* [clearance sale] is a term used in business and accounting: *Solde débiteur.* GRAND *solde de fourrures. Soldes* SENSATIONNELS.

544 SOUILLON [sloven (a sloppy, untidy man), slattern (a slovenly, untidy woman)]. This noun is of both genders: *Ma servante Mélanie qui est pourtant* UN SOUILLON (M. Aymé). UNE SOUILLON *ahurie* (Fr. Mauriac).

545 STEPPE. The gender of this noun is indecisive, but for the French Academy and for most authors, it is feminine: UNE *steppe immense* (J. Romains). *On retrouve* LA *steppe* (G. Duhamel). *Dans* LE *steppe natal* (P. Loti).

546 SUISSE [Swiss]. To designate a Swiss woman, people usually say: *une Suissesse.* At times you will hear *une Suisse,* but you are cautioned not to use it.

547 THERMOS. The final *s* in this word is pronounced. This noun is of both genders but the masculine prevails: *Cherche* LE *thermos* (J. Cocteau). *Le panier, le cabas,* LE *thermos* (Colette). *Deux thermos* PLEINES *d'alcool* (A. Malraux). UNE *thermos* REMPLIE *de thé* (J. Kessel).
　People also say *une bouteille thermos: Tu trouveras le lait dans la* BOUTEILLE THERMOS (H. Troyat).

548 VIEILLARD [old man]. The feminine form, *une vieillarde* (which is not recognized by the French Academy), is taken with a nuance of scorn, according to Littré; at times it is used otherwise: *Avant six mois, je t'aurai cassée comme* UNE VIEILLARDE (J.-P. Sartre). *La mort de la première prieure,* VIEILLARDE *sainte (. . .) est d'une grande beauté* (R. Kemp).

549 VILLES *(noms de~)* [names of cities]. For the gender of the names of cities, usage is completely wavering. We shall have to content ourselves with the following observations:
　　(1) Many people use the feminine when the name of the city ends in a silent syllable *(-e* or *-es): Narbonne est* BELLE (Hugo). *Athènes s'est* REBÂTIE (R. Kemp).
　　(2) The predicate adjective is most often written in the femi-

nine form: *Madrid était* PLEINE *de chiens magnifiques* (A. Malraux).

(3) With *tout* + the name of the city, and with *le tout* + the name of the city (meaning the elite society of. . .), the masculine form is always used: TOUT *Antioche s'étouffait au théâtre* (A. France). TOUT *La Rochelle fut* MENACÉ *d'envahissement* (M. Maeterlinck). LE TOUT-PARIS *méprise le reste du monde* (J. Benda).

Examples of indecision in usage: *Constantinople* INTOLÉRANTE (Nerval). *Constantinople déjà* FROID (Id.). CE *Venise* (M. Proust). CETTE *Venise* (Id.). UN NOUVEAU *Lourdes* (or UNE NOUVELLE *Lourdes*) (R. Kemp).

II. SINGULAR / PLURAL

550 ABSOUTE [absolution]. *Une absoute* is the series of prayers recited around the coffin after the service of the dead. Do not use this word in the plural, which is a confusion arising from the influence of the word *les funérailles* or *les obsèques*, which are used only in the plural. Do not say: LES ABSOUTES *seront dites en telle église*. . .Say: L'ABSOUTE *sera dite*. . . *Elle va rester ainsi, prostrée, jusqu'à* L'ABSOUTE (H. Bazin).

551 AGAPE(S) [agape, love-feast]. In the *Dictionnaire de l'Académie*, 8th ed., 1935, the form is given only in the plural, *agapes:* LES AGAPES *des premiers chrétiens.* AGAPES *fraternelles.*

The singular form, *agape*, is not rare: L'AGAPE *suit la communion sainte* (Chateaubriand). *Tous les baptisés se réunissaient pour* LA FRATERNELLE AGAPE (Daniel-Rops). *Mes oncles achevaient maintenant leur* AGAPE (A. Malraux).

552 AÏEUL. *Un aïeul* [grandfather], *une aïeule* [grandmother]. The plural, *les aïeuls:* the paternal grandfather and the maternal grandfather, or the grandfather and the grandmother: *Ses deux* AÏEULS *assistaient à son mariage* (Ac.).

Les aïeux are the ancestors: *C'était la mode chez nos* AÏEUX (Ac.).

Ordinarily, people say: *les bisaïeuls* (or, at times, *les bisaïeux)* [great-grandparents]; *les trisaïeuls* (or, at times, *les trisaïeux)* [great-great-grandparents]: *Nos* BISAÏEUX (A. Maurois). *Jusqu'à nos* TRISAÏEUX (Destouches).

553 AIL [garlic (Botany: allium)]. The plural form, *aulx*, is becoming outdated and currently people say: *des ails,* a form which is also constant in botany.   *Il y a des* AULX *cultivés et des* AULX *sauvages* (Ac.).   *Il aidait sa mère à tresser les* AULX (Colette).

554 BERCAIL [sheepfold; fold (*rentrer au bercail,* to return to the fold)]. The plural of *le bercail* is *les bercails,* which is used rarely: *Conduire tous les nourrissons vers les mêmes* BERCAILS (Ph.-H. Simon).

555 BÉTAIL [cattle, livestock]. *Le bétail* has no form in the plural. As for form, *bestiaux* is the plural of the old noun *bestial* or *bestiail.* As for meaning, *bestiaux* designates all the animals on a farm, including the small as well as the large ones.

556 CIEL [sky]. The plural of *le ciel* is *les cieux* when it designates the immense space where the stars move, or "the heavens": *L'immensité des* CIEUX (Ac.).   *Le royaume des* CIEUX (Id.).

The plural of *le ciel* is *les ciels* when it means: a bed canopy, part of a painting representing the sky, a quarry roof, the atmosphere, a particular aspect of the sky of a region: *Des ciels de lit. Ce peintre fait bien les ciels* (Ac.).   *Des ciels de carrière. Les beaux ciels sans nuages* (A. Maurois).   *Des aviateurs combattant dans tous les ciels* (Charles de Gaulle).

In the meaning of "climate," *le ciel* is *les ciels* in the plural or, much more frequently, *les cieux: Un de ces* CIELS *perfides qui caressent et brûlent la peau tendre des citadins* (A. France).   *Le soleil de vingt* CIEUX *a mûri votre vie* (Hugo).

557 CISEAU. *Un ciseau* is a chisel: CISEAU *de maçon,* CISEAU *de sculpteur.*

Les ciseaux is a pair of scissors: *Mettre les* CISEAUX *dans une étoffe* (Ac.). In this last meaning, the singular (*le ciseau*) is somewhat frequently used: *On n'a point encore mis le* CISEAU *dans cette étoffe* (Littré).   *Quand elle donnait dans le drap le coup de* CISEAU (J. Green).   *Il coupait ses poils au* CISEAU (J. Giono).

Note the following singular and plural forms of other nouns. Certain nouns of objects that are made of two similar parts easily permit the singular or plural in order to designate the single object:

CULOTTE *de drap* (Ac.); *porter des* CULOTTES (Id.).

Être en CALEÇON (Ac.); *porter des* CALEÇONS (Id.).

PANTALON *large* (Ac.).; *Malgré des* PANTALONS *trop courts. . .* (M. Barrès).

Apportez la TENAILLE (Littré); *Arracher un clou avec des* TENAILLES (Ac.).

Couper de la tôle avec une CISAILLE, *avec des* CISAILLES.

Porter un BERMUDA *ou des* BERMUDAS (*Robert*, Suppl.).

Raser sa MOUSTACHE (Ac.); *porter des* MOUSTACHES *(Dictionnaire général).*

Let us observe, along with Marcel Cohen in his book *Toujours des regards sur la langue française* (p. 182), that in Paris ordinary usage is: *caleçon, culotte, pantalon* normally in the singular.

558 DIRECTIVE(S). The French Academy recognizes only the plural form of this noun: *Des* DIRECTIVES *furent données par le général en chef.*

The singular is, however, fairly frequently used: *Sans tenir compte d'aucun mot d'ordre, d'aucune* DIRECTIVE (Fr. Mauriac). *Ce qu'il faut déduire de cette* DIRECTIVE (É. Henriot). *Je donnai comme* DIRECTIVE. . . (Charles de Gaulle).

559 ÉMAIL [enamel]. The ordinary plural of *un émail* is *des émaux: Les* ÉMAUX *doivent être très fusibles* (Ac.). *Un dais composé d'*ÉMAUX *translucides* (A. France).

A modern plural, *des émails*, is suitable when designating certain beauty products (for fingernails, for example) or certain products used in various industries (paint, automobile body work, etc.): *Une gamme complète d'*ÉMAILS *pour les ongles.*

560 ÉTAL [butcher's stall, marketplace stand or booth]. The plural of *un étal* is normally DES ÉTAUX: *Ce boucher a plusieurs* ÉTAUX (Littré). *Devant les* ÉTAUX *de boucherie* (M. Druon).

Because the plural form, *étaux*, is a homonym of the plural of *un étau* [a vise], the form *étaux* has been supplanted in modern usage by *des étals: Les* ÉTALS *des bouchers* (A. France). *Sur les* ÉTALS *du marché* (É. Henriot).

561 FLEUR(S) *(en~)* [in blossom, in bloom, in flower]. This term can be used in the singular or plural: *Un arbre en* FLEUR (Ac.). *Les marronniers en* FLEUR (A. Arnoux). *La Vie en* FLEUR (A. France). *Plantes en* FLEURS (Ac.). *À l'ombre des jeunes filles en* FLEURS (M. Proust). *Les orangers en* FLEURS (A. Suarès).

561bis**FRAIS** [expenses, costs, outlay]. Normally, this word is always in the plural: LES FRAIS *d'un voyage* (Ac.). *Faire* SES FRAIS (Id.). *À* SES FRAIS *et dépens* (Id.).

G. Duhamel used it, on the fringe of normal usage, in the singular: *Pour vous éviter* LE *moindre* FRAIS (in *L'Archange de l'aventure*, p. 48).

562 IDÉAL [ideal]. The plural of *un idéal* has two forms: *des idéaux* and *des idéals*. The form *idéaux*, according to the Academy, is used in the technical language of philosophy and mathematics. The form *idéals* is used in the language of literature, fine arts, and morals.

As a matter of fact, both plural forms are in ordinary use: *Les* IDÉAUX *d'origine historique* (P. Valéry). *Des* IDÉAUX *politiques* (Daniel-Rops). *De tous les* IDÉALS *tu composais ton âme* (Hugo). *Et toujours leurs* IDÉALS *se heurtèrent* (M. Barrès).

563 MAIN(S) *(en~)*. This expression can be used in the singular or in the plural, as in: *en main(s) propre(s), prendre en main(s)* [i.e., to take charge of]: *Je lui ai remis cette lettre* EN MAIN PROPRE (Ac.). *Remettre une lettre* EN MAIN(S) PROPRE(S) *(Robert).* PRENDRE EN MAIN *les intérêts, la cause de qqn* (Ac.). PRENDRE EN MAIN(S) *l'éducation d'un enfant.*

Ordinarily, use the plural in such expressions as *en bonnes mains, en mauvaises mains, en mains sûres*. Use the singular [*main*] in the expression *une poignée de* MAIN [a handshake]: *Il lui donna une cordiale poignée de* MAIN (Ac.). *Se séparer avec force poignées de* MAIN *(Robert).*

564 MATÉRIAU [material]. *Le matériau* is a revised singular form, done at the end of the 19th century, based on the plural form *matériaux*, whose singular was *matérial* in Old French: *Le seul* MATÉRIAU *du pays est l'argile* (Daniel-Rops). *Le* MATÉRIAU *est solide* (J. Giraudoux).

565 MESURE(S). You may use the singular or plural in the expression *un costume fait sur mesure(s)* [a suit custom-made]. But since the tailor takes the customer's measurements, the plural *sur* MESURES is more logical than the singular *sur* MESURE.

566 OEIL [eye]. The usual plural of *un oeil* is *des yeux: Des* YEUX *bleus. Les* YEUX *du pain, du fromage, du bouillon. Tailler à deux* YEUX, *à trois* YEUX.

There is a plural form, *des oeils*, in certain compound nouns: *Des oeils-de-boeuf* (windows), *des oeils-de-chat* (precious stones), *des oeils-de perdrix* (soft corns on feet); also in the vocabulary of trades and crafts or of the navy when *un oeil* designates an opening, a hole, a buckle, etc.: *Les* OEILS *de ces grues, de ces marteaux, de ces étaux*, etc.

The familiar expression, *entre quatre yeux*, meaning *tête à tête*, [a private conversation; "between us two, our four eyes"] is generally pronounced *entre quatre-**z**-yeux* or *entre quat'-**z**-yeux*—which is explained, according to Martinon, by the fact that for the general public *un oeil* has no plural form other than *zyeux*.

567 PAIN D'ÉPICE(S) [gingerbread]. The Academy writes this as *pain d'épice*, but it is also often written as *pain d'épices: Lorsque je me suis vu représenté en* PAIN D'ÉPICE (H. Bordeaux). *Les boutiques de* PAIN D'ÉPICES (A. Maurois).

568 SARRAU [overall, child's smock]. The traditional plural of *un sarrau* is *des sarraus*. There is some hesitation, at times, in usage and you will find the plural form, *des sarraux:* SARRAUX *de toile jaune* (Nerval). *Des* SARRAUX *noirs* (V. Larbaud). *Nous enfilâmes des* SARRAUX (G. Duhamel).

569 TÉMOIN [witness]. Normally, *un témoin* does not change in form in the expression *prendre à témoin* [to call to witness] or when the word *témoin* is at the beginning of a sentence: TÉMOIN *les blessures dont il est encore tout couvert* (Ac.). *Je les ai pris tous* À TÉMOIN (Id.).

   Usage, however, tends to vary: *Je vous prends* À TÉMOINS, *Messieurs* (M. Genevoix). TÉMOINS *les codes les plus cruels* (A. Suarès).

570 TÉNÈBRE(S) [darkness, gloom, obscurity]. Bescherelle, Littré, *Dictionnaire général*, the French Academy, the *Grand Larousse encyclopédique*, *Robert*, and *Lexis* list only the plural form, *ténèbres*.

   However, the form in the singular, *la ténèbre*, is found: *Aucune* TÉNÈBRE *ne recouvrait la terre* (Fr. Mauriac). *Dans la* TÉNÈBRE *liquide* (P. Claudel). *Alain ne vit plus devant lui qu'*UNE TÉNÈBRE *immense* (L. Martin-Chauffier). *Je marche sur ma* TÉNÈBRE (J. Cocteau).

570^{bis}TOILETTES. In the plural, this word is used to mean "a rest room": *Aller aux* TOILETTES. [In Belgium, it is generally used in the singular: *Aller à* LA TOILETTE.]

571 TRAVAIL [work]. The usual plural of *le travail* is *les travaux: Les* TRAVAUX *d'Hercule. Les* TRAVAUX *des champs.*

   The plural form, *les travails*, is used when it designates a kind of frame, sling, or device used to subdue horses, cattle, etc., in order to shoe them or to submit them to certain operations.

Plurals of Proper Nouns

572 When proper nouns are used to name:
(1) Peoples of the world, certain illustrious families in history,

they vary in the plural: *Les Italiens, les Horaces, les Tarquins, les Bourbons, les Stuarts.*

(2) Entire families (except the illustrious family names just mentioned above), they are invariable: *Les Oberlé, les Roquevillard, les Boussardel.*

(3) Several individuals designated by the same name, they are invariable: *Les deux Corneille. Les Goncourt.*

It is the same for names of machines, automobiles, airplanes, etc.: *Je te donne dix* CHRYSLER *pour une Voisin* (M. Achard). *Plusieurs* CARAVELLE.

For the names designating several cities or several countries, there is much hesitation in usage: *Il y a deux* FRANCE (A. Hermant.) *Il y a deux* VILLENEUVE (Id.). *On aura l'image de deux* FRANCES (P. de La Gorce). *Faire la jonction des deux* MAROC (A. Maurois). *Il y a deux* MAROCS (P. Hamp).

(4) Individuals considered to be types, they often vary in the plural: *Les* CICÉRONS *modernes. Ce sont les* MÉCÈNES *qui font les* VIRGILES (É. Henriot).

But they often remain invariable: *Les* GOLIATH *sont toujours vaincus par les* DAVID (Hugo). *Les* JÉRÉMIE *de la finance* (A. Maurois). *Pasteur (. . .) est sans doute une figure pour les* PLUTARQUE *de l'avenir* (G. Duhamel).

(5) An individual whose name is preceded, for emphasis, by the plural article, even though it is a matter of a single personnage, they are invariable: *Les* BOSSUET, *les* BOURDALOUE, *les* FLÉCHIER *ont illustré la chaire chrétienne au XVIIᵉ siècle.*

(6) Titles of books, newspapers, etc., generally they are invariable: *Acheter deux* ÉNÉIDE. *En feuilletant des vieux* MONDE ILLUSTRÉ (M. Bedel).

At times, however, they are variable: *Tandis que je feuilletais de vieux* MAGASINS PITTORESQUES (Fr. Mauriac).

(7) Works of art designated either by the subject represented or by the name of the author are, according to the whims of usage, variable or invariable: *Les* ANNONCIATIONS *des peintres chrétiens* (J. de Lacretelle). *Dans les* DESCENTES DE CROIX (G. Duhamel). *Un certain nombre de* VERTUMNE *et de* POMONE (F. Funck-Brentano). *On peint des* ENFANT JÉSUS *et surtout des* CHRIST EN CROIX (S. de Beauvoir). *Des* CALLOTS *accrochés au mur* (É. Estaunié). *Un certain nombre de* COROTS (A. Maurois). *Il avait été revoir les* TITIEN (Flaubert). *L'un des plus beaux* COROT *du monde* (Fr. Jammes).

(8) Several countries, provinces, streams, etc. having the same name, they vary: *Les deux* AMÉRIQUES, *les deux* FLANDRES, *les*

deux NÈTHES.   *Bibracte était la ville la plus industrieuse des* GAULES
(C. Jullian).

Plurals of Compound Nouns

Principle. In compound nouns, only the *nouns* and the *adjectives*
can be written in the plural, and that is done when common
sense indicates it.

General Examples

573 Noun + noun; noun and adjective: Both elements are written
in the plural: *Des choux-fleurs, des oiseaux-mouches, des avocats-con-
seils; des coffres-forts, des arcs-boutants, des grands-pères, des francs-
tireurs.*

If the second noun (with or without a preposition) is a complement of the first noun, only the first noun is variable: *Des chefs-
d'oeuvre, des timbres-poste, des arcs-en-ciel, des appuis-main.*

574 Verb + direct object: Only the direct object may change to the
plural; since there is no precise rule, the meaning must be taken
into account: *Des tire-bouchons, des pèse-lettres, des couvre-lits. Des
cache-poussière, des rabat-joie, des porte-monnaie.*

575 Invariable word + noun: Only the noun may change to the plural: *Des avant-projets, des arrière-boutiques, des haut-parleurs, des
contre-attaques.*

576 Elliptical or ready-made expressions: No element changes: *Des
on-dit, des coq-à-l'âne, des manque à gagner, des passe-partout, des
pince-sans-rire, des ouï-dire.*

577 Foreign words: They do not change: *Des nota bene, des post-scrip-
tum, des statu quo, des vice-rois, des ex-ministres, des volte-face, des
pick-up.*

Certain compound nouns formed from foreign words are con-
sidered as really Gallicized: *Des* FAC-SIMILÉS (Ac.).   *Deux grands*
IN-FOLIOS (A. Chamson).   *Pour se rapprocher de la famille des* EX-
VOTOS (J. Romains).

According to the English plural: *Des boy-scouts, des music-halls,
des negro-spirituals, des pipe-lines, des pull-overs, des snack-bars, des
week-ends, des skate-boards.*

When the first element ends in *-o* or *-i*, that element does not change to the plural: *Des électro-aimants, des pseudo-prophètes, les Gallo-Romains, les Anglo-Saxons, des tragi-comédies.*

578 Onomatopoeic elements: Sometimes the last element alone changes to plural by adding *s*: *Crépitements,* TIC-TACS (Maeterlinck). *Déjà* TAM-TAMS *et calebasses à grelots retentissent au loin* (H. Troyat). *Deux à trois* PING-PONGS (Fr-Régis Bastide).
   Usage varies: *Des* TIC-TAC (*Robert;* id. Dournon). *De vieux* TEUF-TEUF (Dournon). *Course de* TEUF-TEUF or *de* TEUFS-TEUFS *(Petit Robert).* *Des* FROUS-FROUS or FROU-FROUS *(Grand Larousse de la Langue française).* *Des* FRIC-FRAC (Dournon). *Une série de* FRIC-FRAC(S) *(Robert,* Supplement).

Some Special Cases

579 À-CÔTÉ [savings set aside]. *Il gagne tant, sans compter les* À-CÔTÉS *(Petit Robert).*

580 À-COUP: *Cet enfant travaille par* À-COUPS (Ac.).

581 APRÈS-MIDI [afternoon]. The Academy writes: *des après-midi.* But often you will find among authors: *des après-midi: Trois* APRÈS-MIDIS (A. Siegfried). *Ces sombres* APRÈS-MIDIS (Fr. Mauriac).

582 BONHOMME [good old chap, simple-minded man] **and GENTILHOMME** [nobleman].
   These two words, as well as the titles *madame, mademoiselle, monseigneur,* and *monsieur,* change to the plural each of the compound elements: *Des bonshommes, des gentilshommes, mesdames, mesdemoiselles, messeigneurs (nosseigneurs), messieurs.*
   The plurals: *des monsieurs, des madames, des mademoiselles, des monseigneurs* are used at times in irony or badinage: *Les simples* MONSEIGNEURS (La Fontaine). *Des jambes de grosses* MADAMES (Fr. Mauriac).

583 BOY-SCOUT. According to the English plural, *des boy-scouts.* At times, you will come across the plural form des *boys-scouts: Dans notre jardin sont venus camper des* BOYS-SCOUTS (A. Maurois). *Les défilés de* BOYS-SCOUTS (P.-H. Simon). *Nous étions redevenus, irrémédiablement, des* BOYS-SCOUTS (J. Dutourd).

584 CHÊNE-LIÈGE [cork-oak]. For the Academy, the plural is *des chênes-lièges,* which is the plural form currently used: *Des forêts de* CHÊNES-LIÈGES (M. Pagnol).

Nevertheless, more than one author—because of the interpretation *chêne à liège*—writes the plural as *des chênes-*LIÈGE: *À travers des bois de* CHÊNES-LIÈGE (M. Genevoix). *Les interminables rangées de* CHÊNES-LIÈGE (J. Green).

585 CLIN D'OEIL [wink]. In the plural: *des clins d'*OEIL: *De rapides clins d'*OEIL (E. Jaloux). *Les demi-sourires et clins d'*OEIL (R. Martin du Gard).

The following is also used: *des clins d'*YEUX: *Faisant force clins d'*YEUX (Hugo). *Colonnes de clins d'*YEUX *qui fuyaient aux éclairs* (G. Apollinaire). *Ils accueillirent mon ami par des clins d'yeux et des sourires narquois* (M. Pagnol).

At times you will find *un clin d'yeux: Comme* UN CLIN D'YEUX *d'intelligence* (V. Larbaud).

586 GARDE [guard]. In compound nouns, add *s* to the noun *garde* in the plural if the compound noun designates a person [i.e., if *garde* is equivalent to *gardien(ne)*]; it does not change when the compound designates a thing: *Des gardes-barrière, des gardes-chasse, des gardes-malade(s). Des garde-fous, des garde-boue, des garde-robes.*

587 GRAND-MÈRE [grandmother]. In compound words that are feminine (*grand-mère, grand-tante, grand-messe*, etc.), the adjective *grand*, traditionally, does not change to the plural: *Des costumes dignes de nos* GRAND-MÈRES (G. Duhamel). *Une de ses* GRAND-TANTES (A. Chamson).

But people also write: *des grands-mères, des grands-tantes*, etc.: *Le nom du gâteau que mangeaient nos* GRANDS-MÈRES (G. Duhamel). *Rien ne vaut la bonne suée de nos* GRANDS-MÈRES (A. Chamson). *Avec nos pieuses* GRANDS-MÈRES (H. Bazin).

588 GUET-APENS [ambush]. In the plural: *des guets-apens* (pronounced: *ghè-ta-pan*): *On parle, on va, l'on vient; les* GUETS-APENS *sont prêts* (Hugo). *Des* GUETS-APENS (Ac.).

589 LIEU-DIT [place, locality]. The Academy does not write this word with a hyphen. In the plural: *des lieux-dits, des lieux dits.*

At times it is written as one word: *lieudit;* its plural, then, according to *Robert*, is: *des lieuxdits.*

590 PETIT-BEURRE [butter cookies]. In the plural: *des petits-beurre: Tandis que je déballais à mon tour les oranges, les* PETITS-BEURRE (M. Arland).

591 REINE-CLAUDE [greengage]. The spelling *des reines-Claude* was the one used by the French Academy (7th ed., of its *Dictionnaire*, 1878) and it is still the same form listed in *Larousse du XXe siècle*. But that spelling has been abandoned and today the adopted plural form is: *des reines-claudes*, which is recommended by Littré. This new spelling is found in the 8th edition of the *Dictionnaire de l'Académie* (1935), in *Robert, Grand Larousse encyclopédique, Grand Larousse de la Langue française*, and *Lexis*.

Evidently, the spelling *reine-claude* does not change in the expression *des prunes de reine-claude*.

592 SOUTIEN-GORGE [brassière, bra]. *Larousse du XXe siècle* writes: *des soutien-gorge;* you do come across this form and Le Gal considers it most frequently used. He cites: *Hommes (. . .) affligés de* SOUTIEN-GORGE *féminins* (Colette).   *L'usage des soutien-gorge* (P.-A. Lesort).

But his opinion does not seem to be founded: the spelling *des soutiens-gorge* (which is more logical) certainly prevails and it is listed in *Grand Larousse encyclopédique, Grand Larousse de la Langue française, Petit Robert,* and *Lexis: Devant le rayon des* SOUTIENS-GORGE (M. Arland).   *Des* SOUTIENS-GORGE (M. Toesca).   *Y compris les* SOUTIENS-GORGE (J. Kessel).   *Une marque de* SOUTIENS-GORGE (R. Le Bidois).

Plurals of Foreign Nouns

Principle. Nouns borrowed from foreign languages follow the French rule in forming the plural when frequent use of them has really Gallicized them: *Des accessits, des autodafés, des bénédicités, des vivats, des scénarios, des macaronis, des guérillas, des meetings.*

593 NOMS LATINS [Latin nouns].   (1) The following Latin words do not change in spelling in the plural:

admittatur	*exequatur*	*minus habens*
alter ego	*extra*	*miserere*
amen	*forum*	*nota bene*
ana	*Gloria*	*Pater*
Avé	*intérim*	*stabat*
confiteor	*Kyrie*	*Te Deum*
credo	*Magnificat*	*vade-mecum*
deleatur	*mea culpa*	*veto*
exeat		

(2) **Addenda:** *Un addenda, des* ADDENDA (Littré).

Addendum is used at times when it is only a matter of a single addition; but to follow the Latin, in that way, is somewhat pedantic.

(3) **Déficit:** Hardly anyone ever writes this in the plural as *des déficit.*

The word has certainly been Gallicized and the normal plural today is to write: *des déficits,* which is recommended by Littré and which is listed in *Robert* and the *Grand Larousse encyclopédique: Le poker et les siestes remédiaient aux* DÉFICITS (Cl. Farrère).

(4) **Desideratum:** This Latin word is used especially in its plural form: *des desiderata* (Ac.).

(5) **Duplicata, triplicata:** These words are invariable: *On lui a envoyé les* DUPLICATA *de plusieurs dépêches* (Ac.). Littré states, with good reason: "It is not understood why the Academy writes an *s* on *des opéras* but does not also write: *des duplicatas, des triplicatas.*"

(6) **Errata:** This collective noun is invariable, designating the list of misprints in a publication; people say *un errata,* even if there are several misprints or just one: *Il a fait* UN ERRATA *fort exact* (Ac.). *J'ai fondu l'*ERRATA *avec la table* (Stendhal). *Les* ERRATA *sont nécessaires dans les livres (Dictionnaire général).*

But there is some hesitation in actual usage: some people say, for just one error: *un erratum;* plural: *des errata.* Some people (Marcel Cohen, for example) even say *un erratum* at all times, whether there is just one misprint or more than one.

(7) **Maximum, minimum:** The Latin plural ending *-a* is used especially in scientific language: *Déterminer les* MAXIMA *et les* MINIMA *d'une fonction* (Ac.). *Nous distinguerions encore deux couleurs principales, leurs* MAXIMA, *leurs* MINIMA (Taine).

The Latin plural form is also used for scholarly words ending in *-um: Des moratoria, des postulata, des preventoria, des sanatoria, des ultimata.* . . .

These plurals ending in *-a* have something pedantic about them; in current language, people will say: *des maximums, des minimums, des moratoriums* (better still: *des moratoires*), *des postulatums* (better still: *des postulats*), *des préventoriums, des aériums, des sanatoriums* (or: *des sanas*), *des ultimatums, des referendums, des consortiums, des criteriums* (better still: *des critères*), *des solariums,* etc.

Maximum, minimum, optimum, extremum, as adjectives:

(a) In the feminine, they ordinarily keep the form ending in

-um: La température maximum (A. Hermant).   *La dépense minimum (Dictionnaire général).   Pression optimum, extremum.*

Especially in technical language, there is a form ending in *-a,* as in Latin: *Pression maxima, température minima* (Ac.).   *L'indemnité maxima* (J.-P. Chabrol).   *Poussée optima, extrema.*

(b) For the plural: ending in *-ums* or *-a: Des prix maximums* or *maxima.   Recettes maxima* (A. Maurois).   *Conditions optimums* or *optima.   Des pressions extremums* or *extrema.*

(c) The Academy of Sciences (Paris) recommends using the adjectives *maximal, minimal, optimal, extrémal* whose feminine (in *-ale*) and plural masculine (in *-aux*) raise no difficulties.

(8) **Quantum:** (Latin neuter sing., *quantus,* meaning how great, how much). In the plural, *quanta: La théorie des* QUANTA *de lumières, qu'on appelle des photons, a été très féconde en optique* (Ac.).

(9) **Quota:** It takes an *s* in the plural: QUOTAS *d'importation (Robert).*

594 NOMS ITALIENS [Italian nouns]. The words *bravo* (assassin), *carbonaro, condottiere, graffito, lazarone, libretto, pizzicato, scenario, soprano* are ordinarily formed in the plural in *-i: Bravi, carbonari,* etc.

The Italian plurals *concetti, confetti, graffiti, lazzi, mercanti* are used as singular nouns: *un confetti, un lazzi,* etc.; Gallicized, they take an *s* in the plural: *Ses* LAZZIS *sont des flammèches* (Hugo).   *Pons crachait des* CONFETTIS (A. Chamson).

Certain terms in music, adverbs by nature, remain invariable when they indicate movement or nuances: *Des crescendo, des smorzando.*

If they designate the musical airs themselves, they take an *s* in the plural: *De beaux* ANDANTES, *des* ADAGIOS, *des* ALLÉGROS (Ac.).

595 NOMS ANGLAIS [English nouns].   (1) English nouns ending in *-man* change to the plural in the English way by changing *-man* to *-men: Un gentleman, des gentlemen; un policeman, des policemen; un cameraman, des cameramen; un sportsman, des sportsmen.*

English nouns ending in *-y* change to *-ies* in the plural, as is done in English: *Un baby, des babies; un dandy, des dandies; une lady, des ladies; un whisky, des whiskies.*

These nouns ending in *-man* or in *-y* often form the plural in the French way: *Jeunes clubmans* (A. Daudet).   *Un de ces dandys* (A. Billy).   *Des whiskys à l'eau* (J. Romains).

(2) **Flash:** In the plural, the form is: *des flashes.*

(3) **Match:** The plural is formed in the English way: *aux* MATCHES *de boxe* (R. Rolland). *Une organisation de* MATCHES (R. Martin du Gard).

Plural in the French way: *J'assistais à des* MATCHS *de foot-ball* (A. Maurois). *Pas de grands* MATCHS *en perspective* (P. Morand).

(4) **Miss:** The plural is formed in the English way: *De jeunes* MISSES (Th. Gautier). *Chez les* MISSES *Mapleson* (A. Hermant).

In the French way: *Les deux* MISS *pensionnaires* (A. Gide). *Les jeunes* MISS (R. Dorgelès).

(5) **Sandwich:** English plural, *des sandwiches: L'assiette de petits* SANDWICHES (Colette). *Elle avait déjà préparé ses sandwiches* (A. Maurois).

More than one author writes: *des sandwichs,* in the French way: *Ils mordaient à grandes bouchées dans deux* SANDWICHS (R. Martin du Gard). *Deux ou trois* SANDWICHS (A. Gide). *De petits* SANDWICHS (A. Billy).

(6) **Speech:** English plural: *Il y eut quelques* SPEECHES *amusants (Petit Robert).* In the French way: *Des speechs.*

596 NOMS ALLEMANDS [German nouns].

(1) **Leitmotiv:** German plural: *des leitmotive: Deux* LEITMOTIVE *que l'on retrouve de siècle en siècle* (R. Kemp).

At times, the Gallicized form of the word is used, *leitmotif* (or *leit-motif,* with a hyphen). In the plural: *Un des* LEIT-MOTIFS *du volume* (A. Thérive).

(2) **Lied:** The German plural, *lieder,* is used especially in the language of musicians: *Il écrivit pour elle deux ou trois* LIEDER (G. Duhamel).

In current usage, people ordinarily say, *des lieds: Les bateliers chantaient des* LIEDS *sentimentaux* (A. Maurois).

(3) **Mark** and **pfenning:** According to German usage, they do not change in the plural: *La pièce de vingt* MARK (*Grand Larousse encyclopédique*). *Le mark est divisé en cent* PFENNIG (Id.). But these nouns, in current French usage, take an *s* in the plural: *Deux cent mille* MARKS (A. Lanoux). *Le menu du matin coûtait 60* PFENNIGS (J. Mistler).

CHAPTER 2

ARTICLES

597 SUR LES DEUX HEURES [at around two o'clock]. *Les, des* are used in front of the hour (when telling time), in front of days, etc., in order to mark approximation or latitude: *Sur* LES *une heure* (Littré). *Vers* LES *une heure* (A. Chamson). *Vers* LES *six heures. Samson déjà a tué dans* LES *deux mille adultes* (J. Giraudoux). *Marius rentre à présent à* DES *une heure du matin!* (Hugo).

With *midi* and *minuit*, you can use *le* or *les* or *des*: *Sur* LE *midi* (Littré). *Sur* LE *minuit* (P. Claudel). *Vers* LES *midi un quart* (H. Lavedan). *Je pars vers* LES *minuit* (J. Giono). *Rentrer jusqu'à* DES *minuit.*

598 *Minuit* was, formerly, feminine. In modern usage, LA MINUIT (or LA *mi-nuit*) is archaic: *Je vous revois vers* LA *minuit.* . . (G. Duhamel). *Il sortait et vadrouillait jusqu'à* LA *mi-nuit* (Montherlant).

599 LE MIDI, CE MIDI. People say *à midi* [at noon], meaning at the hour of noon, this day: *On a beaucoup parlé de vous,* À MIDI, *chez les gens avec qui j'étais* (G. Duhamel). *Cette vieille servante de mon grand-père qui, du fond de mon enfance, m'apporte,* À MIDI *et le soir, une soupe parfumée* (Fr. Mauriac).

Le midi (corresponding to *le matin, le soir*) and *ce midi* (corresponding to *ce matin, ce soir*) are criticized. Some authors write: *Dans les premières heures qui suivirent* LE MIDI *du 10 décembre* (Stendhal). LE MIDI *du second jour, (. . .) la servante introduisit un enfant porteur d'une lettre* (G. Duhamel). *Nous l'attendons pour* CE MIDI (A. Gide). Compare: *Chaque midi* (Maupassant). *L'autre midi* (Cl. Farrère).

600 ACCUSER (LA) RÉCEPTION [to acknowledge receipt]. The French Academy points out only *accuser réception,* without the definite article *la: Accuser réception d'une lettre, d'un paquet. Accusez-moi réception.* But you may use the definite article: *Accuser* LA *réception* or *accuser réception d'une lettre, d'un paquet* (Littré). *Je vous prie de m'accuser* LA *réception de cette lettre* (Stendhal).

601 AVOIR (LE) DROIT DE + infin. [to have (the) right + infin.]. The article is optional: *Avoir droit de voter* or LE *droit de voter* (Ac.).

602 (LA) NOËL [Christmas]. People say elliptically [by omitting the word "fête"]: *la Noël: À l'approche de* LA *Noël* (Littré). *Peu avant* LA *Noël* (H. Queffélec).
But you may do without the definite article *la: Mais à Noël, qui peut savoir que l'hiver est fini?* (Alain.) *À quelques jours de Noël* (F. Gregh). *La veille de Noël* (Ac.).

603 LE HERNANI, LA BRINVILLIERS. The definite article in front of a proper noun of a person is used, at times, in order to express contempt: *Le chef,* LE *Hernani / Que devient-il?* (Hugo.) LA *Montespan (. . .) a certainement consulté les diseuses de bonne aventure et même probablement* LA *Voisin pour se conserver l'amour du roi* (M. Garçon).
Similarly, in popular usage (not always with denigration): LA *Léontine s'éloigna dans l'ombre* (M. Barrès). *Vous vous rappelez,* LE *Gaëtan, comme il montait à cheval?* (M. Arland.)

604 ÈS. Pronounce the *s*. This word is an old form; it is a contraction of *"en les";* it is found in some set expressions: *Docteur* ÈS *lettres,* ÈS *sciences; licence* ÈS *lettres.*
At times it is used to express irony or badinage: *Il n'y a pas de canton qui n'ait sa douzaine de docteurs* ÈS *vignes* (R. Bazin). *Le professeur* ÈS *idées générales* (Fr. Jammes).
To use *ès* followed by a noun in the singular would indicate a lack of understanding of the etymology of *ès: docteur ès pédagogie.*
As for *ès qualités* = in the capacity of (as) exercising the function with which a person is charged, note: *Ici le ministre ne pouvait parler, intervenir* ÈS *qualités (Petit Robert).* To use the singular, *qualité,* would be improper (influence of the expression *en qualité de*): *Le conseil ne siège plus* ÈS QUALITÉ (H. Bazin).

605 PARLER (LE) FRANÇAIS [to speak French]. In practical use, the definite article is optional: *Elle parlait* LE FRANÇAIS *sans accent* (A. Malraux). *Nous nous tutoyions lorsque nous parlions* ALLEMAND, *mais nous ne parlions que* FRANÇAIS (A. Hermant).

If it has to do with a particular kind of French, the article is needed: *Elle parle* UN FRANÇAIS *d'autrefois* (J. Green).

606 L'ARTICLE et les noms propres italiens [The article and Italian proper nouns].
(a) People say: *Dante,* without the definite article: *De beaux vers de* DANTE (Sainte-Beuve).   *La Béatrice de* DANTE (Montherlant).   But also, fairly often: LE *Dante;* (but this is not very regular because in Italian the definite article is never placed in front of a masculine first name; *Dante* is the abbreviation of the first name, *Durante): Il n'est rien que* LE *Dante n'exprimât* (Voltaire).   *Tout autant que* LE *Dante* (Flaubert).   *Le menton* DU *Dante* (Colette).
(b) What has just been said also applies to *Titien* (= the Italian first name, *Tiziano;* family name, *Vecellio): Vélasquez vénérait Titien* (A. Malraux).   *L'ambre* DU *Titien* (A. France).
(c) People say: *l'Arioste, le Corrège, le Véronèse, le Tintoret, le Pérugin,* at times *le Vinci.*
(d) The definite article has been placed in front of the proper names of famous actresses or singers: *La Champmeslé, la Malibran*—but today this Italianism is outdated.

607 LE PLUS, LE MOINS, LE MIEUX [the most, the least, the best]. In these expressions, followed by an adjective or a participle, the definite article *le* remains invariable if the comparison is made between the different degrees of a quality considered in the same being or object: *C'est au milieu de ses enfants qu'une mère est* LE *plus heureuse* (i.e., happy in the highest degree).   *C'est souvent lorsqu'elle est* LE *plus désagréable à entendre qu'une vérité est* LE *plus utile à dire* (A. Gide).

However, agreement is made with the noun expressed or understood when there is a comparison between different beings or objects: *Cette femme est* LA *plus heureuse des mères, la mère* LA *plus heureuse* [she is being compared to the other mothers]. *Une population qui est* LA *plus sobre et* LA *plus nombreuse du monde* (P. Valéry).   *Les questions qui paraissent* LES *plus dangereuses se trouvent un jour résolues par les circonstances* (A. Maurois).
(1) A practical way to tell the difference: if the adjective allows *de tous, de toutes* after it, then the definite article is variable [it changes]; if the adjective allows *le plus (le moins, le mieux) possible* after it, then the definite article is not variable [it does not change].
(2) It would be desirable to observe the distinction which has just been explained, but in current usage and at times in literature, there is a strong tendency to vary the article in all cases: *L'hiver, c'est la saison où les nuits sont* LES *plus longues* (J. Giono).   *Les*

points où la citadelle est LA *plus battue en brèche* (A. Thérive).   *C'est en hiver que ces jardins sont* LES *plus beaux* (É. Henriot).

608 DE BON TABAC [(some) good tabacco]. In front of a group "adjective + noun," instead of using *du, de la, de l', des,* written or careful language uses the simple *de* in order to show the partitive meaning: *J'ai* DE *bon tabac* (Ac.).   DE *jolies maisons blanches* (Vigny).   *Ils burent (. . .)* DE *mauvais thé* (É. Henriot).

But the spoken language and often the written language use *du, de la, de l', des:* DU *bon tabac.*   DE LA *bonne encre et* DU *bon papier* (A. Gide).   DES *petites pierres* (A. Chamson).

609 (1) People use *du, de la, de l', des* if the adjective forms a unit with the noun: DES *grands-pères,* DES *jeunes gens,* DE LA *bonne volonté, dire* DES *bons mots.*

(2) In front of a group "adjective + plural noun," when the partitive idea is reinforced by *bien,* at times you will find *bien de:* *Cette contrée renferme* BIEN DE *fertiles prairies* (Littré).   *J'ai une jugeote qui rend* BIEN DE *petits services* (J. Giono).   But current practice is to use *bien des: J'ai pris* BIEN DES *petits verres* (A. Daudet).   BIEN DES *jolies têtes souriaient* (Th. Gautier).   BIEN DES *petits services* (M. Proust).

(3) In this use, if the adjective is *autres,* people always say *bien d'autres* (never: *bien des autres*): *J'ai vu sous le soleil tomber* BIEN D'AUTRES *choses* (Musset).

(4) When the noun is represented by *en,* if it is a matter of expressing the partitive idea, careful language uses the simple *de:* *Du vin? j'en ai* DE *bon; de la bière? j'en ai* DE *bonne. Des fleurs? il y en a* DE *blanches,* DE *rouges. . . .* But current practice is to use *du, de la, de l', des: Du vin? j'en ai* DU *bon; de la bière? j'en ai* DE LA *bonne.   Des fleurs? il y en a* DES *blanches,* DES *rouges. . . .*

610 ARTICLE PARTITIF et la négation [Partitive article and negation]. In negative sentences certain distinctions must be made:

(a) If the negation is absolute, that is to say, if the noun can be preceded by *aucun* or *aucune quantité de,* just *de* is used: *Je n'ai pas* D'*argent.   Vous ne m'avez jamais fait* DE *peine* (M. Proust).

(b) If the negation is not absolute, that is to say, if the sentence, despite the negative construction, implies (as far as the noun is concerned) an affirmative idea, then the following are used: *du, de la, de l', des: Je n'ai pas* DE L'*argent pour le gaspiller* [that is, "I have some money, but not for wasting it"].   *Je ne prendrai point* DE LA *peine pour rien* (Montesquieu).   *Il n'a* DE LA *bonté que dans la tête* (Diderot).

If the noun is modified by an adjective and if the negation

does not bear on the noun but rather on the adjective, use *du, de la, de l', des: Madame, je n'ai point* DES *sentiments si bas* (Racine). *C'est même une des raisons qui font que la dictature n'a pas* DES *causes uniformes* (J. Bainville). *Il ne boit pas* DE L'*eau pure, mais une potion odieusement contaminée.*

611 The article is repeated in front of two adjectives joined by *et* or by *ou*, when these adjectives qualify different beings or objects, even though they may be designated by a single noun: *Il y a* UNE *bonne et* UNE *mauvaise honte* (Ac.). *Dans* LA *bonne ou* LA *mauvaise fortune.*

612   If the coordinate adjectives are placed after the noun, there are four possible constructions:
(1) *La langue latine et la langue grecque* (this is the usual construction): *Le chat domestique et le chat sauvage* (Ac.).
(2) *La langue latine et grecque: La syntaxe latine et française* (A. Maurois).
(3) *La langue latine et la grecque: L'infanterie allemande et l'espagnole* (Voltaire).
(4) *Les langues latine et grecque: Les statuaires grecque et chinoise* (A. Malraux).
[See also entry no. 649.]

613 **ENTRE (LES) DEUX** [between the two, between both]. In order to express the idea of "moderately," "middling," "so-so," or the idea of "neither good nor bad," you may use *entre deux* or *entre les deux: Ce mouton est-il dur ou tendre?* ENTRE DEUX (Ac.). *Est-elle laide?* ENTRE LES DEUX (Littré).

614 **TOUS (LES) DEUX** [both, the two]. The article is optional in the expressions *tous les deux, tous les trois, tous les quatre: Faut-il les tuer* TOUS LES DEUX? (Mérimée.) TOUS DEUX *sont morts* (Hugo). TOUS LES TROIS, *vous paierez les frais* (R. Benjamin). *Ils se retrouveraient comblés* TOUS TROIS (M. Arland). *J'ai pris la liberté de les alerter* TOUS LES QUATRE (J. Giraudoux). TOUS QUATRE *étaient fort émus* (A. Hermant).
    According to the French Academy, the article is required beyond the number four. This opinion is too absolute; people tend to follow the statement made in Littré, which is: "beyond the number four up to and including ten, the article is rarely left out; beyond ten, it is always used": *Y seront-ils* TOUS LES CINQ? (Hugo.) *Et* TOUS CINQ *se sont endormis pour toujours* (Nerval). *Ils sont là,* TOUS LES DIX (Hugo).

CHAPTER 3

ADJECTIVES

I. MASCULINE / FEMININE

615 The following have only one form for both genders:

adverse	*gnangnan (gnian-*	*riquiqui (rıkiki)*
angora	*gnian)*	*rococo*
bath (argot fam.)	*kaki*	*rosat*
bengali	*mastoc*	*snob*
capot	*olé olé*	*standard*
chic (fam.)		

616 AQUILIN [aquiline, Roman]. Rare in the feminine form: *Un nez d'une noble courbe* AQUILINE (Th. Gautier).

617 AVANT-COUREUR [forerunner]. This word is not used in the feminine. The feminine form *avant-courrière* is borrowed from the word *avant-courrier*.

618 BEL, NOUVEL, FOL, MOL, VIEIL. These masculine singular adjectives are used immediately in front of a masculine singular noun beginning with a vowel or a mute *h: Un bel arbre* [a beautiful tree], *un nouvel habit* [a new suit], *un fol espoir* [a foolish hope], *un mol oreiller* [a soft pillow], *un vieil usage* [an old usage].

But people will say: *Ce drap est* BEAU *et bon* (Littré). *Un* NOUVEAU *et rare moyen* (Id.). *Un homme* MOU *et efféminé* (Ac.). VIEUX *et usé* (Littré).

Nevertheless, this observation is not absolute: In front of a word beginning with a vowel sound, people frequently use these adjectives in the form ending in -*l: Un* BEL *et pathétique récit* (G. Duhamel). *Mon or, si* BEL *et si clair* (Montherlant). *Un nez* MOL *et enfoncé* (A. Thérive). *Un* NOUVEL *et fâcheux événement* (Ac.). VIEIL *et illustre dramaturge* (M. Druon).

The old masculine forms *fol* and *mol* are still found occasionally, even in front of a word beginning with a consonant sound or at a pause: *Un* FOL *gaspillage* (G. Duhamel). *La vieille Périne (. . .) le tenait pour un peu* FOL (L. Martin-Chauffier). *Le devoir des amis d'un mort n'est pas d'accompagner sa mémoire de* MOLS *gémissements* (Montherlant).

At times, *vieux* is used in place of *vieil* when in front of a noun beginning with a vowel sound: *Un* VIEUX *usurier* (Montesquieu). *Un* VIEUX *appareil* (A. Gide).

619 CHÂTAIN [chestnut brown color]. When this adjective is next to a feminine noun, it can be taken as a substantive and in that case it is invariable: *Trois petites frisettes* CHÂTAIN (A. Billy). *Une jolie moustache* CHÂTAIN (M. Pagnol).

The feminine form, *châtaine*, is used today: *Avec ses longues tresses châtaines* (Hugo). *Une grande chevelure châtaine* (Colette). *Une courte moustache châtaine* (M. Druon). *Elle restait blonde, avec plus de beauté, mais moins d'éclat que sa soeur, qui devenait châtaine* (Ph. Hériat).

620 COI [quiet, silent]. *Coi* in the feminine is *coite*. The word is used especially in the familiar expressions *se tenir coi (coite)* [to remain quiet, still], *demeurer* or *rester coi (coite)* [to remain quiet, still]: *Là où les grandes personnes demeurent* COITES (Fr. Mauriac).

621 FAT [conceited, vain, foppish]. The Academy gives only the masculine for this word. The feminine, *fate*, is listed in Littré and you come across it sometimes: *Cette émigration* FATE *m'était odieuse* (Chateaubriand). *Dans une attitude à la fois très* FATE *et très gênée* (Alain-Fournier).

622 FORT [strong]. *Fort* is invariable in the expressions **se faire fort de** [to undertake], and **se porter fort pour** [to answer for]: *Elle se fait* FORT *d'obtenir la signature de son mari* (Ac.). *C'étaient de mauvaises herbes; elle se faisait* FORT *de les arracher* (R. Rolland). *Elles se portent* FORT *pour nous.*

That is the traditional use, but, as Littré points out, it is only an archaism which, moreover, has long and often been repudiated. Nowadays, it is not uncommon for authors to regard *fort* as variable (in gender and number) in the expressions *se faire fort de* and *se porter fort pour: Quand la "Libre Parole" se fit* FORTE *de prouver. . .* (M. Barrès). *Je me fais* FORTE *d'avance de son acceptation* (É. Estaunié). *Catherine se faisait* FORTE *de convaincre peu à peu l'enfant* (G.-E. Clancier).

623   Similarly, *court* [short] is invariable in the expressions *demeurer court*, *rester court*, *se trouver court* (all of which have the meaning "to stop short" in the sense of lacking recall, finding oneself at a loss for words or means): *Elle est demeurée* COURT *après les premiers mots de son compliment* (Ac.). *Je tremblais de les voir rester* COURT (A. Hermant).

624   **GRAND** [big, large, great (general meanings; this word has other meanings, depending on how it is used)]. The adjective *grand* remains invariable in gender in the expressions **pas grand-chose** [not much], **grand-croix** [Grand Cross (decoration)], **avoir grand-faim** [to be very hungry], **avoir grand-soif** [to be very thirsty], **avoir grand-honte** [to feel deep shame], **avoir grand-hâte** [to be in a great hurry], **avoir grand-peine** [to be in great pain], **avoir grand-peur** [to be in great fear], **avoir grand-pitié** [to have great pity], **grand-maman** [grandma], **grand-mère** [grandmother], **grand-messe** [high mass], **grand-tante** [great-aunt]. These are all expressions that are true compound nouns.

625   In these expressions, the adjective *grand* (when next to a feminine noun) is a survival of something that used to be done where *grand* had only one form for both genders. When it became general usage to show the feminine form of all adjectives by adding a final -*e*, it was astonishing to find that *grand* plus a feminine noun appeared in countless groups of words (. . .*mère*, . . .*tante*, . . .*messe*, . . .). In order to make all things regular, an apostrophe was added to the adjective *grand* in order to show that feminine *e* had dropped—but actually, in these feminine compound nouns, the feminine *e* was never there in the first place.

The apostrophe was dropped and a hyphen was put in its place in the 8th edition of the *Dictionnaire de l'Académie* (1935).

626   **GROGNON** [grumbler, grouch]. The feminine form of *grognon* is *grognonne*, or it is invariable (may remain *grognon* in the feminine): *Humeur* GROGNONNE (Ac.). *Femme grognon (Larousse du XXᵉ siècle).*

627   **HÉBREU** [Hebrew]. When it is a question of things, the feminine form is *hébraïque* (which is the same form in both genders): *Langue* HÉBRAÏQUE. *Université* HÉBRAÏQUE *de Jérusalem.*

When it has to do with persons, the feminine form *juive* or *israélite* is used (= pertaining to the community, to the Jewish religion).

628 IMPROMPTU. For the Academy, the adjective *impromptu* is invariable. Undoubtedly, it is fairly frequent not to vary it in the feminine: *Une confrontation* IMPROMPTU *avec les chefs-d'oeuvre* (A. Chamson). But more than one good author makes it agree in the feminine (in gender and number): *Des besognes impromptues* (R. Martin du Gard). *Redoutant une visite impromptue* (M. Druon). *Des vers impromptus* (Voltaire). *Il y a souvent des crimes dans la montagne et ils sont toujours* IMPROMPTUS (J. Giono).

629 IVROGNE, MULÂTRE, NÈGRE, SUISSE [drunkard, mulatto, Negro, Swiss]. These words, when used as adjectives, have one form for both genders: *Femme* IVROGNE, *servante* MULÂTRE; *la reine* NÈGRE (A. Maurois); *femme* SUISSE.

630 LAÏQUE [lay, secular; layman, laywoman]. Whether as an adjective or a noun, *laïque* is of both genders: *Habit* LAÏQUE, *enseignement* LAÏQUE, *école* LAÏQUE. *Un* LAÏQUE, *une* LAÏQUE.
   The masculine may also be written as: *Un* LAÏC *(Robert)*.

631 LAPON, LETTON, NIPPON [Lapp (Laplander), Lett (Lettonian, Latvian), Nipponese]. To obtain the feminine form of these words, either as adjectives or nouns, at times the letter *n* doubles, at times it does not; there is hesitation in usage: *La race* LAPONE (Littré). *Deux soeurs* LAPONNES (A. Bellessort). *La forêt* LETTONE (M. Bedel). *La police* NIPPONE (P. Morand). *Les trompettes* NIPPONNES (Cl. Farrère).

632 MAÎTRE et TRAÎTRE [master and traitor]. Taken as adjectives, in feminine they are: *maîtresse, traîtresse: La* MAÎTRESSE *branche* (Ac.). *Une âme traîtresse* (Id.).
   However, *traître*—and *maître* in popular usage—are sometimes left invariable in gender: *La pieuvre est* TRAÎTRE (Hugo). *La rive est* TRAÎTRE, *abrupte* (M. Genevoix).

633 MELLIFLU(E) [mellifluent, mellifluous (flowing with honey)]. It is astonishing that Littré, the *Dictionnaire général*, the Academy, the *Grand Larousse encyclopédique*, Robert, and Dournon list only the form *melliflue* for this adjective. (The Academy says that the form of this adjective, *melliflue*, is the same for both genders.) [The *Grand Larousse de la Langue française* and *Lexis* give *melliflue, -e* or *melliflue*.]
   There is no doubt, however, that the masculine form, *melliflu*, is good and that it comes from the Latin *mellifluus* (from *mel*, Latin; *miel*, French; honey, English; and from *fluëre* in Latin,

meaning "to flow")—exactly like the word *superflu,* which comes from the Latin, *superfluus;* English, superfluous. Thus, mention of the masculine form, *melliflu,* is completely right, as pointed out by Bescherelle, La Châtre, Poitevin, and *Larousse du XXe siècle: Discours* MELLIFLUS (Bescherelle).

634 MORMON [Mormon]. Feminine form is *mormone.*

635 RIGOLO [funny, comical, droll]. This word is used familiarly in slang. Its feminine form is: *rigolote;* it is somewhat rarely written as *rigolotte* (with two *t*'s): RIGOLOTE *chanteuse* (M. Harry). *De jolies histoires* RIGOLOTTES (J.-P. Chabrol).

636 SAUVEUR [saver, savior, saviour, saving]. For the feminine form of the adjective *sauveur,* the neologism, *salvatrice,* is used: *Quelque doctrine salvatrice* (G. Duhamel).
    Another neological form, but not used much, is *sauveuse: Une rigueur (. . .) pourtant* SAUVEUSE (P. de La Gorce).

637 VAINQUEUR [victorious]. As an adjective, this word has no feminine form. To obtain a feminine form, you can borrow from *victorieux* the form *victorieuse.*

II. SINGULAR / PLURAL

638 The following do not change in the plural:

bath (argot fam.)	*melba*	*rococo*
capot	*kaki*	*rosat*
chic	*mastoc*	*standard*
gnangnan (gnian-	*olé olé*	*sterling*
gnian)	*riquiqui (rikiki)*	

Examples: *Nous sommes demeurés* CAPOT (Littré). *Des chaussettes* KAKI (A. Maurois). *Ces potages* STANDARD (J. Romains). *Cinquante livres* STERLING (Ac.). *Toutes les femmes* CHIC *de Saïgon* (Cl. Farrère).

639   For the plural of *chic,* there is some indecision; you often find it with an *s: Des gens* CHICS (M. Proust). *Dans des bals* CHICS (Montherlant). *Chez les maîtresses de maison les plus* CHICS (H. Troyat).

640 ADJECTIFS EN *-AL* [Adjectives ending in *-al*]. Generally, these adjectives change the ending -*al* to -*aux* to form the plural: *Brutal*, *brutaux*.

Few of them form the plural in -*als*: *Mendiants* BANCALS, *termes* CAUSALS, *rocs* FATALS, *sons* FINALS, *paysages* NATALS, *combats* NAVALS, *systèmes* TONALS, *conflits* TRIBALS.

641 (1) *Banal*, a feudal term, is *banaux* in the masculine plural: *Fours*, *moulins* BANAUX. In ordinary usage, it is *banals*, but often, it is also *banaux*: *Après des compliments* BANALS (Ch. de Gaulle). *Des pastiches assez* BANALS (M. Brion). *Quelques mots* BANAUX (R. Rolland). *Une mosaïque originale d'éléments* BANAUX (J. Rostand).

(2) *Marial* is an adjective that is sometimes written as *mariaux*, sometimes as *marials* in the plural; there is some hesitation about this: *Grand Robert* gives *mariaux*, but *Petit Robert* gives *marials*, which is the form that prevails: *Textes* MARIALS (P. Laurentin). *Sanctuaires* MARIALS (H. du Manoir).

642 ANGORA. This word is invariable if you consider that the omission of the word "breed" in understood elliptically: *Des chats* ANGORA (Littré). *D'adorables chattes* ANGORA (P. Loti).

But almost always the word *angora*, as an adjective or noun, follows the normal rules of agreement: *Les trois chats* ANGORAS (J.-L. Vaudoyer). *Chats, chèvres, lapins* ANGORAS *(Robert)*.

Special Observations

643 MEILLEURS VOEUX [best wishes]. The greetings *meilleurs voeux, meilleurs souhaits*, etc., are criticized by certain theorists of good language; they say that what we wish to express is not wishes that are better [*meilleurs* = the comparative] than other wishes but rather *les meilleurs* (the best possible), which is the superlative. Without doubt, to be strictly correct, the definite article or a possessive would be required: *Les meilleurs voeux de. . .*, *mes meilleurs voeux*. But the expressions *meilleurs voeux, meilleurs souhaits*, etc., are so frequently used, especially during the Christmas and New Year season, that it would be difficult to change them. Along with André Thérive (see his *Procès de langage*, p. 115), we can—even though they are so brief that they lack courtesy—accept them as set forms, as stereotypes. Compare: *Meilleures amitiés de votre vieil ami* (H. de Balzac). But it would always be better to prefer to say or to write: *les meilleurs voeux de. . .* , *mes meilleurs voeux*.

644 (1) *Plus meilleur*, a redundant comparative, is used in popular language. Do not say: *Plus ce vin vieillira, plus il sera meilleur.* Say: *Plus ce vin vieillira, meilleur il sera* (or: *plus il sera bon)* [The more this wine ages, the better it will be].

(2) *Meilleur*, no matter what certain purists say, can be modified by *beaucoup: Ce vin est beaucoup meilleur* (Ac.).

645 PLUS BON, in principle, cannot be said.

Nevertheless, *bon* can be used with *plus* when both words are separated by a verb: PLUS *une oeuvre est* BONNE, *plus elle attire la critique* (Flaubert).

Similarly, when *bon* is taken to mean "simple, trusting": *Vous êtes bon de croire cela! Et vous, vous êtes encore* PLUS BON *de croire ceci.*

Note that, in the following sentences, *plus* and *bon* do not have between them the relationship existing in the comparative *plus bon: Il est bon plus que juste* [*plus* ties in with *que: plus que*. . .]. *Cette phrase sera plus ou moins bonne selon que*. . . (Littré) [*plus ou moins* = adverbial locution: more or less]. *On ne saurait être plus bon enfant, plus bon vivant, plus bon apôtre* [*bon enfant, bon vivant,* etc. = compound nouns].

Note also that in expressions like *bonne foi, bon mot, bon vivant, bonne volonté*, etc., if *bon* is, for the meaning, absolutely insepara- ble from the noun, the expression can take *meilleur: C'est le meil- leur bon vivant que j'aie vu. Un de vos meilleurs bons mots.* But if the group "*bon* + noun" is not absolutely indissoluble, then *bon* fits in poorly with *meilleur*; for example, you would say: *Avec la meil- leure volonté du monde*. . . (rather than: *avec la meilleure bonne vo- lonté*. . .).

646 PIRE, PIS [worse, worst]. *Pire* (from Latin, *pejor*, the compara- tive of *malus*, meaning *mauvais* in French; English, bad)—much less currently used than *plus mauvais*—belongs to the same family as *pis* (Latin, *pejus*, neuter of *pejor*).

Both words are used as adjectives or nouns: *C'est bien la* PIRE *peine* (Verlaine). *Pour les vieillards, c'est bien* PIRE (A. Maurois). *Il n'y a rien de* PIS *que cela* (Ac.). *En mettant tout au* PIS (Id.). *En mettant tout au* PIRE (Fr. Mauriac). *Le* PIS *du destin* (La Fon- taine). *Ce qu'il y a de* PIS (Diderot). *Ce qu'il y a de* PIRE (A. Ar- noux).

647 ANTÉRIEUR,   EXTÉRIEUR,   INFÉRIEUR,   INTÉRIEUR, POSTÉRIEUR, SUPÉRIEUR [anterior, exterior, inferior, interior, posterior, superior]. Etymologically, these words are comparatives; the words *infime, intime, minime, ultime* are etymologically superlatives. All may descend to the level of simple positives and lend themselves to a variation of more or less: *Il serait* TRÈS INFÉRIEUR *à ces Iroquois* (Voltaire).   *Une salle* PLUS *intérieure* (J. Romains).   *Aide-major de classe* TRÈS INFIME (A. Daudet).   *Un incident* TRÈS MINIME (G. Duhamel).

648   Certain adjectives that express a high degree or an absolute idea may, occasionally, allow variations in more or in less. For example:

absolu	*éternel*	*indispensable*
achevé	*excellent*	*parfait*
divin	*extrême*	*suprême*
énorme	*immense*	*total*
essentiel	*impossible*	*universel*

Examples: *Une catastrophe* PLUS ABSOLUE (Montherlant).   *L'ouvrage* LE PLUS ÉNORME (Michelet).   *Dans* LA PLUS EXCELLENTE *acception de ces deux mots* (E. Fromentin).   *Les mots* LES PLUS INDISPENSABLES (Nerval).   *À partir d'une ruine* SI TOTALE (Fr. Mauriac).

III. AGREEMENT OF ADJECTIVE

General rule: Agreement in gender and number with the noun or pronoun to which the adjective refers.

649 NOMS JOINTS PAR *ET* [nouns joined by *and*].
   (1) If the adjective qualifies several nouns joined by *et*, it is written in the plural: *Un livre et un cahier* NEUFS.

   When the qualified words are of different genders, the adjective is written in the masculine plural: *Une tête et un buste* HUMAINS (A. France).

   When the adjective has, for both genders, very different pronunciations, it is generally the masculine noun that is placed next to the adjective for harmony in sound: *Une tête et un buste* HUMAINS (rather than *un buste et une tête* HUMAINS).
   (2) At times, if the adjective refers to several abstract nouns, the agreement is made only with the closest: *Tant elles* [*les lettres*] *étaient mortifiantes pour la vanité et la jalousie* PERSANE (Montesquieu). *Un goût et une aise* NOUVELLE (J. Giraudoux).

   At times, the meaning demands agreement with the closest noun: *Venez avec votre père et votre frère aîné.*

(3) Several adjectives in the singular may refer to the same noun, expressed only once, in the plural: *Organiser les deuxième et troisième positions* (J. Romains). *Les statuaires grecque et chinoise* (A. Malraux). *Du XVe au XVIIe siècles* (J. Rostand).

For various possible constructions, see entry no. 612.

650 NOMS JOINTS PAR *COMME, AINSI QUE,* etc. [nouns joined by *comme, ainsi que,* etc.]. The adjective referring to nouns joined by a conjunction of comparison agrees with the first: *L'aigle a le bec, ainsi que les serres,* PUISSANT *et acéré.*

But the agreement is made with the ensemble of nouns if the conjunction has the meaning of *et: Il avait la main ainsi que l'avant-bras tout* NOIRS *de poussière.*

651 NOMS SYNONYMES ou EN GRADATION [synonymous nouns or nouns in gradation]. Agreement is made with the closest noun: *Il a montré un courage, une énergie peu* COMMUNE. *Une vigueur, un acharnement* ÉTONNANT. *Il a conservé tout* ENTIÈRE *l'habileté, le talent qu'il avait.*

652 NOMS JOINTS PAR *OU* [nouns joined by *ou*]. Ordinarily, the idea of conjunction prevails and agreement of an adjective is made with the group of nouns: *Par une ambition ou une rancune* INDIGNES *de son grand cœur* (J. Bainville).

The adjective agrees with the last noun if the idea of disjunction prevails; this agreement is required when the adjective obviously qualifies only the last noun: *Autour d'eux une indifférence ou une hostilité* PROFONDE (J. et J. Tharaud). *Pour écouter (. . .) parfois aussi un pianiste ou un flûtiste* RENOMMÉ (M. Brion). *Une statue de marbre ou de bronze* DORÉ.

653 When the adjective follows a noun which functions as a determinate complement of another noun, agreement is made with the one of the two nouns that indicates common sense: *Du poisson de mer* FRAIS. *Deux bouteilles de vin* ALGÉRIEN.

654 A number of adjectives (especially short adjectives found in usual expressions) are used adverbially. They are obviously invariable: **coûter cher, voir clair, chanter faux, sentir bon, raisonner juste, filer doux, s'arrêter court,** etc.: *Les cuivres, ciselés* FIN (P. Loti). *Roide moustache, coupée* COURT (Montherlant). *Arbres posés droit* (Saint-Exupéry).

At times, these adjectives are attributes or detached (disjunctive) adjectives, in which case they are variable: *Il avait les cheveux coupés* COURTS (G. Duhamel). *La route s'allongea,* DROITE *et boueuse* (Cl. Farrère).

655 Certain nouns taken adjectivally are invariable when they are felt to be elliptical expressions: *Des manières* CANAILLE [that is to say, similar to those of *une canaille*] (Littré). *Leur nage* [des grenouilles] *allègre et* BON ENFANT (M. Genevoix). *Les pantoufles* BON ENFANT *de la facilité collective* (J. d'Ormesson). *Des étoffes* BON TEINT.

But if they are not felt as elliptical expressions, they vary: *Des paroles* FARCES (Littré). *Des hommes* GÉANTS *sur des chevaux* COLOSSES (Hugo). *Dans les meetings* MONSTRES (J. et J. Tharaud). *Une Allemagne* (. . .) BONNE ENFANT (A. Siegfried). *Des clins d'oeil* CANAILLES (R. Sabatier).

656 MOTS DÉSIGNANT UNE COULEUR [words designating a color].
  (1) The simple adjective agrees, but the compound adjective does not: *Des étoffes* BRUNES. *Des étoffes* BRUN CLAIR [that is, *d'un brun clair*].
  (2) The noun (simple or compound) remains invariable: *Des étoffes* MARRON [that is, *de la couleur du marron*]. *Des favoris* POIVRE ET SEL [that is, *de la couleur du poivre et du sel*].
  However, *écarlate* [scarlet], *mauve* [pale bluish purple], *pourpre* [purple], and *rose* [pink], because they have become real adjectives, are variable: *Des rubans* ÉCARLATES, MAUVES; *des étoffes* POURPRES, ROSES.

657 ADJECTIFS COMPOSÉS [compound adjectives].
  (1) Formed from two adjectives, when both of them qualify the same noun, they both vary: *Des filles* SOURDES-MUETTES. *Des paroles* AIGRES-DOUCES.
  Adjectives taken from a compound word: the first element is invariable: *La cour* GRAND-DUCALE, *les officiers* GRAND-DUCAUX. *Les théories* LIBRE-ÉCHANGISTES. *Populations* EXTRÊME-ORIENTALES. *Origine* FRANC-COMTOISE (R. Martin du Gard). *Diverses loges* FRANC-MAÇONNES (É. Henriot).
  (2) Formed from an invariable word and an adjective, obviously the adjective alone varies: *L'*AVANT-DERNIÈRE *page. Rayons* ULTRA-VIOLETS. *Les maigres vaches* NORD-AFRICAINES (M. Genevoix).
  (3) Formed from two adjectives whose first has an adverbial value, the first element is invariable: *Des personnes* HAUT

PLACÉES *(Robert)*. *Trois enfants* MORT-NÉS (J. Rostand). *Personnes* COURT-VÊTUES.

658 Note: In certain cases, following an old usage, both elements vary: *Des roses* FRAÎCHES CUEILLIES (Ac.). *Les deux pages* GRANDES OUVERTES (J. Romains). *Les yeux et la bouche* LARGES OUVERTS (J. Cocteau). *Ils sont arrivés* BONS PREMIERS.

Special Observations

659 AVOIR L'AIR [to look, to seem, to appear].
   (a) If we give to the word *air* the meaning of "look, mien, appearance, physiognomy," the adjective agrees with *air*: *Elle a l'air* FAUX (Ac.). *C'est drôle, comme les gens ont l'air* CONTENT (R. Rolland).
   (b) If we take *avoir l'air* as a synonym of *paraître* [to appear], the adjective agrees with the subject: *Ils n'ont point l'air* INDIGENTS (Taine). *Elle n'avait pas l'air trop* FÂCHÉE (A. Maurois).

660 DEMI, SEMI, MI [half, semi, mid].
   (a) **Demi** in front of the noun is invariable and is joined to it by a hyphen: *Une* DEMI-*douzaine*. *Toutes les* DEMI-*heures* (Ac.).
   After the noun, it is joined by *et* and agrees in gender only: *Deux pommes et* DEMIE. *Il est dix heures et* DEMIE.
   People write: *midi et* DEMI (Ac.); *à minuit et* DEMI (Id.). However, among the best authors, you will frequently find: *midi et* DEMIE, *minuit et* DEMIE: *Il est bientôt midi et* DEMIE (M. Genevoix). *À minuit et* DEMIE (A. France). *Vers minuit et* DEMIE (J. Romains).
   (b) **Demi** and **semi**, when in front of an adjective, are invariable and are joined to it by a hyphen: *Ses ais* DEMI-*pourris* (Boileau). *Je suis* DEMI-*morte!* (E. Rostand.) *Populations* SEMI-*nomades*.
   À demi is used in the same way but the hyphen is dropped: *La statue était* À DEMI *voilée* (Ac.).
   Semi, in front of a noun, is invariable and it is joined to it by a hyphen: *Les* SEMI-*voyelles*.
   (c) **Mi** is always invariable and is joined by a hyphen to the word with which it forms a body: *La* MI-*carême*. *Les yeux* MI-*clos*. *À* MI-*hauteur*. [See also entry no. 460.]

661 ÉGAL (n'avoir d'~que) [to have as equal only . . ., to be equal only . . .]. As for agreement on the word *égal*, as a substantive adjective, usage is indecisive.

At times, agreement is made with the subject of *avoir*: *Edmont, dont le dévouement n'avait d'ÉGAL que la conscience scientifique* (A. Dauzat). *Avec un intérêt qui n'a d'ÉGAL que l'attention de mon petit chien* (Ch. Maurras).

At other times, agreement is made with the second related term: *Avec un tact et une souplesse qui n'ont d'ÉGALE que sa superbe loyauté* (Cl. Farrère). [Molière] *n'a d'ÉGAUX en puissance sereine que Montaigne et Shakespeare* (A. Suarès).

662 D'égal à égal [as equal, as an equal]. Each of the two terms may remain invariable: *Elle parle à Dieu presque d'ÉGAL À ÉGAL* (J. Green).

But you can also make each term agree with the word to which it refers: *Au milieu de merveilles qu'il traitait d'ÉGAL À ÉGALES* (J. Giraudoux).

663 Sans égal [without equal]. Agreement is made with the word to which *égal* refers: *Une imprudence sans ÉGALE* (Ac.). *Des beautés sans ÉGALES.*

Sans égal, with a masculine plural, remains invariable, according to *Grand Larousse de la Langue française*: *Des chagrins sans ÉGAL.* This opinion does not appear to be well founded. There appears to be nothing that would prevent anyone from saying or writing: *Des chagrins, des malheurs, des champions, des apprêts. . .sans ÉGAUX.*

664 DES PLUS, DES MOINS, DES MIEUX [(among or between the) most, least, best]. The adjective in relation to one of these three expressions agrees almost always with the plural noun logically raised by *des* (= among the. . ., between the. . .): *Notre souper fut des plus SIMPLES* (Th. Gautier). *Ce travail est des plus DÉLICATS* (Ac.). *Quoique latiniste des moins SÛRS de soi* (P. Valéry). *Un toast des mieux RÉDIGÉS* (A. Thérive).

In cases when it is a question of a single person or a single thing, the adjective is sometimes written in the singular. In that event, *des plus, des moins, des mieux* are taken in the meaning of *très, très peu, tout à fait bien*: *La situation était des plus EMBARRASSANTE* (G. Duhamel).

This singular form is also logically required when the adjective refers to a neuter pronoun: *C'était, en effet, des plus INTÉRESSANT* (P. Vialar).

665 FEU [deceased, the late. . .]. *Feu,* meaning "someone who has been dead for a short time," is hardly ever used except in literary, juridical, or administrative language. Its agreement varies when it is placed between the article (or the possessive) and the noun: *La* FEUE *reine* (Ac.). *Les* FEUS *rois de Suède et de Danemark* (Id.). *Toute votre* FEUE *famille* (J.-P. Sartre).

In other cases, it is invariable: *J'ai ouï dire à* FEU *ma soeur. . .* (Montesquieu). FEU *mes oncles* (Littré).

In current usage, people use *pauvre* or *défunt*: *Ton* PAUVRE *arrière-grand-père me disait. . .* (Fr. Mauriac). DÉFUNT *mon père aussi en était adepte* (R. Martin du Gard). DÉFUNTE *ma mère* (G. Bernanos).

666 FIN. When *fin* is taken adverbially in the meaning of "completely," it is invariable according to modern syntax; but often it does take agreement, according to old syntax: *Nous sommes seuls,* FIN *seuls* (J. Richepin). *Quand elle était* FIN *prête* (H. Duvernois). *Ils sont rentrés à l'aube, tous* FIN *saouls* (G. Bernanos). *Elle [une balle] était* FINE *bonne, celle-là* (G. Duhamel). *Aussi* FINS *saouls les uns que les autres* (R. Vercel).

667 FRANC DE PORT. This expression is outdated. Today, people say: *affranchi* [postpaid, postage paid, postmarked] for a letter and *franco* for a package. It takes no agreement if the expression refers to the verb: *Recevoir* FRANC DE PORT *une lettre et un paquet* (Ac.). It does take agreement if it refers to the noun: *Recevoir une caisse* FRANCHE DE PORT (Ac.).

668 HAUT et BAS [up or high, down or low]. Taken adverbially, these words are invariable in: *J'en viendrai à bout* HAUT *la main* (Ac.). HAUT *les mains!* BAS *les armes!*

669 DE GUERRE LASSE [for the sake of peace and quiet]. The adjective is always in the feminine. This is explained, it would seem, by the fact that the letter *s* on the word *las* [tired, weary] used to be pronounced at a pause and it was believed that the word was feminine: *Le chauffeur, de guerre* LASSE, *avait sans doute accepté de charger un piéton persuasif* (J. Cocteau).

670 IL N'Y A DE. . .QUE [there is only. . ., there is nothing but . . ., the only "thing" that is. . .is. . .(this or that)]. When an adjective is related to *il n'y a de. . .que, il n'y a pas plus. . . que, tout ce qu'il y a de. . .,* (ceci or cela) [this or that] *n'a de. . .*

que, it is often written in the masculine singular—actually, it is
in the neuter: *Il n'y a de* VRAI *que la richesse* [The only thing that is
real is wealth] (Musset). *Il n'y a pas plus* DOUILLET *que les
hommes* (J. Giraudoux). *Toute émotion n'a d'*EXQUIS *que sa surprise*
(A. Gide).

But it can also agree with the substantive element which the
thought gives to it as support: *Il n'y a de* PURS *que l'ange et que la
bête* (P. Valéry). *C'est une mort tout ce qu'il y a de plus* NATURELLE
(P. Vialar). *Ce sont des gens tout ce qu'on fait de plus* GENTILS
(A. Chamson).

671 MEILLEUR MARCHÉ [better buy, the best buy]. In sentences
like *Elle cherche le* MEILLEUR *marché des cotonnades* and *je voudrais des
chaussures* MEILLEUR *marché,* the adjective *meilleur* must be in the
masculine singular because it refers to *marché.*

672 NOUVEAU [new, newly]. This word is invariable in: *Les* NOU-
VEAU-NÉS (Littré). *Une petite fille* NOUVEAU-NÉE (Colette). *D'autres
beautés* NOUVEAU-NÉES (Ch. Maurras). *Des vins* NOUVEAU *percés*
(Littré) [this is little used; *nouvellement* is ordinarily used].

It is variable in front of a past participle taken as a substantive
in: *Des* NOUVEAUX *mariés* (Ac.). *Une* NOUVELLE *convertie* (Littré).
Il y eut un court colloque entre les NOUVELLES *venues* (R. Martin du
Gard).

To form the adjectives corresponding to *Nouveau-Québec, Nou-
velle-Zélande,* etc., *nouveau* (or *nouvelle*) is changed to *néo,* which
is invariable: *Les mines* NÉO-QUÉBÉCOISES, *les Alpes* NÉO-ZÉLAN-
DAISES.

673 NU [naked]. The word is invariable in *nu-tête, nu-bras, nu-jambes,
nu-pieds, nu-pattes: Elle s'était levée* NU-*jambes,* NU-*pieds* (Maupassant). *Aller* NU-*tête.*

It is variable after a noun: *Aller la tête* NUE. *Il lui parle tête* NUE
(Ac.). *Marcher pieds* NUS (Id.).

Nue-propriété changes, in the plural, to *des nues-propriétés; des
nus-propriétaires.*

The adverbial locution, *à nu,* is invariable: *Mettre un membre,
une plaie* À NU (Ac.). *D'abord leurs escoffions* [= *coiffes*] (headdress)
ont volé par la place / Et, laissant voir À NU *deux têtes sans cheveux, /
Ont rendu le combat risiblement affreux* (Molière).

674 PASSÉ et PRÉCIS [past and exactly]. In telling time, after indicating the hour, these two words agree with *heure(s),* or *midi,* or
minuit: Il est dix heures PASSÉES, *dix heures* PRÉCISES. *À une heure*

vingt PASSÉE, *à une heure et demie* PRÉCISE, *à deux heures et demie*
PASSÉES, *ou* PRÉCISES.   *À midi* PASSÉ, *à minuit* PRÉCIS.

675 PLAIDER COUPABLE, PLAIDER INNOCENT [to plead guilty,
to plead innocent]. In the expression *plaider coupable,* which
means "to recognize the guilt by undertaking to excuse it or to
extenuate it," and in the expression *plaider innocent,* which means
"to plead innocence," the words *coupable* and *innocent* remain,
generally, invariable: *Les accusés y ont* [dans un procès], *grande
nouveauté, plaidé non* COUPABLE (L. Martin-Chauffier). *Ils plaident*
INNOCENT.

Making no agreement can be explained by the fact that the adjective seems to be treated as if it qualified a neuter complement
implied in the verb: *Ils plaident* COUPABLE (or: INNOCENT) = . . .
something guilty (something innocent).

However, having the adjective agree would not be illogical: *Ils
plaident* COUPABLES (or: INNOCENTS) = . . . that they are guilty
(or: . . .that they are innocent).

676 POSSIBLE. According to the traditional rule, this word is invariable after a superlative (*le plus, le moins,* etc.), in which case it
refers to the impersonal pronoun *il,* understood: *Il lui adressait les
compléments les plus justes* POSSIBLE (Flaubert) [that is to say, *les plus
justes qu'il était possible*]. *Je pose le moins de questions* POSSIBLE
(J. Green).

It is variable in other cases, and it refers, therefore, to the noun:
Vous pouvez tirer sur tous les gibiers POSSIBLES (Mérimée).
(1) It would be a good thing to observe this distinction, but authors often neglect to and they make the word *possible* agree in
sentences containing a superlative: *Il voulait lui donner le plus de
choses* POSSIBLES (J. Giono).   *Il fait charger le plus de machines* POS-
SIBLES *sur des péniches* (A. Maurois).
(2) When *possible* is placed immediately after *le plus, le moins,*
etc., it is invariable: *Voir le plus* POSSIBLE *de gens de toutes sortes*
(M. Achard).

677 PROCHE [near, close]. *Proche,* as an adjective, means "which
is within short distance, either in time or in space": *Rappelez-
vous les faits: ils sont encore* PROCHES.   *Nos plus* PROCHES *voisins.*

Proche, as an adverb (equal to *près*) and *proche de* are somewhat
archaic: *Mes amis demeurent ici* PROCHE.   *Ces gens habitent* PROCHE
DE *chez moi,* PROCHE *l'église.*

678 SEC. The expression *en cinq secs,* meaning "very rapidly, in a jiffy," is often written as *en cinq* SEC [*faire quelque chose en cinq sec:* to do something in a jiffy, "in one shake of a lamb's tail"]: *Je te joue cela en cinq* SEC *ou* SECS (Littré).   *Les marier en cinq* SECS (Colette).   *Régler une affaire en cinq* SEC (Ac.).

679 SEUL À SEUL [alone, privately]. Each of these two adjectives may remain invariable: *La vieille fille (. . .) laissait les époux* SEUL À SEUL (Daniel-Rops).

But one may also have each adjective agree with the noun to which it refers: *C'était la première fois qu'il se trouvait* SEUL À SEULE *avec Élise* (R. Boylesve).   *Elle parlerait* SEULE À SEUL *avec Nicolas* (H. Troyat).

IV. NUMERALS

680 SEPTANTE, HUITANTE, NONANTE [seventy, eighty, ninety]. These are old forms which have been replaced by *soixante-dix, quatre-vingts, quatre-vingt-dix.* Nevertheless, *septante* and *nonante* are still used in Belgium, in the French-speaking part of Switzerland, and in the eastern part of the Vosges. *Huitante* is used in the French-speaking part of Switzerland except in Geneva; it is in general use (even in Geneva) in official services, e.g., army, telephones, etc.

Certain authors sometimes use *septante* and *nonante* to give a provincial flavor to a sentence: *Félicité, la mendiante aveugle de* NONANTE *ans* (A. Arnoux).   *Il était encore bel homme, malgré ses* SEPTANTE-*deux ans* (É. Henriot).

681 ET in numerals. The conjuction *et* is used in numbers only to join *un* to tens [except in *quatre-vingt-un* (Ac.)] and in *soixante et onze.* People say: *vingt* ET *un, cent trente* ET *un, à soixante* ET *onze ans,* etc.

Do not use *et* (because it would be archaic) in: *Cent un, cent deux, trois cent un, mille deux cent cinq, mille un,* etc.: *Dans cent un ans* (Ac.).   *Trois cent un coups de canon* (H. Troyat).   *Mille un fagots* (Littré).

(1) People say, in an indeterminate meaning, *mille et un* [= a great number]: *J'entends bien qu'il ne s'agit pas ici des* MILLE ET UNE *démarches de l'humble vie quotidienne* (G. Duhamel).   Similarly, people use *cent et un* (but somewhat rarely; instead, say: *cent et cent* or just *cent*).

(2) People say *mille et trois* when speaking of Don Juan's conquests.

(3) People say, with *et: Cent* ET *quelques, mille* ET *quelques*—or even: *cent* ET *des, mille* ET *des: Je ne possédais que cent* ET *quelques francs. Une dette de cinq cents* ET *des francs.*

682 TRAIT D'UNION [hyphen]. In compound numerals used as adjectives, people use the hyphen between the elements below one hundred except when they are joined by *et: Trente-huit; soixante-dix-sept; mille deux cent trente-cinq francs.*

As for ordinals, usage is somewhat indefinite: *La deux centième année* (Ac.).   *Le numéro quatre-centième* (Littré).   *La deux-millième place* (Id.).

683 UN [one].   (1) Generally, people say: *page* UN, *page trente et* UN, *strophe vingt et* UN, etc.; but you can also say: *page* UNE, *strophe vingt et* UNE, etc.

(2) People say: *vingt et* UN *mille livres de rente, trente et* UN *mille cartouches, quarante et* UN *mille tonnes,* etc.; Littré says that *un* has no bearing on the feminine noun but rather on *mille.* But, along with Thérive, it can be claimed that in these expressions the agreement of *un* is with the feminine noun.

(3) When telling time, people say: *Il est trois heures* UNE; *à dix heures moins* UNE, *à six heures vingt et* UNE, etc. Martinon allows the use of *un* in the masculine, in cases like these, but current usage calls for *une.*

684 DEUX OU PLUSIEURS [two or several]. *Deux ou plusieurs* is justified as well as *un ou plusieurs: plusieurs,* as a matter of fact, is essentially a comparative and the expression boils down to "two or a greater number": *La société est un contrat par lequel* DEUX OU PLUSIEURS *personnes conviennent de mettre quelque chose en commun* (Civil Code).

Plusieurs may be used as a pronoun: PLUSIEURS *pensent que. . .* (Littré).   *Ceci nous fut redit par* PLUSIEURS (A. Gide).

685 VINGT et CENT [twenty and one hundred]. *Vingt* and *cent* take an *s* when they are multiplied by another number and they end the numeral used as an adjective: *Quatre-*VINGTS *francs.   Mutilé à quatre-*VINGTS *pour cent* (J. Mistler).   *Trois* CENTS *mètres.   Nous étions cinq* CENTS.   But: *quatre-*VINGT*-deux francs.   Trois* CENT *quinze mètres.   Nous étions cinq* CENT *trente.   Les* VINGT *livres reçus.   Tous les* CENT *mètres.*

(1) The idea of a multiplier is sometimes expressed in an indefinite way: *Je fis quelques* CENTS *mètres* (Alain-Fournier).

(2) *Vingt* and *cent*, used for *vingtième* or *centième*, are invariable: *Page quatre*-VINGT (Ac.).   *Chant premier, vers deux* CENT (Id.).

(3) *Cent*, used for "*centaine*," is a noun, and it varies in the plural: *Deux* CENTS *d'oeufs, de fagots* (Littré).   Similarly, when it designates certain monies [one hundredth of a principal unit]: *Deux dollars cinquante* CENTS [here, pronounce CENTS as in the singular English word: "cent"].

686 MILLE [(one) thousand]. This word is invariable as an adjective: *Deux* MILLE *hommes.   Quatre* MILLE *cinq cent dix francs.   Le chiffre des* MILLE.

When stating the date of the years in the Christian era, traditionally, the written word is *mil* if this word begins the date and is followed by one or several other numbers: *L'an* MIL *sept cent* (Ac.).   MIL *huit cent onze!* (Hugo).

But: *Aux environs de l'an* MILLE (É. Henriot).   *Quand l'an deux* MILLE *arrivera* (A. Rousseaux).

The rule that has just been given is precarious; in particular, the spelling *l'an mil* is frequent: *Depuis l'an* MIL (P. Loti).   *Vers l'an* MIL (M. Barrès).   You also find: *l'an deux* MIL: *La grande peur de l'an Deux* MIL (F. Gregh).

Mille [mile], is a noun when it designates "a mile" and it takes an *s* in the plural: *Ce navire parcourt tant de* MILLES *à l'heure* (Ac.).   *À deux mille* MILLES *de tout secours* (H. Bazin).

The rule also applies to the English word, *mile: Battre le record des dix* MILES.   *Les 500* MILES *d'Indianapolis.*

People write: *Des* MILLE *et des cents* [i.e., a lot of money]; *Plusieurs* MILLE *d'épingles.   Deux* MILLE *de paille.*

Millier, million, milliard, milliasse, billion, etc., are nouns, and they take an *s* in the plural. (Note that they do not prevent the agreement of *vingt* or *cent*): *Des* MILLIERS *de gens.   Quatre-vingts* MILLIONS *de francs.   Deux cents* MILLIARDS *cinq cent mille francs.*

687 ZÉRO [zero] is a noun and takes an *s* in the plural: *Deux* ZÉROS.

It is not used as an adjective. Nevertheless, people do say: *zéro faute, zéro franc, zéro centime, zéro degré, zéro heure: L'usage tend à s'introduire de numéroter les heures de 0 heure à 24* (Ac.).

688   *Autres, derniers, mêmes, premiers, prochains.* . .are placed after a noun denoting a number: *Les* DIX AUTRES *vers* [the *other ten* verses], *les* DEUX DERNIÈRES *strophes* [the *last two* stanzas], *les* TROIS MÊMES *chiffres* [the *same three* figures], *les trois premières* voitures [the *first* *three* automobiles], *les* DEUX PROCHAINES *semaines* [the *next two* weeks].

Nevertheless, when a group is considered to be a unit (e.g., when you count by 10s, by 100s, etc.), these adjectives are placed in front of the indicated amount: *Les* PREMIERS *cent francs; les* DER-NIERS *mille francs que je vous donne.   Les* PROCHAINS *mille exemplaires que vous m'enverrez.   Pendant les* MÊMES *cinq années* (Ch. de Gaulle).

V. POSSESSIVE ADJECTIVES

689 MON, TON, SON [my, your, his / her / its]. These possessive adjectives are used instead of *ma, ta, sa* in front of a feminine word beginning with a vowel or a mute *h*: MON *erreur,* TON *âme,* SON *habitude,* SON *aimable réponse.*

However, in front of *huitaine, huitième, ululation, yole, Yolande* and *onzième,* people use *ma, ta, sa:* MA *huitaine d'oeufs,* TA *huitième victoire,* SA *ululation,* SA *yole.*   SA *Yolande* (Fr. Mauriac).   *Dans* SA *onzième année* (Ac.).

As for *ouate, hyène,* there is some hesitation: *En* SA *ouate d'azur* (J. Laforgue).   *Dans* SON *ouate* (Ph. Hériat).   TA *hyène* or TON *hyène.*

Similarly, with the article or with *de: Acheter de* L'*ouate* (Ac.).   *De* LA *ouate* (Id.).   *Une couverture* D'*ouate* (Id.).   *Turban* DE *ouate* (R. Martin du Gard).   *L'hyène* (Ac.).   *La hyène* (Flaubert).

690 BATTRE SON PLEIN [to be at its height]. This expression is used in referring to the tide at the moment it reaches its maximum height and remains stationary for a time. In current language, the expression has the metaphorical meaning of "to be complete, to be at its peak."

In this sense, *plein* is a noun preceded by a possessive adjective. Thus, people say: *En état de transe, je bats* MON *plein* (A. Gide).   *Les grèves russes battent* LEUR *plein* (H. Troyat).

691 The following words are ordinarily used with no possessive adjective in a direct address, when speaking in an affectionate and trusting familiarity: *père, papa, grand-père, grand-papa, bon-papa, mère, maman, grand-mère, grand-maman, bonne-maman, oncle, tante, parrain, marraine: Mère, je propose que nous continuions nos adresses* (R. Bazin).   *Écoutez, tante Henriette, je vais vous parler franchement* (A. Maurois).

Frère, soeur, cousin, cousine may also do without the possessive adjective.

The possessive adjective is used with *bru, gendre, neveu, nièce*.

When immediately in front of a first name, the possessive adjective expresses a deep tenderness: *Mon Victor, je suis heureuse . . .* (R. Bazin).

692 USAGES MILITAIRES [military uses]. A military person, when speaking to his / her superior says, with *mon: mon général, mon colonel, mon capitaine, mon lieutenant* (and, in France: *mon adjudant*, but in Belgium: *adjudant*); without *mon: sergent, caporal*.

When talking directly to a marshal: *Monsieur le maréchal*.

A military person, when speaking to a military person of lower rank, states the rank without *mon: Colonel, capitaine, adjudant*, etc.

When addressing an officer, a civilian does not use, in principle, *mon: Général, lui dit Clemenceau, voici pourquoi nous vous avons appelé* (A. Maurois).

If there is any intimacy in the relationship, occasionally *mon cher* is used, or *cher: Je compte, mon cher général, que vous serez des nôtres*.

Often, men of a social rank lower than that of an officer use *mon*, especially if they have been in the military. Women must never use the *mon;* nevertheless, a young woman addressing an officer older than she is or who is of a higher rank, will say: *Monsieur le général, Monsieur le colonel, . . .* or merely *Monsieur*.

693   The possessive adjective is, generally speaking, replaced by the definite article when the relationship of possession is clearly indicated by the general meaning of the sentence, particularly in front of nouns designating parts of the body, articles of clothing, or the mind: *Il lève LA tête, ouvre LES yeux, étend LES bras, me tire par LA manche. Il perd LA mémoire*.

This rule is not absolute. If there is only the slightest desire to indicate personal "ownership," the possessive adjective is used: *Il étend SES bras* (Diderot).   *Il la tire familièrement par SA manche* (M. Prévost).   *J'ai mal dans MES jointures* (Colette).

On the other hand, the possessive adjective is called for when it is necessary to avoid ambiguity, when it is a question of a habitual thing, or when the noun is qualified or specified by an object: *Donnez-moi VOTRE bras (dit le médecin).   Elle a SA migraine* (A. France).   *Un Saxon étendu, SA tête blonde hors de l'eau* (A. Daudet).   *Ils t'ont coupé TES beaux cheveux, TES cheveux d'ange blond*.

694 CHACUN et le possessif [*chacun* and the possessive].

(a) When *chacun* refers to a plural in the first or the second person, *notre, nos, votre, vos* are used: *Nous suivions chacun* NOTRE *chemin* (Lamartine). *Nous avons chacun* NOS *soucis. Vivez chacun de* VOTRE *côté* (Ac.). *Vous vous retirerez (. . .) chacun dans* VOS *États* (Hugo).

The rule allows some latitude; in particular, *chacun de son côté* is frequently used: *Nous sommes tous partis, chacun de* SON *côté* (G. Duhamel). *Nous sommes six cents (. . .) chacun sur* SON *cheval* (A. de Châteaubriant).

(b) When *chacun* refers to a plural in the third person, the following are used, depending on the required form: *son, sa, ses,* or *leur(s): Les deux clercs écrivaient, chacun à* SA *table* (Hugo). *Rien d'impossible à ce que deux ou plusieurs de ces variétés (. . .) gardent chacune* SES *caractères particuliers* (A. France). *Ils gagnèrent* CHACUN *leur place* (Hugo).

695   When each one of the possessors owns only one object, use the following—according to the point of view envisaged:

(a) the singular forms *notre, votre, leur* if, among the group of possessors, the individual is in mind: *Mes compagnons, ôtant* LEUR *chapeau goudronné. . .* (Chateaubriand). *Nous ôtons* NOTRE *manteau.*

(b) the plural forms *nos, vos, leurs* if the plurality or the variety of detail is envisaged: *Ils prirent* LEURS *manteaux et* LEURS *chapeaux* (M. Brion). *Nous pouvons encore nous appeler par* NOS *noms* (M. Arland).

Use the singular or plural, depending on the number, in sentences like the following: *Ils sortent avec leur(s) femme(s): Nous laissons* NOS *chères compagnes* (La Fontaine). *Ils aimaient* LEURS *femmes* (Montesquieu). *Des hommes brillants venus à Balbec sans* LEUR *femme* (M. Proust). *Sur cinq hommes mariés (. . .) trois avaient déjà retrouvé* LEUR *femme* (A. Chamson).

VI. INDEFINITE ADJECTIVES

696 AUCUN and NUL. These two words are normally used in the singular. They are written in the plural when they refer to nouns that have no singular or that, in the plural, have a special meaning: AUCUNS *frais.* NULLES *funérailles.* AUCUNS *apprêts!* (Hugo.) *Elles non plus ne toucheraient* AUCUNS *gages* (J. Schlumberger).

They are also found in the plural—in addition to the two examples which have just been pointed out—but they appear to be archaic and they stem from common usage: AUCUNES *choses ne méritent de détourner notre route* (A. Gide). *On ne doit surcharger* NULLES *créatures* (A. France).

However, the plural is perfectly justified when the sentence implies (as far as the noun is concerned) an idea of plurality or some sort of connection, comparison, resemblance, opposition, etc.: NULS *pépiements d'oiseaux n'égayaient cette solitude* (H. Lavedan). NULS *chefs ne s'affrontaient* (Ch. Péguy). AUCUNES *familles n'étaient plus unies que ces deux-là.*

697 AUTRE [other].

(1) In front of an indication of time, *l'autre* refers to a more or less recent past; at times, also, it may refer to a near future: *J'étais* L'AUTRE *jour dans une société où je me divertis assez bien* (Montesquieu). *Mes infirmités me rendent si faible! Cependant, j'aurais pu vivre jusqu'à* L'AUTRE *hiver, encore!* (Flaubert.)

(2) After *l'un et l'autre* as an adjective, the noun is written in the singular or plural: *L'un et l'autre* CRIME (J. Lemaitre). *Sur l'une et l'autre* RIVE (M. Arland). *Dans l'une et l'autre* ATTITUDES (Daniel-Rops). *L'une et l'autre rives du Rhin* (J. Kessel).

(3) When using *l'un ou l'autre* or *ni l'un ni l'autre* as adjectives, the noun is written in the singular: *Il me faut déserter l'un ou l'autre* RIVAGE (M. Jouhandeau). *Ni l'un ni l'autre* ESCADRON *n'arriva* (Michelet).

(4) The adjective *autres*, in front of a plural noun whose generic meaning encompasses several nouns that precede, is used in sentences like: *Il collectionne les papillons, fourmis, mouches et* AUTRES INSECTES. *De menus objets de menuiserie, tels que bagues, ronds de serviettes, coquetiers, manches d'ombrelles et* AUTRES *agréables* BABIOLES (É. Henriot).

If, in sentences like these, the plural noun that ends the series does not encompass the terms that precede, the effect is vulgar or playful and, regrettably, collides with common sense: *Ces doctes traités, essais, précis, mémoires et* AUTRES DISCOURS *qui vont désormais orner votre solitude* (G. Duhamel). *Le "cha-cha-cha," le "be-bop," et* AUTRES "CHARLESTONS" *sont des danses gaies* (P. Daninos).

(5) *Autre* is added as a term to underline or oppose the pronouns *nous* and *vous: Nous ne ferons pas cela,* NOUS AUTRES. *Vous ne comprenez jamais rien,* VOUS AUTRES!

Eux autres belongs to popular or very familiar language: EUX AUTRES, *ils ont discuté, avec le patron* (J. Giono).

(6) *Entre autres* [among others] is an expression which is most often related to a noun or pronoun expressed before or after it: *J'ai vu les plus beaux tableaux de Rome,* ENTRE AUTRES *"la Transfiguration" de Raphaël* (Ac.).   *J'ai visité* ENTRE AUTRES *musées celui du Louvre.*

But, no matter what certain theorists of language think, *entre autres* is also used in an absolute sense, as a substitute for "for example" or "in particular": *Je me souviens,* ENTRE AUTRES, *que M. Dubois nous récitait (. . .) de certains vers de Voltaire ou de lui* (Stendhal).   *Corps dur et solide, de la nature des rochers, qu'on emploie,* ENTRE AUTRES, *pour bâtir* (Littré).   *Je lis ceci* ENTRE AUTRES: *"Monsieur, au cours d'un voyage . . ."* (A. Hermant).

(7) The plural of *un autre* is *d'autres:* D'AUTRES *vont maintenant passer où nous passâmes* (Hugo). Do not say: *Des autres vont. . . .*

(8) *Un autre* and *d'autres,* as real subjects, attributes, or direct objects, are supported by the pronoun *en* which precedes: *Je rapporte ce livre; il m'*EN *faudrait un autre; donnez-m'*EN *un autre, donnez-m'*EN *d'autres.   Votre habit est usé, il faut* EN *acheter un autre* (Ac.).   *Tu* EN *aimes un autre?* (A. Daudet).

However, at times they can do without the support of the pronoun *en: Quant à ses chansons, (. . .) elles célébraient d'autres que Gabrielle* (Nerval).   *Et si j'aimais un autre, tu m'aimerais toujours?* (R. Rolland.)   *L'auteur de cette lettre—combien d'autres ai-je reçues!—tuerait volontiers le général de Gaulle* (A. Malraux).

698 CERTAIN. The meaning of *certain* is indicated by its position:

Un succès CERTAIN means a success that is assured, incontestable. *Un* CERTAIN *succès* is a success that is partial, incomplete, not well defined.

Un certain + a proper noun indicates that the person is not well known; at times, it expresses disdain: *Le personnage intéressant de la foire était* UN CERTAIN *Nissim Tobler* (J. et J. Tharaud).   UN CERTAIN *Chose m'a téléphoné.*

The following, in the plural, have no difference in meaning: *certaines choses, de certaines choses; à certaines heures, à de certaines heures,* etc.: *Il y a* CERTAINES *choses,* DE CERTAINES *choses pour lesquelles on éprouve de la répugnance* (Ac.).

699 CHAQUE [each]. In principle, this word must be immediately followed by a noun: CHAQUE *âge a ses plaisirs.*

700   In familiar, commercial, or popular language, it is used in an absolute way, without any noun expressed after it: *Ces cravates coûtent tant de francs* CHAQUE. *Passer dans trois cabarets et boire plusieurs verres dans* CHAQUE.

At times, this is found even in literary language: *Les carrosses de louage (. . .) taxés cinquante-deux livres par an* CHAQUE (Hugo). *Trois secteurs, trois jours dans* CHAQUE (M. Genevoix). Nevertheless, until now, it has not been accepted as good usage. In careful, polished language, people say, for example: *Ces cravates coûtent douze francs* CHACUNE (Ac.), or: *douze francs (LA) pièce*, or: *douze francs* L'UNE. *Les cartons coûtaient alors deux sous* PIÈCE (A. Chamson).

701 CHAQUE followed by a numeral and a noun may serve to indicate a period of time, for example: *chaque huit jours*. Purists protest this use and want us to say: *de huit (jours) en huit jours*, or *tous les huit jours*.

It must be noted, however, that the condemned construction is rather common in literary usage: *Il est bien juste que pour* CHAQUE *mille francs je vous donne vingt-cinq francs* (Sévigné). CHAQUE *dix minutes* (M. Barrès). *On recense seulement une fois* CHAQUE *quatrième année* (Cl. Farrère). *Soixante-dix avions* CHAQUE *vingt-quatre heures* (J. Kessel). CHAQUE *huit jours* (M. Druon).

702 Entre chaque, entre chacun [between each, between each one]. These are used even in literary language (despite what purists say) in the meaning of "in each interval of the series stated." Some people consider that it would be more logical to use *après* instead of these.

Nevertheless, *entre chaque* and *entre chacun* are old terms and many excellent authors use them: ENTRE CHASCUNE *tour* (Rabelais). ENTRE CHAQUE *tilleul* (Diderot). ENTRE CHAQUE *tableau* (Chateaubriand). ENTRE CHAQUE *tige de blé* (Hugo). ENTRE CHAQUE *phrase* (A. Chamson). ENTRE CHACUNE *de ses phrases* (Th. Gautier). ENTRE CHACUNE *de ces démarches* (J. Kessel). [See also entry no. 793.]

703 MAINT [many a]. *Maint* is used as an adjective in the singular and often in the plural: *Je l'ai rencontré en* MAINTE *occasion* (Ac.). *Maintes gens vous diront que. . .*(Id.). MAINTES ET MAINTES *fois j'en avais entendu parler* (J. de Lacretelle).

After *maint et maint*, the noun is written in the singular and, at times, in the plural: *Je fis mainte et mainte* REMARQUE (G. Duhamel). *J'ai reçu maint et maint* CONSEILS (J. et J. Tharaud).

As a pronoun, *maint* is archaic: *Une philosophie dont se réclame*

MAINT *d'entre eux* (J. Benda). *Un assez grand nombre de mythes dont* MAINTS *n'ont aucune chance de se réaliser bientôt* (Daniel-Rops).

704 **MÊME** [same, very (same)]. This word is an adjective and is variable when it is:
(a) in front of the noun and it expresses identity, resemblance: *Les* MÊMES *fautes ne méritent pas toujours les* MÊMES *châtiments.*
(b) immediately after a noun or pronoun; in this position, it strongly underlines what the noun or pronoun denotes: *Les Romains ne vainquirent les Grecs que par les Grecs* MÊMES (Ac.). *Merci des livres que vous m'offrez; ce sont ceux-là* MÊMES *que je désirais. Dieu est la sagesse* MÊME, *la miséricorde* MÊME (Ac.).

705 (1) *Même,* used in this way after one of the personal pronouns *moi, toi, soi, nous, vous, lui, eux, elle(s),* is joined to it by a hyphen: *Nous-mêmes, eux-mêmes,* etc.
   There is no hyphen after a demonstrative pronoun: *Ceci même, cela même, ceux mêmes.*
(2) *Nous-même* and *vous-même* (without final *s*), when *nous* or *vous* designates only one person: *Nous*-MÊME, *maire soussigné, avons constaté le fait.*
(3) *De même* is invariable and is sometimes used as an attribute in the meaning of "similar": *Les femmes ne sont pas* DE MÊME (A. France).

706 *Même* [even] as an adverb is invariable when it indicates an extension, in which case it means "also, up to and including, besides, in addition" and always supposes an idea of gradation: *Sa femme, ses enfants, ses amis* MÊME *se sont dévoués pour lui* (Ac.). *Les plus sages* MÊME (Id.). *Les domestiques* MÊME *étaient insolents* (L. Daudet).
(1) In many cases, *même* placed after a noun or a demonstrative pronoun can be considered as an adjective or adverb: *Ces murs* MÊMES [i.e., these walls themselves] *ont des oreilles,*—or: *Ces murs* MÊME [these walls also; i.e., even these walls] *ont des oreilles. Les malheurs* MÊME(S) *n'ont pas abattu son orgueil. Ceux* MÊME(S) *que cet homme avait sauvés l'ont trahi.*
(2) *Même* can be recognized as functioning as an adverb in this way and could be placed in front of the article, the determinate, or the demonstrative pronoun: *Les domestiques même étaient insolents* [i.e., *même les domestiques. . .*(even the servants)]. *Ceux* MÊME *qu'il avait sauvés l'ont trahi* [i.e., *même ceux qu'il avait sauvés . . .*(even those whom he had saved)].
(3) When *même,* as an adjective, comes after several coordinated

nouns by using *et* or in a reversed order, it agrees with the group of nouns if it bears on each one of them: *Le premier-né ce fut la douceur et la patience* MÊMES (J. Supervielle).

At times, however, it remains in the singular, according to the agreement discussed in par. (2) in entry no. 649. *Elle était la bizarrerie et la bonne humeur* MÊME (Alain-Fournier).

(4) *Même* [the same thing] is a noun in the example, *Cela revient au* MÊME, and in the familiar phrase, *C'est du pareil au* MÊME.

(5) *Quand même* [even so] is used familiarly in the meaning of "it must be admitted" or "one would agree": *Une nuit de réflexion, c'est* QUAND MÊME *trop peu* (G. Duhamel).

707 QUEL QUE [whatever, no matter what]. This is written in two words when it is followed by the verb ÊTRE or one similar to it, either immediately after it, or with an intermediary pronoun, such as *il, elle, en.* . . . *Quel* agrees, therefore, with the subject of the verb: QUELS *que soient les humains, il faut vivre avec eux* (Gresset). QUELLE *qu'en puisse être la difficulté, je remplirai ma tâche.*

If there is more than one subject, synonymous with the first, agreement is made with the closest: QUELLE *que soit votre valeur, votre mérite, restez modeste.*

If there are subjects connected by *ou*, agreement is made with both subjects or with the closest, depending on whether the idea dominating is one that connects or separates: QUELS *que soient leur qualité ou leur mérite* (Montherlant). QUEL *que fût le temps ou la saison* (H. de Régnier).

708 QUELQUE [some, a few]. Aside from the expression *quelque* . . . *que*, this simple adjective, *quelque*, is variable when it refers to a noun: *Dans* QUELQUES *jours.*

Et quelques [and then some] can appear after a number used as a noun (most often equal to or higher than twenty) to indicate that the number is a little beyond what is stated: *Nous étions à cette réunion quarante* ET QUELQUES (Ac.). *J'avais dans ma bourse cent* ET QUELQUES FRANCS (J. Vallès). At times, it is in the singular: *Quand on a vingt ans* ET QUELQUE (James de Coquet). *Le train de dix heures* ET QUELQUE.

709 Quelque [whatever, whichever, however, no matter how, etc.], in the expression QUELQUE. . .QUE, is written as one word. As for its agreement, we must note:

(1) In front of a noun, it is an adjective and is variable: QUELQUES *raisons* QUE *vous donniez, vous ne convaincrez personne.*

(2) In front of a simple adjective, it functions as an adverb and is invariable: QUELQUE *bonnes* QUE *soient vos raisons*, . . .

(3) In front of an adverb, it functions as an adverb and is invariable: QUELQUE *habilement* QUE *vous raisonniez*, . . .

(4) In front of an adjective followed by a noun, it functions as an adverb and is invariable if it modifies the adjective; this may be ascertained in the following way: the noun is an attribute and the subordinate verb is, therefore, *être* or one similar to it: QUELQUE *bonnes raisons que soient ces témoignages*, . . .

If not, it refers to the noun and is therefore variable: *Quelques bonnes raisons que vous alléguiez*, . . .

A simple, practical way to figure out the distinction pointed out in par. 4 above: If you remove the adjective in front of the noun, you can tell if *quelque* still has a reason for being there:

(a) *Quelque [bonnes] raisons que soient ces témoignages* . . . : after removing the adjective *(bonnes)*, the sentence loses its meaning; this shows that the support for *quelque* is certainly the adjective *bonnes;* therefore, *quelque* serves as an adverb to modify the adjective.

(b) *Quelques [bonnes] raisons que vous alléguiez* . . . : after removing the adjective *(bonnes)*, the sentence keeps its general meaning; this shows that *quelques* preserves the support of the noun *(raisons);* therefore, it agrees with it.

Another practical means to figure out the function of *quelque* explained in par. 4 above: *quelque* is an adjective when you can replace it with *quel que soit le. . ., quelle que soit la. . ., quel(le)s que soient les. . . ."*

Quelque is an adverb and is invariable when, in front of a number used as a noun, it means "about"; even in the expression *quelque peu: Falcone marcha* QUELQUE *deux cents pas dans le sentier* (Mérimée). *Un loup* QUELQUE PEU *clerc* (La Fontaine).

710 QUELCONQUE [ordinary, commonplace, some sort of]. This adjective can have the meaning of "mediocre, banal," or it may even indicate scorn; it allows different degrees of meaning: *Le papier de la lettre est* QUELCONQUE (P. Bourget). *Ce petit salon très sobrement meublé, très* QUELCONQUE *en somme* (P. Loti). *On la trouverait [la cuisine] plus* QUELCONQUE *si elle était moins parcimonieuse* (M. Proust). *Il a été attaqué par de* QUELCONQUES *voyous* (Montherlant).

It can, especially in didactic style, be placed between a numeral and a determinate object designating a totality: *Prenons un* QUEL-

CONQUE [Let's take any] *de ces nombres. Considérons deux* QUEL-
CONQUES *des points d'une droite.*

At times, it is preceded by a reinforced adverb, like *tout à fait*
[completely] or *généralement: Pensions et autres dettes* GÉNÉRALE-
MENT QUELCONQUES (Stendhal). *Toute pensée* GÉNÉRALEMENT
QUELCONQUE *peut être "suprême pensée"* (P. Valéry). *Je suppose
(. . .) que les coordonnées d'un point soient des fonctions continues,
d'ailleurs* TOUT À FAIT QUELCONQUES (H. Poincaré).

711 TOUT, adjectif [**all,** as an adjective, having different meanings,
depending on the phrase: all, all of. . ., a whole. . ., etc.].

(1) *Tout* is an adjective and agrees with the noun that follows in
such expressions as: TOUTE *une affaire, c'est* TOUTE *une histoire,*
TOUTE *une révolution,* etc.

(2) *Tout* is invariable in front of a person's name denoting the
whole of the works done by the person named: *Il a lu* TOUT
Madame de Ségur.

As for *tout* in front of a title (or an expression designating a
painting, a sculpture, etc.), there is need to distinguish:

According to whether the article (or the determinate) is considered to be part of or not part of the title, *tout* is variable or
invariable: *J'ai lu* TOUS *les "Martyrs,"* or: TOUT *"Les Martyrs";*
. . . TOUTES *les "Précieuses ridicules,"* or: TOUT *"Les Précieuses ridicules."*

When the title does not contain an article, *tout* is invariable:
J'ai lu TOUT *"Athalie,"* TOUT *"Émaux et Camées."*

In order to avoid certain odd effects or certain ambiguities,
you can, instead of using *tout,* use *en entier,* which does not
change.

(3) *Tout* in front of the name of a city is invariable, whether the
inhabitants are designated, whether you are talking about the
city itself in a concrete sense, or whether it has to do with the
elite society of the city; in this last case, use a capital letter and
a hyphen: TOUT *Antioche s'étouffait au théâtre* (A. France). TOUT
Rome serait détruit. Le TOUT-PARIS *méprise le reste du monde*
(J. Benda).

(4) In **tout à tous, tout à chacun,** *tout* agrees with the word to
which it refers; however, if the expression refers to a masculine
plural, *tout* is invariable: *Elle était* TOUTE *à chacun et* TOUTE *à tous*
(J.-K. Huysmans). *Pasteurs charitables qui se sont faits* TOUT *à
tous* (Bossuet).

(5) The following expressions may be written in the singular or
plural: **toute affaire cessante, en tout cas, en toute chose, tout
compte fait, de tout côté, de toute façon, en tout genre, en**

tout lien, de toute manière, à tout moment, en toute occasion, de toute part, en tout point, toute proportion gardée, à tout propos, de toute sorte, en tout sens, en tout temps, etc.

In certain expressions, common sense indicates whether the singular or plural is appropriate: à **toute allure, de tout coeur, à toute force, à toute heure, à toute vitesse; à tous crins, à tous égards, à toutes jambes, en toutes lettres, de toutes pièces,** etc.

(6) In **tout le premier** (meaning *le premier de tous*), *tout* is variable: *Nous avons cru à cette nouvelle, nous* TOUS *les premiers* (Ac.). *Bette,* TOUTE *la première,. . .est une de ces exagérations* (Sainte-Beuve).

(7) A popular or very familiar construction: *C'est* TOUT *espions, dans ce pays* (R. Dorgelès). *C'est* TOUT *voleurs!* (M. Genevoix.) At times, *des* is inserted: *C'est* TOUT *des mensonges!*

In standard French: *Ce sont* TOUTES *fables que vous contez là* (Littré). *Je dois plaider l'agrément, la beauté,* TOUS *arguments qui me discréditent* (H. Bordeaux).

712 Tout used as a noun is written *touts* in the plural: *Plusieurs* TOUTS *distincts les uns des autres* (Ac.).

713 Tout, adverb

(1) *Tout* is an adverb when it means "completely, entirely" or when it belongs to the locution *tout. . .que,* expressing concession: *La ville* TOUTE *entière. Des fillettes* TOUT *de blanc vêtues. Une veste* TOUT *usagée. Elles sont* TOUT *en larmes,* TOUT *étonnées,* TOUT *hébétées.* TOUT *habiles et* TOUT *artificieux qu'ils sont* (Ac.).

It varies in gender and number in front of a feminine word beginning with a consonant or an aspirate *h: Elles sont* TOUTES *penaudes,* TOUTES *honteuses.* TOUTES *hardies qu'elles sont,* TOUTES *hautaines qu'elles paraissent.*

(2) In front of feminine adjectives beginning with a semivowel (*oisive, ointe, ouateuse,* etc.), *tout* may vary or remain invariable: *Des mains* TOUT(ES) *oisives, une peau* TOUT(E) *huileuse, des étoffes* TOUT(ES) *ouateuses.*

(3) According to Littré, *tout. . .que,* structured with a feminine noun denoting a thing and beginning with a consonant or an aspirate *h,* is invariable: *Ce coeur se réveille,* TOUT *poudre qu'il est* (Bossuet). But there is no reason why a person would not apply the common rule in this case: *Ces belles boules. . .sont battues, Monsieur l'abbé, battues,* TOUTES *boules bretonnes qu'elles sont* (L. Veuillot).

(4) **Tout au début** competes with **au tout début** (which J. Green

gives as "an example of contemporary gibberish"); you will also find **le tout début.** Strange as these constructions may seem, in usage they are placed in certain positions: *Au* TOUT DÉBUT *(Petit Robert).* *Nous n'en sommes qu'au* TOUT DÉBUT *du XXe siècle* (J. Roy). *C'était le* TOUT DÉBUT *du printemps* (A. Chamson).

(5) *Tout,* invariable, reinforces a noun in **être tout yeux, tout oreilles; être tout feu, tout flamme;** and in the commercial terms **tout laine, tout soie,** etc.

Aside from these cases, there is some hesitation in usage as to the syntactic value of *tout,* reinforcing a noun:

(a) adverb: *La vie n'est pas* TOUT *roses* (A. France).   *Jeanne d'Arc fut* TOUT *piété et patriotisme* (G. Hanotaux).

(b) adjective, agreeing with the noun that follows: *Mon père était* TOUTE *intelligence,* TOUTE *clarté* (É. Henriot). *[Ses yeux] étaient à présent* TOUTE *prière et respect* (M. Genevoix).

(c) adjective, agreeing with the subject: *La nature l'y forcera, qui est* TOUTE *alternances, qui est* TOUTE *contractions et détentes* (Montherlant).

(6) Generally speaking, *tout* is an adverb and is invariable in: **tout d'une pièce, tout de travers, tout d'une traite, tout d'un bloc, tout d'une haleine, tout d'une venue,** etc.: *Esther s'était levée* TOUT *d'une pièce* (Aragon).   *Ces gens* TOUT *d'une pièce* (G. Duhamel).   *Lui-même, d'ailleurs, m'avait raconté l'histoire* TOUT *d'une traite* (J. de Lacretelle).   *Il a la jambe* TOUT *d'une venue* (Littré).

It is not incorrect to treat *tout* as an adjective: *Cette colonne, cette table de marbre est* TOUTE *d'une pièce* (Ac.).   *Une randonnée faite* TOUTE *d'une traite.*

(7) Modern French has formed substantive expressions, for example, **la toute jeunesse** from **tout jeune** and **la toute enfance** from **tout enfant:** *Dans la* TOUTE JEUNESSE (G. d'Houville). *Depuis sa* TOUTE ENFANCE (J. de Lacretelle).

(8) People say: **tout de son long** (i.e., stretching out on the floor, on the ground, in bed) or **de tout son long:** *Au lieu de m'affaler* TOUT DE MON LONG (J. Green).   *Couché* DE TOUT MON LONG (A. Daudet).

(9) **Tout** followed by **autre** is an adjective and is variable if it refers to the noun that follows; in that case, it means "any or no matter which, etc." and it can be close to the noun: TOUTE *autre vue* [i.e., *toute vue autre* or *n'importe quelle vue autre*] *eût été mesquine* (J. Bainville).

It is an adverb and invariable if it modifies the adjective *autre;* in that case, it means "entirely," and you could not separate it from *autre: Une* TOUT *autre idée* [i.e., *une idée entièrement autre*] *vint traverser mon esprit* (Nerval).   *Il y a de* TOUT *autres aspects* (P. Valéry).

(10) In certain cases, you have to look at the meaning in order to recognize the value of *tout:*

Elles exprimaient TOUTE *leur joie* [i.e., *leur joie entière*].   *Elles exprimaient* TOUTES *leur joie* [i.e., *toutes ces personnes exprimaient leur joie*].   *Demandez-moi* TOUTE *autre chose* [i.e., *toute chose autre*].   *Vous demandez* TOUT *autre chose* [i.e., *tout à fait autre chose*].

(11) **Tout** and a negation.

In sentences like *Tout. . .n'est pas . . .*, the negation ordinarily bears on the word *tout: Tout ce qui reluit n'est pas or* [i.e., *non pas tout ce qui reluit est or*].   *Toutes les taupes ne sont pas prises par le taupier* (Hugo).

At times, the negation falls on the verb of the second part of the sentence: *Tous ceux qui se soumettront ne seront pas punis* [i.e., AUCUN *de ceux qui se soumettront* NE SERA PUNI]. *Tous les grands panneaux de la voûte n'existent plus* [i.e., *aucun panneau ne subsiste*] (Th. Gautier).

When it is desired to have the negation bear on the second part, it is preferable (in order to avoid ambiguity) to use *aucun, nul, pas un, personne. . .: Tous les champs n'ont pas été ravagés* could mean: "not all the fields were destroyed"; if you wish to say: "the fields, such as they all are, escaped destruction," you should say: *Aucun champ n'a été ravagé.*

714 TEL [such, such a. . ., like. . ., etc.]. In the construction *tel que* [such as], as in the sentence: *Il périssait,* TEL QU'*une fleur* (Fénélon), you can, in modern usage, say the same elliptically with just *tel: Il périssait,* TEL *une fleur.*

As for agreement, usage is indecisive:

(a) Agreement with the noun or pronoun following: *Il vivait là . . .* TELLE *une plante* (G. Duhamel).   *Une pièce où les mots sautent,* TELLES *des puces de mer* (R. Kemp).

(b) Agreement with the other term of comparison: *Soudain le vent expira,* TEL *une bête hors d'haleine* (É. Estaunié).   *La matière brute, pondéreuse, que l'usine européenne malaxera,* TELLE *un ogre jamais rassasié* (A. Siegfried).

715 Tel quel is used in the meaning "such as it is. . ., such as they are" or "mediocre": *Je vous rends vos livres* TELS QUELS.   *Deux chambres* TELLES QUELLES (Mérimée).

To convey this meaning, do not say: *J'ai laissé les choses telles que.*

716 Tel, in expressions such as **croire tel, considérer comme tel, en**

tant que tel, etc., agrees with the noun to which it refers as an attribute: *Ce sont des savantes; du moins, je les crois* TELLES [i.e., *telles que des savantes*]. *Cette comédie est un chef-d'oeuvre; les critiques la considèrent comme* TELLE.

717 Tel que [such as] can announce an enumeration or an example that develops or illustrates a synthetic term; agreement is made with the synthetic term: *Plusieurs langues,* TELLES QUE *le grec, le latin, l'allemand, etc., divisent les noms en trois genres* (Ac.). *Quelques-uns avaient servi dans l'ancienne armée,* TELS QUE *Louis Davout* (Heredia). *Ce ne sont pas les poissons carnivores,* TELS QUE *le brochet, que le sang attire le plus* (P. Gascar).

At times the *que* of *tel que* may be omitted, but there is indecision regarding agreement: *Les algébristes qui,* TELS *Barrès, résolvaient les problèmes de la guerre sur le papier* (G. Duhamel). *Les peintres de la Renaissance,* TEL *Véronèse* (R. Huyghe).

718 After **tel et tel** or **tel ou tel** [such and such], the noun is most often written in the singular: *Il m'a dit telle et telle* CHOSE (Ac.). *Il reprenait telle ou telle* OEUVRE (Fr. Jammes).

With the noun in the plural: *Elle s'acharnait à interpréter tel et tel* DÉTAILS (R. Rolland). *Tel et tel* VIVEURS *aimaient à ne se coucher qu'après l'aube* (H. Queffélec).

Tels et tels or *tels ou tels,* in the plural: *Si* TELS ET TELS *portraits venaient à disparaître* (E. Fromentin). *La présence de* TELS OU TELS *hommes* (Fr. Mauriac).

719 Un tel [so-and-so] is used as a pronoun, in place of a person's name in order to designate a person whom you cannot or do not wish to name precisely: *C'est monsieur* UN TEL, *madame* UNE TELLE *qui m'a conté le fait* [Mr. So-and-So, Mrs. So-and-So told me the fact].

In this use, *un tel* has been used in the past with things; in modern usage, people use just *tel,* as an adjective without *un: Il m'a parlé de* TEL *livre qu'il venait de lire. J'ai promis de partir* TEL *jour, à* TELLE *heure.* Do not say: ". . .d'un tel livre. . ." and do not say: "partir *un tel* jour, à *une telle* heure."

4

PRONOUNS

720   In principle, a noun cannot be represented by a pronoun if it has not been determined, that is to say, if it has not been preceded by an article or a determinative. That is why you would not say, for example: *J'ai confiance en vous, et* ELLE *est fondée. J'ai obtenu satisfaction,* QUE *j'attendais avec impatience.*

Formerly, usage was very free: *Allez lui rendre hommage et j'attendrai* LE SIEN (Corneille).   There are still some authors who at times use a pronoun representing a noun with neither an article nor a determinative: *Elle a d'abord perdu connaissance et ne* L'*a reprise que chez le pharmacien* (A. Gide).   *Il s'adresse à moi en hébreu,* QUE *je ne parle pas* (J. Kessel).

In practice, do not take such liberties unless you use a considerable amount of discernment.

I. PERSONAL PRONOUNS

721   The pronoun representing a collective or generic noun in the singular sometimes agrees with the plural noun suggested by it: *Il articulait chaque syllabe et* LEUR *donnait une valeur musicale très sensible* (P. Valéry).   *Jamais il n'eût tourmenté un chat inutilement. Il* LES *respectait* (H. Troyat).

722   The pronoun representing a title, such as *Majesté, Excellence,* etc., agrees with the title: *Votre Majesté partira quand* ELLE *voudra* (Voltaire).

If the title is followed by a noun which is a part of it, it is with the noun that the pronoun agrees: *Sa Majesté le roi viendra-t-*IL? (A. Hermant).   *J'ai eu l'honneur d'être reçu par Sa Sainteté le pape*

Léon XIII en audience particulière. Ce qu'IL a bien voulu me dire . . .
(F. Brunetière).

723 ILS [they]. Especially in familiar language, the pronoun *ils* is
used as an indefinite, often with a scornful meaning: ILS *ont encore
augmenté les impôts!* ILS *font tout ce qu'ils peuvent pour nous embêter.
Qu'est-ce qu'*ILS *ont encore inventé?* ILS, *ce sont, suivant les cas, si-
multanément, l'État, le gouvernement ou le Parlement, la majorité et
l'opposition, mais surtout les bureaux.* ILS, *ce sont ceux qui décident*
(A. Peyrefitte).

724   The following two constructions are current in popular or familiar French: *Nous l'avons fait nous deux mon frère; nous l'avons fait
avec mon frère.* At times, they are also found in literary language:
Nous l'avons fait à nous deux le roi (Hugo).   *Quel voyage d'artistes
vous allez faire, vous deux Guerard!* (Flaubert.)   *Nous en parlions,
avec Léo, avant que tu n'entres* (J. Cocteau).   *On ne s'ennuie pas nous
deux mon mari, comme Claudel prétend qu'il faut dire* (P.-H. Simon).

In careful, polished French, you would say: *Nous l'avons fait,
mon frère et moi,* or: *Mon frère et moi, (nous) l'avons fait,* or: *Je l'ai
fait avec mon frère.*

725 UNE LETTRE À MOI TRANSMISE [a letter transmitted to me].
Be careful not to say: *une lettre me transmise, nous transmise, vous
transmise, leur transmise.* The indirect object personal pronoun in
front of a participial adjective must be one of the stressed pronouns, *moi, toi, soi, lui, elle, nous, vous, eux, elles.* Furthermore,
it must be preceded by *à: Une grande enveloppe* À MOI *adressée*
(P. Loti).   *L'argent* À LUI *confié* (Alain).   *Dans une lettre* À NOUS
adressée (J. Benda).

It is possible to have a similar construction with the present
participle or verbal adjective *appartenant* [belonging]: *Les immeubles
à elle* APPARTENANT (Civil Code).   *Domaines à lui appartenants*
(Littré).

However, in modern usage, most often people simply use,
without *à,* one of the unstressed forms, *m', t', lui, nous, vous,
leur: La source* LUI *appartenant* (P. Arène).   *Il se délectait de la voir
manier   un   objet* LUI *appartenant* (H.   Troyat).   *Les   biens*
M'*appartenant,* NOUS *appartenant.*

726   The pronoun *le* may be used optionally as an object in comparative clauses beginning with *autre, autrement aussi, plus, moins,
mieux,* etc.: *Il est autre que je croyais,* or: *. . . que je ne croyais,* or:

. . . *que je ne* LE *croyais* (Ac.).   *Il n'est pas aussi pauvre qu'on croit,*
or: . . . *qu'on* LE *croit.*

727   When verbs that are coordinate or placed side by side have the
same personal pronoun as an object, that pronoun is repeated for
the sake of clarity if it is a direct object on the one hand and an
indirect object on the other: *Il* ME *blesse et* ME *nuit. Il* NOUS *jugera et*
NOUS *dira que.* . . . *Il* VOUS *a jugés et* VOUS *a dit que.* . . .

At times excellent authors, in sentences of this sort, ascribe to
the pronoun (expressed only once in front of the first verb) the
double function of direct object and indirect object: *Elle le trouva
dans sa cuisine, où il* S'*était introduit, et accommodé une vinaigrette*
(Flaubert).   *Il* M'*a pris par le cou et demandé pardon* (G. Duhamel).   *Nous* NOUS *sommes roulés dans les champs, arraché les cheveux* (J. Vallès).

728   In familiar language, the personal pronoun in the 1st or 2nd
person (in the form of an indirect object) sometimes expresses the
desire to take action on the part of the speaker; at other times,
the presence of the pronoun serves to invite the listener or reader
to become interested and involve himself / herself in it: *Qu'on* ME
l'égorge tout à l'heure (Molière).   *Sa personne entière* VOUS *avait une
bonhomie relevée par un grain de folie* (A. France).   *Regardez*-MOI *cette
misère* (A. Thérive).

At times, in popular usage, people use two expressive conjunctive pronouns: *Avez-vous vu comme je* TE VOUS *lui ai craché à la
figure?*

729   When an affirmative imperative has two personal pronoun objects (one direct, the other indirect), it is the direct object pronoun
that is placed in front of the other: *Dites*-LE-*moi. Ces lettres, envoyez*-LES-*lui; rends*-LES-*nous.*
   (1) At times, you will find the direct objects *le, la, les* after the
       indirect object pronoun: *Rends*-NOUS-LES (Hugo).   *Épargnez*-
       NOUS-LA (É. Augier).   *Dis*-NOUS-LE (Ph. Hériat).
   (2) You can say: *Tiens*-TOI-LE *pour dit* (Ph. Hériat), but ordinarily
       people say: *Tiens*-LE-TOI *pour dit* (A. Gide).
          In the 1st and 2nd persons of the plural, you may use the
       reversed order and say: *Tenons*-LE-NOUS, *tenez*-LE-VOUS *pour dit.*
       But ordinarily people say: *Tenons*-NOUS-LE *pour dit. Tenez*-VOUS-
       LE *pour dit* (J. Cocteau).

730   At times, people still place the personal object pronoun of the

infinitive in front of the main verb, but this is an archaic construction; it is found especially with verbs like *pouvoir, aller, vouloir,
devoir, falloir, venir, savoir, oser, croire, penser,* etc.: *Le président de
cette société* LE *vint voir* (Hugo). *On* LES *peut vaincre*
(Maupassant). *Je pensais* M'*aller coucher* (G. Duhamel). *Il ne s'est
pas voulu dédire* (A. Suarès). [See also entry no. 755.]

731   The pronouns *le, la,* and *les* are used as attributes, representing either a noun preceded by the definite article or a determinative, or a proper noun: *Je me regarde comme la mère de cet enfant; je*
LA *suis de coeur* (Ac.). *Le président, oui je* LE *suis; la présidente, je*
LA *suis; les préposés, nous* LES *sommes. J'ai été cette pauvre chose-là.
Tu* LA *seras toi aussi* (Montherlant). *Êtes-vous Jeanne Durand? Oui,
je* LA *suis.*

   The use of *la, les* as attributes in spoken French is not common.
For example, instead of saying: *Votre mère, je* LA *suis,* in spoken
French you will hear: *Votre mère, oui, je suis votre mère.* And in
answer to a question like, *Êtes-vous la mère?* in spoken French you
will hear: *Oui, c'est moi* or: *Non, ce n'est pas moi.*

732   With *c'est,* the personal pronoun attribute in the 3rd person is
lui, elle(s), eux, placed after the verb: *Ma mère, oui, c'est* ELLE.
Mes parents? Ce sont EUX. *Est-ce votre maison? Oui, c'est* ELLE.

   With names of animals or things, classical French used as attributes in the 3rd person *le, la,* and *les* before the verb: *Ne* LES *sont-
ce pas là* [vos tablettes]? *Oui, ce* LES *sont là elles-mêmes*
(Boileau). Littré still gives: *Est-ce là votre voiture? Oui, ce* L'*est.
Est-ce là votre maison? Ce* LA *fut.* These constructions are not in use
in spoken French (except for the set form *il les est* when telling
time: *Dix heures? il* LES *est déjà!*).

733   People use the neuter object pronoun *le* (equivalent to *cela*) in
order to represent either an adjective or participle or a noun without a definite article or determinative: *Êtes-vous chrétienne? Je* LE
suis (Voltaire). *J'étais mère et je ne* LE *suis plus* (A. Maurois).
Comme si trop de paroles n'avaient pas été dites qui auraient dû L'*être*
(J. Green). *Il y a des monstres; nous ne* LE *sommes pas*
(É. Henriot). *Nous sommes des hommes libres, et nous entendons* LE
rester (Ch. de Gaulle).

734   The following is an "absolute" rule, according to Littré:
The neuter pronoun *le* cannot be used as a preceding direct object of an active verb merely by making it function as a passive
with that meaning understood; therefore, instead of saying *Je le*

traiterai comme il mérite de L'*être,* we should repeat the verb and put it in the passive form: *Je le traiterai comme il mérite d'être traité.*

Such a rule would be logical, without doubt. However, there are many good authors, classical as well as modern, who are not concerned with such a rule: *Si nous établissons la confiance comme elle* L'*est déjà de mon côté* (Sévigné).   *On paya alors avec cet argent tous ceux qui voulurent* L'*être* (Voltaire).   *En ne la traitant pas comme elle mérite de* L'*être* (Fr. Mauriac).   *Me consoler? Je ne voulais pas* L'*être* (M. Genevoix).

735   At times, *en* is used as a direct object in place of an indeterminate noun, without an article, or preceded by an indefinite article or partitive: *J'appelle "histoires" ce qui n'*EN *est pas* (G. Duhamel). *On appelle cela de la poésie. Eh! bien sûr c'*EN *est!* (P. Vialar).

736   The neuter pronoun object *le* may be used in place of an adjective of any gender or any number: *Elle était chrétienne. Son père et sa mère* L'*avaient été* (É. Henriot).   *Si le père n'était pas exact à l'ouvrage, la fille* L'*était pour deux* (R. Bazin).   *Ses tantes étaient pieuses; lui ne* L'*était pas. Si son oncle n'était pas pieux, ses tantes* L'*étaient.*

737 SOI [oneself]. When *soi* represents a person, it generally agrees with the subject that is indeterminate or merely suggested: *Heureux qui vit chez* SOI! (La Fontaine).   *Chacun travaille pour* SOI (Ac.).   *Rester* SOI, *c'est une grande force* (Michelet).

However, with *chacun, aucun, celui qui,* the following are used: *lui, elle(s), eux: C'est tout un monde que chacun porte en* LUI! (Musset.)   *Ceux qui se jugent les plus maîtres d'*EUX-*mêmes* (L. Daudet).

738   People generally use *lui, elle(s),* or *eux* (either alone or reinforced by *même*) in a reflexive sense to represent a subject with a precise determined meaning, whether it is about persons or things: *Racine avait contre* LUI *toute la vieille génération* (J. Lemaitre).   *Mlle Cloque revint doucement à* ELLE (R. Boylesve).   *Les sauterelles étaient parties; mais quelle ruine elles avaient laissée derrière* ELLES! (A. Daudet.) *Le mont Icare. . .laissait voir derrière* LUI *la cime sacrée du Cithéron* (Chateaubriand).

In this case, classical writers used *soi (-même);* this use is found fairly often among modern authors, notably in the set locutions *en soi, de soi: Elle pensait à* SOI (Cl. Farrère).   *Elle se repliait sur* SOI-*même* (E. Jaloux).   *Le feu s'était de* SOI-*même éteint* (Flaubert).   *Cette foule n'est pas mauvaise en* SOI (Michelet).   *Cela va de* SOI.

739 Soi-disant [so-called, self-styled, would-be]. According to the Academy (communiqué dated Feb. 18, 1965) and to purists, this term is applied only to persons who are able to talk and, therefore, capable of "saying about themselves" this or that: *De* SOI-DISANT *docteurs* (Ac.). *La plupart des femmes* SOI-DISANT *artistes* (A. Hermant). Otherwise, *prétendu* should be used: *Accorder de* PRÉTENDUES *faveurs. La copie de* PRÉTENDUES *instructions secrètes* (Chateaubriand).

That is very logical; nevertheless, *soi-disant* is used by excellent authors when referring to things: *Dans le* SOI-DISANT *état de simple nature* (Diderot). *Un* SOI-DISANT *contrepoison* (Hugo). *Les choses* SOI-DISANT *sérieuses* (Flaubert). *Péchés* SOI-DISANT *mortels* (Fr. Mauriac). *La* SOI-DISANT *angine de poitrine* (A. Maurois). *Une* SOI-DISANT *expérience* (Ac.), under the entry *empirique*.

On the other hand, SOI-DISANT (in the meaning of "pretending") is in full use in good usage, which Littré allows: *Valdo jouait* SOI-DISANT *pour faire travailler Cécile* (G. Duhamel).

740 (1) *Soi-disant que* is used in popular or very familiar language: *Agnès s'est allongée:* SOI-DISANT *qu'elle voulait dormir* (G. Cesbron).

(2) Be careful of the spelling: Do not write *Soit-disant*. Also, be careful not to show any agreement on *soi-disant: Une* SOI-DISANT *protectrice; de* SOI-DISANT *duchesses.*

741 À PART [aside (from)]. This expression can be followed by *moi, toi, soi, lui, elle, nous, vous, eux, elles* in order to form adverbial locutions, such as *à part moi, à part toi*, etc.: *Nous nous le disions, chacun* À PART SOI (M. Arland). À PART ELLE, *elle songeait. . .* (R. Boylesve). À PART NOUS. . ., *nous rêvons un peu* (G. Duhamel).

742   The pronouns *en* and *y* most often take the place of nouns of animals, things, and abstract ideas: *J'aime beaucoup Paris et j'*EN *admire les monuments* (Ac.). *Cette maladie est dangereuse; il peut* EN *mourir* (Id.). *Elle aime beaucoup son petit chien et ne s'*EN *séparerait pour rien au monde. Ce vase est brisé: n'*Y *touchez pas. La défiance? Je n'*Y *suis pas enclin.*

However, when speaking of animals or things, instead of *en* or *y*, people sometimes use *lui, à lui, de lui, à elle(s), d'elle(s), à eux, d'eux*, expecially when there is personification or to avoid ambiguity: *Ces vacances! Il jouissait d'*ELLES (V. Larbaud). *Pour amortir les secousses du volant. . ., il s'était cramponné* À LUI *de toutes ses* *forces* (Saint-Exupéry).   *Le sentiment de la possession des choses m'est d'ailleurs inconnu; je jouis* D'ELLES (J. Benda).   *Le cheval rua et le charretier* LUI *donna un coup de fouet* (Littré).   *Ces arbustes vont périr si on ne* LEUR *donne de l'eau* (Ac.).

743   Among the French classical writers, *en* and *y* could refer to persons; this use, which is less frequent among modern writers, has not been abandoned: *Pascal plaisait peut-être à quelques femmes; il* EN *était admiré* (Fr. Mauriac).   *C'est un véritable ami; je ne pourrai jamais oublier les services que j'*EN *ai reçus* (Ac.).   *C'est un homme équivoque; ne vous* Y *fiez pas* (Id.).

744   Regarding the use of *y*, you will find in Littré: *Vous n'y irez pas?* And in the works of Faguet: *Il y irait non seulement de l'empire, mais de la vie.* But, in principle, *y* is omitted for the sake of euphony when in front of the forms *irai* and *irais: Avez-vous été à Paris? J'irai* (Ac.).   *Quand il irait de tout mon bien* (Id.).

745   *Je n'en peux rien* [I can't help it; I'm not responsible for it] is used currently in Belgium and in eastern France in the meaning of *Je n'en suis pas responsable.* This provincialism could, according to the case at hand, be replaced by: *Ce n'est pas (de) ma faute; il n'y a pas de ma faute; je ne suis pas en faute; je ne suis pas fautif; ce n'est pas à moi qu'en est la faute; je n'y suis pour rien; je n'y peux rien.*

746   *Je n'y peux* (or: *puis*) *rien* means either "It's not my fault" or "It's not up to me to oppose that, to prevent it, to remedy it, or to change anything about it": *Ce n'était pas sa faute! Il n'y pouvait rien* (Flaubert).   *Je n'y peux rien; je n'ai pas d'éducation* (J. Kessel).   *Elle n'y pouvait rien; elle l'aimait* (J. Green).   *Le paysan reçoit la grêle ou la gelée, et n'y peut rien* (Alain).

747   *Je n'en peux* (or: *puis*) *mais. . .* [I can't; I'm unable to, but . . .] is an archaic construction; it may indicate a nonresponsibility, inability, or (but very rarely) an exhaustion: *L'incroyable et sotte Affaire du collier compromettait la reine qui n'en pouvait mais* (A. Maurois).   *Je me souviens d'une nuit, à Chambord, où les vociférations, les fanfares de "son et lumière" n'en pouvaient mais contre ces cris sauvages* [des cerfs] (M. Genevoix).   *Rapporté par Alain, qui n'en peut mais d'admiration* (J. Benda, cited by Baiwir).

748 C'EN EST FAIT [That's the end! That does it!]. People say: *C'en* *est fait! Je m'expatrie!* [That does it! I'm leaving the country! (I'm going to expatriate myself!)] (Littré) [= it's been decided irrevocably].

In classical usage, the expression was without *en: C'est fait de moi* [= I'm finished, all washed up], *c'est fait de ta vie* [your life is through], etc.: *S'il m'échappait un mot, c'est fait de votre vie* (Racine). Other writers did use *en: C'en est fait de moi, de ta vie,* etc.: *C'en est fait d'Israël* (Racine). Nowadays, this last construction supplants the other: *Si je pense à toi, c'en est fait de mon repos* (Colette). *C'en est fait de nous* (Ac.).

749 EN AGIR [to act. . ., to behave. . .]. This expression has justly been condemned by Racine and Bouhours, as Littré affirms, because one cannot say *agir de.* For Littré and for purists, instead of saying *Votre frère* EN *a mal agi envers moi,* we should say: *Votre frère a mal agi envers moi* or: *. . . en a mal usé. . . .*

Despite the logic, *en agir* has become firmly implanted in good usage: *C'est ainsi qu'on* EN AGIT *dans toute la terre* (Voltaire). *Elle n'*EN AGIRAIT *pas si familièrement avec moi* (Musset). *Je connais trop les bienséances pour* EN AGIR *autrement* (Nerval).

750 IMPOSER, EN IMPOSER. According to the French Academy, *imposer,* taken in its absolute significance, means "to inspire respect, admiration, fear." *En imposer* (although often used in the meaning just given for *imposer*) means exactly: "to delude, to deceive, to impose upon."

This distinction is not founded; the best authors use one and the other expression in the first meaning as well as in the second.

(a) Idea of respect, of fear: *La majesté du sacerdoce m'*IMPOSAIT (Chateaubriand). *Il ne s'*EN *laissait nullement* IMPOSER *par la majesté royale* (J. et J. Tharaud).

(b) Idea of deceit: IMPOSONS *quelque temps à sa crédulité* (Voltaire). *Ma débile raison s'*EN *laissait* IMPOSER *par mes désirs* (A. Gide).

751 SE PRENDRE à quelqu'un. This expression means "to attack someone": *Il ne faut pas se prendre à plus fort que soi* (Ac.).

752 S'en prendre à qqn means to make someone feel responsible for some fault: *Je m'*EN *prendrai à vous de tout ce qui pourra arriver* (Ac.).

753 S'Y RETROUVER [to find (get) one's bearings]. This expression is used in familiar language in the meaning of "to cover one's monetary outlay": *Le patron a des frais, mais il s'*Y *retrouve* (Robert).

754   The pronouns *y* and *en,* when in contact with other pronouns, are placed after them: *Ne nous* EN *parlez pas. Je vous* EN *récompenserai. Il est tombé dans le fossé, retirez-l'*EN. *Retirez-les-*EN (Littré).   *Souviens-t'*EN (Hugo).   *Menez-nous-*Y (Littré).

755 (1) After an imperative form of a verb, the constructions *m'y* and *t'y* are avoided and it is preferable to say *y-moi, y-toi: Mènes-y-moi* (Littré).   *Confies-y-toi* (Id.).   These last constructions are not used much.

(2) When using *s'agir,* the object pronouns *y* or *en* are inserted between *s'* and the verb form: *Je n'ai pas voulu qu'il s'*EN *soit agi* (Littré).   *Je fus frappé par un curieux passage. Il s'*Y *agit de louer la science* (A. Gide, cited by Damourette and Pichon).

(3) People say: *Je veux* EN *parler. Je peux* Y *aller.* Nevertheless, in literary language, people do write: *J'*EN *veux parler; j'*Y *peux aller. Qu'*EN *vas-tu faire?* (Colette).   *Rien de condamnable ne s'*Y *pouvait découvrir* (A. France).   [See also entry no. 730.]

(4) When a verb has *y* and *en* as objects at the same time, *y* is placed in front of *en: Il s'*Y EN *donna* (Littré).   *Mettant de l'orgueil dans une chose où jamais il n'aurait dû* Y EN *entrer* (G. Sand).

II. DEMONSTRATIVE PRONOUNS

756 CE [it, as a subject]. The *e* in *ce* drops and an apostrophe is added *(c')* in front of any form of the verb ÊTRE beginning with a vowel *(ce* becomes *ç',* with a cedilla, in front of the vowel *a)* and in front of the pronoun *en* or in front of *aller* followed by an infinitive: C'est *bien;* C'*eût été,* Ç'*a été,* Ç'*aurait été,* C'*eût été difficile:* C'*en est fait. La grande affaire* ç'*allait être les colis* (Fr. Nourissier).

757 CE is used as a subject in front of the verb ÊTRE (at times preceded by *devoir, pouvoir, aller);* it is also found, but somewhat rarely, in front of *sembler, paraître, devenir, pouvoir, avoir,* etc.: CE *serait un grand bonheur.* CE *devait être bien agréable.* CE *pourrait être grave.* Ç'*allait être gai* (J.-L. Vaudoyer).   CE *lui avait semblé un jeu* (R. Rolland).   CE *nous parut un travail tout aisé* (G. Duhamel).   CE *devient une grande difficulté* (M. Barrès).   CE *resta longtemps le grand secret de nos adolescences* (Alain-Fournier).   CE *ne veut pas dire du tout qu'on soit généreux* (La Varende).

758   When the subject of the verb ÊTRE is *ce,* the infinitive following (if there is one), is introduced by *de* or *que de,* at times by just *que* (which is archaic): *C'est beau* D'*être la puce d'un lion* (Hugo).   *C'est imiter quelqu'un* QUE DE *planter des choux* (Musset).   *C'est une grande erreur* QUE *faire une confiance illimitée à la méchanceté des hommes* (Montherlant).

759   *Ce*, used as the subject of the verb ÊTRE, forms the Gallicisms *c'est. . .qui, c'est. . .que;* these are used to emphasize any element of thought (except the verb in a personal mode): C'EST *moi* QUI *suis Guillot* (La Fontaine).   C'EST *demain* QUE *nous partirons* (Ac.).   C'EST *en badinant* QUE *je l'ai dit.*

760   If the object that is placed in the forefront—through the use of *c'est. . .que*—is object of a preposition, you have to insert the preposition and its object between *c'est* and *que: C'est* À VOUS *que je parle. C'est* DE LUI *qu'il s'agit. C'est* POUR VOUS *que je m'attendris.*

The following are archaic constructions: *C'est vous* À QUI *je parle. C'est lui* DONT *il s'agit. C'est vous seul. . .*POUR QUI *mon coeur s'attendrit* (Fénelon).   *On eût pu croire que c'était moi* DE QUI *l'absence la faisait souffrir* (R. Boylesve).   *C'est votre coeur* OÙ *j'aspire* (H. Bosco).   *C'est* À *sa table* À QUI *l'on rend visite* (Molière).   *Ce n'est pas* D'*épées* DONT *ils ont besoin, mais de foi* (Fr. Mauriac).

761   The following are archaic expressions: *ce durant, ce pendant* (or *cependant = pendant cela* [during that]), *ce néanmoins, ce nonobstant, nonobstant ce: Ils sentent. . .que vos armées,* CE DURANT, *leur feront une terrible retraite* (M. Barrès).   *Et si la guerre éclatait,* CE PENDANT (Cl. Farrère).   *Et* CE NÉANMOINS, *les ordres reçus étaient des ordres* (Id.).

762 ÇA [that; *ça* is a popular contraction form of *cela*]. When in front of a verb form, the vowel *a* in *ça* does not drop: ÇA *a passé en un clin d'oeil* (Flaubert).   *Oh!* ÇA *arrive* (J. Giono).   ÇA *a été dur, par ce froid de chien?* (J. Kessel.)

Ça, as a subject of a compound form of the verb ÊTRE, is used in popular or familiar language; in careful, polished language, *ce* or *cela* is used: ÇA *a été une belle fête* (J. Giono).   ÇA *aurait été tellement plus chic* (St. Passeur).

(1) In Belgium, popular or current French uses *ça* even in front of the simple forms *est* or *était*: ÇA *est beau;* ÇA *était possible.*

(2) In familiar language *ça* is used as a subject in the simple tenses as well as in compound tenses when, between *ça* and the verb, a personal pronoun, or *ne*, or either of the two helping verbs *devoir* or *pouvoir*, is inserted: ÇA *m'est agréable;* ÇA *n'est pas possible;* ÇA *doit être;* ÇA *peut être dangereux.*

The same is done with *tout ça* or with the verb forms *soit, sera, serait: Tout* ÇA *est ridicule; il faut que* ÇA *soit vrai;* ÇA *sera,* ÇA *serait magnifique.*

763 **CELUI, CELLE(S), CEUX.** According to the opinion of Littré, the Academy's notice dated Feb. 18, 1965, and purists in general, these pronouns cannot be followed by an adjective, nor a present or past participle, nor an object introduced by a preposition other than *de.* Therefore, sentences like the following would not be correct French: *Ces livres sont intéressants, surtout ceux relatifs à la préhistoire.   Les raisons données par autrui et celles trouvées par nousmêmes.   Diverses preuves et même celle par l'absurde.* These must be corrected by saying: . . .*ceux qui sont relatifs. . . ; . . .et celles qui ont été trouvées. . . ; . . .et même la preuve par l'absurde.*

Nevertheless, Littré allows *celui, celle(s), ceux* + adjective or participle, when the adjective or participle is part of a group of words, set off by commas as an incidental thought, followed by *qui, que,* or *dont: Votre exemple et celui, si généreux, qu'a donné votre lettre.   Ma lettre et celle, écrite par mon ami, qui vous sera remise.*

In good modern usage, there is no question that *celui, celle(s)* and *ceux* can take after them—in spite of what purists say— a participle (either present or past), or an object introduced by any preposition, or even (but this does not happen often) an adjective:

(a) *La blessure faite à une bête et* CELLE FAITE *à un esclave* (Montesquieu).   *Il lui envoya des vers aussi beaux que* CEUX OFFERTS *à Judith* (A. Maurois).   *Il n'est pas de plus grands crimes que* CEUX COMMIS *contre la foi* (A. France).   *Comme* CEUX CACHANT *un secret* (A. Gide).

(b) *La distinction. . .est aussi confuse que* CELLE ENTRE *forme et contenu* (A. Malraux).   *Tous les jeunes gens en rouge se réunissent. L'un à côté de l'autre, ils vont former une lettre, puis* CEUX EN *vert formeront une autre lettre, puis* CEUX EN *jaune, une autre* (Montherlant).   *Je n'ai pas parlé de la plus malaisée des patiences:* CELLE ENVERS *soi-même* (A. Maurois).

(c) *Tout ceci se passa dans un temps moins long que* CELUI NÉCESSAIRE *pour l'écrire* (Th. Gautier).   *Les régions dont je parlais ne sont pourtant pas inhabitées; ce sont* CELLES SUJETTES *à d'importantes évaporations* (A. Gide).

764   *Faire celui, celle(s), ceux* + a relative clause is used in the meaning of "to play a role or to appear to be like *celui, celle(s)* or *ceux*": *Et tu feras celui qui passait par hasard* (M. Pagnol).   *Le chien qui fait celui qui boite pour n'être pas battu* (Montherlant).

765   Do not say: *Il y en a de ceux. . . , de celles. . . , j'en connais de ceux. . . , de celles. . .* , with a relative pronoun. Omit *de ceux, de celles* and just say simply: *Il y en a. . . , j'en connais. . . .*

III. RELATIVE PRONOUNS

766 QUI [who, which, whom]. *Qui* is used as a subject or prepositional object.

(a) **As a subject,** it applies to persons, animals, or things: *L'homme* QUI *travaille; le chien* QUI *aboie; la maison* QUI *nous abrite.*

Qui is used without an antecedent in certain proverbs, in dogmatic or oracular sentences, in locutions such as *qui plus est, qui mieux est, qui pis est,* and after *voici* and *voilà:* QUI *vivra verra. Comprenne* QUI *pourra. Il est compétent et,* QUI *mieux est, très consciencieux. Voici* QUI *me plaît* (Ac.).   *Voilà* QUI *est beau* (Id.).

In the familiar expression *comme qui dirait* [as one would say], the pronoun *qui* means *si l'on* or *si quelqu'un,* which is a survival of an old usage: *Sa coiffure attira nos regards, c'était comme* QUI *dirait un turban* (Littré).

Aside from this familiar expression, the use of *qui,* as an indefinite and suppositive pronoun, is rare: *Bah!* QUI *prévoirait tous les risques, le jeu perdrait tout intérêt* (A. Gide).

(b) **As a prepositional object,** *qui* applies to persons or personified things, at times also to animals: *L'homme à* QUI *je parle, pour* QUI *je travaille. Rochers à* QUI *je me plains* (Ac.).   *Un chien à* QUI *elle fait mille caresses* (Id.).   *Les rossignols de* QUI *l'on crève les yeux* (M. Barrès).

As a prepositional object referring to things, *qui* may be justified when the idea of personification is acceptable; but when it is not, the use of *qui* is a capricious archaism or a peculiarity of style: *La dorure du baromètre, sur* QUI *frappait un rayon de soleil* (Flaubert).   *Des murs solides et sur* QUI *les balles les plus violentes ne marquent pas* (J. Cocteau).

767   *Qui* may be used in an absolute way, in the meaning of *celui qui, celle qui: Aimez* QUI *vous aime* (Ac.).   *Il le raconte à* QUI *veut l'entendre.*

Tout qui is not correct French. Instead of saying: *Tout qui a voyagé dans ce pays en est revenu enchanté,* say: *Quiconque a voyagé . . . ,* or: *Tous ceux qui. . . .*

768 QUI or **QU'IL** [elision of *que* + *il*]. With verbs that can be used impersonally, there is sometimes hesitation between using *qu'il* (an impersonal construction) and *qui* (a personal construction):

(1) With *falloir*, **qu'il** is required: *Il ne sait ce* QU'IL *lui faut* (Ac.).

(2) With *advenir, arriver, rester,* you may use *qu'il* or *qui: Voici ce* QU'IL *advint* (É. Henriot). *Tout ce* QUI *adviendra. Quoi* QU'IL *arrive, je ferai mon devoir* (Ac.). *Quoi* QUI *arrivât dans sa vie. . .* (Montherlant). *Tout ce* QU'IL *vous reste à découvrir* (G. Duhamel). *Le peu d'énergie* QUI *lui reste* (R. Martin du Gard).

(3) With *plaire*, a distinction can be made, which is hardly taken into consideration in practice: *Choisis ce* QUI *te plaît = ce qui te donne du plaisir; Choisis ce* QU'IL *te plaît = ce qu'il te plaît de choisir, ce que tu voudras. Je dis ce* QUI *me plaît* (G. Duhamel). *Vous pouvez me dire tout ce* QU'IL *vous plaira* (M. Arland).

(4) With other verbs, such as *convenir, importer, prendre, résulter, se passer,* etc., the choice is somewhat free, but it seems that *qui* is used most often: *Faites ce* QUI *convient, ce* QUI *importe* (or: *ce* QU'IL *convient, ce* QU'IL *importe*). *Qu'est-ce* QUI *vous prend?* (or: *. . .*QU'IL *vous prend?*) *Tout ce* QUI *se passe* (or: *. . .*QU'IL *se passe*).

769 QUOI [meaning *which*]. This pronoun is found fairly often in literary usage (it is an archaism), instead of *lequel* [*which*], in order to represent the name of a thing, masculine or feminine, singular or plural, with a precise and definite meaning: *Je m'asseyais sur une de ces bornes à* QUOI *l'on amarre les bateaux* (Fr. Mauriac). *Une vapeur bleue à travers* QUOI *jouait la lune* (É. Henriot). *Cette case, vers* QUOI *convergeaient les regards de presque tous les joueurs* (A. Malraux). *Un cocktail à* QUOI *elle était conviée* (J.-L. Curtis).

You will find this same use in *pourquoi* (or *pour quoi*) used (now becoming outdated) in the meaning of *pour lequel: C'est le motif* POURQUOI *je vous interroge* (A. Hermant). *Là serait peut-être la raison* POUR QUOI *son travail sur les Souris n'a jamais été publié* (J. Rostand).

770 Comme quoi is used familiarly in the meaning of *comment* [how] or *disant que* [saying that]: *Prouvez-lui* COMME QUOI *il se trompe* (Ac.). *Quand Germain raconta* COMME QUOI *il avait été forcé de ramener la petite Marie. . .*(G. Sand). *Faites-lui un certificat* COMME QUOI *son état de santé nécessite du repos (Robert).*

771 LEQUEL, as a subject, is used instead of *qui*, especially to avoid ambiguity: *Un homme s'est levé au milieu de l'assemblée,* LEQUEL *a parlé d'une manière extravagante* (Ac.).

Lequel is frequently used in literary language, even when there is no ambiguity; it is generally used to represent the antecedent more noticeably: *Il rencontra un médecin de sa connaissance* LEQUEL *était aux gages de madame de Sablé* (A. France). *Alors Simon la saisit par une de ses mains,* LAQUELLE *s'arracha aussitôt à cette étreinte* (J. Green).

Lequel is currently used in juridical or administrative language: *On a entendu trois témoins,* LESQUELS *ont dit . . .* (Ac.).

There is no objection to the use of *lequel* after a proper noun: *Damien avait une sympathie particulière pour Jean-Pierre,* LEQUEL *était employé de banque* (Daniel-Rops).

772 LEQUEL as an object is most often introduced by a preposition, which contracts to *duquel, auquel;* it refers to a noun denoting a thing, an animal, or, less frequently, a person: *La patrie, pour* LA-QUELLE *chacun doit se sacrifier, exige ce nouveau sacrifice* (Ac.). *Un petit chien,* AUQUEL *elle fait mille caresses. Un homme dans* LEQUEL *je crois voir plusieurs Marius* (Montesquieu).

773 (1) In literary usage, but rarely in current practice, *lequel* can be introduced by *en: Le monde* EN LEQUEL *nous avions placé toutes nos aveugles espérances* (G. Duhamel).

(2) After *parmi,* it is *lequel* (and not *qui,* which would create cacophony) that is used as a relative pronoun object: *Là, il connut des jeunes gens instruits, parmi* LESQUELS *Maucroix* (É. Faguet).

(3) *Lequel,* in modern usage, is rare as a nonprepositional object: *J'ai cédé, me dit-il, à un mouvement de fureur, il est vrai;* LAQUELLE *je ne pouvais tourner que contre moi* (A. Gide).

774 DONT is used as an equivalent of an object introduced by *de;* it may represent persons, animals, or things: *Dieu,* DONT *nous admirons les oeuvres* (Ac.). *La maladie* DONT *il est mort* (Id.). *La maison, le bétail* DONT *vous êtes propriétaire.*

Dont, indicating the means or the instrument, is archaic: *Ces pêcheurs sont armés d'une baguette pointue* DONT *ils piquent adroitement leur proie* (A. France).

775 *Dont,* in a relative clause completed by another clause, may be used in the meaning of *au sujet duquel* ["regarding which," "about which"]: *Un luxe* DONT *j'imagine aujourd'hui qu'il devait être affreux* (Fr. Mauriac). *Celui* DONT *nous savons qu'un feu étrange le dévore* (M. Bedel).

776 In principle, the noun in the relative clause, which has *dont* as a determinative object, does not receive the possessive adjective; you would not say: *L'enfant dont son jouet est cassé;* that would create a pleonasm because the idea of possession is shown, on the one hand, by *son* and, on the other, by *dont* [= *de qui*]; you would say: *L'enfant dont* LE *jouet est cassé. Un homme dont* LE *corps a l'habitude d'aider* LA *pensée* (J. Romains).

The following rule is not absolute: in certain cases, the possessive may be called for in order to achieve perfect clarity in the sentence: *Cette malheureuse créature, dont la mort prématurée attriste* SA *famille* (E. Hello).

777 In principle, *dont* cannot depend on a noun introduced by a preposition. You would not say, for example: *Un livre dont on ignore la date de la publication; un poète dont on célèbre le centenaire de la naissance; cet enfant dont vous veillez sur la conduite.* You should say: *Un livre de la publication* DUQUEL *on ignore la date; un poète de la naissance* DUQUEL (or: DE QUI) *on célèbre le centenaire; cet enfant sur la conduite* DUQUEL (or: DE QUI) *vous veillez.*

778 (1) These last sentences are not easily enunciated. It is, therefore, understandable why more than one author is not concerned with the rule of grammarians (which appears plausible only if *dont* depends on the prepositional object and, at the same time, on the subject of the relative clause): *L'autre,* DONT *les cheveux flottent sur les épaules. . .*[les épaules *de qui,* les cheveux *de qui*] (A. France). *Ce garçon. . .*DONT *l'énergie se lit dans les yeux bleus* (J. and J. Tharaud).

(2) A noun, as a prepositional object in relation to *dont,* at times takes the possessive adjective (which is generally clearer), and at other times it takes simply the article: *Celui dont les larmes ont effacé l'histoire de* SES *péchés* (Massillon). *Osymanduas, dont nous voyons. . .de si belles marques de* SES *combats* (Bossuet). *Ceux dont les soucis ont dévoré les premières années de* LA *vie* (J. Green). *La propre maison dont elle ignorait le nom* DES *locataires* (R. Rolland). *Un écrivain dont l'oeuvre. . .est à peu près inséparable de* LA *vie* (M. Arland).

779 At times, you will find, after *dont* and the subject of the relative clause, a personal pronoun representing the antecedent, but this sort of thing is not recommended: *Quelques-uns de ses amis,* DONT *les parents ne manqueront certainement pas de* LES *accompagner* (É. Henriot).

780 Instead of saying: *Les auteurs dont le talent* LEUR *a valu du succès,* *dont les oeuvres* LES *ont rendus illustres,* you should say: . . . À QUI *leur talent a valu du succès,* . . .QUE *leurs oeuvres ont rendus illustres.*

781   After *dont,* you cannot have the pronoun *en* referring to the same antecedent as its own; exception: *il y en a, il en est.* You would not say, for example: *Des épreuves* DONT *j'*EN *supporte le poids.* But you would say: *Ces épreuves,* DONT *il y* EN *a une* (or: DONT *il* EN *est une*) *que j'ai supportée difficilement.*

782   *Dont* can serve as the complement of a number used as a noun or of an indefinite numeral, direct objects: *Puis on répandit devant eux des saphirs* DONT *il fallut choisir quatre* (Maupassant). *Ceci n'ira pas sans de terribles conséquences,* DONT *nous ne connaissons encore que quelques-unes* (A. Camus).

783   After a numerical indication, *dont,* in the meaning of *parmi lesquels* [among which], can introduce a relative clause in which the verb *être* is used elliptically: *Il avait huit enfants,* DONT *six filles* (É. Faguet). *Trois juges,* DONT *moi, décerneront les prix* (J. Green).

784   In a relative clause, *dont* can be a complement of the subject, on the one hand, and of the object, the attribute, or the circumstantial object, on the other: *Il plaignit les pauvres femmes* DONT *les époux gaspillent la fortune* (Flaubert). *Vous avez un âge* DONT *l'ingénuité est à la fois un attrait et une faiblesse. Un calepin. . . *DONT *l'élastique détendu s'enlevait en courbe longue sur la reliure* (R. Bazin).

785   The relative clause that expresses the idea of emanating (coming) from, remoteness or distance, parentage or lineage, or deduction is at times introduced by *dont,* at other times by *d'où.* The following distinction is made:
(a) In speaking of persons, descent, extraction, or lineage, *dont* is used: *Le sang des demi-dieux* DONT *on me fait sortir* (Voltaire). *L'archidruide* DONT *elle était descendue* (Chateaubriand).
(b) In speaking of things, *d'où* is used: *La chambre* D'OÙ *je sortais* (Colette). *L'armoire minuscule* D'OÙ *il avait sorti les lettres* (A. Gide). *Une harmonie* D'OÙ *résulte le bonheur* (Montesquieu).
   (1) This distinction has nothing absolute about it, as you can see from the following examples: *La famille* D'OÙ *il est sorti* (Ac.). *La race* D'OÙ *ils tirent leur origine* (Dictionnaire

générale).   Dans l'allée sombre et étroite DONT *elle était sortie*
(Musset).   *Cette lampe* DONT *coulait une lumière d'huile* (Saint-
Exupéry).

(2) In interrogative sentences or without any antecedent expressed, *d'où* is used: D'OÙ *descend-il, lui qui se dit noble? Rappelez à cet orgueilleux* D'OÙ *il est issu.*

786 OÙ, a relative adverb, applies only to things; it is used without
a preposition or in combinations, such as *d'où, par où, jusqu'où*
(rarely: *sur où, pour où, vers où*) and serves to denote the place,
the time, the situation: *Voila* OÙ *j'en suis.   La ville* OÙ *j'habite, d'où
je viens, par où je passe, jusqu'où j'irai.   La Tunisie* POUR OÙ *je partais*
(Montherlant).   *Fongueusemare,* VERS OÙ *revolait sans cesse ma
pensée* (A. Gide).   *Le temps* OÙ *nous sommes* (Ac.).

The following archaic constructions are replaced, in modern
usage, by *auquel, dans lequel, vers lequel,* etc.: *C'est une chose* OÙ *je
suis déterminée* (Molière).   *C'est un mal* OÙ *mes amis ne peuvent porter de remède* (Montesquieu).   *Le but* OÙ *il tend* (Ac.).   *Les affaires*
OÙ *je suis intéressé* (Id.).

IV. INTERROGATIVE PRONOUNS

787 LEQUEL [which, which one], in the interrogative, is used as a
neuter at times; LEQUEL *pèse le plus de cent livres d'or, ou de cent
livres de plume?* (Sévigné.)   LEQUEL *préférez-vous, partir ou rester?*
(Ac.)

The following two examples are archaic because *quel?* is used
instead of *lequel?: On ne savait jamais quel des deux serait vainqueur*
(R. Rolland).   *Quelle, de ces causeries, préférer?* (R. Kemp.)

788 QUI, in the interrogative, is rarely feminine: QUI *cela pouvait-il
bien être, cette femme?* (Aragon.)   *Sais-tu* QUI *est devenue ma cliente?*
(G.-E. Clancier.)

Qui may denote a plural if the sentence contains an attribute
and if the verb is ÊTRE: *Il ne sait pas* QUI *sont les ennemis du roi*
(Mérimée).   QUI *étaient mes prétendants?* (M. Pagnol.)

The interrogative *qui* is sometimes used as a neuter to mean
qu'est-ce qui? (a direct interrogative) or *ce qui* (an indirect interrogative); it is a survival of an old use: QUI *t'amène à cette heure?*
(Musset.)   *Je ne sais* QUI *m'émeut davantage: la colère d'être joué ou le
danger que courait Étienne* (M. Arland).

789 QUE, in the interrogative, may have the value of *"pourquoi? pour quoi? en quoi? à quoi? combien?"*: QUE *tardez-vous?* QUE *vous sert de pleurer?* QUE *n'irions-nous au Rhin?* (Ch. de Gaulle.)   QUE *gagnez-vous par an?* (La Fontaine.)

In an indirect interrogative after *avoir, savoir, pouvoir* used negatively and followed by an infinitive (at times also after *chercher, se demander,* etc. + infinitive), you can use, as an attribute or direct object, *que* or at times *quoi;* the use of *quoi* seems to prevail because it has more substance: *Je ne savais* QUE *répondre* (Chateaubriand).   *Je cherchais* QUE *lui répondre* (G. Duhamel).   *Ne sachant* QUOI *faire* (A. Gide).   *Je n'aurais pas su* QUOI *répondre* (H. Bosco).

V. INDEFINITE PRONOUNS

790 AUCUN [not one, not any] originally had the positive value of *quelque, quelqu'un.* This value was kept in the expressions *aucuns* (outdated), *d'aucuns,* meaning *quelques-uns* or *certains:* AUCUNS, D'AUCUNS *croiront. . .* (Ac.).   *Si parmi vous, pourtant,* D'AUCUNES / *Le comprenaient différemment, / Ma foi tant pis, voilà comment / Nous nous aimâmes pour des prunes* (A. Daudet).

Aucun, taken in an absolute meaning, is little used (normally *personne* is used): *Il n'oubliait la fête* D'AUCUN *de la famille* (R. Rolland).   AUCUNE *n'a jamais été aimée comme moi!* (Flaubert.)

791 AUTRUI [others, other people] is normally used as an object of a preposition: *Le bien* D'AUTRUI. *Ne fais pas* À AUTRUI *ce que tu ne voudrais pas qu'on te fît. Être exigeant* POUR AUTRUI.

At times it is used as a subject or direct object: AUTRUI *nous est indifférent* (M. Proust).   *Là où* AUTRUI *nous croit coupables, nous nous trouvons innocents* (E. Jaloux).   *Il ne faut pas traiter* AUTRUI *comme un objet* (A. Maurois).

792 CERTAIN, in the plural, is used as a subject pronoun in the masculine: CERTAINS *se figurent et prétendent que l'esprit humain est illimité* (L. Daudet).

You sometimes find it in the feminine: *Mariette ne conserve pas tout, comme* CERTAINES (H. Bazin).

You also find it currently used as a complement: *Chez* CERTAINS *même les cheveux n'avaient pas blanchi* (M. Proust).   *J'ai peut-être même aidé* CERTAINS *à s'accrocher à la vie* (A. Chamson).

793 CHACUN [each one] has no plural form. When it means *toute* *personne, sans distinction,* it is always in the masculine: CHACUN *pense à soi* (Ac.).

When it designates "each person" or "each thing" of a totality, a whole, it agrees in gender with the noun or the pronoun to which it refers: *Logez ces voyageurs* CHACUN *à part* (Ac.). CHACUNE *d'elles a refusé* (Id.).

If it refers to nouns of different genders, it remains masculine: *Le mari, la femme ont* CHACUN *son département* (M. Prévost).

In familiar usage, *sa chacune* denotes the woman to whom a man is united in marriage: *Chacun enlaçant* SA CHACUNE, *il nous fut donc permis d'attaquer le rigaudon d'un bon pied* (Y. Gandon).

Un chacun, tout chacun, tout un chacun are used to reinforce the simple *chacun: Celui. . .qui sait les dessous de cartes* D'UN CHACUN (Sainte-Beuve). *Nous. . .recevions les compliments de* TOUT CHA-CUN (Cl. Farrère). TOUT UN CHACUN. . .*peut ici s'asseoir* (Colette). *Cela peut arriver à* TOUT UN CHACUN (M. Druon).

Similarly, as one says *entre chaque,* one can say: *entre chacun.* [See also entry no. 702.]

794 ON [one, someone, somebody, people, etc.], in principle, has an indeterminate value and, as a subject, it always designates one or several persons: ON *guérit comme* ON *se console;* ON *n'a pas dans le coeur de quoi toujours pleurer et toujours aimer* (La Bruyère).

At times, the pronoun subject *on* (because of its effect when conveying irony, scorn, modesty, reproach, etc.) has the value of *je, tu, nous, vous, il(s), elle(s): Et puis, on* [= *je*] *est bourgeois de Gand* (Hugo). *Un couplet qu'on* [= *vous*] *s'en va chantant / Efface-t-il la race altière / Du pied de nos chevaux marqué dans votre sang?* (Musset.)

In particular, it must be noted that the use of *on* for *nous* is very frequent in familiar or popular French: *Quand nous autres,* ON *règle des alésages au dixième de millimètre* (A. Thérive). *Tu ne peux rien me dire de plus précis, maintenant que l'*ON *va se quitter?* (M. Arland.)

When circumstances indicate clearly that one is talking about a woman, the attribute or the apposition is written in the feminine: *Qui regrette-t-on quand on est si* BELLE? (Musset.) *Eh bien! petite, est-on toujours* FÂCHÉE? (Maupassant.)

Similarly, when circumstances indicate clearly that it is a matter of several persons, the attribute or the apposition is written in the plural; nevertheless, the verb remains in the singular: *On n'est pas des* ESCLAVES *pour endurer de si mauvais traitements* (Ac.). *On dort* ENTASSÉS *dans une niche* (P. Loti).

If it is necessary to express (by using a personal pronoun) an object referring to *on*, use *nous* or *vous* (according to the meaning intended) or *se* or *soi* if the object has a reflexive value: *Qu'on hait un ennemi quand il est près de* NOUS! (Racine.)   *Quand on se plaint de tout, il ne* VOUS *arrive rien de bon* (J. Chardonne.)   *Ce n'est pas* SOI *qu'on voit* (La Fontaine).   *On n'ose plus* SE *demander si cela* VOUS *plaît* (M. Proust).

795   Generally speaking, in written French, *l'on* is a substitute considered "elegant" for the simple *on;* it is used for euphony (so say grammarians, but that is not a very strong reason because *l'on* is not at all obligatory); *l'on* is used after *et, ou, où, que, qui, quoi, si, lorsque: Jamais le sol n'en avait été défriché et* L'ON *y avait semé des pierres* (Chateaubriand).   *Le Monde où* L'ON *s'ennuie* (Pailleron).   *Les rossignols de qui* L'ON *crève les yeux* (M. Barrès).   *Le dos, avec quoi* L'ON *repose* (G. Duhamel).   *Si* L'ON *nous entendait* (Ac.).   *Il faut que* L'ON *consente* (Id.).   *Lorsque* L'ON *était occupé à une grande guerre* (Montesquieu).

796 (1) *L'on* is found in other positions in addition to those just indicated above; in particular, it is found at the beginning of a sentence or a group of words: *Éloi pardonne; mais* L'ON *ne devrait pas avoir à pardonner* (M. Arland).   *Spontanément* L'ON *acclama l'orateur* (H. Bordeaux).   L'ON *m'apporta tous les papiers d'Ellénore* (B. Constant).
(2) Generally, *l'on* is avoided after *dont* or in front of a word beginning with the letter *l*: *Les livres dont* ON *parle; si* ON *les lit.* In front of a word beginning with *con-*, it is preferable to use *que l'on* in place of *qu'on: Ce que* L'ON *conçoit bien.*

797 PERSONNE [no one (anyone)]. As a pronoun, *personne* is masculine singular. In certain cases, it keeps its original positive meaning: *Y a-t-il* PERSONNE *d'assez hardi?* (Ac.)   *Il a parlé sans que* PERSONNE *le contredît* (Id.).   *Je suis meilleur juge que* PERSONNE (É. Augier).
Most often *personne* has the negative value of *nul être humain: L'avenir n'est à* PERSONNE. *Qui vient? Qui m'appelle?* PERSONNE (Musset).

798 (1) When the context or circumstances indicate clearly that *personne* expresses the idea of *aucune femme* [no woman, not any woman] the feminine form is used for the words which, for agreement, are related to it: *Personne n'était plus* BELLE *que Cléopâtre* (Jullien, in Littré).   *Personne n'est plus que moi votre* SERVANTE, *votre* OBLIGÉE (Littré).

(2) In literary language, you find *personne autre* [no one else]: *Elle n'aimait* PERSONNE AUTRE (R. Rolland). But in current usage, *personne d'autre* is used: *Je n'ose m'adresser à* PERSONNE D'AUTRE (M. Barrès).

799 AUTRE CHOSE, grand-chose, quelque chose, peu de chose. These are all neuter combinations where the word *chose* has lost its value as a noun and its etymological gender: *Autre chose de grand. Pas grand-chose de bon. Quelque chose de fâcheux.*

800 (1) *Autre chose* [something else], as an attribute, is placed at the beginning of a sentence and at times it is repeated at the beginning of the second term of the comparison: AUTRE CHOSE *est la culture,* AUTRE CHOSE *la conduite de la vie* (M. Brion).

(2) In familiar French, *pas grand-chose* [not much of anything] is used as a noun in both genders; it is invariable, and it means *homme ou femme de peu, gens de peu: C'était une* PAS GRAND-CHOSE (É. Henriot).

(3) *Quelque chose* [something] is sometimes used as a noun: *Je ferai ce que je dois, et même un petit* QUELQUE CHOSE *en plus* (Fr. Mallet-Joris).

(4) You must be careful to keep *chose* as a feminine noun in: *Toute autre chose me plairait mieux. Quelque chose que je lui aie dite, quelques choses que je lui aie dites, je n'ai pu le convaincre* (Ac.). *Il y a toujours . . . quelque chose urgente qui doit être faite* (A. Maurois).

801 QUELQU'UN [someone]. In an indeterminate way, this pronoun designates a person, man or woman (*quelqu'une* in the feminine is rare): QUELQU'UN [man or woman] *est venu.* QUELQU'UN *qui était content, c'était ma tante. Si* QUELQU'UNE *savait quelque chose d'une autre,. . . qu'elle avertisse la Mère Supérieure* (A. Chamson).

When *quelqu'un* is related to *en* or a plural, or a collective, it is used for persons and things in both genders and both numbers: *J'en connais* QUELQUES-UNS *à qui ceci plaira.* QUELQU'UNE *de vos compagnes* (Littré). *De ces découvertes* QUELQUES-UNES *seulement sont connues.*

802 (1) *Quelqu'un* is used with *de: Quelqu'un* DE *grand, quelqu'un* DE *bien informé. Entre les nouvelles qu'il a débitées, il y en a quelques-unes* DE *vraies* (Ac.). However, if the adjective is followed by a complement, it can be simply placed side by side: *Comme quelqu'un absorbé par une passion profonde* (Th. Gautier).

Quelqu'un d'autre [anyone else] is used, but in literary language, *quelqu'un autre* is also used: *Tu aurais épousé quelqu'un autre* (E. Jaloux).

(2) *Quelqu'un,* an invariable attribute in gender and number, at times can mean "a notable person" ["a somebody"]: *Il s'adressait l'éternel reproche de n'avoir pas su être* QUELQU'UN (Maupassant). *Mme Monge est* QUELQU'UN. . . (R. Kemp).

803 **QUICONQUE** [whoever, anyone who, etc.]. This pronoun properly means *celui, quel qu'il soit, qui: Et l'on crevait les yeux à* QUICONQUE *passait* (Hugo).

In the meaning of "no matter who," "anyone who," it is, despite purists, acceptable today: *Travailler en de telles conditions eût découragé* QUICONQUE (M. Genevoix). *Plus que* QUICONQUE, *elle avait droit au voyage* (H. Troyat).

Do not say: *Tout quiconque le connaît l'aime.* Say: *Quiconque le connaît. . . .*

804 **RIEN** has kept, in certain cases, its original positive meaning of *quelque chose: La bonne vieille est loin de* RIEN *soupçonner* (J. Green).

But ordinarily it has the negative value of *nulle chose* [nothing, not anything]: *Je veux* RIEN *ou tout* (Racine).

805 (1) People say: *rien de tel* (archaic form is *rien tel*), *rien d'autre* (less often: *rien autre*), at times also: *rien autre chose* [they all have the general meaning of "nothing like," "nothing else like," "none such"]: *Je ne vis jamais* RIEN DE TEL (Ac.). *Il n'est* RIEN TEL *que ces doux et ces humbles pour aller droit et haut* (Sainte-Beuve). RIEN D'AUTRE *nulle part que ces trois choses effarantes* (P. Loti). *Il n'a trouvé* RIEN AUTRE (A. Malraux). *Elle ne possède* RIEN AUTRE CHOSE (Maupassant).

(2) *Rien,* used as a noun, takes an *s* in the plural: *Il dit toutes sortes de* RIENS (G. Duhamel).

But *rien du tout* [nothing at all, a nothing, a zero], *rien qui vaille* [nothing that is worth it, a worthless. . .], used as nouns in order to designate a person or thing without any value, do not change in the plural.

806 **Rien moins que, rien de moins que.** As a strict rule, the following distinction is made: *rien moins que* [not at all, in no way, by no means] is negative and means *nullement: Il tremble; il n'est* RIEN MOINS *qu'un héros* [= *il n'est nullement un héros* (he's no hero)]. *Rien de moins que* [nothing less than] has a positive meaning and conveys *pas moins que* [not less than]: *Quelle fermeté! Il*

n'est RIEN DE MOINS QU'*un héros* [What firmness! He is nothing less than a hero] [= *il est bel et bien un héros* (he is handsome and quite a hero)].

Among authors, this distinction is far from being observed; it would be best to adhere to it.

807   Ne. . .pas rien, rebuffed by purists, is nevertheless current, not only in familiar language, but also in literary usage: *Cette indépendance* NE *me coûte* PAS RIEN (J. Renard). *J'ai ceci, dit-elle, et ceci à revoir. Ce* N'est PAS RIEN (A. Hermant).

808   With **UN,** followed by a complement designating a whole, the article is optional: L'UN *de vous,* UN *de vous. Henri IV fut* L'UN OU UN *des plus grands rois de France* (Littré).

Today, it would be considered archaic to use *l'un* adjectively in front of a noun. Do not say: *L'une main ne sait pas ce que l'autre donne.* Say: *Une main ne sait pas.* . . .

809   L'un ou l'autre. Used as a pronoun or adjective, this expression still has a disjunctive meaning (between this or that, between this one or that one); it also has the indeterminate and vague meaning of *tel ou tel* ["such and such"]: *Vous avez deux amis influents:* L'UN OU L'AUTRE *avait bien essayé de la voir seule à seul* (H. Bordeaux). *Florence se divisa en deux camps pour* L'UN OU L'AUTRE *rival* (R. Rolland).

L'un ou l'autre cannot be used in the meaning of "two or three, a few." Do not say: *Il reste l'une ou l'autre faute dans votre devoir.*

CHAPTER 5

VERBS

I. TRANSITIVE / INTRANSITIVE

810 AIDER qqn, AIDER à qqn [to help someone]. Attempts have been made to distinguish between these two constructions. For the Academy, for example, AIDER À QQN indicates momentary (temporary) help and most often the aid is accompanied by physical effort. This distinction and certain others are not observed in usage. It should be noted that *aider à qqn* is completely outdated: *Le marquis* LUI *avait aidé à remonter* (La Varende). *Aidez-*LUI *à soulever ce fardeau* (Ac.).

811 AVOIR qq.ch. à qqn / OBTENIR qq.ch. à qqn [to get, to obtain, or to provide something for someone]. People ordinarily use the causal *faire* with either of these two expressions: *On lui* FERA AVOIR, *on lui* FERA OBTENIR *une place.*

Sometimes they are used without *faire: J'ai besoin de deux notaires et d'un témoin, je pense. Voulez-vous bien vous charger de me les* AVOIR? (Marivaux.) *Aulard se flattait de nous* AVOIR *du papier à bon compte* (Vercors). *Le crédit de la reine* OBTINT *aux catholiques ce bonheur singulier et presque incroyable* (Bossuet).

812 CONSENTIR qq.ch. [to consent, to agree to]. This expression is found in legal language or the language of diplomacy: *Consentir un traité* (Ac.). *Consentir une vente, un prêt, un délai.* The following is also said: *Vérité consentie par tout le monde.*

When used currently, *consentir qq.ch.* has an archaic stigma; ordinarily, people say *consentir à qq.ch.: Nous sommes tous résolus à consentir des sacrifices* (G. Duhamel). *Consentir une explication* (M. Prévost).

813 DÉBATTRE [to debate]. This direct transitive verb means to examine something with someone in a contradictory way: *Débattre une question, une cause, une opinion* (Ac.).   Do not say: "débattre *d'*une question."

814 DÉBLATÉRER [to shout insults at, to hurl abuse at]. Do not say: *déblatérer qqn* or *qq.ch.* Say: *déblatérer contre* or *sur. . .: Frédéric se soulageait en déblatérant* CONTRE *le pouvoir* (Flaubert).   *Il a déblatéré* SUR *l'impôt,* SUR *les pauvres* (Hugo).

815 DÉBUTER, DÉMARRER [= *commencer*]. These two verbs (which mean to begin, to commence, to start, to start off) cannot be used with a direct object, as noted in the communication dated Nov. 5, 1964, of the French Academy. Do not say: *débuter un programme, une émission, une séance,* etc.; *démarrer sa carrière*.

816 DISPUTER qq.ch. This verb means to contest something in order to obtain or to preserve it: *Disputer un prix, une chaire de professeur* (Ac.).   *Les deux armées se disputèrent longtemps la victoire* (Id.).

Disputer qqn, in the meaning of "to quarrel with someone" is condemned by the Academy (its communiqué dated Jan. 13, 1969).   Nevertheless, this construction is mentioned as familiar by Littré, in *Robert,* and attested by certain writers: *Après ce désastre, les deux garçons se mirent à* DISPUTER *leur soeur* (A. Chamson).

Se disputer (= *se quereller* [to quarrel]), rejected by Littré and admitted by the French Academy as being familiar, is current in today's usage: *Deux hommes* SE DISPUTAIENT (P. Valéry).

817 EMPÊCHER qq.ch. à qqn. This expression is archaic. Normally, people say: *défendre qq.ch. à qqn* or *interdire qq.ch. à qqn,* or *défendre à qqn de faire qq.ch.* or *interdire à qqn de faire qq.ch.,* all of which mean "to prohibit someone from doing something": *Le travail de chaque jour* LUI *empêchait de s'abandonner aux soucis du lendemain* (A. Chamson).   *Ils* LUI *empêchaient de voir le mendiant* (G.-E. Clancier).

818 ÉQUIVALOIR [to equal, to be equivalent (to)]. This verb requires the preposition *à* in front of the second term related to the equality. Do not say: *Cette chose équivaut telle autre*; say: *Cette chose équivaut* À *telle autre. Cette réponse équivaut* À *un refus* (Ac.).

819 ÉVITER qq.ch. à qqn [= *le lui épargner*]. This expression means "to spare someone from something." Although *éviter qq.ch. à qqn* is rejected by Littré and unaccepted by the Academy, it is never-theless attested by many excellent authors: *Il est impossible de* VOUS ÉVITER *toutes sortes de peines* (Diderot).   *Vous* M'ÉVITEREZ *une course* (Flaubert).   *Cela* M'ÉVITERAIT *beaucoup de souffrances* (A. Maurois).

820 **HABITER** [to inhabit, to live in]. This verb is used as a direct transitive or intransitive: *Habiter Paris, habiter la province, habiter la campagne* (Ac.).   *Habiter à la ville, à la campagne, habiter dans un vieux quartier* (Id.).

821 **HÉRITER** [to inherit (from)]. This verb is used with *de* in front of the direct object of the person: *Il a hérité* DE *son oncle* (Ac.).

When *hériter* has only a thing as the direct object, people say: HÉRITER DE QQ.CH. or HÉRITER QQ.CH.: *Il a hérité* D'*une maison* (Ac.).   *Nous avons hérité* DES *croyances d'un autre siècle* (A. Chamson).   *Pour hériter la dot* (A. Thérive).   *Il hérite une belle maison* (J. Green).

When this verb contains the direct object of the person and, at the same time, the thing inherited, people say: HÉRITER QQ.CH. DE QQN: *Il avait hérité de l'oncle Paul ses amitiés et ses dégoûts* (É. Henriot).

If you said *hériter de qq.ch. de qqn*, the double *de* would not sound pleasant to your ear; also, this construction is found only rarely. But if one of the objects is *dont* or *en*, it is not shocking: *Un secret* DONT *j'ai hérité* DE *mes pères* (Nodier).   *L'Italie n'a pas inventé la mosaïque; elle* EN *hérita* DES *Grecs* (Cl. Roger-Marx).

822 **IGNORER de qq.ch.** [to be unaware of something, to know nothing about something]. This construction, which is archaic to-day [*de* is not used now], has been preserved especially in juridi-cal style and in "playful" language [badinage, banter]; it is found in the negative with the pronoun *en*: *Il annonça ses intentions, afin que personne n'*EN *ignorât* (Littré).   *Je voudrais que nul n'*EN *ignore* (A. Gide).

823 **INVECTIVER** [to rail at, to inveigh against, to hurl abuse at]. Parallel to the classical construction, *invectiver contre qqn*, the di-rect construction *invectiver qqn* is used today: *Ils invectivent* CONTRE *tout* (A. Suarès).   *Il invectivait volontiers les royalistes du département* (A. France).

824 **MOQUER qqn** [to mock someone]. This verb, used in the active

voice, is found in literary usage: *À une heure. . .où l'action* MOQUE *la pensée* (A. Gide). *Il arrive qu'on* MOQUE *Flaubert de jouer au crucifié* (R. Kemp).

Être moqué, se faire moquer [to be mocked] are current: *Thalès aussi* FUT MOQUÉ D'*une servante* (Alain). *Vous vous* FEREZ MOQUER (Ac.).

825 OBÉIR [to obey], **DÉSOBÉIR** [to disobey]. Although these verbs no longer take a direct object today, they can be used in a passive construction: *Votre Altesse* SERA OBÉIE (Stendhal). *L'ordre de mobilisation* FUT OBÉI (P. Gaxotte). *Je savais. . .que ses larmes* N'AURAIENT PAS ÉTÉ DÉSOBÉIES (B. Constant). [Of course, notice that *obéir* and *désobéir* take the preposition *à* in front of an object: *Paul obéit à ses parents*].

826 OBSERVER [to observe], **REMARQUER** [to notice]. In careful, polished French, people say, using *faire* as a causal helping verb: *Je vous* FAIS OBSERVER *que. . ., je vous* FAIS REMARQUER *que. . .*— and not: *Je vous observe. . ., je vous remarque que. . .*: *Je vous* FAIS OBSERVER *que vous vous trompez* (Ac.). *Je vous* FERAI REMARQUER *que . . .* (Id.).

The constructions *je vous observe que. . ., je vous remarque que. . .*, accepted by A. Thérive and which, according to Brunot, are "perhaps not unpardonable," are current in spoken French and are at times found in literature: *Je vous observe que le général Marchand est sur les lieux* (Stendhal). *Condillac* REMARQUE: *La Bruyère paraît aimer ce tour* (Littré).

827 PALLIER [to palliate, to extenuate]. Etymologically, this verb means "to cover with a pallium, a pall" [i.e., with a cloak, a coat]. It is used in an absolute sense or with a direct object: *Ces remèdes ne font que pallier (Dictionnaire général). Pallier la honte d'une défaite* (A. Gide).

The construction *pallier à qq.ch.* seems to be entering the language, but you should avoid it; it was condemned by the French Academy in its notice dated Nov. 5, 1964. Examples not to imitate: *Pallier* À *toutes les distractions* (H. Bordeaux). *Pallier* À *toute défaillance du service* (H. Bazin).

828 PARDONNER qqn, for **pardonner à qqn** [to pardon someone], which is the normal construction, is generally reputed to be incorrect, notably by Littré and the Academy.

However, the construction *pardonner qqn*, which is old, is not, in modern usage, as rare as it is believed: *Frédéric l'eût pardonnée* (Flaubert). *Pardonnez un amant* (J. Bainville). *Il les a tous pardonnés.* (A. Chamson).

The passive form is regularly used: *Vous êtes pardonné.*

829 PERCUTER [to percuss, to sound, to strike, to crash into]. This verb is used as a direct transitive in the language of medicine, mechanics, and also in current language: *Percuter la poitrine d'un malade (Robert).* *Mobile qui percute un autre corps* (Id.).

According to *Robert,* people say familiarly and incorrectly: *Voiture qui percute un arbre.*

As an intransitive verb, *percuter* is used in the meaning of "to collide with, in an explosive burst" and, by extension, in the language of journalists, in the meaning of "to come into violent contact with" (a wall, a tree, a vehicle, etc.): *Obus qui vient percuter contre le sol, contre un mur (Robert).* *L'avion percuta contre le sol* (Id.). *Voiture qui percute contre un arbre (Grand Larousse encyclopédique).*

Along with André Goosse, we may observe that a newspaper like *Le Figaro* prefers to use *heurter* (a tree), or *s'écraser contre* (a tree), or *se jeter sur* (a tree) in place of *percuter* (a tree).

830 PRÉJUGER [to prejudge]. People say, according to classical usage: **préjuger qq.ch.**: *Je ne veux point préjuger la question* (Ac.).

But in today's use, the indirect construction **préjuger de qq.ch.** is in competition with the direct construction: *Pour préjuger* DE *mon acquiescement* (M. Barrès). *Je ne préjuge pas* DE *la réponse* (Ch. de Gaulle).

831 PRENDRE, REPRENDRE [to grip, to catch (an illness), to seize]. These verbs are used to indicate the first attacks of an illness, the first reactions to feeling, sentiments, etc.; they allow a direct or indirect construction: *L'accès* LE *prit à telle heure* (Ac.). *Qu'est-ce qui* LES *prend?* (H. Troyat.) *La fièvre, la goutte,* etc. LUI *a pris,* LUI *a repris* (Ac.). *Qu'est-ce qui* LEUR *prend?* (M. Jouhandeau.) *La fantaisie* LEUR *a pris d'aller à Genève* (Sévigné).

832 SE RAPPELER [to recall, to remember]. According to strict usage, this verb is used with a direct object: *Je me rappelle* CE FAIT; *je me* LE *rappelle; le fait* QUE *je me rappelle.*

The following are very current in popular language: *je me rappelle* DE *ce fait, je m'*EN *rappelle* (influence of *je me souviens* DE. . ., *je m'*EN *souviens*). This construction is entering literary usage:

Que l'on veuille bien se rappeler DE *ma ridiculissime éducation* (Stendhal).   *Te rappelles-tu* DE *Jeanne Fréron?* (J.-L. Vaudoyer).

833 **RÉPONDRE** [to respond] is a direct transitive verb in the following expressions: *répondre une requête, une pétition, un placet, un mémoire* (all of which are used in juridical language) and *répondre la messe* [to state the responses in mass].

These expressions allow the passive construction: *La pétition n'a pas encore été répondue* (Ac.).

Parallel to the usual construction *répondre à une lettre* [to answer a letter, to respond to a letter], we must note the archaic construction *répondre une lettre* (= y faire réponse) [i.e., to make a response to it]: *Ma lettre est aisée à répondre* (Stendhal).

People do say, in the passive: *une lettre répondue* (= to which a person has given an answer): *Le dossier des lettres non répondues* (G. Marcel).

834 **RÉUSSIR qq.ch.** [to succeed (in doing) something]. This construction is in general use today: *Je ne réussis plus que des ébauches* (A. Gide).   *Réussir un beau dessin* (Saint-Exupéry).   *Depuis qu'il a réussi cette affaire* (M. Pagnol).

When speaking about examinations, people say: *réussir à un examen* or *réussir un examen: J'ai réussi* À *mes examens* (H. Bordeaux).   *Je réussis mes examens* (P. Vialar).

People usually say: *être reçu, être refusé, échouer à un examen* [to fail an exam];—*subir un échec* [to undergo a failure, to fail]. Familiarly: *être recalé*, or *retoqué*, or *collé*, or *blackboulé à un examen, rater un examen* [all of which mean: to fail, to flunk, to make a mess of an exam].

835 **SORTIR** [to take out]. This verb can be used with a direct object: *Sortez la voiture de la remise* (Littré).   *Cela n'a pas suffi à me sortir de ma torpeur angoissée* (M. Prévost).   *Je sortis l'infirmier de son lit* (L. Martin-Chauffier).

People currently say, especially in familiar language, *se sortir (d'une difficulté)* [to get oneself out of a difficulty], *s'en sortir: Disant n'importe quoi pour* SE SORTIR *d'affaire* (M. Garçon).   *Comment allait-elle* S'EN SORTIR? (Aragon).

In juridical language, *sortir* is used in the meaning of "to produce," "to obtain": *La sentence* SORTIT, SORTISSAIT *son plein et entier effet.*

836 **VITUPÉRER** [to vituperate, to rail]. People say: *vitupérer qqn* or

qq.ch.: Il vitupère la misère humaine (H. Bordeaux).   *Il vitupérait le Prince et la Monarchie* (A. Chamson).

Vitupérer contre seems to be penetrating the language: *Un furieux en tout cas, qui vitupère* CONTRE *l'univers* (R. Kemp).   *Il . . . vitupérait volontiers* CONTRE *les Jésuites* (M. Pagnol).

837 VIVRE. This verb is used transitively to mean "to live, to spend, to endure, to lead, to experience" in living out one's life: *Après les nuits d'angoisse que je venais de vivre* (H. Bosco).   *Il a vécu une existence bien dure* (Ac.).   *Un apôtre, prêtre ou laïque, s'il vit vraiment sa foi. . .* (Fr. Mauriac).   *Vivre sa vie.*

838   Certain intransitive verbs are at times used transitively with a direct object expressing the same idea as that contained in the radical of a verb: *Jouer gros jeu. Dormez votre sommeil* (Bossuet). *Bien! aimez vos amours et guerroyez vos guerres!* (Hugo.) *S'il peut arriver à suer sept sueurs, il sera guéri!* (H. Troyat.)

Analogous constructions: *trembler la fièvre, grelotter la fièvre, brûler la fièvre, trembler le frisson.*

839   Expressions such as *dit-il* [he said], *répondit-il* [he replied], etc. are often replaced by verbs whose meaning can superimpose the idea of *dire: Si, si,* SOUPIRA-*t-elle* (A. Thérive).   *Paris est odieux,* MAUGRÉE-*t-il* (G. Duhamel).

But if the meaning of the verb does not lend itself naturally to the superimposition of the idea of *dire,* such use would not be permitted. Sentences like the following are not good to imitate: *Du secours! sursauta la visiteuse* (A. Billy).   *Pardon! s'étrangla le bonhomme* (R. Dorgelès).

II. CONJUGATION

General Observations

840   Verbs ending in **-cer:** write a cedilla under the *c* in front of *a* and *o: J'avançais, nous plaçons.*

841   Verbs ending in **-ger:** add an *e* after the *g* in front of *a* and *o: Je nageais, nous changeons.*

842   Verbs ending in **-yer:** the *y* changes to *i* in front of a mute *e; Il nettoie. Qu'ils appuient.*

(1) Verbs ending in **-ayer:** this change is optional: *Je paye* or *je paie. Nous balayerons* or *nous balaierons.*

(2) Verbs ending in **-eyer:** always keep the *y: Je grasseye, il grasseyera.*

843 Verbs ending in **-guer** (pronounce as *gai*) and in **-quer** (pronounce as *ké*): keep the *u* in their conjugation; the *u* belongs in the radical: *Distinguer, nous distinguons, je distinguais, nous distinguions. Fabriquer, nous fabriquons, je fabriquais, nous fabriquions.*

844 Verbs that have a mute *e* in the syllable next to the last: the mute *e* changes to *è* in front of a mute syllable: *Semer, je sème, nous sèmerons.*

845 Verbs ending in **-eler** or in **-eter:** Most of these verbs double the *l* or *t* in front of mute *e: Bourreler, je bourrelle. Harceler, je harcelle. Souffleter, je soufflette. Voleter, je volette.* [See also entry no. 330 regarding acceptable modifications in spelling.]

According to the French Academy, the following verbs—instead of doubling *l* or *t*—change *e* to *è:*

celer	démanteler	dégeler	peler	crocheter
déceler	écarteler	regeler	acheter	fureter
receler	geler	marteler	racheter	haleter
ciseler	congeler	modeler	corseter	

Je cisèle, il martèle; j'achète, il halète.

Interpeller keeps the double *l* in its complete conjugation: *Nous interpellons, j'interpellais, en interpellant,* etc. In the oral flexion of this verb there is, ordinarily in front of a final stressed syllable, the *e* in *peler,* but at times also the *e* in *sceller.* [Analogous observation for *Montpellier.*]

846 Verbs that have *é* in the syllable next to the last: *é* changes to *è* in front of a final mute syllable; therefore, in the future and conditional they keep *é,* but that *é* is pronounced open: *altérer, j'altère, j'altérerai; espérer, j'espère, j'espérerais.*

(1) For verbs of this type, there is a distinct tendency to write *è* (instead of *é*) in the future and conditional—which makes sense because of the pronunciation: *Je ne blasphèmerai pas les morts* (G. Bernanos).   *Le déjeuner complèterait le tout* (P. Vialar).

(2) Also, note that verbs ending in **-éer** always keep *é: agréer, j'agrée, j'agréerai; créer, je crée, je créerais.*

847 Verbs ending in **-uer** or **-ouer:** Certain grammarians have recommended the use of the dieresis sign [the two dots] *(ï)* on the vowel *i* on the first two persons in the plural (*nous* and *vous* forms) of the imperfect indicative and the present subjunctive, but the dieresis is not used: *Nous évoluions* (not *nous évoluïons*), *que vous saluiez, nous nous dévouions, vous louiez.*

Let's look at the verb *arguer* (pronounce the vowel *u*). Littré writes: *j'arguë, tu arguës, il arguë.* That is very plausible. Let us notice, however, that in conjugating *arguer*, authors very often do not use the dieresis sign: *Évariste. . .*ARGUA*. . .* (A. Gide). *Il n'en* ARGUE *pas. . .* (A. Thérive). *Ils* ARGUENT *des bénéfices qu'ils pourraient retirer. . .* (Aragon).

848 Verbs whose present participle ends in **-iant, yant** (except for *ayant*), **-llant** [the double *ll* is pronounced like the *y* in the English word *yes*], or in **-gnant:** in the first two persons in the plural (the *nous* and *vous* forms) of the imperfect indicative and the present subjunctive, make sure that you write *i* **after the** *i* or *y,* **after the** double *ll,* or **after the** *gn: Nous criions, que nous envoyions, nous travaillions, que vous régniez.*

849 AVOIR and **ÊTRE.** Contrary to all other verbs that end in *-e* in the third person singular of the present subjunctive, these two verbs have a final *t: Qu'il ait, qu'il soit.*

In the first two persons of the plural in the present subjunctive, there is no *i* after *y: Que nous ayons, que vous ayez, que nous soyons, que vous soyez.*

850 BÉNIR in the past participle:
(a) *bénit, bénite:* these two forms are used uniquely as an adjective when speaking of things consecrated by ritual benediction: *pain bénit* [holy bread, i.e., bread that has been blessed], *eau bénite* [holy water, i.e., water that has been blessed]; *un chapelet bénit, une branche bénite.*
(b) *béni, bénie:* these forms are used in cases when it is not a matter of ritual benediction: *Un peuple* BÉNI *de Dieu* (Ac.). *Ce roi est* BÉNI *par son peuple* (Littré). *Qui a vu le pays basque veut le revoir. C'est la terre* BÉNIE (Hugo).

Even when it is a matter of a ritual benediction, *béni* and *bénie* are used when each is applied to persons and each time that it is **a verb form,** not an adjective: *Soyez donc en paix, ma fille, lui dis-je. Et je l'*AI BÉNIE (G. Bernanos). *Un curé catholique* AVAIT BÉNI *le mariage* (A. Maurois). *Prends cette médaille. Elle* A ÉTÉ BÉNIE *par le pape* (A. France). *Le prêtre nous* A BÉNIS (H. Troyat).

851 FLEURIR [to flower, to blossom]. When this verb means "to produce flowers" or "to decorate with flowers," in the imperfect indicative the verb form is *fleurissais* and the present participle or verbal adjective is *fleurissant: Les cerisiers* FLEURISSAIENT. *Voyez ces cerisiers* FLEURISSANT *dans le verger. Les prés* FLEURISSANTS (Ac.).

In the figurative meaning of "to prosper" or "to be in honor," the verb form is *florissait* (from the old verb, *florir*) or *fleurissait* in the imperfect indicative, and almost always *florissant* as a present participle or verbal adjective: *Les sciences et les beaux-arts* FLEURISSAIENT OU FLORISSAIENT *soue le règne de ce prince* (Ac.). *Ce style roman qui* FLEURISSAIT *encore en Aquitaine au XII*ᵉ *siècle* (A. France). *Raoul pouvait citer tel parlementaire de sa famille,* FLORISSANT *sous la Régence* (J. Green). *Un règne* FLORISSANT, *une santé florissante.*

852 HAÏR drops the dieresis sign in the singular of the present indicative and the imperative [command form]: *je hais, tu hais, il hait; hais.*

853 DÛ, REDÛ, MÛ, CRÛ (from *croître*), **RECRÛ** (from *recroître*).   These forms have the circumflex accent mark only in the masculine singular: *L'argent* DÛ; *il est* MÛ *par l'intérêt; le fleuve a* CRÛ, RECRÛ.

(1) Without the circumflex accent mark: *La somme* DUE, *les honneurs* DUS; *ils sont* MUS, *elles sont* MUES *par l'intérêt; la rivière est* CRUE (Ac.).

(2) Without the circumflex accent mark: *accrue, décru, ému, promu, recru* [this last one, meaning "very tired"].

854   Verbs ending in **-indre** and in **-soudre** keep the *d* only in the simple future and the present conditional; BE CAREFUL! there is no *d* in the singular of the present indicative or the imperative [command form]: *peindre, je peins, il peint; peins—je peindrai, je peindrais.* Also, note: *résoudre, je résous, il résout; résous—je résoudrai, je résoudrais.*

In verbs ending in **-indre,** the consonants *-nd-* change to *-gn* [*gn* is pronounced like the first *n* in the Enlgish word, onion] when in front of a vowel: *peindre, nous pei*GN*ons, je pei*GN*ais, pei*GN*nant,* etc.

855   Verbs ending in **-aître** and in **-oître** have a circumflex accent mark on the *i* of the stem each time this vowel is followed by a *t: paraître, il paraît, je paraîtrai, nous paraîtrions; accroître, il accroît, j'accroîtrai, nous accroîtrions.*

(1) Without circumflex accent: *je parais, il paraissait, paraissant,* etc.; *j'accrois, il accroissait, que j'accroisse,* etc.

(2) *Croître* has a circumflex accent mark not only when *i* is followed by a *t,* but also each time when the form may be confused with a corresponding form of *croire* (except for *crus, crue, crues*): *je croîs, tu croîs, il croît en sagesse; je crûs, tu crûs, il crût, nous crûmes, vous crûtes, ils crûrent en science.*

856 Notice the following in the third person singular in the present indicative: *il clôt, il gît, il plaît (il déplaît, il complaît),* which take the circumflex accent mark.

The French Academy does not use the circumflex in *il éclot, il enclot.*

857 In certain constructions where the subject *je* is placed in the inverted form, when the first person singular of the verb form ends in *e,* that *e* is replaced by *é* (which, moreover, is pronounced as if it were *è*): *parlé-je? puissé-je réussir! Eussé-je échoué, dussé-je y perdre ma fortune. Pourquoi me fussé-je retenu?* (P.-H. Simon.)

858 Notice that in *va-t'en, souviens-t'en, retourne-t'en,* etc. there is one hyphen and one apostrophe—not two hyphens! The *t'* is really the *te* with the *e* dropped and an apostrophe added because *en* begins with a vowel. Because that apostrophe is needed, no second hyphen is used. Compare *va-t'en* and *allez-vous-en.*

859 The second person singular of the imperative [command], when the verb form ends in a mute syllable (even for *va*), is written without final *s: Marche! Travaille! Ouvre! Souffre! Sache-le!, Veuille me suivre. Va au diable!*

860 However, this second person singular of the imperative—when it ends in a mute syllable (even for *va*) takes a final *s* in front of the pronouns *en* or *y* when not followed by an infinitive: PLANTES-*en;* CHERCHES-*en les raisons; des fleurs,* OFFRES-*en à ta mère;* VAS-*y;* PENSES-*y.*

861 (1) However, in front of the pronouns *en* or *y* followed by an infinitive, and in front of the preposition *en,* there is no final *s* and no hyphen: OSE *en dire du bien;* DAIGNE *en agréer l'hommage.* VA *y mettre ordre.* VA *en savoir des nouvelles* (Ac.). *Ce mal,* LAISSE *y porter remède.* VA *en paix.* PARLE *en maître.*

(2) In the expression *à Dieu vat!* (written, at times, as *adieu-va!* or *à Dieu-va!*), the *t* in *vat* is very likely the same as the one which

is added in popular language to *va* + a vowel, for example, as in: *Malbrough s'en va-t-en guerre.*

862   The third person singular of the imperfect subjunctive always has a circumflex accent on the desinent vowel: *Qu'il plantât, qu'il finît, qu'il reçût, qu'il vînt.*

Auxiliary verbs

863   The following verbs are conjugated with **être:**
(1) All reflexive verbs: *il* S'EST BLESSÉ; *ils* SE SONT TROMPÉS.
(2) Some intransitive verbs which, for the most part, express a movement or change in state:

aller	*naître*	*tomber*
arriver	*partir*	*venir*
décéder	*repartir*	*intervenir*
devenir	*rentrer*	*parvenir*
échoir	*rester*	*revenir*
entrer	*retourner*	*survenir*
mourir	*sortir*	

864   The following are conjugated with **avoir:** *circonvenir, contrevenir, prévenir,* and *subvenir.*

Disconvenir, in the meaning of *ne pas convenir de* [not to agree on, not to agree about] is conjugated with **être:** *Il n'*EST *pas* DISCONVENU *de cette vérité;* but when *disconvenir* means *ne pas convenir à* [not to suit, not to please] it is conjugated with **avoir:** *Cette mesure* A DISCONVENU *à bien des gens.*

865   Certain verbs used intransitively are conjugated with **avoir** when they express an action and with **être** when they express the state resulting from an accomplished action. For example:

aborder	*crouler*	*divorcer*
accoucher	*croupir*	*échouer*
accroître	*déborder*	*éclater*
alunir	*décamper*	*embellir*
atterrir	*déchoir*	*empirer*
augmenter	*décroître*	*enchérir*
baisser	*dégeler*	*enlaidir*
camper	*dégénérer*	*expirer*
cesser	*déménager*	*faillir*
changer	*dénicher*	*grandir*
chavirer	*descendre*	*grossir*
crever	*diminuer*	*maigrir*
croître	*disparaître*	*monter*

paraître	*recroître*	*sortir*
passer	*redescendre*	*stationner*
périr	*résulter*	*trébucher*
pourrir	*ressusciter*	*trépasser*
rajeunir	*sonner*	*vieillir*
récidiver		

Example: *Les prix* ONT *augmenté l'an dernier. Les prix* SONT *augmentés maintenant.*

866 (1) As a matter of fact, many of these verbs are conjugated only with **avoir:** *Il* A CHANGÉ, *il* A GRANDI, *il* A EMBELLI, etc.; they are conjugated with **être** when the past participle is used as a simple adjective: *Il* EST CHANGÉ, *il* EST GRANDI, *il* EST EMBELLI, etc.

On the other hand, several of these verbs (for example, *descendre, monter, passer, ressusciter.* . .) are conjugated with **être,** it seems, if no distinction is made between the action and the state: *Où le père n'*EST *pas* PASSÉ, *l'enfant imaginaire passera* (Fr. Mauriac). *Quand* SERA PARU *le second tome.* . . (R. Kemp).

(2) Several of these verbs call for the helping verb **avoir,** evidently, when they are used transitively in the active voice: *On* A MONTÉ *le piano. Il* A MONTÉ *l'escalier* (Ac.). *On* A SORTI *la voiture. Ils* ONT AUGMENTÉ *les impôts.*

867 Besides **avoir** and **être,** which are auxiliary verbs par excellence, there are certain verbs which are semiauxiliary when, followed by an infinitive, they are used to mark certain nuances in time or mode, or different aspects of the development of an action:

aller	*—à*	*laisser*
s'en aller	*—après à*	*paraître*
devoir	*—en train de*	*sembler*
être en passe de	*—pour*	*passer pour*
—en voie de	*faillir*	*pouvoir*
—sur le point de	*manquer de*	*sortir de*
être près de	*faire*	*venir à*
—loin de	*ne faire que (de)*	*vouloir*

Examples: *Je vais partir, je dois partir. Il est en passe d'être nommé, en voie de réussir. Cela n'est pas pour durer. Il a failli, il a manqué de tomber. Laissons dire les sots. L'hiver semble finir, paraît finir. Il pouvait être dix heures. Nous sortions de dîner. Un homme vint à passer. La blessure semble vouloir se fermer.*

868 (1) *S'en aller*, with an infinitive, is hardly ever used except in the first person singular of the present indicative: *Je* M'EN VAIS *faire moi-même au lecteur les honneurs de ma personne* (Taine).

(2) Note the following distinction between *ne faire que de* + infin. and *ne faire que* + infin.: the first one indicates a very near past, e.g., *Je ne fais que d'arriver; laissez-moi respirer.* The second one indicates the continuity, the repetition, or the restriction, e.g., *Il ne fait que bâiller* [= *il bâille continuellement*]: *Le pauvre enfant ne faisait que descendre de sa chambre et y remonter* (Musset). *Je ne fais qu'exécuter les ordres que j'ai reçus* (Ac.).

(3) *Vouloir* can be used to indicate an action which is near completion and, as such, the action is presented as if it depended on the willingness of the subject—a willingness that at times lends itself to things: *On dirait que cet enfant* VEUT *faire une rougeole. Une blessure qui ne* VEUT *pas guérir* (Musset). *Il* VEUT *pleuvoir.*

(4) *Voulons-nous . . . ?* with an infinitive can be used to express the idea of "to be willing to, to be inclined to": *Voulons-nous faire une promenade? Voulons-nous . . . faire provisoirement le point de la période considérée?* (M. Cohen.)

Special Observations

869 ACCOURIR [to run up to], **APPARAÎTRE** [to appear]. These two verbs are conjugated with **avoir** or with **être**: *J'*AI ACCOURU *vers vous* (Voltaire). *Je* SERAIS ACCOURU *vers vous* (A. Gide). *Enfin le soleil* A APPARU (J. de Lacretelle). *Le spectre qui lui* AVAIT APPARU, *qui lui* ÉTAIT APPARU (Ac.).

870 CONVENIR. The traditional rule is the following:

(a) **convenir à** means "to suit, to please, to be appropriate to" and it is conjugated with **avoir**: *Cette maison m'*A CONVENU (Ac.). *Ce régime lui* AURAIT CONVENU *parfaitement* (A. Hermant).

(b) **convenir de** means "to agree on, to recognize the truth of, to agree about, to come to an agreement" and it is conjugated with **être**: *Il* EST CONVENU *lui-même de sa méprise* (Ac.). *Je ne voulais pas manquer à ce dont nous* ÉTIONS CONVENUS *ensemble* (P.-H. Simon).

(1) The distinction is arbitrary; modern usage allows *convenir de* to be conjugated with **avoir**: *Bien que de cela il n'*EÛT *jamais* CONVENU (Montherlant). *Nous* AVONS CONVENU *de nous retrouver le 14* (A. Chamson).

(2) As for the verb *disconvenir*, see entry no. 864.

871 COURIR [to run]. This intransitive verb is conjugated with **avoir:** J'AI COURU *ici à tout hasard* (Fr. Mauriac).

The auxiliary verb **être** is not used much, but it is equally correct (Littré).

872 DEMEURER. When this verb means "to inhabit," "to live in," "to delay" (i.e., "to be long, to be late in doing something"), "to take time to get something done" it is conjugated with **avoir:** *Pendant le temps que j'*AI DEMEURÉ *à Paris* (M. Donnay).   *Sa plaie* A DEMEURÉ *longtemps à guérir* (Ac.).   *Il n'*A DEMEURÉ *qu'une heure à faire cela* (Id.).

This verb is conjugated with **être** when it means "to remain in some place, to remain in a certain state": *Mon cheval* EST DEMEURÉ *en chemin* (Ac.).   *Il* EST DEMEURÉ *muet* (Id.).

873 ÉCHAPPER is conjugated with **avoir** when it means "not to be noticed, not to be grasped, i.e., when something *escapes* you": *Cette distinction m'*AVAIT ÉCHAPPÉ (Nodier).

In other cases, this verb is conjugated with **avoir** or **être** when it applies to what a person has said because of imprudence, carelessness: *Cela lui* AVAIT ÉCHAPPÉ; *il n'avait pas réfléchi* (Fr. Mauriac).   *Son secret lui* EST ÉCHAPPÉ (Sainte-Beuve).   *Cela m'*AVAIT, *m'*ÉTAIT ÉCHAPPÉ *de la mémoire* (Ac.).   *Les quelques habitants qui* ÉTAIENT ÉCHAPPÉS *aux massacres* (R. Ikor).

874 ÉCLORE [to bloom (flower)]. According to most grammarians and dictionaires, this verb is always conjugated with **être:** *Ces fleurs* SONT ÉCLOSES *cette nuit* (Ac.).

However, it is sometimes conjugated with **avoir** when the action (not the state) is considered: *Les fleurs* ONT ÉCLOS *pendant la nuit* (Nyrop).   *Puis une tendre idylle* AURAIT ÉCLOS (J. Dutourd).

875 REPARTIR [to retort (to reply)]. When this verb means "to retort," it is always conjugated with **avoir:** *Jamais!* A-*t-il* REPARTI *vivement.*

876 RESTER. When this verb means "to continue to be in one place, situation," it is conjugated with **être:** *On me pressait de partir, mais je* SUIS RESTÉ *encore deux jours à Paris. Je* SUIS RESTÉ *debout deux heures durant.*

Archaic constructions: J'AI RESTÉ *six mois entiers à Colmar* (Voltaire).   *Il ne m'*A RESTÉ *qu'à m'immoler* (Chateaubriand).   *Je n'y* AI RESTÉ *que peu de jours [dans une maison]* (A. Hermant).

877 S'AGIR [to be a question of, to be a matter of]. The impersonal expression *il s'agit* is conjugated with **être:** *Je n'ai pas voulu qu'il* S'EN SOIT AGI (Littré). *Il* S'ÉTAIT AGI *de déclarer la déchéance de Louis XVI* (Chateaubriand). *Quand il* S'EST AGI *de prendre une décision.* BE CAREFUL! Do not say: *Quand il a s'agi de.* . .

878 TOMBER [to fall] is ordinarily conjugated with **être:** *Ce secours nous* EST TOMBÉ *du ciel* (Ac.). *Ils* SONT TOMBÉS *l'un sur l'autre avec impétuosité* (Id.). *Cette pièce* EST TOMBÉE *à la première représentation* (Id.).

Archaic constructions where the auxiliary verb **avoir** is used to indicate the action, not the state: *Ce grand courage* A TOMBÉ *tout à coup* (Ac.). *Comme une toile d'araignée sur laquelle la pluie* A TOMBÉ (Hugo). *Pendant la nuit la neige* AVAIT TOMBÉ (M. Arland).

Irregular Verbs and Defective Verbs

Preliminary remark: When the **future** tense is used, the **conditional** is also used. Similarly, if the **passé simple** tense exists, the **imperfect subjunctive** also exists. If the **past participle** exists, you can form the **compound tenses.**

879 ABATTRE [to knock down, to strike down, to dishearten]. Conjugated like *battre.*

ABSOUDRE [to absolve]. Pr. Ind.: *j'absous, tu absous, il absout, nous absolvons, vous absolvez, ils absolvent.* Imperf. indic.: *j'absolvais.* Passé s. [there are no forms in this tense]. Fut.: *j'absoudrai.* Imper.: *absous, absolvons, absolvez.* Pr. subj.: *Que j'absolve.* Imperf. subj. [there are no forms in this tense]. Pr. part.: *absolvant.* Past part.: *absous, absoute.*

ABSTENIR (s'~) [to abstain]. Like *tenir,* but **être** is used in the compound tenses.

ABSTRAIRE [to abstract]. Like *traire.*

ACCOURIR [to run up to]. Like *courir.*

ACCROIRE [to impose upon, to delude, to humbug]. Used only as an infinitive, preceded by the verb *faire: Il m'en fait accroire.*

ACCROÎTRE [to increase, to make greater]. Pr. ind.: *j'accrois, tu accrois, il accroît, nous accroissons, vous accroissez, ils accroissent.* Imperf. indic.: *j'accroissais.* Passé s.: *j'accrus, tu accrus, il accrut, nous accrûmes, vous accrûtes, ils accrurent.* Fut.: *j'accroîtrai.*

Imper.: *accrois, accroissons, accroissez.* Pr. subj.: *Que j'accroisse.*
Imperf. subj.: *Que j'accrusse.* Pr. part.: *accroissant.* Past part.: *accru, accrue* [see entry no. 853, note (2)]. In the compound tenses, it takes **avoir** or **être** according to the nuance in thought [see entry no. 865].

ACCUEILLIR [to welcome, to greet]. Like *cueillir.*

ACQUÉRIR [to acquire]. Pr. ind.: *j'acquiers, tu acquiers, il acquiert, nous acquérons, vous acquérez, ils acquièrent.* Imperf. indic.: *j'acquérais.* Passé s: *j'acquis.* Fut.: *j'acquerrai.* Imper.: *acquiers, acquérons, acquérez.* Pr. subj.: *Que j'acquière, que tu acquières, qu'il acquière, que nous acquérions, que vous acquériez, qu'ils acquièrent.* Imperf. subj.: *Que j'acquisse.* Pr. part.: *acquérant.* Past part.: *acquis, acquise.*

ADJOINDRE [to adjoin]. Like *craindre.*

ADMETTRE [to admit, to allow]. Like *mettre.*

ADVENIR [to occur, to come to pass, to happen]. Like *tenir*, but is used only in the infinitive form and in the third persons, and takes **être** in the compound tenses. *Advenant* is used in contracts, etc. in the meaning *s'il arrive* [if it occurs, if it happens].

ALLER [to go]. Pr. ind.: *je vais, tu vas, il va, nous allons, vous allez, ils vont.* Imperf. indic.: *j'allais.* Passé s.: *j'allai.* Fut.: *j'irai.* Imper.: *va* (for *vas-y*, see entry no. 860), *allons, allez.* Pr. subj.: *Que j'aille, que tu ailles, qu'il aille, que nous allions, que vous alliez, qu'ils aillent.* Imperf. subj.: *Que j'allasse.* Pr. part.: *allant.* Past part.: *allé, allée.* The compound tenses are formed with **être.**

S'EN ALLER [to go away]. Like *aller: je m'en vais*, etc. Notice the imper.: *Va-t'en, allons-nous-en, allez-vous-en.* In the compound tenses, the auxiliary **être** is placed between *en* and *allé: je m'en suis allé*, etc.

The construction *je me suis en allé* (cf. *je me suis enfui*) tends to be spreading and is even found in literary usage: *Ceux qui me condamnent de* M'ÊTRE EN ALLÉ (Voltaire). *Le gentilhomme. . .s'était à coup sûr en allé* (Th. Gautier).

En allé, when taken adjectivally, is somewhat frequently used: *Son épaule sentit le froid de cette tête* EN ALLÉE (M. Genevoix).

APERCEVOIR [to perceive]. Like *recevoir.*

APPARAÎTRE [to appear]. Like *paraître.*

APPAROIR. This verb is used primarily in juridical language and it means "to be evident, to be manifest, to appear to be." A term used by lawyers, judges and barristers. It is used only as an infinitive and impersonally in the 3rd person of the present indic.: *Il a fait apparoir de son bon droit. Ainsi qu'il appert de tel acte.*

APPARTENIR [to belong (to), to pertain (to)]. Like *Tenir.*

APPENDRE [to suspend]. Like *rendre.*

APPRENDRE [to learn]. Like *prendre.*

ASSAILLIR [to assail, to assault]. Pr. ind.: *j'assaille, tu assailles, il assaille, nous assaillons, vous assaillez, ils assaillent.* Imperf. ind.: *j'assaillais, nous assaillions. Passé s.: j'assaillis.* Fut.: *j'assaillirai.* Imper.: *assaille, assaillons, assaillez.* Pr. subj.: *Que j'assaille, que nous assaillions, que vous assailliez, qu'ils assaillent.* Imperf. subj.: *Que j'assaillisse.* Pr. Part.: *assaillant.* Past part.: *assailli, assaillie.*

ASSEOIR [to seat]. Pr. ind.: *j'assieds, tu assieds, il assied, nous asseyons, vous asseyez, ils asseyent* (or: *j'assois, tu assois, il assoit, nous assoyons, vous assoyez, ils assoient*). Imperf. indic.: *j'asseyais, nous asseyions* (or: *j'assoyais, nous assoyions*). Passé s.: *j'assis.* Fut.: *j'assiérai* (or: *j'assoirai*). Imper.: *assieds, asseyons, asseyez* (or: *assois, assoyons, assoyez*). Pr. subj.: *Que j'asseye, que nous asseyions, qu'ils asseyent* (or: *Que j'assoie, que nous assoyions, qu'ils assoient*). Imperf. subj.: *Que j'assisse.* Pr. part: *asseyant* (or: *assoyant*). Past part.: *assis, assise.*

ASTREINDRE [to compel, to force, to subject, to tie down]. Like *craindre.*

ATTEINDRE [to attain, to reach]. Like *craindre.*

ATTENDRE [to wait, to wait for]. Like *rendre.*

ATTRAIRE [to attract]. Like *traire,* but is hardly ever used except in the infinitive form.

AVOIR [to have]. Pr. ind.: *j'ai, tu as, il a, nous avons, vous avez, ils ont.* Imperf. indic.: *j'avais, tu avais, il avait, nous avions, vous aviez, ils avaient.* Passé s.: *j'eus, tu eus, il eut, nous eûmes, vous eûtes, ils eurent.* Fut.: *j'aurai, tu auras, il aura, nous aurons, vous aurez, ils auront.* Imper.: *aie, ayons, ayez.* Pr. subj.: *Que j'aie, que tu aies, qu'il ait, que nous ayons, que vous ayez, qu'ils aient.* Imperf. subj.: *Que j'eusse, que tu eusses, qu'il eût, que nous eussions, que vous eussiez, qu'ils eussent.* Pr. part.: *ayant.* Past part.: *eu, eue.*

880 BATTRE [to beat, to hit, to strike]. Pr. ind.: *je bats, tu bats, il bat, nous battons, vous battez, ils battent.* Imperf. indic.: *je battais.*

Passé s.: *je battis.* Fut.: *je battrai.* Imper.: *bats, battons, battez.*
Pr. subj.: *Que je batte.* Imperf. subj.: *que je battisse.* Pr. part.: *battant.* Past part.: *battu, battue.*

BOIRE [to drink]. Pr. ind.: *je bois, tu bois, il boit, nous buvons, vous buvez, ils boivent.* Imperf. indic.: *je buvais.* Passé s: *je bus.* Fut.: *je boirai.* Imper.: *bois, buvons, buvez.* Pr. subj.: *Que je boive, que tu boives, qu'il boive, que nous buvions, que vous buviez, qu'ils boivent.* Imperf. subj: *Que je busse.* Pr. part.: *buvant.* Past part.: *bu, bue.*

BOUILLIR [to boil]. Pr. ind.: *je bous, tu bous, il bout, nous bouillons, vous bouillez, ils bouillent.* Imperf. indic.: *je bouillais, nous bouillions.* Passé s: *je bouillis.* Fut.: *je bouillirai.* Imper.: *bous, bouillons, bouillez.* Pr. subj.: *Que je bouille, que nous bouillions, que vous bouilliez, qu'ils bouillent.* Imperf. subj.: *Que je bouillisse.* Pr. part.: *bouillant.* Past part.: *bouilli, bouillie.*

BRAIRE [to bray (donkey)]. This verb is hardly used except in the infinitive form and in the 3rd persons of the present indicative, future, and conditional: *Il brait, ils braient. Il braira, ils brairont. Il brairait, ils brairaient.* The following forms are rare: Imperf. indic.: *il brayait, ils brayaient.* Pr. part.: *brayant.* Past part.: *brait* (in the compound tenses: *il a brait,* etc.—without a feminine form).

BRUIRE [to rustle (leaves), to buzz (insects), to hum (machine)]. This verb is hardly used except in the infinitive form, in the 3rd person sing. of the present indic.: *Il bruit;* in the 3rd persons of the imperf. Indic.: *il bruissait, ils bruissaient (il bruyait, ils bruyaient* are archaic); and as a pr. part.: *bruissant (bruyant* is now used only as an adjective).

You will find: *Des eaux vives* BRUISSENT *partout alentour* (P. Loti). *Les peupliers. . .*BRUISSENT *toujours* (É. Henriot.) *Quelque chose. . .*BRUISSA *sous la table* (Saint-Exupéry). *Parmi les robes qui* BRUISSÈRENT (Cl. Farrère). *On entendait des voix* BRUISSER (H. Barbusse). Those are risky forms; theoreticians of good language generally consider that *bruire* is not used (or is barbarous) in the passé simple, in the compound tenses (*j'ai brui*), and in persons other than the 3rd; they also consider that *bruisser,* with a complete conjugation, is to be condemned. For the French Academy (its notice dated Nov. 13, 1969), "the verb *bruisser* does not exist."

881 CEINDRE [to gird on, to buckle on, to belt on]. Like *craindre.*

CHALOIR [to have any importance]. This verb is no longer used except impersonally in the following expressions: *Il ne m'en chaut;*

il ne m'en chaut guère; peu me chaut [little do I care; I couldn't care less!]

CHOIR [to fall]. This verb is no longer used except in poetry or in badinage in the infinitive form. In the future: *je cherrai*, and as a past participle: *chu, chue.*

CIRCONCIRE [to circumcise]. Like *suffire*, but the past part. ends in -*s: circoncis, circoncise.*

CIRCONSCRIRE [to circumscribe]. Like *écrire.*

CIRCONVENIR [to circumvent]. Like *tenir.*

CLORE [to close, to shut]. This verb is used only in the infinitive form and in the following verb forms: Pr. ind.: *je clos, tu clos, il clôt,* (*ils closent* is rare).   Fut. (a rare tense): *je clorai, tu cloras,* etc.   Imper.: *Clos.*   Pr. subj. (rare):   *Que je close,* etc.   Past part.: *clos, close.*

COMBATTRE [to combat, to fight]. Like *battre.*

COMMETTRE [to commit]. Like *mettre.*

COMPARAÎTRE [to appear (a verb used in juridical language: *faire comparaître devant* means "to appear, to bring before")]. Like *connaître.*

COMPAROIR [to appear (a verb used in juridical language, which is now archaic and has been replaced by *comparaître*)]. It is used only in the infinitive form. *Comparant* is used as an adjective or noun.

COMPLAIRE [to please, to gratify]. Like **plaire.**

COMPRENDRE [to understand]. Like *prendre.*

COMPROMETTRE [to compromise]. Like *mettre.*

CONCEVOIR [to conceive]. Like *recevoir.*

CONCLURE [to conclude]. Pr. ind.: *je conclus, tu conclus, il conclut, nous concluons, vous concluez, ils concluent.* Imperf. indic.: *je concluais, nous concluions.* Passé s.: *je conclus.* Fut.: *je conclurai.* Imper.: *conclus, concluons, concluez.* Pr. subj.: *Que je conclue, que nous concluions.* Imperf. subj.: *Que je conclusse.* Pr. part.: *concluant.* Past part.: *conclu, conclue.*

CONCOURIR [to compete, to concur]. Like *courir.*

CONDESCENDRE [to condescend]. Like *rendre.*

CONDUIRE [to conduct, to drive, to guide, to lead]. Pr. ind.: *je* *conduis, tu conduis, il conduit, nous conduisons, vous conduisez, ils conduisent.* Imperf. indic.: *je conduisais.* Passé s.: *je conduisis.* Fut.: *je conduirai.* Imper.: *conduis, conduisons, conduisez.* Pr. subj.: *Que je conduise.* Imperf. subj.: *Que je conduisisse.* Pr. part.: *conduisant.* Past part.: *conduit, conduite.*

CONFIRE [to pickle, to preserve, to candy (fruits)]. Like *suffire,* except for the past part., which is *confit, confite.*

CONFONDRE [to confound, to mingle, to confuse]. Like *rendre.*

CONJOINDRE [to join (in marriage), to conjoin]. Like *craindre.*

CONNAÎTRE [to know, to be acquainted with]. Pr. ind.: *je connais, tu connais, il connaît, nous connaissons, vous connaissez, ils connaissent.* Imperf. indic.: *je connaissais.* Passé s.: *je connus.* Fut: *je connaîtrai.* Imper.: *connais, connaissons, connaissez.* Pr. subj.: *Que je connaisse.* Imperf. subj.: *Que je connusse.* Pr. part.: *connaissant.* Past part.: *connu, connue.*

CONQUÉRIR [to conquer]. Like *acquérir.*

CONSENTIR [to consent]. Like *mentir.*

CONSTRUIRE [to construct]. Like *conduire.*

CONTENIR [to contain]. Like *tenir.*

CONTRAINDRE [to constrain, to restrain]. Like *craindre.*

CONTREDIRE [to contradict]. Like *dire,* except in the 2nd person plural present indicative and the imperative, where you have: *contredisez.*

CONTREFAIRE [to mimic, to ape, to imitate, to falsify, to forge]. Like *faire.*

CONTREVENIR [to contravene, to infringe, to transgress]. Like *tenir.*

CONVAINCRE [to convince]. Like *vaincre.*

CONVENIR [*convenir à* (to please, to suit); *convenir de* (to agree on, to agree about, to come to an agreement)]. Like *tenir. Convenir* with *à* is conjugated with **avoir** in the compound tenses; *convenir* with *de* is conjugated with **être** in the compound tenses. [See entry no. 870.]

CORRESPONDRE [to correspond (with a person), to connect (rooms, places)]. Like *rendre.*

CORROMPRE [to corrupt, to spoil]. Like *rompre.*

COUDRE [to sew]. Pr. ind.: *je couds, tu couds, il coud, nous cousons, vous cousez, ils cousent.* Imperf. indic.: *je cousais.* Passé s.: *je cousis.* Fut.: *je coudrai.* Imper.: *couds, cousons, cousez.* Pr. subj.: *Que je couse.* Imperf. subj.: *Que je cousisse.* Pr. part.: *cousant.* Past part.: *cousu, cousue.*

882 **COURIR** [to run]. Pr. ind.: *je cours, tu cours, il court, nous courons, vous courez, ils courent.* Imperf. indic.: *je courais.* Passé s.: *je courus.* Fut.: *je courrai.* Imper.: *cours, courons, courez.* Pr. subj.: *Que je coure, que tu coures, qu'il coure, que nous courions, que vous couriez, qu'ils courent.* Imperf. subj.: *Que je courusse.* Pr. part.: *courant.* Past part.: *couru, courue.*

COUVRIR [to cover]. Pr. ind.: *je couvre, tu couvres, il couvre, nous couvrons, vous couvrez, ils couvrent.* Imperf. indic.: *je couvrais.* Passé s.: *je couvris.* Fut.: *je couvrirai.* Imper.: *couvre, couvrons, couvrez.* Pr. subj.: *Que je couvre.* Imperf. subj.: *Que je couvrisse.* Pr. part.: *couvrant.* Past part.: *couvert, couverte.*

CRAINDRE [to fear]. Pr. ind.: *je crains, tu crains, il craint, nous craignons, vous craignez, ils craignent.* Imperf. indic.: *je craignais, nous craignions.* Passé s.: *je craignis.* Fut.: *je craindrai.* Imper.: *crains, craignons, craignez.* Pr. subj.: *Que je craigne, que nous craignions.* Imperf. subj.: *Que je craignisse.* Pr. part.: *craignant.* Past part.: *craint, crainte.*

CROIRE [to believe]. Pr. ind.: *je crois, tu crois, il croit, nous croyons, vous croyez, ils croient.* Imperf. indic.: *je croyais, nous croyions.* Passé s.: *je crus.* Fut.: *je croirai.* Imper.: *crois, croyons, croyez.* Pr. subj.: *Que je croie, que tu croies, qu'il croie, que nous croyions, que vous croyiez, qu'ils croient.* Imperf. subj.: *Que je crusse.* Pr. part.: *croyant.* Past part.: *cru, crue.*

CROÎTRE [to increase]. Pr. ind.: *Je croîs, tu croîs, il croît, nous croissons, vous croissez, ils croissent.* Imperf. indic.: *je croissais.* Passé s.: *je crûs, tu crûs, il crût, nous crûmes, vous crûtes, ils crûrent.* Fut.: *je croîtrai.* Imper.: *croîs, croissons, croissez.* Pr. subj.: *Que je croisse.* Imperf. subj.: *Que je crusse* (it is not understood why the French Academy writes this form without the circumflex accent).   Pr. part.: *croissant.* Past part.: *crû* (plural: *crus*), *crue.* In the compound tenses, it sometimes takes **avoir,** sometimes **être** [see entry no. 865].

CUEILLIR [to gather, to pick, to pluck]. Pr. ind.: *je cueille, tu cueilles, il cueille, nous cueillons, vous cueillez, ils cueillent.* Imperf. indic.: *je cueillais, nous cueillions.* Passé s.: *je cueillis.* Fut.: *je cueil-*

lerai. Imper.: *cueille, cueillons, cueillez.* Pr. subj.: *Que je cueille, que nous cueillions.* Imperf. subj.: *Que je cueillisse.* Pr. part.: *cueillant.* Past part.: *cueilli, cueillie.*

CUIRE [to cook]. Like *conduire.*

883 DÉBATTRE [to debate, to discuss, to dispute, to argue]. Like *battre.*

DÉCEVOIR [to disappoint, to deceive]. Like *recevoir.*

DÉCHOIR [to fall]. Pr. ind.: *je déchois, tu déchois, il déchoit* (the archaic form is *il déchet), nous déchoyons, vous déchoyez, ils déchoient.* Imperf. indic.: (not used). Passé s.: *je déchus.* Fut.: *je déchoirai* (the archaic form is *je décherrai).* Imper.: (not used). Pr. subj.: *Que je déchoie, que nous déchoyions, que vous déchoyiez, qu'ils déchoient.* Imperf. subj.: *Que je déchusse.* Pr. part.: (not used). Past part.: *déchu, déchue.* In the compound tenses, this verb takes **avoir** or **être** [see entry no. 865].

DÉCLORE [to open]. According to the Academy, this verb is used only in the infinitive form. According to Littré, this verb has only the following persons and tenses: Pr. ind.: *je déclos, tu déclos, il déclôt* (no plural forms). Fut.: *je déclorai.* Conditional: *je déclorais.* Pr. subj.: *Que je déclose, que tu décloses, qu'il déclose, que nous déclosions, que vous déclosiez, qu'ils déclosent.* Infin.: *déclore.* Past part.: *déclos, déclose.*

DÉCOUDRE [to unstitch]. Like *coudre.*

DÉCOUVRIR [to discover]. Like *couvrir.*

DÉCRIRE [to describe]. Like *écrire.*

DÉCROÎTRE [to decrease]. Like *accroître.* In the compound tenses, it is conjugated with **avoir** or **être,** according to the nuance in thought. [see entry no. 865].

DÉDIRE (se ~) [to withdraw, to retract, to "unsay," to cancel]. Like *dire,* except in the 2nd person plural of the present indic. and imper.: *Vous vous dédisez; dédisez-vous.* In the compound tenses, it is conjugated with **être.**

DÉDUIRE [to deduce, to infer]. Like *conduire.*

DÉFAILLIR [to become feeble, to weaken, to lose strength]. Like *assaillir.* According to the Academy, this verb is hardly ever used except in the plural of the present indicative, in the imperfect indicative, the passé simple, the passé composé, in the infinitive form, and in the present participle form.

DÉFAIRE [to undo]. Like *faire.*

DÉFENDRE [to defend, to forbid]. Like *rendre.*

DÉMENTIR [to give the lie to, to belie, to contradict, to refute]. Like *mentir,* but it has a past participle form in the feminine: *démentie.*

DÉMETTRE [to dislocate, to put out of joint, to dismiss]. Like *mettre.*

DÉMORDRE [to let go, to give in, to depart from]. Like *rendre.*

884 DÉPARTIR [to distribute, to dispense, to assign, to divide]. Like *mentir,* but its past participle form, *départi,* has a feminine: *départie.*

In literature, you will at times find this verb conjugated like *finir: L'être humain . . . se purifie inconsciemment au contact de ce que lui* DÉPARTISSENT *le ciel, la terre, la ville* (Colette). *Mon père. . .se* DÉPARTISSANT *pour une fois de sa réserve. . .* (É. Henriot).

Advice: Stick to the general usage.

DÉPEINDRE [to depict, to describe, "to paint"]. Like *craindre.*

DÉPENDRE [to take down; to depend, to be dependent]. Like *rendre.*

DÉPLAIRE [to displease]. Like *plaire.*

DÉSAPPRENDRE [to unlearn, to forget how to]. Like *prendre.*

DESCENDRE [to descend, to go down]. Like *rendre.* In the compound tenses, it takes **avoir** or **être,** depending on the nuance in thought. [see entry no. 865].

DESSERVIR [to clear the table]. Like *servir.*

DÉTEINDRE [to remove the color from a fabric]. Like *craindre.*

DÉTENDRE [to loosen, to relax, to unbend]. Like *rendre.*

DÉTENIR [to detain]. Like *tenir.*

DÉTORDRE [to untwist]. Like *rendre.*

DÉTRUIRE [to destroy]. Like *conduire.*

DEVENIR [to become]. Like *tenir,* but in the compound tenses it is conjugated with **être.**

DÉVÊTIR [to unclothe, to undress qqn]. Like *vêtir.*

DEVOIR [to owe, to have to, ought to, should, must]. Pr. ind.: *je* *dois, tu dois, il doit, nous devons, vous devez, ils doivent.* Imperf. indic.: *je devais.* Passé s.: *je dus.* Fut.: *je devrai.* Imper. (very seldom used): *dois, devons, devez.* Pr. subj.: *Que je doive, que nous devions.* Imperf. subj.: *Que je dusse.* Pr. part.: *devant.* Past part.: *dû* (pl.: *dus*), *due.*

DIRE [to say, to tell]. Pr. ind.: *je dis, tu dis, il dit, nous disons, vous dites, ils disent.* Imperf. indic.: *je disais.* Passé s.: *je dis.* Fut.: *je dirai.* Imper.: *dis, disons, dites.* Pr. subj.: *Que je dise.* Imperf. subj.: *Que je disse.* Pr. part.: *disant.* Past part.: *dit, dite.*

DISCONVENIR. Like *tenir.* In the compound tenses, in the meaning of *ne pas convenir de* [not to agree on, not to agree about], it is conjugated with **être:** *Il n'EST pas DISCONVENU de cette vérité.* In the meaning of *ne pas convenir à* [not to please, not to suit, not to fit], it is conjugated with **avoir:** *Cette mesure A DISCONVENU à beaucoup de gens.*

DISCOURIR [to discourse]. Like *courir.*

DISJOINDRE [to disjoin, to sunder, to separate]. Like *craindre.*

DISPARAÎTRE [to disappear]. Like *connaître.*

DISSOUDRE [to dissolve]. Like *absoudre.*

DISTENDRE [to distend, to strain (a muscle), to stretch (the skin)]. Like *rendre.*

DISTRAIRE [to distract]. Like *traire.*

DORMIR [to sleep]. Pr. ind.: *je dors, tu dors, il dort, nous dormons, vous dormez, ils dorment.* Imperf. indic.: *je dormais.* Passé s.: *je dormis.* Fut.: *je dormirai.* Imper.: *dors, dormons, dormez.* Pr. subj.: *Que je dorme.* Imperf. subj.: *Que je dormisse.* Pr. part.: *dormant.* Past part.: *dormi* [the fem. *dormie* is rare: *Trois nuits mal DORMIES* (Musset)].

885 **ÉBATTRE (s ~')** [to frolic, to gambol, to frisk about]. Like *battre.* It is conjugated with **être** in the compound tenses.

ÉCHOIR [to fall (*à*, to)]. Used only as an infin. and in the following forms: Pr. ind.: *il échoit* (*il échet* is archaic), *ils échoient.* Passé s.: *il échut.* Fut.: *il échoira, ils échoiront* (*il écherra, ils écherront* are archaic forms). Condit.: *il échoirait, ils échoiraient* (*il écherrait, ils écherraient* are archaic forms). Pr. part.: *échéant.* Past part.: *échu, échue.* The compound forms are conjugated with **être.**

ÉCLORE [to hatch, to bloom, to burst]. According to the Academy, this verb is hardly used except as an infin. and in the 3rd persons in some tenses: *Il éclot* (it is not understood why the French Academy writes this form without a circumflex accent), *ils éclosent. Il est éclos. Il éclora. Il éclorait. Qu'il éclose. Éclos.* According to Littré, *éclore* has the following tenses: Pr. ind.: *j'éclos, tu éclos, il éclôt, nous éclosons, vous éclosez, ils éclosent.* Imperf. indic.: *j'éclosais.* Fut.: *j'éclorai.* Conditional: *j'éclorais.* Pr. subj.: *Que j'éclose.* Past part.: *éclos, éclose.* In the compound tenses, it is conjugated with **être** (at times, with **avoir**; see entry no. 874).

ÉCONDUIRE [to reject, to send packing]. Like *conduire.*

886 ÉCRIRE [to write]. Pr. ind.: *j'écris, tu écris, il écrit, nous écrivons, vous écrivez, ils écrivent.* Imperf. indic.: *j'écrivais.* Passé s.: *j'écrivis.* Fut.: *j'écrirai.* Imper.: *écris, écrivons, écrivez.* Pr. subj.: *Que j'écrive.* Imperf. subj.: *Que j'écrivisse.* Pr. part.: *écrivant.* Past part.: *écrit, écrite.*

ÉLIRE [to elect, to choose]. Like *lire.*

EMBOIRE [to coat with oil or wax in order to prevent the metal (that one is casting) from sticking to the mould; to imbibe]. Like *boire.*

ÉMETTRE [to emit]. Like *mettre.*

ÉMOUVOIR [to move, to touch, to affect (emotionally)]. Like *mouvoir,* but the past part. *ému* is written without a circumflex accent.

EMPREINDRE [to impress, to imprint, to stamp, to mark]. Like *craindre.*

ENCEINDRE [to surround with a ring, an enclosure of walls]. Like *craindre.*

ENCLORE [to enclose, to close in]. Pr. ind.: *j'enclos, tu enclos, il enclot* (it is not understood why the French Academy writes this form without a circumflex accent), *nous enclosons, vous enclosez, ils enclosent.* Imperf. ind. (rare): *j'enclosais.* Passé s.: (there is no form).   Fut.: *j'enclorai.* Imper.: *enclos.* Pr. subj.: *Que j'enclose.* Imperf. subj.: (there is no form).   Pr. part. (rare): *enclosant.* Past part.: *enclos, enclose.*

ENCOURIR [to incur]. Like *courir.*

ENDORMIR [to lull to sleep]. Like *dormir.*

ENDUIRE [to coat (with), to plaster (with)]. Like *conduire.*

ENFREINDRE [to infringe, to transgress, to offend against]. Like *craindre.*

ENFUIR (s'~) [to flee, to run away, to fly (off, away)]. Like *fuir.* In the compound tenses, it takes **être.**

ENJOINDRE [to enjoin]. Like *craindre.*

ENQUÉRIR (s'~) [to inquire, to make inquiries, to ask (about)]. Like *acquérir.* In the compound tenses, it takes **être.**

ENSUIVRE (s'~) [to ensue, to come after, to follow]. Like *suivre,* but it is used only as an infin. and in the 3rd persons of each tense. In the compound tenses, it takes **être.** When the object is the pronoun *en,* you can say *s'en ensuivre;* but *s'en suivre* is also used: *Il s'en est suivi quelques propos un peu vifs* (Vigny). *Pour ce qui s'en suivra* (Cl. Farrère).

ENTENDRE [to hear]. Like *rendre.*

ENTREMETTRE (s'~). [to intervene]. Like *mettre.* In the compound tenses, it is conjugated with **être.**

ENTREPRENDRE [to undertake]. Like *prendre.*

ENTRETENIR [to keep up, to maintain, to foster]. Like *tenir.*

ENTREVOIR [to catch a glimpse, to foresee]. Like *voir.*

ENTROUVRIR [to half-open, to draw slightly aside (drapes, curtains)]. Like *couvrir.*

887 ENVOYER [to send]. Pr. ind.: *j'envoie, tu envoies, il envoie, nous envoyons, vous envoyez, ils envoient.* Imperf. indic.: *j'envoyais, nous envoyions.* Passé s.: *j'envoyai.* Fut.: *j'enverrai.* Imper.: *envoie, envoyons, envoyez.* Pr. subj.: *Que j'envoie, que nous envoyions.* Imperf. subj.: *Que j'envoyasse.* Pr. part.: *envoyant.* Past part.: *envoyé, envoyée.*

ÉPANDRE [to spread, to pour out (a liquid)]. Like *rendre.*

ÉPRENDRE (s'~) [to fall in love, to become infatuated (with)]. Like *prendre.* In the compound tenses, it is conjugated with **être.**

ÉQUIVALOIR [to be equivalent (to), to amount (to)]. Like *valoir,* but the past part. *équivalu* has no feminine form.

ÉTEINDRE [to extinguish, to put out, to blow out]. Like *craindre.*

ÉTENDRE [to stretch out, to spread, to hang out]. Like *rendre.*

ÊTRE [to be]. Pr. ind.: *je suis, tu es, il est, nous sommes, vous êtes,* *ils sont.* Imperf. indic.: *j'étais, tu étais, il était, nous étions, vous étiez, ils étaient.* Passé s.: *je fus, tu fus, il fut, nous fûmes, vous fûtes, ils furent.* Fut.: *je serai, tu seras, il sera, nous serons, vous serez, ils seront.* Imper.: *sois, soyons, soyez.* Pr. subj.: *Que je sois, que tu sois, qu'il soit, que nous soyons, que vous soyez, qu'ils soient.* Imperf. subj.: *Que je fusse, que tu fusses, qu'il fût, que nous fussions, que vous fussiez, qu'ils fussent.* Pr. part.: *étant.* Past part.: *été* (with no feminine form).

ÉNTREINDRE [to embrace, tu hug, to squeeze]. Like *craindre.*

EXCLURE [to exclude]. Like *conclure.*

EXTRAIRE [to extract]. Like *traire.*

888 **FAILLIR** [to fail, to miss (almost)]. This verb is hardly ever used except as an infinitive and in the passé simple, future, conditional, and in compound tenses. Pr. ind. (archaic): *je faux, tu faux, il faut, nous faillons, vous faillez, ils faillent.* Imperf. indic. (archaic): *je faillais, nous faillions.* Passé s.: *je faillis.* Fut.: *je faillirai* (archaic: *je faudrai*).   Pr. subj. (archaic): *Que je faille, que nous faillions.* Imperf. subj. (archaic): *Que je faillisse.* Pr. part. (archaic): *faillant.* Past part.: *failli, faillie.* In the meaning of *faire faillite* [to go bankrupt], *faillir* is conjugated like *finir.*

FAIRE [to do, to make]. Pr. ind.: *je fais, tu fais, il fait, nous faisons, vous faites, ils font.* Imperf. indic.: *je faisais.* Passé s.: *je fis.* Fut.: *je ferai.* Imper.: *fais, faisons, faites.* Pr. subj.: *Que je fasse.* Imperf. subj.: *Que je fisse.* Pr. part.: *faisant.* Past part.: *fait, faite.*

FALLOIR [to have to, to be necessary (must)]. This is an impersonal verb [which means that it is used only in the 3rd person with *il* as the subject]. Pr. ind.: *il faut.* Imperf. indic.: *il fallait.* Passé s.: *il fallut.* Fut.: *il faudra.* Pr. subj.: *Qu'il faille.* Imperf. subj.: *Qu'il fallût.*   Pr. part.: (there is no form).   Past part.: *fallu* (without a feminine form).

FEINDRE [to feign, to simulate, to sham]. Like *craindre.*

FENDRE [to split, to crack]. Like *rendre.*

FÉRIR (= frapper) [to strike]. This verb is used only in the infin. form in the expression *sans coup férir* [without striking a blow], and as a past participle: *féru, férue,* used as an adjective and properly means: "wounded, struck by something," and in the figurative meaning of "infatuated, smitten (with), in love."

FLEURIR [to blossom, to bloom, to flower]. In its proper meaning, this verb is conjugated like *finir*. In its figurative meaning of "to prosper," the verb form is often *florissait* in the imperfect indicative and almost always *florissant* as a present participle. The verbal adjective is always *florissant* [See entry no. 851].

FONDRE [to melt, to thaw]. Like *rendre*.

FORFAIRE [to forfeit, to fail (in something)]. Hardly ever used except as an infinitive and in the compound tenses: *J'ai forfait à l'honneur*, etc.

FRIRE [to fry]. Hardly ever used except as an infinitive, in the singular of present indicative: *je fris, tu fris, il frit*. As a past participle: *frit, frite*. And in the compound tenses: *j'ai frit, j'avais frit*, etc. Rare: Fut.: *je frirai*. Condit.: *je frirais*. Imper. sing.: *fris*. The other verb forms are supplied by using the tenses of the verb *faire* plus the infinitive *frire: Nous faisons frire*, etc.

FUIR [to flee, to run away]. Pr. ind.: *je fuis, tu fuis, il fuit, nous fuyons, vous fuyez, ils fuient*. Imperf. indic.: *je fuyais, nous fuyions*. Passé s.: *je fuis*. Fut.: *je fuirai*. Imper.: *fuis, fuyons, fuyez*. Pr. subj.: *Que je fuie, que tu fuies, qu'il fuie, que nous fuyions, que vous fuyiez, qu'ils fuient*. Imperf. subj. (rare): *Que je fuisse*. Pr. part.: *fuyant*. Past part.: *fui, fuie*.

889 GEINDRE [to whine, to whimper]. Like *craindre*.

GÉSIR (= être couché) [to lie down, to be lying down]. Used only in the Pr. ind.: *je gis, tu gis, il gît, nous gisons, vous gisez, ils gisent;* and in the imperf. indic.: *je gisais*, etc.; as a pr. part.: *gisant*. [The following form is ordinarily used on tombstones: *Ci-gît. . .* (Here lies. . .)].

890 HAÏR [to hate]. Pr. ind.: *je hais, tu hais, il hait, nous haïssons, vous haïssez, ils haïssent*. Imperf. indic.: *je haïssais*. Passé s.: (rare): *je haïs, nous haïmes, vous haïtes, ils haïrent*. Fut.: *je haïrai*. Imper.: *hais, haïssons, haïssez*. Pr. subj.: *Que je haïsse*. Imperf. subj. (rare): *Que je haïsse, que tu haïsses, qu'il haït*. Pr. part.: *haïssant*. Past part. *haï, haïe*.

891 IMBOIRE [to imbue]. An archaic verb which is conjugated like *boire;* only its past participle has lasted: *imbu, imbue*, which is used especially as an adjective.

INCLURE [to enclose, to include]. Hardly ever used except as a past part.: *inclus, incluse* (not: *inclue*) which is most often preceded by *ci-* [*ci-inclus* (herewith enclosed)].

INDUIRE [to induce]. Like *conduire.*

INSCRIRE [to inscribe]. Like *écrire.*

INSTRUIRE [to instruct, to teach, to inform (of)]. Like *conduire.*

INTERDIRE [to forbid, to prohibit]. Like *dire*, except in the 2nd person plural of the present indicative and the imperative, where you have: *interdisez.*

INTERVENIR [to intervene]. Like *tenir.* It takes the auxiliary **être.**

INTRODUIRE [to introduce]. Like *conduire.*

ISSIR (= sortir) [to come (from) in the sense of the blood origin of a family]. This verb has survived only as a past participle: *issu, issue,* which is used alone or with **être:** *Un prince issu du sang des rois.   Il est issu d'une famille noble.*

892 **JOINDRE** [to join]. Like *craindre.*

893 **LIRE** [to read]. Pr. ind.: *je lis, tu lis, il lit, nous lisons, vous lisez, ils lisent.* Imperf. indic.: *je lisais.* Passé s.: *je lus.* Fut.: *je lirai.* Imper.: *lis, lisons, lisez.* Pr. subj.: *Que je lise.* Imperf. subj.: *Que je lusse.* Pr. part.: *lisant.* Past part.: *lu, lue.*

LUIRE [to shine, to gleam, to glimmer]. Pr. ind.: *je luis, tu luis, il luit, nous luisons, vous luisez, ils luisent.* Imperf. indic.: *je luisais.* Passé s.: (little used): *je luisis.* Fut.: *je luirai.* Imper.: *luis, luisons, luisez.* Pr. subj.: *Que je luise.* Imperf. subj. (little used): *Que je luisisse.* Pr. part.: *luisant.* Past part.: *lui* (with no fem. form).

894 **MAINTENIR** [to maintain, to keep up, to hold up]. Like *tenir.*

MAUDIRE [to curse]. Pr. ind.: *je maudis, tu maudis, il maudit, nous maudissons, vous maudissez, ils maudissent.* Imperf. indic.: *je maudissais.* Passé s.: *je maudis.* Fut.: *je maudirai.* Imper.: *maudis, maudissons, maudissez.* Pr. subj.: *Que je maudisse.* Imperf. subj.: *Que je maudisse.* Pr. part.: *maudissant.* Past part.: *maudit, maudite.*

MÉCONNAÎTRE [to misunderstand, to misinterpret, to refuse to recognize]. Like connaître.

MÉDIRE [to speak ill (of), to cast aspersions (on)]. Like *dire*, except in the 2nd person plural of the present indicative and in the imperative, where you have: *médisez.* The past part. *médit* has no feminine form.

MENTIR [to lie, (not to tell the truth)]. Pr. ind.: *je mens, tu mens,* *il ment, nous mentons, vous mentez, ils mentent.* Imperf. indic.: *je mentais.* Passé s.: *je mentis.* Fut.: *je mentirai.* Imper.: *mens, mentons, mentez.* Pr. subj.: *Que je mente.* Imperf. subj.: *Que je mentisse.* Pr. part.: *mentant.* Past part.: *menti* (without a fem. form).

MÉPRENDRE (se~) [to be mistaken (about)]. Like *prendre.* In the compound tenses, it is conjugated with **être.**

MESSEOIR [to be unbecoming (to)]. Used only as an infin.; it is used in the same tenses as **seoir** [See entry no. 907].

METTRE [to put, to place]. Pr. ind.: *je mets, tu mets, il met, nous mettons, vous mettez, ils mettent.* Imperf. indic.: *je mettais.* Passé s.: *je mis.* Fut.: *je mettrai.* Imper.: *mets, mettons, mettez.* Pr. subj.: *Que je mette.* Imperf. subj.: *Que je misse.* Pr. part.: *mettant.* Past part.: *mis, mise.*

MORDRE [to bite]. Like *rendre.*

MORFONDRE (se~) [to feel dejected or melancholy]. Like *rendre.* In the compound tenses, it is conjugated with **être.**

MOUDRE [to grind, to mill]. Pr. ind.: *je mouds, tu mouds, il moud, nous moulons, vous moulez, ils moulent.* Imperf. indic.: *je moulais.* Passé s.: *je moulus.* Fut.: *je moudrai.* Imper.: *mouds, moulons, moulez.* Pr. subj.: *Que je moule.* Imperf. subj.: *Que je moulusse.* Pr. part.: *moulant.* Past part.: *moulu, moulue.*

MOURIR [to die]. Pr. ind.: *je meurs, tu meurs, il meurt, nous mourons, vous mourez, ils meurent.* Imperf. indic.: *je mourais.* Passé s.: *je mourus.* Fut.: *je mourrai.* Imper.: *meurs, mourons, mourez.* Pr. subj.: *Que je meure, que tu meures, qu'il meure, que nous mourions, que vous mouriez, qu'ils meurent.* Imperf. subj.: *Que je mourusse.* Pr. part.: *mourant.* Past part.: *mort, morte.* In the compound tenses, it is conjugated with **être.**

MOUVOIR [to move, to stir, to set in motion]. Pr. ind.: *je meus, tu meus, il meut, nous mouvons, vous mouvez, ils meuvent.* Imperf. indic.: *je mouvais.* Passé s.: (rare): *je mus.* Fut.: *je mouvrai.* Imper.: *meus, mouvons, mouvez.* Pr. subj.: *Que je meuve.* Imperf. subj. (rare): *Que je musse.* Pr. part.: *mouvant.* Past part.: *mû* (pl.: *mus*), *mue.*

895 **NAÎTRE** [to be born]. Pr. ind.: *je nais, tu nais, il naît, nous naissons, vous naissez, ils naissent.* Imperf. indic.: *je naissais.* Passé s.: *je naquis.* Fut.: *je naîtrai.* Imper.: *nais, naissons, naissez.* Pr. subj.: *Que je naisse.* Imperf. subj.: *Que je naquisse.* Pr. part.: *naissant.* Past

part.: *né, née.* In the compound tenses, this verb is conjugated with **être.**

NUIRE [to harm]. Like *conduire,* but the past participle is *nui* (without a *t*) and has no feminine form.

896 **OBTENIR** [to obtain]. Like *tenir.*

OCCIRE (= tuer) [to kill, to slay]. Is used only in badinage in the infin. form and as a past part.: *occis, occise,* and in the compound tenses.

OFFRIR [to offer]. Like *couvrir.*

OINDRE [to anoint]. Like *craindre,* but is hardly ever used except as an infinitive and past part.: *oint, ointe.*

OMETTRE [to omit]. Like *mettre.*

OUÏR [to hear]. This verb is hardly ever used except as an infinitive and past part.: *ouï, ouïe,* especially in: *J'ai ouï dire* [I have heard tell. . .].

OUVRIR [to open]. Like *couvrir.*

897 **PAÎTRE** [to graze (on), to feed (on)]. Pr. ind.: *je pais, tu pais, il paît, nous paissons, vous paissez, ils paissent.* Imperf. indic.: *je paissais.* Passé s.: (there is no form). Fut.: *je paîtrai.* Imper.: *pais, paissons, paissez.* Pr. subj.: *Que je paisse.* Imperf. subj. (no form). Pr. part.: *paissant.* Past part. (no form).

PARAÎTRE [to appear]. Like *connaître.*

PARCOURIR [to pass through, to go through, to proceed through (or over)]. Like *courir.*

PARFAIRE [to perfect]. Like *faire.*

PARTIR [to leave]. Like *mentir,* but its past participle, *parti,* has a feminine form, *partie.* In the compound tenses, *partir* is conjugated with **être.**
   Partir was formerly used in the meaning of "partager" [to divide, to share], and it is now used in that meaning only in the expression, *avoir maille à partir avec qqn* [to have a bone to pick with someone]. [*une maille* = a coin valued at about a penny]. The past participle, *parti,* in terms of heraldry (blazon, coat of arms), is used either concerning the shield divided perpendicularly in equal parts or an eagle with two heads.

PARVENIR [to reach, to attain, to come (to), to succeed

(in),]. Like *tenir*, but the compound tenses are formed with **être**.

PEINDRE [to paint]. Like *craindre*.

PENDRE [to hang]. Like *rendre*.

PERCEVOIR [to perceive]. Like *recevoir*.

PERDRE [to lose]. Like *rendre*.

PERMETTRE [to permit]. Like *mettre*.

PLAINDRE [to pity, to feel sorry for]. Like *craindre*.

PLAIRE [to please]. Pr. ind.: *je plais, tu plais, il plaît, nous plaisons, vous plaisez, ils plaisent.* Imperf. indic.: *je plaisais.* Passé s.: *je plus.* Fut.: *je plairai.* Imper.: *plais, plaisons, plaisez.* Pr. subj.: *Que je plaise.* Imperf. subj.: *Que je plusse.* Pr. part.: *plaisant.* Past part.: *plu* (without a feminine form).

898 PLEUVOIR [to rain]. Pr. ind.: *il pleut.* Imperf. indic.: *il pleuvait.* Passé s.: *il plut.* Fut.: *il pleuvra.* Pr. subj.: *Qu'il pleuve.* Imperf. subj.: *Qu'il plût.* Pr. part.: *pleuvant.* Past part.: *plu* (no fem. form).

POINDRE [to dawn, to sting]. In the meaning of "commencer à paraître" [to begin to appear, to dawn], this verb is conjugated like *craindre*, but is hardly ever used any more except as an infinitive and in the 3rd person singular of the pr. ind. and fut.: *Le jour point; le jour poindra.* In the meaning of "piquer" [to sting], it is hardly ever used except in the proverbial locution: *Oignez vilain, il vous poindra; poignez vilain, il vous oindra* [i.e., Bless a villain and he will curse you; curse a villain and he will bless you; or, Anoint a villain and he will sting you; sting a villain and he will anoint you; or, One must treat a rough person roughly if one wishes respect].

PONDRE [to lay (an egg)]. Like *rendre*.

POURFENDRE [to split in two, to strike hard at, to lunge at]. Like *rendre*.

POURSUIVRE [to pursue]. Like *suivre*.

POURVOIR [to provide]. Like *voir*, except in the Passé s.: *je pourvus;* in the Fut.: *je pourvoirai;* in the Condit.: *je pourvoirais;* and in the Imperf. subj.: *Que je pourvusse.*

899 POUVOIR [to be able, can]. Pr. ind.: *je peux* (or: *je puis*) *tu peux,* *il peut, nous pouvons, vous pouvez, ils peuvent.* Imperf. indic.: *je pouvais.*   Passé s.: *je pus.* Fut.: *je pourrai.* Imper. (no form).   Pr. subj.: *Que je puisse.* Imperf. subj.: *Que je pusse.* Pr. part.: *pouvant.*   Past part.: *pu* (with no fem. form).

PRÉDIRE [to predict, to foretell]. Like *dire,* except in the 2nd person plural of the pres. ind. and imperative, where you have: *prédisez.*

PRENDRE [to take]. Pr. ind.: *je prends, tu prends, il prend, nous prenons, vous prenez, ils prennent.* Imperf. indic.: *je prenais.* Passé s.: *je pris.* Fut.: *je prendrai.* Imper.: *prends, prenons, prenez.* Pr. subj.: *Que je prenne, que tu prennes, qu'il prenne, que nous prenions, que vous preniez, qu'ils prennent.* Imperf. subj.: *Que je prisse.* Pr. part.: *prenant.* Past part.: *pris, prise.*

PRESCRIRE [to prescribe]. Like *écrire.*

PRESSENTIR [to have a presentiment or a foreboding or an inkling of] Like *sentir.*

PRÉTENDRE [to claim, to assert, to maintain]. Like *rendre.*

PRÉVALOIR [to prevail]. Like *valoir,* except in the pr. subj.: *Que je prévale, que tu prévales, qu'il prévale, que nous prévalions, que vous prévaliez, qu'ils prévalent.* The past part., *prévalu,* has no fem. form.

PRÉVENIR [to anticipate, to forestall, to ward off, to warn]. Like *tenir.*

PRÉVOIR [to foresee]. Like *voir,* except in the fut.: *je prévoirai;* and in the Condit.: *je prévoirais.*

PRODUIRE [to produce]. Like *conduire.*

PROMETTRE [to promise]. Like *mettre.*

PROMOUVOIR [to promote]. Used only as an infin., as a present part.: *promouvant,* and in the compound tenses. The past part., *promu,* is written without a circumflex accent.

PROSCRIRE [to proscribe]. Like *écrire.*

PROVENIR [to derive, to issue (from)]. Like *tenir,* but in the compound tenses, it is conjugated with **être.**

900 **QUÉRIR** (or **querir**) [to look for]. Used only as an infin. after *aller, venir,* and *envoyer.*

901 **RABATTRE** [to turn down, to press down]. Like *battre.*

RAPPRENDRE [to learn again, to relearn]. Like *prendre*.

RASSEOIR [to seat again]. Like *asseoir*.
The infinitive *rassir* has been formed from the past part., *rassis*, when speaking of bread and certain pastries: *Ce pain commence à* RASSIR, *à* SE RASSIR *(Petit Robert)*. The past part. in the fem. form, used familiarly, is: *rassie*.

RAVOIR [to get back, to recover]. Hardly ever used except as an infin., in the future, and the conditional: *je raurai, je raurais*, belonging to familiar language.

RÉAPPARAÎTRE [to reappear, to appear again]. Like *connaître*.

REBATTRE [to beat again]. Like *battre*.

902 **RECEVOIR** [to receive]. Pr. ind.: *je reçois, tu reçois, il reçoit, nous recevons, vous recevez, ils reçoivent.* Imperf. indic.: *je recevais, nous recevions.* Passé s.: *je reçus.* Fut.: *je recevrai.* Imper.: *reçois, recevons, recevez.* Pr. subj.: *Que je reçoive, que nous recevions, que vous receviez, qu'ils reçoivent.* Imperf. subj.: *Que je reçusse.* Pr. part.: *recevant.* Past part: *reçu, reçue.*

RECLURE [to isolate, to shut in]. Used only as an infin. and as a past part.: *reclus, recluse.*

RECONDUIRE [to escort, to accompany, to take someone back to some place]. Like *conduire*.

RECONNAÎTRE [to recognize]. Like *connaître*.

RECONQUÉRIR [to reconquer, to win back]. Like *acquérir*.

RECONSTRUIRE [to reconstruct]. Like *conduire*.

RECOUDRE [to sew again, to resew]. Like *coudre*.

RECOURIR [to run again, to run back]. Like *courir*.

RECOUVRIR [to cover again, to re-cover, to cover up]. Like *couvrir*.

RÉCRIRE [to rewrite, to write out again]. Like *écrire*.

RECROÎTRE [to grow again]. Like *accroître*. For the past part.: *recrû* (pl.: *recrus*), *recrue*, see entry no. 853. In the compound tenses, *recroître* is conjugated with **avoir** or **être** [see entry no. 865].

RECUEILLIR [to collect, to take in or to give shelter to someone]. Like *cueillir*.

RECUIRE [to bake again, to cook or roast again]. Like *conduire*.

903 **REDESCENDRE** [to bring down again, to take down again, to come or go down again]. Like *rendre*. In the compound tenses, it takes **avoir** or **être,** according to the nuance in thought [see entry no. 865].

REDEVENIR [to become again]. Like *tenir,* but the compound tenses are conjugated with **être.**

REDEVOIR [to owe still, to owe a balance of]. Like *devoir.*

REDIRE [to say or to tell again, to repeat]. Like *dire.*

RÉDUIRE [to reduce]. Like *conduire.*

RÉÉLIRE [to re-elect]. Like *lire.*

REFAIRE [to redo, to do again, to do over again]. Like *faire.*

REFENDRE [to split]. Like *rendre.*

REFONDRE [to remelt, to melt again, to recast]. Like *rendre.*

REJOINDRE [to rejoin, to join or to connect together again]. Like *craindre.*

RELIRE [to read again, to reread]. Like *lire.*

RELUIRE [to shine, to glisten, to gleam, to glow]. Like *luire.*

REMETTRE [to remit, to put back, to replace]. Like *mettre.*

REMORDRE [to bite again, to take another bite]. Like *rendre.*

RENAÎTRE [to be born again]. Like *naître,* but it has no past participle and, therefore, has no compound tenses.

RENDORMIR [to put to sleep again, to lull to sleep again]. Like *dormir,* but the fem. form of the past participle is used: *rendormi, rendormie.* In the compound tenses, *se rendormir* is conjugated with **être.**

RENDRE [to render, to return (something), to restore, to give back]. Pr. ind.: *je rends, tu rends, il rend, nous rendons, vous rendez, ils rendent.* Imperf. indic.: *je rendais.* Passé s.: *je rendis.* Fut.: *je rendrai.* Imper.: *rends, rendons, rendez.* Pr. subj.: *Que je rende.* Imperf. subj.: *Que je rendisse.* Pr. part.: *rendant.* Past part.: *rendu, rendue.*

RENTRAIRE [to sew torn fabric invisibly]. Like *traire.*

RENVOYER [to return, to throw, to send back, to postpone, to dismiss, to send away]. Like *envoyer.*

904 REPAÎTRE [to feed, to graze]. Like *paître*, but it has a passé s.: *je repus:* an imp. subj.: *Que je repusse;* and a past part.: *repu, repue.*

RÉPANDRE [to pour out, to spill, to scatter, to spread, to diffuse]. Like *rendre.*

REPARAÎTRE [to reappear, to appear again]. Like *connaître.*

REPARTIR [to leave again, to set out again, to start off again]. Like *partir.* The compound tenses take **être.**

REPARTIR [to reply, to retort]. Like *partir,* but the compound tenses take **avoir.** Do not confuse this verb with *répartir,* meaning *partager* [to share, to divide], which is conjugated regularly like *finir.*

REPEINDRE [to paint again, to repaint]. Like *craindre.*

REPENDRE [to hang again]. Like *rendre.*

REPENTIR (se~) [to repent, to be sorry for, to rue]. Pr. ind.: *je me repens, tu te repens, il se repent, nous nous repentons, vous vous repentez, ils se repentent.* Imperf. indic.: *je me repentais.* Passé s.: *je me repentis.* Fut.: *je me repentirai.* Imper.: *repens-toi.* Pr. subj.: *Que je me repente.* Imperf. subj.: *Que je me repentisse.* Pr. part.: *se repentant.* Past part.: *repenti, repentie.*

RÉPONDRE [to reply, to respond]. Like *rendre.*

REPRENDRE [to take back, to take up again]. Like *prendre.*

REPRODUIRE [to reproduce]. Like *conduire.*

REQUÉRIR [to come or go for, to beg, to ask]. Like *acquérir.*

905 RÉSOUDRE [to resolve, to dissolve]. Pr. ind.: *je résous, tu résous, il résout, nous résolvons, vous résolvez, ils résolvent.* Imperf. indic.: *je résolvais.* Passé s.: *je résolus.* Fut.: *je résoudrai.* Imper.: *résous, résolvons, résolvez.* Pr. subj.: *Que je résolve.* Imperf. subj.: *Que je résolusse.* Pr. part.: *résolvant.* Past part.: *résolu, résolue.* (Another form of the past part.: *résous,* meaning "changed," is rarely used; its fem. form *résoute* is almost never used.)

RESSENTIR [to feel, to experience, to feel deeply]. Like *mentir,* but its past part., *ressenti,* has a fem. form: *ressentie.*

RESSERVIR [to serve again, to be able to be used again]. Like *servir.*

RESSORTIR [to come out of a place where one has just entered, to come or go out again]. Like *mentir*, but the compound tenses take **être**. Do not confuse this verb with *ressortir*, meaning "to be under the jurisdiction (of), to be amenable (to)," which is conjugated regularly like *finir: Ces affaires ressortissent, ressortissaient à tel tribunal.*

In the meaning of "to be under the jurisdiction (of) or to be amenable (to)," *ressortir* takes *à: Dans toutes les questions qui ressortissent* à *la souveraineté collective* (Hugo). Certain authors incorrectly conjugate it like *sortir* and at times use *de* with it. Examples that you should not imitate: *Cela* RESSORTANT *au domaine moral* (P. Léautaud). *Quelque chose qui. . .*RESSORT *plutôt* DU *style* (M. Cohen).

RESSOUVENIR (se~) [to recall again, to remember again]. Like *tenir*, but the compound tenses take **être**.

RESTREINDRE [to restrict, to curtail]. Like *craindre*.

906 **RÉSULTER** [to result]. Used only as an infin. and in the 3rd person in the other tenses. In the compound tenses, it is conjugated with **avoir** when the action is emphasized: *Du mal en* A RÉSULTÉ; and with **être** when the state is emphasized: *Il en* EST RÉSULTÉ *du mal.*

RETEINDRE [to dye again, to redye]. Like *craindre*.

RETENDRE [to bend again, to stretch again]. Like *rendre*.

RETENIR [to retain, to keep, to detain]. Like *tenir*.

RETORDRE [to twist, to wring out (laundry)]. Like *rendre*.

RETRADUIRE [to retranslate, to translate again]. Like *conduire*.

RETRAIRE [to draw again, to milk again (milk from a cow)]. Like *traire*.

REVALOIR [to return like for like, to pay back in kind]. Like *valoir*.

REVENDRE [to sell again, to resell]. Like *rendre*.

REVENIR [to come back, to return]. Like *tenir*, but the compound tenses take **être**.

REVÊTIR [to clothe again, to reclothe]. Like *vêtir*.

REVIVRE [to relive, to live again]. Like *vivre*.

RIRE [to laugh]. Pr. ind.: *je ris, tu ris, il rit, nous rions, vous riez, ils rient.* Imperf. indic.: *je riais, nous riions.* Passé s.: *je ris, nous* *rîmes, vous rîtes, ils rirent.* Fut.: *je rirai.* Imper.: *ris, rions, riez.* Pr. subj.: *Que je rie, que nous riions.* Imperf. subj. (rare): *Que je risse.* Pr. part.: *riant.* Past part: *ri* (without a fem. form).

ROMPRE [to break]. Pr. ind.: *je romps, tu romps, il rompt, nous rompons, vous rompez, ils rompent.* Imperf. indic.: *je rompais.* Passé s.: *je rompis.* Fut.: *je romprai.* Imper.: *romps, rompons, rompez.* Pr. subj.: *Que je rompe.* Imperf. subj.: *Que je rompisse.* Pr. part.: *rompant.* Past part.: *rompu, rompue.*

ROUVRIR [to open again, to reopen]. Like *couvrir.*

907 SAILLIR [to gush out, to spurt out, to stand out]. Hardly used except as an infinitive and in the 3rd persons: pr. ind.: *il saillit, ils saillissent.* Imperf. indic.: *il saillissait, ils saillissaient.* Passé s.: *il saillit, ils saillirent.* Fut.: *il saillira, ils sailliront.* Imper. (no form). Pr. subj.: *Qu'il saillisse, qu'ils saillissent.* Imperf. subj.: *Qu'il saillît, qu'ils saillissent.* Pr. part.: *saillissant.* Past part.: *sailli, saillie.*

   Saillir, meaning "bulging," [*être en saillie*], is used only in the 3rd persons: pr. ind.: *il saille, ils saillent.* Imperf. indic.: *il saillait, ils saillaient.* Passé s.: *il saillit, ils saillirent.* Fut.: *il saillera, ils sailleront.* Imper. (no form). Pr. subj.: *Qu'il saille, qu'ils saillent.* Imperf. subj.: *Qu'il saillît, qu'ils saillissent.* Pr. part.: *saillant.* Past part.: *sailli* (without a fem. form).

SATISFAIRE [to satisfy]. Like *faire.*

SAVOIR [to know]. Pr. ind.: *je sais, tu sais, il sait, nous savons, vous savez, ils savent.* Imperf. indic.: *je savais.* Passé s.: *je sus.* Fut.: *je saurai.* Imper.: *sache, sachons, sachez.* Pr. subj.: *Que je sache.* Imperf. subj.: *Que je susse.* Pr. part.: *sachant.* Past part.: *su, sue.*

SECOURIR [to help, to succor, to aid]. Like *courir.*

SÉDUIRE [to seduce]. Like *conduire.*

SENTIR [to feel, to smell]. Like *mentir,* but its past part., *senti,* does have a fem. form: *sentie.*

SEOIR (= *convenir* [to suit, to be becoming]). Used only as a present part. and in the 3rd persons. It has no compound tenses. Pr. ind.: *il sied, ils siéent.* Imperf. ind.: *il seyait, ils seyaient.* Passé s.: (no form). Fut.: *il siéra, ils siéront.* Condit: *il siérait, ils siéraient.* Imper.: (no form). Pr. subj.: (rare): *Qu'il siée, qu'ils siéent.* Imperf. subj. (no form). Pr. part.: *seyant.* (*Séant* is used as an adjective: *Il n'est pas* SÉANT *de faire cela*).

Seoir (= *être assis, siéger*) [to sit, to sit down, to be on the bench (judge)]. Is hardly ever used except as a pr. part.: *séant;* and as a past part.: *sis, sise.* No compound tenses. **Se seoir** (= *s'asseoir*) [to sit down]. This verb is used only in poetry and in familiar language in the imperative [command]: *sieds-toi, seyez-vous.*

908 SERVIR [to serve]. Pr. ind.: *je sers, tu sers, il sert, nous servons, vous servez, ils servent.* Imperf. indic.: *je servais.* Passé s.: *je servis.* Fut.: *je servirai.* Imper.: *sers, servons, servez.* Pr. subj.: *Que je serve.* Imperf. subj.: *Que je servisse.* Pr. part.: *servant.* Past part.: *servi, servie.*

SORTIR. Like *mentir,* but its past participle, *sorti,* has a fem. form: *sortie.* In the compound tenses, *sortir,* as a transitive verb, is conjugated with **avoir:** *J'ai sorti la voiture* [I took the car out].

As an intransitive verb [no direct object], it is conjugated with **être:** *Je suis sorti(e) de bonne heure.*

Sortir, as a term in law, meaning "to produce," is conjugated like *finir,* but is used only in the 3rd persons: pr. ind.: *La sentence sortit son effet, les sentences sortissent leur effet,* etc. In the compound tenses, this verb is conjugated with **avoir** when used transitively [with a direct object].

SOUFFRIR [to suffer]. Like *couvrir.*

SOUMETTRE [to submit]. Like *mettre.*

SOURDRE [to well, to well up, to spring (water)]. Hardly ever used except as an infin. and in the 3rd persons of the pr. ind.: *il sourd, ils sourdent.* The following forms are archaic: imperf. indic.: *il sourdait.* Passé s.: *il sourdit.* Fut.: *il sourdra.* Condit: *il sourdrait.* Pr. subj.: *Qu'il sourde.* Imperf. subj.: *Qu'il sourdît.* Pr. part.: *sourdant.*

SOURIRE [to smile]. Like *rire.*

SOURSCRIRE [to subscribe]. Like *écrire.*

SOUSTRAIRE [to take away, to remove, to subtract]. Like *traire.*

SOUTENIR [to support, to hold up]. Like *tenir.*

SOUVENIR (se~) [to remember]. Like *tenir.* In the compound tenses, it is conjugated with **être.**

SUBVENIR [to help, to assist, to relieve]. Like *tenir.*

909 SUFFIRE [to suffice, to be sufficient]. Pr. ind.: *je suffis, tu suffis, il suffit, nous suffisons, vous suffisez, ils suffisent.* Imperf. indic: *je* *suffisais.* Passé s.: *je suffis.* Fut.: *je suffirai.* Imper.: *suffis, suffisons, suffisez.* Pr. subj.: *Que je suffise.* Imperf. subj.: *Que je suffisse.* Pr. part.: *suffisant.* Past part.: *suffi* (with no fem. form).

SUIVRE [to follow]. Pr. ind.: *je suis, tu suis, il suit, nous suivons, vous suivez, ils suivent.* Imperf. indic.: *je suivais.* Passé s.: *je suivis.* Fut.: *je suivrai.* Imper.: *suis, suivons, suivez.* Pr. subj.: *Que je suive.* Imperf. subj: *Que je suivisse.* Pr. part.: *suivant.* Past part.: *suivi, suivie.*

SURFAIRE [to overrate, to praise too highly]. Like *faire.*

SURPRENDRE [to surprise]. Like *prendre.*

SURSEOIR [to postpone, to stay (an execution)]. Pr. ind.: *je sursois, tu sursois, il sursoit, nous sursoyons, vous sursoyez, ils sursoient.* Imperf. ind.: *je sursoyais, nous sursoyions.* Passé s.: *je sursis.* Fut.: *je surseoirai.* Condit.: *je surseoirais.* Imper.: *sursois, sursoyons, sursoyez.* Pr. subj.: *Que je sursoie, que nous sursoyions.* Imperf. subj.: *Que je sursisse.* Pr. part.: *sursoyant.* Past part.: *sursis, sursise.*

SURVENIR [to happen, to take place]. Like *tenir.* In the compound tenses, it is conjugated with **être.**

SURVIVRE [to survive]. Like *vivre.*

SUSPENDRE [to suspend, to hang up]. Like *rendre.*

910 **TAIRE** [to say nothing about, to keep secret (a name); to suppress, to hush up]. *je tais, tu tais, il tait, nous taisons, vous taisez, ils taisent.* Imperf. indic.: *je taisais.* Passé s.: *je tus.* Fut.: *je tairai.* Imper.: *tais, taisons, taisez.* Pr. subj.: *Que je taise.* Imperf. subj.: *Que je tusse.* Pr. part.: *taisant.* Past part.: *tu, tue.*

TEINDRE [to dye, to stain]. Like *craindre.*

TENDRE [to stretch, to strain, to tighten]. Like *rendre.*

TENIR [to hold]. Pr. ind.: *je tiens, tu tiens, il tient, nous tenons, vous tenez, ils tiennent.* Imperf. indic.: *je tenais.* Passé s.: *je tins, nous tînmes, vous tîntes, ils tinrent.* Fut.: *je tiendrai.* Imper.: *tiens, tenons, tenez.* Pr. subj.: *Que je tienne, que nous tenions.* Imperf. subj.: *Que je tinsse.* Pr. part.: *tenant.* Past part.: *tenu, tenue.*

TISTRE or **TÎTRE** (= *tisser*) [to weave]. Used only as a past part.: *tissu, tissue,* and in the compound tenses. It is hardly ever used, except in its figurative meaning: *C'est lui qui* A TISSU *cette intrigue.*

TONDRE [to clip (hair); to shear (sheep)]. Like *rendre*.

TORDRE [to twist]. Like *rendre*.

TRADUIRE [to translate]. Like *conduire*.

TRAIRE [to draw (milk); to milk (a cow)]. Pr. ind.: *je trais, tu trais, il trait, nous trayons, vous trayez, ils traient.* Imperf. indic.: *je trayais, nous trayions.* Passé s.: (there is no form). Fut.: *je trairai.* Imper.: *trais, trayons, trayez.* Pr. subj.: *Que je traie, que nous trayions.* Imperf. subj. (there is no form). Pr. part.: *trayant.* Past part.: *trait, traite.*

TRANSCRIRE [to transcribe]. Like écrire.

TRANSMETTRE [to transmit]. Like mettre.

TRANSPARAÎTRE [to show through]. Like *connaître*.

TRESSAILLIR [to thrill, to shiver, to shudder, to tremble]. Like *assaillir*.

911 VAINCRE [to conquer, to vanquish, to defeat, to master, to get the better of]. Pr. ind.: *je vaincs, tu vaincs, il vainc, nous vainquons, vous vainquez, ils vainquent.* Imperf. indic.: *je vainquais.* Passé s.: *je vainquis.* Fut.: *je vaincrai.* Imper.: *vaincs, vainquons, vainquez.* Pr. subj.: *Que je vainque.* Imperf. subj.: *Que je vainquisse.* Pr. part.: *vainquant.* Past part.: *vaincu, vaincue.*

VALOIR [to be worth]. Pr. ind.: *je vaux, tu vaux, il vaut, nous valons, vous valez, ils valent.* Imperf. indic.: *je valais.* Passé s.: *je valus.* Fut.: *je vaudrai.* Imper.: *vaux* (rare), *valons, valez.* Pr. subj.: *Que je vaille, que tu vailles, qu'il vaille, que nous valions, que vous valiez, qu'ils vaillent.* Imperf. subj.: *Que je valusse.* Pr. part.: *valant.* Past part.: *valu, value.*

VENDRE [to sell]. Like *rendre*.

VENIR [to come]. Like *tenir*, but in the compound tenses, it is conjugated with **être**.

VÊTIR [to clothe]. Pr. ind.: *je vêts, tu vêts, il vêt, nous vêtons, vous vêtez, ils vêtent.* Imperf. indic.: *je vêtais.* Passé s.: *je vêtis.* Fut.: *je vêtirai.* Imper.: *vêts, vêtons, vêtez.* Pr. subj.: *Que je vête, que nous vêtions.* Imperf. subj: *Que je vêtisse.* Pr. part.: *vêtant.* Past part: *vêtu, vêtue.*

The forms with -iss-, which were somewhat frequently used formerly, are still found at times: *Ils achètent les habits des pestiférés, s'en* VÊTISSENT (Montesquieu). *Il se* VÊTISSAIT *de la nuit* (Hugo).

VIVRE [to live]. Pr. ind.: *je vis, tu vis, il vit, nous vivons, vous* *vivez, ils vivent.* Imperf. indic.: *je vivais.* Passé s.: *je vécus.* Fut.: *je vivrai.* Imper: *vis, vivons, vivez.* Pr. subj: *Que je vive.* Imperf. subj: *Que je vécusse.* Pr. part: *vivant.* Past part: *vécu, vécue.*

VOIR [to see]. Pr. ind.: *je vois, tu vois, il voit, nous voyons, vous voyez, ils voient.* Imperf. indic.: *je voyais, nous voyions.* Passé s.: *je vis.* Fut.: *je verrai.* Imper.: *vois, voyons, voyez.* Pr. subj.: *Que je voie, que tu voies, qu'il voie, que nous voyions, que vous voyiez, qu'ils voient.* Imperf. subj.: *Que je visse.* Pr. part.: *voyant.* Past part.: *vu, vue.*

912 **VOULOIR** [to want]. Pr. ind.: *je veux, tu veux, il veut, nous voulons, vous voulez, ils veulent.* Imperf. indic.: *je voulais.* Passé s.: *je voulus.* Fut.: *je voudrai.* Imper.: *veuille, veuillons, veuillez* (*veux, voulons, voulez* are used only to express a command to arm oneself in firm willingness). Pr. subj.: *Que je veuille, que tu veuilles, qu'il veuille, que nous voulions, que vous vouliez, qu'ils veuillent.* Imperf. subj.: *Que je voulusse.* Pr. part.: *voulant.* Past part.: *voulu, voulue.*

The old forms *que nous veuill(i)ons, que vous veuill(i)ez* are found, at times, in contemporary use: *Que vous le* VEUILLEZ *ou non* (R. Rolland).   *Sans que nous* VEUILLIONS *écouter* (M. Genevoix).

As for *ne pas en vouloir à,* there is an imperative modeled on the subjunctive: *ne m'en* VEUILLE *pas* (J. Giraudoux).   *Ne m'en* VEUILLEZ *pas* (A. Thérive).   But there is another imperative, modeled on the indicative, which is somewhat frequent: *Ne m'en* VEUX *pas de fuir* (Hugo).   *Ne m'en* VOULEZ *pas* (M. Barrès).

III. MODES (MOODS)

Various Observations

913 **AIMER** + infin. [to like + infin.]. There are three possible constructions: AIMER LIRE (which is the most frequent), AIMER À LIRE, or AIMER DE LIRE: *Il aime contrarier* (Ac.).   *J'*AIME À *prier à genoux* (Chateaubriand).   *Il n'*AIMAIT *pas* DE *prêcher sur les toits* (A. Hermant).

914 **ARRÊTER** [to stop]. In the meaning of *cesser* [to cease], this verb is used currently with *de* + infin: *Ils n'arrêtaient pas* DE *fumer* (Fr. Mauriac).

915 COMMENCER [to begin, to commence]. This verb takes an object by using *à* or *de* in front of the infinitive. The following verbs also take the preposition when followed by an infinitive: *continuer, contraindre, s'efforcer, s'ennuyer, faire attention, forcer, obliger, solliciter: Nous* COMMENÇÂMES À *parler* (A. Gide). *Quand la nuit* COMMENÇA DE *tomber* (P. Loti). *Le paysan français* CONTINUE À *nourrir le tisserand français* (A. Maurois). *Je* CONTINUE DE *lire ma lettre* (G. Duhamel).

916 DEMANDER [to ask (for)] + infin. If the two verbs have the same subject, use **demander à:** *Il* DEMANDE À *parler* (Littré).

In the opposite case, use **demander de:** —*Je vous* DEMANDE DE *m'écouter* (Ac.).

When *demander* has an indirect object, *demander de* is generally used, even if the two verbs have the same subject: *Il me* DEMANDA, *un jour,* DE *se servir du téléphone* (G. Duhamel).

Do not say: *demander* POUR *entrer,* POUR *téléphoner,* etc.

917 ESPÉRER + infin. [to hope + infin.]. The ordinary use is: *J'espère réussir.* The use of *de* is now somewhat frequent in literature: *Ce secret du génie, je n'espère pas* DE *le comprendre.* (Alain).

918 IL FAIT BON, IL FAIT CHER, IL FAIT DANGEREUX, etc., + infin. [It is good (to). . ., It is expensive (to). . ., It is dangerous (to). . . , etc., + infin.]. Normal construction is without a preposition: *Alors, il fera bon vivre* (A. France). *Il fait cher vivre dans cette ville* (Ac.). *Il fait beau voir que. . .* (Id.).

The construction with *de* is formed by analogy with the expression *Il est bon de. . .*and it is fairly frequent: *Il fait bon* DE *vivre* (M. Arland).

919 FEINDRE + infin. [to feign (pretend) (to)]. Ordinary construction: *Feindre* D'*être gai,* D'*être en colère* (Ac.).

The construction without *de* is rare: [*Le renard*] *feignit vouloir gravir* (La Fontaine). *Elle feignit ne pas comprendre* (Fr. Mauriac).

920 NE PAS LAISSER DE + infin. [not to allow (to). . ., not to let go. . ., not to let things go. . .]. The ordinary construction is: *Il ne faut pas laisser* D'*aller votre chemin* (Ac.).

The construction with *que de* is out of date, but is used by some authors: *Cette situation . . . ne laisse pas* QUE DE *prêter à réflexion* (P. Claudel).

921 MANQUER (de) + infin. [almost, nearly]. People say: *Il a man-

qué D'*être tué* (Ac.).   For Littré, to say *Il a manqué tomber* is faulty. This construction, without *de,* is perfectly correct today: *Elle avait manqué mourir* (Flaubert).   *J'ai manqué glisser* (J. Giraudoux).

Manquer à faire une chose [to fail to do something] means "not to do something, not to succeed in doing it": *On mésestime celui qui* MANQUE À *remplir ses devoirs* (Littré).

922 NIER (de) + inf. [to deny (to)]. With or without *de,* as you choose: *Elle a d'abord nié* D'*être en commerce avec les rebelles* (A. Chamson).   *Il nie avoir approuvé la phrase funeste* (J. Kessel).

923 S'OCCUPER à *faire une chose* [to be busy doing something]. This means to work at something or to make it the object of one's activity: *Il y a vingt ans que je m'occupe* À *faire des traductions* (Montesquieu).   *Tout le jour il s'occupe* À *lire* (Ac.).

S'occuper de + infin. [to be busy (with)]. This construction indicates a more attentive activity, including preoccupations, concerns, figuring, etc.: *Il s'occupe* DE *détruire les abus* (Ac.).   *Il ne s'occupe que* DE *gérer sa fortune* (Id.).

924 PLAIRE [to please, to be pleasing (to)]. After the impersonal expression *il me plaît, il te plaît,* etc., the dependent infinitive is introduced by *de: Il me plaît* DE *faire ceci* (Ac.).

Outdated construction: *Jusqu'au jour où il te plaira me marier* (É. Augier).

925 PRÉFÉRER + infin. [to prefer (to)]. Ordinary construction: *Il préfère mourir* (Littré).   The construction with *de,* somewhat outdated, is nevertheless maintained in literary usage: *Il semblait préférer* DE *rester seul* (A. Hermant).   *D'autres préfèrent* DE *rester debout* (J. Rostand).

926 PRENDRE GARDE à *faire une chose* [to take care, to be careful, to be sure to do something]. This means to take care to do it, to pay attention to doing it: *Prenez garde* À *éviter les cahots* (M. Druon).

Prendre garde de + infin. made negative [to be careful not to. . .]. This has the same meaning as the one above: *Qu'il prenne garde* DE *ne pas la confondre* [*la gloire*] *avec le succès* (J. Green).

Prendre garde de + infin. without a negation [be careful not to. . ., watch out (for). . .]. This means to make an effort to avoid something: *Prenez garde* DE *tomber* (Ac.).   [See entry no. 1036].

927 PRÊT à + infin. [ready to]. People say, in the active form of the infinitive: *vêtement prêt à porter, manuscrit prêt à imprimer, etc.: De bons troupeaux de moutons prêts à tondre* (Nodier). *Quarante stères de bois* PRÊT À SCIER (H. Bazin).

You can also say, in the passive form: *prêt à être porté, prêt à être imprimé,* etc.: *Il a laissé sa caisse toute* PRÊTE À ÊTRE MONTÉE (A. Chamson).

928 SE RAPPELER + infin. [to remember, to recall]. Ordinary construction is: *Je me rappelle avoir vu, je me rappelle avoir fait telle chose* (Ac.).

The construction with *de* is outdated: *Je me rappelle* D'*avoir aimé les femmes* (La Varende).

If the infinitive expresses an action yet to be accomplished, *de* is necessary: *Rappelle-toi bien* D'*employer tout ce que tu as d'esprit à être aimable* (Stendhal).

929 REGRETTER de + infin. [to regret + present part.]. The normal construction is: *Je regrette de lui avoir parlé trop durement* (Ac.).

Avoir regret, with *de* or *à* [to regret]: *J'ai regret* DE *n'avoir pas acheté ce domaine* (Ac.). *J'ai regret* À *le dire* (Id.).

Avoir le regret, avoir du regret, with *de* [to regret]: *J'ai le regret* DE *vous apprendre que. . .* (Ac.). *J'ai du regret* DE *vous voir dans l'erreur* (Id.).

Être au regret, with *de* [to regret, to feel sorry about]: *Je suis au regret* D'*avoir dit,* D'*avoir fait cela* (Ac.). [See entry no. 392].

930 RESTER + infin. [to remain (what is left to do)]. In the meaning of "to remain, to be left to do," use *à: Ce qui reste à faire . . . . Il reste encore* À *prouver que . . .* (Ac.). In the meaning of "to stay, not to go," use *à* or no preposition: *Restez ici à dîner* (Ac.). *Restez à souper* (J. Giono). *Vous restez dîner avec nous* (É. Henriot). *Il lui faut rester travailler à Paris* (Id.). *Il faudrait . . . que je reste coucher à la ferme* (H. Troyat).

Archaic construction: *Il me restait* D'*attendre* (H. Bosco). *Il lui restait* DE *prendre congé* (Ph. Erlanger).

931 JE NE SACHE PAS. The expressions *je ne sache pas* [I do not know], *je ne sache point* [I do not know at all], *je ne sache rien* [I know of nothing, I don't know of anything], *je ne sache personne* [I know no one, I know of no one, I do not know anyone] are used only in the 1st person singular or 3rd person with the subject *on*. They are used to express an extenuating affirmation: *Je ne*

SACHE *pas que vous ayez rien à vous reprocher* (Marivaux). *Je ne*
SACHE *rien de si beau* (Ac.).   *On ne* SACHE *pas qu'elle ait jamais pro-*
testé autrement (A. Billy).

The following locutions *que je sache* [as far as I know], *que tu*
saches [as far as you know], *que nous sachions, que vous sachiez* are
used to indicate (if the fact mentioned is not real) that you are not
aware of it: *Il n'a point été à la campagne,* QUE JE SACHE
(Littré).   [See also entry no. 1267.]

932 JE NE SAURAIS [I would not know how . . .], used with just
ne, not *pas,* can be an equivalent of *je ne puis (pas)* [I cannot]: *Je*
ne SAURAIS *faire ce que vous me dites* (Ac.).   *Les hommes ne* SAU-
RAIENT *se passer de religion* (G. Duhamel).

933 SOUHAITER + infin. [to hope, to expect]. With *de* or no
preposition: *Les renseignements que je souhaite* D'*obtenir*
(G. Duhamel).   *Tout politicien souhaite plaire* (A. Maurois).

If *souhaiter* has an indirect object *(je te souhaite . . ., je souhaite*
à mon ami . . ., etc.), the infinitive after the verb form of *souhaiter*
is preceded by *de: Je vous souhaite* D'*arriver jusque-là* (M. Druon).

934 SE SOUVENIR + infin. [to remember]. With or without *de: Je*
me souviens D'*avoir dîné chez un Grand d'Espagne* (Fr. Mauriac).   *Je*
me souviens avoir lu, cependant, qu'à Port-Royal on n'était pas triste
(J. Green).

935 TÂCHER + infin. [to try (to)]. Ordinary construction: with *de: Je*
tâcherai DE *vous satisfaire* (Ac.).

The construction with *à* is frequent in literary use (but for the
Academy, it is becoming outdated): *Il n'est point exceptionnel qu'on*
tâche À *se racheter de ses oeuvres par ses jugements* (J. Rostand).

IV. PRESENT PARTICIPLE

936   The form ending in *-ant* is a **present participle** and it is invariable in all cases where it expresses an action.

Examples of principal cases: *Les troupes* COUVRANT *la retraite.* . . .
Des discours PLAISANT *à chacun.* . . .   *Nous marchions ne* SONGEANT
à rien. . . .   *Clarté* FUYANT *toujours.* . . .   *Deux amis* SE RENCON-
TRANT. . . .   *Les difficultés vont* (EN) CROISSANT. . . .   *De* SOI-
DISANT *prophètes.* . . .

937   The form ending in -*ant* is a verbal adjective and it is variable when it expresses (by using a simple qualifier) a state, a quality more or less permanent.

Examples: *La plaine* VERDOYANTE. . . . *Des gazons toujours* RE-NAISSANTS. . . . *Elles attendaient, pâles et* TREMBLANTES. . . . *Des personnes bien* PENSANTES. . . .

938   There are a certain number of present participles that are distinctly different from corresponding qualifiers ending in -*ent* or -*ant* because of their spelling:

Present participle	Qualifier	Present participle	Qualifier
abstergeant	*abstergent*	*équivalant*	*équivalent*
adhérant	*adhérent*	*excellant*	*excellent*
affluant	*affluent*	*expédiant*	*expédient*
coïncidant	*coincident*	*extravaguant*	*extravagant*
communiquant	*communicant*	*fatiguant*	*fatigant*
compétant	*compétent*	*influant*	*influent*
confluant	*confluent*	*intriguant*	*intrigant*
convainquant	*convaincant*	*naviguant*	*navigant*
convergeant	*convergent*	*négligeant*	*négligent*
déférant	*déférent*	*précédant*	*précédent*
déléguant	*délégant*	*provoquant*	*provocant*
détergeant	*détergent*	*somnolant*	*somnolent*
différant	*différent*	*suffoquant*	*suffocant*
divaguant	*divagant*	*vaquant*	*vacant*
divergeant	*divergent*	*violant*	*violent*
émergeant	*émergent*	*zigzaguant*	*zigzagant*

939 (1) The present participle is variable, according to an old usage, in certain expressions used in juridical language: *les* AYANTS *cause, les* AYANTS *droit, toute(s) affaire(s) cessante(s), tous empêchements* CESSANTS, *deux requêtes* TENDANTES *à même fin, la partie* PLAIGNANTE, *la Cour d'appel* SÉANTE *à Paris, maison à lui* APPARTENANTE [in ordinary usage, people say: *maison à lui* APPARTENANT, or: *maison lui* APPARTENANT (see entry no. 725)].

(2) **Battant** (or **flambant**) **neuf** [brand new]. In these expressions, the form ending in -*ant* is most often invariable [and *neuf* is treated at times as an adjective, at other times as an adverb]: *La jolie demeure du comte de Chalon, tout* BATTANT NEUF

(É. Henriot). *Des Saint-Cyriens* FLAMBANT NEUFS (H. Troyat). *Des bâtiments* FLAMBANT NEUF (A. Chamson).

With agreement: *Deux édifices gothiques* BATTANTS NEUFS (L. Veuillot). *Avec des habits* FLAMBANTS NEUFS (A. Dumas père).

(3) Agreement or no agreement in: *à dix heures sonnant (es)*, or: *battant(es)*, or familiarly: *toquant(es)*, or: *tapant(es)*, or popularly: *pétant(es)*: *À sept heures* SONNANTES (A. France). *À l'heure* TO-QUANTE (Colette). *À dix heures* TAPANTES (H. Bosco). *À neuf heures* SONNANT (Hugo). *À neuf heures* TAPANT (A. Hermant).

(4) **S'agissant de** [having to do with] is used in the meaning of *s'il s'agit de* [if it has to do with], *comme il s'agit de* [as (if) it has to do with], *quand il s'agit de* [when it has to do with]: *C'est "lepus" qu'il fallait mettre,* S'AGISSANT *ici* DU *lièvre* (A. Hermant). *On le comprend surtout,* S'AGISSANT DE *la troupe nouvelle* (M. Arland).

V. AGREEMENT OF THE PAST PARTICIPLE

Basic Rules

940 (1) As an epithet: agreement in gender and number with the modified word: *Des enfants* ABANDONNÉS.

(2) With **être**: Agreement with the subject: *Ces champs seront* LA-BOURÉS *au printemps. Mes tantes sont* ARRIVÉES *hier.*

(3) With **avoir**: Agreement with the *preceding* direct object; no agreement with the direct object when it follows the verb or when there is no direct object: *Les champs qu'on a* LABOURÉS; *ces champs, je les ai* LABOURÉS. *Mes tantes sont là; je les ai* AMENÉES *en voiture.*

On a LABOURÉ *ces champs. J'ai* AMENÉ *mes tantes en voiture. Elles ont* RÉFLÉCHI.

Special Cases

941 ATTENDU, COMPRIS, etc.

The past participles *attendu, compris (non compris, y compris* [including,]), *entendu, excepté, ôté, ouï, passé, supposé, vu* are invariable as prepositions when they are placed *in front of* the noun or pronoun: ATTENDU *ses moeurs solitaires, il était à peine connu d'elles* (Musset). *Tout le monde consentait à s'en mêler,* Y

COMPRIS *les personnes les plus âgées* (P. Loti). *Rien ne remuait,* EXCEPTÉ *les flammes* (Hugo). PASSÉ *les grilles de la Porte-Maillot, je trouve la plus noire solitude* (M. Barrès).

They vary [*i.e.,* they agree] when they *follow* the word to which they refer or when they precede it only by the inverted form: *Les indications* Y COMPRISES (Ac.). *Les passagers ont tous péri, cinq ou six* EXCEPTÉS (Id.). *Déjà* COMPRISES *au compte précédent, ces sommes n'ont pas dû figurer ici* (Littré).

942 (1) You find, somewhat often, in literary usage, certain past participles other than those of the traditional series which are used invariably [i.e., no agreement] when in front of a noun serving as a complement ("object"): *Il n'était séant de trotter qu'une fois* DÉPASSÉ *la limite rituelle* (Cl. Farrère). *Notre première rencontre—*OUBLIÉ *les quelques lignes et les extraits que lui consacrent les manuels scolaires—eut lieu chez un bouquiniste* (M. Chapelan). VENU *la fin de l'hiver, la troupe tout entière partit pour l'Angleterre* (G. Duhamel).

(2) Contrary to what has just been stated, it often happens that *passé* agrees with the noun that follows: PASSÉES *les grandes épreuves des invasions sarrasines et normandes, la population des campagnes s'était accrue* (P. Gaxotte). PASSÉES *les courses de feria, il me faudra revenir* (Montherlant).

943 L'ÉCHAPPER BELLE, la bailler, la manquer belle, or **la manquer bonne**. In these expressions (which have survived from the language of players of a game that nowadays is known as tennis), the pronoun *la* was used to take the place of the noun *balle* [ball]. The fact that the past participle is invariable in such expressions as *Il l'a* ÉCHAPPÉ *belle,* [He had a narrow escape] *il me l'a* BAILLÉ *belle,* or *il me l'a* BAILLÉ *bonne,* [He tried to put something over on me; He tried to lead me to believe] *il l'a* MANQUÉ *belle* [It was a sure miss] is explained by an old use that permitted the participle to remain invariable when it did not complete the clause. Nowadays, we can continue to leave the participle invariable, but it is perfectly acceptable to make the agreement: *Il l'a* ÉCHAPPÉE *belle; il me l'a* BAILLÉE *bonne.*

944 FINI [finished, completed]. When *fini* is at the beginning of a sentence, it agrees with the subject if you consider that the auxiliary **être** has been omitted: FINIE *la vie glorieuse, mais* FINIS *aussi la rage et les soubresauts* (A. Camus).

At times, *fini* at the beginning of a sentence may be considered as referring to the pronoun *ce* (or *cela*) understood, and you leave it invariable: FINI, *les bibelots sur la courtepointe!* (La Varende.)

945 ÉTANT DONNÉ [considering, seeing that. . .]. This expression traditionally agrees with the noun that follows, but, in modern usage, it is often left invariable: *Étant* DONNÉE *la modestie de mon grade. . .* (G. Duhamel). *Étant* DONNÉES *les circonstances présentes* (Saint-Exupéry). *Étant* DONNÉ *la menace allemande* (J. Benda). *Je n'ose rien dire étant* DONNÉ *les surprises de la pellicule* (J. Cocteau).

946 CI-ANNEXÉ, CI-JOINT, CI-INCLUS [herewith]

(a) These expressions are variable when they are considered as epithets or attributes: *Les feuilles* CI-ANNEXÉES, CI-JOINTES, CI-INCLUSES. *Je vous envoie* CI-JOINTES, CI-INCLUSES *mes factures, trois factures.* *Vous trouverez* CI-INCLUSE *la copie que vous m'avez demandée* (Ac.). *Ci-incluses, ces pièces sont en sûreté.*

(b) They are invariable when they are given the function of an adverb (compare: *ci-contre, ci-dessus,* etc.): *Trouvez* CI-JOINT *les 2.000 francs que nous vous devons* (H. Bazin). *Vous trouverez* CI-INCLUS *une lettre de votre père* (Ac.). *Je vous envoie* CI-ANNEXÉ, CI-JOINT, CI-INCLUS *mes factures, trois factures.*

(c) If one can write, taking into consideration a choice between an adverbial function or a qualifying function: *Je vous envoie* CI-ANNEXÉES, CI-JOINTES, CI-INCLUSES—or: CI-ANNEXÉ, CI-JOINT, CI-INCLUS—*les pièces que vous avez demandées,* then usage consistently gives these expressions an adverbial function:

(1) when they are at the beginning of a sentence [except in cases when they are there merely as detached adjectives: CI-INCLUSES, *ces pièces seront en sûreté*]: CI-JOINT *l'expédition du jugement* (Ac.). CI-JOINT *les factures, trois factures;*

(2) when, in the body of the sentence, they precede a noun without an article or without a demonstrative or possessive determinative: *J'ai l'honneur de vous transmettre* CI-JOINT *copie de la réponse* (Stendhal). *Vous recevrez* CI-INCLUS *copie de. . .* (Ac.).

947 COÛTÉ, VALU, PESÉ, *etc.*

(a) As for these past participles, the agreement is not influenced when what is considered to be an adverbial complement (e.g., price, value, weight, etc.) is not taken as a direct object: *Les trois mille francs que ce meuble m'a* COÛTÉ (Ac.). *Ce cheval ne vaut plus la somme qu'il a* VALU *autrefois* (Id.). *Elle songea aux années qu'elle avait* VÉCU *ensuite* (J. de Lacretelle). *Les dix grammes que cette lettre aurait* PESÉ; *les vingt minutes que j'ai* MARCHÉ, COURU. *Les deux heures que j'ai* DORMI, *que j'ai* REPOSÉ.

(b) Certain intransitive verbs may become transitive; their past participle, then, is variable: *Les efforts que ce travail m'a* COÛTÉS

[= *causés*] (Ac.).   *La gloire que cette action lui a* VALUE [= *pro-
curée*] (Id.).   *Les paquets que j'ai* PESÉS [= placed on the
scale].   *Les dangers que j'ai* COURUS [= *affrontés*[.   *Les heures
qu'il avait* VÉCUES [= *passées*] *loin de Dieu* (A. France).   *Ses con-
victions, il les a* VÉCUES [= *traduites en actes*, i.e., put into ac-
tion].

948 VERBES IMPERSONNELS [impersonal verbs].
The past participle is always invariable [no agreement]: *Les chal-
eurs qu'il a* FAIT. *Les inondations qu'il y a* EU. *Quels soins il a* FALLU!

949 DIT, DÛ, CRU, PU, SU, etc. [These are past participles, re-
spectively, of *dire, devoir, croire, pouvoir, savoir*]. These past participles are invariable when the direct object is an infinitive or a
clause understood after them: *J'ai fait tous les efforts que j'ai* PU [un-
derstood: *faire*].   *Il n'a pas obtenu les résultats qu'il avait* CRU, *qu'il
avait* PENSÉ, *qu'il avait* PRÉVU [understood: *qu'il obtiendrait*].

950 PAST PARTICIPLES + attribute of an object.
(a) Agreement with the object if it precedes: *Tant de choses que
j'avais* CRUES *éternelles* (Stendhal).   *Une affreuse barbe de chèvre,
qu'on eût* DITE *postiche* (R. Martin du Gard).   *C'était de bonnes
jumelles, qu'il eût* VOULUES *meilleures encore* (M. Genevoix).
Tous ceux qu'il avait FAITS *grands* (L. Bloy).
(b) Also, the past participle is very often invariable: *L'armée qu'on
avait* CRU *si forte* (J. et J. Tharaud).   *Ces meubles qu'on eût* DIT *usés
à force d'être frottés* (J.-J. Gautier).   *Merveille des départs que je n'ai
jamais* VOULU *tristes* (A. Gide).

951 PAST PARTICIPLE in relation to the pronoun l'.
The past participle is invariable if the pronoun *l'* is neuter
and is equivalent to *cela: Une étude moins difficile que je ne l'avais*
PRÉSUMÉ, CRU, PENSÉ [= *que je n'avais présumé, cru, pensé* CELA;
that is to say: *qu'elle était difficile*]. *L'étape est beaucoup plus longue que Labarbe ne vous l'avait* DIT (A. Gide).
   In certain cases, *l'* can take the place of a noun and it can
take agreement, in which case it is a matter of interpretation:
Fermina Márquez n'était pas telle qu'il se l'était IMAGINÉE (V. Larbaud) [you could also write: *qu'il se l'était imaginé*; that is to say:
qu'il s'était imaginé qu'elle était].

**952 PAST PARTICIPLE and a collective noun or a noun indicat-
ing a portion or fraction.**
(a) Agreement is called for by the collective noun or by its com-

plement, according to whether it is one or the other which is most striking in thought: *La foule d'hommes que j'ai* VUE *commença à se disloquer.* *Un groupe de quelques manifestants que la police a* RELÂCHÉS *après vérification d'identité de chacun d'eux.* *Une partie du linge fut* VOLÉ *(Marivaux).* *Plus de la moitié du travail était* TERMINÉE *(H. Troyat).* *La moitié du village est* BRÛLÉ(E). *Le quart de la récolte fut* PERDU(E).

(b) **Le peu** + [the little +] complement. Agreement of the past participle is called for by *le peu* if this expression dominates the thought: otherwise, agreement is called for by the complement: *Le peu de confiance que vous m'avez* TÉMOIGNÉ *m'a ôté le courage* (Littré). *Ses doigts perdaient le peu d'assurance qu'ils auraient* EU (J. Romains). *Le peu de confiance que vous m'avez* TÉMOIGNÉE *m'a rendu le courage* (Littré).

953 PAST PARTICIPLE and an adverb of quantity.

Agreement with the complement: *Que de craintes nous avons* EUES! *Autant de batailles il a* LIVRÉES, *autant de victoires il a* REMPORTÉES. *Jamais tant de vaisselle ne fut* CASSÉE (J. Cocteau). *Trop de haine lui fut* TÉMOIGNÉE.

At times, the adverb of quantity dominates the thought and calls for agreement: *Un peu d'animation était* REVENU *au village* (R. Martin du Gard). *Trop de patience serait* REGARDÉ *comme une faiblesse. Moins d'application aurait été* BLÂMÉ.

954 PAST PARTICIPLE and antecedents joined by a conjunction of comparison.

A distinction must be made between the following:

(a) The idea of "in addition to": *C'est ma tante ainsi que mon oncle que j'ai* INVITÉS. *C'est l'un comme l'autre que j'ai* FÉLICITÉS.

(b) The idea of disjunction ["separated" or "not joined"]: The first antecedent calls for agreement: *C'est sa vertu, autant que son devoir, que nous avons* ADMIRÉE.

955 PAST PARTICIPLE and antecedents joined by *ou* / *ni*.

Note the following distinction:

(a) The idea of "in addition to": *La peur ou la misère, que les moralistes ont* CONSIDÉRÉES *comme restreignant notre liberté, ont fait commettre bien des fautes. Ce n'est ni l'or ni la grandeur que cet homme a* RECHERCHÉS.

(b) The idea of disjunction ["separated" or "not joined"]: Agreement is called for by the second antecedent: *C'est son salut ou sa perte qu'il a* RISQUÉE. *Est-ce une louange ou un blâme qu'il a* MÉRITÉ?

Ce n'est ni Pierre ni Paul qu'on a NOMMÉ *colonel de ce régiment.   Ce n'est ni un abricot ni une pêche que j'ai* MANGÉE.

956 PAST PARTICIPLE in relation to *un des, une des, un de, une de.*
A distinction must be made according to meaning or intention:
(a) Agreement is called for by the plural antecedent: *Un des premiers plaisirs que j'aie* GOÛTÉS *était de lutter contre les orages* (Chateaubraind). *Voici un des plus beaux romans que j'aie* LUS *depuis longtemps* (E. Jaloux). *C'est une des plus belles actions qu'il ait* FAITES (Littré). *Voici un de ceux que vous avez* SAUVÉS.
(b) Agreement is called for by the singular noun which is in the thought: *Johnny se souvenait particulièrement d'une de ces images qu'il avait* VUE *dans le livre de messe d'une petite fille* (V. Larbaud). *On transporta le blessé chez un de ses amis, qu'on avait* INFORMÉ *en toute hâte de l'accident. J'appris à connaître ma tante qui était certainement une des meilleures femmes que la terre ait* PORTÉE (J. Green).

957 PAST PARTICIPLE + infinitive.
(a) There is agreement if the direct object pronoun refers to the past participle: *Les violonistes que j'ai* ENTENDUS *jouer* [*j'ai entendu qui?*—QUE, that is to say, *les violonistes, qui jouaient*]. *Les marins que j'ai* VUS *partir. Des hommes que l'on avait. . .*ENVOYÉS *combattre* (J. Dutourd). *Ces douleurs, je les ai* SENTIES *monter jusqu'à l'épaule.*
(b) The past participle is invariable if the direct object pronoun which precedes refers to the infinitive: *Les airs que j'ai* ENTENDU *jouer* [*j'ai entendu quoi?*—JOUER QUE, that is to say, *jouer les airs*]. *Les marins que j'ai* VU *décorer. Les hommes que j'ai* ENVOYÉ *chercher. Une société qu'il avait* ESPÉRÉ *réformer* (A. Maurois). *La matière. . . que j'ai* CHERCHÉ *à pétrir* (M. Barrès).
   Practical ways to figure this out: (1) Insert the pronoun (or the noun that is replaced) between the past participle and the infinitive, then reverse the infinitive either by the present participle, or by a relative clause in the imperfect tense, or by the expression *en train de* [in the process of]. If the sentence keeps its meaning, make the agreement: *Les marins que j'ai* VUS *partir: J'ai vu les marins partant / . . .qui partaient / . . .en train de partir.*
(2) If the infinitive allows after it an agent serving as a complement introduced by *par*, then the past participle is invariable: *Les marins que j'ai vu décorer* [*par le préfet*].
(3) If the preceding direct object pronoun performs the action indicated by the infinitive, make the agreement.

958 (1) **Fait,** immediately followed by an infinitive, is always invariable: *Je les ai* FAIT *chercher partout* (Ac.). *Cette femme s'est*
FAIT *peindre* (Id.).

(2) When **laissé** is followed immediately by an infinitive, agreement is often made when the direct object refers to the participle: *On les a toutes* LAISSÉES *aller* (Ac.).

But you can, along with Littré, regard the rule as not absolute; if there is reason, when you wish, you may see a Gallicism
in the locution, in which case *laissé* remains invariable: *Reprenez
la cognée où nous l'avons* LAISSÉ *tomber* (R. Rolland). *On les a*
LAISSÉ *entrer* (J. Cocteau).

(3) **Participles indicating opinion** + infinitive. These participles
(**dit, affirmé, cru, pensé,** etc.) do not take agreement: *Ces
lettres que vous m'avez* DIT *être de madame d'Ange* (A. Dumas,
fils). *Des sublimités qu'on a* RECONNU *être des fautes de copiste*
(A. France).

(4) **Eu, donné, laissé** + à + infinitive. In certain cases, the
meaning imposes no agreement (when the past participle is related to the infinitive): *Les volcans que j'ai* EU *à nommer. La comète
qu'on m'a* DONNÉ *à décrire. La somme que vous m'avez* LAISSÉ *à
chercher.*

But in a general way, authors freely opt for either agreement
or no agreement: *Tous les blessés que j'avais* EUS *à traiter* (G. Duhamel). *La leçon que je lui ai* DONNÉE *à étudier* (A.). *Dans les
pages que j'avais innocemment* DONNÉ *à lire* (J. Roy). *Les problèmes qu'il
nous a* LAISSÉS *à résoudre* (A. Salacrou). *La seule turpitude que les doc-
trinaires et les républicains lui eussent* LAISSÉ *à désirer* (L. Bloy).

959 PAST PARTICIPLE preceded by *en.*

The simplest and most practical rule is not to make an
agreement on the past participle when it is preceded by the
pronoun *en,* neuter and partitive, whether or not this pronoun is related to an adverb of quantity (*beaucoup, combien, tant,
trop, plus,* etc.): *Voyez ces fleurs, en avez-vous* CUEILLI? (Littré). *Ses imprudences à lui, s'il en a* COMMIS, *furent élevées*
(H. Bremond). *J'en ai tant* VU, *des rois!* (Hugo). *Tu m'as dit
que les romans te choquent; j'en ai beaucoup* LU (Musset).

But usage is very indecisive and authors often make an
agreement: *Conquérir autant de royaumes que j'en ai* PERDUS
(A. France). *Les fleurs, il n'en avait jamais* VUES (M. Proust). *Ma
mère? mais jusqu'alors je n'en avais point* EUE (M. Arland).

960 PAST PARTICIPLE of reflexive verbs.

Preliminary remark: In order to find the direct object of reflexive or reciprocal verbs, substitute the auxiliary **avoir** in place of the auxiliary **être**. Examples: *Elle* S'EST COUPÉE *au doigt* (*Elle a coupé qui?*—SE, that is to say, *elle-même;* the direct object *precedes* the past participle and, therefore, the past participle agrees with it). *Elle s'est coupé les ongles* (*Elle a coupé quoi?*—LES ONGLES; the direct object *follows* the past participle and, therefore, the past participle does not agree with it).

961 (a) **Reflexive or Reciprocal.** Agreement with the direct object if it precedes: *Elles se sont* BLESSÉES [= *elles ont blessé* SE, that is to say, *elles-mêmes* (themselves)]. *Pierre et Paul se sont* BATTUS, *puis se sont* RÉCONCILIÉS [= *ils ont battu* SE, *ont réconcilié* SE, that is to say, *eux-mêmes* (themselves)]. *Les peines qu'il s'est* IMPOSÉES [= *il a imposé* QUE, that is to say, *les peines* (the pains, hardships)]. *Ils se sont* IMAGINÉ *qu'on les persécutait* [= *ils ont imaginé quoi?*—*qu'on les persécutait* (That they were being persecuted)]. *Les choses qu'ils se sont* IMAGINÉES [= *ils ont imaginé quoi?*—QUE, that is to say, *les choses* (the things)].

962 (1) Past participle of a reflexive verb + infinitive [see also entry no. 958 (2)]: *Elle s'était* LAISSÉE *mourir* (A. Bellessort). *Elle s'était* LAISSÉ *murer dans ce tombeau* (P. Loti). *Elle ne s'est pas* SENTIE *mourir* (M. Arland). *Elle s'est* SENTI *piquer au cou.*

(2) The past participle of the following verbs takes no agreement. However, for *se plaire, se déplaire, se complaire,* see entry no. 963, par. 3.

se convenir	*se déplaire (déplaire à soi)*	*se sourire*
se nuire	*se complaire*	*se succéder*
s'entre-nuire	*se mentir*	*se suffire*
se parler (parler à soi)	*se ressembler*	*se survivre*
se plaire (plaire à soi)	*se rire*	*s'en vouloir*

Examples: *Ils se sont* NUI; *ils se sont* PLU *l'un à l'autre; elles se sont* RI *de ces difficultés; les rois qui se sont* SUCCÉDÉ; *ils s'en seraient* VOULU.

(3) With *se persuader que,* agreement of the past participle is optional: *Ils se sont* PERSUADÉ(S) *que l'occasion était bonne* [= *ils ont persuadé* EUX *que . . .* / or: *ils ont persuadé* À EUX *que . . .*].

(4) Participle of a reflexive verb + the attribute of a reflexive pronoun: Agreement is generally made with the reflexive pronoun: *Cosette s'était toujours* CRUE *laide* (Hugo). *Elle s'était* RENDUE *intéressante* (J.-J. Gautier).

(5) Hanse, Thomas, Robert, and *Grand Larousse de la Langue française* claim that, for *se faire l'écho de,* the past participle *fait*

does not take agreement. But it is not understood why it would not take agreement [See entry no. 950(a)]: *Les Goncourt se sont* FAITS *l'écho de certaines de ses confidences* (A. Billy).

963 (b) Reflexive verbs whose reflexive pronoun is neither a direct object nor an indirect object: Agreement is made with the subject: *Elles se sont* APERÇUES *de leur erreur.   Ils se sont* DOUTÉS *de la chose.   Elles s'y sont* PRISES *adroitement.   Elles se sont* TUES.

There are four exceptions where the past participle does not take agreement: *se rire, se plaire* [= *se trouver bien*), *se déplaire* [= *ne pas se trouver bien*), *se complaire* [= *se délecter en soi*): *Elles se sont* RI *de ces projets.   Elles se sont* PLU, DÉPLU *dans ce lieu.   Les travaux où elles se sont* COMPLU.

It is not rare, however, to find authors who make an agreement on the past participle of *se plaire, se déplaire, se complaire: Elle s'était* PLUE *à éveiller l'amour* (A. Maurois).   *Presque jamais les hommes ne s'étaient* COMPLUS *à un aspect aussie barbare . . .* (Aragon).

964 (c) Passive reflexive verbs. Agreement is made with the subject: *La bataille s'est* LIVRÉE *ici.   La langue latine s'est* PARLÉE *en Gaule.*

965 It is sometimes difficult to determine whether the reflexive pronoun influences the agreement on the past participle. The past participle of each of the reflexive verbs in the following list always takes an agreement. Subsidiarily, it can be observed that, with the exception of *s'arroger*, the past participles of verbs that are only in the form of reflexive verbs always agree.

s'absenter	*se blottir*	*s'échapper*
s'abstenir	*se cabrer*	*s'écouler*
s'acharner	*se carrer*	*s'écrier*
s'acheminer	*se chamailler*	*s'écrouler*
s'adonner	*se connaître à*	*s'efforcer*
s'affaiblir	*se dédire*	*s'embusquer*
s'agenouiller	*se démener*	*s'emparer de*
s'apercevoir de	*se départir de*	*s'empresser*
s'approcher	*se désister*	*s'en aller*
s'arrêter	*se disputer (avec)*	*s'endormir*
s'attacher à	*se donner de garde*	*s'enfuir*
s'attaquer à	*se douter de*	*s'ennuyer*
s'attendre	*s'ébahir*	*s'enorgueillir*
s'avancer	*s'ébattre*	*s'enquérir*
s'aviser de	*s'ébouler*	*s'en retourner*

s'en revenir	*s'ingénier*	*se prosterner*
s'ensuivre	*s'ingérer*	*se railler de*
s'entendre à	*s'insurger*	*se ratatiner*
s'envoler	*s'invétérer*	*se raviser*
s'éprendre de	*se jouer de*	*se rebeller*
s'escrimer	*se lamenter*	*se rebiffer*
s'étonner	*se lever*	*se recroqueviller*
s'évader	*se louer de*	*se rédimer*
s'évaltonner	*se mécompter*	*se réfugier*
s'évanouir	*se méfier de*	*se réjouir*
s'évaporer	*se méprendre*	*se rengorger*
s'éveiller	*se moquer*	*se repentir*
s'éverteur	*s'opiniâtrer*	*se résoudre à*
s'extasier	*s'oublier*	*se ressentir de*
se fâcher	*se pâmer*	*se saisir de*
se féliciter	*se parjurer*	*se sauver*
se formaliser	*se plaindre*	*se servir de*
se gausser de	*se prélasser*	*se soucier de*
se gendarmer	*se prendre à*	*se souvenir de*
se hâter	*s'y prendre*	*se suicider*
s'immiscer	*se presser*	*se taire*
s'infatuer	*se prévaloir de*	*se targuer*
s'infiltrer	*se promener*	*se tromper, etc.*

966 **Practical rule,** according to Brunot in his *La Pensée et la Langue,*
p. 355; Every reflexive verb conjugated with *être* has an agreement on the past participle with its subject: *Elles se sont* LAVÉES;
les récoltes se sont VENDUES; *elles se sont* COMBATTUES; *elles se sont*
ÉVANOUIES.

Exception: If the reflexive pronoun *se* does not function as a
direct object and if the verb can be converted by the past participle and used with *avoir,* then apply the rule of past participles
with *avoir: La tâche qu'elles se sont* IMPOSÉE, i.e., [= *qu'elles* ONT
IMPOSÉ *à elles*]; *elles se sont* CROISÉ *les bras* [= ONT CROISÉ *les bras à
elles*].

VI. AGREEMENT OF THE VERB

Basic Rules

967 (1) Agreement in number [singular or plural] and person [1st,
2nd, or 3rd] with the subject, whether expressed or implied.

(2) Several subjects: the verb is in the plural.

(3) Subjects of different persons: the 1st person has priority over the other two; the 2nd person has priority over the 3rd: *Pierre, et toi, et moi* TRAVAILLONS. *Pierre et toi* TRAVAILLEZ.

One Subject

968 THE SUBJECT AS A COLLECTIVE NOUN + its comple-ment.

Agreement is made with the collective noun if the persons or objects are considered as a unit in their totality: *Une multi-tude de sauterelles* A *infesté ces campagnes* (Littré). *La foule des vivants* RIT *et* SUIT *sa folie* (Hugo).

Agreement is made with the complement of the collective noun if the persons or objects are considered in detail in their plurality: *Une multitude de sauterelles* ONT *infesté ces campagnes* (Littré). *Quand une bande d'étourneaux* APERÇOIVENT *un geai. . .* (Chateaubriand).

969 (1) **La plupart** + a complement in the 3rd person: Agreement is made with the complement. If the complement is implied or understood, it is presumed to be in the plural: *La plupart des gens ne* FONT *réflexion sur rien* (Ac.). *La plupart du monde* PRÉTEND . . . (Id.). *La plupart* SONT *persuadés que le bonheur est dans la richesse* (Id.).

(2) **Moitié, tiers, douzaine,** etc.: Agreement is made with the quantitative term if that is what you wish to emphasize; if not, agreement is made with the complement: *La moitié des députés* A *voté pour, et l'autre moitié contre le projet de loi* (Littré). *Une quin-zaine de francs* SUFFIRA or *suffiront.* *La moitié des caves de la section n'*ONT *pas encore été fouillées* (A. France). *Pendant un an, une douzaine de bonnes se* SUCCÉDÈRENT (J. Chardonne).

(3) **Le reste de, ce qui reste de, ce qu'il y a de,** etc. + plural noun: The verb is in the singular or the plural, according to the idea: *Le reste des naufragés* A *péri* or: ONT *péri* (Littré). *Il y a de ces années de désertion où tout ce qu'on a d'amis* DISPARAÎT (Mus-set). *Ce qui restait d'élèves* BATTAIENT *la semelle dans la cour agrandie* (M. Pagnol).

(4) **La plupart, beaucoup, certains,** etc. + *de nous, de vous, d'entre nous, d'entre vous:* The verb is in the 3rd person plural: *La plupart d'entre nous* ÉTAIENT *trouvés trop légers* (A. Cham-son). *La moitié d'entre nous* AVAIENT *l'air de chiens savants* (P. Gaxotte).

At times, however, the thought stops at the group desig-nated by *nous* or *vous;* the agreement, therefore, is made with one of these pronouns: *La plupart de nous n'étions que des enfants* (Cl. Farrère).   *Plusieurs d'entre vous* SEREZ *des chefs.*

(5) **Le peu** + complement: Agreement is made with *le peu* if this expression dominates the thought; if not, agreement is with the complement: *Le peu de qualités dont il a fait preuve l'*A *fait éconduire* (Ac.).   *Le peu de dents que j'avais* EST *parti* (Voltaire).   *Le peu de services qu'il a rendus* ONT *paru mériter une récompense* (Ac.).   *Le peu de cheveux qu'il avait* ÉTAIENT *gris* (Hugo).

970 ADVERB OF QUANTITY + **complement.** Agreement is with the complement; if the complement is not expressed, it is presumed to be in the plural: *Combien de gens* S'IMAGINENT *qu'ils ont de l'expérience par cela seul qu'ils ont vieilli!* (Littré.)   *Peu de paroles* SUFFISENT *au sage* (Id.).   *Peu* SAVENT *comme vous s'appliquer ce remède* (Corneille).

971 (1) After **plus d'un,** the verb is often written in the singular, but it is not rare to write it in the plural—and that is even a rule if *plus d'un* is repeated or if reciprocity is expressed: *Plus d'un se* RAPPELA *des matinées pareilles* (Flaubert).   *Plus d'une brebis galeuse s'*ÉTAIENT *glissées dans les rangs des apôtres bourgeois* (R. Rolland).   *Plus d'un se* SENTAIENT *las* (Fr. Mauriac).   *Plus d'une anguille, plus d'un barbeau, plus d'une truite* SUIVAIENT *le courant* (F. Fabre).   *Plus d'un fripon se* DUPENT *l'un l'autre.*

(2) After **moins de deux,** the verb is in the plural: *Moins de deux mois* ONT *suffi . . .* (M. Prévost).

(3) The adverb of quantity may be stressed with intensity; if so, agreement is made with it: *Beaucoup de cierges* VALAIT *mieux* (Flaubert).   *Tant de bravades* AVAIT *poussé l'homme à bout de résistance* (M. Garçon).

972 THE PRONOUN ce. When the verb **être** has *ce* as its subject, it is ordinarily written in the plural when the attribute is a plural noun or a pronoun in the 3rd person plural; the singular form of the verb is also used but more in familiar language than in literary usage: *Ce* SONT *de braves enfants* (Ac.).   *Ceux qui vivent, ce* SONT *ceux qui luttent* (Hugo).   *Ce* SONT *eux qui ont développé l'irrigation* (A. Siegfried).   However: *Ce n'*EST *pas des visages, c'*EST *des masques* (A. France).   *L'enfer, c'*EST *les Autres* (J.-P. Sartre).

973 (1) The expression *C'est eux* is very current and it prevails over *Ce sont eux* in negative or interrogative clauses: *C'*EST *eux qui pillent* (Ch. Péguy).   *Je crois que c'*EST *elles qui m'ont porté se-*

cours (Colette). C'EST *eux que je salue* (A. Camus). *Ce n'*EST *pas eux qui touchent les commissions* (P. Vialar). EST-*ce bien eux?*

(2) Always say: C'EST *nous; c'*EST *vous.*

(3) Say: *Ce* DOIT *être* or *ce* DOIVENT *être; ce* PEUT *être* or *ce* PEUVENT *être; ce ne* SAURAIT *être* or *ce ne* SAURAIENT *être,* when the attribute is a plural noun or a pronoun of the 3rd person plural.

(4) If the plural complement inserted in the Gallicism *c'est. . . que* is not an attribute of *ce* (and notably when it is introduced by a preposition), the verb of the Gallicism must remain in the singular: C'EST *pour eux que je travaille* (Littré). C'EST *des malades qu'ils prient que l'on ait pitié* (G. Duhamel). Be careful not to say, for example: *Ce sont sur ces gens-là qu'il faudrait se régler; ce sont d'eux qu'il faut parler, ce sont des aveugles que je veux parler.*

(5) With the subjects *ceci, cela, (tout) ce* + a relative clause, the verb **être** (when followed by a plural attribute) agrees as if the subject were *ce* and you may use the plural or the singular: *Ceci* SONT *plutôt des souhaits vagues* (J.-J. Rousseau). *Tout cela* SONT *des "peut-être"* (Stendhal). *Ce que vous dites là* SONT *tout autant de fables* (Littré). *Ceci* EST *des souhaits* (Littré). *Tout cela n'*ÉTAIT *que des cas particuliers* (Montesquieu).

In practice, people ordinarily insert *ce: Tout cela, ce sont des atouts dans votre jeu* (A. Maurois). *Ce que vous dites là, ce sont tout autant de fables.*

(6) The verb **être** (when it has the pronoun *ce* as its subject) remains in the singular in *si ce n'est* (= *excepté*), *fut-ce, fût-ce, ne fût-ce que;* the same is true in certain constructions where the plural would sound odd (for example: *furent-ce, eussent-ce été, c'eussent été): Si ce n'est eux, quels hommes eussent osé l'entreprendre?* (Littré). FUT-*ce mes soeurs qui le firent?* (Id.). *Les mauvais riches,* FÛT-*ce les pères, prennent une assurance sur l'avenir, en prodiguant les dons* (A. Suarès).

(7) When the attribute of *ce* is a plural numeral, the verb *être* is in the plural if the attribute is thought of as being a plurality; but in the singular if it is considered as expressing a whole, a total quantity: *Ce* FURENT *quatre jours bien longs* (Maupassant). *On me doit 10.000 francs, mais ce* SONT *10.000 francs fictifs* (J. Green). However: C'EST *onze heures qui sonnent* (Littré). C'EST *quarante francs jetés à l'eau* (P. Mille).

974   When the attribute of the subject *ce* consists of more than one noun of which the first at least is in the singular, the verb *être* can be singular or plural: C'EST *la gloire et les plaisirs qu'il a en vue* (Littré). *Ce* SONT *l'esprit et le coeur qui remportent les victoires* (Ch. de Gaulle).

But the plural is called for when the multiple attribute develops a plural or collective noun which precedes: *Il y a cinq parties du monde; ce* SONT: *l'Europe, l'Asie,* etc.

975 RELATIVE PRONOUN qui. A verb, whose subject is the relative pronoun *qui,* is in the same number [singular / plural] and in the same person [1st, 2nd, 3rd] as the antecedent: *C'est moi qui* SUIS; *c'est moi qui* IRAI. But be careful: use the 2nd person when the antecedent is a person to whom you are speaking directly: *Jeune homme qui m'*ÉCOUTES, *crois-moi.   Ah! maudit animal, qui n'*ES *bon qu'à noyer* (La Fontaine).   *Toi qui* SÈCHES *les pleurs des moindres graminées* (E. Rostand).   *Il est dommage. . .que ce ne soit pas moi qui* AIE *fait les deux rencontres* (J. Romains).

976 (1) When *qui* is preceded by an attribute referring to a personal pronoun of the 1st or 2nd persons, the attribute calls for an agreement:

    (a) If it is preceded by the definite article or if it contains a demonstrative idea: *Vous êtes l'élève qui* A *le mieux répondu. Nous sommes les jardiniers qui* ENTRETIENNENT *le parc.   Je suis celui qui* TIENT *le globe* (Hugo).

    (b) If the main clause is negative or interrogative: *Vous n'êtes pas un homme qui* AIME *la flatterie.   Êtes-vous un homme qui* SAIT *réfléchir?   Es-tu celui qui* PEUT *quelque chose pour son bonheur?* (M. Barrès).

(2) As for affirmative statements, usage varies when the attribute is preceded by the indefinite article or when it is or contains *le seul, le premier, le dernier, l'unique,* etc.: *Je suis un homme qui ne* SAIT *que planter des choux* (A. France).   *Je suis un paresseux qui ne me* PLAIS *qu'à dormir au soleil* (M. Aymé).   *Vous êtes le seul qui* CONNAISSE (or: *qui* CONNAISSIEZ) *ce sujet* (Littré).

    Usage is also indecisive when the attribute is *deux, dix,* etc., *beaucoup, plusieurs,* or when it is a proper noun without a determinative: *Nous sommes deux, plusieurs, quelques-uns qui vous* DÉFENDENT, or: *qui vous* DÉFENDONS. *Je suis Pierre, qui vous* A *écrit,* or: *qui vous* AI *écrit.*

(3) After *un des, une des, un de, une de,* the relative pronoun *qui* refers (according to the meaning) at times to the plural noun, at times to *un* or *une*—which can, in this case, be replaced by *celui, celle: Observons une des étoiles qui* SCINTILLENT *au firmament* [the action of twinkling (*scintiller*) refers to the plurality of the stars].   *Je vous enverrai un de mes ouvriers qui* FONT *ce genre de travail.   Un de ceux qui* LIAIENT *Jésus-Christ au poteau* (Hugo). *Vincent possédait une de ces montres qui se* REMONTENT *toutes seules*

(G. Duhamel). *Je suis allé remercier un des laboureurs qui nous* AVAIT *envoyé des roses* (Fr. Mauriac). *J'allais justement chez une de ces femmes, qui* HABITE *rue Pauquet* (J. Romains). *Je vous enverrai un de mes ouvriers, qui* FERA *la réparation.*

977 SENTENCES WITH ÊTRE + attribute.

In sentences like *Sa nourriture est* (or *sont?*) *des fruits,* normal usage is to have the verb agree with the term that precedes the verb **être**: *Le signal* ÉTAIT *deux fusées* (Voltaire). *Le lit ordinaire de M. de Pontchâteau* ÉTAIT *des fagots* (Sainte-Beuve).

An agreement that is nowadays archaic: *L'effet du commerce* SONT *les richesses* (Montesquieu). *Le reste* SONT *des horreurs* (M. Proust).

978 NUMERICAL EXPRESSION.

When a plural subject is a numerical expression, the verb is in the plural or singular, depending on—in the thought of the person who is speaking or writing—whether the subject is considered as a plurality of units or as a whole, that is, a single total unit: *Cinquante francs ne* SUFFISAIENT *pas pour acquitter sa dette* (Hugo). *Quatre heures* APPROCHAIENT (M. Arland). However: *Cinquante domestiques* EST *une étrange chose* (Sévigné). *Dix-huit ans n'*EST *pas encore l'âge ingrat des Allemands* (A. Hermant). *Seize cent mille francs de gain* ÉTAIT *encore une jolie somme* (Zola).

(1) A fractional expression as subject: The agreement of the verb is with the first element: *Trois heures et demie* VENAIENT *de sonner* (R. Martin du Gard). *Dix heures et quart* SONNÈRENT (J. Green). *Une pomme et demie me* SUFFIT (Littré).

(2) *Midi* and *minuit* call for the verb in the singular: *Midi* EST *sonné* (Littré). *Quand minuit* EUT *achevé de sonner* (A. Gide).

979 PERCENTAGE AS A SUBJECT.

When the subject is a percentage, for example, *vingt pour cent* [twenty percent] / *de la population,* the verb sometimes agrees with the first element of the subject—in which case it is considered as a plurality of hundredths; at other times, it agrees with the second element. Usage varies: *90% de notre production* PARTENT *pour l'étranger* (A. Maurois). *Un eugéniste a calculé que 10% de sang frais* DEVIENDRAIENT *nécessaires à chaque génération* (H. Bazin). However: *Vingt pour cent de la population s'*EST *abstenue* (A. Dauzat). *Le curé nous dit que dix pour cent de la population* ASSISTE *à la messe* (J. Green).

If the percentage is preceded by the article *les* or by a plural determinative, obviously the verb is in the plural: *Les 20%, ces 20% du bénéfice seront répartis de la façon suivante.*

980 PLURAL TITLE.

(a) When a title begins with an article (or a determinative) in the plural, or when it is preceded by an article (or a determinative) in the plural, the verb may be written in the plural or in the singular; usage varies: *Les "Variations"* SONT *le maître livre de Bossuet* (É. Faguet). *Les "Feuilles d'automne"* PARURENT *au lendemain de la Révolution de 1830* (A. Bellessort). *"Les Employés"* SONT *d'une langue excellente* (A. Gide). *"Les Fossiles" sont* (or *est*) *un chef-d'oeuvre* (Flaubert). *"Les Dieux ont soif"* EST *un livre d'une maîtrise absolue* (A. Thibaudet). *"Le Rouge et le Noir"* VAUT *pour tous les temps* (J. de Lacretelle).

(b) A title without an article (or a determinative) at the beginning—the verb is in the singular: *"Guerre et Paix"* EST *la plus vaste épopée de notre temps* (R. Rolland). *"Nuits de guerre"* SUIVIT *l'année d'après* (M. Genevoix).

981   Usage varies regarding agreement in gender with the adjective, the past participle, or the pronoun in sentences of this type: *"Athalie" est belle* (Sainte-Beuve). *La "Légende des siècles" ne doit être* PRISE *que pour un volet d'un triptyque* (A. Thibaudet). *"Volupté" est* ÉCRIT *dans l'ombre de Lamennais* (Id.). *Il ne s'arrête qu'à janvier 1919 avec "l'Atlantide" dont il parle pour* LA (*or* LE) *louer comme il faut* (F. Strowski).

More Than One Subject

982 A SINGLE CONCEPT.

When there is more than one subject, each in the singular and joined in a single concept, the verb is in the singular: *Quand le Prince des pasteurs et le Pontife éternel* APPARAÎTRA. . . (Bossuet). *Admirer la pensée de Proust et blâmer son style* SERAIT *absurde* (J. Cocteau).

983 SUBJECTS THAT ARE SYNONYMOUS OR EXPRESSED IN A GRADUAL PROCESS OR IN DEGREES.

In such a case, the verb agrees with the subject nearest to it: *Et un dégoût, une tristesse immense l'*ENVAHIT (Flaubert). *Brusquement une plaisanterie, un mot, un geste me* GLACE (M. Arland).

984 SUBJECTS SUMMED UP OR ANNOUNCED BY ONE WORD.
When there is more than one subject summed up or announced by one word, the verb agrees with the word that sums up or announces the various subjects: *Remords, crainte, périls, rien ne m'*A *retenue* (Racine). *Tout, trottoirs mouillés, chaussées fangeuses, plaques d'égout luisantes, rails resplendissants,* REFLÉTAIT *la couleur chaude du ciel* (E. Jaloux).

985 SUBJECTS JOINED BY ainsi que [as well as], **comme** [like, as], **avec** [with], etc.
(a) If the conjunction is copulative (= the idea of in addition to, linking), the verb agrees with the whole [subject]: *Le français ainsi que l'italien* DÉRIVENT *du latin* (Littré). *Aussi bien l'oncle Mathieu que tante Philomène n'*ÉTAIENT *pour moi que sons* (H. Bosco). *La voix non plus que la silhouette ne lui* ÉTAIENT *connues* (A. de Châteaubriant). *Le murmure des sources avec le hennissement des licornes se* MÊLENT *à leurs voix* (Flaubert). *L'une comme l'autre* GARDENT *peu de loisir disponible pour l'aventure* (M. Prévost). *Tant le sol boueux que l'eau m'*ÉTAIENT *présents* (H. Bosco).
(b) If the conjunction expresses clearly an idea of comparison, agreement is made with the first term of the comparison: *Le français, ainsi que l'italien,* DÉRIVE *du latin* (Littré). *Son visage, aussi bien que son coeur,* AVAIT *rajeuni de dix ans* (Musset). *Le manque d'air ici, autant que l'ennui,* FAIT *bâiller* (A. Gide). *L'un comme l'autre* EST *pris au jeu* (Id.). *La religion, comme la politique,* A *ses Brutus* (A. Hermant). *Renée, pas plus que Gilbert, n'*ÉTAIT *retournée chez les Guillaume* (M. Arland).
The same is true if the preposition *avec* serves to join the main subject: *Le travail avec ses servitudes lui* INSPIRA *de bonne heure un grand dégoût* (M. Garçon).

986 SUBJECTS JOINED BY moins que [less than], **plus que** [more than], etc.
In such a case, the verb agrees with the first subject: *La gloire, moins que les richesses toutefois,* SÉDUIRA *toujours les hommes. Votre honneur, plus que vos intérêts, vous* DÉFEND *d'agir ainsi. La bonté et non l'habileté* DOIT *être le principe de toute politique* (A. Maurois).

987 NON SEULEMENT [not only] . . . **MAIS** [but] . . .
In such a case, the verb ordinarily agrees with the closest subject: *Non seulement notre dignité à l'intérieur, mais notre prestige à l'étranger en* DÉPEND (J. Giraudoux).

At times, agreement is made with the whole [subject]: *Non seulement sa chambre ou sa cellule, mais sa table même* ÉTAIENT *toujours bien rangées* (Comte d'Haussonville, cited by Brunot).

988 TANTÔT. . . TANTÔT. . . [sometimes. . . sometimes. . .]; **PARFOIS. . . PARFOIS. . .** [at times. . . at times].

When there is more than one subject in the 3rd person singular, arranged in such a way as to express an alternative, agreement of the verb is:

(a) with the closest subject, if the idea of disjunction [separated, not connected] prevails: *Tantôt l'un, tantôt l'autre* PRENAIT *la parole* (H. Bosco). *Parfois la sottise, parfois la puissance de l'esprit* S'OBSTINE *contre le fait* (P. Valéry). *Soit le pape, soit Venise* MET-TRAIT *sans grande peine la main sur Rimini* (Montherlant).

(b) with the whole group [of subjects], if the idea of conjunction [connection] prevails: *Tantôt la peur, tantôt le besoin (parfois la peur, parfois le besoin; soit la peur, soit le besoin)* FONT *les mouvements de la souris. Soit l'Angleterre, soit la Hollande* FURENT *toujours assez fortes pour interdire aux Français l'accès d'Anvers* (Ph. Erlanger).

If one of the subjects is in the plural, the verb is in the plural. If the subjects are not all in the same person, the verb is in the plural, in the person that has priority.

989 SUBJECTS JOINED BY ou / ni.

When there is more than one subject in the 3rd person singular joined by **ou** [or] / **ni** [neither], agreement of the verb is:

(a) with the closest subject if the idea of disjunction prevails: *La douceur ou la violence en* VIENDRA *à bout* (Ac.). *Ni crainte ni respect ne m'en peut détacher* (Racine).

(b) with the whole group [of subjects] if the idea of conjunction [connection] prevails: *La peur ou la misère* ONT *fait commettre bien des fautes* (Ac.).

   (1) At times, the meaning separates the subjects: *Pierre ou Paul* SERA *colonel de ce régiment. Ni Pierre ni Paul ne* SERA *colonel de ce régiment. Le père, ou la mère plutôt, du petit Publius* VOULUT *que ce garçon étudiât* (É. Henriot).

   (2) If one of the subjects is in the plural, the verb is in the plural: *Les menaces ou la douceur en* VIENDRONT *à bout. Ni les menaces ni la douceur n'en* VIENDRONT *à bout.*

   (3) If the subjects joined by *ou / ni* are not in the same person, the verb is written in the plural and in the person which has priority: *Lui ou moi* FERONS *cela* (Littré). *Maître Gépier, ou toi, en* AURIEZ *entendu parler* (J. Romains).

990 TEL OU TEL [such and such], **NI L'UN NI L'AUTRE** [neither one nor the other].

With *tel ou tel, ni l'un ni l'autre* (used as pronouns or adjectives), the verb is in the singular or plural, depending on the idea which prevails (disjunction or conjunction): *Je sais bien que tel ou tel* EST *avare* (H. de Régnier).   *Telle ou telle innovation n'*ÉTAIT *pas repoussée* (Mérimée).   *Je. . .ne sais comment* ONT *réagi tel ou tel de mes exigeants confrères* (G. Marcel).

Ni l'un ni l'autre n'y EST *pour rien* (R. Rolland).   *Ni l'un ni l'autre escadron n'*ARRIVA (Michelet).   *Ni l'un ni l'autre n'*ONT *su ce qu'ils faisaient* (Vigny).   *Ni l'une ni l'autre solution ne* CONVIENNENT.

991   When the expression *ni l'un ni l'autre* is used in a conjunctive meaning, it sometimes happens that the verb is in the 1st person plural, in which case the meaning is *ni moi ni l'autre,* or in the 2nd person plural, in which case the meaning is *ni toi ni l'autre: Ni l'un ni l'autre n'*ÉTIONS *plus capables de piège* (J. Cocteau).   *Je vous plains tous deux; ni l'un ni l'autre ne* POURREZ *réussir.*

992 L'UN OU L'AUTRE, L'UNE OU L'AUTRE [one or the other].
Used as pronoun or adjective, these generally indicate a disjunction and call for the verb in the singular: *L'une ou l'autre* AVAIT-*elle un sentiment pour moi?* (M. Proust.)   *L'un ou l'autre projet* SUPPOSE *de la fatuité* (M. Prévost).

At times, the meaning is conjunctive and the verb is written in the plural: *L'un ou l'autre* MANQUENT *forcément dans toutes les anthologies que nous connaissons* (A. Thérive).

993 L'UN ET L'AUTRE, L'UNE ET L'AUTRE [one and the other].
Used as pronoun or adjective, most often these indicate an idea of "in addition to" and the verb is written in the plural; this is required if the sentence implies an idea of joining, resemblance, or comparison. . .: *L'un et l'autre me* SEMBLAIENT *identiques* (J. Romains).   *L'un et l'autre sont venus* (Ac.).   *L'une et l'autre affaire se* TIENNENT (É. Henriot).   *L'un et l'autre seuil lui* ÉTAIENT *fermés* (H. Bosco).

If the meaning is disjunctive, the verb is in the singular: *L'un et l'autre* APPROCHA (La Fontaine).   *L'une et l'autre saison* EST *favorable* (Ac.).   *L'un et l'autre y* A *manqué* (Id.).

994   It goes without saying that if the noun is in the plural [see entry no. 697 (2)], the verb also is in the plural: *Il semble que l'un et l'autre documents* AIENT *été débattus* (P. de La Gorce).

995 REPETITION OF **CHAQUE, TOUT, NUL, PAS UN, AUCUN.**
Agreement of the verb is made with the closest subject or with
the whole group: *Chaque canonnier, chaque soldat, chaque officier*
s'ATTELAIT, TIRAIT, ROULAIT, POUSSAIT *les redoutables chariots*
(Vigny). *Chaque personne, chaque milieu* ONT *leur manière de voir*
(M. Arland). *Nul écrivain, nul artiste . . . ne me* DÉMENTIRA
(M. Barrès). *Nul chemin de fer, nulle usine, ne* SONT *venues dissiper
la lourde mélancolie de ce canton* (Fr. Jammes).

996 (1) This rule applies even when the subjects are coordinate:
Chaque homme et chaque femme AVAIT or AVAIENT *un bouquet*
(Littré).
(2) In sentences like the following, it is preferable to write the
verb in the singular: *Rien de grand, rien de noble ne l'*ÉMEUT.
Tout ce qui chante, tout ce qui fleurit au printemps me PLAÎT. *Ceci
et cela me* PLAÎT.

997 N'ÉTAIT, N'EÛT ÉTÉ. Most often, agreement is made according to number [singular or plural]: N'ÉTAIENT [Were it not for
. . .] *les lampadaires électriques qui étoilent le Jardin, cette nuit serait
très sombre* (Cl. Farrère). N'EUSSENT *été* [Had it not been for. . .]
les fumées des toits, le village eût semblé désert (J. et J. Tharaud).
No agreement: *Tu n'entendrais même rien du tout, n'*ÉTAIT [if it
weren't for] *les briques des faîtes* (G. Bernanos).

998 PEU IMPORTE [little does it matter. . .], **QU'IMPORTE?** [what
does it matter. . .?]   Agreement or no agreement of the verb:
Peu IMPORTENT *les mobiles* (M. Barrès).   *Peu* IMPORTE *les noms* (Vercors).   *Qu'*IMPORTENT *ces folies?* (Musset.)   *Qu'*IMPORTE *ces pierres
de taille?* (Ch. Péguy).

999 RESTE [remaining, what there remains, what there is left]. When
this verb is at the beginning of a clause, the verb may agree or
not agree: RESTENT *les bijoux* (A. Chamson).   RESTAIT *ces gens de
Poitiers* (J. de Lacretelle).

1000 SOIT [let us suppose]. Agreement or no agreement: SOIENT *deux
grandeurs égales* (Taine).   SOIT *quatre catégories* (H. Bremond).

1001 TEL ET TEL [such and such]. With *tel et tel* (used as pronoun or
adjective), the verb is in the plural, at times in the singular: *Tel et
tel se* SERONT *révélés* (É. Henriot). *Les chiffres des recettes
qu'*AVAIENT *faites telle et telle pièce* (R. Rolland). *Tel et tel* IRONISE
parfois (R. Kemp).

1002 VIVE [long live. . .!]. In exclamations, *vive* ordinarily agrees with the subject or subjects (3rd person) placed after it: VIVENT *les gens d'esprit!* (Hugo.)   VIVENT *les patriotes!* (Renan.)   VIVENT *la Champagne et la Bourgogne pour les bons vins!* (Ac.)

But *vive* is often considered to be an interjection and it remains invariable: VIVE *les gens d'esprit!* (Littré.)   VIVE *les nouilles, malgré tout!* (R. Martin du Gard.)

CHAPTER 6

ADVERBS

1003 AINSI [thus, so, in this way, like that]. The old expression used to be *par ainsi*. Vaugelas [1585–1650] already noted, during his time, that this locution *(par ainsi)* was hardly ever used. It is at times found in modern literature: *Vous vous êtes égalés* PAR AINSI *aux hommes les plus grands* (J. Romains). *Ils entendaient,* PAR AINSI, *sauvegarder leur liberté* (G. Duhamel). *Je mettais des semelles d'amiante dans mes souliers, qui* PAR AINSI *devenaient trop étroits* (Colette).

1004 ALENTOUR [around, round about]. When this adverb is not preceded by the preposition *de*, it is at times written as *à l'entour*, but this spelling is archaic: *Ces ombrages* À L'ENTOUR *sont pleins d'ombres* (É. Henriot).

Instead of saying *autour de* [around], people sometimes say *à l'entour de*, which is an old expression: *Oh! mets tes bras* À L'ENTOUR DE *mon cou!* (Hugo).

1005 -AMMENT, -EMMENT. The ending *-amment* and the ending *-emment* are used on adverbs which come from their adjective forms ending in *-ant* or *-ent: vaillant*, an adjective, becomes *vaill*AMMENT, an adverb; *prudent*, an adjective, becomes *prud*-EMMENT, an adverb.

Exceptions: *lentement, présentement, véhémentement.*

1006 ASSEZ BIEN [fairly well]. This locution indicates the manner in which something is done; *assez* expresses an attenuation, for example, compare: *très bien, fort bien, moins bien. . .: Cela est* ASSEZ BIEN (Ac.). *Ce comédien joue* ASSEZ BIEN.

Do not use *assez bien* or *assez bien de* to indicate quantity or number. For example, do not say: *Il y a assez bien de fautes dans ce devoir. Il y avait assez bien de monde au spectacle.* And do not say: *Il a assez bien neigé.* In such sentences, use just the simple word *assez* or, somewhat familiarly, you may use: *pas mal, pas mal de* [see entry no. 1044].

Placement of *assez:* Parallel to the expression *Il a assez d'argent,* usage allows *Il a de l'argent assez: Il avait du stock assez pour tenir jusqu'à octobre* (Aragon).

1007 AUSSI, SI [such (a), so, as]; **AUTANT, TANT** [so, so much, as].
(1) *Si* may be used for *aussi* and *tant* may be used for *autant* in negative or interrogative sentences: *Nulle part, Monsieur, je n'ai trouvé* SI *bon accueil qu'à Paris* (Taine). *Il n'est pas* SI *riche que vous* (Ac.). *Est-il* SI *pauvre que vous le dites? Rien ne m'a* TANT *fâché que cette nouvelle* (Ac.).
(2) In front of passive participles: If the participle has a true verbal value, regular use is made of *tant* or *autant,* but *si* is not rare in modern usage: *Cette femme* TANT *aimée. . .* (Ac.). *Cette femme* SI *aimée. . .* (M. Proust). *La gravité ardente, d'ailleurs* SI *admirée par elle, de Shelley* (A. Maurois).

If the participle has the value of an adjective, *si* or *aussi* may be used: *Un homme* SI *éclairé,* SI *rangé* (Littré). *La fête n'est pas* SI *animée* (or: *aussi animée*) *qu'on l'espérait.*
(3) To express the idea of "also, likewise": In affirmative sentences, like the following: *Vous le voulez, et moi* AUSSI (Ac.). Negative sentences: *Vous ne le voulez pas, ni moi* NON PLUS (Littré).

With *ne. . . que* [only]: *Il lit incessamment, je ne fais* NON PLUS *que lire,* or: *je ne fais* AUSSI *que lire* (Littré).

Note the use of *aussi* in sentences where the thought stops on the identity of the situation, on a positive fact: *Moi* AUSSI, *Aline, je n'ai plus rien* (Fr. Mauriac).
(4) *Tant* is used to express a quantity that a person does not want or cannot be precise about: *Dans ce journal, on paie* TANT *la ligne* (Ac.).

An error frequently heard in Belgium: The use of *autant,* in this meaning, for *tant: Cet ouvrier gagne autant par jour. Les frais montent à autant.* You must say: *. . .gagne* TANT *par jour;. . . montent à* TANT.

1008 AUTREMENT [more, far more]. Instead of saying *Il ira plus loin,* or *Il ira beaucoup plus loin,* or *Il fera bien mieux,* you may add an effective nuance to the statement by saying: *Il ira* AUTREMENT *loin, Il ira* AUTREMENT *plus loin, Il fera* AUTREMENT *mieux. Je suis bien sûr que ton mari s'y entendait* AUTREMENT *mieux que moi* (J. Kessel).

1009 BEAUCOUP [much, a great deal]. People say: *Il est* BEAUCOUP *plus savant.* Or: *Il est* DE BEAUCOUP *plus savant.* Or: *Il est plus savant* DE BEAUCOUP. *Il est le plus riche* DE BEAUCOUP. Or: *Il est* DE BEAUCOUP *le plus riche.*

1010 BIEN (merci~) [thank you very much]. In order to reinforce the word *merci,* which is a term of politeness used to thank someone, people say: *grand merci* (popular during the classical period), or: *merci bien,* or: *merci beaucoup,* or: *merci mille fois,* or: *mille mercis.*

1011   Do not say: *Tu n'aimes pas cela? Moi,* BIEN. And do not say: *Je ne sortirai pas aujourd'hui; demain,* BIEN. Say: . . .*moi* OUI (at times, OUI BIEN), or: . . .*moi* SI: *Je ne crois pas.* . .*que notre grand'mère ait été très malheureuse; notre mère,* OUI (A. Maurois). *Tu n'y pense jamais? Moi,* SI (Daniel Rops).

1012 BIEN VOULOIR; VOULOIR BIEN + inf.
    Some people maintain that **vouloir bien** is more of an imperative and is suitable between persons whose relationship is that of superior rank to lower rank; they also maintain that **bien vouloir** is used between persons whose relationship is that of lower rank to superior rank. In the language of authors, either construction is used freely: *Je vous supplie instamment de* VOULOIR BIEN *m'instruire si j'ai parlé de la religion comme il convient* (Voltaire). *Je vous prie, Monsieur l'Intendant général, de* VOULOIR BIEN *me donner vos ordres* (Stendhal). *Je vous prie de* BIEN VOULOIR *sortir* (Fr. Mauriac). *Je vous prie de* BIEN VOULOIR *cesser les leçons que vous donniez à mon fils* (P. Guth).

1013 CE QUE [how. . .!]. This is used as an adverb of intensity or quantity, especially in exclamatory sentences: CE QUE *tu peux être mauvaise!* (Fr. Mauriac.) *C'est inouï* CE QU'*un mot peut vite devenir une image!* (A. Chamson.)
    Popular construction: QU'EST-CE QU'*on peut ne se connaître guère!* (G. Conchon.)

1014 COMBIEN. [This adverb ordinarily means "how much" or "how many," but it has special meanings, as in the following examples] . . .
    When speaking of the day of the month, in everyday language people say: *Le combien est-ce? Nous sommes le combien?* But in correct, careful French, people say: *Quel jour du mois avons-nous? Quel jour est-ce aujourd'hui?* (Ac.). *Quel jour sommes-nous?* (G. Duha-

mel.) *À quel jour du mois sommes-nous?* (Hugo.) *Quelle date avons-nous aujourd'hui?* (St. Passeur.)

1015 (1) The following expressions are little used or outdated: *Quel est le quantième?* (Littré.) *Quel quantième du mois avons-nous? (Dictionnaire général.) Quel jour est-il aujourd'hui?* (Ac.) *Le quantième est-ce?* (Martinon.)

(2) *Combientième, combienième,* and *tous les combien* belong to popular or very familiar language: *C'est la* COMBIENTIÈME (or: COMBIENIÈME) *fois que je le dis? Tu changes de chemise* TOUS LES COMBIEN?

1016 DAVANTAGE [more]. This adverb cannot modify an adverb. Do not say: *Marchons davantage lentement.* Say: *Marchons plus lentement.*

It is rarely used with an adjective: *Il dut faire un effort pour n'être pas* DAVANTAGE *odieux* (Montherlant).

Davantage + de + a noun (which is a classical construction) is still frequent in literary language: *Ils n'en récoltèrent pas* DAVANTAGE DE *gratitude* (J. Cocteau). *Il eut des admirateurs, il compta* DAVANTAGE DE *détracteurs* (J. Chastenet).

Davantage que, which was used during the classical period, has regained great favor in contemporary literary usage: *Elle causait peut-être* DAVANTAGE QUE *les deux autres* (P. Loti). *Ce manque d'égards la blessait* DAVANTAGE QU'*une trahison* (H. Troyat).

Davantage is at times used in the meaning of "the most," which is a survival from classical usage: *Je ne sais de sa leçon ce qui me transporte* DAVANTAGE—*cette loi des oppositions ou le choix même des sujets* (Aragon).

1017 DEBOUT [standing] is always invariable: *Ils restent* DEBOUT. It can be used as an adjective: *Dans la position* DEBOUT. *Dix places* DEBOUT.

1018 DE SUITE [in succession] / **TOUT DE SUITE** [immediately, at once]. The traditional meaning of these two adverbial expressions, according to the Academy, is as follows: *de suite* means "without interruption," "one after the other": *La Russie a été gouvernée par cinq femmes* DE SUITE (Voltaire). *Faites-les marcher* DE SUITE (Ac.). *Tout de suite* means "without delay, at once": *Envoyez-moi de l'argent* TOUT DE SUITE (Littré).

This distinction is purely conventional. It does not prevent some authors from frequently using, in their literature, *de suite* in the meaning of "at once": *On ne comprend pas* DE SUITE *un mot semblable* (P. Loti). *Allez* DE SUITE *vous restaurer* (A. Gide).

1019 ENTRE-TEMPS [meanwhile]. According to the Academy, this adverb is written with a hyphen. At times, you will find some authors who write it as: *entre temps* or *entretemps*. This word is a modification of the old form *entretant* or *entre tant*, which some authors have attempted to revive: *Après avoir*, ENTRE TANT, *publié les Mémoires d'un touriste* (É. Henriot). ENTRETANT, *nous continuions à nous occuper de notre plaquette* (Fr. de Miomandre).

1020 EXCESSIVEMENT [excessively]. Strictly speaking, this adverb means "in an excessive manner, in an excessive way," "to an inordinate degree:" *Il est* EXCESSIVEMENT *gros* (Ac.). *Boire* EXCESSIVEMENT (Id.).

But in ordinary usage—even literary—it is not rare to find *excessivement* used in the meaning of "very, extremely," without any unfavorable nuance: *Le cardinal Fesch. . ., toujours* EXCESSIVEMENT *pieux* (Stendhal). *Le talent chez les pornographes est* EXCESSIVEMENT *rare* (R. Kemp).

1021 EXPRÈS [expressly, on purpose]. Its reinforced forms are: *tout exprès, expressément. Exprès* means "with formal intention": *Laissez tomber* EXPRÈS *des épis* (Hugo). *Il est venu* TOUT EXPRÈS *pour me voir* (Ac.).

Archaism: *Le disciple direct de Flaubert, Maupassant, a décrit* PAR EXPRÈS *un monde grossier et bas* (A. Thérive).

1022 INCESSAMMENT. This adverb is outdated in the meaning of "continually": *Il travaille* INCESSAMMENT (Ac.). In ordinary usage, it means "without delay, very soon": *Il doit arriver* INCESSAMMENT (Ac.).

1023 LÀ CONTRE or **LÀ-CONTRE** [**contre cela:** against that]. This adverbial locution is not accepted by the Academy; however, it is in use: *On ne peut pas aller* LÀ CONTRE (Molière). *Aucune illusion ne tient* LÀ CONTRE (G. Bernanos). *Tout son être se soulevait* LÀ-CONTRE (M. Genevoix).

1024 MOINS (de~; en~) [less]. *De moins* and *en moins* express the idea of lack, need, or diminution: *Il y a dans ce sac dix francs* DE MOINS [i.e., ten francs are lacking, are needed] (Littré). *Il avait un billet* DE MOINS *dans son portefeuille* (Ac.). *J'ai reçu* EN MOINS *trois francs* (Littré). *Beau profit, une jambe* EN MOINS! (É. Henriot).

1025 (1) Do not say: *Il y a dix francs trop peu* (or: *de trop peu*).
(2) A somewhat outdated construction: *J'ai trouvé cent francs* DE

MANQUE *dans ce sac d'écus* (Bescherelle).   *Un grain chromosomique de trop ou* DE MANQUE (J. Rostand).

(3) *Moins de, moins que* + a number.   Normal construction: *Cela coûtera* MOINS DE *cent francs* (Ac.).   With a more mathematical value: *Il ne m'avait pas fallu* MOINS QUE *ces sept années . . . pour mettre au point cet énorme livre* (F. Gregh).

(4) With *à demi, à moitié,* etc., you have a choice: *Cela est* MOINS D'*à demi fait,* MOINS QU'*à demi fait.*

1026 NAGUÈRE / JADIS. Make a distinction between these two adverbs: *naguère* [= *Il n'y a guère. . .* (there is hardly. . ., scarcely)] means "a short time ago." On the other hand, *jadis* means "a long time ago, formerly": *C'est aux choses de* JADIS *bien plus qu'à celles de* NAGUÈRE *qu'elle* [*ma mémoire*] *aime d'appliquer sa volonté de résurrection* (G. Duhamel).   *Charlemagne* JADIS *visitait les écoles.*

Examples that you should not follow: *Là fut* NAGUÈRE, *il y a trois siècles, un des plus beaux palais du monde* (J. et J. Tharaud, *Marrakech,* p. 88).   *Come le fit* NAGUÈRE *la Révolution française* (Ch. de Gaulle, Discours et Messages, volume I, p. 314).

1027 NE is generally accompanied by an auxiliary element, such as in: *ne. . .pas, ne. . .point, ne. . .guère, ne. . .plus, ne. . .rien,* etc.

1028   The restriction marked by *ne. . .que* cannot bear on a verb expressed in a personal mode in the simple tenses; for example, it is impossible to restrict the second clause in the following sentence by using *ne. . .que: Il ne tuera pas le sanglier, il le blessera.* You must resort to using *seulement* or *ne faire que:. . .il le blessera* SEULEMENT, or: *. . .il* NE FERA QUE *le blesser.* In the compound tenses, *ne. . .que* is possible: *Il* NE *l'a* QUE *blessé.   Ils* N'*auront* QUE *perdu leur temps* (J. Cocteau).

1029   *Ne. . .que* is at times associated with *seulement,* which reinforces the idea of restriction: *Je* N'*ai* SEULEMENT QU'*à dire ce que vous êtes* (Marivaux).   *Simon* NE *faisait* SEULEMENT QUE *renouer son lacet* (M. Druon).

1030   *Ne. . .pas que, ne. . .point que* are condemned by Littré and purists, but they have been incontestably received in good usage: *Il* N'*y avait* PAS QUE *les forêts* (Hugo).   *Il* N'*y a* POINT QUE *le vice à peindre* (Fr. Mauriac).   *L'homme* NE *vit* PAS QUE *dans les forêts* (A. Maurois).

By a curious shifting, certain verbs at times take the negation which, logically, does not bear on them: *Il* NE *faut* PAS *qu'il périsse* [that is to say, *il faut qu'il ne périsse pas*]. *Il* NE *veut* PAS *que les petits enfants aient froid* (A. France.)

1031   In a clause that expresses a particular goal or aim, be careful, when using *pour que*, where you place the two elements of the compound negation; you must not insert any other words between *pour* and *que*: *Sors,* POUR QU'*on* NE *te voie* PAS.

Popular constructions: *Sors, pour* NE PAS *qu'on te voie,* or: *Sors, pour* PAS *qu'on te voie. Pour* NE PAS *qu'on le plaigne* (G. Cesbron). *Il leur avait coupé leurs bretelles pour* PAS *qu'ils se cavalent* (R. Vercel).

1032 NE is used alone (with neither *pas* nor *point*) in proverbs, with *ni* repeated, after *ce n'est pas que,* after *non (pas) que,* after *que* meaning *pourquoi?* or in a relative clause in the subjunctive after a negative or interrogative clause: *Il* N'*est pire eau que l'eau qui dort. Ni l'or ni la grandeur* NE *nous rendent heureux* (La Fontaine). *Ce n'est pas qu'il* NE *faille quelquefois pardonner* (Littré). *Non qu'il* NE *soit fâcheux de le mécontenter* (Ac.). QUE *ne parliez-vous? Il n'est pas d'homme, y a-t-il un homme qui* NE *désire être heureux?*

Here are other examples (where, moreover, *ne pas* or *ne point* may be used if you wish to reinforce the negation); *Il* NE *cesse de parler; il* N'*ose parler; il* NE *peut parler. Il* NE *sait quoi inventer. Se je* NE *me trompe. Je* N'*ai d'autre désir que de vous être utile. Il y a deux ans que je* NE *l'ai vu. Ceux qui venaient* NE *daignaient s'asseoir* (Michelet).

1033   Be careful not to omit *n'* after *on* in sentences like the following: *On* N'*est pas plus aimable. On* N'*a rien sans peine. Des promesses, on* N'*en a tenu aucune.*

Practical way to remember this: In place of the subject *on*, substitute another subject which does not end in the letter *n* (e.g., *l'homme, il, je,* etc.): *L'homme* N'*est pas plus aimable.*

1034 NE "expletive." The use of *ne* (called "expletive") has never been fully fixed in use. In literary usage, this particle is often optional; in spoken French, people generally do not bother to use it.

Principal cases:
1035 (1) After verbs expressing **fear,** used affirmatively, when there is something that you are afraid to see happen, use *ne: Je craignis que mes soins* NE *fussent mauvais* (A. France). *Je crains*

qu'il NE *vienne* (Ac.).   *Je tremble qu'il* NE *succombe* (Littré).

If it is a matter of expressing an effect that you are afraid may not happen, use *ne pas: Je tremble qu'il* NE *réussisse* PAS.

After verbs of fear used negatively, do not use *ne: Je ne crains pas qu'il fasse cette faute* (Littré).

1036 (2) After verbs expressing **hindrance, impediment,** or **precaution,** the use of *ne* is optional: *J'empêche qu'il* NE *vienne, qu'il vienne. Je n'empêche pas qu'il* NE *fasse, qu'il fasse ce qu'il voudra. Évitez qu'il* NE *vous parle* (Ac.).   *La main empêchait qu'on vît la bague* (Colette).   *Tout cela n'empêcha pas que l'erreur ait eu la vie dure* (P. Gaxotte).

Prenez garde [meaning *évitez* (avoid)] *qu'on* NE *vous trompe; prenez garde* [meaning *ayez soin* (take care)] *qu'on* NE *vous trompe* PAS. *Prenez garde* [meaning *évitez* (avoid)] *de tomber; prenez garde* [meaning *ayez soin* (take care)] *de ne pas tomber. Prenons garde* [meaning *remarquons* (let us notice)] *que ce point est important, que ce point* N'*est* PAS *négligeable.*

1037 (3) After verbs expressing **doubt** or **negation,** used affirmatively, do not use *ne: Je doute fort que cela soit* (Ac.).   *Il nie qu'il se soit trouvé dans cette maison* (Littré).

If the sentence is negative or interrogative, *ne* is optional: *Je ne doute pas qu'il* NE *vienne bientôt,* or: *qu'il vienne bientôt. Doutez-vous que cela* NE *soit vrai?* (Littré.)   *Doutez-vous que je sois malade?* (Ac.).   *Il n'est pas douteux que la règle* NE *doive s'y étendre* (Littré).   *Il n'est pas douteux que les grands États modernes aient fait . . . des efforts ordonnés* (G. Duhamel).   *Je ne nie pas que cela* NE *soit ingénieux, que cela soit ingénieux. Niez-vous que cela* NE *soit beau, que cela soit beau?*

1038 (4) In **comparative clauses** (that is to say, after *autre que, plus que, mieux que, plutôt que,* etc.), the use of *ne* is optional: *Il est autre que je croyais, que je* NE *croyais* (Ac.).   *Il agit autrement qu'il parle* or *qu'il* NE *parle* (Id.).   *Paris était alors plus aimable qu'il* N'*est aujourd'hui* (A. France).   *[La ville] nous croyait plus nombreux que nous l'étions* (Chateaubriand).   *Il n'est pas plus grand que vous* N'*êtes* (Hugo).   *On ne peut pas être plus heureux que je le suis* (A. Chamson).   *Quel mortel fut jamais plus heureux que vous l'êtes?* (Voltaire.)   *Est-on plus heureux que vous* NE *l'êtes?*

In negative or interrogative sentences where a comparison

of equality is indicated by *aussi, si, autant,* or *tant,* do not use *ne: Votre mère n'est pas aussi malade que vous croyez* (A. Daudet). *La vie n'est jamais romanesque autant qu'on l'imagine* (J. de Lacretelle). *Est-il aussi pauvre qu'on le croit?*

1039 (5) **Conjunctive locutions.**

(a) After **avant que,** the use of *ne* is optional: *J'irai le voir avant qu'il parte,* or: *avant qu'il* NE *parte* (Ac.).

(b) After **sans que,** do not use *ne* [according to the notice dated February 17, 1966, issued by the French Academy]: *Je ne puis parler sans qu'il m'interrompe* (Ac.). *La tête tourna sans que le corps remuât* (Hugo).

Some authors write *ne* after *sans que* when the main clause has a negative meaning or when the subordinate clause contains a negative term: *Onde sans cesse émue / Où l'on ne jette rien sans que tout* NE *remue* (Hugo). *La journée s'écoulait sans que personne* NE *vînt* (H. Troyat). *Elle était grande sans que nul* NE *puisse dire qu'elle l'était trop* (A. Chamson).

(c) After **à moins que,** you may omit *ne,* but most often it is used: *Il n'en fera rien, à moins que vous* NE *lui parliez* (Ac.). *À moins que l'instituteur ait maintenu son refus* (Fr. Mauriac).

(d) After *que*—when used in place of *avant que, sans que, à moins que, de peur que*—you must use *ne: Il n'aura point de cesse que vous* NE *lui ayez donné ce qu'il demande* (Ac.). *Tu ne bougeras pas d'ici que tu* N'*aies demandé pardon* (G. Sand). *Sortez vite, qu'on* NE *vous voie.*

1040 (6) After **il s'en faut que, peu s'en faut que,** the *ne* is optional: *Il s'en faut de dix francs que la somme entière y soit,* or: N'*y soit. Peu s'en fallut qu'il tombât, qu'il* NE *tombât.*

1041 **NON** [no, not]. People say: *pourquoi* NON?—which is a classical expression, or else: *pourquoi pas?: Eh bien oui, l'orgueil. Pourquoi* NON? (R. Martin du Gard). *Mon esprit se plie facilement à ce genre de travail; pourquoi* PAS? (Chateaubriand).

Similarly: moi *non,* moi *pas: Tu partiras? Moi* NON; or: *moi* PAS; or: PAS *moi.*

In contemporary usage, people use *non* interrogatively as an equivalent to *n'est-ce pas?* [isn't that so?] or *n'est-il pas vrai?* [isn't that true?]: *Mermoz a tout de même le droit d'avoir une belle bagnole,* NON? (J. Kessel.) *C'était gentil,* NON? (A. Maurois.)

Be careful of where you place such words as *non seulement* . . . or *mais* . . . in order to obtain logical balance when you use

these words in place of terms expressing opposition: *Il perdit* NON
SEULEMENT *sa fortune,* MAIS *sa réputation. Il est* NON SEULEMENT
courageux, MAIS *même téméraire.*

Awkward constructions to avoid: *Non seulement il perdit sa fortune, mais sa réputation. Non seulement il est courageux, mais même
téméraire. L'attente est non seulement bénévole, mais elle est déjà
récompensée* (Colette).

1042 PAREIL. This word is used in popular or very familiar language
in the adverbial meaning of "similar, similarly": *Tu fais* PAREIL
(J. Giono). *Nous nous entendions bien, nous pensions* PAREIL (P. Vialar).

1043 PARTOUT [everywhere]. *Tout partout* [all over, everywhere, all
over the place] is an old expression: *Le jugement doit* TOUT PAR
TOUT *maintenir son droit* (Montaigne). *Tout partout* has survived
in popular usage.

1044 PAS MAL. This expression is used in familiar language in the
meaning of "passably, fairly, rather well, middling" or "many, a
lot (of), much". It used to be associated with *ne* but it is now used
without the negation, especially when it is preceded by a preposition, in which case *ne* is never used: *Il n'y avait* PAS MAL *de curieux à ce spectacle* (Littré). *Je ne mets* PAS MAL *d'eau dans mon vin*
(Hugo). *Nous avons avalé* PAS MAL *de poussière* (A. France). *J'ai
parlé avec* PAS MAL *de gens.*

In negative clauses, if the verb is in a compound tense, *pas mal*
is placed between the auxiliary verb and the past participle: *Un
petit minois qui ne m'a* PAS MAL *coûté de folies* (Marivaux).

1045 PEUT-ÊTRE [perhaps, maybe]. Some theoreticians have claimed
that it is negligent in style to use *peut-être* with the verb **pouvoir,**
especially in a group, such as: . . . *peut peut-être.* Their scruples
are not well founded: PEUT-ÊTRE *alors* POURRONS-*nous essayer*
(A. Daudet). *Vous* POURRIEZ PEUT-ÊTRE *aussi le convoquer lui-même*
(Daniel-Rops). *On* PEUT PEUT-ÊTRE *le consoler* (M. Druon). *Je*
PEUX PEUT-ÊTRE *y aller* (B. Clavel).

1046 PILE is taken adverbially to mean "abruptly, (stop) short, precisely" in popular or familiar language: *Nous devons nous arrêter*
PILE (A. Maurois). *À neuf heures* PILE, *qu'il pleuve, qu'il vente, elle
se carapatte* (H. Troyat).

1047 PLEIN [full]. In familiar French, people use *plein, tout plein* in the meaning of "much, many" or "very": *Vous avez* TOUT PLEIN *d'amis* (Diderot). *Il y avait* PLEIN *d'étoiles au ciel sombre* (M. Proust). *Il y a* TOUT PLEIN *de monde dans les rues* (Ac.). *Je l'aime déjà* TOUT PLEIN (Th. Gautier). *Il [un chien] est mignon* TOUT PLEIN (J. Romains).

Plein is used familiarly to mean "everywhere on": *Il a des flocons* PLEIN *les cheveux* (H. Bazin).

1048 PLUS [more]. In order to indicate a comparison by using *plus* in front of a numeral, normally use *plus de: Il a fait* PLUS DE *deux lieues à pied* (Ac.).

1049 (1) *Plus que* has a sort of mathematical value: *Cette lampe éclaire trois fois plus. . .et même* PLUS QUE *trois autres* (A. Thérive). *Dix, c'est* PLUS QUE *neuf.*
(2) With *à demi, à moitié,* etc., you may choose from: *plus de, plus que: Cela est* PLUS D'*à demi fait,* PLUS QU'*à demi fait* (Ac.). *Un problème* PLUS D'*aux trois quarts,* PLUS QU'*aux trois quarts résolu.*

1050   Plus tôt, plutôt. Distinction between these two is: *plus tôt* [earlier] is the opposite of *plus tard* [later]. *Plutôt* indicates preference: *Vous auriez dû arriver* PLUS TÔT. PLUTÔT *souffrir que mourir* (La Fontaine).

1051   Ne . . . pas plus tôt que [. . .no sooner. . .]. This is the spelling for this locution, adopted by the French Academy, that is generally used: *Il n'eut pas* PLUS TÔT *aperçu son père* QU'*il courut à lui. Il ne fut pas* PLUS TÔT *dans son fauteuil* QU'*il s'endormit* (Aragon).

In use, there is some indecision about this and you will find more than one author writing *plus tôt* as one word: *Édouard n'eut pas* PLUTÔT *prononcé ces paroles qu'il en sentit l'inconvenance* (A. Gide).

1052 PRESQUE [almost]. When *presque* is used in a group, such as in *presque tout, presque tous, presque chaque, presque aucun, presque chacun,* etc., and if these are associated with a preposition, *presque* is generally placed between the preposition and the term indicating a quantity: *Dans* PRESQUE *toutes les contrées. . .* (Diderot). *Le ressort de* PRESQUE *tous les drames* (É. Henriot). *Sans* PRESQUE *aucun moment de fatigue ou d'ennui* (A. Gide).

Here is another construction, which is not incorrect: PRESQUE *pour toutes les femmes* (Diderot). PRESQUE *à chaque phrase* (J. Green). *Abandonné* PRESQUE *de tous* (Daniel-Rops).

1053   What has just been explained above also applies to *à peu près:*
Dans À PEU PRÈS *tous les cas,* À PEU PRÈS *dans tous les cas.* À PEU
PRÈS *sur toutes les questions, sur* À PEU PRÈS *toutes les questions.*

1054 SITÔT, SI TÔT. The Academy writes *sitôt* as one word without
making a distinction; that is based on a certain usage: *Quoi donc,*
elle devait périr ˋSITÔT [so soon]! (Bossuet.)   SITÔT *que de ce jour / La*
trompette sacrée annonçait le retour (Racine).   *Toutes fragiles fleurs*
SITÔT *mortes que nées* (Hugo).   *Je n'arriverai pas sitôt* [as soon, as
early] *que vous* (Ac.).

It is logical to write *si tôt* [so early, as early] in two words each
time that you wish to express the opposite of *si tard* [so late, as
late] and also in *pas de si tôt* [not so early, not as early]. Many
authors do this: *On ne m'attendait pas* SI TÔT (Colette).   *Il ne se*
couchera pas de SI TÔT (J. Cocteau).

1055 TANTÔT [soon, presently, by and by, just now, a little while
ago]. When *tantôt* marks a moment of duration, it indicates either
a near future or a recent past: *Il y a assez longtemps que je n'avais lu*
Thucydide. J'y jetais TANTÔT *un coup d'oeil* (Montherlant).   *Un livre*
dont je ferai moi-même TANTÔT *un examen impartial* (G. Duhamel).

1056 (1) To use *tantôt* to mean *bientôt* is archaic: *Il est tantôt nuit*
(Ac.).   *Depuis tantôt deux ans, il ne lui avait pas écrit* (P. Loti).
(2) When *tantôt* is used with a verb in the future or in the past,
the French Academy gives it only one meaning—that of *cet*
après-midi [this afternoon]: *Je l'ai vu ce matin, et je le reverrai en-*
core TANTÔT (Ac.).
(3) In several regions of France, and at times also in Paris, you
will hear: *le tantôt* [= *l'après-midi*], *ce tantôt, au tantôt, l'autre*
tantôt, etc.: *Je viendrai sur* LE TANTÔT (*Dictionnaire général*).   *Le*
quignon de miche qu'on lui avait passé LE TANTÔT (A. de
Châteaubriant).   *Ils sont restés encore comme* CE TANTÔT, *la*
bouche pleine, à écouter (J. Giono).

1057 TOUT À COUP / TOUT D'UN COUP. Make a distinction between these two. *Tout à coup* means "suddenly": *Ce mal l'a pris*
TOUT À COUP (Ac.).   *Tout d'un coup* means "all of a sudden": *Le*
crédit tomba TOUT D'UN COUP (Voltaire).

1058 (1) In actual usage, the two expressions are often confused and
tout d'un coup may have the meaning of *tout à coup:* TOUT
D'UN COUP, *elle poussa un cri* (J. Green).
(2) *Du coup* [at the same moment, at the same time], a neological

expression, has a meaning close to that of *du même coup* [at the same moment]: *Elle aussi! cria M. Seguin stupéfait, et* DU COUP *il laissa tomber son écuelle* (A. Daudet).

1059 TRÈS [very]. You can say: **avoir très faim, très soif, très envie; faire très plaisir, très attention,** etc. The same is true with *assez, bien, trop, extrêmement, ne. . .guère.* . . . In these expressions, the adverb of quantity modifies not just the single noun but the whole verbal locution: *J'ai* TRÈS *faim* (M. Proust). *Comme j'avais* TRÈS *froid* (A. France). *Hélène avait* TRÈS *peur* (G. Duhamel). *C'est* TRÈS *dommage* (J. Giraudoux). *Antoine n'avait que* TROP *raison* (R. Martin du Gard). *Avoir* EXTRÊMEMENT *faim* (Ac.).

Do not use *très* to modify a verb in a compound tense. Do not say: *Un tableau que j'ai très admiré.* Say: *Un tableau que j'ai beaucoup admiré.*

1060 TROP [too, too much, too many]. To indicate a measure of excess, say: *de trop* or, at times, *en trop*: *Vous m'avez donné cent francs* DE TROP (Ac.). *Recevoir dix francs* EN TROP (*Grand Larousse encyclopédique*). *Tu as bu un verre* DE TROP? (J. Green.)

Without *de* or *en*: *beaucoup trop, un peu trop, bien trop.*

1061 TROP as an attribute with **être.** The following distinctions are made:

(a) To express the idea of an inopportune, inconvenient, or useless presence: *Je crois que nous sommes* DE TROP *dans cette petite fête de famille* (Flaubert). *Il faut retrancher ce qui est* EN TROP (Ac.).

(b) To express the idea of an excessive quantity, use *trop, de trop*: *Ils étaient* TROP, *il ne pouvait rien contre eux* (R. Rolland). *Cinq minutes ne sont pas* DE TROP (R. Bazin).

1062 (1) Do not say: *trop de bonne heure.* Say: *de trop bonne heure.*

(2) Do not say: *Il a trop de bon sens* QUE *pour agir ainsi.* In good French *que* is not used: *Il a trop de bon sens pour agir ainsi* (Ac.). The same is true for the following where *que* should not be used: *assez que pour, suffisant que pour, insuffisant que pour, suffisamment que pour, insuffisamment que pour, trop peu que pour.*

1063 VITE [quickly, quick]. This word is used as an adverb in general usage, but it is also used as an adjective in the language of sports and, at times, in literature: *Ces chevaux étaient très* VITES (A. France). *L'Amérique est le pays le plus* VITE *du monde* (P. Morand). *Il a le pouls fort* VITE (Ac.).

1064 VOIRE, in the meaning of "really, truly," is archaic. In ordinary usage, this word means "and even": *L'Académie peut se permettre des hardiesses,* VOIRE *des fantaisies* (H. Bremond).

Voire même is condemned by certain purists as being pleonastic, but that is not so if you take *voire* in its basic meaning of *vraiment.* It is current in literary language: *Les couteaux et les pipes,* VOIRE MÊME *les chaises, avaient fait leur tapage* (Musset).   *Ce remède est inutile,* VOIRE MÊME *pernicieux* (Ac.).

1065 Y COMPRIS [including]. In a neological use, *y compris* at times is followed by a preposition or a subordinate conjunction: *La liberté ne survivrait pour personne dans le monde,* Y COMPRIS *pour les État-Unis* (Ch. de Gaulle).   *Craignons les Grecs,* Y COMPRIS *lorsqu'ils font des offrandes aux dieux.*

CHAPTER 7

PREPOSITIONS

1066 A preposition is frequently used as an adverb: *Les uns attendent les emplois, les autres courent* APRÈS (Ac.). *Ils avaient moins de patience qu'*AVANT (P. Guth). *La gloire est soumise à des perspectives. Impossible de tricher* AVEC (J. Cocteau).

Generally speaking, in literary language it is preferable to use a preposition with an object pronoun: *J'ai vos lettres; je voyage* AVEC ELLES (J.-L. Vaudoyer).

1067 Ordinarily, *à, de,* and *en* are repeated in front of each object: *Il écrit* À *ses parents et* À *son oncle.*

Here are some examples of principal cases where these prepositions are not repeated in front of each object: *École* DES *arts et métiers. Se mettre* À *aller et venir. Adresses* DES *amis et connaissances. Un délai* DE *trois ou quatre mois.*

1068 There is repetition also with *ni l'un ni l'autre* or *l'un ou l'autre: Je n'irai ni* CHEZ *l'un ni* CHEZ *l'autre. Il devait combattre* AVEC *l'un ou* AVEC *l'autre* (Fustel de Coulanges).

1069 (1) With *l'un et l'autre:* CHEZ *l'un et* CHEZ *l'autre* (A. France). CHEZ *l'un et l'autre* (P. de La Gorce).

(2) Repetition is optional with *autre, autre chose* + *que, ce dont . . . c'est, ce à quoi . . . c'est, excepté, hormis, sauf, y compris: Je ne puis me montrer* À *d'autres qu'*À *vous* (Voltaire). *Le miel était mangé, mais* PAR *d'autres que* PAR *elle* (A. Chamson). *Ce* DONT *elle rêvait, c'était* D'*élégance* (A. Billy). *Ce* À *quoi je parviens le plus difficilement à croire, c'est* À *ma propre réalité* (A. Gide). *Abandonné* DE *tous, excepté* DE *sa mère* (Hugo). *Des hommes libres* DE *tout, sauf* DE *leurs femmes* (Colette). *Ne parlez pas de cela* À *d'autres que vos amis* (Littré). *Ce* DONT *je suis redevable. . . . ,*

c'est l'apaisement de notre conscience (Fr. Mauriac).   *Ce* À *quoi il faut toujours revenir, c'est l'organisation.* . . (Ch. Du Bos).   *Accorder l'amnistie* AUX *rebelles, excepté les chefs, sauf les chefs, y compris les chefs.*

À

1070   **À bas de** [at the base of]. People say: *sauter* À *bas du lit* [to leap out of bed; in other words, to jump (out of bed) so that your feet are at the base of the bed]. People also say: *sauter* À *bas de son cheval* [to jump off one's horse]. Or, in the same meaning, you may use: *en bas du lit, en bas de son cheval: Il le mit* À *bas de son cheval* (Ac.).   *Jean se jeta* EN *bas de son lit* (M. Prévost).

Do not say: *sauter bas du lit;* and do not say: *tomber bas de l'échelle.*

1071   **À bicyclette, en bicyclette** [on a bicycle, by bicycle]. The two constructions are good: *Elle arrive* À *bicyclette* (G. Duhamel).   *Apprendre à monter* À *vélo* (A. Arnoux).   *Un très grand nombre de voyageurs se déplacent* À *motocyclette,* À *vélomoteur,* or À *scooter* (A. Siegfried).   *Leur père est passé* EN *bicyclette* (A. Gide).   *Quand je me promenais* EN *motocyclette* (A. Maurois).   *Il était* EN *vélo* (Fr. Mauriac).   *Aller* EN *scooter.*

1072   (1) With an article or what takes the place of it: *Monter* SUR *une bicyclette* (A. Hermant).   *Il partit* SUR *sa bicyclette* (Colette).
(2) People say: *aller* EN *skis* (which is an opinion offered by Dauzat); Or, people most often say: *à ski* or *à skis: Les promenades* À SKI (H. Troyat).   *Il descendait* À SKIS *les pentes des Tatras* (M. Blancpain).

1073   **À bon marché** [cheap, cheaply]. With or without *à,* as in *acheter bon marché,* or: *acheter* À *bon marché, vendre* À *bon marché (Dictionnaire général).   Avoir une chose à bon marché* Ac.).   *Il acheta le cheval bon marché* (Voltaire).   *Vendre bon marché* (Littré).

When used with the value of an adjective, with or without *à: Avec leurs articles à bon marché* (A. Chamson).   *Des livres bon marché* (Fr. Mauriac).

1074   **Adresses** [addresses]. Some people like to write on an envelope, in front of the destination: *À Monsieur.* . .   In ordinary usage, the preposition is not used: *Monsieur X.* . .

1075   **D'ici** . . . [from here. . . , from now. . . from this moment

. . . , etc.]. This expression may be followed by *à* or not: *D'ici* À
8 ou 10 jours (Stendhal). *Nous verrons bien des choses d'ici* À *ce
temps-là* (Ac.). *D'ici* À *Angkor* (P. Benoit). *D'ici* À *peu. . .*
(A. Hermant). *D'ici quelques mois* (M. Prévost). *D'ici une heure*
(J. Green). *D'ici peu de temps* (G. Marcel).

Always (or almost always) without *à*: *D'ici là, j'aurai arrangé
votre affaire* (Ac.).

D'ici is placed after a complement of time or distance: *À quatre
pas d'ici* (Corneille).

1076 **Dix à douze personnes** [ten to twelve persons] **dix ou douze
personnes** [ten or twelve persons]. The traditional distinction is:
(a) If an intermediary quantity is supposed, use *à* or else *ou: Des
groupes de quatre à dix hommes* (A. Maurois). *Vingt à trente personnes* (Ac.). *Je resterai quatre à cinq jours* (Mérimée). *Une fillette de sept ou huit ans* (Th. Gautier). *Les murailles délabrées ont
ici cinq ou six pieds d'épaisseur* (P. Loti).
(b) If there is no possible intermediary quantity, use *ou: Sept ou
huit chèvres* (La Fontaine). *Il vit cinq ou six arbres* (Stendhal). *Elle a élevé sept ou huit petits frères* (A. France).

1077 (1) Some authors follow this rule somewhat freely: *Treize à
quatorze personnages principaux* (Diderot). *Ils vous tueront sept
à huit hommes* (Stendhal). *Il n'y avait là que cinq à six personnes* (A. Billy).
(2) In cases like the following, where the approximate evaluation
is indicated by means of two numbers joined by *à*, the first
number can be introduced by *de*—but the *de* is not often used:
Ils étaient de vingt à vingt-cinq (Ac.). *Des volumes assez communs
coûtaient 7 à 8 francs* (A. Billy).

1078 **Être à lundi** [to be Monday, etc.; used with a personal pronoun as subject or with the indefinite pronoun subject *on*]. You
have a choice, either *être lundi* or *être à lundi: On était* AU *sa-
medi* (Flaubert). *Nous sommes* À *demain* (A. Dumas fils). *Il lui
tardait presque d'être* À *dimanche* (Fr. Mauriac). *Nous étions le 6 mai*
(A. France). *Nous sommes mardi!* (J. Giraudoux.)

1079 **Aller au coiffeur** [to go to the hairdresser, to the barber], **aller
au médecin** [to go to the doctor, etc.]. This construction is especially used in popular or familiar language: *Il vaut mieux aller au
boulanger qu'au médecin (Larousse du XXᵉ siècle). Maman allait le
moins possible "au boucher"* (Fr. Mauriac).

In careful, polished French, use *chez: Il vaut mieux aller* CHEZ LE BOULANGER *que* CHEZ LE MÉDECIN (Littré).   *Un matin qu'elle devait se rendre* CHEZ LE COIFFEUR. . .(Colette).

Aller à l'évêque, aller au ministre; these, for example, are equivalent to saying: *s'adresser à l'évêque, s'adresser au ministre,* etc. [that is to say, to go to talk to the bishop, to go to talk to the minister, etc.].

Aller au bois, à l'eau, etc.; these mean "to go get provisions consisting of wood, water, etc."

1080   **Se confier à, se confier en, se confier dans, se confier sur** [to confide in, to trust (to, in), to put faith in]. The usual constructions are with *en* or *à: Il s'est confié* EN *ses amis* (Ac.).   *Se confier* EN *ses forces,* EN *la bonté de quelqu'un* (Id.).   *Homme, personne de confiance, à qui l'on se confie entièrement* (Littré).

Se confier dans or *se confier sur* are somewhat rare.

1081   (1) People say: *se fier à qqn, à qq.ch.* or *se fier sur qqn, sur qq.ch.* [to rely on]—*avoir confiance, mettre sa confiance en* or *dans,* or at times *à—prendre confiance en: Se fier aveuglément* À *quelqu'un* (Ac.).   *Se fier* SUR *ses propres forces* (Id.).   *Avoir confiance, prendre confiance* . . . EN *quelqu'un* (Id.).   *Mettre sa confiance* EN *Dieu* (Id.).

(2) *Se fier en* is outdated.

1082   **À la bouche** [in one's mouth]. People say: *la pipe, la cigarette* À *la bouche* rather than EN *bouche: Avec des cigares à la bouche* (Flaubert).   *Avec sa pipe à la bouche* (M. Bedel).   *Son garçon d'épées, cigarette à la bouche* (Montherlant).   *Il fit le geste de la jeter* [*une cigarette*], *la regarda et la remit en bouche* (A. Thérive).   *Tandis qu'il s'asseyait par terre devant l'âtre, pipe en bouche* (Vercors).

1083   **À nouveau; de nouveau.** According to the Academy, *à nouveau* means "in a completely different way": *Ce travail est manqué; il faut le refaire* À NOUVEAU [over again].   *De nouveau* means "once more," "again": *On l'a emprisonné* DE NOUVEAU.

Modern authors use *à nouveau* in the meaning of "once more," "again": *Comme il tournait* À NOUVEAU *le corridor* . . . (A. Gide).   *Il pleuvait* À NOUVEAU (Aragon).

1084   **Hier matin** [yesterday morning], **hier (au) matin** [yesterday (in the) morning], **hier soir** [yesterday evening, last night], **hier au soir** [yesterday in the evening, last night]. The use of the preposition is optional: *Hier* AU MATIN (Ac.).   *Torlonia est parti hier* AU

SOIR (Chateaubriand). *Le dimanche* AU MATIN (P. Mac Orlan). *On résolut de partir un mardi matin* (Maupassant). *Elle est partie et revenue dimanche soir* (Flaubert). *Hier matin* (Ac.). *À dix heures, hier soir* (G. Duhamel).

1085 (1) The following must be used with *au: La veille* AU *soir* (Flaubert). *Le 22 juillet* AU *matin* (P. de la Gorce). *Même le 22* AU *soir, il était trop tard* (R. Martin du Gard).

(2) You may use the singular or plural: *Tous les jeudis* MATIN (J. Romains). *Tous les jeudis* SOIR (A. Thérive). *Les dimanches* MATINS (V. Larbaud). *Tous les samedis* SOIRS (M. Jouhandeau).

(3) With or without *à: hier (à) midi, aujourd'hui (à) midi, le lundi (à) midi,* etc.

(4) If you wish to give an indication of the general time of day, say: *au matin, au soir,* or *le matin, le soir: La diane* AU *matin fredonnant sa fanfare* (Hugo). *Le matin, elle fleurissait. . . ;* LE *soir, nous la vîmes séchée* (Bossuet).

1086 **Avoir affaire à, avoir affaire avec, avoir affaire de.** [Affaire is also written as: *à faire*]. The distinctions are:

(a) *avoir affaire à qqn* or *avoir affaire avec qqn* means "to have to talk to someone," "to have some matters to talk to the person about." The only real difference between these two constructions is, according to Littré, that *à* is more general.

(b) *avoir affaire de* means "to have need to (of)": *Qu'ai-je affaire* DE *l'estime de gens que je ne puis estimer?* (A. Gide.)

1087 **C'est à moi à, Cest à moi de** + infin. According to the French Academy, *C'est à vous à parler* means "your turn to speak has come up." *C'est à vous de parler* means "it is appropriate at this time for you to speak." But practical usage does not follow this distinction: *C'est au temps* À *aguerrir les troupes* (Voltaire). *À vous* DE *jouer, capitaine* (A. Daudet).

1088 **Chaque fois, à chaque fois** [each time, at each time]. The use of the preposition is optional in *(à) chaque fois, (à) la première fois,* etc.: *Chaque fois qu'on lui parle* (Ac.). *À chaque fois que l'heure sonne* (Hugo). *La première fois que je l'ai vu. À la deuxième fois, j'ai laissé mon chien courir sur lui* (M. Arland).

1089 **Mal à la tête** [headache], **froid aux pieds** [cold feet], etc. Do not omit *à: Bonsoir, j'ai mal* À *la tête* (A. France).

1090 **Être (à) court** [to be short (of), to lack]. In classical usage, no *à: Être court de mémoire* (Ac.).   *Nous étions courts d'ameublements* (A. Gide).

In modern usage: *à court: Ils étaient* À *court de vivres* (Mérimée).   *Se trouvant à court d'argent* (Villiers de l'Isle-Adam).   *Tu n'es jamais* À *court d'arguments* (A. Maurois).

À court used in an absolute sense: *Le page ne semblait jamais* À COURT (La Varende).   *Bédier n'était jamais* À COURT (J. Tharaud).

1091   **À la perfection, dans la perfection; en perfection** (to perfection].   You have a choice: *Elle danse* À LA PERFECTION (Ac.).   *Elle nageait* DANS LA PERFECTION (R. Bazin).   *Cet ouvrier travaille* EN PERFECTION (Ac.).

1092   **Être (à) quatre.** Make the following distinction: *Nous étions quatre* means that you envisage merely the numerical aspect of the group. If you use the preposition *à*, as in *Nous étions* À *quatre*, you indicate a consideration for the tie or bond that holds together a social group, a community of interests, or efforts, or situation, etc.: *Nous partîmes cinq cents* (Corneille).   *Ils soulevèrent ce fardeau* À *quatre* (Littré).   *Ils fonderaient* À *eux deux une maison de banque* (Balzac).   *De très pauvres gens qui vivent* À *six dans un logement de deux pièces* (G. Duhamel).

1093   **Au point de vue, du point de vue; sous le point de vue** [from the point of view]. The three constructions are good, except that the third one is somewhat outdated: *Se mettre* À *un point de vue* (Ac.).   AU *point de vue esthétique, je vote pour le liseron* (G. Duhamel).   *Tout regarder* DU *point de vue moral* (H. Bremond).   *Ayant pris la question* SOUS *ce point de vue* (Baudelaire).

1094   (1) Archaic: *Les chrétiens ne le regardent pas [le mariage]* DANS *ce point de vue* (Montesquieu).
(2) After *point de vue*, the noun complement is regularly introduced by *de: Au point de vue* DE *la structure* (P. Valéry).   *Revoir sous le point de vue* DU *style un ouvrage* (Flaubert).
It is fairly current not to use *de: Au point de vue idées* (O. Mirbeau).   *Du point de vue métier* (H. Bremond).

1095   **À pied** [on foot (**aller à pied:** to walk)]. People say: *aller à pied, venir à pied: J'aimerais autant aller à pied* (G. Sand).   *Il regagnait* À PIED *le ministère* (É. Estaunié).

1096   (1) Archaic: *Ils s'en allèrent* DE *pied à Turin* (La Varende).
(2) *Marcher à pied*, at times criticized as being pleonastic, adds to the verb *marcher* a certain amount of precision, a certain pictur-

esque flavor. This construction has been used by good authors: *Il fallut qu'Aman marchât* À PIED *devant Mardochée* (Bossuet). *On marcherait* À PIED *et l'on coucherait sous la tente* (A. Chamson).

The same observation can be made for *la marche à pied*, an expression allowed by Dupré in *Encyclopédie du bon français*.

1097   À terre, par terre [on the ground]. Aside from certain established expressions (**aller ventre à terre** [to go at full speed, lickety-split] and **mettre pied à terre** [to dismount from a horse, to get off or out of a vehicle, etc.]), people use freely *à terre* or *par terre: Se jeter à terre, par terre* (Ac.).   *Il se couchait à terre* (R. Rolland).

1098   Croire; croire à; croire en. The following distinctions can be made. As for *croire à* and *croire en*, the distinction is more theoretical than practical and authors are hardly concerned about it:

(a) *Croire qqn* or *qq.ch.* means "to regard the person or the thing as truthful, veracious, trustworthy": *Croyez-vous cet homme-là?* (Ac.)   *Il ne croit point les médecins* (Id.).   *Il croit cette histoire* (Id.).

(b) *Croire à qqn, à qq.ch.* means "to have faith in the person's or the thing's veracity, power, existence." The expression indicates, essentially, an adherence in mind: *Croire* AUX *astrologues* (Ac.).   *Je ne crois pas* À *la médecine* (Hugo).   *Benjamin Constant ne croit pas* À *Dieu* (A. Suarès).

(c) *Croire en qqn* means "to have total confidence in his/her existence, power, and words." The expression indicates, essentially, a feeling in one's heart: *Croyez-vous* EN *Dieu?* (G. Bernanos.)   *Il faut arriver à croire* EN *l'homme* (R. Martin du Gard).

1099   Se méprendre à; se méprendre sur [to be mistaken about]. You have a choice: *Je ne me méprends pas* À *vos serments d'amour* (Hugo).   *Il ne se méprenait pas* SUR *la tristesse de Margot* (Musset).

1100   Mettre à jour; mettre au jour. The traditional distinction is: *Mettre à jour* means "to make known one's correspondence, accounts, etc." *Mettre au jour* means "to produce, to give birth to, to divulge, 'to take the lid off' ": *Le terre fouillée pour mettre* AU *jour les ruines de Ninive* (Littré).   *Mettre* AU *jour la perfidie de quelqu'un* (Ac.).

It would be a good thing to observe this distinction, but among authors the observation is shaky: *mettre à jour* is often used for *mettre au jour: La source dissimulée sous les galets que les travaux ont mis* À *jour . . .* (G. Bernanos).   *Ces égouts mis* À *jour . . .* (P. Morand).   *On vient de mettre* À *jour (à droite) les premiers Sphinx mâles* (J. Cocteau).   *J'admire qu'on n'ait pas plus tôt mis* À *jour l'imposture* (Étiemble).

1101   Clef à la porte, clef sur la porte [key in the door]. You have a choice: *La clef est* à *la porte; votre belle-mère y est!* (Balzac.)   *La clef était* à *la serrure* (É. Estaunié).   *La clef était* SUR *la porte* (G. Duhamel).   *La clef est* SUR *la serrure* (Montherlant).

At times: DANS *la serrure: Elle voyait les panneaux de la porte et la clef* DANS *la serrure* (J. Green).

1102   À raison de; en raison de [by reason of, because of, in consideration of]. Either of these two locutions can mean *à proportion de* or *à cause de, en considération de: On paya cet ouvrier à raison de l'ouvrage qu'il avait fait* (Ac.).   *Cet employé, à raison de ses bons services, vient de recevoir une gratification* (Littré).   *Il doit être payé en raison du temps qu'il y a mis* (Id.).   *On s'irrite moins en raison de l'offense reçue qu'en raison de l'idée qu'on s'est formée de soi* (Chateaubriand).

1103   Ne servir à rien; ne servir de rien [to serve no purpose]. You have a choice: *Cela ne sert à rien (Dictionnaire général).   Il ne sert à rien de s'emporter* (Ac.).   *Les titres ne servent de rien pour la postérité* (Voltaire).

For the sake of harmony, say: *ne servir* à *rien* DE . . . rather than *ne servir* DE *rien* DE . . . Also say: *ne servir* DE *rien* à . . . rather than *ne servir* à *rien* à . . . .

1104   Réfléchir à; ~ sur. In the meaning of "to think at length," *réfléchir* allows both constructions: *J'ai réfléchi* à *ce que vous m'avez dit,* SUR *ce que vous m'avez dit* (Ac.). *Je vous prie de réfléchir* SUR *cette affaire* (Id.).

1105   Rêver à; rêver de; rêver sur [to dream of]. Note the following distinctions:
(a) *rêver de* means "to dream (to see in a dream) while sleeping": *Je n'ai fait que rêver de vous toute la nuit* (Hugo).
(b) *rêver à* or *rêver de* means "to imagine, to think vaguely, to desire": *Vous rêviez à des choses extraordinaires, à des voyages interplanétaires* (G. Duhamel).   *J'ai passé une bonne partie de la journée à rêver de toi* (Flaubert).   *Je me prenais à rêver d'une vie enfin délivrée d'artifices* (M. Arland).
(c) *rêver à* or *rêver sur* means "to meditate deeply": *J'ai longtemps rêvé sur cette affaire, à cette affaire* (Ac.).   *Dans le train, il rêva sur cette rencontre* (É. Henriot).

1106 (1) In the various meanings indicated above, *rêver* is also used as a direct transitive verb: *J'ai rêvé une chute, un incendie* (Ac.). *Le traité de grammaire que je rêve* (A. Hermant).   *Il faudrait rêver quelque incident pour cela* (Molière).

(2) *Rêver de* + infin.: *Renoncer aux belles missions que j'avais rêvé d'accomplir* (J. de Lacretelle).

1107   Cent km à l'heure; cent km par heure [100 kilometers an hour]. When you use *par*, the expression suggests a purely technical characteristic. In current usage, people say *à l'heure: Vous vous représentez une véritable voiture . . . qui fait du cent vingt à l'heure* (A. Hermant).

1108 (1) In ordinary usage, people do not use the preposition *à* or *par*, but in writing, a hyphen is used: *à cent kilomètres-heure: Les voitures passent à près de cent kilomètres-heure* (G. Duhamel). *À 60 kilomètres-heure* (P. Daninos).
(2) With the definite article, no *à* is used: *Terres à 5 francs l'hectare* (A. Daudet). *Je payais les enfants un franc l'heure* (V. Larbaud). *Cette étoffe coûte vingt francs le mètre* (Ac.).
(3) Popular use is with *de* + definite article: *Elle demandait dix sous de l'heure* (G. Duhamel). *Pour réussir à gagner cent quarante francs de l'heure* (J.-P. Chabrol).

1109   Comparer à; comparer avec [to compare to (with)]. Along with Littré, the following distinction can be made which, however, leaves some latitude: *comparer à* is used when you wish to find an equal relationship: *Corneille comparait Lucain à Virgile* (Littré). *Comparer l'obéissance militaire à celle qu'exige l'Église* (A. Gide).   However, *comparer avec* is used when you are making a methodical comparison for the purpose of finding similarities and differences: *Nous comparerons la traduction avec l'original* (Ac.).

1110   Confronter à; confronter avec [to confront with]. These two constructions are good: *Confronter les témoins à l'accusé* (Ac.). *Nous fûmes confrontés à de pressants problèmes d'embouteillage* (Vercors). *Confronter deux étoffes l'une* AVEC *l'autre* (Littré). *Confronter les témoins* AVEC *l'accusé* (Ac.).   *L'homme qui se cherche et qui se trouve confronté* AVEC *les passions* (P. Gaxotte).

1111   Participer à; participer de. Make a distinction between these two terms: *participer à* means "to participate, to have a hand or share in, to be a party to: *On l'accusa d'avoir participé à la conjuration* (Ac.); *participer de* means "to partake (of)": *Une affection participant* DE *l'habitude,* DE *la compassion et* D*'une indifférence bienveillante* (Maupassant).

APRÈS
1112   Attendre après [to wait for] indicates the need that a person has for the person or thing that is being awaited, or it may indi-

cate an impatience: *J'attends après le médecin, après des nouvelles* (Littré). *Et que je n'attende pas après vous, quand nous serons prêts* (A. Salacrou).

When *attendre* means "to stay in a place expecting someone or something to come, to be there where you are waiting," *attendre après* is not correct. Do not say: *J'attendrai après vous jusqu'à trois heures; j'attends après mon bus.* Say: *Je vous attendrai. . . ; j'attends mon bus.*

1113   Chercher après qqn or **qq.ch.** [to look for someone or something]. This is a popular or familiar expression. In good, careful French, you should say: *Je vous cherchais* (Ac.). *Je cherche ma plume* (Id.).

1114   Courir après [to run after]. *On courut inutilement après le voleur* (Ac.). Instead of saying *il court après moi, il court après eux,* etc. [which is correct], people use the following familiar way: *il me court après, il leur court après,* etc. People also say: *courir sus à qqn.*

1115   Crier après [to cry out against]. The following constructions imply an idea of anger, of scolding, etc.: *crier, s'emporter, jurer, être furieux,* APRÈS *qqn.* [= *contre qqn* (against someone)]: *S'emporter* APRÈS *quelqu'un* (Littré). *Salomé eut beau crier* APRÈS *lui; impossible d'avaler un morceau* (R. Rolland).

1116   Demander après. This construction is parallel to the ordinary term *demander qqn* [to ask for someone] (= to look for someone in order to talk to the person); *Qui demandez-vous? On vous demande,* etc. In familiar usage, people say *demander après qqn* [to ask for someone]: *Il entre de nouveau et demande* APRÈS *Gallimard* (P. Léautaud) *Je me rendis à sa librairie, demandai* APRÈS *lui* (Vercors).

1117   Par après. This locution became outdated in the 17th century. It is no longer used in France but it has remained current in Belgium. Do not say: *Il est devenu par après un très honnête homme.* And do not say: *Travaillons d'abord; nous nous amuserons par après.* Instead of saying *par après,* say merely *après* [after, afterward], or *ensuite,* or *par la suite,* or *dans la suite.*

1118 AUSSITÔT, SITÔT [soon after, immediately after, right after]. In spite of purists, these are used as prepositions in the meaning of *dès* [as soon as, soon after]: AUSSITÔT *le déjeuner, on partit en gondole* (P. Loti). *Promettant une réponse* AUSSITÔT *mon retour*

(P. Arène). SITÔT *le dessert, elle emmenait Gise dans sa chambre* (R. Martin du Gard).

AVEC

1119   When used adverbially, *avec* [with], is hardly ever used except when speaking of things: *Il a pris mon manteau et s'en est allé* AVEC (Ac.).

If you are talking about persons or animals, careful French uses an object. Do not say: *Nous allons à la ville; est-ce que vous venez avec? Je pars pour Paris; viens-tu avec?* Say: . . .*est-ce que vous venez* AVEC NOUS? Say: . . .*viens-tu* AVEC MOI? *Il y a le petit chien; ils jouent gravement* AVEC LUI (J. Renard).

1120   **Avec deux *n* / par deux *n*** [with two *n*'s]. You have a choice between *avec deux. . . / par deux. . . .   Ce mot s'écrit* AVEC *deux n*, or: *Ce mot s'écrit* PAR *deux n: Il nous faisait écrire notre vieux nom en deux mots,* AVEC *un H majuscule* (G. Duhamel). *Elle écrit catégorie* PAR *un th* (Flaubert).

1121   **Causer avec; causer à** [to chat with]. *Causer* À *qqn* is equivalent to "to talk to him / her" and such an expression is used in popular or very familiar French. This construction is at times found in literary language: *On trouve toujours dans cette ville des gens* À *qui causer* (Flaubert).   *Le vin dont nous entendons tout à coup la Vierge se mettre à causer* À *son fils* (P. Claudel).   [See also entry no. 100.]

In careful, polished French *causer* AVEC *qqn* is used: *Je cause volontiers* AVEC *lui* (Ac.).

1122   **Communiquer avec; communiquer à** [to connect to, to adjoin . . .].   People use either of the two indifferently: *Cette pièce communique* AVEC *telle autre*, or: *Cette pièce communique* À *telle autre: Cette porte qui communique* AVEC *votre pièce à vous* (J. Romains).   *Cette chambre communique* AVEC *telle autre par un corridor* (Ac.).   *Cette porte communique* À *un corridor* (Littré).   *Un bureau communiquant* AU *salon . . .* (A. Thérive).

1123   **Dîner avec qq.ch.; dîner de qq.ch.** The theoretical distinction given by Littré is the following: *Déjeuner, dîner, souper* AVEC is used when talking about persons with whom someone has eaten. *Déjeuner, dîner, souper de* is used when talking about the food that someone has eaten: *Dîner* AVEC *des amis; dîner* D'*un potage et* DE *légumes.*

Frequent usage, even in literary language, is: *déjeuner, dîner, souper avec* [such and such food]: *Et déjeunions en hâte* AVEC *quelques oeufs frais* (Molière). *Il dînait* AVEC *du pain et des pommes de terre* (Hugo). *Nous avions déjeuné. . .*AVEC *des sandwiches et des fruits* (P.-H. Simon).

1124 Divorce, divorcer (d') avec. You have a choice: *Ces femmes qui ont divorcé* AVEC *la terre pour s'unir au ciel* (Chateaubriand). *Ayant enfin divorcé* AVEC *un mari atroce* (P. Loti). *L'héroïne avait divorcé* D'AVEC *un mari indigne* (R. Rolland). *Ce divorce* D'AVEC *une ombre* (É. Henriot).

You also find *divorcer* DE and at times SE *divorcer* with reciprocity stated: *Elle a divorcé* DE *mon père* (H. Troyat). *Ces époux* SE *sont divorcés* (Bescherelle).

1125 Se fâcher avec; se fâcher contre. *Se fâcher* AVEC *qqn* means "to have a falling out with a person": *Il saisit l'occasion d'une brouille pour se fâcher* AVEC *ses amis* (G. Duhamel). *Se fâcher* CONTRE *qqn* means "to become angry at someone": *Je me suis fâché tout rouge* CONTRE *lui* (Flaubert).
(1) *Se fâcher* SUR *qqn* is a Germanism.
(2) Popular or very familiar: *se fâcher* APRÈS *qqn: Sont-elles fâchées* APRÈS *Cathie? s'inquiéta le père* (G.-E. Clancier).

1126 Faire connaissance avec; faire connaissance de; faire la connaissance de [to meet (for this first time after being introduced)]. All three constructions are correct: *Il a fait connaissance* AVEC *un tel* (Ac.). *Je fis connaissance* DE *M. Viennet* (A. Hermant). *Shelley fit* LA *connaissance de l'institutrice* (A. Maurois).

1127 Fiancer avec, marier avec; fiancer à, marier à [to become engaged to, to marry off to]. Both constructions are good: *Fiancé* AVEC *une jeune fille charmante. . .* (E. Jaloux). *Fiancée* AU *baron de Plane. . .* (P. Bourget). *Son père l'a marié* À *la fille. . . ; Son père l'a marié* AVEC *la fille d'un de ses amis* (Ac.).

1128 Identifier avec; identifier à [to identify with]. You have a choice: *Un auteur dramatique doit s'identifier* AVEC *les personnages qu'il fait agir et parler* (Ac.). *En s'identifiant* AU *héros du roman* (J.-P. Sartre).

1129 CHEZ can mean "in the home, office, place, or country of. . ." or "in the person, in the work or the thought of, in the society of. . .": CHEZ *mes parents. C'est* CHEZ *lui une habitude. J'ai lu* CHEZ *un conteur de fables. . .* (La Fontaine).

Chez takes only nouns of animated beings as an object. You would not say: *Cela ne s'observe pas chez les minéraux.*

DANS, EN

1130 **With nouns of seasons.** People say: *au printemps, en été* (Rare: *à l'été*), *en automne* (at times: *à l'automne*), *en hiver* (rare: *à l'hiver*). Note the following: EN *plein été,* EN *plein hiver.* With the definite article: *dans le printemps, dans l'été,* etc. Without a preposition: *Ces peuples-là dorment l'hiver, veillent l'été* (H. Bosco).

1131 **Dans le journal.** People say: DANS *le journal* [in the newspaper], SUR *un registre* [on a register] (at times: DANS *un registre* [in a register]): *Il se rappelle avoir lu* DANS *un journal.* . . (A. France). *On parlait de lui* DANS *le journal* (Fr. Mauriac).   *Nous inscrivons volontiers notre signature* SUR *les registres des hôtels où nous passons* (É. Henriot).   *Votre nom, que j'ai lu* DANS *les registres de ma paroisse* (J. Green).

  (1) According to Littré, say: *lire* SUR *un journal,* SUR *une page* if you have the newspaper or the page spread open in front of you. Otherwise, it is incorrect to say: *J'ai lu cela* SUR *le journal.*

  (2) With *à: On l'inscrivit* AU *registre de l'église Notre-Dame* (É. Estaunié).

  (3) With *sur: Écrivez cela* SUR *votre agenda* (Littré).   *Il chercha le numéro* SUR *l'annuaire* (G. Bernanos).

1132 **En enfer.** People say: AU *ciel,* EN *enfer,* EN *purgatoire* (rare: AU *purgatoire*), EN *paradis* (rare: AU *paradis*).   To express a more concrete topographical value, say: DANS *le ciel,* DANS *l'enfer,* DANS *le purgatoire.*   *On entendait aller et venir* DANS *l'enfer* (Hugo).

1133 **En, dans** + names of countries, provinces, etc.
  Generally speaking, if it is a matter of pointing out the location or direction, the following distinctions are made:

  (1) Use AU with masculine names beginning with a consonant: *Être, aller* AU *Pérou,* AU *Canada,* AU *Maroc,* AU *Pakistan.*

    With *Danemark, Luxembourg, Portugal, au* is most often used, but *en* may also be used: *Retourner* AU *Danemark* (G. Duhamel).   *Aller* AU *Luxembourg* (A. Maurois).   *Puisque je n'ai pas été* AU *Portugal* (P. Valéry).   EN *Danemark* (L. Bloy).   *Il se rendit* EN *Luxembourg* (S. de Beauvoir).   *Se faire roi* EN *Portugal* (Sainte-Beuve).

  (2) Masculine names beginning with a vowel and feminine names, use *en: Être, aller* EN *Iran,* EN *Uruguay;* EN *Allemagne,* EN *Espagne,* EN *France,* EN *Chine.*

(3) Names of islands. Use *en* for feminine names of large islands: EN *Sardaigne*, EN *Sicile*, EN *Nouvelle-Guinée*. But: À *Malte*, À *Chypre*, À *Terre-Neuve*, À *Cuba*, À *Madagascar*, À LA *Martinique*, À LA *Réunion*.

(4) Names of provinces. General use is with *en* for French or foreign provinces: EN *Picardie*, EN *Normandie*, EN *Berry*, EN *Lorraine*, EN *Brabant*, EN *Lombardie*, EN *Piémont*. But also: DANS LE *Berry*, DANS LE *Poitou*, DANS LE *Brabant*, DANS LE *Piémont*, DANS LA *Calabre*, etc.

(5) Names of *départements*. Use *en* for names formed with two elements joined by *et:* EN *Seine-et-Marne*, EN *Saône-et-Loire*. But: DANS LE *Var*, DANS LES *Vosges*, DANS LE *Gard*, DANS LE *Lot*, DANS LA *Moselle*, DANS LE *Cher*, etc. Note that usage generally allows *dans* + the definite article, no matter what the name of the *département* is.

1134 **Dans Paris, à Paris.** When saying DANS *Paris*, a person envisages a circumscribed territory: *Les taxis roulaient* DANS *Paris* (Aragon). *L'armée entra ainsi* DANS *Alger* (J. Roy).

À Paris simply indicates the place, as opposed to another place: *Nous irons* à *Paris tous les deux.*

1135 (1) People normally say: *à Avignon, à Arles*, etc.: *De retour à Avignon* (Chateaubriand). *De quoi aller à Avignon* (J. Giono). *Je vais à Aix* (A. Chamson).

En Avignon, en Arles, etc. have a provincial tint: *En Avignon, le pont ne l'avait point frappé* (R. Kemp). *Son voyage de noces. . .l'avait conduite jusqu'en Alès* (J.-P. Chabrol). *J'ai été joué à Orange et en Arles* (Montherlant).

(2) Some authors have attempted to show a preference for the old construction *"en* + name of city" with names of cities whose first letter is a vowel: *Il ne parvint pas,* EN *Alger, à servir autant qu'il le souhaitait* (R. Kemp). *Rose. . .s'était. . . installée* EN *Amiens* (G. Duhamel).

1136 **En l', en la** are found in certain locutions already established: *en l'air, en l'état, en l'an. . ., en la personne de,* etc. Except for these examples, at times you will find in literature: *Dîner* EN LA *compagnie des nouveaux venus* (Flaubert). EN LA *société de ces bergers* (P. Loti).

1137 **En le, en les** are found but they are criticized; for example, Dauzat has described these constructions as "individual fantasies, literary eccentricities." EN LE *présent sujet* (Montherlant). EN

LE *miroir de leur esprit* (A. Gide).   EN LES *jours de deuil* (G. Duha-mel).   The usual construction is: *dans le, dans les.*

1138   Dans la rue. Examples: *La façon dont il devait se comporter* DANS *la rue* (M. Proust).   *Je ne veux pas qu'on nous voie porter des valises* DANS *la rue* (Montherlant).   *Jouer, courir,* DANS *la rue.*   Similarly: *Les grands élèves et les gamins éparpillés* DANS *la cour neigeuse* (Alain-Fournier).

1139 (1) Do not say: *se bien comporter* EN *rue,* which is an archaism used in Belgium and Switzerland; and do not say: *jouer* SUR *la rue, courir* SUR *la rue,* SUR *la cour.*

(2) People do say: EN *pleine rue, de rue* EN *rue, avoir pignon* SUR *rue, avec vue* SUR *la rue.*

(3) The expressions *jeter qqn à la rue, dans la rue, mettre qqn à la rue, dans la rue* all mean "to drive someone out, to reduce some-one to misery": *Le père Baptiste, le vieux tourneur, que l'on jette* À *la rue, après l'avoir mis en prison* (A. Billy).   *Quand ils t'auront jeté* DANS *la rue, il ne te restera plus un kopek* (M. Achard).

Être à la rue, dans la rue are also used to mean "to be without a roof over one's head."

(4) The following are used: *demeurer dans une rue, dans* or *sur une avenue, sur un boulevard, sur une place.*

When indicating the address of a residence or a place, ordi-narily the preposition is omitted: *Il habite rue Vaneau, boulevard Voltaire.*

1140   Dans le but [for the purpose of. . .] means *en vue de,* or *afin de,* or *à dessein de,* etc. Although condemned by purists, *dans le but* has received the sanction of good usage: DANS LE BUT *de rompre une majorité* (Chateaubriand).   *Tu as pris,* DANS UN BUT *sublime, une route hideuse* (Musset).   *Il a dépensé* DANS CE BUT *des sommes énormes* (G. Bernanos).   *J'aurais honte de m'introduire en secret chez les autres, et* DANS UN BUT *strictement personnel* (M. Pagnol).   *Elle vient de provoquer cette scène* DANS UN DOUBLE BUT (H. Bazin).   [See also entry no. 87].

1141   Dans un fauteuil; sur un fauteuil [in an armchair]. Both are used: *Je m'assis* DANS *un fauteuil* (Musset).   *M. Henriot s'asseyait* SUR *un fauteuil de paille* (M. Arland).

People generally say: SUR *un canapé,* SUR *un divan,* SUR *un sofa.*

1142   En chambre. *Un ouvrier* EN *chambre* is a worker who works at home, not in a studio or shop.

Instead of saying *être en chambre* or *rester en chambre*, you should say rather: *être* DANS *sa chambre, garder la chambre.*

1143   **En deux heures** [within two hours]. People say: *faire un travail* EN *deux heures* and not: SUR *deux heures: J'ai fait le trajet* EN *trois heures et demie* (A. Siegfried).

1144   **En or** [made of gold]. People say: *une montre* D'*or, une table* DE *marbre;* but you can also say: EN *or,* EN *marbre,* etc.: *Dans l'armoire* EN *noyer* (Hugo).   *Une comète* EN *fer forgé* (A. France).
In a figurative meaning, always use *de: Mon âme* DE *cristal* (Hugo).   *Une santé* DE *fer.*

1145   **En place; à sa place** [in place; in its place]. People say: *mettre qq.ch.* EN *place* or À *sa place,* at times EN *sa place: Elle remit tout* EN *place* (J.-L. Vaudoyer).

1146 (1) *Remettre qqn à sa place* means "to make the person feel that he / she has overstepped the boundaries": *Elle l'avait remis à sa place de son ton le plus sec* (R. Dorgelès).
(2) *Être en place* means "to be in the employ, to have a responsibility which gives authority, consideration." It is also used when speaking of a household worker who performs services: *Elle prit ses guenilles d'habits. . . et partit* EN PLACE (Ch. Péguy).

1147   **En semaine** [work day week]. This expression is used—as opposed to Sunday—for a work day: *Nous sommes* EN *semaine* (A. Daudet).   EN *semaine, il travaille comme quatre* (O. Mirbeau).

1148   **En tête à tête** [privately, a private conversation]. This expression has been rejected by purists because they allow only *tête à tête,* without *en;* but it has been accepted into usage by some best authors. It is at times written as *en tête-à-tête: Il les avait laissés* EN *tête-à-tête* (Flaubert).   *Vivre* EN *tête à tête* (A. Thérive).

DE

1149   **Appréhender** is used with *de* + an infinitive and its complement. Do not say, for example: *Il appréhende vous déplaire.* Say: *Il appréhende* DE *vous déplaire* (Ac.).

1150   **D'avance; par avance; à l'avance** [in advance]. Ordinary classical usage is *d'avance* or *par avance: Payer* D'*avance, payer* PAR *avance* (Ac.).   PAR *avance, j'acceptais tout* (G. Duhamel).
In modern usage, *à l'avance* [although condemned by Littré

and not accepted by the Academy] is currently used: *M. Mérimée s'y est pris* À L'AVANCE (Sainte-Beuve). *Un jour fixé* À L'AVANCE (A. Chamson). *Coup préparé* À L'AVANCE (Ac., listed under *coup*).

1151 **De par.** This is an archaic construction which means *de la part de* [on behalf of]: DE PAR *le roi des animaux* (La Fontaine). Modern usage: (1) DE PAR *le monde* means *quelque part dans le monde* [somewhere in the world], *dans toute l'étendue de la terre* [in the whole expanse of the earth]: *Il a* DE PAR *le monde un cousin qui a fait une grande fortune* (Ac.). (2) *de par* (in a causal sense) also has the meaning of "because of, on account of": *Il était,* DE PAR *sa complexion, franc du service militaire* (G. Duhamel).

1152 **De** (or **par**) + object indicated by an agent.
There is no strict rule regarding the use of the prepositions *de* or *par* introducing the object expressed by an agent with a verb in the passive. Let us observe, generally speaking, that *de* is used especially when you wish to express the state that exists; *par* is used when you wish to express the action: *J'étais craint* DE *mes ennemis et aimé* DE *mes sujets* (Fénelon). *Abandonné* DE *tous, excepté* DE *sa mère* (Hugo). *La charrue était tirée* PAR *deux boeufs. La peinture m'était enseignée* PAR *ma soeur* (P. Loti).
In addition: *de*, with verbs taken in a figurative meaning: *Il était accablé* DE *honte; par*, with verbs taken in their proper meaning: *Il était accablé* PAR *la charge.*
De with an object not accompanied by a determinative: *La place était encombrée* DE *curieux; par* with an object accompanied by the definite article or a determinate word: *La place était encombrée* PAR *les curieux,* PAR *les curieux du voisinage.*

1153 **Deux jours (de) libre** [two free days]. With or without *de*, but the construction with *de* detaches the adjective and presents it with the value of an attribute: *Il y eut cent hommes* DE *tués* (Littré). *Encore une journée* DE *perdue* (Fr. Mauriac). *Un cheval qui n'a que les pattes de devant* DE *mauvaises* (J. Renard). *Il y eut cent hommes tués* (Littré). *Il n'y a eu que trois élèves admis sur dix* (Ac.). *J'ai donc une main libre* (G. Duhamel).

1154 **À travers, au travers de** [through, across]. *À travers* never takes *de; au travers* always takes *de: Il sourit* À TRAVERS *ses larmes* (A. Hermant). *Il avait longtemps marché* AU TRAVERS DE *la ville* (A. Gide).

1155   Qualifier (de) fou [to qualify as. . . , to describe as. . . , to call. . . , to term. . .]. With or without *de: Qualifier quelqu'un* DE *fourbe* (Littré). *Cette innocence que j'ai qualifiée. . .* DE *fonctionnelle* (P. Valéry). *Un fait qualifié crime* (Ac.). *Des froidures qu'il n'est pas exagéré de qualifier sibériennes* (G. Duhamel).

1156   De demain en huit [a week from tomorrow]. Classical usage requires *de:* DE *mardi en huit* (Ac.). *Il est probable que* D'*aujourd'hui en quinze j'arriverai à Paris* (Flaubert).

Familiar usage, without *de: Elle peut être ici dimanche en huit* (Fr. de Croisset). *Jeudi en huit* (Martinon).

1157   C'est (de) ma faute [It's my mistake, It's my fault]. The traditional construction is without *de* (Littré, the French Academy, *Dictionnaire général*): *Est-ce ma faute, à moi?* (Ac.) *Si l'entreprise a échoué, ce n'est pas ma faute* (Id.). *Ce n'est pas ta faute* (Hugo). *Tout est ma faute* (J. Cocteau).

In modern usage, *de* is used: *C'était* DE *ma faute* (Diderot). *Ce n'est pas* DE *ma faute* (A. France). *C'est* DE *votre faute* (M. Arland). *Tout est* DE *ma faute* (H. Troyat).

1158 (1) With *il y a,* you must use *de: Il y a, il n'y a pas* DE *ma faute.* (2) In the following expressions, the object of *faute* is introduced by *de: C'est la faute* DE *Bilboquet* (Nerval). It is popular to use *à: C'est la faute* À *Voltaire* (in Hugo).

1159   Le mot (de) gueux [the word *gueux*]. In order to present a word which is generally in italics or in quotation marks, the use of *de* is optional: *Le mot* DE *gueux est familier* (Ac.). *Je ne sais pourquoi je me sers de ce terme maladie* (Nerval).

1160   Province de, province du [province of. . .]. There seems to be a certain tendency to say or to write: *province* DU *Brabant,* DU *Hainaut,* DU *Limbourg,* DU *Luxembourg,* DE LA *Flandre orientale.* There is nothing incorrect in this use [since people can say: *province* DU *Finistère* (Ac.)], but it would be better to use the simple *de: province* DE *Brabant,* DE *Hainaut,* DE *Limbourg,* DE *Luxembourg,* DE *Flandre orientale.* [Compare: *le canton* DE *Vaud, le royaume* DE *Belgique.*]

1161   Comme de juste [as is proper]. This locution, banned by purists (who want us to say *comme il est juste),* is now among better usages: *Habillé* COMME DE JUSTE *à l'européenne* (A. Hermant). COMME DE JUSTE, *la porte était fermée* (J. Romains).

1162 *Comme de bien entendu* [of course, naturally] is popular or very familiar: *Il n'y avait personne,* COMME DE BIEN ENTENDU (J. Giono). [Compare: *la chanson à succès* (Arletty, Michel Simon . . .): *Elle était jeune et belle / Comme de bien entendu.* . .]

1163 **Si j'étais (de) vous** [If I were you]. People use *de: Quand je serais* DE *vous, je ne le ferais pas davantage* (Littré). *Si j'étais* DE *vous, Madame, j'irais chez M. Guillaumin* (Flaubert). *Si j'étais* DE *toi,* DE *lui,* D'*elle, je n'agirais pas ainsi.*

(1) *Que de* is an archaic construction: *Voilà un bras que je me ferais couper tout à l'heure, si j'étais* QUE DE *vous* (Molière).

(2) *Si j'étais vous* means *Si j'étais la personne que vous êtes: Si j'étais vous,. . .je ne sourirais pas* (J. Green).

1164 **On dirait (d') un fou** (or: *on jurerait, on croirait.* . . , etc.) [One would say a madman (or: one would swear, one would think. . . , etc.).]. With *de* or without; without *de* is more current: *On dirait* D'*un fou* (Ac.). *Le vent remue si doucement les feuilles qu'on jurerait* D'*un bruit de pas* (Fr. Mauriac). *On dirait un fou* (Ac.).

1165 **(De) crainte de, (de) crainte que** [for fear that. . .]. People say: *de crainte de, de crainte que:* DE *crainte d'être surpris* (Ac.). DE *crainte qu'on ne vous trompe* (Id.).

De may be omitted: *Crainte de malheur* (Ac.). *Elle n'avait pas montré cette lettre à Mme Dandillot, crainte que celle-ci n'en prît une mauvaise impression* (Montherlant). *Ils confectionnaient leurs paquetages, crainte de n'être pas prêts à temps, au matin, pour partir* (J. Dutourd).

1166 **Aimer mieux souffrir que (de) mourir** [to prefer to suffer than to die]. As in the case with *préférer* (see entry no. 1237), after *aimer mieux* or *il vaut mieux,* the use of *de* is optional in front of an infinitive whose second term contains the comparison: *Il aime mieux faire cela que* DE *faire autre chose* (Littré). *Saint Louis aimait mieux mourir que pécher* (Id.).

(1) Parallel to *Il aime mieux souffrir* QUE (DE) *mourir,* you may have: . . . PLUTÔT QUE (DE) *mourir.*

(2) Bescherelle notes that *aimer mieux. . .que* + *infinitive* indicates a preference in taste: *J'aime mieux danser que chanter;* and that *aimer mieux que de* + *infinitive* indicates a preference in will, willingness: *J'aime mieux lui pardonner* QUE DE *le réduire au désespoir.*

1167 **De, as a nobiliary particle.** This particle is used only to join

the name to the first name, to the title of nobility, or to titles such
as *monsieur, madame, mademoiselle, monseigneur, maréchal*, etc., or
to those of relatives such as *frère, oncle, tante*, etc.: *C'est Alfred* DE
Musset qui l'a dit; le comte DE *Vigny fut élu; monsieur* DE *Pourceaugnac
se fâche*.

But without *de: C'est Musset qui le dit; Vigny fut élu; Pourceaugnac
se fâche*.

(1) According to Littré, keep the *de*, even without a first name,
qualification, or title: (a) in front of names of one syllable or of
two syllables with a mute *e*: DE *Thou*, DE *Sèze*; (b) in front of
names beginning with a vowel or a mute *h*: *À moi* D'*Auvergne;
l'"Armorial" de* D'*Hozier*.

But usage, in this regard, varies. You will find no *de* used
with names of one syllable or two with a mute *e*: *À dîner chez*
MUN (M. Barrès).   MAISTRE *justifie sans doute l'ordre établi* (A. Camus).   A number of authors keep the *de*, without considering the number of syllables or the first letter of the name:
Voilà DE *Vigny à l'Académie* (Sainte-Beuve).   *J'ai lu* DE *Bonald*
(L. Bloy).   *Les frères* DE *Goncourt* (É. Henriot).

(2) The nobiliary particles *du* or *des* are not omitted: *Les jolis vers
de* DU *Bellay* (A. Daudet).   *La terre de* DES *Lourdines* (A. de
Châteaubriant).

1168   **Merci** [thank you], **remercier de, remercier pour** [to thank for
. . .]. You have a choice: *Merci* DE *votre obligeance* (Ac.).   *Je vous
remercie* DE *vos bonnes intentions* (Stendhal).   *Mille remerciements* DE
toutes vos bontés (L. Veuillot).   *Merci* POUR *les fleurs*
(M. Arland).   *Soyez remercié* POUR *cette nouvelle* (G. Bernanos).

With an infinitive used as an object, *de* is needed: *Merci* DE *porter
cette lettre* (G. Duhamel).   *Je vous remercie* DE *m'avoir fait lire votre
bel ouvrage* (M. Barrès).

1169   All that applies also to *reconnaissant* [grateful], *reconnaissance*
[gratefulness], *gratitude, rendre grâce(s)* [to give thanks].

Savoir gré [to be grateful for] uses only *de*.

1170   **Féliciter de; féliciter pour; féliciter sur** [to congratulate
(someone) on]. People say: *féliciter de qq.ch.*, at times *sur qq.ch.: Je
l'ai félicité* DE *son discours* (Hugo).   *J'ai raconté l'histoire et l'on m'a
félicité* POUR *cette malice* (J. Giono).

Féliciter sur is fairly outdated: *Je la félicite sur ses succès*
(Diderot).   *Après avoir félicité ses hôtes sur l'excellence de leur café*
(A. Billy).

Use *de* with an infinitive object: *Je me félicite* D'*avoir fait un si bon choix.*

1171 **En face, près, proche, vis-à-vis** [Opposite, near, close, facing] + a noun of place.

The object is ordinarily introduced by *de* but it is often omitted: *En face le pont de la Tournelle* (Flaubert). *Près l'escalier* (A. Gide). *Proche la paroisse de Saint-Nicolas* (Sainte-Beuve). *Francine d'Aubigné . . . demeurait vis-à-vis la maison de Scarron* (A. France).

1172 (1) In the language of diplomacy, *près* (without *de*): *Ministre, ambassadeur du roi* PRÈS *la cour de. . .* (Littré). *Notre ambassade* PRÈS *le Saint-Siège* (Montherlant).

(2) *Vis-à-vis de* may be used in the meaning of *envers* [toward], *à l'égard de* [with regard to]: *Rien n'égale l'impertinence de cet enfant* VIS-À-VIS DE *ses parents* (Ac.). Somewhat rarely when talking about things: *N'avoir* VIS-À-VIS DE *l'argent qu'une âpreté simplement aryenne* (Montherlant).

1173 **Retour de** [returning from]. The traditional construction is DE *retour de: L'abbé de Bonnevie est ici,* DE *retour de Rome* (Chateaubriand).

In modern usage, people frequently say *retour de: Des officiers anglais,* RETOUR DE *Pantellaria, apportent quelques renseignements* (A. Gide). *Déjeuné avec Gide,* RETOUR D'*Algésiras* (J. Green).

1174 **Il s'en faut (de)** [There is needed / there is lacking]. After *il s'en faut* and *il s'en manque,* the object indicating what is lacking or needed is generally introduced by *de* and it does not matter if it is a question of a difference in quality or quantity: *Il s'en faut* DE *moitié que le vase ne soit plein* (Ac.). *Il s'en faut* DE *dix francs que la somme entière n'y soit* (Id.). *Il s'en faut* DE *beaucoup qu'il soit laid* (G. Sand). *Il ne s'en est pas fallu* DE *l'épaisseur d'un cheveu* (Littré). *Il ne s'en est fallu que* D'*un moment* (Voltaire). *Il s'en faut, il s'en manque* DE *peu que le tableau ne soit réussi, que la dette ne soit éteinte.*

But you may omit *de: Il s'en fallait beaucoup que la ville de Paris fût ce qu'elle est aujourd'hui* (Voltaire). *Il ne s'en est pas fallu l'épaisseur d'un cheveu* (Id.). *Il s'en faut cent sous* (Littré). *Il s'en fallait peu qu'il n'eût achevé* (Ac.). *Il s'en manque dix francs, peu, beaucoup.*

1175 (1) Without *de: Il ne s'en est guère fallu* (Ac.). *Il s'en faut bien, il s'en manque bien. Peu s'en faut. Tant s'en faut. Bien s'en faut* (Littré).

(2) The locution *loin s'en faut* (influenced by *loin de là*) cannot be justified structurally and it is not found listed in any dictionary.

1176   Au prix de [in comparison to] is an archaic expression. For Littré, it is used only for things or persons which can be appraised or be given a value, and one would therefore say: *Mes malheurs ne sont rien* AUPRÈS DE *ceux qui m'attendent*—and not: *au prix de. . .*

Authors hardly take this observation into account: AU PRIX DES *terreurs qu'elle avait ressenties, son inquiétude présente n'était rien* (J. Green).   *Tout cela est peu de chose* AU PRIX DE *la réquisition scandaleuse à laquelle sont soumis les Français. . .* (Fr. Mauriac).

1177 DEPUIS. In order to express "at which point from" in relation to a given place, people say: DE *ma fenêtre, je vois le village. Émission transmise* DE *Paris.*

In modern usage, this *de* [from] is frequently replaced by *depuis: La nuit,* DEPUIS *sa fenêtre, il regardait leur manège* (M. Arland).   DEPUIS *la porte, . . . elle vérifie qu'on ne peut rien voir* (M. Genevoix).   *La collinette forestière qu'elle voyait* DEPUIS *son lit* (Daniel-Rops).

In a notice dated May 20, 1965, the French Academy condemned such usage.

1178 DURANT [during]. The following is a distinction made between the meaning of *durant* and *pendant*, although it is not strictly observed: *durant* implies an idea of duration; *pendant* implies a limited portion of duration: *Annibal, victorieux* DURANT *seize ans. . .* (Bossuet).   *C'était* PENDANT *l'horreur d'une profonde nuit* (Racine).

1179 ENDÉANS. This old locution, meaning "within (a certain length of time)," has remained current in Belgium, notably in the language of business and government administration: *Le versement doit être fait* ENDÉANS *les cinq jours.*

In normal French: *dans cinq jours, dans le* (or: *dans un*) *délai de cinq jours.   Dans l'intervalle de trois ans* (Civil Code).

The use of *sous* in this meaning is outdated: SOUS *cinq jours: L'arrêt est exécutoire sous trois jours* (Hugo).   *Il me la promet* [une somme] *sous huit jours* (Vercors).

1180 ENTRE PARENTHÈSE(S), PAR PARENTHÈSE [parenthetically]. The two constructions are good: ENTRE *parenthèses, je tiens à signaler que. . .* (Ac.).   ENTRE *parenthèse, nous pourrions aller faire un tour à la cuisine* (A. Chamson).   PAR *parenthèse, j'ajouterai telle* *chose* (Ac.). *Voilà* PAR *parenthèse qui constitue un précédent intéressant à considérer* (É. Henriot).

1181 ENVIRON [around]. This word, which was used as a preposition during the classical period, has kept its place in literary usage: ENVIRON *le début du XIXe siècle* (A. Hermant). ENVIRON *le XVe siècle* (Colette). *Cette excellente femme était née* ENVIRON *1800* (É. Henriot).

Aux environs de, denoting an approximate period of time, has been wrongfully criticized: AUX ENVIRONS DE *1900. . .* (A. Maurois). AUX ENVIRONS DE *1700. . .* (J. Green).

1182 HORS. People say *hors de pair* or *hors pair* [unrivaled, unequaled]: *Ce premier livre est* HORS DE PAIR (É. Henriot). *Cuénot fut un professeur* HORS PAIR (J. Rostand).

(1) *Hors,* meaning "except," is used without *de: Nul n'aura de l'esprit,* HORS *nous et nos amis* (Molière). If the object is an infinitive, *de* is optional: HORS DE *le battre, il ne pouvait le traiter plus mal* (Ac.). [*Gens*] *qui ne savaient rien,* HORS *cultiver les champs* (J. Boulenger).

(2) Do not say: *hors cause.* Say: *hors* DE *cause* [irrelevant (questions)]: *Être hors* DE *cause* (Littré). *Mettre hors* DE *cause* (Ac.).

1183 JUSQUE [until, up to, even]. *Jusque* is used with a preposition (*à, chez, vers, dans, sur, sous,* etc.): JUSQU'À *la mort,* JUSQUE SUR *le toit,* etc.

It is used without a preposition with adverbs such as *ici, là, où, alors, tard* and with certain adverbs of intensity modifying an adverb of time or of place: *jusqu'ici, jusque-là,* etc.: *Pour faire durer* JUSQU' *assez tard ma soirée* (J. Romains). JUSQUE *bien avant dans la nuit* (A. Daudet). JUSQUE *tout récemment* (A. Siegfried).

Do not omit *à* in: *jusqu'à Paris, jusqu'à deux heures, jusqu'à demain, jusqu'à hier, jusqu'à maintenant, jusqu'à près de dix heures, jusqu'à quand,* etc.: *De Paris jusqu'à Rome* (Ac.). *Jusqu'à demain, jusqu'à hier* (Littré). *Depuis le milieu de la nuit jusqu'à maintenant* (J. Green). *Jusqu'à près de midi* (A. Gide). *Jusqu'à quand souffrirez-vous que. . .* (Ac.).

1184 (1) At times, without *à* in familiar language: *Jusqu'hier même* (A. Siegfried). *Jusqu'hier, jusque demain, jusque maintenant* (in Martinon, *Comment on parle en français,* p. 488, note). *Jusque Halle* (P. Gaxotte). *Les Blancs paient ça jusque six cents dollars* (R. Gary).

(2) People say: *jusqu'à aujourd'hui* or *jusqu'aujourd'hui: J'ai différé*

JUSQU'AUJOURD'HUI or JUSQU'À AUJOURD'HUI *à vous donner de mes nouvelles* (Ac.).

(3) *Au jour d'aujourd'hui* is a popular pleonasm which is also found in literary usage: *Jusqu'au jour d'aujourd'hui* (A. Chamson). *Au jour d'aujourd'hui* (A. Hermant).

(4) At times, *jusque* is written as *jusques* when in front of a word beginning with a vowel, especially in poetry: *Et les bois étaient noirs jusques à l'horizon* (Vigny). *Jusques après Pâques* (Flaubert). *Jusques et y compris la peur* (M. Druon).

(5) *Jusqu'à* + an object. An ambiguous statement: *Il prête jusqu'à ses valets* (meaning: *il prête même ses valets?* or does it mean: . . . même à ses valets?*).   *Jusqu'à* + an indirect object is plausible when the sentence clearly indicates that there is an indirect object: *Il fait sa cour à tout le monde,* JUSQU'AU *chien du logis* (Ac.).

1185 OUTRE. Most often, this word means *en plus de* [in addition to, besides]. People say: OUTRE *cette somme, il a reçu une forte indemnité* (Ac.).

But, in spite of purists, you can also say EN *outre de:* EN OUTRE DE *mes vieilles dettes* (Chateaubriand).   EN OUTRE DU *bon vouloir* (Musset).   EN OUTRE DE *la gloire* (A. France).

Similarly, *en plus de* is used: EN PLUS DE *sa mauvaise tête* (J. Romains).   EN PLUS DES *huit heures de travail* (A. Maurois).

1186 PARMI [among]. This word is most often followed by a plural object, but it can also take a collective singular object or if its use implies a certain expanse [e.g., grass, a field, the sky]: PARMI *les douceurs d'un tranquille silence* (Boileau).   *Il se mêla* PARMI *eux* (Ac.).   PARMI *le cortège* (Chateaubriand).   PARMI *la foule* (Ac.). *Des frémissements* PARMI *l'herbe* (A. Gide).

POUR

1187 Parier pour [to bet]. Do not say: Je parie *pour* cent francs qu'il *en est ainsi.* Say: *Je parie cent francs. . . Je parie cent contre un que vous vous trompez* (Ac.).

People do say: parier POUR, or *parier* SUR *qqn, parier* POUR *tel cheval, parier* SUR *tel cheval: La France pariera* POUR *l'homme* (G. Bernanos).   *Parier* SUR *un cheval,* POUR *un cheval* (Ac.).

1188   The object of the person to whom you propose the bet is introduced by *contre* or *avec: Parier* CONTRE *la personne qui le propose* [le pari] (Ac.).   *Mon oncle avait parié dix mille francs contre un sou* AVEC *sœur Marie-Henriette. . .* (Fr. Mauriac).

Familiar use: *Je* TE *parie qu'elle va traverser en ligne droite* (A. Dhôtel).

1189 Partir pour [to leave for]. With an object indicating the goal or destination, *partir* POUR, at times *partir* VERS are used: *Il est parti* POUR *l'Aquitaine* (Hugo). *Son frère partit* POUR *l'Amérique* (Colette). *Je partis tout seul* VERS *les collines enchantées* (M. Pagnol.) *Ils partirent* VERS *la campagne* (B. Clavel).

Purists condemn using *partir* with *à, en, chez, dans, ailleurs, là,* etc. This construction is fairly frequent, even in literary usage: *Hippolyte partit à Neufchâtel* (Flaubert). *Cinq soeurs de Saint-Charles partiront à Coblence* (M. Barrès). *Pour cent Vénitiens qui partaient* EN *Asie.* (J. Giono). *Il partait* CHEZ *les ombres* (J. Cocteau). *Nous partions* DANS *le Midi* (L. Daudet). *Nous partions* LÀ-BAS (J. et J. Tharaud).

1190 (1) These last constructions are logical when *partir* indicates the place where a person has arrived: *Gontran étant parti* AU *Casino. . .* (Maupassant). *Antonine était, depuis deux mois déjà, repartie* DANS *sa province* (G. Duhamel).

(2) The following use of *partir en* is correct: *partir* EN *voyage,* EN *vacances,* EN *promenade,* etc.: *Je pars* EN *voyage* (A. Gide). *Il fallait bien partir* EN *vacances* (M. Arland). *Parti* EN *mission* (J. Kessel).

1191   Pour cent [percent]. People say: *prêter à cinq* POUR *cent.* In popular language: *. . . à cinq* DU *cent.*

1192   Pour de bon [for good]. The classical construction is: *Parlez-vous* TOUT DE BON? (Molière).

The modern construction is POUR *(tout) de bon:* *Y aller* POUR *tout de bon* (Littré). *Partir* POUR *de bon* (G. Duhamel).

1193 (1) *Pour de vrai* [for good, once and for all] is used in familiar language, but you also find it even in literary language: *ils ne se sont pas demandé si Baudelaire souffrait* POUR *de vrai* (J.-P. Sartre).

(2) Popularly: *pour de rire* [for fun, for joking]: *Un architecte, c'est un type qui construit des maisons. Des vraies, pas* POUR *de rire!* (R. Ikor.)

1194   Qu'est-ce là pour un homme? [What kind of man is he?]. This construction is a Germanism. French constructions are: *Quel homme est-ce là? Quel genre d'homme est-ce?* (A. Billy). *Quel* *homme est-ce?* (Fr. Jammes). *Quelle espèce d'homme est-ce?* (Th. Gautier).

1195   **Raisons, motifs pour; raisons, motifs de** + infin. [reasons, motives for + present participle; reasons, motives + infin.]. Both constructions are good: *Je n'avais point eu de motif* POUR *refuser* (B. Constant). *J'avais d'autres raisons* POUR *lui résister* (Fr. Mauriac). *Vous n'avez pas de raisons* DE *vouloir la mort de cet homme?* (Hugo). *Quand on a des raisons* DE *se méfier* (M. Aymé).

1196   **Soigner pour** [to care for]. People say: SOIGNER or TRAITER *qqn* POUR *telle maladie;* at times: DE *telle maladie: Je soignais,* POUR *la même sorte de blessure, un jeune paysan* (G. Duhamel). *Il soigna sa femme* D'*une horrible petite vérole* (H. de Régnier).

1197   **Tenir (pour)** + attribute [to consider (as) + attribute]. You can say: *Je le tiens un grand homme, je tiens cela négligeable* or: *Je le tiens* POUR *un grand homme, je tiens cela* POUR *négligeable: Je vous tiens de ce jour sujet rebelle et traître* (Hugo). *Je tiens ces deux opinions également soutenables* (Ac.). *Je tiens* POUR *un malheur public qu'il y ait des grammaires françaises* (A. France). *Je le tiens* POUR *honnête homme* (Ac.).

1198   **Train pour Paris, train de Paris.** Theoretically, *le train pour Paris* is the one which is going to Paris. *Le train de Paris* is the one which is coming from Paris. But, in practice, hardly anyone takes this distinction into consideration. Brunot says "The train *d'*Italie is the train which is going *toward* Italy as well the one which is coming *from* that country." *Demain, avant de prendre le train* DE *Paris, je confierai ce manuscrit à la poste* (P.-H. Simon).

1199   **PRÈS DE / PRÊT À** + **infin.** Make a distinction between these two: *près de* means "on the point of": *Je la vis* PRÈS D'*expirer* (Musset); *prêt à* means "ready to": *La mort ne surprend point le sage / Il est toujours* PRÊT À *partir* (La Fontaine).

1200   **QUANT À / TANT QU'À** [as for]. Regular usage is: QUANT À MOI, *je partirai.* Popular language uses *tant qu'à* for *quant à.* At times, that is found in literary language: TANT QU'À *toi, il sera beau de t'être fait un parti de toi-même* (Chateaubriand). TANT QU'À *moi, j'aurais cru que mon arme aurait fait long feu* (A. Chamson).

1201   In popular language and, at times, in literary language, *tant qu'à* + infin. has taken on the meaning of "supposed or as-

sumed that things are pushed as far as . . .": TANT QU'À
marcher, autant se diriger du côté de la délivrance (A. Gide).   You
will especially find the following constructions: *tant qu'à faire,
tant qu'à faire que (de)* + inf. [if it comes to that]: TANT QU'À
FAIRE, *mieux vaut que vous me laissiez vous présenter à ma nièce*
(J. Schlumberger).   TANT QU'À FAIRE *que de me dépayser, il vaut
mieux y aller bon coeur bon argent* (J. Giono).

Opposed to those constructions, you have the following regular construction: *"à tant faire que (de)* + infin.": À TANT FAIRE
QUE *s'offrir au Seigneur, ne faut-il pas se donner tout entier?* (Daniel-Rops).

1202   **QUITTE À** [even if, at the risk of]. If you take *quitte à* as being
a prepositional locution, *quitte* is invariable: *Quand l'un d'eux est
obligé d'abattre une bête mangeable, tous lui en achètent,* QUITTE *à jeter
le morceau* (Flaubert).

If the word *quitte* retains its value of an adjective, it is variable:
Nous devons nous contenter de ce que la vie réelle nous offre, QUITTES
à la magnifier (V. Larbaud).

Use the plural in the expression *Nous sommes* QUITTES [We are
even (we are quits; not indebted)]; use the singular in *Nous
sommes* QUITTE À QUITTE.

1203   **SANS** (n'être pas ~ + infin.).   Note well the meaning that results from the negative elements in *Vous n'êtes pas sans ignorer
. . .,* whose meaning is *Vous n'êtes pas non ignorant . . .;* the first
negation *ne pas* does away with the second *sans* or *non,* and the
result is: *vous ignorez. Vous n'êtes pas sans savoir . . .* = *vous n'êtes
pas non sachant . . .* = *vous savez . . . .*

1204   **SOUS LE RAPPORT DE** [with regard to]. Although criticized by
Littré and by purists, this expression is in good usage: *Cette voi-
ture est excellente* SOUS LE RAPPORT DE *la commodité, de la vitesse*
(Ac.).

1205   *Rapport à* [= because of, on account of, relative to the subject
of . . .] belongs to popular language: *Si madame voulait me donner
un congé de huit jours,* RAPPORT À *ma femme qui a le mal du pays* (É.
Estaunié).

SUR
1206   **Aller sur ses dix ans** [going on ten (years of age)]. People do
say: *Cet enfant va* SUR *quatre ans,* SUR *ses quatre ans* (Ac.).   *Elle marchait* SUR *ses vingt ans* É. Henriot).

Somewhat rare: *Frankie marchait* VERS *ses neuf ans* (G. Conchon).

1207   **D'accord sur** [in agreement on]; **d'accord de; d'accord en; d'accord avec.** People say: *d'accord* SUR *qq.ch.*, DE *qq.ch.* (outdated), EN *qq.ch.*, AVEC *qq.ch.*: *Après un échange d'idées* SUR *lesquelles ils étaient tombés d'accord* (R. Martin du Gard).   *Il était d'accord* SUR *tout* (H. Troyat).   *On croira, Madame, que vous êtes d'accord* DE *tout ce qui se passe* (Chateaubriand).   *Quoiqu'ils paraissent n'être d'accord* EN *rien* (Fénelon).   *La forme du corps et le tempérament sont d'accord* AVEC *la nature* (Buffon).   *Rester en accord* AVEC *quelque chose de permanent* (A. Maurois).

When the object designates a person, say *d'accord* AVEC [in agreement with], *en accord* AVEC: *Je suis d'accord* AVEC *vous. En accord* AVEC *d'autres pays américains* (G. Duhamel).

1208   **Blaser, blasé.** People say: *"être blasé* [to be indifferent], SE BLASER SUR *qq.ch.* or DE *qq.ch.* [to become indifferent to, to grow weary of something]: *La mauvaise vie qu'il a menée l'a blasé* SUR *tout* (Ac.).   *Nous commençons par être un peu blasés* SUR *les prouesses de la biologie* (J. Rostand).   *Blasé* DES *danses viles* (P. Verlaine).   DE *rien facilement je ne me blase* (H. Bosco).

(1) Rarely: *Aussitôt le même bien-être élémentaire l'enveloppait . . .* CONTRE *lequel elle ne se blasait pas* (M. Genevoix).

(2) *Blaser, blasé de* + infin.: *J'étais déjà blasé* DE *piétiner la neige durcie* (A. Hermant).

1209   **Propre sur soi** [*être propre sur soi* / to keep one's body and clothing clean] is perfectly correct: *La santé demande qu'on soit propre* SUR *soi* (Littré).   *Être propre* SUR *soi* (Ac.).

1210   **Sur la côte** [on the coast]. People say *être* SUR *la côte, aller* SUR *la côte: c'est* SUR *la Côte d'Azur que nous achevâmes de passer l'hiver* (A. Gide).   *Elle aurait pu aller à la montagne, ou plutôt* SUR *la Côte d'Azur* (Montherlant).   *Avec nos vacances* SUR *la Côte basque* (P. Daninos).

1211   (1) With *partir: Partir* POUR *la côte d'Azur,* VERS *la côte d'Azur,* SUR *la côte d'Azur.*
(2) Rare and obsolete: À *la côte: Pierre . . . se noya* À *la côte d'Afrique* (Chateaubriand).   *Faire naufrage* À *la côte* (Littré).

1212   **Sur le plan / au plan** [on the level (of) . . .]. People say: SUR *le plan des principes,* SUR *le plan moral* [= *au point de vue* . . .]: *Faire* *son salut* SUR le plan spirituel (A. Maurois). SUR *le plan des idées, ils sont indulgents* (M. Aymé).

Neological construction: AU *plan . . . .: La biologie n'est pas seulement,* AU *plan de la science pure, l'étude de progrès de la vie* (P.-H. Simon).

1213 **Vivre sur; vivre de** [to live on]. When speaking of things that provide the means to live, people say: *vivre* SUR or *vivre* DE: *Vivre* SUR *son revenu (Dictionnaire général). Il nous faudra vivre* SUR *notre capital* (Fr. Mauriac). *Vivre* DE *son bien,* DE *ses rentes* (Ac.).

In a figurative meaning, *sur* is generally used: *Vivre* SUR *sa réputation* (Littré). *Il vécut jusqu'à la fin* SUR *un vieux fonds de culture assez sommaire* (H. Bremond).

1214 VOICI; VOILÀ [here is, here are; there is, there are (when pointing out)]. The theoretical distinction is the following: *voici* [= *vois* ICI] implies the idea of relative proximity: *Me* VOICI. VOICI *des fruits, des fleurs, des feuilles et des branches* (Verlaine); *voilà* [= *vois* LÀ] implies the idea of relative distance: VOILÀ *tous mes forfaits; en voici le salaire* (Racine).

1215 (1) In practice, this distinction is hardly observed and *voilà* has clearly supplanted *voici:* VOILÀ *l'histoire. Vous savez qui je suis? rien, une fille du peuple,* etc. (Hugo). VOILÀ *mon excuse: l'intérêt* (Th. Maulnier). *Tenez,* VOILÀ *pour vous.*

(2) Do not use the following archaic construction: *le voici, le voilà* QU'IL *vient.* Say: . . .QUI *vient: Le voilà* QUI *vient par ici* (J. Giraudoux); or else (without the personal pronoun in front of *voici* or *voilà*): *Voici, voilà qu'il vient.*

(3) When presenting or offering a thing, people say: *Voulez-vous me donner ce livre?*—VOICI (or: VOILÀ), *monsieur.* At times, especially to attract attention more effectively: *s'il vous plaît: Édouard saisit aussitôt la salière et la tendit à bout de bras, en inclinant le buste*—S'IL VOUS PLAÎT, *Monsieur* (G. Duhamel, cited by Ph. Baiwir).

CHAPTER 8

CONJUNCTIONS

1216 CAR EN EFFET [for in fact, for in effect]. This construction is generally redundant. The expression, condemned by the French Academy in a notice dated Nov. 13, 1969, is justified, however, when *en effet* has the strong meaning of *dans la réalité* or when it serves to reinforce *car:* CAR EN EFFET, *la seule immensité de cette douleur lui aurait donné le coup de la mort* (Bossuet, cited by R. Le Bidois).   CAR EN EFFET *il n'y a que deux états dans la vie: le célibat et le mariage* (Chateaubriand).

1217 DEMEURANT (au~) [on the while, after all] = *au reste, pour le reste* [besides, what is more, furthermore, moreover]. This expression has been favored in literary usage: *Il est un peu vif, mais,* AU DEMEURANT, *bon garçon* (Ac.).   AU DEMEURANT, *forte tête et grande âme* (A. Maurois).

ET

1218   **Nombres complexes** [complex numbers]. Do not use *et* to connect two consecutive elements in complex numbers: *Cette poutre a trois mètres vingt centimètres de long.   Un homme de cinq pieds six pouces* (Ac.).

When it is a matter of a number of years plus a number of months (plus a number of days), use *et* to join the last element: *Il y a aujourd'hui trois cent quarante-huit ans six mois* ET *dix-neuf jours* (Hugo). *Âgé de soixante-dix-huit ans trois mois* ET *vingt-quatre jours* (É. Faguet).

1219   **Indication d'heure, de mesure** [indication of time, of measure]. When the fraction is *demi,* you should use *et: Trois heures* ET *demie; cinq mètres* ET *demi.* With all other fractions, you may use *et,* but most often it is not used: *Midi* ET *un quart* (Littré). *Une* *aune* ET *un tiers* (Id.). *Il était midi un quart* (M. Barrès). *Il est quatre heures trois quarts* (M. Pagnol). *Un mètre trois quarts* (Ac.).

1220 (1) If there is only a single quarter, people say *et quart* (without *un*): *Vers onze heures* ET *quart* (É. Estaunié). *Un mètre* ET QUART (Ac.). Less often: *un quart*: *Vers huit heures* UN QUART (P. Mille). *Deux heures* UN QUART (Ac.).

If there is subtraction, people say: *moins le quart*: *Après le coup de cloche de midi moins* LE QUART (M. Arland). *À sept heures moins* LE QUART (J. Cocteau). Less often: *moins un quart*: *Trois heures moins* UN QUART (Ac.). *À six heures moins* UN QUART (Chateaubriand).

(2) Do not say: *Il est deux heures quart*. And do not say: *le quart pour deux heures*.

(3) People do say (especially when speaking of the ringing of a clock): *le quart de, la demie de, les trois quarts de, le quart avant, le quart, la demie, les trois quarts après*: *L'horloge de Carfax sonna le quart de midi* [= *midi et quart*] (A. Hermant). *La demie de minuit* [= *minuit et demi*] *sonna* (Maupassant). *Les aiguilles marquaient la demie de onze heures* (A. Arnoux). *Le quart avant midi sonna* (M. Genevoix). *La demie après onze heures* (C. Farrère). *Comme les trois quarts après onze heures sonnaient* (Stendhal).

1221 **Et donc** [and therefore] "is no longer used" declares Littré. It is still found: *Je sais que les demoiselles sont bien plus à craindre que les dames, étant nécessairement plus spontanées,* ET DONC *plus moqueuses* (P. Valéry). *Elle devait avoir vingt-deux ans,* ET DONC *elle était majeure* (G. Duhamel).

1222 **ET / OU** [and / or]. The double conjunction *et / ou,* influenced by the English and / or, and indicating the possibility of an addition or a choice, has recently been introduced into business and technical language: *Cette machine broie les agglomérés* ET / OU *leurs chutes. Nous attendons monsieur le directeur* ET / OU *son adjoint.*

1223 **NI** [neither]. People say: *Sans force* NI *vertu* (Littré). But you can also say: *Sans force* ET SANS *vertu* (Littré). *Je restais sans force* ET SANS *parole* (A. Gide).

You can have *ni sans . . . ni sans, ne pas sans . . . ni sans: Le spectacle ne serait ni sans intérêt ni sans charme* (Hugo). [*Ces vers*] *ne sont pas sans tendresse ni sans grâce* (J. Lemaitre).

1224 *Et ni (même)* [And neither (even)] is sometimes found: ET NI *la jeune femme allaitant son enfant* (Mallarmé). ET NI *votre air bête et*

NI *ces yeux tard venus* (P. Valéry). *Je ne parle pas pour toi* ET NI
MÊME *pour moi* (G. Duhamel).

QUE and locutions

1225   **À ce que, de ce que.** Certain verbs such as *aimer, conclure,
consentir, demander, faire attention, prendre garde, s'attendre, tâcher,*
etc. are used with *à ce que* [instead of the simple *que*] not only in
spoken French but also in the writings of good authors: *Il aime* À
CE QU'*on le considère comme un bon ouvrier* (J.-J. Gautier). *L'avocat conclut* À CE QUE . . . (Ac.). *Je consens volontiers* À
CE QU'*il vienne avec nous* (Mérimée). *Je demande* À CE QU'*on
m'oublie* (Flaubert). *Elle ne faisait pas toujours attention* À CE QU'*il
n'y eût personne dans la chambre voisine* (M. Proust). *M. de Maupassant prend garde* À CE QUE *son peintre ne soit jamais un héros* (A.
France). *Il s'attend* À CE QUE *je revienne* (Ac.).

The simple *que* [instead of *à ce que*] is also used: *aimer que, consentir que, demander que,* etc.

1226   Similarly, *de ce que* is often used instead of just *que* with verbs
of feeling, for example: *s'affliger, s'étonner, se féliciter, frémir, se
glorifier, s'indigner, s'irriter, se plaindre, se réjouir, être heureux,
être fier, être fâché, être content. . .*, etc.: *Je me félicitai d'abord*
DE CE QU'*on me laissait en paix* (J. Green). *Il s'étonne* DE CE QU'*il
ne soit pas venu* (Ac.). *Irrité* DE CE QUE *je sois tourmenté*
(M. Prévost). *La maréchale se plaignait* DE CE QUE *sa robe fût
chiffonnée* (A. Maurois).

The simple *que* [instead of *de ce que*] is also used: *s'affliger que,
s'étonner que, se plaindre que,* etc.

1227   When a comparison is indicated by *même*, you may omit the
conjuction *que* and the demonstrative pronoun, for example, as
in such sentences as, *Suivez le même chemin (que celui) que j'ai
suivi; vous aurez les mêmes droits (que ceux) dont j'ai parlé: Suivez
le même chemin que j'ai suivi; vous aurez les mêmes droits dont j'ai
parlé. On vous fera le même traitement qu'on lui a fait* (Littré).

1228   At times, logical syntax produces *que* twice, the first introduced by the main verb, the other by an adverb or a comparative term; thus, theoretically you would have a construction
which was formerly used: *J'aime mieux qu'il lise* QUE QU'*il joue.*

To avoid using *que* twice consecutively, you may, according
to the case:

(1) replace the second *que* by using *si*: *J'aime mieux que vous alliez
   à Paris que* SI *vous perdiez votre temps chez vous* (Littré). *Il vaut*

mieux tuer le diable que SI *le diable nous tue* (Stendhal).

Archaic: *Il vaut mieux tuer le diable* QUE NON PAS QUE *le diable vous tue* (Littré).

(2) use a single *que: Il ne manquait plus* QU'*elle vous vît arriver* (A. Dumas fils). *Il ne demandait pas mieux* QU'*un de ses fils fût baptisé* (A. Bellessort).

(3) resort to using *que de* + infin., or *plutôt que de* + infin., or *plutôt que* + subjunctive: *J'aurais mieux aimé que mon frère se fît tuer* QUE DE *se conduire sans bravoure* (M. Barrès). *J'aimerais mieux qu'il se fasse tuer* PLUTÔT QUE DE *trahir. J'aime mieux qu'il se fasse tuer* PLUTÔT QU'*il trahisse.*

At times, after *que de* or *plutôt que de,* you may use *voir* + infin.: *J'aime mieux qu'il se fasse tuer que de le voir* (or, *plutôt que de le voir*) *trahir.*

1229 **Au début que** [in the beginning when . . .]. Do not say: AU DÉBUT QUE *nous habitions ici . . .*. Say, for example: *Dans les premiers temps où . . .,* or *dans les premiers temps que . . .*.

For Littré, *maintenant que* and *à présent que* are "compound conjunctions [of a sort] which mean *en ce temps où* [at this time when] and are formed like *pendant que* and *alors que.*" By analogy, it would seem that the locution *au début que* could be acceptable along with those compound conjunctions, even though no references to dictionaries or citations of authors are given here. Compare: AU COMMENCEMENT QUE *l'évêque avait seul entre les mains tout le revenu de son église* (Massillon, in Littré).

1230 **Autre chose que** [other than]. In negative or interrogative clauses after *autre, autre chose, rien,* the second term of the relationship is generally introduced by *que: Il n'a pas* (or: *a-t-il . . .?*) *d'autres amis* QUE *vous: il n'entend pas autre chose* QUE *le silence; il n'entend rien* QUE *le silence.*

It may also be introduced by *sinon* or by *si ce n'est: Il n'a pas d'autre ressource* SINON *une petite place* (Littré). Or: *. . .* SI CE N'EST *une petite place. Il ne me reste plus autre chose à faire,* SINON *de m'écrier avec le prophète . . .* (Bossuet).

1231 **Cependant que** [while] has the same meaning as *pendant que,* but it is archaic and uniquely literary: *Mais,* CEPENDANT QU'*il rompait la cire du cachet, il avait remarqué une légère accélération des mouvements de son coeur* (A. Hermant).

1232 **De façon à ce que, de manière à ce que** [so that, in a way that, in such a way that]. These conjunctions are parallel to *de* *façon que, de manière que,* which are classical locutions, easier to use, and recommended in carefully polished language. They are current, even in literary language: *Il s'arrangea* DE FAÇON À CE QUE *Josiane allât à la baraque Green-Box* (Hugo). *Remettez-vous vite,* DE FAÇON À CE QUE *nous ne nous irritions pas l'un l'autre* (A. Maurois). *Un double portique, disposé* DE MANIÈRE À CE QU'*on trouvât de l'ombre à toute heure du jour* (A. France).

1233 **Informer que** [to inform that] and not *de ce que: J'ai à vous informer* QUE . . . *l'Administration* . . . *a reçu une forme différente* (Stendhal). *La Radio informe les habitants* QUE *les fenêtres éclairées font d'excellentes cibles* (F. Gregh).
The same with: *avertir que, instruire que, faire part que.*

1234 **Malgré que** [though, although]. People do use *malgré que* with *en avoir,* as in *malgré que j'en aie* [for all I can do], *en dépit que j'en aie, quoi que j'en aie* [= in spite of myself]: MALGRÉ QU'IL EN AIT, *nous savons son secret* (Ac.). EN DÉPIT QU'ON EN AIT, *elle se fait aimer* (Molière). *Revenant toujours,* QUOI QU'IL EN EÛT, *à la rue des Serpents* (Montherlant).
Malgré que, in the meaning of *bien que* [although] (but with an idea of opposition) is condemned by Littré, by purists in general, and not recognized by the Academy; nevertheless, this conjunction has found a solid place for itself in usage, even in literature: MALGRÉ QUE *Gertrude lui ait déclaré* . . . (A. Gide). MALGRÉ QUE *le soir tombe* (J. Romains).

1235 **Pour autant que** [as much as, as far as]. Although this conjunction is not recognized by Littré or by the Academy, it is used in a restrictive meaning and has the value of *autant que* [as far as, as much as, as near as], *à proportion que* [in proportion as], *dans la mesure où* [insofar as]: POUR AUTANT QUE *je le sache, ils étaient d'une très honnête et probablement très loyale piété* (G. Duhamel). *Je cherche à me représenter tes sentiments,* POUR AUTANT QUE *je puisse* (M. Druon). POUR AUTANT QUE *je me souvienne* (Vercors).

1236 (1) *Pour autant* [for as much, for so much, for so many], in a causal and adversative meaning, is very much alive in present usage: *Le problème de la vie n'est pas résolu* POUR AUTANT (É. Henriot). *Nous connaissons assez cette pensée, si chère à plusieurs modernes. Mais est-elle vraie* POUR AUTANT? (J. Guitton.)
(2) *D'autant que* [the more so as, all the more so because] is used in the meaning of *d'autant plus que* [all the more . . . as; doubly

so . . . as]: *J'avais un faible pour la psychologie,* D'AUTANT QUE *j'y croyais avoir quelques aptitudes* (A. Hermant).

1237   **Préférer** + two infinitives (see also entry no. 1166).

Classical usage is: *préférer souffrir* PLUTÔT QUE (DE) *mourir: Il préférait m'admirer* PLUTÔT QUE *m'approuver* (H. Bordeaux). *Il préférait deviner les êtres* PLUTÔT QUE DE *les interroger* (J. de Lacretelle).

Modern usage, frequently found among a number of excellent authors, is: *préférer souffrir* QUE (DE) *mourir: Il préfère tout louer* QUE DE *faire son choix* (E. Jaloux).   *Elle a préféré mourir* QUE DE *vivre ainsi* (Fr. Mauriac).   *On préférait prévenir* QUE *châtier* (J. Kessel).

1238   (1) With the second infinitive not expressed: *Il préfère y étaler son intelligence* QUE *ses dons* (M. Achard).   *Je préfère me tromper par l'action* QUE *par l'inertie* (R. Ikor).

(2) At times you will find *préférer à* with two infinitives: *J'ai préféré ne pas vous voir à vous voir comme cela* (Montherlant).

1239   **Que du contraire** [on the contrary]. Do not say: *Il n'est pas insensible,* QUE DU CONTRAIRE. Say: . . . *au contraire, bien au contraire, tout au contraire.*

Do not say, as is sometimes said in Belgium: *Vous avez suivi un chemin* CONTRAIRE to mean *vous vous êtes trompé de chemin* [you took the wrong road]; *contraire* is not used to mean *faux* [false], *inexact, erroné* [erroneous].

1240 Se rendre compte que [to realize]. Although rebuffed by certain purists, this locution is attested by a number of excellent authors: *Elle se rendait compte* QU'*elle était ridicule* (R. Rolland).   *Elle se rendit compte* QU'*elle avait été spirituelle et caustique en pure perte* (V. Larbaud).

Se rendre compte de ce que (which is clumsy) is much less frequent: *Et non le roi, pensa Mortier, qui tout d'un coup se rendit compte* DE CE QUE *le Duc allait lui rester sur les bras* (Aragon).

1241   **Surtout que** (= *surtout parce que* [especially because], *d'autant (plus) que* [all the more . . . as; doubly so . . . as]), generally condemned by purists, nevertheless is, as Thérive says, "irreproachable." It is finding its place more and more in literary usage: *Ce que vous m'en dites m'agrée en tous points,* SURTOUT QUE *la villa n'est point humide* (Fr. Jammes).   *Édith n'irait pas se vanter d'une chose pareille!* SURTOUT QUE *je sais très bien que tu ne fais rien de mal* (M. Achard).   *Leurs dents étaient blanches et pointues, in-*

quiétantes en quelque sorte, SURTOUT QU'*ils les montraient en jeunes rongeurs* (J.-P. Chabrol).

1242   Tâcher que [to try (to), to attempt (to)] is well established in usage: TÂCHONS QUE *nos âmes ne soient pas englouties devant Dieu* (Hugo).   TÂCHEZ QU'*on ne vous voie pas* (A. France).

Tâcher à ce que is rare: *Tâchant à ce que le contenu en demeurât invisible à la foule, elle ouvrit l'écrin* (O. Mirbeau, cited by Sandfeld).

1243   Tant (il) y a que [the fact remains that . . ., all the same . . .]. This is used familiarly and in literary usage in the meaning of *quoi qu'il en soit* [however that may be], *avec tout cela, enfin: Jolie enfant ou non,* TANT Y A QUE *c'est une excellente femme* (Diderot).   *Je ne sais pas bien ce qui donna lieu à leur querelle,* TANT IL Y A QU'*ils se battirent* (Ac.).

1244   Veiller à ce que [to see to (it) that . . . , to attend to, to look after]. This is the normal construction: *Le magistrat doit veiller* À CE QUE *l'esclave ait sa nourriture et son vêtement* (Montesquieu). *Veillez* À CE QUE *toutes les persiennes soient bien closes* (Fr. Mauriac).

Veiller que is somewhat rare: *Veille* QU'*il* [un secret] *demeure en toi dans sa fraîcheur première* (M. Bedel).

1245 PAR AILLEURS can mean *par une autre voie* [by (through) another way, road, path]: *Il faut faire venir vos lettres* PAR AILLEURS (Littré).

Also, it very frequently means "besides," *d'autre part* [on the one hand . . . on the other hand], *d'un autre point de vue, pour le reste: Je l'ai trouvé très irrité et,* PAR AILLEURS, *décidé à se retirer* (Ac.).   *Cela lui était,* PAR AILLEURS, *indifférent* (A. Malraux).   *C'était,* PAR AILLEURS, *un brave homme* (H. Bosco).

1246 PAR CONTRE [on the other hand]. This term is rejected by purists, ignored by the Academy, but unquestionably accepted by the best authors: PAR CONTRE, *je ne suis plus trop rassuré en face de moi-même* (A. France).   PAR CONTRE, *quand quelqu'un te livrera une de ces impressions obscures, ne la rejette pas* (G. Duhamel).   *Les aliments ne sont touchés qu'avec des gants de caoutchouc.* PAR CONTRE, *à table, on se sert avec les doigts* (P. Morand).   *J'étais malade de honte et prêt à pleurer.* PAR CONTRE, *mon père exultait d'une joie tapageuse* (H. Troyat).

1247 QUOIQUE / QUOI QUE. The distinction between these two is:

quoique = *bien que* [although]: QUOIQU'*il soit jeune, il est très réfléchi* (Ac.).

Quoi que = "quelque chose que" [whatever, no matter what]: *Restons fermes,* QUOI QU'*il arrive.*

1248 (1) *Quoique ça* (= *malgré cela*) [in spite of that] belongs to popular language: *Mais* QUOIQUE ÇA, *c'est tout de même un collège* (A. Daudet).

(2) *Bien que* [although] is at times used incorrectly for *quoi que* [whatever, no matter what]: *L'âme humaine n'est point partout la même,* BIEN QU'*en dise M. Levallois* (Flaubert). *Aucune femme,* BIEN QU'*elles prétendent, n'étant indifférente à la beauté physique et à la gloire . . . (Maupassant).*

1249 **SOIT** [be, (so) be it]. In order to indicate an alternative, you can have *soit . . . soit; soit . . . ou; soit que . . . soit que; soit que . . . ou que* [whether; whether . . . or; whether . . . whether; *etc*]; SOIT *raison,* SOIT *caprice,* / *Rome ne l'attend pas pour son impératrice* (Racine). SOIT *rapide disparition du mal* OU *sursaut de volonté* (H. Bordeaux). SOIT QU'*il le fasse,* SOIT QU'*il ne le fasse pas* (Ac.). SOIT QU'*elle ne comprît pas* OU *qu'elle ne voulût pas comprendre . . .* (Th. Gautier).

1250 The following is an archaic use: SOIT *en paix* OU SOIT *en guerre* (Ronsard). *Soit qu'il l'accorde* OU SOIT *qu'il le refuse.* For Littré, the use of *ou* is nothing more than "a pleonasm which does not merit condemnation."

CORRECT FRENCH IN SUBORDINATE CLAUSES

I. USE OF MOODS (MODES)—PRINCIPLES

1251 Use:
(a) **the indicative** when the statement is made on the level of reality, placed in one of the three periods in duration of time [past, present, future].
(b) **the conditional** when you wish to indicate a hypothetical future. According to most modern linguists, this mood is nothing more than a sector of the indicative mood. Thus, for each use of the indicative there is a corresponding use of the conditional when the action is placed in the realm of a hypothetical future: *Je crois que tu* RÉUSSIRAS. / *Je crois qu'en changeant de méthode tu* RÉUSSIRAIS.
(c) **the subjunctive** when you indicate that the fact is placed not on the level of reality but rather in the realm of things that are simply envisaged, things that do not exist or do not yet exist, and thoughts that are expressed with a certain amount of drive or feeling that come from within yourself, from your heart and soul, for example, thoughts that express volition, desire, regret, joy, fear, etc.

Noun Clauses

1252 Use the subjunctive:
(1) after impersonal expressions that indicate possibility, impossibility, doubt, negation, necessity, approval, disapproval, or expressions that indicate some stirring in your heart and soul: *Il est possible, impossible, douteux, nécessaire, important, exclu, bon, juste, urgent que cela se* FASSE. *Il faut, il importe, il est temps, il vaut mieux qu'on* PARTE.
(2) after verbs of opinion or perception when the subordinate fact is simply envisaged in the mind, not in reality. That is the case after forms that are negative, interrogative, conditional (introduced by *si* [if])—or, after verbs expressing negation, doubt, uncertainty (*nier, douter, contester, démentir*, etc.): *Je ne crois pas qu'il le* FASSE. *Pensez-vous qu'il le* FASSE? *Si vous jugez que cela* SOIT *possible . . . Je nie, je doute, je conteste que cela* SOIT.
(3) after verbs that express volition, command, interdiction or prohibition, hindrance or impediment: *Je veux, j'ordonne, je commande, j'exige, je demande, je défends, je permets, je consens, je souhaite, j'empêche qu'on* FASSE *cela.*
(4) after verbs expressing a feeling, a stirring of the heart and soul (joy, grief or pain, fear, regret, etc.) and after nouns or adjectives of the same type as these verbs (*la crainte que, la peur*

que, heureux que, surpris que, etc.): *Je regrette, je m'étonne, je me réjouis, je suis heureux, content qu'il le* FASSE.

Special Observations

INDICATIVE, CONDITIONAL, SUBJUNCTIVE, INFINITIVE

1253   Use the **indicative** if the subordinate fact is real after **il n'est pas douteux** (*contestable, discutable,* etc.) **que, il n'y a pas de doute que, il ne fait pas de doute que, il est hors de doute que, sans doute que, nul doute que, c'est dommage que, il est possible que, il est de fait que.**

Use the **conditional** if the fact is hypothetical or eventual: *Il n'est pas douteux qu'il* VIENDRA, *qu'en insistant il* VIENDRAIT.

1254   After **il suffit que,** use the **subjunctive,** rarely the **indicative** which is archaic: *Il suffit que vous le* DISIEZ *pour que je le croie* (Littré). *Il me suffit que vous l'*AIMEZ (Molière).

1255   After impersonal expressions indicating certainty, plausibility or result, use:

(a) **the indicative** when these expressions are used affirmatively: *Il est certain, sûr, probable, vraisemblable, évident qu'il viendra. Il y a apparence, il me paraît, il s'ensuit que cela se* FERA. *Il y a une chance sur trois qu'il* EST *Italien* (P. Valéry).

However, after *il est probable, il est vraisemblable, il est exact, il y a apparence, il y a des chances,* the subjunctive is not impossible: *Il est donc probable . . . qu'il lui* AIT *parlé* (M. Pagnol). *Il est vraisemblable que . . . cette nécessité-là* SOIT *devenue inutile* (E. Jaloux).

(b) **the conditional** if the subordinate fact is hypothetical or eventual: *Il est certain, sûr, évident, probable, vraisemblable qu'en changeant de méthode, il* RÉUSSIRAIT.

(c) **the subjunctive** when these impersonal expressions are used in negative, interrogative, or conditional clauses—or, more generally, when the fact is merely envisaged in the thought: *Il n'est pas certain, sûr, évident qu'il* VIENNE. *Est-il vrai, sûr, certain qu'il* PARTE? *Tous ont l'accent de Paris, s'il est vrai que Paris* AIT *un accent* (Fr. Jammes).

At times, however, you have the **indicative:** *Il n'est pas sûr que je* PARTIRAI. *Est-il certain que vous* VIENDREZ? *S'il est vrai qu'on ne* PEUT *rien lui reprocher, ne le condamnons pas.*

1256   After **il arrive que, il advient que, il se fait que, il se peut que, il se trouve que, il survient que,** use the **subjunctive** when the fact is visualized in the thought (generally when these expressions are used in negative, interrogative or conditional clauses): *Il n'arrive (n'advient, ne se fait, ne se peut, ne se trouve, ne survient) jamais que cela se* FASSE. *Arrive-t-il, advient-il, se fait-il, se peut-il, se trouve-t-il, survient-il que cela se* FASSE? *S'il arrive (advient, se fait, se peut, se trouve, survient) qu'on* AIT *ce malheur. . . .*

Use the **indicative** if the subordinate fact is real; the **conditional** if it is hypothetical or eventual: *Il arrive (advient, se fait, se peut, se trouve, survient) que l'on* PERDE *tout ce qu'on a,—que l'on* SOUHAITERAIT *changer de situation.*

1257 **Il semble que** [it seems that] (with or without an indirect object: *me, te, lui . . .*):
(a) Taken affirmatively, it is followed by the **indicative** or the **conditional** (an eventual fact), or by the **subjunctive:** *Il (me) semble que vous* AVEZ *raison, que vous* DEVRIEZ *partir, que vous* AYEZ *raison.*
(b) Taken negatively or interrogatively, it is followed by the **subjunctive:** *Il ne (me) semble pas qu'on* DOIVE *partir.   (Vous) semble-t-il qu'on* PUISSE *partir?*
(c) Followed by an adjective used as an attribute, it takes the same mode as the impersonal expression *il est . . .* formed with the adjective: *Il (me) semble évident que vous* AVEZ *raison, que vous* AURIEZ *raison si . . .   Il (me) semble douteux que vous* AYEZ *raison.*

1258 What has just been said above also applies to *il (me, te . . .) paraît que* with one reservation, however: when used in the affirmative, this expression takes after it only the **indicative** or the **conditional** (not the subjunctive): *Il (me) paraît que vous* AVEZ *raison, que vous* DEVRIEZ *partir.*

1259 After **(il) m'est avis que** [it is my opinion that . . ., in my opinion . . .], the **indicative** is used or the **conditional** (an eventual fact): *(Il) m'est avis que le temps* VA *changer.   M'est avis que ce* SERAIT *une sage précaution de les avertir* (J. Green).

1260 After **il s'agit que** (a rare construction) [*il s'agit de* (it is a matter of, it is a question of) is the usual term], the **indicative** is used when a reality is indicated or the **conditional** when an eventuality is indicated; the **subjunctive** is used if a necessity is expressed: *Il s'agit que Rome* A *besoin d'un maître* (Voltaire). *Il s'agit que nous* PÉRIRIONS *si . . .   Il s'agit que la participation* DEVIENNE *la règle et le ressort d'une France renouvelée* (Ch. de Gaulle).

1261   After **(il) n'empêche que** [it does not prevent . . ., there's no keeping from . . ., etc.[, the **indicative** is used or, if an eventual fact is expressed, the **conditional** is used: *Il n'empêche qu'en la saluant . . . je ne* PUS *me défendre d'un mouvement de retrait* (É. Henriot). *N'empêche que je* SUIS *un équipage de défaite* (Saint-Exupéry). *N'empêche que l'entreprise* PÉRICLITERAIT *si. . .*
At times the subjunctive is used: *Il n'empêche . . . que nous* APPROCHIONS *de l'objectif qui est le nôtre* (Ch. de Gaulle).   This is an improper use.

1262   After verbs of opinion or perception, the subordinate clause introduced by **que** takes the **indicative** if the fact is real, the **conditional** if the fact is hypothetical, the **subjunctive** if the fact is simply envisaged in the thought; in many cases, this occurs after a main clause which is negative, interrogative, or conditional. Examples:
Je crois, j'affirme, je déclare, je vois, je sais, je sens que nous RÉUSSIRONS; *que nous* RÉUSSIRIONS *en procédant autrement. Je ne crois pas, je ne vois pas que nous* PUISSIONS *réussir. Croyez-vous, estimez-vous que nous* PUISSIONS *réussir? Si vous croyez, si vous estimez que nous* PUISSIONS *réussir, dites-le.*

1263   After a main clause that is negative, interrogative or conditional, a verb expressing opinion or perception calls for the **indicative** after it if a reality is indicated; the **conditional** if an eventuality is expressed: *Nous ne savions pas que la ville* ÉTAIT *si distante* (A. Gide).   *Croit-on que nous* SOMMES *sur un lit de roses?* (Colette.)   *Je ne crois même pas que l'on* POURRAIT *lui reprocher une distraction* (G. Duhamel).   *Si je pensais que Guillaume* SERAIT *plus heureux. . ., je fuirais avec lui loin de Paris* (A. Maurois).

1264   **Espérer que** [to hope that], **se flatter que** [to flatter oneself that], when used in the affirmative normally take the **indicative** after them or the **conditional** if an eventual fact is expressed; at times, also, they are followed by the **subjunctive** (when the idea of *croire* [to believe] is expressed): *J'espère qu'il* VIENDRA *bientôt* (Ac.).   *Je me flatte que vous* ÊTES *quitte de votre accès de goutte* (Voltaire).   *J'espère qu'il* POURRAIT *payer un peu mes dettes* (Stendhal).   *Il se flatte qu'avec un peu de chance il* RÉUSSIRAIT.   *Murs d'argile . . ., espérant qu'enfin vous* CÉDIEZ, *je vous longe* (A. Gide).   *Je me flattais donc qu'elle* SENTÎT *la disproportion de l'honneur que je lui avais fait* (A. Hermant).
When these verbs are used negatively or interrogatively, they

generally take the **subjunctive** after them, at times the **indicative,** or the **conditional:** *Je n'espère pas que vous le* FASSIEZ (Littré). *Je ne me flatte pas que ces pages* PUISSENT *avoir beaucoup de lecteurs* (É. Henriot). *Il n'espère pas qu'il* ENTENDRA *de nouveau l'ordre mystérieux* (G. Bernanos). *On n'espère pas qu'il* MANQUERA *l'oeuf* (J. Renard). *Espérez-vous que je le* FASSE, or *que je le* FERAI? (Littré.) *Espères-tu que je le* FERAIS *sans toi?*

1265   What has just been explained above also applies to *à l'espoir que* and *l'espérance que* [in the hope that].

1266   **Ignorer que** [not to know that, to be unaware that], in tne affirmative, negative or interrogative often takes the **subjunctive** after it; if the fact is real, it takes the **indicative;** if it is eventual, the **conditional:** *J'ignorais qu'il* FÛT *arrivé* (Ac.). *Il n'avait pas ignoré que Félicité* EÛT *un amant* (A. France). *Ignorais-tu qu'il* FÛT *de retour? Il ignorait que j'*AVAIS *donné ma démission* (Chateaubriand). *Vous n'ignorez pas qu'elle* EST *riche* (G. Sand). *Ignorez-vous qu'il* EST *malade?* (G. Bernanos). *Je n'ignore pas qu'il se* TIRERAIT *d'embarras sans moi.*

1267   **Je ne sache pas que** [I do not know that . . .], **on ne sache pas que** [one does not know that . . .] require the **subjunctive** in the clause that follows: *Je ne sache pas que mettre tout en doute, préalablement,* VAILLE *mieux que tout croire* (H. Bosco). *On ne sache pas qu'elle* AIT *jamais protesté autrement* (A. Billy). [See also entry no. 931.]

1268   **Nier que** [to deny that], **douter que** [to doubt that], **contester que** [to contest, to challenge that], **démentir que** [to give the lie to, to contradict that], **disconvenir que** [not to agree that], **dissimuler que** [to conceal the fact that] are generally followed by the **subjunctive;** by the **conditional** if an eventual fact is expressed: *Je nie (je ne nie pas, nieras-tu?), je doute (je ne doute pas, doutes-tu?), je conteste (je ne conteste pas, contestes-tu?) qu'il* AIT *raison. Je ne nie pas que la liberté ne* SOIT *pour une nation le premier des biens* (A. France). *Nierez-vous que notre religion* SOIT *belle?* (R. Martin du Gard.) *Doutez-vous que cela ne* SOIT *vrai?* (Littré.) *Elle ne doute pas qu'elle* FERAIT *mieux encore* (J. Renard). *Je doute qu'ils vous* LAISSERAIENT *jouer contre votre propre monnaie* (G. Bernanos).

When used negatively or interrogatively, these verbs are followed by the **indicative** if the reality of a fact is emphasized: *Je ne doute pas qu'il* FERA *tout ce qu'il pourra* (Littré). *Tu ne nieras pas que* *tu m'*AS *forcé la main* (G. Marcel). *Je ne me dissimule pas qu'il y* AURA *du tirage!* (H. Bernstein.) *Douterais-tu que cette main . . .* A *tué Cragnasse?* (Ch. Silvestre.)

1269   After **on dirait que** [one would say (or think) that], **on aurait dit (on eût dit) que** [one would have said (or thought) that], **vous diriez (auriez dit, eussiez dit) que** [you would say or think (you would have said or thought) that] (= *il semble, il semblait que)* [(= it seems, it seemed that)], the **indicative** is ordinarily used if a reality is envisaged; the **conditional,** if an eventual fact is expressed. Examples:

On dirait que son cou GROSSIT (R. Boylesve). *On aurait dit que ma présence* ÉTAIT *attendue* (É. Estaunié). *On eût dit qu'il* S'AGISSAIT *de son propre corps* (P. Valéry). *On dirait que, sans mon avis, vous n'*OSERIEZ *rien entreprendre.*

The **subjunctive** after these expressions (in use during the classical period) is used today: *On dirait qu'il* ROUGISSE *de sa nature secrète* (M. Arland). *On eût dit que les sons échappés de ce souffle* FUSSENT *émis comme un signal* (H. Bosco).

1270   **Oublier que** [to forget that] is followed by the **indicative,** or the **conditional** (an eventual fact), or the **subjunctive** (only when used in the affirmative if a fact is envisaged in thought): *J'ai oublié qu'il* DEVAIT *venir me chercher* (Ac.). *N'oubliez pas que je vous* ATTENDS (Id.). *Oubliez-vous qu'elle* DÉPEND *d'une mère vaine et inflexible?* (G. Sand.) *Il avait oublié qu'elle* EXISTÂT (J. Kessel). *J'oublie que vous* PRENDRIEZ *bien un rafraîchissement. N'oubliez pas (oubliez-vous?) que je* DEVRAIS *partir à dix heures.*

1271   After **promettre que** [to promise that] (= *s'engager à faire . . .)* [(= to commit oneself to doing . . ., to undertake to do . . .)], the **indicative** is used (one of the tenses in future time): *Je vous promets bien que je* FERAI *tout mon possible* (Ac.). *Je ne vous promets pas (promettez-vous?) que tout se* PASSERA *bien.*

When it means "to affirm" or "to assure," **promettre que** takes the **indicative** or the **conditional,** or the **subjunctive,** according to the nuance in thought: *Je vous promets qu'il* SERA *puni* (Littré). *Vous me promettez que vous ne vous battez pas aujourd'hui?* (A. Dumas fils.) *Je vous promets que je ne l'*AI *pas épargné* (Deharveng). *Je vous promets qu'ils* [les pronoms] *ne* SAURAIENT *troubler ma digestion* (A. Hermant). *Je ne vous promets pas que la balance* SOIT *exacte* (Id.).

1272   After **s'attendre que** [to expect that], when in the affirmative, the **indicative** or the **subjunctive** is used, depending on the shade of difference in the thought expressed: *Je m'attends que vous* VIENDREZ *demain* (Ac.). *Je m'attendais qu'il* ALLAIT *m'éviter* (Musset). *Je m'attendais que M. Lancelot* JETÂT *les hauts cris* (A. Hermant).

When used in the negative or interrogative, it is followed by the **subjunctive,** rarely by the **indicative:** *Ne vous attendez pas que je le* FASSE (Littré). *Vous attendez-vous que je le* FASSE? *On ne s'attend point que les Athéniens . . .* METTRONT *en fuite la nombreuse flotte du grand roi* (Voltaire, cited by Deharveng).

1273   **S'attendre à ce que** [to expect that] is frequently used and it normally takes the **subjunctive** after it, somewhat rarely the **indicative:** *Il s'attend à ce que je* REVIENNE (Ac.). *Il ne s'attendait pas à ce que l'incinération* FÛT *si longue* (J. Schlumberger). *Vous attendez-vous à ce qu'il* PARTE? *Je m'attends à ce que Paris* VA *avoir le sort de Varsovie* (Flaubert).

1274   **Admettre que** [to admit, to allow that], **mettre que** [to suppose, to grant, to assume that], **comprendre que** [to understand that, to admit that, etc.], **concevoir que** [to conceive, to imagine that], **supposer que** [to suppose that].

(a) When used in the affirmative, they are followed by the **indicative** if the fact is placed on the level of real things; the **conditional** if the thought expresses something that would happen eventually; the **subjunctive** if the thought expresses a potential possibility or something unreal.

Examples:

J'admets qu'il en EST *ainsi* (Littré). *Mettez que je n'*AI *rien dit* (Ac.). *Vous comprenez que cela* DOIT *m'inquiéter* (Id.). *Tu peux concevoir que je ne* CÉDERAI *pas. Je suppose que le mage* CROYAIT *en lui-même* (Alain).

Tu admettras qu'un autre plan CONVIENDRAIT *mieux. Mettons qu'avec mon aide il* RÉUSSIRAIT. *Vous comprendrez qu'en changeant de méthode nous* RÉUSSIRIONS. *Je conçois qu'il* FAUDRAIT *un peu de relâche. Je suppose que tu* FERAIS *bien ce travail.*

J'admets qu'il y AIT *six mille graines semées qui germent* (Littré). *Mettons que cela* SOIT *vrai* (Ac.). *Elle comprendra que nous* SOYONS *restés ici* (M. Genevoix). *Je conçois qu'il n'*AIT *pas été satisfait de votre conduite* (Ac.). *Je suppose que vous* FASSIEZ *le voyage de Paris en Bretagne* (Nodier).

(b) When used in the negative or interrogative, these verbs require the **subjunctive:** *Je n'admets pas, ne mettons pas, je ne comprends pas, je ne conçois pas, ne supposez pas (admettez-vous . . . .?*

mettrons-nous . . .? comprends-tu . . .? conçois-tu . . .? supposes-tu . . .?) que cela se FASSE.

1275   After **supposé que** and **à supposer que,** meaning *dans la supposition que,* the **subjunctive** is always used: *Supposé que l'inoculation* AIT *été parfaite* (Voltaire).

1276   Certain verbs of decision or resolution, used with **que,** are followed by the **indicative** if the thought is expressed on the level of reality. For example: **arrêter** [to stop, to delay, to hold up], **commander** [to order], **convenir** [to agree, to acknowledge, to admit], **décider** [to decide], **établir** [to establish], **exiger** [to insist], **ordonner** [to command], **prescrire** [to prescribe, to ordain], **régler** [to rule, to regulate], **résoudre** [to resolve]. Examples:

J'arrête que l'exécution AURA *lieu demain* (Hugo).   *Le tribunal a décidé que la donation* ÉTAIT *nulle* (Ac.).   *Les juges ordonneront. . . que les parties intéressées* SERONT *appelées* (Civil Code).

But when these verbs express merely the general idea of *vouloir* [to want, to will], they are followed by the **subjunctive:** *Ils convinrent que cela* FÛT *fait* (Littré). *L'empereur Trajan ordonna que des quintuplés* FUSSENT *élevés aux frais de sa cassette particulière* (J. Rostand).

1277   **Consentir** [to consent], **dire** [to say, to tell], **écrire** [to write], **être d'avis** [to be of the opinion . . .], **faire savoir** [to inform, to notify], **prendre garde** [to take care, to watch out (not) to], **prétendre** [to claim, to maintain], **signifier** [to signify, to mean]. When these verbs are used with **que,** they express either a simple opinion or a will; if they express a simple opinion, they call for the **indicative** or **conditional;** if they express a will, they call for the **subjunctive.** Examples:

*Je consens (= j'accepte comme vrai) que le haut clergé n'*EST *pas coupable* (A. Gide).   *Je dis qu'il* VIENT, *qu'il* VIENDRAIT *si . . .   Prenez garde (= remarquez)* [notice], *monsieur, que vous vous* ADDRESSEZ *à un officier ministériel* (M. Donnay).   *Je consens (= je veux bien)* [I am willing] *que vous le* FASSIEZ (Ac.).   *Prenez garde qu'on ne vous* VOIE (Id.).

1278   **Entendre que,** in the meaning of *percevoir par l'ouïe* [to hear, "to know from hearing"], requires the **indicative:**   *J'entends qu'on* VIENT.   In the meaning of *vouloir* [to want], it is followed by the **subjunctive:** *J'entends qu'on m'*OBÉISSE (Littré).   In the meaning of *avoir comme intention* [to intend], it is sometimes followed by the *indicative: J'entends bien que mes trois fils* SERONT *agiles, adroits, robustes, si la vie me prête assistance* (G. Duhamel).

1279 **Le ciel permit que** [The sky (heaven) permitted that], **le malheur veut que** [misfortune wants that], **le hasard voulut que** [chance wanted that], **je veux bien que** (= *j'admets que*), etc. After any of these, the **indicative** is at times used or the **conditional** in order to express ascertainment or establishment of a real or eventual fact. Examples:

La légende veut qu'à Bagdad il RENCONTRA *l'illustre El Ghazali, et qu'en le voyant, celui-ci . . .* AURAIT *dit . . .* (J. and J. Tharaud). *Le malheur veut que les spécialistes ne* SAVENT *pas toujours écrire* (J. Green). *Je veux donc bien que toute règle de justice* EST *vaine si l'on n'aime point* (Alain).

If **vouloir** [to want, to will] truly means the idea of will (volition), the **subjunctive** is used: *Le ciel voulut que, dans sa route, il* RENCONTRÂT *le médecin du village* (Musset). *Le sort voulut que ces paroles* FUSSENT *prophétiques* (H. Bordeaux).

1280 Certain verbs of feeling are used with *que* or with *de ce que;* when used with *que,* they call for the **subjunctive:** *Je me réjouis, je m'étonne, je me plains qu'il* AIT *fait cela.* When used with *de ce que,* they are generally followed by the **indicative** or **conditional** (an eventual fact), but the **subjunctive** is not incorrect: *On s'étonne de ce qu'il n'y* A *presque jamais de changement* (Montesquieu). *Il . . . se plaignait à d'autres de ce que je ne l'*AIMAIS *pas* (B. Constant). *Il s'étonne de ce qu'il ne* SOIT *pas venu* (Ac.). *Madame de la Hotte se réjouissait de ce que sa fille* ÉPOUSÂT *un beau garçon* (R. Boylesve). *Je vais être obligé de me plaindre de ce que la mariée* SOIT *trop belle* (P.-H. Simon).

1281 When the subordinate clause introduced by **que** in an inverted position is at the beginning of the sentence, its verb is generally written in the **subjunctive:** *Qu'on* PUISSE *agir sur lui par cette crainte, Napoléon en est certain* (J. Bainville). *Qu'il* AIT *refusé les rubans va de soi* (A. Maurois).

If you want to emphasize the reality of a fact or to indicate its eventuality, the **indicative** or **conditional** is used: *Que l'homme* EST *né pour le bonheur, certes toute la nature l'enseigne* (A. Gide). *Que tu* RÉUSSIRAIS *en changeant de méthode, c'est bien certain.*

1282 If the clause is introduced by **que** and is placed in relation to expressions such as **d'où vient, de là vient, l'important est,**

l'idée que, le fait que, etc., the verb is in the **indicative,** the **conditional,** or the **subjunctive**—according to the nuance in thought: *D'où vient que le temps de notre petite enfance nous APPARAÎT si doux?* (G. Bernanos.) *De là vient que la prison EST un supplice si horrible* (Pascal). *L'essentiel est qu'on VIENT à votre secours* (R. Rolland) *L'idée que Poil de Carotte EST quelquefois distingué amuse la famille* (J. Renard). *Le fait que nous VIVONS à l'époque industrielle n'empêche pas que . . .* (Ch. de Gaulle).

Other examples: *D'où vient qu'en réfléchissant tu CHANGERAIS d'opinion? L'essentiel est qu'avec votre aide nous RÉUSSIRIONS. Je note le fait que tu CHANGERAIS d'opinion si les circonstances se modifiaient. D'où vient que je ne SOIS jamais interrogé sur son âge?* (M. Arland.) *Le pire était qu'à rêver sans cesse, il OUBLIÂT la moitié du temps de boire et de manger* (M. Aymé). *L'idée qu'il PUISSE risquer sa vie pour moi m'est intolérable* (A. Gide). *Le fait que Stiopa se SOIT déjà remis à écrire . . . est un mauvais signe* (H. Troyat).

1283   After expressions like **apparemment que, bien sûr que, peut-être que, probablement que, sans doute que,** etc., the **indicative** or **conditional** is used, according to the meaning conveyed: *Apparemment qu'il VIENDRA* (Ac.)., or: *qu'il VIENDRAIT si. . . Peut-être qu'il le DIT* (Corneille), or: *qu'il le DIRAIT si. . . Probablement que, sans doute que nous le REVERRONS,* or: *que nous le REVERRIONS si. . .*

1284   A subordinate infinitive clause dependent on a verb of perception, or **faire,** or **laisser:**
(a) Infinitive without a direct object: *Je LE vois venir, je LE regarde venir, je L'entends venir. Je LE ferai venir, je LA ferai venir, je LES ferai venir; je LE laisse partir, je LA laisse partir, je LES laisse partir. Je vois venir MON AMI, je fais venir MON AMI, je laisse venir MON AMI. Elle déclara . . . que rien ne LA ferait renoncer à son nouvel état* (A. Decaux).
(b) Infinitive with a direct object: *Je LE vois* or *je LUI vois planter un arbre; je LES entends* or *je LEUR entends fermer la porte.*

After *faire* or *laisser: Je fais, je laisse bâtir ma maison* **à** (or **par**) **cet architecte.** *Je LUI fais* or *je LE fais bâtir ma maison; je LUI laisse* or *je LE laisse bâtir ma maison.*

Relative Clauses

1285 (a) The verb in a subordinate relative clause is in the **indicative** when a certain fact is expressed that is real; in the **con-**

ditional when a hypothetical (imaginary) fact is expressed: *J'ai trouvé un médecin qui* A *pu me guérir, un conseiller que la raison* CONDUIT. *Je vois peu d'hommes qui* SONT *contents de leur sort. Est-il un trésor qui* VAUT *le sommeil? Si je retrouve le livre qui vous* A *plu, je vous l'enverrai. Donnez-moi la liste des livres qui vous* PLAIRAIENT.

(b) Generally speaking, the verb in a subordinate relative clause is in the **subjunctive** when the thought indicates a goal to be attained, an intention, a consequence, or when the idea conveys a certain doubt, some uncertainty; in particular, that is usually the case after a main clause which is negative, interrogative, or conditional: *Je cherche un médecin qui* PUISSE *me guérir, un conseiller que la raison* CONDUISE. *Je vois peu d'hommes qui* SOIENT *contents de leur sort. Est-il un trésor qui* VAILLE *le sommeil?* (A. France.) *S'il rencontre alors un sujet qui l'*ÉMEUVE. . . (J. Lemaitre).

1286   After **le seul** [the only], **le premier** [the first], **le dernier** [the last], **l'unique** [the one and only], **le suprême** [the supreme], and after a superlative or an expression of analagous value, the verb in the relative clause is in the **indicative** if the reality of the fact is emphasized, if a certainty is expressed. But it is in the **conditional** if the eventuality is indicated: *C'est le seul poste, l'unique poste que vous* POUVEZ *(que vous* POURRIEZ*) remplir. Voilà le seul plaisir, le plus grand plaisir que j'*AI *(que j'*AURAIS*) goûté. C'est une des grandes erreurs qui* SOIENT *parmi les hommes* (Molière).

But the verb is in the **subjunctive** if the main clause contains some sort of measure of restraint or temperament, either by expressing a certain doubt in thought or by a desire to avoid a cutting, sharp tone: *C'est le seul poste, l'unique poste que vous* PUISSIEZ *remplir. Voilà le seul plaisir, le plus grand plaisir que j'*AIE *goûté.*

1287   At times, but not necessarily, the verb is in the **subjunctive** in the relative clause if it depends on the main clause which is in the subjunctive: *Je doute, je ne crois pas qu'il prenne le remède qui* CONVIENNE (or, according to the meaning: *qui convient, qui conviendrait*). *Quel que soit le coup que je* REÇOIVE (Musset). *Rieux n'était pas même sûr que ce fût elle qu'elle* ATTENDÎT (A. Camus).

1288   When the verb in the relative clause (introduced either by **où** or by a relative pronoun preceded by a preposition) implies the idea of *pouvoir, devoir,* or *falloir,* it is at times in the **infinitive** form: *Il indique l'endroit où* PRATIQUER *la plaie* (J. de Pesquidoux). *Il cherchait une main à quoi s'*ACCROCHER (Cl. Farrère).

1289   A relative clause is at times related to a noun clause that functions as a direct object: *Une grâce // que je crains // qu'on ne m'accorde pas* (Montesquieu). *Le mal // que personne ne peut contester // qui existe* (É. Faguet). *Ce démon // que tu dis // qui t'assiste* (A. Hermant).

These constructions may appear to be awkward. In modern usage, at least for certain sentences, it is preferable to use the **infinitive** form or even a construction using **dont** (= *au sujet duquel*): *Cet enfant que je dis* AVOIR VU, DONT *je dis que je l'ai vu.* In certain cases, an incidental clause may be used; for example, instead of saying *Une feuille // qu'on dit // qui paraît toutes les semaines* (Voltaire); or, instead of saying *D'un mot // que je suppose // que vous allez comprendre* (A. Camus), you could certainly say: *Une feuille qui paraît,* DIT-ON, *toutes les semaines. D'un mot que,* JE LE SUPPOSE, *vous allez comprendre.*

At times in literary language, in order to give to the relative clause a special prominence, it is placed before the antecedent: *Elle me montra,* QUI JOUAIT, *dans son jardin, un de ces ânes charmants de Provence, aux longs yeux résignés* (M. Barrès).

Conditional / Adverbial Clauses

1290   **Après que** [after . . .] logically takes the **indicative** form of the verb in its clause or the **conditional** if an eventual fact is expressed: *On cherche ce qu'il dit après qu'il* A *parlé* (Molière). *Après que vous* AUREZ *parlé, il parlera* (Ac.). *Comme un miroir qui garderait l'image après que l'objet* AURAIT *disparu* (Hugo).

In today's usage, **après que** is, annoyingly, often followed by the **subjunctive:** *Longtemps même après qu'elle m'*AIT *quitté* (J.-P. Sartre). *Une demi-heure après qu'il* AIT *été tué* (Montherlant). *Peu de temps après que j'*EUSSE *retrouvé la paix* (Fr. Mauriac). *Trois quarts d'heure après que des coups de feu* AIENT *été tirés* (Ch. de Gaulle).

In the French Academy's notice dated Nov. 19, 1964, the following statement is made: *"Après que* normally takes the indicative."

1291   The following indicate time or place and they take the **indicative,** the **conditional,** or the **subjunctive** according to the nuance in thought expressed: **Aussi loin que** [as far as], **d'aussi**

(or **de si**) **loin que** [as far away as], **au** (or **du**) **plus loin que** [as far back as, as far away in the distance as]. Examples:
  Mes pères, aussi loin que nous POUVONS *remonter. . .* (Renan). *Aussi loin que la vue* ALLAIT, *tout était nu* (Maupassant). *Du plus loin, d'aussi loin que je l'*AI *aperçu, j'ai couru au-devant de lui* (Ac.). *Nous n'apprendrions rien là-dessus, aussi loin que nous* REMONTERIONS. *Du plus loin qu'il me* SOUVIENNE, *la chose était ainsi* (Ac.). *Aussi loin que* PORTÂT *sa vue, elle n'apercevait que la forêt* (J. Green). *Au plus loin que ma vue* PUISSE *s'étendre, je n'aperçois rien* (Ac.).

1292 **Loin que, bien loin que** [far from] (= tant s'en faut que [far from it]) always take the **subjunctive:** *Et loin qu'à son crédit* NUISE *cette aventure. . .* (Molière). *Bien loin qu'il se* REPENTE, *il s'obstine dans sa rébellion* (Ac.).

1293 After **jusqu'à ce que** [until, until such time as], the **subjunctive** is generally used: *Je verrai cet instant jusqu'à ce que je* MEURE (Hugo). *Il avait combattu jusqu'à ce qu'il* FÛT *tué* (A. Malraux).
    But you may use the **indicative** or the **conditional,** according to whether you wish to emphasize the reality of a fact or indicate its eventuality: *Je m'étais fait un grand magasin de ruines, jusqu'à ce qu'enfin. . .je m'*ÉTAIS *trouvé une ruine moi-même* (Musset). *L'étoile. . .les précédait jusqu'à ce que, venant au-dessus du lieu où était l'enfant, elle s'y* ARRÊTA (A. France). *N'attendriez-vous pas à employer leur éloquence jusqu'à ce qu'ils* AURAIENT *leur nécessaire?* (Fénelon.)
    Instead of using **jusqu'à ce que,** in order to indicate a real fact, **jusqu'au moment où** is ordinarily used with the **indicative:** *Les danseurs frappaient le sol du pied. . .jusqu'au moment où. . .ils* S'ÉCROULAIENT (Y. Gandon).

1294 The present subjunctive **vienne** [from *venir*] is at times used to express the idea of "when such a thing will come, will happen" or "if such a thing comes or happens": VIENNE *l'été, le rossignol s'arrête* (G. Duhamel). VIENNE *la tempête, on double les amarres* (Alain). VIENNENT *les heures troubles, il s'épuise. . .* (É. Estaunié).

1295 After **non que** [not that], **non pas que** [not that], **ce n'est pas que** [it's not that], **faute que** [because of a lack, because of a failure to, for failure to], the **subjunctive** is normally used: *Non qu'il ne* SOIT *fâcheux de le mécontenter* (Ac.). *Non pas*

*que j'*ADMETTE *la compétence d'un écrivain à juger de son oeuvre*
(P. Bourget).   *Ce n'est pas que je* CRAIGNE *les hommes* (G. Sand).
Faute que l'État MÎT *les choses en ordre, il payait les déficits* (Ch. de
Gaulle).

These expressions (except for *faute que*) are at times followed by
the **indicative** (if a real fact is expressed) or the **conditional** (if an
eventual fact is indicated): *Ce n'est pas qu'il* EST *mauvais*
(A. France).   *Ce n'est point qu'il* RECHERCHAIT *une intrigue* (J. Giraudoux).   *Ce n'est pas que je n'*AURAIS *rien à dire des grèves en cours*
(Fr. Mauriac).   *Non pas que cela* AURAIT *changé quelque chose*
(E. Triolet).

1296   **Du moment que** (= *puisque*, or: *depuis que*) [since] normally
takes the **indicative** or **conditional:** *Du moment que vous me* CON-
VENEZ, *. . .il est nécessaire que vous sachiez exactement ce que
j'attends de vous* (É. Estaunié).   *Du moment que je l'*AI *connu, je l'ai
aimé* (Ac.).

     Du moment où is rare: *Du moment où l'archidiacre eut aperçu cet
inconnu, son attention sembla se partager entre la danseuse et lui*
(Hugo).

1297   **Pour** [in order, for], with a past or passive infinitive construction (at time present), can indicate the cause, often with a joint
idea of concession: POUR ÊTRE *plus qu'un roi, tu te crois quelque
chose* (Corneille).   POUR DORMIR *dans la rue, on n'offense personne*
(Racine).   POUR AVOIR OUBLIÉ *ces choses, l'apprenti sorcier a perdu la
tête* (A. Maurois).   *Je recevais maintenant des remontrances* POUR
ÊTRE *mal peigné* (P. Loti).   POUR ÊTRE *plus lyrique, on finit par ne
plus être précis du tout* (A. Gide).

1298   A relationship of cause (reason) can be expressed by using
a clause where an attribute is combined with **que** or
comme: *Les assistants,* ÉBLOUIS QU'*ils sont, se regardent furtive-
ment entre eux* (G. Duhamel).   *Vous ne le croiriez peut-être pas,
. . .* ENTÊTÉ COMME *vous l'êtes des préjugés de l'Orient* (Montesquieu).

1299   **Pour,** followed by an infinitive of purpose (goal), with the in-
sertion of a noun (or a personal pronoun) as subject, forms a construction which was used in Old French and which is found in
juridical language and in certain dialects of the Walloons in the
northeastern part of France, Savoy: *Le propriétaire peut exiger que
les meubles. . .soient vendus,* POUR LE PRIX EN ÊTRE PLACÉ. . . (Civil
Code, art. 603).

1300   After **bien que** [although], **quoique** [though, although], **encore que** [though, although], you may have a present participle or a past participle with **ayant** or **étant:** BIEN QU'ÉCRIVANT *un latin très élégant. . . ,il n'a pas le goût vif des Lettres anciennes* (Sainte-Beuve).   QUOIQUE AYANT COMMENCÉ *fort jeune l'étude des langues de l'Orient, je n'en sais que les mots les plus indispensables* (Nerval).   BIEN QU'ÉTANT REPARTI *vers l'aube. . .* (P. Benoit).

1301   After **bien que** [although], **quoique** [though, although], **quoi que** [whatever, no matter what], **encore que** [though, although], **malgré que** [though, although], **pour . . . que** [however . . . that], **si . . . que** [however . . . that], **pour si . . . que** [however . . . that], **pour aussi . . . que** [however . . . that], **quel que** [whatever, no matter what], **quelque . . . que** [whatever . . . that], the **subjunctive** is normally used: Examples:

Bien que je SACHE, *quoique je* PRENNE, *quoi que tu* DISES, *encore qu'il* VIENNE, *malgré qu'il le* FASSE, *pour grand qu'il* SOIT, *si mince qu'il* SOIT, *quel qu'il* SOIT, *quelque puissant qu'il* PARAISSE. Those are examples of general usage, which should properly be followed.

Some authors, however, at times use the **indicative** after these expressions in order to emphasize the reality of a fact, or the **conditional** to indicate an eventual fact (exceptionally after *quel que* or *quelque . . . que*): *Bien qu'elles* CRIAIENT (R. Rolland). *Quoique, pour un musicien,* C'EST *merveilleux* (Fr. Mauriac). *Encore que précisément ici je ne* VOIS *pas trop. . .* (A. Gide). *Pour petite qu'elle* EST, *elle est précieuse* (A. France). *Bien que sa corruption ne lui* NUIRAIT *point* (Chateaubriand). *Quoique je* SERAIS *furieux que vous me réveilliez* (M. Proust). *Encore que j'*AURAIS *droit à des félicitations* (P. Léautaud). *Quelles que* FURENT *les instances du marquis* (Diderot). *Quelque harcelé qu'il* SERA (La Varende). *Quelque désir que j'en* AURAIS (J. Dutourd).

1302   **Au lieu que** [whereas] is used with the **indicative** or with the **conditional,** depending on whether the reality of a fact is expressed or an eventual fact is indicated; with the **subjunctive** if the fact is merely considered in the thought: *Cet élan des pensées qui semble dépasser le but, au lieu qu'il l'*ATTEINT *à peine* (Alain). *Il ne songe qu'à ses plaisirs, au lieu qu'il* DEVRAIT *veiller à ses affaires* (Ac.). *Les Turcs vont de l'abstrait au concret, contrairement à nos races. . .chez qui l'objet évoque, au lieu que l'objet* NAISSE *d'une longue évocation* (J. Cocteau).

1303   After **alors (même) que** [when, (even) when, even though], **lorsque** [while], **lors (même) que** [though, even though], **quand (même)** [when, all the same, for all that, just the same], **cependant que** [while, whereas], **tandis que** [while, whereas], the **indicative** (a real fact) is used or the **conditional** (an eventual fact): *Votre santé est bonne, alors que, lorsque, cependant que, tandis que, quand la mienne ne l'*EST *pas ou du moins* POURRAIT **être meilleure.** *Quand tu* SERAIS *sac, je n'approcherais pas* (La Fontaine).

1304   **Tout. . .que** [although, though], as an adversative conjunction, is followed by the **indicative** or the **conditional** (an eventual fact), or, most often, by the **subjunctive** in modern usage: *Tout enfant que j'*ÉTAIS, *le propos de mon père me révoltait* (Chateaubriand).   *Toute mariée que je* SERAIS, *. . .je ne me fierais pas à moi* (Marivaux).   *Tout simple qu'il* SOIT, *il a déjà deviné* (Fr. Mauriac).   *Zéphyrin, tout savetier qu'il* FÛT, *visait au luxe* (Fr. Jammes).

1305   In sentences where a dependent clause indicates opposition or supposition and the verb is in the conditional or imperfect or pluperfect subjunctive, the main clause is connected to it by a simple juxtaposition or it is preceded by **que:** *Le danger serait (or fût-il) dix fois plus grand, je l'affronterais;* or: *. . .que je l'affronterais.   Voudrait-il (or il voudrait, voulût-il) le faire, il ne le pourrait pas;* or: *. . .qu'il ne le pourrait pas.   Le diable entrerait dans la maison qu'on le laisserait faire* (Hugo).

1306   **Des fois que, quelquefois que, un coup que** [all of which convey the meaning of "whenever, sometimes when. . . , now and then when. . ."] are used popularly with the **conditional:** *Je reste là un moment, des fois que vous m'*APPELLERIEZ (C. Bourniquel).   *Il faut attendre encore un peu, quelquefois qu'il* IRAIT (in Brunot).

The same is true of *(une) supposition que* [assuming that. . .] used with the **conditional** or **subjunctive:** *Une supposition qu'une femme* VOUDRAIT *se débarrasser de son mari* (G. de La Fouchardière).   *Supposition que tu* SOIS *en retard* (M. Genevoix).   *Une supposition que ce garçon* AIT EU *l'idée d'écrire tous les jours une petite lettre à son père* (M. Pagnol).

1307   After **si** [if], indicating an unreal fact in the past, you may have four combinations, as follows: *Si j'avais cherché, j'aurais trouvé; si j'eusse cherché, j'eusse trouvé; si j'avais cherché, j'eusse trouvé; si j'eusse cherché, j'aurais trouvé.*

1308   After the constructions **si c'était. . . qui** (or **que**) [if it were
. . . , what if it were. . .], **si ç'avait été. . . qui** (or **que**)
[(what) if it had been. . .], **si ç'eût été. . . qui** (or **que**) [(what)
if it had been. . .], the imperfect or the pluperfect is used,
either in the **indicative** or the **subjunctive:** *Si c'était moi qui*
AVAIS *fait cela* (Ac.).   *Comme si ç'avait été la roue de la fortune qui*
GLISSAIT *sur ces rails* (J. and J. Tharaud).   *Si c'était à sa citadelle*
*qu'on m'*ENVOYÂT (Stendhal).   *Si c'était lui qui* VÎNT *demain?*
(Musset.)   *Si c'était le diable qui* EÛT ÉCRIT *cette phrase généreuse*
(É. Henriot).

1309   Good French does not permit the use of the **conditional**
which popular language willingly uses after **si** [if] or **si que**
[what if. . . , how about. . .], in phrases such as: *Si tu vou-*
drais, on travaillerait ensemble (Fr. Carco).   *Si j'aurais su, j'aurais*
refusé.   Si qu'on marcherait un peu?

1310   In **s'il en fut** [if ever. . . , if ever there was (one)]. Do not
write *fut* as *fût*. **S'il en fut** is a set simple past: *Campement*
délicieux S'IL EN FUT, *où nous terminons le jour* (P. Loti).
   However, the verb is at times not used in its set form: *Un*
coquin s'il en EST (Littré).   *Ordre impératif s'il en* AVAIT *jamais* ÉTÉ
(Cl. Farrère).

1311   **Sinon** or **si ce n'est** [if not] are used elliptically to indicate opposition or negation: *Cette maison est une des plus belles,* SINON *la*
plus belle, SI CE N'EST *la plus belle du quartier.   Autant de piétons dans*
les rues, SINON *davantage* (R. Martin du Gard).
   Si pas [if not], in sentences of this sort, is a provincialism and it
is sometimes found in the works of French authors: *Il a au moins*
vingt-cinq ans SI PAS *plus* (P. Bourget).   *Il était en passe de devenir*
bienheureux, SI PAS *tout à fait saint* (Aragon).   However, it is better
to use *sinon* or *si ce n'est*.

1312   **Si tant est que** [if indeed] normally takes the **subjunctive:** *Je*
ne manquerai pas d'y aller, si tant est que je le PUISSE (Ac.).   *Ma*
dernière explication s'effondrait, si tant est que j'y EUSSE *jamais cru*
(M. Genevoix).
   It is quite exceptional to find *si tant est que* followed by the **in-**
dicative, in which case the supposition is then considered to have
all the hues of reality: *Il n'est pas impossible que ce soient eux qui*
*aient raison, si tant est que c'*EST *avoir raison que de penser comme*
pensera l'avenir (J. Rostand).

1313   **Pour peu que** [if only, if ever, however little] and **pour si. . .que** [however. . .that] take the **subjunctive:** *Pour peu que votre image en mon âme* RENAISSE. . . (Sully Prudhomme, cited by Le Bidois). *Pour si farceur qu'on* SOIT, *on n'escamote pas une ville* (A. Daudet).

1314   There are times when **si** is followed by a **future** or a **conditional** in sentences where the supposition bears on a subjacent (underlying) verb (*s'il est vrai que* [if it is true that], *si on admet que* [if one admits (grants) that], *si on met en fait que* [if one supposes (to be) in fact that], etc.) Examples:
   Cela vous fera-t-il, cela ne vous fera-t-il pas plaisir? Si cela vous FERA *plaisir, remettons la paysanne en croupe* (Diderot). *Pardon . . . si je ne puis t'aimer, si je ne t'*AIMERAI *jamais!* (R. Rolland.) *Si je ne* VOUDRAIS *pas le nier, je crois du moins qu'il en faut rabattre* (F. Brunetière). *Si jamais batailles* AURAIENT *dû être gagnées, ce sont celles-là* (A. Maurois).
   You can also have the future or the conditional after *si* in sentences containing the following expressions: *je veux être pendu si. . .* [I'll be hanged if. . .], *du diable si. . .* [the devil if. . .], *comme si. . .!* [as if. . .!], etc., where the whole group expresses the thought with a special force. Examples: *Ce que tu es, du diable si je le* SAURAI *jamais. . .* (A. France). *Du diable si je vous* AURAIS *reconnu* (M. Arland).

1315   The **conditional** is used after **au cas où, dans** (or **pour**) **le cas où, dans** (or **pour**) **l'hypothèse où** [in the event of, in the event that. . .]: *Au cas où une complication se* PRODUIRAIT, *faites-moi venir* (Ac.). *Dans le cas où quelqu'un se* PRÉSENTERAIT, *téléphonez-moi.*
   Rarely the **subjunctive:** *Au cas où il en* SOIT *encore temps* (A. Thérive). *Au cas où tu* PRENNES *nourriture en forêt* (M. Bedel).

1316   After **à (la) condition que** or **sous (la) condition que** [on condition that, providing that], the **indicative** or the **subjunctive** is used according to the nuance in thought: *Je vous donne cet argent à condition que vous* PARTIREZ *demain* or *que vous partiez demain* (Littré). *À la condition que vous* DÎNEREZ *chez moi ce soir* (Maupassant). *À condition que ce départ* SOIT *accepté* (M. Prévost).

1317   In conditional clauses beginning with **n'était, n'étaient, n'eût été, n'eussent été,** there is an omission of **si ce** (which is understood) all of which mean "if it weren't for. . ." or "if it had not been for. . .". Examples: N'ÉTAIENT *les hirondelles qui chantent, on n'entendrait rien* (P. Loti). N'EÛT ÉTÉ *sa toilette verte, on l'eût pris pour un magistrat* (A. France).

1318 The restrictive locutions **autant que** [as far as, as much as, as near as] and **pour autant que** [as far as, so long as] are used with the **indicative** or with the **conditional** or with the **subjunctive,** according to the nuance in thought: *Tel est l'âge magique, autant qu'on* PEUT *le décrire* (Alain). *Pour autant qu'elle se* MÊLAIT *de son métier* (P. Valéry). *Je ne lui conseillerais de rester dans ce gâchis qu'autant que le prince lui* DONNERAIT *une somme énorme* (Stendhal). *Jamais, autant que je* PUISSE *dire, elle n'avait vu de piano* (G. Duhamel). *Pour autant que j'en* PUISSE *juger, il y a urgence* (H. Bazin).

1319 **Comme si** [as if, as though] at the beginning of a conditional clause takes the imperfect **indicative** or the pluperfect **indicative;** it may also take the pluperfect **subjunctive,** at times the imperfect **subjunctive:** *Comme s'il* VOULAIT *ordonner à son camarade de les faire remplir* [*les verres*] (M. Prévost). *Comme si quelque souffle* AVAIT PASSÉ *sur eux* (Hugo). *Tu raisonnes là-dessus. . .comme si tu* EUSSES ÉTUDIÉ *les cours d'amour* (Th. Gautier). *C'était comme si ce regard. . .la* SUIVÎT *partout* (J. Green).

   Comme si is frequently used to introduce an exclamatory clause, in which case it may be followed by the conditional [see entry no. 1314]: *Comme si à vingt ans on n'*ÉTAIT *pas un homme!* (Fr. Mauriac.) *Comme s'il se* RÉCONCILIERAIT *jamais avant d'avoir vaincu!* (H. Troyat.)

1320 The **subjunctive** is ordinarily used after a second subordinate clause in the conditional when it is coordinate or simply placed side by side in juxtaposition to the first clause by using **que** as a replacement for **si** or **comme si:** *Si vous reculez quatre pas et* QUE *vous* CREUSIEZ, *vous trouverez un trésor* (La Fontaine). *Si je vais en Égypte et* QUE *j'y* SOIS *tué* (Stendhal). *Comme s'il était arrivé jusqu'au bord même d'un abîme et* QU'*il le* TROUVÂT *à ses pieds* (E. Jaloux).

   But fairly often also, the **indicative** is used: *Si nos sens ne s'opposaient pas à la pénitence et que notre corruption ne s'*OPPOSAIT *pas à la pureté de Dieu. . .* (Pascal). *Si je n'ai pas eu de sentiments humbles et que j'*AI *élevé mon âme* (Bossuet). *Si vous arrivez par le fond du vallon et que vous* DÉBOUCHEZ *brusquement dans* *la cour* (J. Schlumberger). *Comme si la vie leur était une prison, et que, tout à coup, quelqu'un leur* DÉSIGNAIT *une issue* (Fr. Mauriac).

1321 After **comme** [as, like] or after a comparative word followed by **que,** you may use *faire,* a substitute verb for a verb of action which precedes: *Il répondit comme les autres avaient* FAIT (Ac.). *Oserions-nous renier ces indésirables parents et les immoler, comme nous* FAISONS *les autres bêtes. . . ?* (J. Rostand.)

In sentences of this sort, you may also do away with the verb in the comparative clause: *Nous connaissons nos signaux mieux qu'un prêtre son bréviaire* (A. Chamson); or, you may even have the substitute verb *faire* followed by a complement introduced by *de,* or *pour,* or *avec: Ma mère me déshabilla . . . comme elle eût fait* D'*un très petit enfant* (G. Duhamel). *Il l'invita comme il faisait* POUR *ses élèves préférés* (Jér. Tharaud). *Nous l'examinions* [un grain de maïs] *comme un bijoutier fait* AVEC *une pierre* (P. Gascar).

1322 **Sans que** [without] is always used with the **subjunctive:** *Les dents lui poussèrent sans qu'il* PLEURÂT *une seule fois* (Flaubert).

1323 The **indicative** is used or, if an eventuality is indicated, the **conditional** is used with **selon que. . .ou (que)** or **suivant que. . .ou (que)** [according to whether. . . or] if an alternative is offered containing a hypothetical idea or one of conformity: *Selon que vous* SEREZ *puissant ou misérable / Les jugements de cour vous rendront blanc ou noir* (La Fontaine). *Il sera payé selon qu'il* TRAVAILLERA (Ac.). *Suivant qu'on m'*AIME *ou* HAIT, *j'aime ou hais à mon tour* (Corneille). [*La France*] *répondra aussi à ce que l'Afrique lui dira, suivant que l'Afrique* DÉCIDERA *de s'associer à elle, ou suivant que, selon une hypothèse que je rejette absolument, elle se* RE-FUSERAIT *à le faire* (Ch. de Gaulle).

At times, on the fringe of what is normal, the **subjunctive** is used, which is probably an influence of the constructions *soit que. . . soit que* and *soit que. . . ou que* [either. . .or; whether. . .or] which require the **subjunctive:** *À tout le moins avais-je pressenti. . .cette sorte d'enchantement (ou d'envoûtement, selon qu'on* VEUILLE *l'entendre) qui nous jette tout à coup au coeur d'un monde et d'une vie paniques* (M. Genevoix). *L'humour, l'humour d'observation surtout, c'est une certaine disposition d'esprit qui vous fait voir les gens et les choses sous un certain angle, l'angle pouvant tout changer suivant que l'on se* TRAVESTISSE *en major Anglais ou en Français moyen* (P. Daninos).

II. SEQUENCE OF TENSES

A Subordinate Clause in the Indicative

1324 (a) When the main verb is in the **present** or **future,** the verb
in the subordinate (dependent) clause is in the tense called
for by the meaning, as if you were treating it as an inde-
pendent clause:
Examples:

J'affirme [present]
[I affirm]

J'affirmerai [future]
[I shall (or will) affirm]

qu'il TRAVAILLE *en ce moment.* [present]
[that he is working at this moment].

qu'il A TRAVAILLÉ *hier.* [passé composé]
[that he worked yesterday].

qu'il TRAVAILLAIT *au moment
de l'accident.* [imperfect]
[that he was working at the time
of the accident].

qu'il AVAIT TRAVAILLÉ *avant
votre arrivée.* [pluperfect]
[that he had worked before
your arrival].

qu'il TRAVAILLA *la semaine
dernière.* [passé simple]
[that he worked last week].

qu'il TRAVAILLERA *demain.* [future]
[that he will work tomorrow].

qu'il AURA TRAVAILLÉ *avant
deux jours.* [future perfect]
[that he will have worked before
two days].

(b) When the main verb is in a **past** tense, the verb in the subordinate (dependent) clause is in the:

Imperfect or **passé simple** (according to the meaning intended), if
the fact is simultaneous.

Examples:

J'ai affirmé qu'il TRAVAILLAIT. [passé composé. . .imperfect]
[I affirmed that he was working.]

Il se fit qu'à ce moment même il ENTRA. [passé simple. . .passé simple]
[It so happened that at that very moment he entered.]

Il courut à moi au moment même où il me VIT. [passé simple. . .passé simple]
[He ran to me at the very moment when he saw me.]

Conditional or **conditional perfect** (according to the meaning intended,
if the fact is stated in posterior (past) time.

Examples:

J'ai affirmé qu'il TRAVAILLERAIT *demain.* [passé composé. . .conditional]
[I affirmed that he would work tomorrow.]

J'ai affirmé qu'il AURAIT TRAVAILLÉ [passé composé. . .conditional perfect]
   avant deux jours.
[I affirmed that he would have worked
   before two days.]

Pluperfect or **passé antérieur** (according to the meaning intended),
if the fact is stated in anterior time [i.e., prior to past].

Examples:

J'ai affirmé qu'il AVAIT TRAVAILLÉ. [passé composé. . .pluperfect]
[I affirmed that he had worked.]

Dès qu'il EUT PARLÉ, *une clameur s'éleva.*
   [passé antérieur. . .passé simple]
[As soon as he had talked, an outcry soared.]

(1) After a past tense in the main clause, you may use the
   present indicative in the subordinate clause if it expresses
   a fact which is true at all times: *La Fontaine a dit que l'absence*
   EST *le plus grand des maux* (A. Hermant).
(2) After a past tense in the main clause, you may also use in
   the subordinate clause a tense whose use must be explained
   by making clear that the fact in the subordinate clause is
   envisaged in relation to the moment the statement is made:
   Je vous ai promis que je FERAI *désormais tout mon*
   possible. Nous disions que vous ÊTES *l'orateur le plus éminent*
   du diocèse (A. France). *On m'a assuré que cette affaire* AURA
   PRIS *fin avant deux jours. Il chercha tant qu'il* TROUVA. *Vous*
   avez tant travaillé que vous RÉUSSIREZ.

A Subordinate Clause in the Subjunctive

1325 (a) When the main verb is in the **present** or **future,** the verb in the subordinate (dependent) clause is in the:

Present subjunctive in order to indicate simultaneous or posterior time: *Je veux, je voudrai qu'il* ÉCRIVE *sur-le-champ, qu'il* ÉCRIVE *demain.*

Past subjunctive [i.e., the passé composé in the subjunctive form] in order to indicate anterior time: *Je doute qu'il* AIT ÉCRIT *hier, qu'il* AIT ÉCRIT *avant mon départ.*

(b) When the main verb is in a **past** tense, the verb in the subordinate (dependent) clause is in the:

Imperfect subjunctive in order to indicate simultaneous or posterior time: *Je voulais, j'ai voulu, j'avais voulu qu'il* ÉCRIVÎT *sur-le-champ, qu'il* ÉCRIVÎT *le lendemain.*

Pluperfect subjunctive in order to indicate anterior time: *Je voulais, j'ai voulu, j'avais voulu qu'il* EÛT ÉCRIT *la veille; . . . qu'il* EÛT ÉCRIT *avant mon départ.*
  (1) After a present tense in the main clause (when the verb in the subordinate clause is in the subjunctive), it is in the imperfect or pluperfect, according to the case, if the subordinate clause expresses a fact simply possible or submitted to a condition stated or not: *En est-il un seul parmi vous qui* CON-SENTÎT? (Ac.) *On craint que la guerre, si elle éclatait, n'*ENTRAÎNÂT *des maux incalculables* (Littré).
  (2) After a past tense in the main clause (when the verb in the subordinate clause is in the subjunctive), it is in the present if the subordinate clause expresses a present or future fact in relation to the given moment, or even if it expresses a fact that is true at all times: *Il m'a rendu trop de services pour que je le* RENVOIE *en ce moment, pour que je le* RENVOIE *demain.   Qui a jamais douté que deux et deux ne* FASSENT *quatre?*
  (3) After a present conditional in the main clause (when the verb in the subordinate clause must be in the subjunctive), it is in the present or imperfect: *Je voudrais qu'il* VIENNE *or qu'il* VÎNT (Littré).
  (4) The **imperfect subjunctive** is no longer used in spoken

French, except perhaps the two forms *eût* and *fût*. Ordinarily, written French preserves the use of this tense in the verbs *avoir* and *être* and in the third person singular of other verbs; but, generally speaking, the **imperfect subjunctive** is frequently replaced by the **present subjunctive;** similarly, the **pluperfect subjunctive** is often replaced by the **past subjunctive** [i.e., the passé composé in the subjunctive form]: *Elle a exigé que je me* DÉBARRASSE (H. Bordeaux).   *Peu s'en est fallu qu'il ne* SOIT *tué* (Ac.).

1326   **SEQUENCE OF TENSES: A SUMMARY**

Main verb		Verb in the subordinate clause	
		Indicative	*Subjunctive*
	Simultaneous time:	Present	Present
	Posterior (past) time:	Future	Present
Present or **Future**	Anterior time: [prior to past]	Imperfect / Passé simple / Passé composé / Pluperfect	Past
Past	Simultaneous time:	Imperfect / Passé simple	Imperfect
	Posterior (past) time:	Conditional / Conditional Perfect	Imperfect
	Anterior time: [prior to past]	Pluperfect / Passé antérieur	Pluperfect

APPENDIX

GRAMMATICAL AND SPELLING CHANGES ALLOWED

(The Haby Decree)

The *Journal officiel de la République française* of Feb. 9, 1977 contains a decree issued by René Haby, Minister of Education, relative to about thirty grammatical or orthographical allowances. The complete text is reproduced here.

In the *Revue générale* (Brussels), issue of March, 1977, Joseph Hanse published a critical article concerning that decree. In the *Bulletin de l'Académie royale de Langue et de Littérature françaises* (vol. LV, no. 1, pp 1–31), you will find the text of his communication dated March 12, 1977 on the "Modifications orthographiques et tolérances grammaticales" ["Orthographical Modifications and Grammatical Allowances"]. Along with him, people will consider it "dangerous and harmful" to accustom students "to believing that *in all cases* they will be allowed to take liberties which usage (not only literary but also everyday language) continues to proscribe" and people will observe "the errors of fact and not merely of judgment which are numerous in this ministerial decree."

MINISTRY OF EDUCATION

Grammatical and Spelling Changes Allowed

The Minister of Education,

In view of the decree dated Feb. 26, 1901, relative to the simplification in teaching French syntax,

And in view of the opinion of the Council on General and Technical Instruction,

decrees:

Art. 1. The list annexed to the said decree of Feb. 26, 1901 is hereby replaced by the list annexed to the present decree.

Art. 2. The general director of curriculum and of coordination, the director of *lycées*, the director of colleges, and the director of schools are charged, insofar as each one is concerned, with carrying out the present decree.

Done in Paris, December 28, 1976.

RENÉ HABY

ANNEXE

Grammatical and Spelling Changes Allowed

In examinations or competitive tests, which are subordinate to the Ministry of Education and its approval of the grades within the elementary and secondary levels, whether or not it is a matter of special tests in spelling, the cases presented below will not be counted as errors on the part of candidates.

Under each heading, there are one, two, or three articles which are assigned a numerical order. Each article contains one or several examples, followed by a comment enclosed in a frame.

The examples and comments are presented in different forms, according to their purpose.

First type:

In the use of certain expressions, usage allows two possibilities without distinguishing between them any appreciable nuances in meaning.

It appeared useful to mention some of these expressions. Each example is composed of two sentences, each placed under the other. The comment is limited to pointing out the two possibilities offered by the language.

Second type:

For other expressions, usage allows a duality of constructions, but a distinction is made between them in the nuances of meaning; the speaker or writer who has been informed makes his / her preference agree with one or the other according to the meaning desired or suggested.

Under the headings, which treat expressions of this type, two parallel sentences are given for each example, but the comment is based on a particular scheme. In the first place, the comment recalls the two possibilities, making it clear that the choice between the two conveys a particular meaning; in the second place, the comment invites the examiners not to demand of the candidates a perfect perception of nuances in meaning in thought or style, which are at times subtle. The allowance is introduced by a succession of two statements: "Usage allows, according to the intended meaning, . . ." and "It will be allowed. . .in all cases."

Third type:

The third category consists of expressions which grammar, in its present state, requires to contain forms or agreements strictly defined, without necessarily considering every breach of norms as an indication of weakness in judgment. In certain cases, the norms themselves would be difficult to justify strictly, whereas the transgressions may come from a concern for analogical or logical coherence.

Under the headings that illustrate these cases, each example consists of a single sentence, containing within it in parentheses, the written form which advisedly ought not to be sanctioned. According to the nature of the question raised, the comment states simply the allowance or explicitness by recalling the rule.

Among the indications included below, it is fitting to distinguish between those that specify usage and those that propose allowances. The first must be taught. The second will not be taken into consideration, except for the correction of examinations or competitive tests; they are not to be studied in the classroom and, moreover, ought not to be substituted for grammatical or orthographical knowledge which the teaching of French must adhere to developing.

I. The Verb

1. Agreement of the verb preceded by several subjects side by side, more or less synonymous, in the third person singular:
La joie, l'allégresse s'empara (S'EMPARÈRENT) *de tous les spectateurs.*

> Usage requires, in this case, that the verb be in the singular.
> Agreement in the plural is allowed.

2(a). Agreement of the verb preceded by several subjects in the third person singular joined by *comme, ainsi que* and other locutions of equivalent use:
Le père comme le fils MANGEAIENT *de bon appétit.*
Le père comme le fils MANGEAIT *de bon appétit.*

> Usage allows, according to the intended meaning, agreement in the plural or in the singular.
> Either agreement will be allowed in all cases.

2(b). Agreement of the verb preceded by several subjects in the third person singular joined by *ou* or by *ni:*
Ni l'heure ni la saison ne CONVIENNENT *pour cette excursion.*
Ni l'heure ni la saison ne CONVIENT *pour cette excursion.*

> Usage allows, according to the intended meaning, agreement in the plural or in the singular.
> Either agreement will be allowed in all cases.

3. Agreement of the verb when the subject is a collective word accompanied by an object in the plural:
À mon approche, une bande de moineaux S'ENVOLA.
À mon approche, une bande de moineaux S'ENVOLÈRENT.

> Usage allows, according to the intended meaning, agreement with the collective word or with the object.
> Either agreement will be allowed in all cases.

4. Agreement of the verb when the subject is *plus d'un* accompanied or not by a complement in the plural:
Plus d'un de ces hommes M'ÉTAIT *inconnu.*
Plus d'un de ces hommes M'ÉTAIENT *inconnus.*

> Usage allows, according to the intended meaning, agreement in the plural or in the singular.
> Either agreement will be allowed in all cases.

5. Agreement of the verb preceded by *un des. . .qui, un de ceux que, une des. . .que, une de celles qui,* etc.:
La Belle au bois dormant est un des contes qui CHARMENT *les enfants.*
La Belle au bois dormant est un des contes qui CHARME *les enfants.*

> Usage allows, according to the intended meaning, agreement in the plural or in the singular.
> Either agreement will be allowed in all cases.

6. Agreement of *c'est* followed by a noun (or by a pronoun in the third person) in the plural:
CE SONT *là de beaux résultats.*
C'EST *là de beaux résultats.*
C'ÉTAIENT *ceux que nous attendions.*
C'ÉTAIT *ceux que nous attendions.*

> Usage allows the agreement in the plural or in the singular.

7. Sequence of tenses:
J'avais souhaité qu'il vînt (QU'IL VIENNE) *sans tarder.*
Je ne pensais pas qu'il eût oublié (QU'IL AIT OUBLIÉ) *le rendez-vous.*
J'aimerais qu'il fût (QU'IL SOIT) *avec moi.*
J'aurais aimé qu'il eût été (QU'IL AIT ÉTÉ) *avec moi.*

> In a subordinate clause in the subjunctive, which is dependent on a clause whose verb is in a past tense or in the conditional, it will be permitted to allow the verb in the subordinate clause to be in the present, when the strict sequence of tenses would require the imperfect; in the past, when it would require the pluperfect.

8. Present participle and verbal adjective followed by an indirect object complement or by an adverbial complement:
La fillette, OBÉISSANT *à sa mère, alla se coucher.*
La fillette, OBÉISSANTE *à sa mère, alla se coucher.*

J'ai recueilli cette chienne ERRANT *dans le quartier.*
J'ai recueilli cette chienne ERRANTE *dans le quartier.*

> Usage allows, according to the intended meaning, the form in *-ant* to be used without agreement as a form of the present participle or with agreement as a form of the adjective which corresponds to it.
> Either use will be allowed in all cases.

9. Past participle conjugated with *être* in a verbal form having *on* as its subject:
On est resté (RESTÉS) *bons amis.*

> Usage requires that the past participle referring to the pronoun *on* be in the masculine singular.
> It will be allowed to write this participle with agreement in gender and number when *on* designates a woman or several persons.

10. Past participle conjugated with *avoir* and followed by an infinitive:
Les musiciens que j'ai entendus (ENTENDU) *jouer.*
Les airs que j'ai entendu (ENTENDUS) *jouer.*

> Usage requires that the participle be in agreement when the direct object complement refers to the conjugated form and that it remain invariable when the direct object complement refers to the infinitive.
> Absence of agreement in the first example will be allowed. Agreement in the second example will be allowed, except when the past participle of the verb *faire* is concerned.

11. Agreement of the past participle conjugated with *avoir* in a verbal form preceded by *en* as direct object complement of this verbal form:
J'ai laissé sur l'arbre plus de cerises que je n'en ai CUEILLI.
J'ai laissé sur l'arbre plus de cerises que je n'en ai CUEILLIES.

> Usage allows either agreement.

12. Past participle of verbs such as: *coûter, valoir, courir, vivre,* etc., when this participle is placed after an object complement:
Je ne parle pas des sommes que ces travaux m'ont coûté (COÛTÉES).
J'oublierai vite les peines que ce travail m'a coûtées (COÛTÉ).

> Usage allows that these verbs, normally intransitive (without agreement of the past participle), be used transitively (with agreement) in certain cases.
> Either use in all cases will be allowed.

13. Participles and locutions such as *compris (y compris, non compris), excepté, ôté, étant donné, ci-inclus, ci-joint:*
13(a). *Compris (y compris, non compris), excepté, ôté:*
J'aime tous les sports, excepté la boxe (EXCEPTÉE LA BOXE).
J'aime tous les sports, la boxe exceptée (LA BOXE EXCEPTÉ).

> Usage requires that these participles and locutions remain invariable when they are placed before the noun to which they are related and that they vary when they are placed after the noun.
> Agreement in the first example and the absence of agreement in the second will be allowed.

13(b). *Étant donné:*
Étant données les circonstances. . .
ÉTANT DONNÉ *les circonstances. . .*

> Usage allows agreement as well as absence of agreement.

13(c). *Ci-inclus, ci-joint:*
Ci-inclus (CI-INCLUSE) *la pièce demandée.*
Vous trouverez ci-inclus (CI-INCLUSE) *copie de la pièce demandée.*
Vous trouverez cette lettre CI-INCLUSE.
Vous trouverez cette lettre CI-INCLUS.

Usage requires that *ci-inclus, ci-joint* be invariable at the beginning of a sentence or if they precede an indeterminate noun; in other cases, variable or invariable, according to the intended meaning.

Agreement or absence of agreement will be allowed in all cases.

II. The Noun

14. Freedom of number:

14(a):

De la gelée de GROSEILLE.   *Des pommiers* EN FLEUR.
De la gelée de GROSEILLES.   *Des pommiers* EN FLEURS.

Usage allows the singular and plural.

14(b):

Ils ont ôté LEUR CHAPEAU.
Ils ont ôté LEURS CHAPEAUX.

Usage allows, according to the meaning intended, the singular and plural.

Either singular or plural will be allowed in all cases.

15. Double gender:

Instruits (INSTRUITES) *par l'expérience, les vieilles gens sont très prudents* (PRUDENTES)*; ils* (ELLES) *ont vu trop de choses.*

Usage gives the masculine gender to the word *gens,* except in expressions such as: *les bonnes gens, les vieilles gens, les petites gens.*

When an adjective or a participle refers to one of these expressions, or when a pronoun takes its place, it will be permitted to allow this adjective, this participle, this pronoun also to be in the feminine.

16. Masculine nouns of titles or professions applied to women:
Le français nous est enseigné par une dame. Nous aimons beaucoup ce professeur. Mais il (ELLE) *va nous quitter.*

> Whether or not preceded by the word *Madame,* these nouns keep the masculine gender as well as their determinants and the adjectives which accompany them.
> When they are replaced by a pronoun, the feminine gender of that pronoun will be allowed.

17. Plural of nouns:
17(a). Proper nouns of persons:
Les Dupont (DUPONTS). *Les Maréchal* (MARÉCHALS).

> Proper nouns of persons in the plural will be allowed.

17(b). Nouns borrowed from other languages:
Des maxima (DES MAXIMUMS). *Des sandwiches* (DES SANDWICHS).

> Forming the plural of these nouns according to the general rule in French will be allowed in all cases.

III. The Article

18. Article before *plus, moins, mieux:*
Les idées qui paraissent LES PLUS *justes sont souvent discutables.*
Les idées qui paraissent LE PLUS *justes sont souvent discutables.*

> In groups formed with a definite article followed by *plus, moins, mieux* and an adjective or a participle, usage allows, according to the intended meaning, that the article vary or remain invariable.
> It will be allowed to let the article vary or remain invariable in all cases.

IV. The Numeral as an Adjective

19. *Vingt* and *cent* [and *mil* or *mille*]:
Quatre-vingt-dix (QUATRE VINGTS DIX) *ans.*
Six cent trente-quatre (SIX CENTS TRENTE QUATRE) *hommes.*
En mil neuf cent soixante-dix-sept (MILLE NEUF CENTS SOIXANTE DIX
SEPT).

It will be allowed to write *vingt* and *cent*, preceded by
a numeral as an adjective with the value of a multiplier,
in the plural even when they are followed by another numeral as an adjective.

When designating thousand in a date, it will be allowed
to write the form *mille* in all cases.

NOTE: Usage places a hyphen between the elements of
a numeral as an adjective when the elements form a
whole less than one hundred.

It will be allowed to omit the hyphen.

V. The Qualifying Adjective

20. *Nu, demi* preceding a noun:
Elle courait nu-pieds (NUS PIEDS).
Une demi-huere (DEMIE HEURE) *s'écoula.*

Usage requires that *nu, demi* remain invariable when
they precede a noun to which they are connected by a
hyphen.

Agreement will be allowed.

---

21. Plural of *grand-mère, grand-tante,* etc.:
Des GRAND-*mères.*
Des GRANDS-*mères.*

Usage allows either written form.

22. *Se faire fort de* . . ..
Elles se font fort (FORTES) *de réussir.*

Agreement of the adjective will be allowed.

---

23. *Avoir l'air:*
Elle a l'air DOUX .
Elle a l'air DOUCE.

Usage allows, according to the meaning intended, that the adjective agree with the word *air* or with the subject of the verb *avoir.*

It will be allowed to write either agreement in all cases.

VI. The Indefinites

24. *L'un et l'autre:*
24(a). *L'un et l'autre* used as an adjective:
1. *J'ai consulté l'un et l'autre* DOCUMENT.
   J'ai consulté l'un et l'autre DOCUMENTS.
2. *L'un et l'autre document* M'A PARU *intéressant.*
   L'un et l'autre document M'ONT PARU *intéressants.*

---

1. Usage allows, according to the meaning intended, that the noun preceded by *l'un et l'autre* be written in the singular or in the plural.
   Either the singular or the plural will be allowed in all cases.
2. With the noun in the singular, usage allows the verb to be written in the singular or in the plural.

24(b). *L'un et l'autre* used as a pronoun:
L'un et l'autre se TAISAIT.
L'un et l'autre se TAISAIENT.

> Usage allows, according to the meaning intended, that the verb preceded by *l'un et l'autre* used as a pronoun be written in the singular or in the plural.
>
> Either the singular or the plural will be allowed in all cases.

25. *L'un ou l'autre, ni l'un ni l'autre:*
25(a). *L'un ou l'autre, ni l'un ni l'autre* used as adjectives:
L'un ou l'autre projet ME CONVIENT.
L'un ou l'autre projet ME CONVIENNENT.

Ni l'une ni l'autre idée NE M'INQUIÈTE.
Ni l'une ni l'autre idée NE M'INQUIÈTENT.

> Usage requires that the noun preceded by *l'un ou l'autre* or by *ni l'un ni l'autre* be written in the singular; usage allows, according to the meaning intended, that the verb be written in the singular or in the plural.
>
> Either the singular or plural of the verb form will be allowed in all cases.

25(b). *L'un ou l'autre, ni l'un ni l'autre* used as pronouns:
De ces deux projets, l'un ou l'autre me CONVIENT.
De ces deux projets, l'un ou l'autre me CONVIENNENT.

De ces deux idées, ni l'une ni l'autre ne M'INQUIÈTE.
De ces deux idées, ni l'une ni l'autre ne M'INQUIÈTENT.

> Usage allows, according to the intended meaning, that the verb preceded by *l'un ou l'autre* or by *ni l'un ni l'autre* used as pronouns be written in the singular or in the plural.
>
> Either the singular or the plural will be allowed in all cases.

26. *Chacun:*
Remets ces livres chacun à SA *place.*
Remets ces livres chacun à LEUR *place.*

> When *chacun* replaces a noun (or a pronoun in the third person) in the plural and is followed by a possessive, usage allows, according to the meaning intended, the possessive to refer to *chacun* or to the word that *chacun* replaces.
>
> Either will be allowed in all cases.

VII. Même *and* Tout

27. *Même:*
Dans les fables, les bêtes MÊMES *parlent.*
Dans les fables, les bêtes MÊME *parlent.*

> After a noun or pronoun in the plural, usage allows *même*, according to the meaning intended, to be in agreement or not.
>
> Either written form will be allowed in all cases.

28. *Tout:*
28(a). *Les proverbes sont de* TOUT *temps et de* TOUT *pays.*
       Les proverbes sont de TOUS *temps et de* TOUS *pays.*

> Usage allows, according to the meaning intended, the singular or plural.

28(b). *Elle est toute* (TOUT) *à sa lecture.*

> In the expression *être tout à. . .,* when *tout* refers to a feminine word, it will be allowed to leave *tout* as invariable.

28(c). *Elle se montra tout* (TOUTE) *étonnée.*

> Usage requires that *tout,* used as an adverb, agree in gender and number in front of a feminine word beginning with a consonant or aspirate *h* and that it remain invariable in other cases.
>
> It will be allowed to make *tout* agree in gender and number in front of a feminine noun beginning with a vowel or a silent *h*.

VIII. The Adverb *ne* as an Expletive

29. *Je crains qu'il* NE *pleuve.*
    Je crains qu'il pleuve.

    L'année a été meilleure qu'on NE *l'espérait.*
    L'année a été meilleure qu'on l'espérait.

> Usage does not impose the use of the expletive *ne*.

IX. Accents

30. *Accent aigu:*
    Assener (ASSÉNER); *referendum* (RÉFÉRENDUM).

> In certain words, the letter *e,* without an acute accent mark, is pronounced [*é*] at the end of a syllable.
>
> It will be allowed to give it that accent mark—even if it is a word of foreign origin—except in proper nouns.

31. *Accent grave:*
    Événement (ÉVÈNEMENT); *je céderai* (JE CÈDERAI).

> In certain words, the letter *e* with an acute accent mark is generally pronounced [*è*] at the end of a syllable.
>
> The use of the grave accent mark in place of the acute accent mark will be allowed.

32. *Accent circonflexe:*
Crâne (CRANE); *épître* (ÉPITRE); *crûment* (CRUMENT).

It will be allowed to omit the circumflex accent mark on the vowels *a, e, i, o, u* in words where these vowels normally bear this accent mark, except when this allowance would bring about confusion between two words resulting in a homographic form (for example: *tâche / tache; forêt / foret; vous dîtes / vous dites; rôder / roder; qu'il fût / il fut).*

X. Hyphen

33. *Arc-en-ciel* (ARC EN CIEL); *nouveau-né* (NOUVEAU NÉ); *crois-tu?* (CROIS TU?); *est-ce vrai?* (EST CE VRAI?); *dit-on* (DIT ON); *dix-huit* (DIX HUIT); *dix-huitième* (DIX HUITIÈME); *par-ci, par-là* (PAR CI, PAR LÀ).

In all cases, it will be allowed to omit the hyphen, except when its presence avoids ambiguity *(petite-fille/petite fille)* or when it must be placed before and after the euphonic *t* in the third person singular between a verb form and an inverted subject pronoun *(viendra-t-il?).*

OBSERVATION

In examinations or competitive tests, as noted at the beginning of this list, the examiners—who grade their evaluations according to the level of knowledge which they may demand from the candidates—will not count as serious errors those (apart from the cases mentioned above) which bear on subtle grammatical particularities.

COMPREHENSIVE INDEX

This index contains words and expressions in French and English in one alphabetical order because I think it is more convenient for a user to look in one place instead of two for an entry. Also, in this way, cognates and near-cognates in both languages are reduced to a single entry. Key words in other languages are also included, as cited in the text.

The preposition *to* in an English infinitive is omitted; e.g., *to land on the moon* is listed under *land on the moon*.

French reflexive verbs beginning with either *se* or *s'* are all listed in one place under the reflexive pronoun *se*. In this way, you can see at a glance all reflexive verbs in one place.

The abbreviation *ff* after a numbered entry means *and the following*; i.e., consult also the entries that follow the numbered entry that is cited. For the meaning of other abbreviations, consult the list given in the front pages of the book.

Numbers refer to entry numbers.

F

806; no matter how 709; no matter what 707; no matter what, whatever 1247*ff*; no one 797*ff*; no sooner 1051; no way 446

nobiliary particle 1167

Noël, la Noël 602

nom (petit ~) 322, 465

noms composés (plural) 573*ff*; *noms étrangers* (plural) 593; *noms latins* (plural) 593; *noms de nombre* (hyphen) 682; *noms propres* (plural) 572; *noms de villes* 549

non 1041; *non seulement. . ., mais . . .* 1041; (agreement of verb) 987; *non que* (mood) 1295

nonante 680

none such 805

noon (before ~) 49

nosseigneurs 582

not 1041; not any 790; not anyone 797*ff*; not as early, not so early 1054; not indebted, even, quits 1202; not less than 806; not one 790; not to agree that 1268; not to know that 1266

notabilité, notoriété 323

notable, notoire 323

note, noter; cote, coter (a written assignment) 144

noteworthy 323

nothing at all 805; nothing less than 806; nothing like 805; nothing or all 804

noun clauses; *see* clauses

nouns 484*ff*; adjectival use 655; collective 952*ff*, 968*ff*; compound, plurals of 573*ff*; compound (with *entre*) 207; English 595; feminine 485*ff*; foreign 593*ff*; gender 484*ff*; German 596; Italian 594; joined by *ainsi que* 650; joined by *comme* 650; joined by *et* 649; joined by *ou* 652*ff*; Latin 593*ff*; *-oir* ending nouns 316; plural of proper nouns 572*ff*; synonymous nouns 651; the article and Italian proper nouns 606; nouns in gradation 651

nous deux mon frère 724

nouveau-né, nouveau marié, etc. 672; *de nouveau, à nouveau* 1083; *nouvel* 618

nu (agreement) 673; with hyphen 460; *à nu* 673

nuisance 324

nul 696; *nul. . ., nul. . .* (agreement of verb) 995*ff*; *nul doute que* (mood) 1253

number (singular, plural) 550*ff*

numerals 680*ff*, 783; complex numbers 1218*ff*; compound numbers 682; numerical expressions 978; use of *et* 681, 1218*ff*; use of hyphen 682; with *chaque* 701

numéro minéralogique 312

O

oatmeal 337

obéir (vous serez obéi) 825

object pronouns; *see* pronouns

obliger à or *de* + inf. 915

observance, observation 325

observer (for *faire observer*) 826

obsolete 174

obtenir qq.ch. à qqn 811

occire 896

occuper (s' ~) à or *de* + inf. 58, 923

œ (pronunciation) 326

oeil, oeils, yeux 566; *clin d'oeil* (plur.) 585; *entre quatre yeux* 561; *tourner de l'oeil* 224

oeuvre (gender) 526

oeuvrer 327

of course, naturally 1162

officer's military orderly 527

-oir ending nouns 316

-oître ending verbs 855

old-fashioned 174

old man, old woman 548

Olympiade, Olympic games 328

omnibus (train ~) 223

on 794; *l'on* 795, 796

on 1206*ff*; on a bicycle 1071*ff*; on a register 1131; on account of 1151, 1205; on an armchair 1141; on behalf of 1151; on foot 1095*ff*; on purpose, expressly 1021; on the coast 1210; on the contrary 1239; on the ground 1097; on the level of 1212; on the one hand, besides 1245*ff*; on the point of 1199; on the while 1217

once and for all, for good 1192*ff*; once more, again 1083

one 683; one after the other 1018; one and only 1286; one and the other 993; one does not know that. . . 1267; one hundred 685; one or the other 992; one, someone, somebody, people, etc. 794; one thousand 686; one would have said (or thought) that. . . 1269; one would say. . . 1164; one would say or think that. . . 1269; one would swear. . . 1164; one would think. . . 1164; one would think or say that. . . 1269

oneself 737*ff*

only 1007 (3); the only thing that is. . . is. . . 670

onomatopoeic elements in the plur. 578

open a can of worms 286

opera hat 86

opinion, verbs of; *see* verbs

opposite 1171*ff*

Q

T

without equal 663; without interruption 1018

woman author 495; woman doctor 506; woman poet 537

word order 729*ff*, 688

words (capitalization of ~) 294; words (foreign ~) 577

work 526; work day week 1147

worms (open a can of ~) 286

worse, worst 646

would-be 739*ff*

wrecked 99

writer (woman ~); *see* author (woman); *see also* woman

writing 195

Y

y in the following examples:
il s'y agit de 755 (2); *il s'y en donna* 755

(4); *Je n'y peux rien* 746; *Je veux y aller, j'y veux aller* 755 (3); *m'y, t'y, y-moi* 755 (1); referring to names of animals or things 742; referring to persons 743; *s'y retrouver* (i.e., *rentrer dans ses débours*, to find (get) one's bearings; *y compris* 941, 1065

y and *en* 742*ff*, 861; *y* with *irai, irais* 744

yearbook 31

years gone by 33

-*yer* ending verb type 842

yesterday evening (~ morning) 1084*ff*

yeux (entre quatre ~) 561

you know, don't you know . . . 416

your 689; your turn to speak has come up 1087

Z

zero 687